THE CONCERTS REVIEWED
65 YEARS OF THE
PORTLAND YOUTH PHILHARMONIC

Final concert, March 29, 1970 Tour, National Cathedral, Washington, D.C.

THE CONCERTS REVIEWED

65 YEARS

of the PORTLAND YOUTH PHILHARMONIC

Jacob Avshalomov

AMADEUS PRESS
Portland, Oregon

Written and edited by Jacob Avshalomov.

ISBN 0-931340-28-4
Printed in Hong Kong

AMADEUS PRESS
9999 S.W. Wilshire
Portland, Oregon 97225

CONTENTS

65TH ANNIVERSARY SEASON
PORTLAND
YOUTH PHILHARMONIC
JACOB AVSHALOMOV
CONDUCTOR-MUSICAL DIRECTOR
4TH INTERNATIONAL TOUR
MARCH 16-31, 1989
JENBACH, LINZ, AUSTRIA ■ BRATISLAVA, CZECHOSLOVAKIA
BUDAPEST, KECSKEMET, SOPRON, HUNGARY ■ STUTTGART, WEST GERMANY

To
Jacques Gershkovitch,
my mentor and partner
in this lovely work,
and to
the thousands of students
whom it was
our pleasure and privilege
to teach

ACKNOWLEDGMENTS

I want to thank two longtime friends and patrons of the Portland Youth Philharmonic, Dorothy Sherman and Betty Lasselle, for their generosity in providing the funds needed to publish this book. I am especially grateful for their understanding of the importance of such a chronicle.

My heartfelt thanks must here be expressed to my wife, Doris, for generously setting the program pages of 65 seasons. This was done by hand, at her Howlet press, with the enthusiasm and sensitivity of one who played in the Orchestra, along with the writer, as our two sons did later. Living the PJS/PYP life for nearly 40 years enabled her to bring nuances to the program pages that will be appreciated by knowing readers.

The reviews included in this book are intact in all their critical matter. Many have been trimmed of irrelevant and redundant material in the interests of keeping the book a manageable size. Readers who would like to see the complete, original reviews can find photocopies of the entire set deposited in the files of the Oregon Historical Society, the Multnomah County Central Library, and the PYP offices.

My thanks also go to Violet Oulbegian, whose contact with the PJS goes back to the 1950s when she played recitals with the concertmaster and accompanied the all-city high school choir when it sang with us. Now a member of the Board, she ferreted out all the reviews of the Gershkovitch era from the scrapbooks of three decades.

Many people have contributed photos included herein, but some must be recognized: Wes Taft, Jr., who accompanied the 1970 tour; Hugh Ackroyd; Hank Kranzler, 1979 Japan Tour; Jerry Baker, 1984 Tour; and Dick Powers, who has looked in on the Orchestra for many a year.

Fans of the Orchestra who follow every account of it will no doubt notice that they have seen some parts of the narrative sections of this book before. They are condensed restatements from *Music is Where You Make It/II* of beliefs still held and accounts still accurate. Those interested in reading the full story will find it in that book under the same headings as are herein marked with an asterisk (*).

The sites of the early concerts, which were various, are named. After 1926 all regular season concerts were held at the Municipal Auditorium, later called Civic Auditorium. From 1984 on they have been given at the Arlene Schnitzer Concert Hall, except where noted otherwise.

Throughout this book the Orchestra is referred to by both its original name, Portland Junior Symphony (PJS), and Portland Youth Philharmonic (PYP), the name it assumed in 1979—according to the period being discussed.

ABOUT THE AUTHOR

AS CONDUCTOR, has led

U.S. premieres of:
Bruckner—Mass in D
Tippett—A Child of Our Time
Handel—The Triumph of Time & Truth
Sessions—Divertimento

Portland Youth Philharmonic since 1954
European Tour, 1970
Japan Tour, 1979
Spoleto/USA Festival, 1981
New York Philharmonic joint concert
& Third International Tour, 1984
4th International Tour, 1989

Commemorative Concerts
Aaron Avshalomov 90th Anniversary,
Beijing, Shanghai, and Wuhan, China, 1985
Bloch Festival, Newport, Oregon, 1990

AS PROFESSOR

Columbia University, 1946—1954

Visiting Professor:
Reed College, Summer 1948
University of Washington, 1959
Tanglewood, Summer 1960
Northwestern University, Summer 1961
University of Illinois, Summer 1969
Aspen Music School, Summer 1971

AWARDS AND PRIZES

A.M. Ditson Fellowship, Composition, 1946
Ernest Bloch Award, 1948
Guggenheim Fellowship, 1952
N.Y. Music Critics Circle Award, 1953
Naumburg Recording Award, 1956
Honorary Doctorate, University of Portland, 1964
A.M. Ditson Conductor's Award, 1965
Honorary Doctorate, Reed College 1973
University of Oregon Distinguished Services Award, 1975
Honorary Doctorate, Linfield College, 1978
Western Oregon State College Distinguished Services Award, 1981

Scuplture of Jacob Avshalomov created by William Bane for 30th Anniversary, 1984
Governor's Arts Award, 1985
National Foundation for the Arts Award, 1990

LECTURER AND CONSULTANT

Phillips Gallery, Washington, D.C.
Griffith Music Foundation, Newark, NJ
Book-of-the-Month Club Music Series, 1952
Avshalomov Lecture Series, 1958—1971
Ford Foundation Composer Project, 1962
Member, National Council for the Humanities, 1968—1974
National Arts Endowment, Music Planning Section, Co-Chairman, 1977—1979
Spoleto/USA Bloch Festival, 1982, 1984
Pro Musicis Foundation, 1984—1988
Avshalomov Festivals
  College of DuPage 1985
  Portland Youth Philharmonic, 1989

STUDIED WITH

Aaron Avshalomov, Ernest Toch, Bernard Rogers,
Jacques Gershkovitch, Aaron Copland

ENCYCLOPEDIA REFERENCES

Who's Who in America
Who's Who in Music
Baker's Dictionary of Music & Musicians
International Encyclopedia of Music
Musikkens Hvem Hvad Hvor, Copenhagen

Prelude

FLARES & FANFARES

NOVEMBER 7, 1926.

JUNIOR SYMPHONY ORCHESTRA SCORES GREAT TRIUMPH

JANUARY 30, 1927.

JUNIOR SYMPHONY WINS CHEERS WITH SPLENDID MUSIC

Junior Symphony Opening Indicates Astonishing Ability

By HILMAR GRONDAHL, *The Oregonian, December 2, 1973*

FEBRUARY 19, 1939.

BIG OVATION GIVEN JUNIOR ORCHESTRA

SUNDAY OREGONIAN
NOVEMBER 26, 1933

JUNIOR ORCHESTRA AMAZES AUDIENCE

Young Musicians Acclaimed for Masterful Work.

FINE TRAINING SHOWN

Schubert's "Unfinished" Symphony Splendidly Rendered; Part of Program Broadcast.

FEBRUARY 9, 1930

JUVENILE ARTISTS, SOLOISTS, PLEASE GREAT AUDIENCE

"What an orchestra!"

"What an organization!"

"What a lesson for us all!"

Aaron Copland, *February 1964*
Conducting 40th Anniversary Concert

Juniors Open Golden Anniversary Season With Shining Performance

By MARTIN CLARK, *Journal Music Editor, December 3, 1973*

Successo dell' orchestra
Portland Junior Simphony

MUSIKKEN ER, HVOR MAN SPILLER DEN

Jacob Avshalomov, amerikansk komponist og dirigent, fortæller om Portland Junior Symphony, et fremragende ungdomsorkester, der har bragt amatørspillet til sjældne højder

---

Musik in Stuttgart

Erstaunliches Format

REMARKABLE CALIBER

Stuttgart, West Germany
STUTTGARTER NACHRITTEN
March 30, 1989

UTOROK 28. MARCA 1989

Vecernik

Oživili koncertnú sezónu

Mladí hudobníci z Portlandu

Bratislava, Czechoslovakia
VECERNIZ
28 March 1989

THEY ENVLIVENED THE CONCERT SEASON
Young Musicians from Portland

Radost muziciranja

"Vjesnik" Zagreb March 22, 1984

The Joy of Music-Making

Висок ниво музицирања

ISKRENA I SVJEŽA GLAZBA

"Novi List" Rijeka March 25, 1984

Genuine and Vigorous Music

SYMPHONY MAGAZINE

June/July 1984

New Triumphs for the Portland Youth Philharmonic

Among the creations of Western culture, the symphony orchestra is surely one of the most marvelous. Its range of expression extends from poignancy to mischief, from languor to frenzy, from the most subtle to the grandest imaginable utterance. Its literature contains some of the most exalted manifestations of the human spirit. If we can learn how to lend ourselves to it, each work can bring us close to its state of being. Hence, it is fitting that young musicians be introduced to these works as soon as they can cope with the technical demands.

In the recent past we have relied on professionals to set and maintain standards. But today, with the epidemic use of recorded music in all its forms, the prospect of earning an adequate living as a musician steadily wanes. As a result, the number of students who aspire to become professionals diminishes. Still, musical *activity* keeps increasing, even though many musicians earn only a small part of their livelihood from it. But they continue out of *love.* Thus, the true meaning of "amateur" is being restored, and a new assessment of the roles of amateur and professional is needed.

The fact is that the amateur is becoming the standard-bearer for music, especially in terms of the influence he or she wields. If our culture is to thrive, amateurs must be helped to a lofty viewpoint and the habit of serious endeavor. These are best implanted in the young; and so it is that their music-making is as important to us all as it is to them.

For over 65 years the Portland Junior Symphony/Youth Philharmonic has served the cause of music in Oregon, and it has long been the natural avenue of musical achievement for the talented youth of this region. When it was founded in 1924, the idea of a "junior" symphony was unique, and recognition came early in its history, partly as a result of nationwide radio broadcasts. Its reputation has steadily continued to grow, and today it is generally held to be the leading youth orchestra in North America—not only because no other city has a youth orchestra with a record half as long, but also for the quality of its repertoire, the level of its performance, and the scope of its activities.

The civic-minded citizens who gathered round to support the PJS in its formative days stated their purposes early and clearly:

> to encourage appreciation and performance of great orchestral music; present public concerts in yearly series; discover and develop talent in children; stress values in good character; and endeavor to create a cultural and educational asset to the community through greater of love of music.

These aims have been amply fulfilled over the decades. Over 4,000 young musicians have been inspired and trained by the Orchestra. Many of them have gone on to the nation's distinguished ensembles. Many more have become the enlightened amateurs of music among us.

The beginnings of the Orchestra were described in 1938 in *A New West to Explore* by Ronald Russell. In 1959, I picked up the saga in the first edition of *Music*

Is Where You Make It. Both accounts showed that Portland's youth orchestra became everyone's pet, but no one's toy.

Treasured at home, it is even more uplifting to receive the tributes that flow in from abroad and from visitors, since they are free of native pride. Those that have been gathered into these pages raise the question: How did the Orchestra achieve its stature? That is best explained by a detailed examination of its work.

Although every concert fades into silence, and the personnel of the Orchestra changes yearly, something remains—in the experience of the players and in the memory of the audiences. Within the community, an intangible cultural edifice is raised; its presence is sensed by many, but it is only clearly visible in the cumulative record of the work accomplished. *Music Is Where You Make It/II* is such a record.

That account carried the story through the 55th season, giving some history and a detailed account of our working methods, repertoire, and rosters of players and notables, with many photos and letters from far and wide, ranging from the time of the Orchestra's beginnings to 1979.

Now, in celebration of our 65th Anniversary, 1988–89, I feel that a different kind of overview is needed. Our working methods have hardly changed in the past decade, so there is not much to add in that regard. What we have never had before is a chronological listing of all the programs and their reviews from the daily and periodical press. This is what we now have in this book, and the critical notices radiate out from Portland, throughout Oregon, to Seattle, Charleston, South Carolina, Washington, D.C., New York, Bratislava, Budapest, Stuttgart, and Zagreb.

I was inspired to produce such a book by the volume published in 1964 by the Friends of Music in Milan. A copy of it was presented to our son Daniel after the American String Quartet, of which he is the violist, performed there in 1986. That handsome tome lists all their programs and performing artists of the past century!

My aim is to show the consistent enthusiasm that has been lavished on the PJS/PYP throughout its history as it continued to fulfill the mandate of its founding Board of Directors, quoted above.

The 65th Anniversary was a season exemplary of our activities, and we begin with it.

65th
Anniversary Season,
1988–89

Not surprisingly, this double anniversary year became the fullest in the Orchestra's history. The PYP's 65th Anniversary coincided with the 35th Anniversary of my first concert—conducted at the Orchestra's 30th Anniversary in February 1954.

In addition to the usual schedule of a Fall, Winter, and Spring concert, plus several Children's Concerts, there were: a late December concert with an Alumni Orchestra and the Preparatory Orchestra; the Sing-Your-Own Messiah; the 4th International Tour, followed by the Berlioz *Requiem* as the grand finale; and throughout the season a festival of my compositions, which the Association had organized to recognize my creative work done during the 35 years of service to the Orchestra.

There were also two pre-season events, a Waterfront Classics Concert and the opening of the new Performing Arts Center in Newport, Oregon.

Because of heart surgery early in the summer of 1988, it was a bit too soon for me to do the Waterfront Classics Concert at the end of August. The Board agreed that it was appropriate for our son David to conduct that event, since he was coming to Portland in February to lead one of my works at the anniversary concert and was also being considered for the role of Assistant Conductor on the International Tour.

We scooped up a passel of works from the previous season, filled out our roster of players (who were signed up in May) with alums who were about town, and all went down to the beautiful park by the Willamette River to play for the immense crowd which had gathered, estimated to be some 30,000.

In mid September, after holding supplementary auditions and two weeks of rehearsals, aided by my associate Eugene Kaza, we bused over to Newport, at the coast, to help open their new Center. This overnight trip served also as a test run for our coming European Tour.

The Avshalomov festival had three parts, one of which was the presentation of an orchestral work at each of the season's concerts, with a guest conductor. In November, it was Kaza. The second part was an evening of chamber music and songs, in February; the third was a program of my choral music, in April.

In early December the 7th annual Sing-Your-Own Messiah brought seven guest conductors to the platform: All colleagues who had some past connection with the Orchestra or the event.

On the second day of Christmas the concert with an all-alumni orchestra brought fifteen of them into the spotlight: nine in the Menotti *Triplo Concerto a Tre,* four in the Haydn concertante, Roger Kaza as horn soloist in the Saint-Saëns *Morceau de Concert,* and Nancy Malos Johnson as conductor of my *Open Seasame!* which she had commissioned earlier for her youth orchestra in New Zealand.

The first of the two special concerts of my music was given on February 13 at the new Winningstad Theatre. Alyce Rogers sang 18 songs, including a set written for her; Daniel Avshalomov played two works—for viola and piano—

which he had recently recorded for Composers Recordings, Inc. of New York; Harold Gray was the sensitive piano partner to them both. These performances were truly definitive and moving, despite the inhospitable acoustics of the room.

The Orchestra's 65th Anniversary concert was given on February 25. The program contained a major portion of the Tour repertoire. At an intermission ceremony, Ned Look, past-president of the Board, presented me with a souvenir videocassette of events from our recent past and congratulated the Orchestra and the audience, after which we all set our faces toward the future.

The 4th International Tour had been gestating for over three years and was now firmly set for March 16–31, 1989. That left us just three weeks after the Anniversary Concert to get it all together: logistics, passports and visas, customs details, packing lists, travel and cultural briefings, escorts meetings and meshing with their groups, medical forms, and the other inescapable details of group travel. It was all accomplished under the indefatigable leadership of Ernestine Oringdulph, Tour Manager, and Barbara Segerstrom, Orchestra Committee Chairman, together with many other helping hands.

Getting it all together also meant preparing the rest of the scheduled music. I had planned to take the makings of three programs with us, partly to maintain the Orchestra's interest with the variety, and partly to join hands with young guest artists abroad. All the additional music had been performed within the past half year, but the new players had not played it. With hard work we got it ready, taking a spare set of parts in a footlocker in case of a lost folder en route.

Finally, 91 players and 18 adults (escorts, staff, and a few fans) were enrolled in the Tour group. Our arrangements had been made with Friendship Ambassadors of New Jersey, a cultural foundation with many years' experience in shepherding musical groups abroad. The students each paid $1,800 to cover all their expenses for the two-week trip; a handful who needed financial help were sponsored by individual friends of the Association. Then, special packing for the cellos, tips on traveling with other instruments, rental of basses, and some percussion—all had been covered.

On the morning of March 16 we met at the Portland Airport, and set off; United Airlines to Chicago, where we met Denis Hunt of Friendship Ambassadors and continued via Swissair to Zurich—a comfortable flight, full of anticipation.

There we were met by the drivers of three buses and a climate-controlled truck for the instruments, provided by Daimler-Benz through the good offices of their Portland affiliate, Freightliner. This windfall proved to be one of the best benefits of the tour. The buses were comfortable, the truck capacious, with lots of padded blankets, and all four drivers were not only expert, but pleasant and helpful beyond all expectation—becoming friends of the entire group and ardent fans of the Orchestra and our music-making.

The drive through the beautiful Tyrolean mountains was an eye-opener to our students, most of whom had never been abroad. Our first concert was in Jenbach, just outside Innsbruck. Its hall, in the community center, was small, as was the audience: a major soccer match was taking place on the same evening. However, it was typically enthusiastic, calling for several encores with insistent rhythmic applause.

The next day our students were able to see something of Innsbruck, briefed by the Austrian guides provided by Friendship Ambassadors. Strolling through that historic town, the Orchestra members really sensed that they were in Europe.

Our second stop was Linz, and the great Brucknerhaus—where the morning rehearsal was enlivened by our first guest soloist, Endre Hegedus of Budapest, who was to play the Bartok concerto. While David Avshalomov, who had been signed on as assistant conductor, got the Orchestra settled and warmed up on stage, the string principals and I met with the pianist in a practice-room, to get acquainted with his interpretation and to get our signals straight.

Hegedus proved to be a dream of an artist: Brilliant, sensitive, congenial, with a good command of English. It was also evident that he had played a good deal of chamber music so he was accustomed to a most natural give-and-take.

I had told the Orchestra before we left home that when we made music with soloists abroad it was my practice to defer to them in matters of interpretation, tempi, and such; they were our guests; we could always do it *our* way at home. Now, in the practice-room Hegedus was explaining why he took the second theme of the third movement a good bit slower than usual. Despite my complete acquiescence, he continued to make his case, citing his professorial and ethnomusical reasons. The pianist clearly felt as though the door he had thought to lean on had been opened from the other side.

The rehearsal with the Orchestra was very exciting, for us all. And the performance that evening went like a rocket. At least the Bartok did. The rest of the program was not so well received by the local press; and the applause for my *Phases* was slow in coming and tepid when it came. Success in Linz seemed not in our stars.

Between the rehearsal and the concert we made a pilgrimage to the monastery of St. Florian. The tour included a viewing of Bruckner's coffin which rested in a crypt; and behind it was a wall of human skulls. Few of the students will forget that sight. A performance by the resident organist on the "Bruckner organ" gave another definition to the Orchestra's new word, Baroque: it was, alas, overwhelming in volume only.

The next day en route to Bratislava in a mild drizzle we visited another Monastery, that at Melk. There, as St. Florian's, the ceiling paintings, with their tricky perspectives, beguiled our students and adults alike.

The prospect of the border crossing into Czechoslovakia had been giving Denis Hunt some uneasiness, and with good reason. We were detained for over

The Brucknerhaus, Linz, Austria.

four hours, with picky and inconsistent complaints about some of our customs forms and the origins of our cameras. Several of the guards were exactly like the surly Iron-curtain officials portrayed in movies. The students fell silent; the body language of our drivers, pacing the platform, was depressed. We were glad to be released to the tender mercies of whoever was taking care of us in Bratislava.

The trio of guides here, all young women, were very helpful and responsive to our wishes. This was a contrast to the Austrian crew who, while charming, seemed set in their notion of how things should go, and we had to insist on a course-correction more than once.

On this Tour, contact with students had been difficult to arrange because our dates ran into the Easter holidays. However, Friendship Ambassadors had been able to connect with the Music Academy and we were invited to a recital by some of their students. They were between 20 and 30 years of age, postgraduate level, and very good, without being exceptional: A wind quartet, a violinist, a cellist, and a baritone singer—who brought grins to our students' faces when he sang Gershwin's "I Got Plenty o' Nothin'," which appears in our *Porgy and Bess Suite.*

No plans had been made for the two groups of students to mingle; but as both sides lingered after the program I simply spoke up and invited them to greet each other, and, encouraged by Ernestine Oringdulph, they did so, gravitating toward their instrumental counterparts, groping in whatever language they could, and taking snapshots. Most of the Slovakian musicians showed up at our concert expressing much appreciation afterward.

The Music Academy faculty was also represented: One gave a short history of music in Bratislava, with a stand-up translation by Ika, one of our guides. The academy rector was there to greet us—a reserved, hollow-eyed gentleman leaning on his cane—as well as a cheerful lady professor of violin, who spoke good English and had written a history of violin-making.

The Orchestra was most eager to get to the Philharmonic Hall, or Redouta, as they call it. It is a beautiful, 18th-century-style building, seating about 900, with interior walls of wood painted white and gold. The stage space was right in the room—no proscenium, no wings, all one ceiling. The sound was scrumptious! Risers were in place: space was a little tight for us, but no matter. A TV crew was on hand to tape part of the rehearsal and they interviewed some of the students, an escort, and me. A radio reporter who followed on their heels had to be corrected rather firmly when she tried to put words into my mouth—concerning our Orchestra and its traditions. The stagehands were helpful; reps of the concert management, Slovkoncert, were in attendance. They all really seemed to have been awaiting us. Later, we learned that we were the first American performing group to appear in the city in 20 years.

While the Orchestra was getting set on stage, I met with our guest artists, a violinist and a harpist, for the Ravel *Tzigane.* The violinist was a charmer, full of spirit and style, but with only a few words of English. Between those and a little Russian and German we managed. What I had not anticipated was that he and the harpist had not rehearsed beforehand—their coordination being tricky. Early in our planning for the tour I had decided not to carry a harp with us—too cumbersome. So we asked the host cities to invite a local harpist, thinking we could in this way join hands with two artists in each city. But now I found myself spending the better part of the hour putting *them* together.

At the concert both our guests did splendidly, and so did our appropriately reduced orchestra. It had been a year since we had performed the piece in Portland and now had had only two rehearsals to warm it up before leaving home.

Inspired by the sound they produced in those acoustics and by the warmth of our welcome in the packed hall, the Orchestra outdid themselves. The Sibelius Symphony, especially, went well and we took eight curtain calls, playing three encores.

At our postconcert refreshment we were joined by the cultural attaché who had come from Prague, representing the Ambassador. He spoke appreciatively to us and from him the students got their first glimpse of the meaning of our tour in the larger picture. All of which nearly erased the memory of the border crossing!

The next day there was another, into Hungary. But, as anticipated, it was easy, barely an hour's wait. Somehow even the countryside seemed greener here, the people more open, the stores better provisioned. But the road signs were baffling: long words with lots of syllables adding up to nothing recognizable.

Before Budapest, one last vignette from Bratislava: On the morning of our departure, as we waited in the lobby for the buses, our first bassoonist, Kristi Millspaugh, was trying her second-year Russian on a group of Soviet visitors. She introduced me to them, and we exchanged pleasantries. Meanwhile a dour-looking woman sat silent among the group. Minutes later, as we were about to depart, the woman rushed out asking where the young lady was who had been chatting with them. I found Kristi, whereupon the woman presented her with an embroidered handkerchief, a hug, and a tear. One never knows what lies behind an impassive face.

In Budapest, the first evening being free, many of our group went to other Festival events: The opera, Bartok's *Bluebeard's Castle;* others went folk-dancing; still others attended an orchestral concert and had a preview of the hall where we were to play. One group went to a Dizzy Gillespie concert. When several of them stayed behind to chat with him and told him who they were, he astonished them (and later me) by asking, "Oh, isn't that Jake Avshalomov's outfit?"

Vigado Hall is right downtown, near the river. Its concert room is a converted ballroom with high ceilings, alabaster pillars, acoustic panels rising from the back wall—all making for a rather bath-tubby sound when empty, but not bad when full. Luckily, we again had a good house.

For the third time, I met with our guest musicians, and again they had not rehearsed. A different surprise was also in store for me: Neither the violinist nor the harpist were the ones originally assigned to us. This harpist was not as good as the one in Bratislava; the violinist was a much "straighter" player, technically cleaner than the Slovakian but without his swagger.

The Orchestra members were keyed up for this concert, it being at the prestigious Budapest spring festival whose invitation had triggered the entire tour. As sometimes happens, they were a little over anxious, so it was not our best performance. Still, it was good enough to elicit eight curtain calls and four encores.

In Budapest we made a new and unexpected friend—the house manager of Vigado Hall, who had been assigned by the Festival director to assist us not only here but also at our two other concerts in Hungary. Boros Janos, a teddy-bear of a man, was so helpful and courteous, and he hit it off so well with, David, who was in charge of logistics, that he immediately entered the charmed circle of our drivers.

The concert at Kesckemet was a runout, about two hours away. The hall, somewhat reminiscent of Jenbach, was also in a community center, housing a variety of arts activities. The stage here was small and the lighting poor. Boros ran interference for us with the local crew and we got settled, more or less. The audience, as in Jenbach, was small but enthusiastic, and would only let us stop after giving several encores.

The next day a five-hour bus ride brought us from Budapest to Sopron, an historic city near the Austrian border, barely an hour from Vienna. We were to perform in the Ferenc Liszt Hall. Here things really needed rearranging to accommodate an orchestra of our size. And again Boros worked miracles with the house crew.

This was David's program. The Orchestra was very responsive to him and gave what was surely the Tour's best performance of Dvorák's "New World" Symphony. The review from Sopron, with its sociological comment, is one which the reader must be sure to note. But perhaps the nicest encomium came from Boros Janos. After the concert I invited him and his wife to have supper with us, which they had to decline. When I gave my heartfelt thanks from us all, he said (in basic German for my sake): "Es is nicht schwer gute menschen zu hilfen" (It is not hard to help good people). With such a send-off it is easy to understand the warm feelings we all had for Hungary.

The crossing back into Austria was smooth, and soon we were back in the hands of our original guides. In Vienna we had a free day, which the whole entourage enjoyed immensely. The entertainment ranged from the Opera Ballet to go-carts, with fine strolls in the Schoenbrunn Palace Gardens. The weather was perfect and everyone was relaxed enough to begin thinking wistfully about the Tour's approaching end.

The drive to our final concert city, Stuttgart, was daylong. We arrived just before dinner time and were to be quartered (or halved) in two hotels. The second contingent was told that there would be a meeting at our other hotel following dinner.

Before we sat down, John van Buren appeared. He is a cheery, bushy-haired Portland-born composer now living, composing, and teaching in Germany. In the months during which we wrestled the Stuttgart arrangements into place John was very helpful. It was he who secured the Beethovensalle for our concert, connected us with the Russ Concert Agency, arranged the loan of the necessary instruments, and served as liaison with the executives at Daimler-Benz. Now he brought the good news that the house would be practically full!

After dinner the second contingent began to troop in. As I saw the flute section slip by with their instruments, my suspicions were confirmed when they broke into a four-part "Happy Birthday" to me: It was my 70th. A beautiful cake, the size of a small auto tire, had been contrived with the help of relatives of one of our players. Moved and delighted, I told them that I could not think of a happier way to celebrate this milestone in my life.

The next afternoon the Orchestra was invited to a reception at the Daimler-Benz auto museum where they had a wonderful time seeing the historic cars, and had a group photo taken surrounding one of the most famous models. At

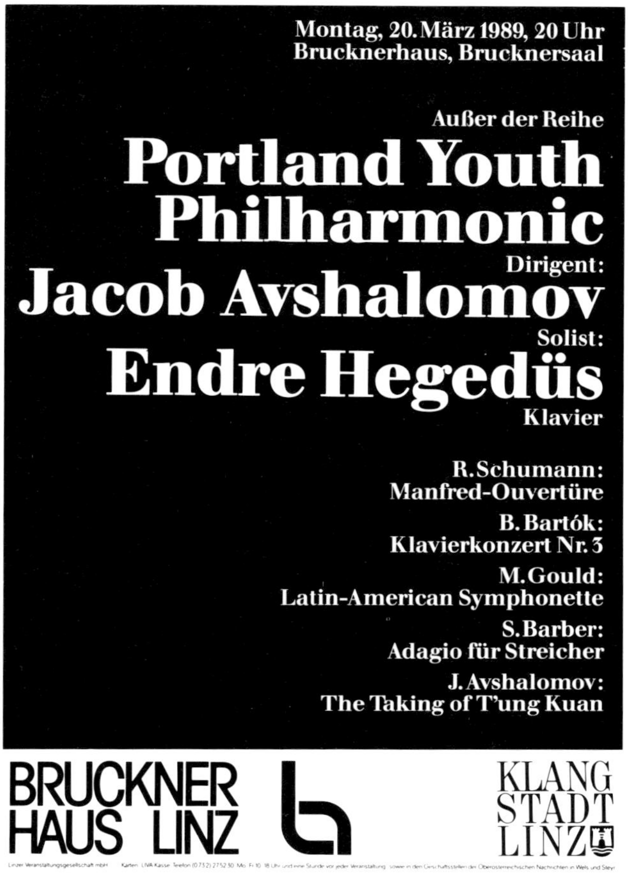

Concert poster in Stuttgart, West Germany.

five o'clock there was an even more elaborate reception for over 200 guests of the corporation and our leadership. There were speeches from both sides, a sumptuous buffet, after which I was driven back to the hotel to dress for the concert while the party continued until curtain time.

The Beethovensalle of the Liederhalle is a modern theater, with a curious curved sweep to the seating plan, and a stage completely surrounded with wood, but with one cement side wall. It is a little austere looking, spacious, with very immediate sound projection—not like any hall we had played in before—very revealing of all details. All part of the liberal education.

We came on stage to see a very full house indeed; a well-turned out audience of 1,900 gave us a warm response, all of which put the Orchestra in its finest fettle. Our only regret was that no recording could be made—technicians being away for the holidays.

Here, as in Bratislava, the U.S. Consul came backstage to thank and compliment us. American students also showed up, as well as relatives of some of our players. It was a rousing climax to the Tour. Everyone felt that they'd given their best. They had been weighed in the balance and found to have given full measure.

High on the Stuttgart reception, there was plenty of time to float back to earth during the exhausting 18-hour trip home. It was and they did.

This had been another dream of a Tour: good and thorough planning had paid off; no serious illness, minor ailments well cared for by our friendly Tour Doc; only one mislaid suitcase, one lost camera; one-and-a-half problem children. Lots of acclaim and satisfaction. Next to catch up on sleep and homework.

Safely back home, we picked up the threads of the season and looked forward to the April 30 program of my choral music. The Oregon Repertory Singers, under the gifted guest director, Ron Jeffers, were joined by a new group, the Choral Cross-ties, organized by Bruce Browne, and the resident choir of the host church, Westminister Presbyterian, under Susan McBerry. In that lovely and resonant room they presented a cross section of my choral works spanning some 40 years. It was a moving experience for me to hear this sound-spectrum of my life and to relate the background of their composition.

Continuing in the choral vein, the Orchestra's grand finale was the Berlioz *Requiem.* This fabulous work calls for—in addition to a large chorus and orchestra—four brass choirs placed at the corners of the hall. The full range of the PYP was brought in to fulfill this requirement. Alumni and selected members of the Prep Orchestra manned the battlements of the Civic Auditorium.

The other work on the program was *Raptures on Madrigals of Gesualdo,* the last of my compositions to be done in the festival. It was splendidly conducted by Donald Thulean, who had premiered it with his Spokane Symphony in 1982.

Thus ended the 65th Anniversary Season, and here begin the reviews earned. Then we turn back to the beginning, with Jacques Gershkovitch's first concert in 1925, and come steadily forward to the 64th Season. Many readers will be astonished to find four or five reviews of the early concerts. These days, when most U.S. cities are reduced to a single newspaper, it is hard to believe that Portland had so many in the 1920s. They all took a passionate interest in the founding and steady progress of this pioneer Orchestra, and in the acclaim it achieved across the nation and beyond. To read their accounts is to rejoice.

65th Anniversary Season

Jacob Avshalomov, Conductor

August 30, 1988

WATERFRONT CLASSICS

Retrospective program from the season

David Avshalomov, Guest Conductor

September 17, 1988

Dedicatory Concerts – Newport Performing Arts Center

Retrospective program

Jacob Avshalomov & Eugene Kaza Conducting

November 12, 1988

SCHUMANN Manfred Overture

BARTOK Piano Concerto NO. 3

Linda Lorati Barker, *Soloist*

AVSHALOMOV The Taking of T'ung Kuan

Eugene Kaza Conducting

BARBER Adagio for Strings

GOULD Latin-American Symphonette

December 2, 1988

7th Annual

SING-YOUR-OWN-MESSIAH

with Guest Conductors: James Day, Mary Margaret Dundore, Jerry Wesley Harris, Ron Jeffers, Ernestine Oringdulph, Gil Seeley, Edwin Snyder

Civic Auditorium

December 26, 1988

CONCERT AT CHRISTMAS

ALUMNI & PREPARATORY ORCHESTRAS

Nancy Malos Johnson Conducting the U.S. premiere of Open Sesame! by Jacob Avshalomov

---

February 13, 1989

Winningstad Theater

AVSHALOMOV FESTIVAL CHAMBER MUSIC PROGRAM

Alyce Rogers, *Mezzo-soprano;* Daniel Avshalomov, *Viola*

Harold Gray, *Piano; & Alumni Winds & Brass*

February 25, 1989

Portland Youth Philharmonic 65th &

Jacob Avshalomov 35th Anniversary Concert

BEETHOVEN Leonore Overture NO. 2

FAURE Elegie for Cello

Brad Ritchie, *Soloist*

MARCELLO Oboe Concerto, C minor

Shannon Sprenger, *Soloist*

AVSHALOMOV Phases of the Great Land

David Avshalomov Conducting

SIBELIUS Symphony NO. 2

March 16–31, 1989

FOURTH INTERNATIONAL TOUR

Austria – Czechoslovakia – Hungary – West Germany

April 30, 1989

AVSHALOMOV FESTIVAL CHORAL PROGRAM

Westminister Presbyterian Church

Oregon Repertory Singers, Ron Jeffers *Conducting*

Choral Cross-ties, Bruce Browne, *Director*

Westminister Presbyterian Church Choir, Sue McBerry, *Director*

May 7, 1989

Civic Auditorium

AVSHALOMOV *Raptures for Orchestra on Madrigals of Gesualdo

Donald Thulean Conducting

BERLIOZ Requiem

Guest Choirs: Portland State University & Choral Cross-ties, Bruce Browne, *Director;* Lutheran Choral Association, Stan Bleything, Director with Alumni & Preparatory Orchestra Brass Choirs

---

* *Portland Premiere*

THE SUNDAY OREGONIAN NOV. 13, 1988

Youth Philharmonic does Jimmy Eoff proud

By PHIL HUNT
of The Oregonian Staff

MUSIC REVIEW

Jimmy Eoff would have been proud. His favorite orchestra, the Portland Youth Philharmonic, played a magnificent concert Saturday night, and Samuel Barber's Adagio for Strings was dedicated to his memory.

On Sept. 18, Eoff died at age 81. He had been a member of the original orchestra under the direction of the late Jacques Gershkovitch and later the assistant conductor to both Gershkovitch and Jacob Avshalomov.

The Barber number is a soaring, eloquent dirge. The orchestra played it so beautifully that it seemed almost inappropriate that there would be applause.

But applause there was throughout the evening, and especially for Linda Lorati Barker, one-time youth soloist with the orchestra in 1971 who returned to perform the demanding Bela Bartok Piano Concerto No. 3.

The second movement is a delightful interlude, like a love duet between the piano and the woodwinds with sounds like birdcalls that are echoed back and forth. Barker was tender when the music cried for a light touch and heavy on the bombastic opening of the third movement and again at the pounding climax.

The Bartok concerto is demanding for the orchestra, as well, and they responded freely to Avshalomov's direction.

In an evening of high points, the performance of one of Avshalomov's own compositions, "The Taking of T'ung Kuan," won a warm response, under the direction of Eugene Kaza, assistant to the conductor.

Based on a Chinese poem about a great battle between "the barbarian horde" and "the army of the House of Han" that took place by the Great Wall in the remote past, the music depicts the two groups at first quietly camped and then moves along with them into battle.

Avshalomov comes from the Russian tradition of composers who were strong on tonal color and orchestration—Nikolai Rimsky-Korsakov, Modest Moussorgsky, Aleksander Borodin—and his composition with its strong use of brass and woodwinds contrasted to the strings is in that tradition. The final clashing dissonance is almost unbelievable.

The program opened with Robert Schumann's "Manfred" Overture, based on a poem by George Gordon Byron. The music is thick, often moody and brooding, with an overlying tension. It requires vigorous action by the entire orchestra.

One small quibble. Avshalomov has moved the cellos away from the front of the stage, behind the viola section. At one point where the cellos were playing alone and in unison, their sound did not carry well.

Avshalomov closed the program with the sophisticated Latin American Symphonette by Morton Gould. The work's four parts are titled: Rhumba, Tango, Guaracha and Conga. The sections are all colorful, and the final is a triumph for percussion and brass, with many jazzy touches. Altogether, it was a satisfying evening.

Jimmy Eoff would have loved it.

THE OREGONIAN FEB. 26, 1989

Preview of program impressive

By DAVID STABLER
of The Oregonian Staff

The flurry of celebrations marking important anniversaries of the Portland Youth Philharmonic and its conductor have tended to overshadow another landmark for the group. In three weeks, the Philharmonic will embark on its fourth international tour, a two-week trip to Hungary, Austria, Czechoslovakia and West Germany.

On Saturday night at the Arlene Schnitzer Concert Hall, the Philharmonic presented a partial preview of what it will play on the tour.

Between the scheduled works on the program, Avshalomov was honored for his 35-year contribution as conductor and music director, and the orchestra was honored for its longevity—65 years—and prestige among youth orchestras in the country. It is the country's first youth orchestra, and, judging by the playing Saturday, it continues to merit its reputation.

Avshalomov led off with Beethoven's "Leonore" Overture No. 2, an adrenalin-filled performance that featured some lovely flute playing by Linda Bailey. Trumpet player Tom Kiso delivered his two offstage horn calls with daring and wonderful tone.

Cellist Brad Ritchie performed Gabriel Fauré's "Elegie" with the orchestra, giving his lines an intensity and a warmth that was a pleasure to hear. He is a mature performer.

Shannon Sprenger stepped up to perform Marcello's Oboe Concerto in C Minor. She played accurately and musically, investing the second movement with smooth, round tones.

Avshalomov's son, David, led the full orchestra in his father's 1959 ode to Alaska, "Phases of the Great Land." The music painted vivid pictures of the frozen north. Klondike fever and the northern lights, then switched to the theme of modern Alaska as a bustling air crossroads.

David Avshalomov, who came from his post with the Santa Monica Chamber Orchestra, will accompany the orchestra to Europe. He has led the orchestra several times in the past.

Jacob Avshalomov returned to conduct the great Second Symphony of Jan Sibelius. It was a concentrated performance that stressed flexibility of phrasing and tone. The ebb and flow of the first movement brought out the themes in a natural, unforced way. The orchestral sound, especially in the final movement, was lush and alive.

Youth Philharmonic alumni shine in concert

By **PHIL HUNT**
of The Oregonian Staff

MUSIC REVIEW

What do talented and dedicated young musicians sound like when they grow up?

A crowd that filled all but the second balcony of Arlene Schnitzer Concert Hall found out Monday night when the Portland Youth Philharmonic Alumni Orchestra, made up of 90 former members, returned home for a grand reunion under the direction of Jacob Avshalomov, the orchestra's longtime conductor and musical director.

There were some flubs, a few sour notes, and obviously a few embouchures that have relaxed over the years. But it was hardly noticeable.

It was a big night for Avshalomov, himself an alumnus whose composition "Open Sesame!" received a vigorous reading under the direction of Nancy Malos Johnson, an alumna who commissioned the work when she was director of a youth orchestra in New Zealand five years ago.

Alumnus Roger Kaza fills in

Avshalomov also shared the podium with another alumnus, Roger Kaza, who filled in for his father, Eugene Kaza, in conducting the Portland Youth Philharmonic Preparatory Orchestra. That group shared the program with the alumni orchestra.

The elder Kaza, who serves regularly as the assistant to Avshalomov and conducts the preparatory group in its weekly rehearsals, underwent an emergency appendectomy, but Avshalomov reported he is recovering.

Roger Kaza led the preps, who range in age from 9 to 18, in "Symphonette" by KcKay. Avshalomov conducted them in Brahms' "Hungarian Dance No. 5" and in Anderson's "Christmas Festival," based on well-known Christmas carols.

Now associated with the St. Louis Symphony, Roger Kaza also was featured a French horn soloist in Saint-Saens' "Morceau de Concert" and showed the technique that has made him an outstanding performer.

The alumni opened the program with Weber's "Euryanthe" Overture, which sounded well-rounded, considering a short rehearsal schedule for many of the musicians, who came from as far as Boston, Honolulu and New Haven, Conn.

Twins Jonathan and Gregory Dubay on violin and cello were joined by oboist Richard Olsen and bassoonist Mary Ellen Harris as they performed the first movement of the Haydn "Quartet concertante" in a delightful reading.

Nine former members of the orchestra were featured in Menotti's "Triple Concerto a Tre." They included Michael Hanson, violin; Steve Price, viola; Andrew Eckard, cello; Pablo Izquierdo, oboe; Todd Kuhn, clarinet; Janice Richardson, bassoon; Linda Barker, piano; Jenny Lindner, harp; and Fred Morgenstern, percussion.

The "Spoleto Brass Quintet"—Steve Conrow and Craig Gibson, trumpets; Dot Rust, horn; David Bryan, trombone; and Michael Grose, tuba—added sparkle to the program with brass arrangements of Handel's "Royal Fireworks" and selections from Bernsteins's "West Side Story." Their rendition of "Maria" was a joy to hear.

THE OREGONIAN MAY 9, 1989

'Amen' fitting conclusion to Philharmonic season

By DAVID STABLER
of The Oregonian staff

The Portland Youth Philharmonic ended its 65th season with a quiet "Amen" Sunday night. It was a fitting finale to a season that took the 100-member orchestra from opening ceremonies at the Newport Performing Arts Center last fall to concerts in four European countries this spring.

Sunday's "Amen" sounded the final note of one of the 19th century's great choral works: the Requiem by Hector Berlioz. The orchestra performed it with 175 singers at the Civic Auditorium.

Jacob Avshalomov conducted with deliberate pacing and loving attention to the work's beauty. With the combined choruses of Choral Cross-Ties, the Portland State University Choir and the Lutheran Choral Association filling the back of the stage, the majestic music emerged in full glory.

Spine-tingling moments came in the terrifying "Dies Irae" as one by one, the four brass choirs joined the performers from distant corners of the hall. With a wave of his hand, Avshalomov cued each group until all four were "spreading a wondrous sound." Then, at last, the timpani began rolling its thunderous charge. Surely, there is no more awe-inspiring description of the Day of Judgement.

Members of the Preparatory Orchestra mixed skillfully with former philharmonic players in the brass choirs.

Choral highlights came in the unaccompanied "Quaerens Me" and the lovely, multi-layered "Offertorium." Ragged and insecure entrances marred the singing in a few other places.

The orchestra played with evident discipline and tenor Bruce Browne sang the "Sanctus" solo ably.

The concert opened with Avshalomov's "Raptures for Orchestra on Madrigals of Gesualdo." Twenty-two members of Choral Cross-Ties san three Renaissance madrigals, accompanied by the orchestra. Donald Thulean of Washington, D.C. conducted. Thulean also conducted the work's premiere in 1982.

The very idea of the piece was delightful: The orchestra's role was to comment on, explain, repeat and enhance each song. First the choir would have a go, singing various lengths of the madrigal as written, then the orchestra would take over.

One reason this worked so well was Gesualdo's clever harmonic writing. Chords shift easily and effortlessly, with sometimes startling results. The orchestra played cleanly, giving the grateful listener another shot at Gesualdo's magic transformations.

STUTTGART, WEST GERMANY
STUTTGARTER NACHRITTEN MAR. 30, 1989

Musik in Stuttgart

REMARKABLE CALIBRE

Portland Youth Orchestra in the Beethovensaal. Though the group has already had six concerts during their European tour (on the occasion of their 65th anniversary), there was no evidence of any fatigue among the roughly 100 young musicians, ages 12–22. This concert, with the sponsorship of Daimler-Benz, was *the only appearance of the Youth Orchestra* in the Federal Republic. The hall was practically sold out; the audience youthful. Both technically and musically the performance demonstrated a remarkable level of achievement; Avshalomov has his young troops well in hand. Among the first-desk players (especially in the woodwind and brass sections) there are some that would do honor to professional orchestras.

The *Adagio for Strings* by Samuel Barber was played with intensity and conviction, demonstrating a fine, homogeneous string tone; after this the players easily got into the swing of Aaron Copland's *Hoedown.*

Gershwin's *Porgy and Bess Suite* and Schumann's *Manfred Symphony,* on the other hand, were somewhat anemic, partly because Avshalomov seemed to lack a feeling for the right tempos.

The most lasting impression was made by the rendition of Sibelius' *Second Symphony;* a moving, tonally beautiful performance, especially by the strings and horns. One forgot that one was listening to a group made up, mostly, of adolescents—not professional musicians.

The orchestra acknowledged the enthusiastic applause by playing a bouquet of encores.

Fleißige Musikarbeiter, viel Dschingderassabum

STUTTGART, WEST GERMANY
STUTTGARTER ZEITUNG MAR. 30, 1989

HARD-WORKING MUSICIANS —LOTS OF TSING-BOOM

The Portland Youth Philharmonic Orchestra in the Liederhalle— America always victorious

The orchestra we heard provides a *jumping-off place for young musicians:* those who win the tough American competitions, who win a place in a good youth orchestra, may soon receive a call to higher levels: Boston, Chicago, or Philadelphia. The Portland Orchestra is 65 years old; it has proved, year after year, that its formula (good training and good follow-up) works well.

For the opening number the son conducted the father: but David Avshalomov could not save the early composition by Daddy Jacob. What we heard was loud, rather than picturesque, program music—picturing the battle for the Chinese mountain pass at Tung-Kuan. Lots of tsing-boom and battle noise—movie music which, in spite of a crescendoing Adagio, would have made a fitting sound track for the battle of Pearl Harbor. The playing, especially by the strings was technically above reproach; yet it could not compensate for the slickness of the interpretation—a quality that characterizes many American orchestras, even where European players provide a "domesticating" influence.

Samuel Barber's neoclassic hit, *Adagio for Strings,* had the refrigerator-cool charm of a model wearing too much makeup. Aaron Copland's *"Hoedown"* from the ballet *Rodeo* came across as a lame, tired little dance, with giggling oboes. Nice and clean, but lacking emotional engagement—that is the way the Portlanders came across.

Schumann's *Manfred Overture,* played at sight, could hardly be effective. Considering the conductor's broad tempos the musicians might have played their heart out, but the result still would not have been impressive.

Sibelius' *Second Symphony* proved that the excellent leading players (especially among the brass) only need inspired conducting in order to shine. Here we heard more than mere machine-like finger dexterity; we heard music that we understood. It was the farewell of these hard-working, highly talented musical workers. Maybe the Portland springboard will catapult them somewhere else where they can develop, and be developed, into artists.

Mirko Weber

AMERIKABOL JOTTUNK...

SOPRON, HUNGARY
KISALFOLD MAR. 27, 1989

WE'VE COME FROM AMERICA

For the closing chords of the Sopron Spring Days the Portland Youth Philharmonic gave a concert as part of their European Tour. In this country we expect youth ensembles to be well-meaning, dilettante groups that play slightly off-key. This orchestra of 91 members, however, thoroughly contradicted all our expectations. They played clearly and with discipline worthy of professionals.

As their leader, 70 year-old Jacob Avshalomov told us, they were very glad to be able to come to our country, being familiar with outstanding Hungarian musicians and our musical traditions through the work of Kodaly and Bartok. Only a small fraction of its members are preparing to become professional musicians—most of them are amateurs. But it is also true that the great orchestras of Boston and New York count on some of them for recruits.

Conducting the concert in Sopron was David Avshalomov, son of the leading Conductor. In him, we came to know an expressive, sure-handed musician: Beethoven's 2nd Leonore overture stayed within European tradition. We have come to expect that musicians from abroad try to "outperform" the musicians of our continent in terms of tempo and interpretation.

Following this, we heard two real American pieces. The movement from Copland's Rodeo Ballet conjured up the folk music of the Wild West. R. Russell Bennett worked the best-known parts of Gershwin's opera, Porgy & Bess, into a well-formed, enjoyable Suite . . . moving the whole audience and making them feel like dancing.

Faure's Elegie, for cello and orchestra is not a demanding piece; rather, it affects the listener with its wistful, dreamy mood. Brad Ritchie, the assistant principal cellist, performed the piece with deep feeling and with clarity, carrying out the brief virtuoso passages flawlessly.

Jacob Avshalomov was born in China. From his Chinese memories he created his symphonic piece, "The Taking of T'ung Kuan". In it we hear (within an American framework) the mystical voice of the Far East, the ancient pentatony, the eerie gongs and clatter of percussion. The Orchestra gave this well-structured, technically demanding work a lucid performance.

After the intermission they played Dvorak's 9th Symphony, "From the New World". The Orchestra did an excellent job in carrying out this difficult task—aside from a few inaccuracies—probably the result of fatigue.

After long applause from the audience, there followed several encores, Barber: Adagio for Strings, Sousa: March, and M. Gould: Tango.

Regarding this excellent concert we have only one serious complaint: all too few Sopron musicians took an interest in it.

Gabor Valtinyi

KEESKÉMET, HUNGARY MAR. 25, 1989

Festival of Young Talent

Portland Youth Philharmonic

Maybe it was coincidence, maybe it was the good idea of the organizers that the final event of the Kecskemét Spring Days turned into a real festival of young talent.

The performers of the concert that took place in the Ferenc Erdei Cultural Center came from the United States, in fact, from its farthest point, the city of Portland in the State of Oregon. The musicians, who are between 12 and 22 years of age, made Kecskemét a station on their international tour—after Linz, Bratislava and Budapest. From the prospectus, which listed their program for the entire tour, I realized that they came prepared with at least three evening's worth of music.

The concert began with Schuman's Manfred Overture, in whose interpretation there was still too much sentimentality. The romantic overture, which demanded a lot from the ensemble both musically and technically, seems to have exceeded the young musicians' preparation. But the next number, Marcello's Oboe Concerto in c minor, was a pleasure to hear, performed by a young lady, as was Director and conductor Jacob Avshalomov's outstanding character-piece titled Phases of the Great Land. The winds sounded nice in the first movement of Dvorak's IX. New World Symphony, and Gershwin's Porgy and Bess suite was a genuine success.

The encore, Gould's *Guaracha,* a rich, lively and witty piece was a real experience.

Publikumspleite für Amis

LINZ, AUSTRIA
OBEROESTERREICHISCHES TAGBLATT MAR. 22, 1989

PORTLAND YOUTH PHILHARMONIC AT THE BRUCKNER HOUSE

Small Audience for Americans

The Portland Youth Philharmonic comes from the northwest state of Oregon in the USA. The Orchestra, composed of young musicians with remarkable ability, performed at the Bruckner House in Linz for a small audience.

A program with considerable variety was prepared for the Fourth International Tour of the Orchestra. Fourteen works, some full symphonies. Jacob Avshalomov, a spirited and mindful maestro who also introduced himself as composer, directed the orchestra. His "Phases of the Great Land", colorfully instrumented, based on folk melodies, but also a nature-based orchestral work—a little trivial and happy-go-lucky, was directed by his son David.

The other American works were the broad "Adagio for Strings" by Samuel Barber and the showy Latin-American Symphonette by Morton Gould. Music full of temperament which we would probably group in the category for entertainment.

However, the evening offered something serious as well. Schumann's Manfred Overture and the wonderful 3rd piano concert of Bartok with Endre Hegedus as outstanding soloist. Especially the deeply expressive 2nd movement and the ravishing finale were extremely successful.

LINZ, AUSTRIA
NEUE KRONENZEITUNG MAR. 22, 1989

KONZERTE KURZ

In its 65th year, the Portland Youth Philharmonic, under the direction of Jacob Avshalomov, undertakes a European Tour, supported by approximately two dozen sponsors.

The hundred musician group included great romantic symphonic works and easy-to-listen-to contemporary American music in the concert program. The musicians from overseas began, in the sparsely seated Bruckner House, with the Manfred Overture which gave an altogether intimidated impression.

Followed by the precisely worked out piano concerto No. 3 by Bartok, with the young Hungarian Endre Hegedus. After the intermission we heard Barber's "Adagio for Strings", some compositions influenced by Chinese impressions of the conductor, Jacob Avshalomov, and Morton Gould's Latin-American Symphonette, a composition particularly refreshing and suitable for young musicians.

LINZ, AUSTRIA
NEUES VOLKSBLATT MAR. 22, 1989

AMERICAN YOUTH ORCHESTRA IN LINZ

Greetings from Portland

Amerikanisches Jugendorchester in Linz

Ein Gruß aus Portland

The young ladies approached the podium in dark blue angel gowns, the young men, in black and white. The Portland Youth Philharmonic, on its European Tour, performed at the Bruckner House in Linz. Today, the pioneers of this orchestra are quite advanced in age, since the orchestra has been in existence for 65 years. Jacob Avshalomov has been conductor since 1954.

A mixed program, some bowing to the European heritage, some presentations of newer American music, promised interesting variety. In the beginning, Robert Schumann's Manfred Overture was a disappointment. The strings played "porridge-like" and non-homogeneous, while the brass had to 'fight' with the intricacies of their instruments. The high levels which the European youth orchestras have established, could not be reached.

The musicians were able to have Hungarian Endre Hegedus for the Third Piano Concerto by Bartok. The 35 year-old felt at home with this work. With a relaxed hand, he led through the piece which Bartok had composed for his wife Ditta. Some nonchalance instead precision did not harm the interpretation.

The second half of the evening was a representation of American music. Works of Jacob Avshalomov, Samuel Barber and Morton Gould gave the young musicians from Portland opportunity to play in lively fashion. In Barber's "Adagio for Strings" they were able to demonstrate 'string culture'.

Večerník

Oživili koncertnú sezónu

BRATISLAVA, CZECHOSLOVAKIA
VECERNIZ MAR. 28, 1989

THEY ENLIVENED THE CONCERT SEASON

—Young Musicians from Portland

On the evening of March 22nd the Portland Youth Philharmonic performed in the Redouta (Philharmonic Hall) and the audience followed with delight the vigor by which the nearly 100 young musicians from the distant State of Oregon showed their musicianship. The mood in the hall was excellent, due to the guests from the USA who demonstrated through expressive music that this kind of art can really build bridges of instant understanding, and due also to the listeners—most of whom were music-loving and music-studying Bratislava youth.

As an overture to this concert there was a mid-morning meeting between members of the Portland orchestra and students of VSMU (College of Musical Arts) who gave an exemplary recital where the American students could appreciate the sophisticated level of our musical college students.

In the evening the full house in the Redouta was an excellent backdrop to a program exhibiting rich dramaturgy. While the origins of the Portland orchestra go back to 1927, the constant regeneration guarantees it perpetual youth. Thus we saw on the stage 13 to 22 year-old musicians led by their conductor, Jacob Avshalomov (who has worked with them since 1954): a dignified, gray haired artist full of youthful energy belieing his age.

He obviously had not only the respect, but also the affection of his charges.

The Portland Youth Philharmonic introduced itself effectively in a repertoire partly American, with works of A. Copland, (Dance from The Suite Rodeo), G. Gershwin (Suite from the Opera Porgy & Bess), and S. Barber's Adagio for Strings. The second part of the program was European. We heard Ravel's concert rhapsody Tzigane—with our violinist Juraj Cizmarovic, and for the orchestra the rather demanding Second Symphony in D major, Op. 43 by J. Sibelius.

The most characteristic features of the orchestra are its inner energy and dynamism of youth. These occasionally substituted for precision and accuracy of individual sections (woodwinds). On the other hand the better coordinated string section attracted us with an affectionate, detailed and expressive presentation of the Adagio for Strings by S. Barber. The more popular quality of the first half of the program also captivated the audience with the rhythmic energy and "authentic" expression of Gershwin's opera suite.

The center of attention in Ravel's Tzigane was the Slovak violinist Juraj Cizmarovic, who was able to present "his" rendition expressively. Considering the instrument he now owns, he preferred the less obvious poetic, supple and elegiac aspects of the piece, with elements of stylized Hungarian music, rather than the overly energetic, passionate features. His performance accorded with the reputation of the young talented violinist, showing the highest artistic standards: precise in details as well as in the larger structural aspects, personal in interpretation, and congruent with the conception of the conductor.

In the Sibelius Second Symphony—extensive in form, challenging in its structure and apt to fall apart if individual beautiful motives were stressed too much—the most notable sections were, again, those which relied on the synchronized work of the strings, broad, romantically agitated music of the Vivacissimo. Jacob Avshalomov, who showed a good understanding of the mentality, capacity and interest of his proteges, stressed mainly the emotional and melodic beauty of the Sibelius, whereas in the Copland, Gershwin, Barber and Ravel works he emphasized youthful energy, natural rhythmic potential of young musicians, and fun, in all the compositions of that evening's program (including several encores).

What may have been not totally precise in details was overcome by an evident zest for playing and an emotional involvement. The Portland Youth Philharmonic was an excellent additional example to our discussion of the influence of superior art on the education of young people and their humanistic development. The admirable organization of the group's tour (publicity materials, audio-visual documentation of their concerts, chaperones, sponsors, etc.) gave us a glimpse of the methods used to form and channel the musical interest of a certain segment of American youth.

The Gershkovitch Era

ORIGINS

The Orchestra's prehistory began in Burns, Oregon, in 1912 where Mary V. Dodge, a Boston-trained violinist, formed a group of children that came to be known as the Sagebrush Symphony. As early as 1915 it had toured eastern Oregon for the Redpath Chatauqua, and a year later it played at the state fair in Salem. Mrs. Dodge and her husband moved to Portland where she continued her devoted work with a new group that gathered around her pupils. At about the time the ensemble had grown to the point where a real conductor was needed, Jacques Gershkovitch and his wife arrived in the city. A graduate of the St. Petersburg Imperial Conservatory, he had been conducting in Tokyo when the great earthquake of 1923 caused them to leave Japan; he hoped to find a post with some professional orchestra in America.

When Mary Dodge saw him guest-conduct the Portland Symphony, she was convinced that he was the man who could make her idea of a complete student orchestra come to life. Going to his home with some of her young players, she asked if he would consider working with her group. He was doubtful, having never worked with children, but she urged him to come hear them, and it was arranged. Her son Glen, then age 12, remembers greeting the Gershkovitches and ushering them up into the attic of the Dodge house where the group was assembled. After hearing them, Gershkovitch said, "I take." Even though he con-

sidered it an interim assignment, he promptly set the tone of serious work and authentic repertoire. Almost without knowing it, he established a tradition. The excitement and determination which gripped those early rehearsals resulted in the historic first concert on Valentine's Day, February 14, 1925. The concert was acclaimed, as the first review attests. The word spread, attracting many recruits. The work of the founding teacher had hitched up to the founding Conductor, and the Portland Junior Symphony's history had truly begun.

From its first concert the Orchestra was greeted with open-mouthed wonder by the public and press. It continued to elicit the same response for the next few decades. And so, while social and political observers in the 1920s worried about the way young people were being brought up in Fascist and Communist countries with regimented, paramilitary activities and massed gymnastics, here in the United States we innocently pursued competitive athletics and music in our public schools. These two pursuits were combined, in fact, in a movement unprecedented in any country, by the matchmaking of the great instrument manufacturing companies of the Midwest where school and college games were cheered on by their bands. This resulted in the most active student musical life in the world which, in turn, culminated in our professional orchestras, which became the standard for the world.

Irvington School Orchestra, which Gershkovitch auditioned and agreed to lead.

In Portland, the development of the PJS was chronicled by an array of local newspapers and journals that few people now living can remember: *The News, The Telegram, The Oregon Journal, Portland Oregonian, Rose City Herald, The Spectator, The Scribe, Music & Musicians, Musical Leader,* and others. As they reported the concern over Amundsen's silence on his North Pole expedition, by plane, speculated on the overthrow of warlord Chang Tso-lin in Peking (my family and I were there at that moment!), and relayed requests from London for U.S. financial support in restoring the Shakespearean theatre at Stratford-on-Avon, the local press also reported the formation of a Board of Directors for the newborn Portland Junior Symphony Orchestra. It had been in existence for nearly a year when some parents of the players realized the need to broaden the Orchestra's scope and formed a committee of seven members to carry on its activities.

GATHERING MOMENTUM

After the Orchestra's second concert in the spring of 1925, a meeting was held in the Central Library which resulted in the formation of a Board of Directors and their statement of purpose quoted earlier. Within the year, Mrs. Dodge's activities were transferred to Los Angeles where her civil-engineer husband's business had taken him.

Gathering momentum, progress was strong for the PJS on at least three fronts: Recognition and praise for the work of the Orchestra and its conductor, support for and expansion of the educational program by auxiliary activities, and fund-raising in various and imaginative ways.

At the beginning of its second season, the PJS played a concert at the Municipal Auditorium for the national convention of the Federation of Music Clubs. A boxed ad in the 1926 *Oregonian* trumpeted the fact that the PJS was one of only four such orchestras in the world, the others being in Berlin, Petrograd, and New York. An editorial suggested that Jacques Gershkovitch, builder and conductor of the PJS, should be endowed as a permanent institution: "These 97 boys and girls, guided by musical genius and his backers, have brought countrywide distinction to Portland." One of the chief backers, Board President John N. Edelfson, was called "the grand man of the PJS" by *The Telegram.*

At the end of the third season, Jacques Gershkovitch, in addition to running the Gershkovitch Conservatory, a Gershkovitch Orchestra, and the PJS, found time to sally forth to New York where he conducted 80 members of the New York Philharmonic in a concert at Town Hall. It was a great success. Back home at a banquet for both the Board and the Orchestra, he reported that he'd heard two youth groups in the East, and they had both needed professional players for their first chairs. He proudly contrasted the tradition of the PJS, with the eastern approach and praised the vision of the Board.

A letter to the editor of *The Journal* urged that the PJS be sent to the Chicago World's Fair. The writer had studied at the conservatories of Leipzig, Frankfurt, and Brussels and noted that, unlike the PJS, the orchestras of all three needed to fill out their ranks with pros.

In 1933 the Central Labor Council heard a talk about "the need for music as a means of softening the harshness of life and filling the leisure hours that result from the scarcity of gainful work." In hopes of offsetting the effects of the Depression the PJS added a fourth concert to its season. As a special attraction, the boy prodigy, Harry Cykman, age 10, was brought from San Francisco to play with the Orchestra.

The Spectator, which ran a pagewide headline, "World Peace Endangered by Hitlerism," also bravely ran a picture of the PJS with a headline of equal size, "Cultural Portland Develops High Ideals in Junior Symphony."

Support for the expansion of the Orchestra's educational program began early, with a lecture at the Central Library on the music of a forthcoming PJS concert. In 1932 the first essay contest was held for school children, with the suggested topic, "What the PJS means to me"..."to Portland,"..."to Oregon." The essay of the second contest's winner, a freshman at Columbia University, was quoted at column length in *The Oregonian.* In later years, various other contests were held, for notebooks, artwork, and program-cover design. One *Sunday Oregonian* pictured *all* the orchestra's principal players. Concerts were given at numerous school assemblies around the city, with the idea that children are inspired by seeing others their own age excel. Reciprocally, articles began appearing in high-school papers at Benson Polytechnic, Commerce, Franklin, Jefferson, and Washington. One article picked up a quote from Haydn on his "Surprise" symphony, "the women will scream" (at the unexpected chords).

In a featured article by Board member Katherine Noyes in *The Spectator,* outlining the value of the PJS, she took pains to emphasize that it was not in competition with the school music groups—an indication that this problem, which became endemic, showed a fever early on. PJS players who also played in their school bands and orchestras were listed in the printed program, as were the private teachers of Orchestra members.

In 1930 student conductors made their first appearance in public: Eugene Linden and Fred Rothchild, both taught by Jacques Gershkovitch. The following year Assistant Concertmaster Geraldine Peterson's *Suite of Oregon Scenes,* was performed at a concert. Beginning in 1936 program notes were written by students, notably Bill Lamont, Joe Karasick, and Roy Stillwell, as well as the present writer.

Money-raising efforts took many forms. A Children's Book Week Tea was sponsored by the Literary Division of the Federation of Women's Clubs, at which PJS members played chamber music. A Silver Tea was held by the Monday Musical Club. The Soroptimists Club attended the first concert of the 1928 season as a group and in a later year adopted the PJS as their "major civic interest." A note in the 1933 programs encouraged the public to send gifts to the scholarship fund instead of flowers to soloists.

In 1927 a request was made to the City Council for the free use of Municipal Auditorium. It was granted because "the Orchestra is important in character-building, and this decision would not create a troublesome precedent due to the distinctly educational nature of the activity." The same request did not fare as well in 1938 when it was turned down because "it might get out of hand."

Entertaining at dinner before the concerts, and sometimes after (when the starting hour was early), became fashionable. But all was not plain sailing: A letter to the Editor of *The Oregonian* deplored the apathy toward support of the Orchestra, and went on to quote *The Saturday Evening Post* on the need for "character building" agencies (clearly a current cause).

One of the most ambitious and successful fund-raisers was the combination of carnival and concert held at the home of Mrs. Edna J. Frank, wife of the head of Meier and Frank Department Store. They lived on an estate called Fir Acres, with a mansion, extensive landscaped grounds, and a swimming pool. Special buses were arranged for and thousands of citizens attended. A circular stressed that it was "NOT A HIGHBROW society party, but a festival for everyone to enjoy." And they did. The event was called "Inspiration Days of 1932," and people paid 25 cents to hear the music and view the famous gardens. Since 1960 the estate has been the site of Lewis and Clark College.

Mrs. Frank was the second President of the PJS Association, and as Edna Holmes (in her second marriage) she continued to be a patron of the Orchestra into her 90s. Her daughter, Dorothy Sherman, served as an equally dedicated President a generation later.

Membership in the Association numbered 600 in 1928, 700 the next season, and in 1928 it leveled off at about 900. In 1934 a big campaign for membership was set for mid September. A speakers committee was organized and chaired by Frank Branch Riley, widely recognized as an "orator." All the papers carried long stories supporting the drive. It was endorsed by the Superintendent of Schools, C. A. Rice, street cars carried signs noting PJS Week, which had been proclaimed by Mayor Carson. He went further, urging citizens to "take a personal part in telling the people of Portland and vicinity of the tremendous value of the PJS to the City, to the Portland Symphony, and to other musical organizations, broadcasting the name of the PJS throughout the world."

Within a year of each other, the CBS, NBC, and Mutual networks had all broadcast a program of the Orchestra's concerts, and these were having a wide effect. Plaudits came in from far and wide: Rockhill, South Carolina; New Haven, Connecticut; New York; and Pasadena, California. The Fresno Bee Radio Playhouse broadcast a PJS concert as part of a program which featured movie stars in a tribute to Admiral Byrd's Antarctic Expedition. Leopold Stokowski wrote

Katherine Noyes asking about ways to model a youth orchestra for Philadelphia along the PJS lines. A pundit on the lecture circuit predicted "Europe will understand America when we have a culture produced by democracy, as distinct from their 'class-culture', and the PJS is a sign of this."

A noted criminologist visiting Portland said, "youths who develop self-discipline through an apprenticeship to trade or hobby are vaccinated against crime for 20 years. Activities such as the PJS will reduce the crime rate for 1938" (a decade away). *The Telegram* editorialized, "the young orchestra doesn't need the word 'junior' any longer; and besides music the students gain discipline, morals and manners, attention, obedience, unselfishness, reliability—all by-products which add up to good citizenship."

But Hilmar Grondahl, longtime music critic for *The Oregonian* and PJS Board member, insisted, "don't dwell too much on the side-benefits of the Orchestra, but rather on the 'musical beauties'."

These, of course, derived from the Orchestra's conductor, Jacques Gershkovitch. One paper headlined, "How Do They Do It?" *The Telegram* congratulated new members of the PJS on their acceptance. After a visit to Portland Moses Menuhin, father of Yehudi, said, "This is a miracle. Those sweet-faced, serious young boys and girls who play in dead earnest possess a refinement and spiritual intelligence unknown among our typically materialistic, prize-fighting, funnysheet-fed youngsters. You in Portland are all fathers to a newborn idea in our American cultural life."

Again, *The Oregonian*: "Mr. Gershkovitch is ever a magnetic, restless and talented master-conductor, with a wise mixture of firmness and kindly good nature, enforcing the needed discipline. He is also a shrewd psychologist. After a grueling rehearsal, when the players are tired and cross he will offer 'a good thought to take home'."

After visiting Portland and hearing the PJS, Mrs. Artie Mason Carter, founder of the Hollywood Bowl, hosted a gathering in Los Angeles to discuss ways of organizing a Junior Symphony there. She quoted the conductor Artur Rodzinski on the Curtis Institute, "Not every city can afford a Curtis, but every city does have a wealth of talent which needs the careful discipline of a well-conducted orchestra." The director of the National Child Welfare Division of the American Legion raved about the PJS and noted, "we don't have one in Indianapolis." *The Scribe* wrote of the many noted musicians who showed an interest in Portland's Junior Symphony: Alfred Hertz, the Conductor of the San Francisco Symphony, Frederick Stock of the Chicago Symphony, Hamilton-Harty, composer in London, Mischa Elman and Mme. Leopold Auer; the dancer La Argentina who extended her stay in Portland for 24 hours so she might listen to a rehearsal of the Junior Symphony.

Meanwhile, Jacques Gershkovitch's remarks were finding their way into the press: "I was in heaven when I conducted the *Russian Easter,* and the children

Opposite. Jacques Gershkovitch.

were with me." Articles began to appear in other cities: *The St. Paul Press* also quoted Gershkovitch, "I talk to them like artists. If you talk to them like children they will never play good. I scold them very much....If they talk too much, I scold them. If they go into the street at intermission, I scold them. If there are too much sweethearts, I scold them. If they chew gum, I scold them. Gum! Hah, that is the worst!" In later interviews Gershkovitch expressed his conviction that the future of music in America depended on young men and women not only as listeners but as active participants.

These comments, in his broken English, revealed what was at the core of Gershkovitch's teaching, and Katherine Noyes, both before and during her presidency, became his chief spokesman. In 1934 she published an article in the Junior League Scribbler's Club on what the PJS meant to the city. Her own convictions became equally known. Upon becoming President of the Association, she expressed the hope that "no economic condition would affect the development of Portland children. The PJS will fit them for any walk of life."

As the 10th Anniversary approached, Katherine Noyes organized committees to celebrate; a charcoal sketch of Jacques Gershkovitch was commissioned from Sidney Bell. A benefit was planned which auctioned off handkerchiefs—some signed—from Heifetz, the Prince of Wales, Norma Shearer, Bing Crosby, and other stars.

The Oregonian noted that few of the original members of the Orchestra remained; over 522 had passed through it, and all of them had had the benefit of Jacques Gershkovitch's teaching. In September 1935 the paper ran a series of 18(!) consecutive articles on the history, purpose, and successes of the PJS.

In the second and third decades, new developments came naturally: the formation of a PJS Chorus reflected Jacques Gershkovitch's background and interest in opera. With the arrival in the city of Ariel Rubstein, another Russian-born musician, who had worked at the opera house in Kiev, he was engaged to train the Chorus. In successive years they presented, in concert form, *Eugene Onegin*, Glinka's *A Life for the Tsar*, *Carmen*, *Faust*, and other operatic favorites. A PJS ballet, under the direction of the Christiansen brothers, was also formed; and they, naturally, presented the "Nutcracker" and other perennials. When auditions for young dance students were announced, the specifications were: Ages 12 to 21; height from 4'10" to 5'5". Before long, 100 students were enrolled in the ballet and 150 in the chorus.

In addition to performances of music by Jacques Gershkovitch's longtime friend, Aaron Avshalomov, my Father, other living composers figured in the programs. Charles Wakefield Cadman was invited to participate in the performance of his *Dark Dancers of the Mardi Gras*. Dent Mowrey's *Danse Américaine* (with a French title!), Emil Enna, Father Dominic, Gerard Gerritson, and other local composers were given a hearing.

Robert Mann, later the founder and leader of the famed Juilliard Quartet,

Concert performance of *Carmen,* 1938.

performed as soloist in 1935 at the age of 13. The reviews foretold a brilliant career for him, and how right they were.

Service clubs began to take an interest. Rotary in West Linn brought the Orchestra in for a concert, hosted by District #101. Students from Prineville came to Portland for a "culture tour", to a concert, to the Historical Museum and the zoo.

Around 1940 the editorials began to get repetitious in their praise and observations about the Orchestra. But an article appeared in the national journal *Current History and Forum.* A pamphlet about the Orchestra, entitled *Whither Youth,* had appeared in the early years. In 1938 Ronald Russell was commissioned to write a more substantial account, and he turned out *A New West to Explore.* It was a handsome little volume, with a very genteel tone. Copies of it lingered in the Association's offices for some years; L. R. Hussa, when President, used them as complimentary copies to spread the word.

New fund-raising methods were devised in a steady stream. The Portland Newcomers Service booklet listed the PJS as an important element of the city. The scholarship program was publicized by listing the 23 recipients in the newspapers. In 1934 three nine-month scholarships to study double-bass were offered with the condition that the recipients would abide by the PJS rules and attend rehearsals and performances for three seasons.

A chain of "coffee hours" was set in motion to benefit both the PJS and the Portland Symphony. Some 54 hostesses each invited four friends, who in turn invited four friends the following week, and the chain continued thus for four weeks. Eleven thousand dollars was raised in this way. It was the first time that the "senior" professional orchestra and the "Junior" student orchestra had collaborated in a joint fund drive. Editorials spoke of "two excellent orchestras."

Another joint effort was a second petition for the free use of the Auditorium to which the City Council responded with only a concession in the rental rate. It was a repeat of the age-old debate between those who wanted the public hall to pay its own way and those who thought it important to support those institutions which were culturally valuable to the community.

A third joint effort was undertaken in January 1952 which promoted a minuscule property tax that would benefit the two orchestras and the municipal band. A "cute" picture of a 12-year-old PJS timpanist delivering a stack of 6,852 petitions to the city auditor appeared in *The Journal.* Members of both orchestras, their Boards, and President Hussa in a letter to the Editor, all worked for the passage of the initiative, but the measure was defeated at the elections that May.

By this time, the problems of the Orchestra and their likely solutions had become perennial. The new members of the PJS were listed in the papers, as well as the players needed. The press noted that not one member had ever been involved in the criminal courts (still true in 1989). Alumni were being traced and a questionnaire circulated to them, gathering evidence of the flock's accomplishments and memories of their days in the Orchestra.

Some unique milestones were also passed. David Campbell, who served for 25 years as commentator for the Children's Concerts, was honored by the invitation to perform as soloist with the Orchestra in the first movement of Tchaikovsky's B-flat Piano Concerto.

Unhappily, Mr. Gershkovitch's health began to fail. A heart attack in 1951 required him to sit out the first two concerts of the season. Eugene Fuerst, a third Russian-emigré conductor who had come to Portland, took the reins temporarily. Jacques Gershkovitch returned for the final concert. But the entire sequence was repeated a year later.

Mr. Hussa, after five years as President, was succeeded by Eugene R. Nudelman—whose daughter was a leading player in the Orchestra. Plans were made to celebrate the 30th Anniversary and invitations were sent in August to Robert Mann and me to participate in that festive season. But Jacques Gershkovitch passed away before he could receive the well-earned honors we were all prepared to bestow. Fuerst, Linden, and I each conducted one of the concerts as the City mourned. The vacancy of the post was announced and 65 conductors applied for it.

Programs & Reviews

1st Through 29th Season

PROGRAM

Opening Concert

of the

Portland Junior Symphony Orchestra

February 14, 1925

at the

Lincoln High School Auditorium

ORCHESTRA

FIRST VIOLINS—Dorothy Cowgill (Concert Master), Ruth Saunders (Assistant Concert Master), Peggy Paladeaux, Erma Eller, Erich Porshman, M. Brockway, Daniel Golden, Margaret Yost, Hestine Hollister, B. Sorensen, John Oliver, Evan Whitlock, Josephine Howard, Maxine Telford.

SECOND VIOLINS—Pauline Wolf (Concert Master), Glen Reeves (Assistant Concert Master), James Eoff, Ellis Vincent, Virginia Reed, Virginia Leihy, Mary Helen Wood, Ruby Norgard, Mildred Collamore, Edwin Lynds, Fay Jaloff, Edward Thompson, Jane Menzies, Dorothy Edlefsen, Alfred Muscovitz, Ruth Van Schoonhoven, Clyde Kincaid.

VIOLAS—Anna May Nolan, Clara Harris, George Jackson.

CELLOS—Brian Hamilton, Eric Taylor, James Babson.

BASS —Thomas Smith, Katherine Palmer.

FLUTES—Joe Newman, Ned Babson.

CLARINET—Junior Brink.

OBOES—J. Berardinelli, Lewis Wallin.

BASSOON—John Sprouse.

TRUMPETS—William Hall, William Sievere, Rowland Rose.

TROMBONES—E. Ragnone, Holden Brink, M. C. Pailthrope.

FRENCH HORN—Thomas McAvoy.

TYMPANI—Robert Dick.

SNARE DRUM—Benton Skibitzke.

BASS DRUMS—Wm. Jones, Alex. Hamilton.

PIANO—Marcus Leopold.

HARP—Frances Pozzi.

1st Season

Jacques Gershkovitch, Director

Lincoln High School Auditorium

February 14, 1925

Symphony (Unfinished) — SCHUBERT

Allegro Moderato

Aria: In Quelle Trine Morbide — PUCCINI

Al mio cor — HANDEL

Miss Corinne Buck, *Soprano*

Miss Olga Ruff, *Accompanist*

Danse Orientale — LUBOMIRSKY

Serenade Melancolique — TCHAIKOWSKY

Le Cygne — SAINT-SAENS

Miss Dorothy Cowgill, *Violinist*

Mr. Marcus Leupold, *Pianist*

Miss Frances Pozzi, *Harpist*

Raymond Overture — AMBROSE THOMAS

Tuesday May 26, 1925

Symphony "Unfinished" — SCHUBERT

(First Movement)

Suite "Peer Gynt" — GRIEG

Danse Orientale — LUBOMIRSKY

Concerto, op. 19 — VIEUXTEMPS

Maxine Telford, *Violinist*

Blythe Owen Cramlett, *Accompanist*

Suite "Caucasian Sketches" — IPPOLITOW-IWANOW

THE OREGONIAN MAY 27, 1925

JUNIOR ORCHESTRA STARS AT CONCERT

Mr. Gershkovitch and Musicians Get Ovation Following First Number Given.

BY C. HILTON-TURVEY.

The Portland junior symphony orchestra gave a remarkable concert last night at the Lincoln high school, directed by Jacques Gershkovitch. Miss Corinne Buck, mezzo-soprano; Miss Dorothy Cowgill, violinist; Miss Frances Pozzi, harpist, assisted in the programme. Miss Olga Ruff and Marcus Leopold accompanied the soloists.

The young orchestra did some astounding work, playing with spirit, musical quality, crisp phrasing and technical skill. The programme began with the "Allegro" of Schubert's B minor symphony, beautifully played. A veritable ovation for orchestra and conductor followed the conclusion of the movement, and a large, handsome basket of flowers was presented to Mr. Gershkovitch by the children.

Peer Gynt Number Given.

"Ase's Death," from the Peer Gynt suite, delighted the audience so much that a repeat was given. In this work the tone was sweet in quality and the pianissimos well sustained, the final chords a mere thread of sound, the whole performance delicately given. The "Danse Orientale" (Lubomirsky) was played with rich color and fine rhythmic values. In the "Raymond" overture (Ambroise Thomas) the young orchestra did extraordinarily artistic work. That these young musicians should be able-to compass the major difficulties of this work and with such beauty of tone and such logical phrasing—this is really amazing!

Portland may well be proud of her junior symphony. Not many cities could show a junior organization to stand comparison with it. Its presence in the community is a notable musical asset. This is not to say that its performance is perfection; that would be too much to expect of young amateurs. There are occasional "holes in the ballad," the wind is sometimes wobbly, and the inner voices are not invariably accurate, but take it by and large, here is a young orchestra capable of great things. The splendid programme last night was a distinct achievement, and congratulations are in order for everybody who helped, in any way, to put it through.

Orchestra Evolved Slowly.

This is the orchestra that evolved from its nucleus the "Sagebrush orchestra" of a few years ago, which was trained and organized by Mrs. Mary Dodge, who accomplished a miracle of love and skill in developing each young player to the high standard necessary for such artistic results. At the end of the programme last night she reluctantly shared in the applause with Mr. Gershkovitch.

Miss Corinne Buck sang an aria from "Manon Lescaut" and sang it extraordinarily well. The mezzo quality of her voice, the mature conception of what she sang, the smooth delivery, the poise and assurance of this youthful singer were surprising to the listener. The "Al mio cor" (Handel) was equally well done, and flowers and a storm of applause followed. Miss Ruff played sympathetic accompaniments.

Miss Dorothy Cowgill made a charming impression with her violin playing, giving "Serenade Melancolique" (Tschaikowsky) with a well-played piano accompaniment by Marcus Leopold, and Saint-Saens' "Le Cygne" to a fragile and silvery harp played by Miss Frances Pozzi. This latter the two young musicians were obliged to repeat.

Orchestra Has Own Board.

The importance of this young people's concert can scarcely be overestimated. As proof of the living, vigorous quality of the organization, it appears that these up-and-coming youngsters have their own official board and that they are learning valuable lessons in the management of their association. Besides their juvenile board, there is an advisory committee of three adults, Robert Robinson, Mrs. Dodge and one other.

The make-up of the printed programme with its multitudinous first-class advertisements shows that there was considerable "digging" and hustling done before the concert.

Concert Without Hitch.

The concert began on time. It went without a hitch. The choice of music, presumably Mr. Gershkovitch's, set a commendably high standard for the juniors to follow in their concerts to come, and he led his juvenile forces with spirit and marked success.

The hall was well filled with an appreciative audience. The ushering was capably done by Campfire girls in blue and white middy suits and blue "tams."

PORTLAND TELEGRAM FEB. 15, 1925

Junior Symphony Is Heard in First Concert

BY SUSIE AUBREY SMITH.

The Portland Junior Symphony orchestra made its debut Saturday night at Lincoln high school in an ambitious program that was much enjoyed by a good sized audience. From the smallest boys and girls in the orchestra—and some of them are surprisingly small—all of the young musicians had good attack and excellent rhythm and gave splendid response to the conductor, Jacques Gershkovitch, who has been in charge of the organization for the last few months.

The opening number was the "Allegro Moderato" from the Schubert "Unfinished Symphony," and was beautifully played. Gershkovitch conducted this and in fact the entire concert in the masterly manner that was evident in the two symphony programs he directed last fall; and he conducted without the musical score.

The other orchestral numbers were "Ase's Death" (Peer Gynt Suite) of Grieg, which was so well liked it had to be repeated; "Danse Orientale" (Lubomirsky) played with splendid verve and atmospheric effect, and the overture "Raymond" of Ambroise Thomas, which the young musicians gave with professional precision and dash.

The program was varied with several solo numbers. Miss Corinne Buck displayed a soprano voice of lovely quality in two solos. Miss Buck sings with assurance, good musical understanding and clear diction. She was accompanied by Miss Olga Ruff. Miss Dorothy Cowgill, violinist, and concert master of the orchestra, gave Tschaikowsky's "Serenade Melancholique" with good tone and technic, accompanied by Marcus Leopold; but her favorite number was "Le Cygne" of Saint Saens, which was a lovely thing with only harp accompaniment by Miss Frances Pozzi.

The orchestra and conductor were given vociferous applause at the end of each number. The junior orchestra is of unusual interest to both musicians and music lovers of the city and has started its career most auspiciously with this first and admirable concert.

OREGON JOURNAL FEB. 15, 1925

JUNIOR SYMPHONY ORCHESTRA GIVES INITIAL CONCERT

Ambitious Program of Classics Amazingly Well Presented; Two Are Soloists Featured.

The premiere concert of the Portland Junior Symphony orchestra, given in the auditorium of the Lincoln high school Saturday night, was an immense success.

The young musicians played an ambitious and exacting program of classics so well that the audience that almost filled the auditorium to capacity broke into storm upon storm of applause.

After the concert hundreds of the thoroughly thrilled audience surged to the stage to congratulate the players and the conductor, Jacques Gershkovitch, who was engaged about two months ago to wield the baton, and Mrs. M. V. Dodge, who originally organized the orchestra.

RESPOND PROMPTLY

The response to the conductor's baton was surprising indeed, and the phrasing and tonal effects such that they would have been credit to an orchestra of seasoned performers. The all-string movement, "Aase's Death," was so exquisitely played that the audience insisted on hearing it again.

The first movement of Schubert's "Unfinished" symphony and the overture to "Raymond" afforded opportunity to display many tonal combinations, and the intonation, while not flawless, was surprisingly good. The brasses and percussion sections were employed with telling effects.

"Dance Orientale" was a happily chosen number to reveal conspicuously the presence of a complete woodwind choir.

OREGON JOURNAL MAY 28, 1925

THEIR TRIUMPH

BROUGHT to their feet by the extraordinary performance of the youthful players, the people in a big audience at Lincoln high Tuesday evening cheered the Portland Junior Symphony orchestra to the echo.

Rarely do juveniles have such triumph. Seldom is an audience stirred and moved by such emotions. Between the excellent character of the music and the amazement of such musical effects by mere children, those in the audience went through an evening of tumultuous feeling.

There were 70 of the young musicians. The average age was somewhere between 15 and 16.

After every number, the youngsters were brought to their feet in response to prolonged and universal applause. And many an auditor sat through the performance with moist eyes in contemplation of the possibilities of the child life of the city and the nation.

This narrative does not pretend to say that musically every note and intonation was perfect. But it is true that laymen and all others than professional musicians or thoroughly experienced critics could see nothing to criticize. To all such, the musical effects were as complete and effective as if rendered by an adult orchestra of experience.

Credit for the concert goes alike to the young performers and to Conductor Jacques Gershkovitch, whose power to inspire musical effort in those under his leadership is extraordinary.

THE OREGONIAN MAY 27, 1925

Junior Symphony Players Demonstrate Talent.

Maxine Telford, Violinist, Is Assisting Soloist.

BY C. HILTON-TURVEY

THE second public concert of the Junior Symphony orchestra, under direction of Jacques Gershkovitch at the Lincoln high school auditorium last night again demonstrated to the audience what talented young folk these are. Maxine Telford, violinist, was the assisting soloist, accompanied by Blythe Owen Cramlett at the piano.

The appearance of the conductor was the signal for wild rounds of applause. The opening number was the first movement of Schubert's "Unfinished" symphony, which the young performers play as if they liked it extremely, showing that good music is quite as attractive to the growing generation as the jazz of which we hear so much.

The Peer Gynt suite was performed with spirit and youthful exuberance and received some of the heartiest applause of the concert. The conductor, being recalled and loudly applauded, invited the orchestra to stand and share the admiring tumult. It was at the end of this suite that a slender young girl, Dorothy Cowgill, concert master, arose and presented a handsome baton to the conductor in the name of the orchestra and "as a token of everlasting gratitude."

Miss Maxine Telford played the Vieuxtemps "Concerto Op. 19," showing technical facility and brilliant style. The andante was perhaps the best played movement of the three. Mr. Cramlett provided a finely conceived performance of the piano part and an elastic blend of tone with the violinist.

The work done by the juniors is all the more commendable when one considers that the multiplicity of their school studies leaves little time for practice. That they stick to it with such zeal and really enjoy playing good music is a matter for congratulation all around.

Before the audience dispersed Mr. Gershkovitch made a short speech which he prefaced by saying that he could not speak much English but that he wanted to ask for increased support for the junior symphony. "These are all Portland children," he said, "and I ask Portland people to help the orchestra along." An enthusiastic audience applauded both conductor and orchestra with evident friendliness and delight.

PORTLAND TELEGRAM MAY 27, 1925

ORCHESTRA IS HIGHLY PRAISED

BY SUSIE AUBREY SMITH.

The Portland Junior Symphony orchestra, Jacques Gershkovitch, conductor, gave its second concert last evening at Lincoln High school before a large and enthusiastic audience. The symphonic selection was the first movement of the Schubert "Unfinished Symphony," which the young musicians played at their first concert. Last night, with an augmented orchestra, they gave this selection in finished style.

Mr. Gershkovitch arranged a program that gave opportunity to all sections of the orchestra to show their skill. "In the Morning" of the "Peer Gynt" suite was especially well played by the wood-winds; "Ase's Death" was beautifully given by the strings and in the last episode, "In the Hall of the Mountain King," the brass and percussion were featured, although all sections of the orchestra did splendid work in working up a big climax. The number had to be repeated in answer to insistent applause.

The young musicians displayed excellent rhythm and musical understanding in all of their playing and Mr. Gershkovitch again demonstrated to a Portland audience his remarkable talents as a conductor.

On behalf of the orchestra members, Dorothy Cowgill, concert master, presented Mr. Gershkovitch with a baton.

Junior Symphony Supplies BIG IDEA

By THE EDITOR

A man handed me a BIG IDEA last night.

I went with Dr. Enna, The News' musical critic, to Irvington school to hear 80 children play Schubert's "Unfinished Symphony," a difficult enough piece for any orchestra.

Jacques Gershkovitch, a newcomer from Russia, conducted.

These children range from 10 to 16 years of age. Some of them took up music for the first time last summer. All of them are, of course, amateurs. Gershkovitch has thus far put them through but six rehearsals. Little boys and girls fiddled and tooted with might and main. A rosy-cheeked lad thumped the traps with enthusiasm and perfect rhythm.

Gershkovitch seemed to have them under perfect control indeed, they seemed hypnotized.

It was when the piece was finished that the man gave me the BIG IDEA. The man was Principal Barr.

"This thing," he said, "is too big for just Irvington grade school."

Let it be, then, the nucleus for a Portland junior symphony orchestra. Every chair in it would be competitive. Every child in Portland with any musical ability at all would want to belong to it. There would spring up in every community, in every grade school, little orchestras whose stars would be graduated into the Portland junior symphony.

And the Portland junior symphony would be a feeder to the big Portland symphony orchestra which plays at the auditorium.

Nothing I can think of would give such an impetus to music as that. Nothing would do so much toward educating the rest of us in music appreciation as that. It would create a situation unique, which would advertise Portland to the world as a musical city.

PORTLAND NEWS MAY 27, 1925

Junior Symphony Gives Wonderful Performance

BY EMIL ENNA

A concert which would have done credit to any professional or mature orchestra was presented by the Portland Junior Symphony orchestra on Tuesday evening in the auditorium of Lincoln high school under the magnetic direction of Jacques Gershkovitch. Maxine Telford, violinist, was the assisting soloist, accompanied by Blythe Owen Cramlett.

Beginning the Junior orchestra was an experiment, but it has flourished and grown, and become so efficient that it is now an educational factor to be reckoned with and supported. It is creating an indelible culture influence on a young generation who will form the nucleus of a future civic orchestra and its supporters. Too much interest and enthusiasm cannot be stimulated.

GERSHKOVITCH BLAZES TRAIL

The program included two numbers which were played on their initial program. The first movement of the "Unfinished Symphony" (Schubert) and "Dance Orientale" (Lubomirsky). These numbers proved a medium whereby one could judge the astonishing results Gershkovitch has achieved in the past few months. He has blazed a trail in musical history of Portland and his enthusiasm and interest, together with artistic interpretation and dynamic conducting, were the dominant features of the program.

The "Peer Gynt" suite (Grieg) was read with intensity and poetic understanding, the orchestra sensitive to his every gesture. Two numbers from "Caucasian Sketches" (Ippolitow-Iwanow) were decidedly interesting.

A spectacular ovation was tendered conductor and orchestra up on the electrifying climax of "In the Hall of the Mountain Kings." The audience rose to its feet, applauding and shouting.

PORTLAND TELEGRAM NOV. 26, 1925

MUSIC PATRONS HEAR SYMPHONY

Junior Orchestra Crowds Hellig With Appreciative Audience.

BY SUSIE AUBREY SMITH.

The first concert of the season given by the Portland Junior Symphony orchestra last night demonstrated the remarkable growth of the orchestra in musical stature since last year. Last night the young musicians, under the splendid leadership of their conductor, Jacques Gershkovitch, included an entire symphony in their program. It was the first time, also, that the junior orchestra had appeared in such a large hall; but the Hellig theater, where the concert was given, was crowded with enthusiastic music patrons.

OPEN WITH MOZART.

The program opened with the Mozart "Symphony in G Minor," which the young musicians, some not yet in their teens, played with surprising finish and musical understanding. When one watched tiny boys and girls handling their violins or horns with the assurance and gravity of professional musicians, one felt a kind of awe and a fuller recognition of the power of music and of the fine qualities of a conductor who can transform such young musicians into such capable artists.

CHRISTMAS THEME CHARMING.

Rebikov's "The Christmas Tree," a charming thing for strings, was charmingly played and drew its full quota of applause. The junior orchestra concluded its program with the march from "Tannhauser," a most ambitious composition for the orchestra, but not at all too ambitious as the young artists proved in their spirited rendition. Their rhythm and attack it excellent, their tone beautiful and the whole musical atmosphere of the concert was quite professional.

At the first concert given by the junior orchestra last season, surprise and wonder were the emotions with which most people listened to their work. Now their audiences listen to the youngsters as they would listen to mature artists; for they realize that these boys and girls are not in any sense "child prodigies," but serious young musicians who deserve serious attention for their work.

PORTLAND NEWS NOV. 26, 1925

JUNIORS WIN NEW LAURELS

Splendid Concert Given by Portland Junior Symphony Orchestra

BY EMIL ENNA

The Portland Junior Symphony orchestra, Jacques Gershkovitch, conductor, presented the first of this season's concerts on Wednesday evening at the Hellig theater, sustaining the brilliancy and reputation of the past season, but gaining new laurels and distinctions, which predict a most unique and prominent position for this city when one considers the dynamic symphonic strides made both in accomplishment and support, as capacity audiences so far have applauded both senior and junior organizations. Such enthusiasm and support is won by the sincerity, magnetism and artistry of the director. All of these Gershkovitch possesses, as well as unusual accomplishment in bringing forth individual talent, and the love and respect of perhaps 75 young people. It is an artistic and cultural organization, from which the members gain unlimited benefit and experience, and the city and sponsors an acquisition of notable fame.

The most outstanding feature of Wednesday evening's program was the lovely, melodic G minor symphony (Mozart).

The symphony was followed by "In the Village" from "Caucasian Sketches," (Ippolitov-Ivanov.) Much of the beauty of this number was due to the viola solo of young Thomas Smith.

"The Christmas Tree" (Rebikov) was a splendid medium to display the development and artistry achieved by the string section under the director's instruction.

The closing number March from "Tannhauser" (Wagner), brought to a brilliant conclusion a most unusual program.

Among most interested listeners in the large audience were Toscha Seidel, distinguished violinist, and Willem Van Hoogstraten, famous symphonic conductor.

OREGON JOURNAL NOV. 26, 1925

Young Players Win New Laurels

By J. L. Wallin

THE Portland Junior Symphony Orchestra gave its first concert of the second season at the Hellig theatre Wednesday night and again amazed by performing symphonic music that puts to test orchestras of the most capable professional performers.

That unusual interest is taken in this unique organization, which is conducted by Jacques Gershkovitch, was demonstrated by the large and distinguished audience. Lower floor, balcony, loges and boxes were occupied practically to the last seat.

Mozart's G Minor Symphony is a most delicate bit of music with no background to conceal imperfections from even musically untrained ears. Its reading was most fascinating and it was exceedingly well played. Painstaking training with uniformly good technic, was demonstrated by the great speed in the final movement.

Applause of the most enthusiastic character followed the completion of the symphony. For the second part of the program Conductor Gershkovitch gave an episode from Ippolitov-Ivanov's "Caucasian Sketches" and it was cleverly done, with fine sense for the picture's atmosphere. Thomas Smith, not yet 14, played the solo passages for viola with the suavest of tone and as graceful phrasing as one could possibly wish, and as reward for his fine work received a real ovation.

The woodwind section, which had already distinguished itself to the symphony, surmounted the difficulties of this number remarkably well, too.

The dainty waltz movement from Rebikov's music drama, "The Christmas Tree," the violins, violas and cellos played with fine silken tone and haunting expression.

The pompous march from Wagner's romantic grand opera, "Tannhauser," brought into action all the resources of the orchestra and gave the audience a thrill that will not soon be forgotten. The clean cut fanfares of the trumpets was a revelation. The grand finale was magnificent and amazingly well balanced.

The Portland Junior Symphony orchestra has become a permanent institution sponsored by the Portland Junior Symphony association with a sustaining and associate membership of more than 500 individuals, who realize the cultural value of this work.

2nd Season

Jacques Gershkovitch, Conductor

Wednesday November 25, 1925
Heilig Theater

Symphony G minor, NO. 40	MOZART
Caucasian Sketch, NO. 2	IPPOLITOV-IVANOV
In the Village	
"The Christmas Tree"	REBIKOV
March from "Tannhauser"	WAGNER

Monday March 22, 1926
The Auditorium

Symphony "Unfinished" B minor	SCHUBERT
Concerto in A minor for Pianoforte & Orchestra – Allegro molto moderato	GRIEG
Jane Hamer Kanzler, *Pianist*	
Suite from Ballet Nutcracker	TCHAIKOVSKY
Symph. Poem, "Danse Macabre"	SAINT-SAENS

JUNIOR SYMPHONY CONCERT DELIGHTS CAPACITY AUDIENCE

Difficult and Exacting Program Splendidly Achieved by Youthful Group Under Direction of Jacques Gershkovitch.

THE Portland Junior Symphony orchestra, Jacques Gershkovitch conductor, presented its first program of the current season last night at the Hellig theater. A capacity audience was present for the performance.

Few orchestras can be credited with a more romantic history than this group of juvenile players. Mrs. M. V. Dodge was responsible for its organization, several years ago, as the junior symphony orchestra of the Irvington grammar school. Mrs. Dodge long ago conceived the idea of bringing the group to the fore, as Portland's own junior symphony. Her ideal came very nearly being realized when the conductorship was entrusted to Jacques Gershkovitch last year, and in the comparatively brief period of his regime the orchestra has developed so manifestly and the public interest in the enterprise has been so greatly augmented that it is safe to say it has now been realized.

High Ideals Attained.

To Mrs. Dodge must be tendered credit for laying the foundations of this bulwark of symphonic music; to Mr. Gershkovitch for erecting the edifice itself.

The Mozart symphony No. 40, in G minor, was immaculate in the hands of these adept youths. Its delicacy, capriciousness and joviality, and its solid harmonic structure were well preserved in the reading of Mr. Gershkovitch. This short menuetto movement was delightful for the distinctive reserve, the dainty interplay of melodic matter that was emphasized by the players.

The rather light number from Ippolitov-Ivanov's Caucasian suite, "In the Village," presented obstacles that were not at once apparent. There is a solo for the viola which involves uncommon intervals and unorthodox progressions. And in the more involved ensemble portions the same progressions and intervals must be even more accurately and subtly performed. It was anything but easy to do. However, there was not a hitch nor a single deviation from the pitch. It was splendid. Master Thomas Smith, the viola soloist, was called to the stand, following the number, to share with the conductor the hearty applause of the audience.

Great Capabilities Shown.

The "Christmas Tree" of Rebikov, a dainty little thing for the muted strings, was nicely played. The Tannhauser march (Wagner) was ambitious, and gave the wind section its first real opportunity for display. It was a glowing number and performed with deliberation and poise.

It should be reiterated that this was no mere performance of amateurs, nor even hardly of ambitious youngsters. It was a performance of a conductor of no little distinction and of great capabilities, and of 75 splendid musicians of practically professional caliber, who simply happen to be quite young.

DEC. 4, 1925

THE SCRIBE

THE PORTLAND JUNIOR SYMPHONY CONCERT

By David Tamkin

The first concert of the Portland Symphony Orchestra under their magnificent Maestro, Jaques Gershkovitch, was an overwhelming success. After hearing the usual "Savanarolic" prophecies of our latent musical talent, it was really unbelievable to know that there exists in Portland a Junior Symphony Orchestra with such sublety of nuance, such remarkable feeling and rhythm, and above all, such precision of attack. Mr. Gershkovitch's magnanimous temperament and music ability must certainly have the desired effect upon these young musicians for the Mozart G Minor Symphony was interpreted with a veritable expression of spontaneous youth plus a most vivid fluency. That mass of symphonic creation was the crowning achievement of the orchestra and their conductor. The purpose of the Portland Junior Orchestra Association can easily be comprehended when they foster and encourage the musical talents of such as Master Thomas Smith. A most brilliant future awaits him as a violinist. May we soon have the pleasure of listening to other performers of the great Portland Junior Symphony Orchestra and their wonderful conductor, Jaques Gershkovitch.

MAR. 23, 1926

THE MUSICAL LEADER

The Portland Junior Symphony Orchestra, Jacques Gershkovitch conductor, gave its second concert of the season at Municipal Auditorium Monday night and attracted a near-capacity audience, which is conclusive evidence of Portland's appreciation of this unique organization and its brilliant conductor. For those Portlanders who have never attended one of these concerts, a splendid spectacle and a great thrill awaits them. This symphonic group, composed of seventy children varying in age between nine and eighteen, playing with musical sense and traditions the symphonies of the great masters, the music of Beethoven, Mozart, Tschaikowsky, Schubert, Grieg, under the baton of this talented Russian, is a valuable asset to the Northwest. One cannot deny to Gershkovitch real genius in the organization and direction of such an ensemble. Throughout the program he conducted without a score, displaying genuine artistic individuality. Perhaps the sensation of the concert (it was all sensational) was the pianistic gift of Jane Kanzler, a pretty young miss of fifteen, who played with orchestra the first movement of Grieg's A Minor Concerto. Extraordinary poise, a goodly amount of style, and a highly developed technic marked this young player as one with a big future. Miss Kanzler received a deluge of flowers and applause. Spontaneous outburst of applause and shouts of "Bravo" greeted Gershkovitch and his young players throughout the evening.

OREGON JOURNAL MAR. 23, 1926

Program Given Before Large Audience

By J. L. Wallin

THE Portland Junior Symphony orchestra's second concert of the season Monday night was a great success, and Conductor Jacques Gershkovitch and the young musicians were overwhelmed with compliments and congratulations.

The concert was in The Auditorium with an attendance that ran close to its capacity, unmistakable evidence of the organization's increasing popularity. A little over a year ago the first concert of the first season was given in the Lincoln high school auditorium, then the orchestra moved to the Hellig only to find the capacity there inadequate.

During each number the audience was held in a spell by the remarkable response of the performers to Gershkovitch's slightest turn of the hand or a vigorous sweep with the baton calling for all the volume of tone available.

Every section did nobly; the intonation was uniformly good, the strings bowed and phrased evenly and the nuances were beautifully balanced.

The program was a popular one and very difficult, too. Tschaikowsky's "Nutcracker" suite with solo passages for nearly all instruments was played with amazing "professionalism," and still it had the freshness of youth that professionalism frequently lacks.

Saint-Saens' "Danse Macabre" (The Dance of the Skeletons) was very spooky.

Both movements of Schubert's "Unfinished" symphony were beautifully phrased and shaded with the solo passages smoothly performed.

Extraordinary was the playing of the first movement of Grieg's A Minor Concerto, with 15-year-old Jane Hamer Kanzler at the piano. The girl, a Washington high school student, played with unbelievable maturity and confidence like an artist in miniature, and the orchestra played the accompaniment marvelously well.

Frances Pozzi played the piano and harp parts in the "Nutcracker" suite with rare ability.

Conductor Gershkovitch conducted the whole program without a score and not a few of the performers played the entire symphony without looking at the printed music.

The orchestra Monday night consisted of 18 first violins. Dorothy Cowgill, concertmaster; 18 second violins, Anna May Nolan, principal; six violas, James Eoff, principal; three double basses, seven cellos, three oboes, three flutes, three clarinets, two bassoons, four trumpets, two horns, four trombones, harp and piano.

Little Miss Kanzler was rewarded with loads of beautiful bouquets and a large bouquet was sent to Conductor Gershkovitch by the members of The Journal Junior orchestra, which attended the concert in a body as guests of the Junior symphony.

PORTLAND TELEGRAM MAR. 23, 1926

YOUNG PLAYERS' MELODY SCORES

Junior Symphonists Provoke Enthusiastic Applause With Concert.

BY SUSIE AUBREY SMITH.

The young musicians of the Portland Junior Symphony orchestra and their conductor, Jacques Gershkovitch, were given a most enthusiastic welcome when they appeared on the stage of the Auditorium last night for their second concert of the season. This is the first time that the junior orchestra has played at the Auditorium, but the large audience quite justified its choosing the largest hall in the city.

The orchestra seems to have taken a large stride in its musical excellence at each succeeding concert. Last night Mr. Gershkovitch offered us a splendid program, with the unusual and thrilling experience of hearing a 15-year-old girl, a member of the orchestra, play part of the Grieg concerto with an orchestra made up of youngsters mostly in their 'teens, and many of them of grammar school age.

PRAISE IS LAVISHED.

Too much praise cannot be lavished on conductor, orchestra and soloist for this performance. The young pianist, Miss Jane Hamer Kanzler, daughter of Judge and Mrs. Jacob Kanzler, displayed a mature poise and assurance—fully justified by her well developed technic, her rich and unforced tone, and that rare attribute even among musicians—real musical taste in interpretation.

CONDUCTOR IS LAUDED.

Mr. Gershkovitch is a conductor with vision and a genius for leadership and he has built up a junior orchestra that Portland should be proud to introduce to the rest of the country.

In this age of triumphant feminism, the girls are demonstrating that they can play as well as the boys. While the boys predominate in the brass and woodwind sections of the orchestra, the concert master is Miss Dorothy Cowgill, an admirable young violinist; its harpist is Miss Frances Pozzi, who did such excellent work in the "Nutcracker Suite" (Tschaikowsky).

PORTLAND NEWS MAR. 23, 1926

YOUNG PLAYERS 'SENSATIONAL'

Junior Symphony Orchestra Displays Artistry and Maturity

PROGRAM

Symphony, "Unfinished," in B Minor .... Franz Schubert
Concerto in A Minor for piano and orchestra (first movement) .... Grieg
"Nutcracker suite" .... Tschaikowsky
Symphonic poem, "Dance of Death" .... Camille Saint Saens

By EMIL ENNA

The program, second of the season, by the Portland Junior Symphony orchestra, Jacques Gershkovitch, conducting, was sensational. Without doubt this organization is our greatest civic attribute. The Portland News was progressive and farsighted in christening this orchestra, it has carefully watched and encouraged the development which resulted in Monday evening's successful program.

To Jacques Gershkovitch, a dynamic conductor, and Mrs. Mary V. Dodge, an instigator and organizer, we are indebted. The program was skillfully selected and artistically performed. Miss Jane Kanzler was the soloist in the Grieg concerto. She is young in years, but mature as a pianist and artist. Her technique is concise and accurate, her phasing poetic and colorful. The Junior orchestra touches the pulse of Portland homes. What greater recompense can a mother ask, the soloist's only teacher, than the ovation Miss Kanzler received Monday evening?

Tribute must be accorded to the splendid orchestral effects achieved by the conductor in the concerto.

The entire program, starting with the "Unfinished Symphony" (Schubert) and ending with Saint Saen's "Dance of Death," was illustrative of the development and progress of the orchestra.

THE OREGONIAN MAR. 23, 1926

JUNIOR ORCHESTRA PLEASES LARGE AUDIENCE AT CONCERT

Director Gershkovitch Carries Young Musicians Through Performance Replete With Thrills.

IT WOULD be difficult to outline a more satisfying program than was presented last night by the Portland Junior symphony orchestra at the public auditorium, Jacques Gershkovitch conducting. Opening with the melodious "Unfinished" symphony, No. 8, in B minor of Schubert, and ending with the curious "Danse Macabre," op. 40, of Camille Saint-Saens, director Gershkovitch carried his players through a performance replete with thrilling climaxes and marked by thorough musicianship.

A vast crowd assembled to witness the performance of this unique and splendid group. It was a much larger crowd than was present at the concert of the same organization given last autumn. The Portland Junior Symphony orchestra demonstrated that it has "arrived" and that the future holds much more in store for it than has been accomplished in the past.

Despite the obvious virtues of the performance of the symphony, the excerpts from the Tschaikowsky "Nutcracker" suite and the "Danse Macabre," the sensation of the evening was the solo performance of the capable young pianist, Jane Hamer Kanzler, in the first movement of the Grieg concerto in A minor, op. 16. Her work was dazzling. She faltered not for a moment and she carried the long solo part in the middle with some force and considerable rapidity. Jane is just 15 and plays like a performer of 30.

The excerpts from the "Nutcracker" suite gave ample opportunity for solo work. The splendid trio of flautists did such beautiful work in "Danse des Mirlitons" (sometimes called "Dance of the Flutes") that the audience broke the silence which had reigned between the previous excerpts, and the three, Ned Babson, Henry Esterly and Tom Galbraith, were compelled to make their own separate bows to the audience.

In the "Dance of the Flowers" the solo work of Frances Pozzi on the harp was particularly worthy of note.

Due credit must be given to the recently acquired French horn division, consisting of William Peterson and Glenn Dodge, for the accuracy and beauty of its work.

Mr. Gershkovitch conducted the entire concert from memory. He gave ample evidence of inspired genius with the polish and discrimination of his reading.

THE OREGONIAN APR. 1926

JUNIOR SYMPHONY PLAYERS END SEASON WITH CONCERT

Jacques Gershkovitch Leads Players Through Work of Beethoven and Compositions of Portland Musicians.

THE Portland Junior Symphony orchestra brought its season to a close with a concert given at the public auditorium last night, Jacques Gershkovitch conducting. The first part of the concert was devoted to the commemoration of the centenary of Beethoven's death; the second to an arrangement and an original composition by Portland musicians.

"The Death of Kin Sei," by A. A. Avshalomoff, possibly attracted the most attention, though its length precluded the possibility of a repetition. This work had its first hearing during a previous concert of the Junior Symphony orchestra, and as at the other occasion, impressed for the originality of invention and depth. Mr. Avshalomoff, in response to many calls from the audience, appeared on the stage.

Beethoven Symphony Played.

Mr. Gershkovitch's arrangement for woodwinds and strings of Tchaikovsky's "At Church" was probably even more enthusiastically received than upon the occasion of its first hearing under his baton.

The concert opened, with the first symphony by Beethoven, and proved itself an admirable vehicle for the display of the talents of this remarkable body of youths, it is nearly the acme of musicianship to catch the spirit of Beethoven. This, it is safe to say, is what Mr. Gershkovitch has inculcated in his players. That the Beethoven symphony was played with such spirit and with such grace, with such emphasis and vigor, was perhaps a more notable achievement than the thrilling rendition of the Rimisky-Korsakov overture, with which the concert closed.

Russian Number Novelty.

"La grande Paque russe" was the single number on the program that was a genuine novelty to patrons of this orchestra.

This composition provided the audience with a variety of thrills. Aside from being the novelty of the evening, it was the sensation of the evening, and the listeners cheered heartily.

The concert was extremely well attended.

3rd Season

Jacques Gershkovitch, Conductor
Municipal Auditorium

Saturday, November 6, 1926

"Italian" Symphony in A, NO. 4	MENDELSSOHN
"Danse Macabre"	SAINT-SAENS
Suite NO. 1, "Peer Gynt"	GRIEG

Saturday January 29, 1927

"Egmont" Overture	BEETHOVEN
"At Church"	TCHAIKOVSKY
Arr. for strings and woodwind by Jacques Gershkovitch	
"Nutcracker" Suite	TCHAIKOVSKY
"Blue Danube" Waltz	JOHANN STRAUSS
"The Death of Kinsei"	A. A. AVSHALOMOFF
First public performance	
"The Christmas Tree"	REBIKOV
For strings alone. Played by request	
"Marche Slav"	TCHAIKOVSKY

Saturday May 21, 1927

Symphony NO. 1, OP. 21, in C	BEETHOVEN
"Danse Macabre"	SAINT-SAENS
"At Church"	TCHAIKOVSKY
By request	
"The Death of Kinsei"	A. A. AVSHALOMOFF
By request	
"La Grande Paque Russe" (The Resurrection)	RIMSKY-KORSAKOFF

OREGON JOURNAL NOV. 17, 1926.

JUNIOR SYMPHONY ORCHESTRA SCORES GREAT TRIUMPH

Large Audience Held in Spell by Youthful Musicians Conducted by J. Gershkovitch.

By Sam Raddon Jr.

One must have been old and cold indeed whose treasure vaults of memory and remembrance of the idyllic were not unlocked by last night's performance of the Portland Junior Symphony orchestra at The Auditorium, the first concert of the organization's third season.

MUSIC THRILLING

The music was thrilling.

Not at all because of the youth of the performers, though most of them were but children. One might close his eyes. The spell remained.

The average person's reaction to music is the music itself; the intangible something that only in perfected direction, organized orchestration and execution stirs in him the nearest thing we know to Godliness.

Perhaps the most spectacular of the numbers was "Danse Macabre" (Dance of Death), Saint-Saens, though in the movements of the "Peer Gynt" suite, probably the more familiar to the casual music lover, wonderfully effective results were achieved in the sweetly smooth gradations of pianissimo, arrested by fortissimo shocks, and concluding with the air "In the Hall of the Mountain King" that virtually brought the audience to its feet demanding an encore.

SYMPHONY SPLENDIDLY DONE

The opening number was the "Italian" Symphony in A major, Felix Mendelssohn also splendidly done.

Jacques Gershkovitch, to whom great credit is due and accorded, proved himself an energetic and gracious, grateful conductor. He afforded his organization equal opportunity to share in the plaudits, and betrayed no small pride in their success.

Although it may be well known, it cannot be over emphasized that in the Junior Symphony Portland has a civic asset of boundless possibility.

CULTURAL ACHIEVEMENT

It is something that the city may well nurse and nourish, for itself, and for the greater glory and preeminence of the city and its culture.

The orchestra, with a membership now of 85, affords its young people an unexcelled opportunity for orchestral training without cost to themselves. The association sponsoring it is pledged not only to encourage appreciation and rendition of orchestral music by the young, but to discover and develop latent talent among the children of Portland and vicinity—a worthy ambition, surely, if ever there was one.

PORTLAND NEWS NOV. 7, 1926

JUNIOR MUSIC CIVIC LAUREL

Symphony Orchestra Wins Praise at Opening Concert

PROGRAM

Symphony in A . . . . Mendelssohn
Danse Macabre . . . . Saint-Saens
Peer Gynt Suite . . . . Grieg

BY EMIL ENNA

The Portland Junior Symphony orchestra made its first appearance of the season at the municipal auditorium on Saturday evening. A most fitting background, for the auditorium belongs to the citizens of Portland and has never been more culturally graced than by the personnel of the Junior Symphony orchestra.

Monuments have been erected in the city to several national characters. A few years hence Jacques Gershkovitch, conductor of the Junior Symphony, will be recognized as having created the greatest monument in Portland. The orchestra is unique and proof of his ability as musician and conductor is evident in the response of the young ensemble. It is neither fair nor just to criticise the orchestra as professional, rather encourage the interest and enthusiasm of its patrons.

Recently a bill was presented by Senator Eddy of eastern Oregon discouraging the cultivation of any arts in the public schools. True to Oregon cultural form, his bill was defeated, but we hope Senator Eddy was present Saturday evening. Surely the performances would explode his theory and induce the school board to grant extra credits to the sincere music students.

Most flattering indeed is the invitation from Chicago for the Junior Symphony orchestra to participate in the biennial program of the National Federation of Music Clubs. While a distinctive civic attribute, the Junior Symphony orchestra is not as yet ready to represent Portland and the cultural center of the northwest as it will be three to five years hence, providing social and civic Portland financially maintains this organization with Gershkovitch as director.

NOV. 25, 1926

THE MUSICAL LEADER

A most valuable asset to the musical life of the Northwest is the Portland Junior Symphony Orchestra, Jacques Gershkovitch, conductor. Monday night this organization composed of about 85 members—ranging in age from eight to eighteen or twenty—played its first concert of this season at the Auditorium before a big audience that was literally swept off its feet by the remarkable playing of the young musicians. Gershkovitch is an inspired conductor! else how could one bring forth such concord of marvelous sounds from an orchestra of children? The program was a difficult one, but under the baton of this gifted temperamental Russian, difficulties vanished and the composer's message, perfect ensemble, intelligent phrasing, remarkable style and finish, proved the genuine worth of this organization. Conductor Gershkovitch was recalled innumerable times to acknowledge the wild enthusiasm which he invariably shared with his young players. This is the third season of the Junior Symphony, and from a modest beginning in the auditorium of the high school where the first concert was given two years ago, it has grown with such strides that now thousands flock to the Public Auditorium to listen and applaud.

* * *

Junior Symphony Concert

By A. AVSHALOMOFF

The Junior Symphony, with Jacques Gershkovitch, conductor, gave its first concert of the season last Saturday night at the Auditorium before a large and enthusiastic audience. Altho the junior orchestra of Portland consists of youthful musicians, yet under the direction of Mr. Gershkovitch it is quite able to bear the criticism given to adult professionals. Mendelssohn's Italian Symphony opened the program, and the first movement showed that the requisites of good orchestral playing were present, namely, "quality and purity of tone, precision, flexibility, nuancing and revelation of the inner voices." The solemn chorus of the Pilgrims (the Andante), the lively scherzo and the difficult and brilliant finale of the symphony were rendered in a masterly way, showing that the conductor's ideas were understood and faithfully carried out. The picturesque and characteristic Dance Macabre (Saint-Saens), which followed the symphony and which was the most difficult number on the program, was poetically interpreted, the clear pure tone of the trumpet which was heard thru fortissimo of the whole orchestra was played with ease and exactness of intonation. The concert master of the first violin in her solo part displayed the elasticity of bowing and beauty of tone which in a violinist is the beauty of his soul. In his work more than any other on the program, the solid sonority of the orchestra, which was maintained from the finest pianissimo to the heaviest fortissimo, manifested itself, and the closing phrase with a trill on the solo and violin and the flute was played with such taste and finesse as to deserve the highest comment. The last on the program was Grieg's Peer-Gynt suite No. 1. Interpretation of Anitra's Dance was full of charm and grace, while "In the Hall of the Mountain King," which brought the program to a close, was played with such extensive gradation of force that it brought forth tremendous applause, which reached its climax in an ovation for the orchestra and its conductor and which had to be repeated. Tho this is not the only junior orchestra in the United States, it is, we believe, the only one which can favorably be compared with some of the symphonies composed of professional musicians and is indeed a high tribute to the city in which it exists and to those who are in charge of it, and reflects great credit to its spirited conductor, who is alone responsible for the interpretation of the works performed. We learn that this orchestra has received an invitation to attend the Chicago convention of American Federation of Music early in the Spring, and to play before the convention, and we hope that Portland will be able to send the Junior orchestra there.

THE SUNDAY OREGONIAN, NOV. 12, 1926

AMBITIOUS CONCERT OPENS JUNIOR SYMPHONY SEASON

Capable Child Musicians, Under Able Leadership of Jacques Gershkovitch, Perform Difficult Compositions Creditably.

THE Portland Junior symphony opened the third consecutive season last night at the public auditorium with a concert which definitely exploded the notion, cherished by many, that "children have no right to play classical music." It was a concert marked by a spontaneity of response to the motions and gesticulations of the orchestra's eminently competent leader, Jacques Gershkovitch. It invariably delights the listener to hear a group of young people perform from the stage. When, as at last night's concert, the young people played in a manner which threatened to rival the performance of a group of hardened professionals, the result was bound to be startling. Which, in truth, it was.

Much Preparation Favored.

Conductor Gershkovitch has observed the theory that fewer concerts providing for more preparation for each individual concert, tends to elevate the musical standards for the separate performance. There was but one work on last night's program repeated from last season, "Danse Macabre" (Saint Saens).

The three excerpts from the Peer Gynt suite, No. 1 (Grieg), were in themselves expressions of what nearly approached the widest variety of effects and moods of the orchestra repertoire. "Ase's Death," the first movement of the suite performed, was sonorously executed, the pathos and restraint being duly emphasized. In "The Hall of the Mountain King," the orchestra worked up to a climax of heroic proportions.

Symphony Opens Concert.

The concert opened with the "Italian" symphony in A major, Op. 90. This is the most ambitious work in the sonata form performed by Mr. Gershkovitch's players to date. The director brought forth the melodic and rhythmic beauties of the work, giving it the flavor of times of the poignantly beautiful and again of sweet succulence.

The concert was extremely well attended, the large patronage rising time and time again to acclaim the talented conductor and his proficient players.

The entire concert was broadcast through station KGW, The Oregonian. This was the first concert of the junior symphony orchestra to be broadcast from the station.

PORTLAND TELEGRAM JAN. 31, 1927

Junior Symphony Plays Ballet by Avshalomoff

BY SUSIE AUBREY SMITH.

The Portland Junior Symphony orchestra took another stride forward in its artistic career in its concert Saturday evening at the Auditorium by giving a first performance of an ambitious and interesting new orchestra composition. This work, "The Death of Kin Sei," by A. Avshalomoff, a Russian composer who has come to make his home in Portland, was composed here.

"The Death of Kin Sei" has that oriental flavor so fascinating to us of the occident. It is a masterly piece of orchestration and of musical writing and is brought up to a dramatic climax characteristic of Russian music. The work was given a splendid reading by Jacques Gershkovitch, conductor of the Junior symphony. Two interesting Chinese harps, additions to the regular orchestra, were played by Frances Pozzi, the regular harpist with the orchestra, and Midori Shoja, a Portland Japanese girl. The composer was called to the stage to share in the applause.

Beethoven's "Egmont" overture and Tschaikowsky's "Nutcracker Suite" were beautifully played. Tschaikowsky's "At Church," arranged by Gershkovitch, and the Rebikov's "The Christmas Tree," were among the best liked selections.

One of the most enthusiastic receptions of the season was given the closing number of the program, Tschaikowsky's dramatic "Marche Slav," which Gershkovitch conducted in a manner to thrill the most blase among his auditors.

DEC. 1926

MUSIC AND MUSICIANS

Junior Orchestra Gives Stirring Concert

The Portland Junior Symphony Orchestra gave its first concert of the season November 6, at the Civic Auditorium under the direction of Jacques Gershkovitch to an audience large and representative. After hearing over eighty boys and girls interpret the best of orchestral music in an artistic fashion it is difficult to be modest in one's assertions.

It is not enough that Portland have a professional symphony orchestra; parents and friends of the coming generation have interested themselves in its development, and there exists the junior organization, founded and sponsored by leading citizens of the city. The playing of the orchestral band of junior musicians last June at the National Federation of Music Clubs' convention mightily moved many of the delegates from all sections of the United States.

The program called for Mendelssohn's "Italian" Symphony in A major, all four movements; Saint Saens' Symphonic Poem "Dance Macabre" and Grieg's Suite No. 1, "Peer Gynt."

The modes of the symphony were unmistakably outlined by the conductor, and the orchestra responded to accelerated and sustained rhythm, with equal facility, though it seemed in the Saltarello Presto finale there was a tendency for these spirited instrumentalists to take the bit in their mouths. The second, third, and fourth movements of the "Peer Gynt" Suite by Grieg brought out the excellent string quality and finally gave the whole orchestra a splendid chance to exhibit its vigor and capacity. Mr. Gershkovitch puts into this group enthusiasm and musicianship which are reflected in the performance, and he shows what can be done with young musicians when properly guided. The Portland Junior Symphony Orchestra Association is well organized and handles the business details of the orchestra. It is headed by John N. Edlefsen, and other officers are Robert Robinson, honorary president; Jacob Kanzler, Mrs. Herman A. Heppner, and Mrs. Florence S. Washburn, vice-presidents; Paul F. Nolan, secretary; Mrs. M. Lloyd Frank, treasurer; and Mrs. Josephine H. Forney, executive secretary.

JUNIOR SYMPHONY PERFORMS PREMIERE OF PORTLAND WORK

"The Death of Kin Sei," Ballet Scene, Under Baton of Jacques Gershkovitch, Bears Pathos in Oriental Guise.

"THE Death of Kin Sei," the concluding scene of the ballet of Ken Nakazawa, Japanese author of this city, which was set to music by A. A. Avshalomoff, Russian musician now residing in Portland, received its first hearing by the Portland Junior Symphony orchestra at its second concert of the season given at the public auditorium last night, Jacques Gershkovitch conducting. The piece, novel for its utilization of characteristic oriental progressions, proved highly pleasing to the occidental ear. Mr. Avshalomoff was called to the platform by Conductor Gershkovitch and the two received prolonged and hearty ovation from the large audience.

Pathos Comes in New Guise.

"The Death of Kin Sei," though strictly classed as program music, made its impression by its absolute musical values. It was sustained, abundantly melodious, and in contrast with the bulk of the program of the evening, anything but noisy. Written in the minor mode, and carrying rhythmic effects ordinarily associated with the east, it conveyed to the listener in a wholly new guise a sense of pathos and tragedy. The effectiveness of the performance was enhanced by the use of two Chinese harps and two Chinese instruments of percussion.

The other novelty of the evening was "At Church," a short pianoforte composition of Tschaikowsky arranged for orchestra by Mr. Gershkovitch.

In contrast with "At Church" was the vivid "Nutcracker Suite" of Tschaikowsky, six of the eight episodes of which were presented by the juniors. Some beautiful solo work in the woodwinds was done in the "Chinese Dance" and in the "Dance of the Flutes." A most even ensemble was maintained in the "Waltz of the Flowers."

The concert opened with the great "Egmont" overture of Beethoven, which, despite its manifold intricacies, received an excellent rendition. The performance of the overture gave evidence of the versatility of Mr. Gershkovitch's musicianship.

It was "Marche Slave" that created the real sensation. Mr. Gershkovitch interpreted this work in a manner which expressed the funereal emotions the composer injected into the work. There was some brilliant display of the brasses toward the close, and with the last cadences the audience staged a demonstration that was most naturally highly gratifying to the conductor who had led his youthful players through such an eventful evening.

JUNIORS WIN HIGH PRAISE

Large Audience Moved to Enthusiasm at Performance

By E. E.

Stupendous is the only term that adequately describes the program of the Portland Junior Symphony orchestra on Saturday evening. The artistry of Jacques Gershkovitch, conductor, will never receive finer tribute than the response of his young people in this symphonic program.

Youth always appeals, but when a conductor can carry grammar and high school students to such artistic heights, the future of American youth is assured. In this Portland stands alone, unique, as the Junior Symphony testifies.

Comparatively few of the Junior orchestra will achieve fame in the musical world, but the future life of each member will be enriched by the experience.

The large audience was moved to demonstrations of enthusiasm which the greatest symphony orchestras could not evoke. Why? Because the present generation demands greater cultural advantages for their children.

Every number from the Beethoven overture "Egmont" to the thrilling "March Slav" (Tschaikowsky) was replete with artistry and deserving of special notice. Novelty was introduced in the number "The Death of Kin Sei" written by A. A. Avshalomoff, a recent Portland resident. It was the first public performance of a masterful work and received the attention and enthusiasm deserved.

The main point is to impress civic Portland of the inestimable value, unlimited possibilities of this orchestra. Portland may be heralded for roses, climate, scenery, but history will tell of the Junior Symphony orchestra, its conductor, founders and supporters.

JUNIOR SYMPHONY WINS CHEERS WITH SPLENDID MUSIC

Conductor Gershkovitch, Composer Avshalomoff and Orchestra Given Great Ovation.

By G. S.

With the precise waving of bows by graceful, girlish arms, a balance of tone which would do credit to any symphonic organization and a mastery of nuance highly artistic, the Portland Junior Symphony orchestra, in its second concert of its third season, Saturday night demonstrated that the youth of its personnel should not longer be held a bar to criticism.

"Egmont," Beethoven's turbulent overture was marked by the particular precision of the woodwind. It was a pleased and somewhat embarrassed group of youngsters which stood up to receive the enthusiastic applause for the very excellent performance.

The perfect waltz, "The Blue Danube," achieved a new distinction. Nothing which Strauss put into it was overlooked, seemingly. The distinctive feature of its rendition was the fine balance maintained at all times between brass and the rest of the instruments during forte passages. One was able to enjoy the composer's composite thought with the brass held in reasonable check.

Orchestra, conductor and composer, A. Avshalomoff, received an ovation following the first public performance of "The Death of Kin Sei," an exotic number from the ballet, "Soul of a Harp." Its flavor was distinctly Oriental.

"The Christmas Tree" (Rebikov) for strings alone, was suave and charming in a playful, youthful manner. It prepared one for the closing selection, "March Slav," with its smashing, fiery determination. The orchestra proved equal to this alternately grim and enthusiastic theme elaborated for the benefit of wounded Russian soldiers.

The Auditorium was well filled. At the close the orchestra was greeted with a hearty cheer, after which they bowed many times as the enthusiastic applause continued.

THE SPECTATOR FEB. 5, 1927

* * *

Portland Junior Orchestra

The second of the Junior Orchestra series for the current season was given on Saturday evening at the auditorium with tremendous success. The children, under the inspired leadership of their conductor, Jacques Gershkovitch, did the best playing of the organization's life and received salvos of applause and bravos for their fine work. The arrangement of Tschaikowsky's "At Church," which Mr. Gershkovitch had made for strings and woodwind, was most impressive and gained recognition for the two choirs which gave it such a beautiful rendition. Six numbers from the Nutcracker Suite were given with good effect and the Rebikov "Christmas Tree" for strings alone was a charming number.

Interest centered in the first performance of "The Death of Kin Sei," one episode of a dramatic ballet "The Soul of a Harp," written by Ken Nakazawa, a Portland author, and set to music by A. A. Avshalamoff. In addition to the usual orchestration, Chinese gongs, drums and harps were used. It was a most interesting number, full of the oriental atmosphere and yet containing much melody. Mr. Avshalamoff was called to the stage to receive the acclaim of both audience and orchestra.

Tschaikowsky's "Marche Slav" brought the concert to a sensational close, when the audience exceeded all bounds of Portland's conservatism and broke into shouts of approval. Mr. Gershkovitch is to be congratulated on the rapid advancement the young people have made. He certainly has a genius for securing the artistic cooperation of the orchestra and is doing a big constructive work for the future of music.

MAY 23, 1927

Ovation Given Conductor and Young Players

By Grant Showerman

The third season of the Portland Junior Symphony orchestra closed gloriously last night, with the youthful musicians at their best, and the main floor and first gallery of The Auditorium filled almost to capacity with enthusiastic music lovers, who time and again were led into spontaneous applause.

Without cavil, the most interesting number was Rimsky-Korsakoff's "Resurrection," it was colorful in the extreme; it afforded every instrument in the orchestra its moment of dominance. It embraces time of a particularly difficult nature, but at every point the young musicians were equal to the demand upon them. From violin to sousaphone each part was effectively rendered.

One could not determine definitely which were favored most by the audience: Saint-Saens' "Danse Macabre," Tschaikowsky's "At Church" or the minuet in Beethoven's No. 1 symphony in C major. Applause was almost as generous for Avshalomoff's "The Death of Kin Sei." A. A. Avshalomoff, the composer, was given an ovation as he appeared with the conductor upon the stage. This was an exotic number employing, among an array of minor instruments, a Japanese harp of bizarre tone. It was a truly Oriental inspiration and instrumentation.

Although each movement of Beethoven's symphony was very creditably played, the minuet stood alone by virtue of the dainty grace of another age.

Jacques Gershkovitch, who has achieved such remarkable results with Portland's young musicians in such a comparatively short time, should be credited with the selection, in his final program, of a bit to suit every palate.

PORTLAND NEWS MAY 23, 1927

Junior Symphony Orchestra Wins New Laurels at Final Concert

By EMIL ENNA

Adding another triumph to their meteoric career, the Portland Junior Symphony orchestra, Jacques Gershkovitch, conductor, gave a brilliant program on Saturday evening at the Auditorium, the final concert of the season.

The Beethoven Symphony evidenced the fact that with sure and sound training Gershkovitch has developed an organization based on profound musicianship. We are all familiar with the fact that the Junior orchestra is capable of doing brilliant things, but the performance given by the Beethoven symphony revealed a steadily maturing symphonic body. One had constantly to keep in mind the youth of the performers interpreting the intricate harmonies with such skill and assurance. Truly the brilliant performance amply repaid the director, founders and supporters, for they have built surely and well.

Gershkovitch conducted the entire program with his usual fire and magnetism, surpassing previous performances of the numbers played on former programs. The Resurrection (Rimsky-Korsakoff) gave splendid balance and impressed one as a huge bridge, spanning the short space of time since the first Junior concert when the audience marveled that a movement from Schubert's Unfinished Symphony might be played by our young people.

That we are civically conscious of the inestimable value of this organization and the untiring efforts and brilliant results Gershkovitch has achieved was emphatically declared by the tumultuous applause, shared by orchestra and director.

PORTLAND TELEGRAM MAY 23, 1927

Junior Symphony Gives Best Concert So Far

By Susie Aubrey Smith

At its last concert of the season Saturday night at the Auditorium, the Portland Junior Symphony orchestra gave another of its interesting programs—interesting because of the excellence of the performance and because of the youthfulness of its personnel. There are 96 young musicians in the orchestra, their ages ranging from seven to twenty years.

In the three years since its organization, the Junior Symphony has gained remarkably in the precision of its attack in the quality and volume of its tone, in clearness of phrasing and in the general finish of its renditions under the capable guiding hand of its conductor, Jacques Gershkovitch.

Saturday night's program was certainly the best ever given by the Junior orchestra. Mr. Gershkovitch is an artist at program arrangement, and he has the unusual faculty of being able to make all parts of a symphony interesting. His reading of Beethoven's First Symphony, which opened the program, was delightful.

Saint-Saens' "Danse Macabre," Tschaikowsky's "At Church," arranged by Mr. Gershkovitch, and so well liked that it had to be repeated, and "The Death of Kin Sei," by A. Avshalomoff of this city, repeated from a former concert, led up to the big thrill of the evening, the rendition of Rimsky-Korsakoff's "La Grande Paque Russe." The audience was most enthusiastic and the Junior Symphony's third season closed most successfully.

JUNIOR SYMPHONY PLAYERS END SEASON WITH CONCERT

Jacques Gershkovitch Leads Players Through Work of Beethoven and Compositions of Portland Musicians.

THE Portland Junior Symphony orchestra brought its season to a close with a concert given at the public auditorium last night, Jacques Gershkovitch conducting.

Of the repeated numbers the original ballet sketch, "The Death of Kin Sei," by A. A. Avshalomoff, possibly attracted the most attention, though its length precluded the possibility of a repetition. This work had its first hearing during a previous concert of the Junior Symphony orchestra, and as at the other occasion, impressed for the originality of invention and depth. Mr. Avshalomoff, in response to many calls from the audience, appeared on the stage.

Beethoven Symphony Played.

Mr. Gershkovitch's arrangement for woodwinds and strings of Tchaikovsky's "At Church" was probably even more enthusiastically received than upon the occasion of its first hearing under his baton. He very obligingly repeated the number in response to popular demand.

The concert opened with the first symphony by Beethoven, a work that had not been heard in its entirety in this city for some time. Nevertheless the first symphony is a great composition, and proved itself an admirable vehicle for the display of the talents of this remarkable body of youths. While Beethoven's music does not present as many technical difficulties for the performer to overcome as do the works of certain other composers, it is nearly the acme of musicianship to catch the spirit of Beethoven. That the Beethoven symphony was played with such spirit and with such grace, with such emphasis and vigor, was perhaps a more notable achievement than the thrilling rendition of the Rimsky-Korsakov overture, with which the concert closed.

Russian Number Novelty.

"La grande Paque russe" was the single number on the program that was a genuine novelty to patrons of the orchestra. It was thoroughly Rimsky-Korsakov, and by the same token brilliant, resounding, and presented soloists in the orchestra with an opportunity to demonstrate individually their artistic prowess. An abundance of crashing climaxes being the nearly inevitable concomitant of the programming of a Rimsky-Korsakov number, this composition provided the audience with a variety of thrills. Aside from being the novelty of the evening, it was the sensation of the evening, and the listeners cheered heartily.

The concert was extremely well attended.

Junior Symphony Concert at Salem Big Event.

Gershkovitch Leads Musicians Through Thrilling Program.

BY AUDRED BUNCH

SALEM, Or., May 8.—(Special.)—Numerous prominent Portland residents were in the audience last night at the Elsinore theater for the extraordinary concert which the Portland Junior Symphony orchestra gave as the concluding feature of National Music week, which has been extensively observed in Salem.

The intrepid Jacques Gershkovitch, conductor of the symphony, electrified the audience from the outset. The 94 young musicians from the little 7-year-old in the second violin section to the dynamic director, stirred the Salem music public as it has seldom been stirred before.

From the first devious and exacting movement of the Beethoven symphony No. 1 and its exultant finale, through the sinister "Danse Macabre," on through the sonorous Tschaikowsky sketch, "At Church," through the weird strains of "The Death of Kin Sei," the ingenious "Music Box," and to the final peerless acclaim of "The Resurrection," the thousand persons in the audience sat in delight. Applause filled every niche of the theater.

At the conclusion of the dramatic Japanese study, Aaron Avshalomoff, the versatile Russian who composed it, received the greeting of Gershkovitch before the footlights.

The musicians returned to Portland on a special train late last night.

MAY 8, 1927

SALEM IS THRILLED BY YOUNG PLAYERS FROM PORTLAND

Junior Symphony Orchestra and Conductor Jacques Gershkovitch Win Great Ovations.

Salem, May 7.—The Portland Junior Symphony orchestra and its conductor, Jacques Gershkovitch, won sensational ovations here tonight in concert at the magnificent Elsinore theatre which wall filled to capacity.

Governor Patterson, Mayor Livesley and many other state and city officials, King Bing of the Cherrians, the May Queen of Willamette university were among those who joined in the tumultuous applause. Quite a number of Portlanders were present too, having come on the special Oregon Electric train that brought the 95 young players who through their unique musical achievements are attracting wide attention to Portland.

The concert was announced as the gala event of Salem's observance of National Music Week, and this indeed it proved to be in every sense of the word.

Skeptics, who came expecting to hear an ordinary children's orchestra, were quickly convinced after the opening strains of Beethoven's symphony No. 1 that they were attending an event they would have missed with regret. The grand pageant "The Resurrection" by Rimsky-Korsakoff, brought the orchestral part of the concert to a thrilling climax.

Throughout the entire program, the undulating waves of exquisite music held the audience in a magic spell, that was broken between each number by storms of applause. Again and again, Conductor Gershkovitch called upon his young performers to join him in acknowledging the plaudits.

4th Season

Jacques Gershkovitch, Conductor

December 3, 1927

Overture: "Egmont"	BEETHOVEN
"The Steppes of Central Asia"	BORODIN
Symphony E minor, NO. 4	BRAHMS
First mvt., Allegro non troppo	
Ballet "Egyptian"	LUIGINI
Solvejg's Song	GRIEG
From "Peer Gynt" Suite no. 2	
Caprice "Italian"	TCHAIKOVSKY

February 25, 1928

Symphony NO. 8 in B minor	SCHUBERT
Russian Folk Songs, op. 58	LIADOV
Ballet "Egyptian"	LUIGINI
Suite "Morning, Noon & Night	*ENNA
"At Church"	TCHAIKOVSKY
Overture "Rienzi"	WAGNER

Wednesday April 11, 1928

Symphony NO. 1, op. 21, in C	BEETHOVEN
Suite NO. 2 "Peer Gynt"	GRIEG
"Toreador et Andalouse"	RUBINSTEIN
"Marche Slav"	TCHAIKOVSKY

* *Portland Premiere*

THE SUNDAY OREGONIAN DEC. 4, 1927

PORTLAND JUNIOR SYMPHONY SHOWS STEADY IMPROVEMENT

Organization of 80 Persons, Mainly Amateurs, Produce Near Furore With "Italian Caprice" at First of Season's Concerts.

BY DAVID L. PIPER

A GROUP of about 80 young people, aroused the enthusiasm of a large audience at the public auditorium last night.

This was the first concert of the junior orchestra's fourth season. And it denoted a steady improvement during the three years of the orchestra's existence. This concert was directed by Jacques Gershkovitch, whose loyalty to his cause, whose resourcefulness and courage have contributed in large measure to the musicianship and the prestige of the organization.

Most of Players Amateurs.

Almost all of the players were amateurs. Two of the first desks, of the viola and violoncello sections, were filled by veteran members of the junior orchestra, but now professionals and members of the Portland Symphony orchestra. Two other desks, the first horn and the first bassoon, were occupied by adult members of the senior orchestra. Two more still, a horn player and a trombonist, were recruited from among the professionals.

Beethoven's "Egmont" overture was the opening number. A symphonic poem by Borodin, "On the Steppes of Central Asia," was the second number. Mr. Gershkovitch appeared to have been more fully at home in this number than in the others, and the result was a reading that was colorful and impressive.

Luigini Ballet Proves Hit.

The Luigini ballet familiar as it was, tuneful as it was, and well adapted as it was to the orchestra, was perhaps the sensation of the evening, though the "Italian Caprice," coming at the end, produced a near furore.

FEB. 21, 1928

Schubert's "Unfinished" Beautifully Played by Symphony Orchestra, Jr.

By J. L. Wallin

I wish Franz Schubert could have heard the Portland Junior Symphony orchestra play his "Unfinished" symphony at The Auditorium Saturday night.

Had he been present in person, I feel, modest and timid as we are told he was, he would have rushed to the stage and shaken hands with Conductor Jacques Gershkovitch and his faithful followers.

The symphony was played beautifully by all sections of the orchestra, which now, in its fourth season, has a membership of 97. With aeolian daintiness, the strings sang with the woodwinds that by this time have developed into an amazingly fine unit. In the fortissimo passages the brasses and batteries entered with splendid feeling for the perfect balance.

The concert was the second of the season's series of three, and the program contained an abundance of delightful variety. Two novelties were included, Eight Songs for orchestra by the Russian composer Anatol Liadov, and Miniature suite by Dr. Emil Enna, pianist-composer and music critic of Portland.

Dr. Enna's miniature suite is a clever little story in three episodes, "Morning, Noon and Night," as its title. A dainty valse for strings alone announces the rising sun at the seashore. The flutes and clarinets, including the bass clarinet, which, by the way, has been added to the orchestra this season, figure prominently in the playful mood of the noonday episode, while the entire instrumentation combines to depict the storm that lends excitement to an otherwise perfect day.

Dr. Enna was not permitted to escape without acknowledging, with Conductor Gershkovitch and the orchestra, the tribute of appreciation carried on huge waves of applause.

OREGON JOURNAL MAY 24, 1927

THEIR LATEST

SOMEBODY ought to endow Jacques Gershkovitch, builder and conductor of the Junior Symphony Orchestra, as a permanent Portland institution.

If you heard the youngsters at The Auditorium Saturday evening, you know why. Musical people in the audience who heard them for the first time hesitated to believe their own eyes and ears.

It is a marvelous thing that has been done here in Portland. These 97 girls and boys, guided by a musical genius and his backers and assistants, have brought a country-wide distinction to Portland as the home of the most conspicuous juvenile orchestra in the United States. They are known in every center where music is cultivated. Their closing concert for the season was far-and-away the best they have yet given. It raised the big audience to a high pitch of enthusiasm and the little players and their conductor were called to their feet many times.

And, to see the scene, brought the flush of pride and a gulp of emotion to many a listener.

5th Season

Jacques Gershkovitch, Conductor

December 15, 1928

Symphony, New World	DVORAK
Adagio: Allegro Molto	
Largo	
Russian Folk Songs, op. 58	LIADOV
Marionetten Trauermarsch	GOUNOD
Melancolie (for strings)	*NAPRAVNIK
Overture Solennelle (1812)	TCHAIKOVSKY

March 2, 1929

Symphony "Italian", op. 90	MENDELSSOHN
Waltz, "Tales of Vienna Woods"	J. STRAUSS
Rondo Cappriccioso	SAINT-SAENS
Dorothy Cowgill, *Violin Soloist*	
Symphonic Poem, "Les Preludes"	LISZT

April 20,1929

Egmont Overture	BEETHOVEN
Symphony No. 6, in C major	*ATTERBERG
Marionetten Trauermarsch	GOUNOD
Melancolie	NAPRAVNIK
Ballet "Egyptian"	LUIGINI

* *Portland Premiere*

JUNIOR ORCHESTRA WINS TRIUMPH IN OPENING CONCERT

Young Musicians Score Brilliant Success in First Appearance of Fifth Season at Auditorium

By J. L. Wallin

The Portland Junior Symphony orchestra won another great triumph Saturday night in its first concert of the fifth season before an audience that ran close to the capacity of The Auditorium. Conductor Jacques Gershkovitch and the young musicians were applauded and applauded again.

This season the orchestra that has attracted national attention because of its unique achievements, is larger than ever with a membership of exactly 100, about 70 of whom constitute the string choir.

The thriller of the program was unquestionably Tschaikowsky's famous festival overture "1812" with which the concert resolved into a really sensational climax. In this overture the orchestra was augmented by some 20 members of Portland's high school bands, who played the extra parts that Tschaikowsky scored for the historic Moscow festival. The many technical difficulties of the overture did not seem to bother in the least the young players. Trumpeters Lewis Johnson, Wesley Stewart Jr., Magar Hyland and David Longtin did some fine pyrotechnics.

But the thing of real tonal beauty perhaps was "Melancolie," by Eduard Napravnik, for string choir alone. Dorothy Cowgill is again the concert master, with Anna May Nolan assistant concert master.

Two movements from Dvorak's symphony "From the New World" formed the first half of the program. They were exceedingly well done. Mary Coin won a big ovation with the English horn solo in the second movement. Tom Galbraith, principal flutist, and Dale Cowan, first clarinetist, since the orchestra was organized, did some outstandingly fine work in the symphony too.

Four numbers from Lliadov's collection of Russian folk songs for orchestra, and Gounod's "Funeral March of a Marionette," completed the program with which Conductor Gershkovitch held the audience at a high pitch of interest from beginning to end.

Following is the personnel of the orchestra:

Assistant to the Conductor—Mrs. M. V. Dodge.

First Violin—Dorothy Cowgill, concert master; Anna May Nolan, assistant concert master; Dorothea Barchus, Helen Becker, Reuben Braunstein, Helen M. Bruce, Jack Buffington, Mary Derrick, D. M. Greenberg, George Hardie, Lewis Hemmila, Phyllis Hogan, C. Honsberger, Arlene Holloway, Chiyoko Makino, Marian Meyer, Bob Morris, Geraldine Peterson, Adella Searle, Tom Smith, Marvin Swire, Audrey Tregaskis.

Second Violin—Glen Reeves, principal; Bernice Barneburg, Kathleen Brady, Mildred Collamore, Leona Davis, Madeline L. Davis, Victor Earll, Harry Hodes, Janet Kalisky, Ralph Kattge, Ramona Lee, Sarah Metzger, Walter Miller, Marjorie Morris, Exelyn Noonan, Leland Numbers, Jane Obee, Margaret Olson, Carlotta Peterson, Bernice Pfenning, Edwin Raudsep, Tarrant J. Rowe, Jane Spies, Dale Stayner, Edward Wagner, Edwin Wall, Elizabeth Willock.

Viola—Edwin Lynds, principal; Joseph Dodd, Ross Hastings, Catherine Heppner, Dorothy Johnson, Jack Knight, Emma L. Lawrence, Lois Lawrence, Alice Southard, Clarence Stevens.

Cello—Elvery Higgins, principal; Mary Davis, Ruth Missildine, Leon Pollock, Bob Renfro, Margie W. W. Taylor, Elizabeth Thornton.

Bass—Hugh Short, principal; Edward McKrill, Rudolph Pearson, Charles West.

Trumpet—Lewis Johnson, Magar Hyland, David Longtin, Wesley Stewart Jr.

Flute—Tom Galbraith, Christian Freer, Marion Goodfellow, Byron Hoyt.

Oboe—Mary Coin, Lewis Wallin.

English Horn—Mary Coin.

Clarinet—Dale Cowen, Donald Burkhart, Fred Ewing Jr.

Bassoon—Ben H. Clay, Paul Nolan Jr.

French Horn—Glen Dodge, V. J. Howell, Lynn Stewart.

Trombone—S. Anderson, David Pitila, Walter C. Schacher, Marjerie Sorber.

Tuba—Drexel Meserve.

Percussion—E. B. Skibitzke, Timpani; Maurice Bush, Snare Drum; Lucille Bowman, Bass Drum; M. Collamore, Cymbals and Tambourine; Fred Rothchild, Triangle; Robert Rowan, Gong and Bells.

Members of high school bands who assisted in the overture were: Omar Bittner, George Burnett, Gordon Finlay, Gerald Lamps, Charles Mason, Charles Merrill, Norman R. Olsen, Roger Olson, Henry Schleyl, Donald Smith, Lane Smith, Frank Willman, Jay Wilson.

J. N. Edleisen, president of the Junior Symphony association, during the intermission spoke in appreciation of Gershkovitch's work.

JUNIOR ORCHESTRA SCORES TRIUMPH IN FINE CONCERT

Enthusiastic, Capacity Audience Won by Artistic Russian Renditions of Symphonic Musicians Directed by Jacques Gershkovitch

NEW musical achievement was won by the young musicians of the Portland Junior Symphony orchestra, Jacques Gershkovitch, conductor, in the first concert of the fifth season of that organization last night in the public auditorium, before an enthusiastic audience that nearly filled the big building. It was a red-letter occasion for the young folk.

The lovely orchestral shadings, the admired ensembles, and other good qualities of this orchestra are due to the great musical ability and personal magnetism of the conductor, Jacques Gershkovitch, who first feels the music in his soul and then brings it out as a message to all others lucky enough to play under his baton. It is almost unbelievable that such exalted symphonic work is that of an organization of 120 members composed principally of Portland grammar and high school children.

Brass Band Formed.

This estimate is based on the playing of this young orchestra in rendering the triumphant Tchaikovsky overture, "Solennele," often called "1812." On this occasion, the symphonic juniors had the assistance of these 13 Portland high school boy musicians.

The "1812" was present with that dramatic fervor so characteristic of a native Russian orchestral conductor—Mr. Gershkovitch—who depicted it as a Russian war-and-peace hymn.

This string choir, especially the first violins, gave exquisite pleasure by fine, alluring tone in the presentation of the Dvorak "New World Symphony," with the familiar song, "Swing Low, Sweet Chariot." Here Dorothy Cowgill and Mary Coin played artistically.

Junior Symphony Scores Success In Fine Program

By SUSIE AUBREY SMITH.

In its first concert of the season Saturday night the Portland Junior Symphony orchestra again scored a big success with music patrons of the city. The lower floor of the Auditorium was practically sold out before the concert and the enthusiasm of the entire audience was of the spontaneous sort that the young musicians of the Junior Symphony always evoke.

Jacques Gershkovitch, conductor of the orchestra, opened with two movements of the Dvorak "New World" symphony, including the favorite largo, which he gave a delightful reading. It was Tschaikowsky's "1812" overture, however, that was really the big number of the program. For this work, the conductor had augmented the orchestra with a group of bandsmen from Portland high schools, as the original score is for symphony orchestra and band. The young musicians gave splendid response to the artistic demands of their conductor and he brought the overture to a thrilling climax.

The excellence of the string section was demonstrated especially in Napravniks' "Melancolie." Contrasted with the melancholy of this was the gay "Marionetten Trauermarsch" of Gounod.

6th Season

Jacques Gershkovitch, Director

December 7, 1929

Symphony No. 1, E b major, op. 26	GOLDMARK
"The Rustic Wedding"	
Concerto No. 1 for Piano	MENDELSSOHN
Andante	
Presto, molto allegro e vivace	
Mollie Dubinsky, *Soloist*	
Celebrated Minuet for strings	BOCCHERINI
Overture, "La Grande Paque Russe" (Easter Night in Russia)	RIMSKY-KORSAKOW

February 8, 1930

Ruy Blas Overture	MENDELSSOHN
Cavatina: "Barber of Seville"	ROSSINI
Lewis Johnson, *Trumpet Solo*	
Ballet Suite, "Raymonda"	GLAZOUNOW
Suite "Coppelia"	DELIBES
Dance of the Automatons; Valse	
The Rising Sun	TORJUSSEN
Orchestrated by Fred Rothchild, Student Conductor	
March, "Tannhauser"	WAGNER

April 5, 1930

Egmont Overture	BEETHOVEN
Symphony No. 3, "Eroica"	BEETHOVEN
Allegro	
Norwegian Dance, No. 2	GRIEG
At Church	TCHAIKOVSKY
Italian Caprice	TCHAIKOVSKY

OREGON JOURNAL APR. 21, 1929

WHEN CHILDREN PLAYED

PORTLAND has had musical successes, many of them. But it has had no musical success more memorable than that of the Junior Symphony Orchestra concert at The Auditorium last Wednesday evening. The boys and girls played and with truly exquisite sensitiveness Beethoven's beautiful Andante cantabile from the symphony in C major.

But it was as much a success of the truly fine conductorship of Jacques Gershkovitch.

Portland's senior Symphony Orchestra is a great musical organization and no comparison is to its disadvantage. Yet with Tschaikowsky's "Marche Slav," no group anywhere could have put into it more spontaneity, vitality, sincerity and the very soul of youth. No wonder it ended amid cheers.

Portland Junior Symphony Orchestra is a sign of the cultural triumphs to be. And it is Portland's!

PORTLAND TELEGRAM APR. 21, 1929

Junior Symphony Scores Success In Last Concert

By SUSIE AUBREY SMITH.

The Portland Junior Symphony orchestra passed another musical milestone Saturday evening in its last concert of the season at the Auditorium. The junior orchestra presented to Portland a new symphony—the composition of Kurt Atterberg, which won the Schubert centennial $10,000 prize. This was the first time the symphony was presented in the West.

For a junior orchestra to undertake the first presentation of a major symphonic work is most unusual in music history. However, the courage of the conductor, Jacques Gershkovitch, was more than justified by the splendid response of his young musicians. The two movements of the Atterberg work, which were given at the end of the first part of the program, were played admirably. The composer has written music that is melodious and interesting and his orchestration is modern and effective. Mr. Gershkovitch brought out the rich musical patterns, the ascending climaxes and the almost Oriental opulence of thematic material in the Adagio in splendid style.

The concert opened with a well rendered performance of Beethoven's "Egmont" overture. As the closing number the Luigini "Egyptian Ballet" was offered. Mr. Gershkovitch led the orchestra through it with his usual artistry.

The audience was enthusiastic in its applause. The concert was, indeed, one of the big musical affairs of the season.

OREGON JOURNAL APR. 21, 1929

Big Ovations Given Young Performers

By J. L. Wallin

THE Portland Junior Symphony orchestra completed its fifth season Saturday night with a concert at The Auditorium that proved a sensational success and that stirred up storms of applause.

The program was by far the most difficult attempted since the memorable event when Conductor Gershkovitch introduced the youngsters in their first ensemble five years ago.

The Atterberg symphony, as it is popularly known, is decidedly modernistic but in classic form, romantic, melodious and thrilling.

This symphony was played for the first time in America last November by the New York Philharmonic, Willem Mangelberg conducting, and its performance here Saturday night was the second in the United States.

The first movement thrilled with its brilliant flourishes in all sections of the orchestra and fascinating effects produced by two harps. Through the first part of the second movement is woven a romantic melody for the clarinet that was beautifully played by Dale Cowan, principal clarinetist.

In the first movement Glen Dodge, principal horn, distinguished himself with a really marvelous recital of the principal theme on the treacherous instrument.

Owing to sudden illness of Tom Galbraith it fell to the lot of Byron Hoyt to move up from second place to principal flute on a moment's notice. He handled the difficult part amazingly well.

The two new harpists were Grace Louise Webb, and Esther A. Palmer.

The program opened with a most fascinating presentation of the descriptive "Egmont" overture by Beethoven. The second half of the concert was devoted to Gounod's humorous and colorful "Marionetten" march, Napravnik's effective poem "Melancolie," for string choir, and the ever popular "Egyptian" ballet suite by Luigini.

Conductor Gershkovitch was called time and again to the platform to acknowledge the plaudits which he, as always, shared graciously with the young performers. The concert marked a new and wide forward step in the orchestra's remarkable career.

The audience was large, with many out-of-town visitors.

ATTERBERG SYMPHONY GIVEN WITH ARTISTRY BY JUNIORS

Young Musicians Under Direction of Jacques Gershkovitch Achieve Success in Performance of Difficult Concert.

BY JOSEPH MACQUEEN.

ALL factors helping in the concert production by the Portland Junior Symphony orchestra, Jacques Gershkovitch, conductor of the splendid and concluding program for 1928–29, heard last night in the public auditorium, are entitled to hearty congratulations. It was a distinct step in spontaneity of musical utterance for that young organization—consisting of about 100 instrumentalists—the members of which are under 18 years old, and practically are either grammar or high school students.

It is inspiring to watch the orchestral performance of so many eager-faced young boys and girls playing there for the artistic love of it.

The Atterberg symphony No. 6 in C major received an inspiring rendition. It has been lately in the storm center of the musical world, and has been in turn derided and lauded. The writer believes that the symphony's message as worked out so skillfully by Mr. Gershkovitch shows that the composition is entitled to a respectful hearing, and that its Portland premier stamps it as a valuable contribution to the exalted music of our time. It is high-class, melodiously pretty, modern without being guilty of discordant dissonance, and novel in ideas.

The orchestral balance observed in this Atterberg symphony was superb.

The overture to "Egmont" (Beethoven) is a bright, cheerful opening number, and it received a good rendition.

The orchestra was resourceful in treatment of the finely-played, gay Gounod's "Marionatten"; and in the somber "Melancholie" (Napravnik). The attractive ballet, by Luigini, "Egyptian," well known and liked here proved a lively number in conclusion.

Mr. Gershkovitch conducted with artistic ability, and with keen sympathy and consideration for the young musicians responsive to his baton. A good deal of the orchestral success won is also due to the consistently faithful work at rehearsals by Mrs. M. V. Dodge, assistant to Mr. Gershkovitch.

The audience was large, enthusiastic, and quick to laud the music treat.

Mr. Gershkovitch plans to leave in May for New York city and other eastern music centers, to take part in symphony orchestral performances during the summer season.

PORTLAND TELEGRAM APR. 21, 1929

THE JUNIOR SYMPHONY.

THE Portland Junior Symphony orchestra brought its fifth season to a close on Saturday night with a performance that would have been remarkable in any case, but from a group of a hundred grammar and high school students, must be counted amazing.

The dignified repertoire which has grown with five years of conscientious rehearsals has given these young people an intimate knowledge of great music that must be a lifetime satisfaction, and they have gained beside, a discipline of patience, of strict obedience, of self-forgetfulness in a united effort, that is the very structure of character.

Portland is tremendously proud of its junior orchestra and The Telegram takes this opportunity to congratulate its members and its sponsors on the work that has been accomplished.

That so much has been done, and so well, is due in largest measure to the masterly leadership of Jacques Gershkovitch, who seems a kindly "Pied Piper," gifted with a magic power that wins children to the same love of music that marks him as an artist.

PORTLAND NEWS APR. 21, 1929

Junior Symphony Closes Season With Fine Concert

By EMIL ENNA

If civic Portland gave one half the response to the Junior Symphony orchestra that its members give to their brilliant, dynamic conductor, Jacques Gershkovitch, we would have an organization unrivalled throughout the nation.

On Saturday evening in the municipal auditorium the Juniors concluded their fifth season with a most brilliant and thrilling program. The principal offering was the Atterberg prize winning symphony, which was a local premiere and the second performance in the United States. The first program of the Juniors, five years ago, featuring a movement of Schubert's Unfinished Symphony, was a revelation. On Saturday evening their presentation of the Atterberg number was a genuine thrill.

The symphony itself as a musical contribution calls forth both praise and criticism, however it is a modern number and most melodic.

The character of the symphony was superseded by the glowing enthusiasm and cultural progress of some 100 students of our grade and high schools. Youth, on the threshold of life, was conveying a glorious and substantial message to parents and friends.

Truly Gershkovitch and sponsors of the Junior orchestra have built exceptionally well.

The overture to "Egmont" (Beethoven), the Luigini ballet "Egyptian," Gounod's happy "Marionatten" and in contrast the Napravnik "Melancholie" were given with mature musicianship and called forth tremendous and enthusiastic ovations for both Gershkovitch and his loyal disciples.

OREGON JOURNAL FEB. 9, 1930

JUVENILE ARTISTS, SOLOISTS, PLEASE GREAT AUDIENCE

Lewis Johnson and Fred Rothchild Thrill Hearers and Are Rewared by Sincere Applause

By J. L. Wallin

Another great triumph was scored by the Portland Junior Symphony orchestra in its second concert of the season Saturday night in The Auditorium before a near capacity audience. Conductor Jacques Gershkovitch and his hundred or so young performers must have felt quite overwhelmed by the barrages of applause that followed each number of the thrillingly presented program.

With Lewis Johnson, principal trumpet, as soloist, and Fred Rothchild, member of the contra-bass section, as student conductor of a number that he himself had orchestrated from the piano score, the concert contained new features to arouse interest in this musical activity that has attracted nation-wide attention. They are students at Washington and Lincoln high schools, respectively.

Johnson, who has been in the orchestra three years, played the brilliant Cavatina from Rossini's opera "The Barber of Seville," with nuances technique and phrasing of a mature artist, and Rothchild called for effects from the orchestra with his baton with real authority and confidence that springs from a perfect conception of the message he wished to convey. The orchestration was colorful, delicate and fascinating.

NEW PIECE GIVEN

The program opened with a dynamic reading by Conductor Gershkovitch of Mendelssohn's "Ruy Blas" overture and closed with an inspirational performance of the well known march from Richard Wagner's opera "Tannhauser."

But the principal offering, from the purely orchestral standpoint, was Alexander Glazounow's ballet suite "Raymonda" which, so far as known has not been presented here before nor anywhere on the Pacific coast.

Nellie Greenwood, piano soloist.

DEC. 8, 1929

JUNIOR MUSICIANS RENDER SYMPHONIC MASTER WORKS

Young Players, Inspired by Jacques Gershkovitch, Give Remarkable Performance; Mollie Dubinsky Scores as Piano Soloist.

BY DAVID PIPER.

THERE are a good many hundred Portlanders who never cease to wonder that one uniquely gifted musician is capable of inculcating no less than 96 youngsters with a very vivid idea of how symphonic music should be played. It awed us, therefore, that Jacques Gershkovitch, while leading the Portland Junior Symphony orchestra in the first concert of its sixth season in the public auditorium last night, brought truly remarkable renditions of some symphonic masterworks from these 96 youngsters.

It is impossible to say whether this was a personal triumph for Mr. Gershkovitch, a collective triumph for the youngsters in the orchestra or an individual triumph for Miss Mollie Dubinsky, the very engaging young pianist who made her initial bow as solo artist during the evening. Paradoxically, Gershkovitch made his biggest sensation while working the least. This was from the playing of the Boccherini "celebrated" minuet, when the leader dispensed altogether with the usual conductorial gesticulations. Indeed, here the sensation was so marked Mr. Gershkovitch was compelled to repeat the piece.

Mr. Gershkovitch elected to open the concert with Goldmark's "Rustic Wedding" symphony, which was ideally adapted to the capabilities of his players. The response by the audience here, too, was emphatic. The concluding number was perhaps the most ambitious ever undertaken by the juniors. Rimsky-Korsakov's concert overture, "The Russian Festival of High Easter," though incorporating a thousand and one technical problems for the players, received a remarkably vivid reading.

The concert was a very big event in the life of Miss Mollie Dubinsky, for this talented young pianist made her first appearance before a legitimate concert audience. Her playing of the second and third movements of Mendelssohn's G Minor piano concerto was the next thing to impeccable.

The Portland Junior Symphony orchestra will be heard twice again during the present season, the next concert being scheduled for February 8.

PORTLAND TELEGRAM DEC. 9, 1929

Junior Symphony Opens Season With Splendid Program

BY SUSIE AUBREY SMITH.

The Portland Junior Symphony orchestra opened its 1929–1930 season Saturday night with a most successful concert at the Auditorium. Junior Symphony audiences are always enthusiastic and Saturday night's program gave special reason for enthusiasm.

For the second time in its history the Junior orchestra presented a young pianist as soloist. Mollie Dubinsky, who won the honor of this appearance in competition, gave the last two movements of the Mendelssohn concerto No. 1 with the orchestra. Miss Dubinsky's playing showed not only excellent training and a splendid technical equipment, but revealed also an interesting personality and a real gift for concert work. She was recalled to the stage several times on the conclusion of the concerto. She is a pupil of David Campbell.

DELIGHTFUL PROGRAM.

Jacques Gershkovitch, conductor of the Junior Symphony, presented an interesting and delightful program, opening with the "Rustic Wedding," symphony of Karl Goldmark. From the augmented string choir Mr. Gershkovitch drew a fine volume of tone, all beautifully smooth. The brass came out splendidly and the youthful musicians in all sections of the orchestra did their usual serious work. The pretty "serenade" and the "Garden" movement of the Goldmark suite were the favorite movements.

In Boccherini's "Celebrated Minuet," the audience had a taste of a "conductorless" orchestra, as Mr. Gershkovitch had the string choir play the piece without the aid of his baton. The remarkably fine training the young musicians have had in orchestra work was evident in their smooth and faultless rendition of this number.

SPLENDIDLY DONE.

For the grand climax of the concert "La Grande Paque Russe" was chosen. It has not only one but many climaxes and many colorful orchestral effects, all of which Mr. Gershkovitch gave us in splendid style. The orchestra members played like veterans and won much applause at the conclusion of this work.

Frederic Rothchild, piano solist and student conductor.

THE OREGONIAN FEB. 9, 1930

JUNIOR, ORCHESTRA SCORES ANOTHER IMPRESSIVE HIT

Musical Youngsters, in Their Second Concert of Season, Prove That Experimental Stage Has Been Passed.

BY DAVID PIPER.

THE already impressive total of successes recorded in behalf of the Portland Junior Symphony orchestra was augmented last night when Jacques Gershkovitch led his centurion of musical youngsters in the second concert of the season. Our junior orchestra is now beyond the experimental stage. There were many earmarks of a mature performance on this occasion, innumerable indications of enhanced musicianship.

The program was almost entirely new, and two of the items were distinctly novel. First, a solo performance starring Lewis Johnson, the orchestra's first trumpeter. This excellent young man exhibited much dexterity. His solo number was Rosina's aria, "Una voce poco fa," from Rossini's "Barber of Seville," transcribed for trumpet and accompanied by the orchestra.

The second half of the evening brought forth an original arrangement of Torjussen's "To the Rising Sun"; and the arranger, Fred Rothchild of the orchestra's double-bass section, led the performance. This excellent young gentleman, by virtue of his really deft baton-wielding, his skilfully contrived orchestration, brought forth thunderous applause. Mr. Gershkovitch led his symphonic centurion in a "first" performance of Glazounov's "Raymonda" ballet suite. This rendition was remarkable for the beauty of the individual cadenzas.

The remaining numbers on the program were Mendelssohn's "Ruy Blas" overture, the dance of the automatons and waltz from Delibes' "Coppelia" ballet suite, and the march from Wagner's "Tannhaeuser." All these Mr. Gershkovitch gave energetic, sympathetic readings.

Following the traditional enter'acte Rabbi Henry J. Berkowitz delivered a diverting, interesting, inspiring address on the mission these juniors have undertaken to perform: on the necessity of whole-hearted support from the community at large.

PORTLAND TELEGRAM FEB. 9, 1930

JUNIORS GIVEN APPLAUSE FOR FINE CONCERT

By SUSIE AUBREY SMITH.

At its second concert of the season Saturday night at the Auditorium, the Portland Junior Symphony orchestra won the applause of an unusually enthusiastic audience and its approval was well deserved by the young musicians and their conductor, Jacques Gershkovitch.

One's sense of wonder at the fine interpretations of the Junior symphony is renewed at each concert it gives, and the novelty of watching girls play the double bass, the cymbals and the bass drum never seems to wear off. Mr. Gershkovitch chose an especially interesting program, which opened with the overture, "Ruy Blas" of Mendelssohn in which the string choir came out exceptionally well. In the entire program the conductor obtained interesting color contrasts and, while working the orchestra up to the big climaxes, did not neglect the smaller musical effects. All sections of the orchestra did splendid work and in the closig march from Tannhauser the brass came out especially well.

Glazounow's ballet suite "Raymonda," was a first performance in Portland. Mr. Gershkovitch gave it an admirable reading, brought it to a brilliant conclusion.

OREGON JOURNAL APR. 8, 1930

AN EVENING OF THRILLS

A BOY of 17 before a concourse of people, facing 100 boys and girls of his own age and under, filled the great hall with the strains and melodies and climaxes of Beethoven's famous overture to "Egmont"—that was a scene Saturday night in The Auditorium that brought a lump into the throat of many a listener.

It was a great moment for all who saw and heard, and a super-moment for Eugene Linden, Jefferson high school boy, who conducted Portland's great Junior Symphony Orchestra.

"It was exciting; my heart was in my throat," said Mrs. Artie Mason Carter, founder of Hollywood Bowl concerts. And she went on to say:

> The thought came to me as I saw those 100 children and heard their wonderful music, expressed in their straightforward way, how it will enrich their lives and the life of every person, child or adult, who is fortunate enough to have the experience I have had at this concert. This is music for music's sake.

Mrs. Carter came from Los Angeles to Portland for the express purpose of hearing in their final concert of the year the Junior Symphony players of which she had heard so much.

The audience was a capacity house, with the largest ticket sale in the history of the orchestra. The progress of the program was a succession of volleys of applause and curtain calls. And the climax of the evening was Tschaikowsky's "Italian" caprice. Its rendition brought an already electrified audience to a high pitch of enthusiasm. Executed by youngsters in their teens and under—and that is a staggering feature of the orchestra's work—the dash and accuracy with which the number was rendered sent thrills through every soul and almost brought the audience to its feet.

THE JEFFERSONIAN APR. 10, 1930

LINDEN DIRECTS JUN. SYMPHONY ORCHESTRA NO.

Many Jefferson Students Appear in Notable Concert

Saturday, April 5, the Junior Symphony Orchestra, under the direction of Jacques Gershkovitch, presented its last concert of the 1929–30 season. The orchestra played a most difficult program, and each selection received a very enthusiastic applause. The selection which interested Jefferson students most was that one which was directed by one of our own students, Eugene Linden, who directed Beethoven's "Egmont Overture." He is a student in the Junior Symphony Class of Conducting, and he showed remarkable talent. One section of the dress circle was reserved for Jefferson students who were there to boost for their classmate. The Jefferson High School Band, of which Mr. Linden is student conductor, attended the concert in full uniform. The blue and gold uniforms made a very impressive showing in the balcony. At the front of the section was placed a large Jefferson banner, which attracted the attention of all those attending the concert.

The last number was Tchaikovsky's "Italian Caprice," a fitting climax to a wonderful evening of music, and was exceptionally well given.

MAY 4, 1930

Radio Concert Brings Many Congratulations

The Portland Junior Symphony orchestra and Conductor Jacques Gershkovitch are still receiving congratulations for the splendid radio concert given on the evening of April 24 over the Western network of the NBC, many of the letters being from distant points.

Writes Mrs. Sarah A. Robinson, from Oakland, Cal. "Last night's broadcast through the Standard Oil company was a rare experience. One expects something near to perfection from men of mature years who have played for long periods, but that a body of young people from the ages of 12 to 18 should achieve such precision of attack and tonal beauty is nothing less than a miracle."

7th Season

Jacques Gershkovitch, Conductor

December 6, 1930

Oberon Overture	WEBER
Symphony NO. 1, in G minor	*KALINNIKOV
Dream Pantomime "Hansel & Gretel"	HUMPERDINCK

Incidental Vocal Solos by
Edythe Wilde, Frances Lynch, Raymond Partipilo

Berceuse	JARNEFELDT
Caprice Brilliant	GLINKA

February 21, 1931

Rosamunde Overture	SCHUBERT
Descriptive, "Baba Jaga" (Witch)	LIADOW
Prelude & Dance, ACT III "The Mastersingers"	WAGNER
Concerto, D minor for Piano Two movements	MOZART

Desda Weinstein, *Soloist*

Suite, "Caucasian Sketches" In the Village Procession of the Sardars	IPOLITOFF-IVANOFF

April 18, 1931

Symphony NO. 8, "Unfinished"	SCHUBERT
Russian Folk Songs, op. 58	LIADOW
Oberon Overture	WEBER
Berceuse	CUI
Scherzo-Caprice	*GERALDINE PETERSON

Composed & orchestrated by the Assistant Concertmaster

Symphonic Poem, "Les Preludes"	LISZT

* *Portland Premiere*

THE OREGONIAN DEC. 7, 1930

JUNIOR SYMPHONY CONCERT HIGHLY SUCCESSFUL EVENT

Youthful Musicians Render Difficult Numbers With Unusual Skill; Three Vocal Proteges Prove Surprise.

BY JOSEPH MacQUEEN.

THE spirit of young America as interpreted in symphony-orchestra expression.

That in a sentence tells the story of last night's fine concert of the Portland Junior Symphony orchestra, Jacques Gershkovitch, conductor, which took place in the public auditorium before a large and highly appreciative audience. From the first moment when the youthful musicians—97 per cent of whom are under 20 years of age, and many of them just little boys and girls—walked on the platform, these attractive players, garbed in dark clothes, were the cynosure of admiring eyes. What followed was a splendid concert in which every one of the 100 executants did his or her best.

Mr. Gershkovitch was ever a magnetic, restless, talented master-conductor. He has a wise mixture of firmness and kindly good nature in dealing with young musical people and in enforcing needed discipline. The orchestra members were in their element, in delineating the romantic adventures of Hansel and Gretel.

The principal number, Symphony No. 1, in G minor (Kalinnikov), an offering with a strong national Russian flavor, has all the elements of the Slav in its texture—seriousness, near melancholy, joy and fine sentiment. The orchestra did some of its best playing at this point. The Finnish Berceuse and Russian caprice formed fitting finales to the enjoyable concert. In this latter the orchestration was helped much by the three trumpeters, David A. Longtin, Gordon A. Finley and Marion Lance. The oboe section, Elsie Foster and Earl Dolan, played smoothly and melodiously. The concert master, Miss Anna May Nolan, played ably in leads.

OREGON JOURNAL DEC. 7, 1930

JUVENILE ARTISTS DELIGHT HEARERS WITH FINE WORK

Great Ovations Follow Colorful Numbers; Conductor's Artistry Evident in Performance.

By J. L. Wallin

Enthusiasm such as is seldom approached at a musical event was aroused when the Portland Junior Symphony orchestra gave its opening concert of the season Saturday night for close to a capacity audience at The Auditorium. The music produced by these 90 or so of talented young performers and their inspired conductor, Jacques Gershkovitch, was so replete with exquisite, colorful and sensitively descriptive effects and such dynamic thrills that the traditional sign of appreciation seemed almost banal. Music such as the slow movement from Kalinnikov's symphony one felt too beautiful, too sacred to be followed by an ovation as it was. In fact, although at times the audience seemed too amazed to break into applause, almost sensational ovations followed each number.

One never imagined the overture to von Weber's "Oberon" so beautiful and so fascinating as this conductor and these youngsters made it.

But still more impressive and beautiful was perhaps the dream pantomime from Humperdinck's fairy opera "Haensel and Gretel" that opened the second part of the program, with the vocal parts sung by Raymond Partipilo, boy soprano, as the sandman, and Edith Wilde and Frances Lynch, sopranos, as the broommaker's two children.

A happy postlude to the pantomine was Jaernefeldt's "Berceuse" for solo violin, woodwind and horn. Anna May Nolan, concertmaster, played the solo.

For the closing number Gershkovitch presented Glinka's Spanish Caprice and with that brought the concert to the thrilling climax that always marks this orchestra's events.

The concert was another glorious triumph for this unique Portland institution that is attracting nationwide attention.

THE SCRIBE DEC. 12, 1930

PORTLAND JUNIOR SYMPHONY CONCERT

BY *MME.* LEAH LEASKA

Saturday night marked the opening of the Portland Junior Symphony Orchestra season under the direction of Jacques Gershkovitch. This series was eagerly anticipated by musical enthusiasts throughout the city, and drew a huge audience who came to pay tribute to the youth of Portland.

Mr. Gershkovitch has a nicely matured group to work with this year—the members have grown a little older and are now capable of finely balanced effects. One hundred of the best juvenile talent in the city showed that they could deliver a program of classics in a meritorious manner that would hold their audience interested throughout. Mr. Gershkovitch has the confidence of these young people and they are willingly guided by his skillful baton.

Symphony No. 1 in G minor (Kalinnikov) was a brilliant achievement. The wonderful "Hansel and Gretel" music held everybody spellbound as did the singing of Raymond Partipilo, 12-year-old Italian boy, also Edith Wilde, soprano, and Frances Lynch, contralto.

By the proper development of our young talent the Portland Junior Symphony orchestra shows that it is doing for the community. The scope of their work is far-reaching and has a certain significant bearing on our citizens of the future. In them is being instilled a love for the best in music, and each child so developed justifies the existence of this splendid organization.

Mr. Gershkovitch and his able board of directors have given the city a group of young artists the people are proud of.

OREGON JOURNAL FEB. 22, 1931

Orchestra and Pianist Given Great Acclaim

By J. L. Wallin

That interest in living music is neither dead nor dying, but to the contrary, sprouting healthily, has been demonstrated forcibly Saturday night when the Portland Junior Symphony orchestra gave its second concert of the season at The Auditorium before close to a capacity audience.

Thousands heard and applauded this unique ensemble of youngsters in their teens who perform with such amazing fidelity, finish and thrilling effects. Ovations following each number were conclusive acclaim of this noble activity, sponsored by the Junior Symphony Orchestra association, now in its seventh year.

The outstanding feature of the concert was undoubtedly the presentation of a 15-year-old Portland girl Desda Weinstein, as soloist in Mozart's D Minor Concerto for piano and orchestra. Two movements, including the interpolated Beethoven cadenza, were done with the delightful and difficult delicacy that characterizes this immortal composer. Conductor Gershkovitch made of the orchestral accompaniment a beautifully subdued background for the solo.

In the magnificent Prelude to Wagner's opera "The Master-singers" and the dances from the same work, the broad, expressive and impressive Wagnerian style was convincingly observed.

The overture to "Rosamunde" by Schubert, originally known as the overture to "The Magic Harp," opened the well balanced program and at once intrigued those who had come for the first time to hear if really an orchestra of children in their teens could arouse such overwhelming enthusiasm with repertoire usually confined to major orchestras.

Much interest centered on Liadow's descriptive symphonic fantasy "Baba Jaga," played here for the first time on this occasion was cleverly done and won rapturous applause.

Two numbers, "In the Village" and "Procession of the Sardar" from Ippolitoff-Ivanoff's "Caucasian Sketches" brought the concert to the usual thrilling close. The duet for English horn and viola in the village scene won individual honors for Elsie Foster and Edwin Lynde.

THE OREGONIAN DEC. 22, 1931

JUNIOR SYMPHONY CONCERT PLEASES LARGE AUDIENCE

Miss Desda Weinstein, Piano Soloist, Gives Creditable Performance of Mozart D Minor Concerto.

BY JOSEPH MACQUEEN.

PORTLAND musical youth, wisely and kindly guided, came into its own triumphant spotlight last night in the public auditorium on the occasion of the second concert this season of the Portland Junior Symphony orchestra, Jacques Gershkovitch, conductor, and Eugene Linden, assistant conductor, in interpreting the glories of great composers like Mozart, Schubert, Liadow, Wagner and Ippolitov-Ivanov.

The large audience by its generous applause placed its approval upon united work of children and conductor.

The concert soloist was Miss Desda Weinstein, pianist—coached in this event by David Campbell—who played with orchestral accompaniment the Mozart D-minor concerto—with one cadenza by Beethoven—is one of the most graceful creations of the eccentric and gifted composer, who lived just 35 years. Miss Weinstein made a modest, graceful platform appearance, and as soloist she played with youthful fire—she is only 15 years old—and with real flowing piano beauty. She has a poetic soul, and in the lighter moods of the composer gave a softly tinted, plastic performance of the concerto's many charms. Her fine piano solo work ever was a silver thread that stood out, while her co-musicians of the orchestra provided splendid accompaniment. She was given floral bouquets carried by seven girl ushers.

Turning to the purely orchestral feature of the event, it was impressive and a quiet joy to which the firm, requisite discipline of this junior symphony orchestra enforced by that friend of musical children, Mr. Gershkovitch. He is in a sense a near-magician, to compel every youthful eye in that orchestra—at a time when we hear so much about youthful scorn of elders and educators generally—to watch and obey the many movements of his busy baton. He makes the young ones believe in their hearts that he is their instructor and friend. Lucky leader.

Unexpectedly good orchestral balance and tonality were noted in the rousing oriental "Procession of the Sardars," by that tuneful Russian genius, Ippolitov-Ivanov. Its central theme is given to the oboe, and it was finely played by Miss Elsie Foster; her fine expression, and her pure, glowing, searching tone deserve to be complimented. The harp music was well played by Mary Lundell.

PORTLAND NEWS FEB. 22, 1931

Junior Concert Receives Praise

By EMIL ENNA

The Junior Symphony orchestra, under the direction of Jacques Gershkovitch were heard at the municipal auditorium in one of the seasons most delightful concerts Saturday evening. Desda Weinstein, pianist, a student of David Campbell, was the soloist.

The program consisted of compositions by Schubert, Liadow, Wagner, Ippolitoff-Iwanoff and Mozart.

Every number on the program was read with the conductors characteristic clearness and technique and the orchestra sensed his message perfectly so that the ensemble was well balanced and pleasing.

It was indeed a highly artistic performance and disclosed the fact that unlimited possibilities lie with the orchestra.

Elsie Foster, first oboist, did some beautiful solo playing in the Ippolitoff-Iwanoff suite. The principal soloist of the evening, Desda Weinstein, played the Mozart piano concerto in D Minor in a highly artistic manner.

Her playing showed the result of natural talent abetted by serious study. Quite outstanding was the fluent technique, excellent tone and splendid interpretation of this youthful pianist.

The large audience thoroughly enjoyed the complete program, much hearty enthusiasm was in evidence.

OREGON JOURNAL FEB. 22, 1931

Young Players' Last Concert Wins Applause

By J. L. Wallin

Somehow when the Portland Junior Symphony orchestra plays Schubert's "Unfinished" symphony one feels that here is something that was written especially for this really marvelous musical organization.

Conductor Jacques Gershkovitch's romantic interpretation of this much beloved work and the spontaneous response of the young players give it a strange charm difficult to explain. They send the message of the lovely themes straight to the hearts of the audience.

History again was written for the orchestra with the premiere performance of the Scherzo from Geraldine Peterson's "Oregon Scenes" suite. This composer is the 17-year-old assistant concertmaster of the orchestra.

The Scherzo proved vividly descriptive of imaginary fairies and gnomes holding high jinks in the Oregon Caves. It is scored for the entire orchestra excepting the top strings. Miss Peterson has already demonstrated as much talent as did many composers whose works are now among the classics.

She acknowledged the ovations with a simplicity of manner that made one feel the pleasure was all hers.

The overture to von Weber's "Oberon" proved a wonderfully graphic synopsis of the story of the opera, with much credit for fine individual work due the horns, the woodwinds and the strings.

Among the smaller numbers was the "Berceuse" by Cesar Cui, a beautiful inspiration charmingly played.

In Liadov's four Russian folk songs, arranged for orchestra, the English born, bassoon and principal cello won admiration with incidental solos.

Conductor Gershkovitch brought the concert and the season to the usual thrilling close with Liszt's deeply emotional symphonic poem "Les Preludes."

John Edlefson, vice president of the Junior Symphony orchestra association, announced that the orchestra will begin its next season without a deficit and expressed the hope for continuation of the public's hearty support.

THE OREGONIAN APR. 19, 1931

PORTLANDERS SAY GOOD-BYE TO JUNIOR SYMPHONY GROUP

Final Concert of 1930–31 Season Rendered at Public Auditorium Before Large Audience.

BY JOSEPH MACQUEEN.

"GOODBY to 1930–31" was eloquently said in glowing music last night by the Portland Junior Symphony orchestra, Jacques Gershkovitch, conductor, at the public auditorium, in a concert which closed the public entertainment events of that young organization for the musical year.

The big number on the program was the Unfinished symphony No. 8 in B minor, of Schubert, in two lovely movements of allegro moderato and andante con moto. It was an ambitious goal for youngsters to reach, but they won out, in strings, woodwind and brass. The sermon-like, prayerful measures of this composition, its full-throated songs of gladness and lovely melodies all were cleverly interpreted with a zeal and a finish that would have done credit to older musicians. The six bass strings, the violoncellos and the French horns did especially brilliant work in etching the fine orchestral coloring. The strings voiced a singing story that fairly glowed with tonal beauty.

The novelty of the performance was the rendition of a scherzo caprice written by the young assistant concertmaster of the orchestra, Miss Geraldine Peterson, a Portland girl, daughter of Mrs. Grace Wilton Peterson and a graduate of Washington high school. She has played in this orchestra six years. She has for three years studied harmony, composition and conducting with Mr. Gershkovitch. The outcome of this busy life of orchestral work is her new scherzo. It is a lively, prettily melodious composition.

The remaining portions of the program are well known. The Liadov Russian folk songs, the Weber overture to "Oberon," a Cui berceuse and the loved Liszt preludes were all brilliantly delineated.

The harp effects were well played by Miss Barbara Frances Jones, 14 years, a student from St. Mary's academy, and who only had two rehearsals with the orchestra.

If Mr. Gershkovitch was energetic and dramatic—he had to be so to get results from so many budding musicians in what educators say is the trying age. His baton was eloquent and impressive.

8th Season

Jacques Gershkovitch, Conductor

November 21, 1931

Symphony NO. 3, "Eroica"	BEETHOVEN
Symphonic Poem, "Call of the West"	*FATHER DOMINIC
Concerto, D major, for Violin Allegro ma non troppo	BEETHOVEN

Anna May Nolan, *Soloist*

Overture, "Russlan & Ludmilla"	GLINKA

February 6, 1932

Rosamunde Overture	SCHUBERT
Eine Kleine Nachtmusic	MOZART
Fingal's Cave Overture	MENDELSSOHN

Fred Rothchild, *Student Conductor*

Invitation to the Dance	WEBER
Concerto, C minor, for Piano Allegro	BEETHOVEN

Mary Bambery, *Soloist*

Prelude & Dance III Act, Die Meistersinger	WAGNER

April 2, 1932

Ruy Blas Overture	MENDELSSOHN
Symphony in G major, NO. 6	HAYDN
Suite NO. 2, "Peer Gynt"	GRIEG
Marche Slav	TCHAIKOVSKY

---

* *Portland Premiere*

THE OREGONIAN NOV. 23, 1931

By Hilmar B. Grondahl

Children Thrill Friends

ONE SELDOM SEES AN AUDIence so actively interested in the performance of its entertainers as we saw in the Auditorium a week ago tonight, while Jacques Gershkovitch led the Junior Symphony through its first programme. To see the faces, or, if not the faces, the posture of the body, showed wrapt attention such as spells musical education.

The audience was interesting, too, from the standpoint of its composition. There were a great many men, faces you see at no other musical functions; and parents, grandparents, and friends bringing children who some day, maybe, will play with the Junior Symphony orchestra. As an educational influence both upon children and parents there seems no doubt of its value.

The orchestra itself, composed of 110 children from quite tender years to legal age, seems unfailingly to thrill with each performance. We realize that the woodwind and brass sections are weak; but so are they with almost all unendowed orchestras. We know that there are few instruments in the entire orchestra made by master craftsmen; but parents are putting their money into lessons, not instruments.

So in spite of these obvious handicaps; immaturity, meager schooling, uncertain orchestral balance, and mediocre instruments we go time after time to hear the Junior Symphony.

Beethoven's Symphony No. 3 (Eroica) was the major work of the concert. This is a tremendous work for any junior orchestra to attempt; under Jacques Gershkovitch this group of youngsters brought out the spirit and intention of its composer.

"The Call of the West", a symphonic poem by Father Dominic of Mt. Angel Monastery was well presented and brought obvious pleasure to the enthusiastic audience.

Perhaps the most spectacular event of the evening was the playing of Beethoven's Concerto in D major for violin and orchestra with Anna May Nolan. Miss Nolan appeared and performed with such perfect ease that she was recalled to the stage several times by full applause.

The concert was concluded with the Overture to "Russian and Ludmilla" (Glinka).

Mr. Gershkovitch deserves great credit for the sane, scholarly and sympathetic way he directs these children.

* * *

OREGON JOURNAL NOV. 23, 1931

Young Players Win Plaudits With Premier

By J. L. Wallin

The Portland Junior Symphony orchestra's first concert of the season Saturday night at The Auditorium was a brilliant success with many impressive features.

Anna May Nolan, who played the solo violin in Beethoven's Concerto, daughter of Mr. and Mrs. Paul Nolan, student at Reed college and member of the Junior orchestra since its organization seven years ago, made the concerto a thing of transcendant beauty with a lovely tone and clean and sure technic. The long cadenza that forms the high point of the first movement, that had been chosen for her debut as soloist, was an exquisite piece of violin virtuosity.

The laurel wreath for Father Dominic was presented by Frederick W. Goodrich, president of the Oregon Music Teachers association, after Conductor Gershkovitch had acknowledged the ovation that followed the performance of the tone poem descriptive of pioneer days in the Willamette valley.

"I have the honor and pleasure to represent the Oregon Music Teachers' association which through its Portland district desires to show its love and respect to the venerable composer, Father Dominic Waedenschwiler."

The principal orchestral number of the program was Beethoven's "Eroica" symphony of which the first, second and third movements were played in a manner that left no room for doubts as to the constant progress of this unique and nationally known ensemble of young performers.

The program was brought to a grand climax with Glinka's brilliant overture to "Russian and Ludmilla."

THE OREGONIAN FEB. 7, 1932

JOY OF YOUTH ENTERS INTO JUNIOR SYMPHONY CONCERT

Eagerness of 93 Boys and Girls to Please in Difficult Music, Inspiration to Those of Audience Who Realize Self-Discipline Task.

BY JOSEPH MACQUEEN.

BRIGHT, cheerful music, played with all the joy of youth, made up a memorable program last night before a large audience, at the second concert of the season of the Portland Junior Symphony orchestra, Jacques Gershkovitch, conductor, at the public auditorium.

On this occasion it is notable that the 93 young people who are playing in that orchestra just now are under 21 years of age, and therefore children, with the single exception of the guest tympani-principal, E. B. Skibitski, formerly a member of that orchestra.

Mr. Gershkovitch was a living magnet of musical attraction to the juvenile orchestral forces committed to his care, and was ever patient, resourceful and dramatic to a finished degree. It was inspiring to watch the eagerness, and the desire to please that came from the youngsters, working under control of his baton. The orchestral phrasing that came from the organization was a joy to hear, in its attention to details creating charming finish and shading of ensemble.

Fred Rothchild won favor as student conductor when he directed the work of the orchestra in interpreting the beauties of the overture "Fingal's Cave" (Mendelssohn). Mr. Rothchild was quiet, competent and inspiring to watch. The orchestra gave him eager support.

The Beethoven concerto in C minor, for piano and orchestra, was heard once more in one movement, the allegro. The solo pianist was Miss Mary Bambery, 16-year-old daughter of Mr. and Mrs. James E. Bambery, who has been coached by Mrs. Ruth Bradley Keiser, and latterly in pianism by Mrs. Frances Striegel Burke. The concerto shone in rich, vivid harmonic detail and colorful keyboard treatment generally. Her technique also is to be commended.

The four selections for full orchestra showed the young orchestra players at their best in illustrating bright, happy music. It was young America—pulsing—eager—filled with the gladness of youth. The Schubert overture, "Rosamunde"; the dignified Mozart serenade, the Weber lovely, gay "Invitation to the Dance," and the Wagner prelude the dance to "Der Meistersingers" all are under this category of orchestral beauty.

It was a treat to watch the cohesive bowing of the strings. The violoncello playing, the strong, musicianly work of the brass, and playing of seven bass viols by juveniles, all did their work in creating worth-while music—really worthy of adults—at this delightful concert.

Applause was hearty.

OREGON JOURNAL FEB. 7, 1932

Audience Is Thrilled at Music Event

By J. L. Wallin

A near-capacity audience in The Auditorium Saturday night was stirred to heights of enthusiasm when the Portland Junior Symphony orchestra gave its second concert of its eighth season under direction of Jacques Gershkovitch.

Sixteen-year-old Mary Bambery won applause that would have warmed the heart of any mature and celebrated artist as soloist in Beethoven's C Minor Concerto for piano and orchestra, of which she played the brilliant Allegro.

This talented girl was chosen for appearance with the orchestra at an audition several weeks ago in which more than a dozen boys and girls demonstrated that the piano is not a dust-gathering relic of the pre-radio period.

Young Miss Bambery rose triumphantly to the occasion with a concert performance both exciting and satisfying and without the slightest noticeable trace of nervousness. With the cadenza near the close of the movement she fired the audience to a real ovation. One almost sensed the large grand doing its best to respond with a rich, round tone to the sensitive touch of the fingers of youth.

Miss Bambery is a pupil of Mrs. Frances Striegel Burke.

Fred Rothchild, 18, principal of the contra-bass section, demonstrated the orchestra's achievement in developing student conductors, with a romantic, rapidly-shifting, reading of Mendelssohn's descriptive "Fingal's Cave" overture.

OREGON JOURNAL FEB. 7, 1932

Junior Symphony Orchestra Presents Fine Concert.

Hundreds Gathered at Fir Acres Applaud Young Musicians.

Hilmer B. Grondahl

FROM a setting unique in the annals of local symphonic concerts, the Portland Junior Symphony orchestra, under student conductors, last night delighted the hundreds who had gathered on broad lawns of "Fir Acres," the Frank estate on Palatine hill, to hear them.

Their platform was a flagstone court on an interior angle in the wings of the old-Norman-style house. Here sat 60 juvenile players. The audience gathered informally on the grass, on stone walls, leaned against tree-trunks or listened as they continued their walk through the gardens.

The program chosen was in two parts. Fred Rothchild, member of the contra-bass section, directed the first part, which included the First Ballet suite by Gluck, Jarnefeldt's "Berceuse" and Mendelssohn's overture to "Fingal's Cave." Eugene Linden, assistant to Jacques Gershkovitch, conductor, led for the first movement of Schubert's "Unfinished" symphony, the Boccherini "Celebrated" minuet and Schubert's overture to "Rosamunde."

There was much in the conducting of both young leaders that showed fine promise of the future. Rothchild, in directing the Mendelssohn work, brought out a breadth of effect that would have been considerable in a larger orchestra. Eugene Linden did his best work in the Schubert overture and achieved an agreeable finish.

This concert was a part of the two-day festival at Fir Acres. The same program will be repeated at 8 o'clock tonight.

APR. 3, 1932

Audience Acclaims Juniors

HAD FRANZ JOSEPH HAYDN BEEN listening among the thousands who thronged the Civic Auditorium last Saturday night, he would probably not have frowned on the way the Portland Junior Symphony Orchestra played his "Surprise" symphony.

To us this symphony No. 6 is the high spot of an unusually successful season, and helps to explain why the last concert of the Junior Symphony Orchestra was its most satisfying musically.

Frankly, we didn't blame the audience for going wild and calling Mr. Gershkovitch back to the stand a half dozen times. We were thrilled.

Next to Haydn, the salient feature was Grieg's "Peer Gynt" suite No. 2, as conducted by Eugene Linden, assistant to Jacques Gershkovitch.

This chap seemed to have the flavor of Grieg and the adventures of Peer well in his mind. His score was well in mind, too.

The audience commended Eugene Linden highly for his work with the baton. "March Slav" (Tschaikowsky) brought the program to a thundering close.

9th Season

Jacques Gershkovitch, Conductor

December 10, 1932

Die Freischutz Overture	WEBER
Symphony in G major, NO. 6	HAYDN
Russian Folk Songs	LIADOW
Concerto, C minor for Piano	BEETHOVEN
Largo & Rondo	
Nellie Greenwood, *Soloist*	
"The Sorcerer's Apprentice"	DUKAS

February 18, 1933

Overture, "Barber of Seville"	ROSSINI
Valse Triste	SIBELIUS
Concerto for Bassoon	MOZART
Andante ma Adagio	
Tempo di menuetto	
Samuel K. Fisher, Jr., *Soloist*	
Praeludium	JARNEFELDT
Concerto in D for Violin	PAGANINI
Geraldine Peterson, *Soloist*	
Ballet Suite, "Raymonda"	GLAZOUNOW

April 8, 1933

Leonore Overture	BEETHOVEN
Concerto for Piano	GRIEG
First movement	
Robert Garretson, *Soloist*	
Sinfonia in Bb major	J. C. BACH
Nocturne	MENDELSSOHN
Resurrection Overture	RIMSKY-KORSAKOW

NEWS TELEGRAM NOV. 1932

YOUNG MUSICIANS OPEN YEAR'S CONCERT SEASON

By EMIL ENNA

The Portland Junior symphony orchestra, Jacques Gershkovitch, conducting, presented the season's first concert at the municipal auditorium Saturday night. Nellie Greenwood, pianist, was the soloist.

The program was replete with brilliancy and contrast which included Weber's overture "Der Freischutz," the Haydn G Major symphony, Russian folk songs by Liadow, Dukas' "The Sorcerer's Apprentice" and the Largo on Rondo from Beethoven's C Minor Concerto.

The response of the orchestra to the conductor's reading was electrifying. Throughout the entire program the orchestra achieved remarkable effects and marked this performance an outstanding one of its career.

The charming youthful soloist, Miss Greenwood, scored a decided success in her performance of the Beethoven piano conceto, showing mature musicianship and clarity of tone and touch. Quite interesting was her fluent technique and fine sense of style. She is a worthy exponent of Marjorie Trotter's instruction.

OREGON JOURNAL FEB. 19, 1933

Concert Wins New Acclaim For Juniors

By J. L. Wallin

Emotional thrills through the medium of amazingly well-played music kept interest at high pitch at the Portland Junior Symphony orchestra's second concert of the season at The Auditorium Saturday night and Conductor Jacques Gershkovitch and the hundred young musicians were rewarded with acclaim that bordered on the sensational.

One can only surmise what Charles de Beriot would have exclaimed had he been there and heard Geraldine Peterson play Paganini's Concerto for violin and orchestra, and its beautifully balanced accompaniment.

ARTIST DISPLAYS POISE

Here a Portland girl, in her teens, did the trick with commendable ease, comforting poise and a freedom and fullness of expression that compared with mature art.

Prolonged acclaim followed also the performance by Samuel K. Fisher Jr. of two movements of Mozart's Concerto for bassoon and orchestra, which by the way was composed when Wolfgang Amadeus was but 18, a year the junior of Saturday night's soloist. Bassoon solos are decided novelties. Young Fisher had the situation perfectly in hand and gave a fine demonstration of the training inspired by the unique orchestra and with the aid of special and individual teachers.

CONDUCTOR WINS NEW LAURELS

While these solos were conspicuous highlights on an altogether attractive program, Conductor Gershkovitch added new laurels to his already large collection with impressive interpretations of the overture to Rossini's opera buffa "The Barber of Seville," Jaernefelt's "Praeludim," Sibelius' "Valse Triste" and Glazounow's both romantic and pompous ballet suite "Raymonda."

FEB. 19, 1933

JUNIOR SYMPHONISTS GIVE THRILLS TO BIG AUDIENCE

Program Broadcast by Radio, Heard and Seen by Thousands of Portland Residents, Wins Accolade.

BY HILMAR B. GRONDAHL.

Again the Portland Junior Symphony orchestra, responding to the baton of Jacques Gershkovitch, its conductor, thrilled thousands who came to hear it at the civic auditorium. But last night its program was made audible to radio audiences of the Pacific coast and the mountain states through a network broadcast.

It was doubtless a source of gratitude to the orchestra that its work should thus be heard and understood outside of the city where it originates, but those who occupied seats in the auditorium knew that the radio audience experienced only a part of what there was to be enjoyed at a performance of this juvenile group.

Strange as it may sound, this orchestra of 100 boys and girls must be seen to be heard. One wishes frequently to reassure himself with open eyes that these are really young amateurs who give this phrase or that orchestral dynamic such a professional finish.

And certainly while either of last night's two soloists was playing, nobody in the audience would have missed witnessing the performance. Samuel Fisher Jr. appeared in a concerto for bassoon and Geraldine Peterson played the solo part of Paganini's concerto for violin and orchestra.

The program opened with the full orchestra in Rossini's overture to "The Barber of Seville." Immediately the conductor and players showed themselves in fine preparation for their program. Here at the outset was one of the most finished performances we have heard the juniors give.

Then came Mozart's concerto for bassoon and orchestra, featuring Samuel Fisher Jr. as soloist. The performance which the orchestra's principal bassoonist gave showed taste and experienced talent. Characteristically Mozartian figures and runs were managed with ease, tone coloring was excellent and the general style of the work was admirably maintained. The orchestra gave excellent support.

Last but far from least in the enjoyment of the audience came the ballet suite from Glazounow's "Raymonda." Here the orchestra had a chance to show the training of all its sections. Especially noteworthy was the fine ensemble and tonality of the brass choir.

There have been some thrilling concerts by the juniors before, but for a high measure of skill and finish from start to finish we haven't heard the equal of last night's concert since the orchestra began playing.

Following the work for solo woodwind Jacques Gershkovitch brought a work which one recalls principally because of its plucked strings, "Praeludium," by Armas Jarnefelt.

OREGON JOURNAL MAY 14, 1933

Youngsters Triumph in Air Concert

By J. L. Wallin

The Portland Junior Symphony orchestra scored the crowning triumph of its nine years of existence in a special concert at The Auditorium Saturday night before an audience of close to 3000; that for enthusiasm has seldom been equaled in the City of Roses, with its high musical standards.

The audience was the largest ever attracted by this unique organization of 110 young musicians conducted by dynamic and musically intensely sensitive Jacques Gershkovitch, and the rousing demonstrations left no room for doubt as to the feeling that this educational and entertaining activity must continue with assurance of hearty public support.

The broadcast over the Columbia national network, through local station KOIN-The Journal, carried the music to hundreds of thousands in the United States and Canada, thereby adding prestige to Portland in many ways.

An added feature was the presentation of Harry Cykman of San Francisco, as soloist in Mendelssohn's E minor concerto for violin, with the orchestra, and a group of shorter numbers to piano accompaniment.

A boy, going on 11, with a remarkably mature musical mind, a marvelous technic and an excellent instrument, held the audience spellbound with his playing, both in the concerto and the group numbers that opened the second part of the program.

In his playing one felt the mastery of Hubey, the famous virtuoso who taught Sigmund Rader, the lad's teacher, who came here with him from San Francisco and who probably was one of the most excited persons in the audience, for the event was a triumph for him as well as his protege and the orchestra.

Mary Bambery, the young Portland girl, who two seasons ago appeared as piano soloist with the orchestra, was the ideal accompanist for the group with piano, of which the difficult and exacting Ballade and Polonaise by Vieuxtemps was on the program.

The orchestral part of the Mendelssohn Concerto was exquisitely performed by every section of the large ensemble and Conductor Gershkovitch was called to the stage time and again.

"Fingals Cave" overture, Sinfonia by J. C. Bach and "The Sorcerer's Apprentice" by Paul Dukas, orchestral numbers of the program, will be remembered as among the most fascinating and emotionally thrilling ever heard here.

Conductor Gershkovitch made an impassioned appeal during the intermission, in behalf of the orchestra, the existence of which, he said, depends largely upon the city's willingness to support.

Mrs. Robert H. Noyes, president, said, "On behalf of the members of the Portland Junior Symphony orchestra and those young people who have received inspiration from a nation-wide recognition of musical training for youth," she said, "the board of directors wish to thank the thousands of Portland citizens who were joined in the belief that the Junior Symphony orchestra under Jacques Gershkovitch should continue to exist as a recognized need at this time.

"There has been a close, spontaneous, thrilling and entirely successful co-operation among all groups of citizenry to fill The Auditorium and thus proclaim to the nation that Portland intends to back her next generation.

THE OREGONIAN MAY 14, 1933

10-YEAR-OLD BOY VIOLINIST THRILLS PORTLAND AUDIENCE

Harry Cykman, Guest Artist of Junior Symphony Orchestra, Appeals to Vast Crowd of Music Lovers at Public Auditorium.

BY HILMAR B. GRONDAHL.

WHILE a radio audience numbering millions listened in on its nation-wide broadcast, the Portland Junior Symphony orchestra, under Jacques Gershkovitch's direction, gave visible as well as audible evidence of effective group musicianship before several thousands in the public auditorium last night. The concert featured as soloist Harry Cykman, 10-year-old violinist of San Francisco.

Master Cykman elected to play the Mendelssohn E minor concerto entire. Mendelssohn was further represented in the overture "Fingal's Cave," which opened the program. Other works played included Johann Christian Bach's sinfonia in B flat major, Paul Dukas' "The Sorcerer's Apprentice" and a group of violin solos with piano accompaniment given by the guest artist and Mary Bambery.

Except for Mr. Gershkovitch, every one on the stage was a minor; 100 youths unified by the orderly boundaries of music. For some cause that is perhaps in the contagion of youthful enthusiasm and ideals, these juveniles played better than should be expected of them. And this extra portion of excellence touched the audience deeply.

There was not the slightest doubt, apparently, from any quarter of the house but that Harry Cykman, playing as he did last night, is destined to ride into that fair province of solo artistry where few are privileged to seek admission. His ease of playing, his sparkling technique, his tone of nice proportion, however small, his style and general musicianship are such as show in few boys so generously. A boy of 10, it was amazing; breath-taking.

Such vigor or response was nowhere so pronounced as when Harry Cykman brought his bow down from the last note of the Mendelssohn violin concerto.

Here was a work of consuming beauty which had had a thrilling performance from a child of prodigious talents.

10th Season

Jacques Gershkovitch, Conductor

November 23, 1933

Symphony NO. 8, B minor	SCHUBERT
Piano Concerto, A minor	SCHUMANN
Patti Greenwood, *Soloist*	
Overture, "Merry Wives of Windsor"	NICOLAI
Elegie for Strings	TCHAIKOVSKY
Overture, "Die Meistersinger"	WAGNER

February 3, 1934

Oberon Overture	WEBER
Sketch, "Steppes of Asia"	BORODIN
Waltz & Elegy [from "Serenade for Strings"]	TCHAIKOWSKY
Polonaise from "Life for the Czar"	GLINKA
Chorus & Orchestra	
"A Night on Bald Mountain"	MOUSSORGSKY
Hallelujah Chorus from "The Mount of Olives"	BEETHOVEN
"Death of Siegfried"	WAGNER
"Tannhauser"-March & Chorus	WAGNER

April 14, 1934

Overture, "Russlan & Ludmilla"	GLINKA
Symphony, "Italian"	MENDELSSOHN
Concerto in D minor for Piano	MOZART
Fred Rothchild, *Soloist*	
Capriccio Espagnol	RIMSKY-KORSAKOV

SPECIAL CONCERT

Jacques Gershkovitch, Conductor

CBS Nationwide Broadcast

May 13, 1933

Fingal's Cave Overture	MENDELSSOHN
Concerto in E minor for Violin	MENDELSSOHN
Harry Cykman, *Guest Soloist*	
Sinfonia in Bb major	J. C. BACH
Ballade & Polonaise	VIEUXTEMPS
Harry Cykman, *Violin;* Mary Bambery, *Piano*	
"The Sorcerer's Apprentice"	DUKAS

June 12, 1934

ROSE FESTIVAL CONCERT

Entry of Queen Beth of Rosaria & Her Royal Court

Fanfare	LINDEN
"Merry Wives of Windsor"	NICOLAI
Berceuse	CUI
Ballet Suite NO. 1, from	GLUCK/MOTTL
"Don Juan," "Orpheus," "Armide," & "Iphigenia in Aulis"	
March & Chorus-"Tannhauser"	WAGNER
Ballet, "Nutcracker" ACT III	TCHAIKOVSKY

Principals: William F. Christensen, Natalie Lauterstein & Janet Reed

THE OREGONIAN NOV. 26, 1933

JUNIOR ORCHESTRA AMAZES AUDIENCE

Young Musicians Acclaimed for Masterful Work.

FINE TRAINING SHOWN

Schubert's "Unfinished" Symphony Splendidly Rendered; Part of Program Broadcast.

BY HILMAR B. GRONDAHL.

For 40 minutes last night an audience of several thousand persons sat amazed at the performance given in the public auditorium by the hundred or more members of the Portland Junior Symphony orchestra as they played the first two numbers on the first concert of their tenth season. For the remaining 30 minutes this audience was joined by the air audience of a broadcasting company's coast-to-coast network. Entirely new to the orchestra's repertoire, and far beyond its capabilities of interpretation not so long ago, was the first movement of Schumann's piano concerto in A minor. This work featured Patty Greenwood, 14-year-old pianist, and proved in some respects to be the evening's high point of interest.

Compositions which went over the broadcasting network were: Nicolai's overture to the "Merry Wives of Windsor," Tchaikovsky's elegie for strings alone, and the preclude to "Die Meister-singer" by Wagner.

Schubert's Symphony Featured.

Under Jacques Gershkovitch's decisive baton, the junior orchestra gave a smooth and felicitous playing of Schubert's great B minor symphony. Melodies were given distinct outline and neat phrasing. Rhythms were emphasized in proper proportion. The audience signified its approval in waves of applause.

Miss Greenwood took her place at the piano and amazed her hearers by reason of her tone, her poetry, her deliberate phrasing and the intensity of certain passages. In some places her part did not sing out above the orchestra but that is a matter of balance which cannot be heard and controlled by a youth of such tender years on her first public appearance.

Gauged by the many curtain calls the girl had given an astonishingly well-proportioned playing of a difficult work. It was particularly in her cadenza that she showed the intensity of her pianistic nature and the variety of her musical equipment.

THE OREGONIAN NOV. 26, 1933

Players Are Well "Feexed" For Junior Symphony Concert

By Grant Showerman

Well, having raised the question as to whether or not Jacques Gershkovitch had properly "feexed" his three clarinet players when they "gobbled" at rehearsal, it is only fair, after the concert, to answer it.

He did.

When he "feexed" them, he fixed them the same as a mechanic would fix an automobile which was firing out of time, one player explained.

Because the players are young, it has been difficult for many to comprehend that this is not a children's orchestra. The scores are not simplified. The young musicians master them as the composer arranged them, if they happen to be modern; or as they have been arranged for modern instrumentation if of the older classics.

The players ask no quarter. They work at their parts until they have mastered them.

The scores last night in every number presented considerable technical difficulty. They were played as smoothly and as intelligently as any musician could wish.

"Isn't it marvelous," commented a middle aged woman. I enjoyed it as much as I used to the Chicago symphony."

Wonderful and marvelous were words frequently heard. The noble chords of Wagner were nobly rendered.

Three thousand Portlanders were thrilled and proud, because the 1933–34 Junior symphony orchestra last night unequivocally demonstrated that it was of the same high class as those of the nine preceding years.

Audience Cheers Players.

After each of the three numbers which went on the air, the audience registered its pleasure in no uncertain terms.

Following the concert Judge Jacob Kanzler introduced Moe Tonkon of the Portland Junior Chamber of Commerce, who read from a parchment scroll bearing the signatures of Governor Meier, Mayor Carson, Amedee M. Smith, president of the Portland Chamber of Commerce; Frank McCaslin, president of the Junior Chamber, and Mrs. Robert H. Noyes, president of the Portland Junior Symphony Orchestra association. This was presented to Conductor Gershkovitch in appreciation of his ten years' service to the orchestra and the community. Hundreds attended the attractive anniversary reception. Hill Military honor guards participated.

THE SCRIBE DEC. 1933

by Hilmar Grondahl

Junior Symphony Plays

The Portland Junior Symphony orchestra is made up of young players under twenty-one. Mostly, they are school children. So their conductor, Jacques Gershkovitch, may have thought for a moment when he came onto the stage to begin the first concert of their tenth season that the trumpet section was up to a prank such as might be expected of lively boys. He had coached the section in no fanfares. To say that he was surprised to have the applause of the audience drowned out by this blare of trumpets is putting it mildly. It must then have occurred to him that this fanfare was the orchestra's own way of signalizing their recognition of his ten years' service as teacher, drillmaster and conductor.

The occasion was one to remember. For ten years this organization of juvenile amateurs has developed. Just how far it has advanced was measured for the audience on November 25th at the Public Auditorium by the inclusion of several numbers played on the first public program years ago. Chief of these was the Schubert B minor symphony. Those who heard the first concert when twenty of the orchestra's thirty-five players were violinists, and many sections were incomplete, would not have recognized the interpretation of the "Unfinished" symphony which flowed from the instruments of more than 100 juniors in an orchestra complete in all sections.

Not only was this tenth anniversary concert celebrated by the replaying of old numbers, and the presentation to Mr. Gershkovitch of a memorial scroll inscribed by the state's governor, the city's mayor, the orchestra association's president, and leaders of commercial life, but it included an enormous reception following the concert, and a coast to coast broadcast of half the program over the Columbia Broadcasting System's network.

Another feature of the evening was the playing of the first movement of Schumann piano concerto in A minor by Patty Greenwood, a girl of fourteen. Her grasp of its poetic ideas was remarkable in a pianist so young. The audience gave her a bewildering number of curtain calls.

THE OREGONIAN FEB. 4, 1934

JUNIOR SYMPHONY MUSIC DELIGHTS LARGE AUDIENCE

Children Play Difficult Works With Ease and Accuracy of Adults; Singing of Chorus of 150 Voices Outstanding.

BY HILMAR B. GRONDAHL.

THE Portland Junior Symphony orchestra under the direction of Jacques Gershkovitch, presented the second concert of its tenth season last night before a large and intensely interested audience at the public auditorium. This concert presented for the first time the Portland Junior symphony chorus of 150 voices.

There is always something inspiring about a concert by the junior orchestra. Last night anyone with the spirit for musical beauty was privileged to dwell to his heart's content upon the music alone. And as an accompaniment to this pleasure he felt the joy of watching these children perform.

The program in its balanced two-section construction was composed of five orchestral works and three choral numbers. For the orchestra alone there was Weber's overture to "Oberon," the "Steppes of Asia" by Borodin, two sections of Tchaikowsky's serenade for strings. From the simplicity of the Tchaikowsky work the orchestra later came to Moussorgsky's picturesque symphonic poem. Much brass and woodwind instrumentation is blended with the strings in this work to establish the weird occurrences which the composer saw transpiring at the congress of witches at the snowy summits of the Bald Mountain.

Something of the dramatic substance of this work seemed to grip the imaginations of these young players, thereby evening off the inherent instrumental difficulties to the point where they were negligible.

The "Death of Siegfried" was even more remarkable in its excellent effect because it is a work replete with the troubles which try many professional orchestras; the bedeviling uncertainties of the brass sections. Through the heavy writing for French horns, trombones, tuba and basses these youths marched with somber and triumphant restraint, producing the best brass choir work that their present season has known.

Last but far from least on this night of well-made music was the singing of the new chorus. Its three numbers were: The polonaise from Glinka's "Life of the Czar," the "Hallelujah" chorus from Beethoven's "Mount of Olives" oratorio, and the march and chorus from Wagner's "Tannhauser." While all sections were of good quality, there are still some adjustments possible in the interest of balance. But the soprano section, which stood out in most of the full ensemble parts, is the most satisfying soprano chorus for freshness of voice that has come to our attention this season.

MIDNIGHT—PORTLAND JUNIOR SYMPHONY.
WABC WHAS WKRC cklw wspd wcco

First Program Of Portland Junior Symphony on CBS, November 25

The opening program of the 1933–34 season by the Portland Junior Symphony, under the direction of Jacques Gershkovitch, will be broadcast direct from the Municipal Auditorium in Portland, Oregon, over WABC and a nationwide Columbia network, Saturday, November 25, from 12:00 midnight to 12:30 a.m. (EST). The concert will be relayed to the Columbia network through the facilities of Station KOIN, Portland.

MUSICAL AMERICA DEC. 25, 1933

Junior Musicians Acclaimed

A fanfare of trumpets brought the audience to its feet when Jacques Gershkovitch appeared on the stage at the tenth anniversary concert of the Junior Symphony, on Nov. 25.

The fine playing of Schubert's Unfinished Symphony and compositions by Nicolai, Tchaikovsky and Wagner emphasized Mr. Gershkovitch's great accomplishment with these young players. Patty Greenwood, youthful pupil of Marjorie Trotter, disclosed rare gifts in the first movement of Schumann's Piano Concerto. The second half of the program was a CBS broadcast over KOIN, the *Oregon Journal* station.

A reception in the wing was held after the concert. A testimonial, signed by Governor Meier, Mayor Carson and Mrs. Robert Noyes, president of the Junior Symphony Society, was presented to Mr. Gershkovitch. To Mrs. Noye's tireless energy can be attributed a marked increase of interest in this organization.

MUSICAL COURIER DEC. 23, 1933

JUNIOR ORCHESTRA MARKS ANNIVERSARY

Marking its tenth anniversary, the Portland Junior Symphony Orchestra (110 juveniles) appeared before 3,000 Oregonians on November 25 and distinguished itself in the first number, Schubert's Unfinished Symphony. Next came Pattie Greenwood, fourteen-year-old pianist. Supported by Conductor Jacques Gershkovitch and the orchestra, she offered the first movement of Schumann's A minor concerto and elicited prolonged applause. The last half of the program, which included the overture to The Merry Wives of Windsor (Nicolai), was broadcast over the CBS network. This enterprising orchestra has a complete instrumentation and all works are played as originally scored. The organization is sponsored by the Portland Junior Symphony Orchestra Association (Mrs. Robert H. Noyes, president; Ruth Isherwood, executive secretary).

OREGON JOURNAL APR. 15, 1934

Orchestra Has Big Success; Season's End

By J. L. Wallin

The Portland Junior Symphony orchestra rounded out its tenth season Saturday night with a concert in The Auditorium that proved a sensational success. As a whole the event must be recorded the climax of the organization's many triumphs to date, and as such a convincing demonstration of the 110-strong ensemble's constant progress.

An outstanding feature was the performance of Mozart's Concerto in D Minor for piano and orchestra with Fred Rothchild as soloist. Young Rothchild, who six years ago joined the orchestra as member of its percussion group, and later advanced to principal of the contra-bass section, amazed the expectant audience with a highly developed musicianship, a dazzling fluency of technic, a fascinating style and a resonant, pearly tone. He had the poise of the mature artist and played the three movements without the slightest detectable flaw.

Fully as amazing was the excellent orchestral accompaniment of Conductor Jacques Gershkovitch, whose every little movement with the stick brought instant response.

Rimsky-Korsakoff's Spanish Caprice formed the second part of the program with the concerto and was given such a thrilling rendition that the crowd called Conductor Gershkovitch to the stage half a dozen times with cheers and applause.

THE OREGONIAN APR. 15, 1934

JUNIOR ORCHESTRA BRINGS THRILLS TO BIG AUDIENCE

Fred Rothchild, Pianist, Adds to Delights of Concert, Last Regular Event of Season Here.

BY HILMAR B. GRONDAHL.

FRED ROTHCHILD, pianist, the 100 or more members of the Portland Junior Symphony orchestra, and their conductor, Jacques Gershkovitch, brought to more than 2000 admiring listeners at the public auditorium last night a concert of more than ordinary programmatic worth which piled thrill upon delight throughout the evening. It was the last regular concert of the season.

The program used included the "Russian and Ludmilla" overture (Glinka). Mendelssohn's Fourth symphony (Italian), the Mozart piano concerto in D minor, and Rimsky-Korsakov's "Capriccio Espagnol."

Fred Rothchild was guest artist in the Mozart work. He has been a member of the orchestra for several years, chiefly in the capacities of principal bass player and student conductor.

Concerto Great Success.

Mozart's D minor concerto was introduced to Portlanders earlier in the season; Mr. Rothchild was prepared both technically and by nature to give a clear projection of the concerto's inner values. His tone was clear, vital and well balanced as to weight. He was deliberate and musical in his phrasings. And his refinement of feeling for the true Mozartian style showed healthy roots. What flowered under his fingers, as a result, was a graceful, living example of Mozart's beauty.

The orchestral counterpart was carefully supervised by Mr. Gershkovitch, and in most places his wish and the result went hand in hand with what the pianist was doing. In the few measures where they pulled a ways apart, the separation was never far enough nor in such pivotal places that the concerto's spirit suffered.

Before the concerto, and before the Italian symphony, the orchestra played that delightful overture to Glinka's imaginative opera. When the moment came for the cello section to sing out its sweetly sentimental theme the youngsters put strong and persuasive bows to their strings. The audience liked it immensely.

Juniors Well Guided.

Almost throughout the course of the Italian symphony last night the juniors were guided by the conductor in moods that were appropriately gay and romantic. In the second movement—sometimes called "The Pilgrim's March"—the violas had one of the rare opportunities which come to them for solo utterance. In the third movement, with its Mozartian folk song of old Venice, the French horns proved themselves fresh in tone and steady in execution, as they also did later in the Spanish caprice. Even the difficult, thinly orchestrated saltarello of the final movement held to the cohesiveness and spirit which are so necessary to make its whirling dance rhythms effective.

This was the finest performance of a symphony that one has heard from the Junior symphony.

Rimsky-Korsakov's "Capriccio Espagnol" brought fresh thrills as the young players reveled in its fantastic orchestral color and holiday spirit. The concert master did some splendid work on her solo violin.

THE OREGONIAN JUN. 14, 1934

SYMPHONY CONCERT LAUDED BY GALVANI

Seaside Mayor Expresses Approval of Junior Player's Work.

"IT WAS the most wonderful event I have ever seen in my long life, and I never expect to see it surpassed."

This is what Mayor William H. Galvani of Seaside had to say yesterday about the Portland Junior Symphony concert and ballet in the public auditorium Tuesday night.

"It was the most wonderful performance I have ever seen in this country or in Europe, and I have known some great artists of music and dancing. Those young persons were not acting like amateurs; they performed like professionals, because of the genius of the conductor, Jacques Gershkovitch," the mayor declared.

Mayor Galvani is in Portland for the festival as a representative of Seaside and upon the invitation of Mayor Carson.

Music and Ballet Amaze Huge Festival Audience

By J. L. Wallin

I would love to go again tonight to see the whole show that the Portland Junior Symphony orchestra presented at The Auditorium Tuesday night as its part of the Rose Festival week celebration and I think all those 5000 persons who wore their hands tired applauding feel the same way about it. A beautiful dream come true. But the plans called for only one performance.

The excellent performance by the 110-piece group of instrumentalists of orchestral numbers that formed the first part of the program amazed those not familiar with past achievements of Conductor Jacques Gershkovitch and his faithful young players, but the overwhelming ovations that followed were mild compared with the storm of applause and shouts of delight let loose as the curtain descended upon the climax and final scene of Tschaikowsky's famous "Nutcracker" ballet that brought the event to a glorious triumph, rich in color, rich in music, full of youth and life.

Speaking of colors, I wish to remark that Tom Huffaker, veteran mechanician at The Auditorium, employed every last ray of light within his reach, with discrimination that puts him into the artist class, and he modestly accepted one of the many curtain calls with Conductor Gershkovitch and Ballet Master William F. Christensen.

The costumes were designed by Harriet Meyer. Mrs. Gershkovitch, I think, had a hand in working out the wonderfully fantastic and effective national costumes that made the trepak one of the big hits.

The trepak was danced by Jeanette Harrow and Robert Irwin, soloists.

Then came the candystick group, Merle Williams, soloist, surrounded by Martha Lang, Zelda Movey, Billy Otis and Marcelle Renoux. Beautiful girls, finely proportioned, graceful in every movement.

Vivian Emery and Don Schaupp made of the Chinese dance, that Tschaikowsky threw in for a bit of humor, a major episode. No burlesque, genuine art down to the finger tips.

A picture one would like to see perpetuated by an artist's hand in oils on canvas was the Arabian scene with Mattlyn Gevurtz as soloist.

The Dance of the Whistle Pipers revealed the tiniest of the large ensemble into their own. With the astonishing precision of the Arabian episode everywhere on the stage at the same time in their glittering costumes, sounding their flutes, in pantomime, exactly in time with the flute players in the orchestra.

Then came the final episode to the enchanting music of the "Waltz of the Flowers," danced by the entire ensemble in such triumphant manner that applause seemingly would not cease. For many minutes the huge crowd joined in a riot of approbation.

No, I have not forgotten the three principals, Christensen himself as the Nutcracker; Natalie Lauterstein as Marie, the girl whose dream is the hub of the fanciful legend and Janet Reed as the Sugar Plum fairy. Who would believe, many will say, such talent can be found in Portland?

Isa Dora Moldovan is credited with fine co-operation in connection with the organization of the ballet.

The orchestral accompaniment was superb, the substantial sort that goes to make a ballet of such magnitude a real success and not a good imitation. All played with the fine tone and smoothness of long seasoned professionals.

Backstage were loads of flowers for the young participants.

The high school chorus helped make the march from Wagner's "Tannhauser" a thrilling offering preceding the ballet.

Queen Beth and her royal court were received with a fanfare scored and directed by Eugene Linden, assistant conductor, who has grown up from the orchestra ranks.

JUNIOR SYMPHONY PROVIDES NIGHT FEATURE OF FESTIVAL

Orchestra, Chorus and Ballet Presented Before Throng in Public Auditorium; Royal Court in Attendance at Event.

BY HILMAR B. GRONDAHL.

ONE of the brightest and most populous spots in all Rosaria last night was the public auditorium, where the Portland Junior Symphony association's orchestra, chorus and ballet appeared before an audience which overtaxed the normal capacity of the large hall and flowed by hundreds into the wings.

Queen Beth of Rosaria with her princesses and royal escorts entered to a fanfare composed by Eugene Linden, assistant conductor of the orchestra. Visiting foreign and native dignitaries helped swell the crowd to nearly 5000.

The occasion was the most brilliant that the hundreds of young people have given, because there was an entirely new and picturesque innovation, the presentation of Tchaikowsky's "Nutcracker" ballet by the newly formed corps of 100 young dancers. This was its coast premiere. Many times enthusiasm for the solo or ensemble dance of the moment swelled to such proportions that it broke into applause which had to die down before the performance could go on.

The first half of the program consisted of a group of orchestral works and the choral march from "Tannhauser." The orchestral compositions were: Niccolai's overture to "The Merry Wives of Windsor," the Gluck-Mottl ballet suite No. 1, and Cesar Cui's berceuse.

The orchestra has seldom played with such effective attention to the minutiae. And the chorus appeared to better advantage than on its initial appearance.

Major interest last night centered on the Tchaikowsky opus with its promise of satisfaction to the eye as well as the ear. This dance will stand as one of the most thrilling cultural contributions to be made so far by the collective efforts of Portland children.

There was a unity and a traditional rightness about the spirit of the ballet which reflects beyond the dancers themselves to the conductor and the ballet master. William Christenson came by his feeling for this particular ballet from his father and his grandfather, the latter being one of the spectators at its first performance under Tchaikowsky's eye more than 40 years ago in Moscow. Mr. Gershkovitch's experience in conducting ballet goes back to his earlier years in Russia.

All these inspiring circumstances evidently made their mark on the kind of effort which went into rehearsals for the performance which thrilled thousands last night had spirit, precision and a high degree of finish.

William Christenson as Nutcracker, Natalie Lauterstein as Marie, and Janet Reed as the Sugar Plum Fairy gave solo episodes which were professionally polished in their technical command and expressiveness. Everyone was worthy of favorable comment from the principal candy-stick down to the forget-me-nots in the "Waltz of the Flowers."

11th Season

Jacques Gershkovitch, Conductor

November 24, 1934

Overture, "Magic Flute"	MOZART
Suite for String Orchestra, op. 5	CORELLI
Concertstueck for Piano	WEBER
Mary Margaret Martin, *Soloist*	
Polonaise, Arietta, Passacaglia	HANDEL/HARTY
Symphony, G minor	MOZART
Prelude, "Die Meistersinger"	WAGNER

February 9, 1935

Rosamunde Overture	SCHUBERT
Suite from "Water Music"	HANDEL/HARTY
Dance of the Buffoons from "The Snow Maiden"	RIMSKY-KORSAKOW
Sinfonia for Double Orchestra, op. 18, NO. 1	J. C. BACH
Andante Cantabile	TCHAIKOVSKY
"Dark Dancers of the Mardi Gras"	CADMAN
Charles Wakefield Cadman, *Pianist*	

March 30, 1935

Overture, "Marriage of Figaro"	MOZART
Waltz from "Eugene Onegin"	TCHAIKOVSKY
Nocturne, "Arlesienne Suite" NO. 2	BIZET
A Night on Bald Mountain	MOUSSORGSKY
"Landsighting"	GRIEG
Jack Randall, *Baritone*, & Chorus	
Praeludium	JARNEFELDT
"Fair Ellen"	BRUCH
Jane Anderson, *Soprano;* Jack Randall, *Baritone*	

June 4, 1935

ROSE FESTIVAL CONCERT

Glazounow – Weber – Bizet – Tchaikovsky – Delibes

OREGON JOURNAL NOV. 25, 1934

Children's Music Is Broadcast Overseas

By J. L. Wallin

The Portland Junior Symphony orchestra opened its eleventh season with a concert Saturday night in The Auditorium that in many respects must be recorded as really marvellous, and in some as the best ever given by this group of 110 juvenile players under direction of the inspired conductor, Jacques Gershkovitch.

A significant feature was the broadcast by CBS from station KOIN-The Journal of two numbers, not only nation-wide but across the seas through short wave connections at New York and Philadelphia. These were heard in London at 5 a.m. Sunday, and among those listening in over there was to be the distinguished English composer, Sir Hamilton Harty, whose transcription of Handel's Polonaise, Arietta and Passacaglia was sent over the air. The other was Mozart's G Minor symphony. Both were beautifully interpreted and exquisitely performed.

The second half of the program was brought to a tremendously thrilling close with the Prelude to Wagner's "Master-singers."

The first half opened with the overture to Mozart's opera "The Magic Flute," followed by a suite by Corelli for strings in three movements, a charming haunting thing of beauty, produced here for the first time.

Then came the highlight of the event, the performance of Maria von Weber's "Concertstueck" for piano with orchestral accompaniment, with Mary Margaret Martin as soloist.

The 14-year-old girl from the union high school at Milwaukie held the audience in a spell from the moment her slender hands first spread over the keyboard until the final flourish that made the large grand sing as if urged on by a Rachmaninoff or a Bauer. A fascinating, musical tone marked her playing throughout and at times, when the score so demanded, it was almost overwhelming yet always perfectly balanced against the smooth orchestral background.

The promising pianist, who is rather tall for her age, scored a complete triumph. She has studied with Ruth Bradley Keiser for a period of five years.

Then "Magic Flute" overture established that the orchestra has an excellent flute section, all girls, and they were heard to fine advantage, too, in Sir Hamilton Harty's transcription which contains many passages for piccolo. The heavier strings, 'cellos and violas, sang with fine phrasing and expression the opening measures of the overture and also the graceful Corelli melodies. The violins, some forty in the two sections, responded with the finest of delicacy to the conductor's baton in the tenderer themes that furnish such charming contrasts in the composition.

It was rousing to hear the clean-cut penetrating tones of the brasses in the Wagner work and the smooth phrasing of the trumpets in the Harty transcription. The woodwind section was exceptionally well in tune, the flutes blending beautifully with the oboes and clarinets. And let us not forget the very excellent performance of the three bassoons.

THE SPECTATOR DEC. 1, 19

Music

By HILMAR B. GRONDAHL

MEMBERS of the Portland Junior Syn phony orchestra with the guidance Jacques Gershkovitch, brought themselv musical credit last Saturday night at the Aud torium before what was said to be the large crowd to assemble for the first concert in the yearly series of three programs.

One of their own age was soloist in Weber musical romance: the "Konzertstuck." This wa Mary Margaret Martin of Milwaukie, Ore. Oth works of the program included two local introdu tions, and such old favorites as Mozart's "Mag Flute" overture, his G minor symphony and th prelude to "Die Meistersinger." The new work were Hamilton Harty's transcription of sever movements from Handel, and a Corelli suite fo string orchestra as arranged by Ettore Pinelli, th Italian composer and critic.

Several factors of improved playing we disclosed on this occasion. First of these is th fine spirit and feeling given to the Mozart sym phony. Another is the disciplined calm an reserved beauty which they read into the sar bande of the Corelli suite. And finally there wa the control, particularly in the brass section.

Perhaps the high mark of interest came wit the appearance of the young soloist, Miss Marti This talented girl was fully aware of the stor behind Weber's concert piece. She proved he self to be equal to all the technical demand assured in her own delineations and flexibly aliv to the indications of the conductor. Her succes with the audience was marked by long an vigorous applause.

OREGON JOURNAL APR. 2, 1935

THEIR VICTORY

A great victory was won in Portland last Saturday night. It was a victory by Jacques Gershkovitch and the boys and girls of the Junior Symphony orchestra.

Beauty mounted to majesty in the spectacle of those youngsters in their teens producing music that choked throats with glad emotion and brought tears of pride and satisfaction to hundreds in the exulting audience in The Auditorium. It is doubtful if such scenes of pride, affection and exaltation have ever been seen in The Auditorium as Portlanders in the seats looked and listened as the big structure was thrilled and sweetened by the climaxes and melodies and concertos and symphonic strains of the masters of music.

In this picture of pictures of Portland life was a 13-year old boy as master of the violin. He is Robert Mann, member of the first violin section of the orchestra and violin soloist for the evening. At only 13 he made the strings of his instrument speak and converse with all lovers of music, particularly with those familiar with violin playing.

A cantata rendered by a chorus on the program was soul-stirring and another victory for Portland youth.

What a master, as a leader of youth, is Jacques Gershkovitch, and what an institution he is in the life of the Rose City!

OREGON JOURNAL FEB. 10, 1935

CADMAN NUMBER TOPS PROGRAM

Composer's Presence Adds to Orchestra's Work

America had its innings at the concert by the Portland Junior Symphony orchestra in the auditorium last night when the ensemble of young American musicians gave an American composition its premier performance in Portland with the composer himself, Charles Wakefield Cadman at the piano.

"Dark Dancers of the Mardi Gras," the Cadman composition, was easily the high spot of the program, producing a performance comparable to that of a professional group, under the direction of Jacques Gershkovitch, conductor.

Mr. Cadman had full recognition for his tantalizingly orchestrated fantasy at its close when the audience called him back again and again with volley after volley of applause.

The symphonic fantasy succeeded beyond expectations in expressing the grotesque, fantastic, erotic, exuberant and almost delirious spirit of the New Orleans carnival.

BACH OPUS APPEALS

In direct contrast to this modern work was the Sinfonia for double orchestra, opus 18, No. 1, written nearly two centuries ago by J. C. Bach, and played last night as a tribute to him on the 200th anniversary of his birth year. The boys and girls of the orchestra gave to this work of simple and beautiful melody great spirituality of feeling.

Tchaikovsky's "Andante Cantabile" was ably and sympathetically performed making of this lovely work a truly "slow song."

The French horn ensemble in the Handel "Water Music," (broadcast last night as part of the usual radio concert held in connection with junior symphony performances) was exceptionally fine in a difficult passage.

RECEPTION FOLLOWS

The overture to Schubert's music for "Rosamunde" and the popular "Dance of the Buffoons," from Rimski-Korsakov's "Snow Maiden," were also included in the program.

A reception for Mr. Cadman followed the concert in the south wing of the auditorium. Rosarians, the Junior Symphony Orchestra association, Mr. and Mrs. Gershkovitch, the Monday Musical club and the Cadman club combined to be hosts to him on this occasion.

OREGON JOURNAL MAR. 31, 1935

Young Artists' Aid Juniors in Final Concert

By J. L. Wallin

The Junior Symphony orchestra's third and final concert of the season at The Auditorium Saturday night developed into the crowning event of the ensemble's series, and Conductor Jacques Gershkovitch and his large group were wildly acclaimed by the near to capacity audience. It was a concert rich in color and filled with thrills.

The first part was broadcast by station KOIN-The Journal over the Columbia National network and in turn relayed across the seas from the Atlantic seaboard.

With the orchestra, in two numbers, appeared the Junior Symphony chorus of approximately 150 young singers, and two vocal soloists, Jane Andrews, soprano, of Vancouver, and Jack Randall, Portland baritone. A third soloist was Robert Mann, 13-year-old violinist.

CHORUS PARTICIPATES

The chorus, trained by the organization's chorus director, Alexander Hull, and vocal soloists participated in Edvard Hagerup Grieg's impressive epic "Landsighting" and in Max Bruch's brilliant cantata "Fair Ellen."

Randall sang with impressive solemnity the incidental baritone solo in the Grieg masterpiece and, with Miss Andrews, carried the solos and duets in the Bruch cantata, in artistic relief, over the solid background of the chorus and orchestra. The lyric quality of Miss Andrews' powerful voice suited admirably her principal part in the cantata.

"Fair Ellen" has not been presented here before in such elaborate manner and under such auspicious circumstances and it brought the concert to a climax and a close amidst overwhelming applause.

In "Landsighting" Conductor Gershkovitch and his group gave a graphic picture of Olaf Tryggveson's return to Norway inspired to introduce Christianity.

Conductor Gershkovitch's interpretation was original, emphasizing more the religious fervor than the warlike spirit of the returning Vikings, from the ominous phrase for solo horn to the glorious climax that ended the first half of the program.

Of the purely orchestral numbers each proved intriguing in its own way. The overture to "The Marriage of Figaro" was daintily Mozartian, the waltz from Tschaikowsky's opera "Eugene Onegin" fascinatingly rhythmic, the nocturne from Bizet's second "L'Arlesinne" suite for strings alone a beautiful dream, while Moussorgsky's fantastic "A Night on Bald Mountain" stirred the imagination. In this the brasses, the woodwind, the harp and the battery figured prominently and effectively.

BOY VIOLINIST ACCLAIMED

After the intermission the boy violinist, Robert Mann, pupil of Edouard Hurlimann, demonstrated his ability by playing superbly two movements from Mozart's concerto in E flat major. Fine poise and a fine performance.

Catherine L. Petersen is the orchestra's new concertmaster, having been promoted to that important position when Geraldine Peterson was awarded a Seattle conservatory scholarship. Marjorie Morris is the new assistant concertmaster.

THE OREGONIAN MAR. 31, 1935

JUNIOR ORCHESTRA ENDS FINE SEASON

The Portland Junior Symphony orchestra and chorus presented a concert last night at the auditorium which was more than a concert. It was a gigantic production, involving some 250 boys and girls, which required skill in staging as well as in directing.

Jacques Gershkovitch, conductor, showed capable handling of the large ensemble. Alexander Hull directed choral rehearsals.

The show piece of the program was the cantata, "Fair Ellen," by Max Bruch, in which two of the featured soloists took part, Jane Andrews, lyric soprano, as Ellen, and Jack Randall, baritone, as Lord Edward.

But in spite of the favor this found with the audience, and the popularity of the ancient Scottish tune, "The Campbells Are Coming," the loveliest and most musicianly part of the concert was Robert Mann's playing of the Mozart concerto for violin in E-flat major with the orchestra.

12th Season

Jacques Gershkovitch, Conductor

November 23, 1935

Symphony No. 7	SCHUBERT
Allegro & Andante	
Suite for Strings	CORELLI
Piano Concerto, G minor	MENDELSSOHN
Mary Lois Ditto, *Soloist*	
Dance of the Buffoons	RIMSKY-KORSAKOV
Caucasian Sketches	IPPOLITOV-IVANOV

February 8, 1936

Overture, "The Magic Flute"	MOZART
Suite in G	BACH/GOOSENS
Baba Jaga	LIADOW
A Stroll in an Ancient Garden	*A. AVSHALOMOFF
Suite No. 2 from "Carmen"	BIZET
Concerto No. 1 for Violoncello	SAINT-SAENS
Betty Harter, *Soloist*	
Die Meistersinger Act III, Excerpts	WAGNER

April 4, 1936

Symphony in G major, "Oxford"	HAYDN
Russian Folk Songs	LIADOW
Violin Concerto No. 4 D minor	VIEUXTEMPS
Catherine Petersen, *Soloist*	
Invitation to the Dance	WEBER
Prelude to "Le Deluge"	SAINT-SAENS
Ballet Music from "Le Cid"	MASSENET

June 6, 1936

Reed College Summer Concert

Overture, "Barber of Seville"	ROSSINI
Valse Triste	SIBELIUS
Nutcracker Suite	TCHAIKOVSKY
Ballet Music, "Le Cid"	MASSENET
Overture, "1812"	TCHAIKOVSKY
with State Champion Jefferson High School Band	

* *Portland Premiere*

OREGON JOURNAL NOV. 24, 1935

Junior Group Presents Fine Musical Event

By J. L. Wallin

Portland's illustrious Junior Symphony orchestra added another triumph to its long list when it gave its first concert of its 12th season Saturday night at The Auditorium, and broadcast two movements from Schubert's Seventh symphony over the nationwide network of the CBS through local station KOIN-The Journal.

One wished that the multitude of invisible listeners could have seen the orchestra in action drawing graceful bows in absolute union and responding to the conductor's baton with marvelous precision.

As invariably at these unique events the intensely interested audience expressed approval and appreciation through long and loud demonstrations of applause that Conductor Jacques Gershkovitch and his over a hundred-strong group of young performers were repeatedly called upon to acknowledge.

Mary Lois Ditto, 15-year-old Portland girl, daughter of Drs. Johnson and Florence Ditto and student at Franklin high school, made a distinct hit as soloist in Mendelssohn's G Minor Concerto for piano and orchestra.

ACCOMPANIMENT GOOD

One marveled at the rich, round tone that welled from the huge grand in response to the wishes of the rather frail looking performer as her slender hands danced over the keyboard. The orchestra provided a nicely sustained accompaniment.

As member of the contra-bass section for three seasons, Miss Ditto grasped the importance of watching and listening; as soloist at the piano came the opportunity to demonstrate individuality, even though guided by her teacher and coached by the conductor. In the second movement her playing was so exquisitely light that a hush fell over the house. She was rewarded with a great ovation and a load of flowers backstage.

PROGRAM BALANCED

The conventional program was neatly balanced and splendidly presented notwithstanding the presence of more than thirty new members admitted since rehearsals began in September.

OREGON JOURNAL NOV. 26, 1935

AND BY PORTLAND YOUTH!

SHE IS only 16. But she electrified a lot of folks.

It happened at The Auditorium Saturday evening. The occasion was the Junior Symphony concert. A piano was brought to the center of the stage. In the background were many boys and girls, composing the orchestra. The 16-year-old came from behind the scenes, seated herself at the piano, and notes began to flood from the instrument.

She made the piano speak to listeners in tones of tenderness, of inspiration, in the thunder tones of the storm, or in the gentle notes of the lullaby. It was artistry in perfection, even though the artist is but a slip of a girl.

With the orchestral accompaniment, the number rose to the heights. And the concert was one of the most attractive in the Junior Symphony's history.

The concerts by these boys and girls are among the biggest things that transpire in Portland.

THE SPECTATOR Feb. 15, 1936

Music

By HILMAR B. GRONDAHL

SEATED within their bright new sound shell, the Portland Junior Symphony orchestra, wtih Jacques Gershkovitch on the podium, gave the crowd of listeners gathered in the Auditorium Saturday night their second program this season. There was a vast audience, unseen, except by the mind's eye, which sat at Columbia Broadcasting system radio bands the country over, and heard a thirty-minute section of the concert.

These innumerable persons shared with those inside the hall, the satisfaction of hearing the world premier of "A Stroll in an Ancient Garden," by Aaron Avshalomoff, a former resident of this city, whose admiration for the Junior Symphony and its conductor led him to dedicate this Chinese tone poem to these friends of earlier days. Its atmospheric fidelity gave it a mood, a tone coloring and a quality of movement that set it apart from ordinary compositions.

It was appropriate that this new work should be broadcast as widely as possible to the world. But it is regrettable that a later feature had not the same chance of pleasing an equal number of people. For had the playing of Betty Harter, as soloist in the Saint-Saens cello concerto in A minor, been a part of the radio broadcast, untold hearers would have joined with the thousands who sat in the Auditorium seats, in marveling that a girl of fourteen should play so surely and so well. She is a musically-endowed girl with a definite sense of what she is up to. Her intelligence is manifest; her unaffected diligence in technical matters, her considered handling of the melodic curve and the small phrase and her realization of the borders of her present development, were simple evidences of the judicious way in which she looks at music.

Her team-mates, under Mr. Gershkovitch's supervision, provided a very creditable counterpart to her solo declarations.

The next best works on the program were Liadow's "Baba Jaga," and the waltz from "Eugen Onegin."

OREGON JOURNAL FEB. 9, 1936

Young Artists Win Applause

Junior Symphony Orchestra Program Broadcast Over Columbia Network.

By J. L. Wallin

The Portland Junior Symphony orchestra's second concert of the season at The Auditorium Saturday night was an event of many highlights, foremost of which was the informal dedication of its new and attractive stage setting.

Of almost paramount interest was the presentation of Betty Harter, 14-year-old Vancouver, Wash., girl as soloist in Saint-Saens' first concerto for cello and orchestra. Her performance proved little less amazing than that of the nationally famous 15-year-old violinist, Ruggiero Ricci, as soloist with the Portland Symphony orchestra Monday night.

Miss Harter, daughter of Mrs. H. C. Harter, and a cello pupil of Sara Jenks, completely captivated the large audience with her lovely musical tone and fluent and sure technique. She had the good fortune of playing on a 164-year-old Cuypers cello brought here for the concert through the efforts of Rudolf F. Schmoll, Portland violin maker.

A third intriguing feature of the event was the American premiere of Aaron Avshalomoff's symphonic composition, "A Stroll in an Ancient Garden." This novelty is based upon Chinese themes and its instrumentation is such as to give a decidedly Chinese atmosphere. The composer made Portland his home a few years ago, and this, his latest work, is dedicated to the Junior Symphony orchestra and its conductor, Jacques Gershkovitch. Avshalomoff has written a number of works that have been played by major orchestras both in the Orient and in the United States. At present he is conductor of the Shanghai Symphony orchestra.

"A special arrangement dedicated to my dearest friend, Jacques Gershkovitch, and his remarkable Junior Symphony orchestra of Portland, Oregon. Would that I could stroll in this garden of blooming youth whose playing still lingers in my memory. Would that I could stroll again to those exciting rehearsals to meet again the many friends I have left behind. Alas, to cross the ocean I cannot—but let us stroll together in this garden of ancient Chinese melody."

Eugene Goosens' arrangement for strings of Johann Sebastian Bach's dance suite was also played in Portland for the first time on this occasion. The noted English conductor has made of this a thing of strong appeal.

A portion of the first part of the program was given world-wide broadcast over the Columbia network from station KOIN-The Journal. Stations at New York and Philadelphia relayed the short wave.

Conductor Gershkovitch, the cello soloist and the orchestra were given rousing ovations.

THE OREGONIAN APR. 5, 1936

JUNIOR PLAYERS WIN HIGH PRAISE

BY HILMAR B. GRONDAHL
Music Editor, The Oregonian

Another example of how well some composers have paid for their honorary doctorates was indicated to Portlanders last night at the public auditorium, where the Portland Junior Symphony orchestra, under the baton of Jacques Gershkovitch, introduced Haydn's G major symphony.

Haydn composed the music and conducted it at Oxford in England nearly a century and a half ago at the ceremonial which made him a doctor of music. Hence the symphony is generally known as "The Oxford."

It is beautiful music from first to last, spirited, friendly, congenial music, with many a pleasant surprise and imaginative contrast. The young musicians played it from their hearts with a sense of their responsibility in putting before their audience music which was old in years but new to local repertories.

All sections played well, but the strings especially moved in commendable unison, displaying a fresh wealth of tone color as they want.

Nation Hears Broadcast

It was this part of the program which was broadcast to the nation over Columbia Broadcasting system's network.

Then followed four Russian folk songs from a group of eight orchestrated by Anatol Liadow, to many in the audience, the high point of the evening: the playing of the Vieuxtempts D-minor violin concerto with Catherine Peterson, this year's concertmaster, in the solo part.

There are some noble lines in this work. These the soloist projected with a cleanly controlled tone of attractive quality.

Her creditable work was roundly applauded by the audience. Mr. Gershkovitch did a skillful thing in fitting a difficult score so smoothly into the soloist's scheme.

OREGON JOURNAL APR. 5, 1936

Soloist Wins High Approval At Concert

By J. L. Wallin

Catherine Petersen, retiring concertmaster of the Portland Junior Symphony orchestra, Jacques Gershkovitch conductor, scored a triumph as soloist when the unique group gave its third and final concert of the 12th season's series Saturday night at The Auditorium. The talented 21-year-old girl played Vieuxtemps' Concerto No. 4 in D Minor for violin and orchestra.

Miss Peterson has been seven years with the orchestra, two as concertmaster. She is the daughter of Mr. and Mrs. Christian Petersen of Laurelhurst, a graduate of Grant high school and a student in short story writing in the extension division of the University of Oregon. She played the customary three movements of the concerto's four musicianly and with comforting ease and fluency. The beautiful slow movement was expressed with a warm, sonorous tone and depth of feeling.

Succeeding her as concertmaster with Marjorie Morris, with Winifred Myers in second chair as assistant.

Orchestral numbers on the program included Haydn's "Oxford" symphony, which was given nationwide broadcast through station KOIN-The Journal over the Columbia network.

The Haydn symphony was beautifully played as no doubt the orchestra management will learn through letters from the invisible audience centered all over the country.

OREGON JOURNAL APR. 7, 1936

Their Victory

Youth on the heights, hearts touched, thoughts inspired, music in perfection, held sway at The Auditorium, Saturday evening.

It was the concluding seasonal concert of the Junior Symphony orchestra. It presented moments and scenes never to be forgotten. It raised the question in the minds of numerous onlookers, Do Portlanders really know what an asset and what an example their city has in the Junior orchestra?

A striking feature was the violin soloist, Catherine Petersen, a Grant high school girl. Many a traveling professional violinist in concerts has displayed less skill and technique. Her renditions called forth enraptured applause.

Solo work on the cello by Betty Harter, the viola by Jean Harter, first violin by Marjorie Morris, and second violin by Dorothy Hutchison, attained professional perfection and aroused boundless enthusiasm.

Generous support of the Junior Symphony should be accorded as recognition of the great service of Jacques Gershkovitch, whose toil, patience and skill with youth have built up this beautiful institution. His work has created here a youth orchestra to challenge and hold the admiration of the nation.

THE SPECTATOR JUN. 13, 1936

By HILMAR B. GRONDAHL

JUPE PLUVIUS raised Ned with the carefully laid plans of men and musicians last Saturday night.

Whatever inclemency there was in the weather left no moody mark on the spirit of the young players, nor dampened, to any degree, the ardor of the audience. The hundred orchestra members bright in the informal clothes and colors of the out-of-doors rather than their customary black and white were undaunted by the eleventh hour change of plans.

What last Saturday's audience missed (and only a few of them knew how much), was the delightful fitness of the Reed College bowl for such an orchestral concert, as those who listened on the morning rehearsal can testify. Here in a verdant amphitheater, with white swans moving quietly over the lake beyond, music seemed an appropriate and unselfconscious part of nature.

The program was made up of compositions familiar to the orchestra and its hearers. It opened with the overture to Rossini's "Barber of Seville," passed through Sibelius' Valse Triste to the "Nutcracker" suite of Tchaikowsky.

The post-intermission part consisted of three movements from the ballet music in Massenet's "Le Cid," and Tchaikowsky's dramatic "1812" overture.

The final work had the thrilling participation of Jefferson high school's prize-winning band, which had been prepared for the occasion by its director, L. E. Wright.

JUN. 7, 1936

Rain Sends Concert Indoors; Juniors Win Ovation

By J. L. Wallin

The Portland Junior Symphony orchestra's first annual summer outdoor concert Saturday night became an indoor event instead because it rained and the full moon refused to come out.

Late in the afternoon when the management found it out of the question to inaugurate the Reed college natural amphitheatre, as planned, with the elaborately prepared program, music racks and other equipment were transferred to the High School of Commerce auditorium which had been engaged for the emergency.

The concert was to have served the dual purpose of presenting Conductor Jacques Gershkovitch and his famous musical ensemble in its first open air concert and formally dedicating the new bowl on the college campus.

The High School of Commerce auditorium shifted into the spotlight instead, for this was its first use for a concert of major proportions. Its large stage accommodated the orchestra and the augmenting Jefferson High School band comfortably and the 2000 seats were more than ample for the audience since the seat sale for the open air amphitheatre was based on a capacity of only 1000.

Conductor Gershkovitch and the young musicians presented the attractive program in the usual and expected thrilling manner and received repeated ovations.

A sensational conclusion was Tschaikowsky's "1812" overture with the trophy winning Jefferson High School band multiplying the volume of the glorious finale.

13th Season

Jacques Gershkovitch, Conductor

November 21, 1936

Coriolan Overture	BEETHOVEN
Symphony NO. 8	BEETHOVEN
Concerto for Two Pianos, Eb	MOZART
Nellie & Pattie Greenwood, *Soloists*	
Air for G String	BACH
Stenka Razin	GLAZOUNOW

February 20, 1937

Merry Wives of Windsor Overture	NICOLAI
Air for G String	BACH
By Request	
Concerto for Harp, C minor	ZABEL
Barbara Jones, *Soloist*	
Piano Concerto in Bb	MOZART
Malcolm Willis, *Soloist*	
"Rustic Wedding" Symphony	GOLDMARK
In the Garden	
Dance	
Introduction & Persian Dances from "Khovanschina"	MOUSSORGSKY

April 24, 1937

Eugene Onegin – In Concert	TCHAIKOVSKY
Excerpts fron Acts I, II, & III	
Aida - In Concert	VERDI
Excerpts from Acts I, II, & III	

The Junior Symphony Chorus & Soloists
Ariel Rubstein, *Chorus Master*

June 8, 1937

ROSE CONCERT UNDER THE STARS

Music by
Glazounow–Thomas–Tchaikovsky–Goldmark
Grieg–Jarnefeldt–Delibes

THE OREGONIAN NOV. 22, 1936

JUNIORS' CONCERT MUSICAL TRIUMPH

Young Symphonists Thrill Large Audience

BY HILMAR B. GRONDAHL
Music Editor, The Oregonian

The happy fusion of youth and ability last night brought to a large audience at the public auditorium a concert of high purpose and sterling musical worth. It was the first program of its 13th season by the Portland Junior Symphony orchestra. Jacques Gershkovitch was the conductor.

Music Highly Enjoyed

Because public performances are not the main purpose of the Portland Junior Symphony orchestra, and never can be, so long as it is fostered primarily for the musical training it gives to youth, the wonder of what unexpected beauties a hundred players may bring to their concert appearances is rather prominent in the minds of this organization's best friends.

Last night provided one of those concerts at which such music poured forth from the stage that the audience could only marvel at its pure tonal loveliness and the arresting rightness of its release.

Young Pianists Please

Such ws the impression created by the Mozart concerto for two pianos and orchestra, which was played on this occasion by Nellie and Pattie Greenwood and the symphony members under Mr. Gershkovitch's baton. It was evident last night that they possess a distinguished singing tone for every melodic use. Their grasp of the true Mozartian style, too, was observable from the start.

The audience was enthusiastic in its approval of the work of the soloists, the orchestra and the conductor.

Programmed works which were broadcast to the nation over the Columbia Broadcasting system included Beethoven's overture to "Coriolanus" and his eighth symphony.

OREGON JOURNAL NOV. 22, 1936

Symphony, Jr. Wins Acclaim

Young Players Open Season With Brilliant Performance; Tribute Paid Wallin

By Susie Aubrey Smith

Enthusiasm was the keynote of Saturday night's concert at The Auditorium, when the Portland Junior Symphony orchestra opened its 13th season under leadership of its popular conductor, Jacques Gershkovitch. The enthusiasm was shared by the audience and the young musicians in an artistic and brilliantly rendered program.

Listening to a concert by the Junior Symphony is always a thrilling experience. Boys and girls in their 'teens—some not yet in their 'teens—playing Beethoven and Bach and Mozart and playing the works of these great composers with perfect rhythm and real feeling for the mood of the music as well as a certain dash that comes, probably, from the buoyancy of youth—it's almost incredible.

Mr. Gershkovitch opened with the overture to Beethoven's "Coriolanus." Then came the Eighth Symphony by the same composer, a particularly happy choice for young people to play. It is exuberant, gay and even jolly music. Mr. Gershkovitch's tempi through the four movements of the symphony were spirited and calculated to bring out all the themes and nuances of the piece. His reading of the Bach "Air for G String," played by the strings alone, was marked by a kind of dignified eloquence, a depth of feeling and a reverence for the immortal music of the composer.

Amazing is the only word that fits the performance of the Mozart concerto in E-flat for two pianos and orchestra. Nellie and Pattie Greenwood, youthful pianists, who were the soloists, exhibited a sureness and cleanness of technique and an understanding of the music that made their playing delightful to listen to. A brilliant future may be predicted for these young artists of the keyboard. Mr. Gershkovitch and his young musicians gave the soloists excellent support.

The last number was Glazounoff's symphonic poem, "Stenka Razine," given in memory of the composer, who died in April of this year, and under whom Mr. Gershkovitch studied at the St. Petersburg conservatory. Glazounoff has used the Volga Boatman song as one of his main themes in this rich and colorful work. Mr. Gershkovitch and his orchestra gave a brilliant rendition of Glazounoff's music and made it a fitting climax to a brilliant program.

Thunderous applause marked the end of the concert, the audience seeming loath to leave.

OREGON JOURNAL NOV. 22, 1936

Count Wallin

Beautiful tribute is paid the late Johan Ludwig Wallin by the board of directors of the Portland Junior Symphony orchestra.

The testimonial appeared on the program of the Junior Symphony concert last night.

"In memory of Johan Ludwig Wallin, a founder of the Portland Junior Symphony orchestra," says the tribute. And it adds:

As a pioneer whose constant interest has been to inculcate in the hearts and minds of children a deep appreciation of music as an integral part of their character development, and as one whose foresight and untiring efforts were a contributing factor in the perpetuation of this association, and whose sudden passing from our midst leaves a place never to be filled . . . we believe that our community as a whole shall forever experience the indelible imprint that his noble and splendid character has left upon our city.

An effective worker in his newspaper calling, a devoted interpreter and exponent of music and musicians, the Junior Symphony, with its portrayals by boys and girls in their teens, was his shrine, his hope, his gospel, and his life objective. He loved the organization, cherished it, adored it and glorified it.

The tribute the association pays him is beautiful and deserved. It is a happy reflection, that life yields personalities who merit such laudation, and that the world does not forget to offer its honors.

THE SPECTATOR FEB. 20, 1937

Music

By HILMAR B. GRONDAHL

TWO young soloists, within the age limits of orchestral membership, enlivened the concert by the Portland Junior Symphony orchestra last Saturday night at the Auditorium. These were Barbara Jones, harpist, and Malcolm Willis, pianist.

Glancing back over recent years in junior orchestra's history, one notices that a change has come over the structure of concerts, especially in so far as it concerns guest artists. Not so many seasons ago it was considered just about all a soloist was capable of, if he or she played a single movement from some familiar concerto. One of the Beethoven piano works came to the audience in two sections: one played at a certain concert by a young girl, the other two at a later concert by another young girl.

Now all this is happily changed. Treating each concerto as a whole, the soloist and the members of the orchestra are allowed to learn the composition as its creator saw it.

Miss Jones came upon the stage in the first half of the program to play Zabel's concerto for harp and orchestra. She was appropriately dressed, graciously poised; a charming addition to the scene. Those of us who knew her playing from earlier appearances anticipated the revealment of sterling musicianship. Her performance exceeded our expectations. Her attack and release were unblurred; her plucking crisp, excellently timed, and rhythmically fluent.

Young Mr. Willis took his place at the piano in the second half of the concert to fulfill the right won in open competition last spring of appearing with the orchestra as soloist in Mozart's earlier B-flat major concerto. He had not the stage presence of the earlier soloist. But he showed some noteworthy characteristics as a pianist. He was secure in his technical resource, discriminative in his handling of tone, and painstakingly accurate in his phrasing. One was surprised at the power in his left hand.

Through these two concertos and the orchestral work, which preceded and followed them, Jacques Gershkovitch exercised his careful direction of the large and youthful ensemble. The audience was particularly eloquent in its applause following the famous Bach air, and the two sections from Goldmark's "Rustic Wedding" symphony.

THE OREGONIAN APR. 25, 1937

JUNIOR SYMPHONY CONCERT TRIUMPH

300 Singers, Players Rouse Enthusiastic Crowd

The 300 young singers and instrumentalists of the Portland Junior Symphony and chorus, appearing last night in selections from the two operas "Eugene Onegin" and "Aida," enjoyed, with their conductor, Jacques Gershkovitch, a gratifying artistic triumph.

An audience, enthusiastic and appreciative, that comfortably filled the public auditorium, paid splendid tribute to orchestra and chorus and the nine soloists who were featured. The big stage of the auditorium presented a sea of eager young faces, sparkling with excitement and happiness, as wave after wave of applause cheered their efforts at the close of each concert.

Each opera was sung in English. Tchaikowsky's "Eugene Onegin," with Harry Steel Jr. in the title role, was presented first. Steel, Grant high school senior and General Motors contest winner last year, acquitted himself with honors, as did his five companions who carried solo parts.

Reception Follows Event

Kathryn Porter had the role of Tatiana, Betty Starr that of Olga, Olga Stolee of Larina and Gladys Berg Vickery of Filipjewna. Dale Baker sang the part of Lenski. During the dance of the reapers Donald Carruth sang, from the chorus, the solo part of the peasant.

Miss Stolee alone had the honor of having solo parts in both operas. In Verdi's "Aida," she had the role of Amneris, in which she sang pleasingly. Esther Lofstedt had the title role of Aida. Michael Gulan had the part of Ramphis, and L. Edwin Beach that of Radames.

The Portland Music Teachers association held a reception for Mr. Gershkovitch and the soloists at the close of the final concert, and many remained to offer personal congratulations.

14th Season

Jacques Gershkovitch, Conductor

November 20, 1937

New World Symphony	DVORAK
Imagery	*HORACE JOHNSON
Piano Concerto No. 2, G minor	SAINT-SAENS
George Beagles, *Soloist*	
Polovetsian Dances	BORODIN

February 19, 1938

Overture, "Barber of Seville"	ROSSINI
Chorus from "Prince Igor"	*BORODIN
For String Orchestra, Arr. Sevitsky	
The Sorcerer's Apprentice	DUKAS
Violin Concerto Op. 26	BRUCH
Warren Signor, *Soloist*	
The Royal Fireworks Music	*HANDEL/HARTY
Mosquito Dance	WHITE
from "Five Miniatures"	
Capriccio Espagnol	RIMSKY-KORSAKOFF

April 13, 1938

Carmen – In Concert	BIZET
Excerpts from Acts I, II & III	
Portland Junior Symphony Chorus & Soloists	

June 14, 1938

Concert for The Oregon Federation of Music Clubs
Retrospective Program from the Season

* *Portland Premiere*

NEWBERG, ORE. GRAPHIC NOV. 25, 1937

GEORGE BEAGLES GETS AN OVATION FOR HIS PLAYING

Noted Oregonian Critic Writer Gives Local Youth Highest Praise Following Jr. Symphony Concert

Hilmad B. Grondahl in Sunday's Oregonian gives high praise to George Beagles, local pianist. We quote as follows:

"Those people who attended concerts by the Portland Junior Symphony orchestra purely on the grounds of entertainment had a thrilling 30 minutes last night at the public auditorium while young George Beagles of Newberg played the Saint-Saens G Minor piano concerto with the ensemble under Jacques Gershkovitch.

"We say 'thrilling' advisedly because it is not generally within the province of youth of this age so fittingly to approximate the precision of greater years nor to infuse music with the subtleties of mood and spirit which are commonly associated with a more mature time.

"The first and second movements of the piano concerto were enough to convey the information that this Newbergian has talent, temperament and taste far beyond the average. He approached his solo essays with authority and projected his statements with assurance. His touch was deliberate yet resilient and his tone clear and ringing in every dynamic degree. His sense of contrast was somewhat extreme but it was nonetheless effective and provided the main evidence that it was not a mature man at the keyboard.

"From first to last the Saint-Saens composition was a young triumph for all concerned."

NEWBERG, ORE., GRPAHIC DEC. 10, 1937

ROTARY CLUB BRINGS ORCHESTRA TO CITY

Because of the efforts of the Oregon City-West Linn Rotary club the Portland Junior Symphony orchestra will present their first program outside of the city of Portland in the senior high auditorium Saturday evening.

OREGON CITY, ORE., ENTERPRISE DEC. 12, 1937

Junior Symphony Concert Pleases 500 Persons Here

By JEAN MAGUIRE

A crowd of 500 last evening wondered why Oregon City doesn't more often have a chance to hear such talent as was displayed by the Portland Junior Symphony orchestra during its concert sponsored by the Rotary club and held at the Oregon City high school.

Opening with the "New World Symphony" with its four inimitable movements and closing with the "Polovetsian Dances," there was demonstrated a wealth of color and precision under the baton of Jacques Gershkovitch.

Accustomed to the "senior" symphony and filled with misgivings many were surprised but all were pleased by the finished product turned out by the young musicians.

The program chosen wasn't easy, hackneyed nor selected as if for a "pop" concert. Rather, Oregon City was given the benefit of the doubt and the selections flattered the listening audience.

A certain fervor or abandon marked their performance, which is missed in the "other symphony," just the same fervor that makes oldsters long for their childhood again.

The soloists performance spoke well for the ages and the total lack of affectation seemed, to us at least, admirable. One faux pas did nothing but endear him to his audience.

"The New World Symphony," always appeals to everyone because of an inbred patriotism, a pride in our country's folk music, and because we have so little choice.

We, at least, left the concert with two firm convictions; one, that radio is a poor substitute for what we heard last night and two, that what we heard was just enough. We left not satiated still but wanting more, a test of a fine performance. We didn't find a chance to fidget.

THE SPECTATOR NOV. 27, 1937

# #

Young Soloist

THE little town of Newberg can take deep satisfaction from the musical stir which one of her younger sons made last Saturday night when he played a piano concerto with the Portland Junior Symphony orchestra. We refer, of course, to George Beagles, the 19 year old pianist who was heard with Jacques Gershkovitch and the ensemble in the second Saint-Saens concerto.

It seems to us that there has not been another concerto performance by this young orchestra and a young soloist, which has reached such heights of congenial interdependence, nor secured so worthy a musical result. Mr. Beagle's work at the keyboard was too assured, too well controlled, too smooth running and musical to be treated as something which could not be done just as satisfactorily on the next night, or the one after that. He knew what he was about every moment: in fact he was so sure of himself that gave his attention to Mr. Gershkovitch's baton in a way which resulted in the best coordination of solo and orchestral factors that this group has ever accomplished.

This was the section drawing the heartiest applause from the audience. There were other good sections such as the two final movements of the "New World" symphony and the dances from "Prince Igor."

OREGON CITY, ORE., COURIER DEC. 14, 1937

Junior Symphony Concert Enjoyed By Many On Sat.

A real musical treat was given to those who attended the concert at the senior high school Saturday evening given by the Portland Junior symphony under the capable direction of Jacques Gershkovitch. It was very noticeable that the audience was greatly impressed by the finished manner in which these young people played the difficult numbers.

"The Star Spangled Banner," played in a spirited manner opened the concert, and after that, the "New World Symphony," by Dvorak with William Lamont as the English horn soloist, was given. Following this, George Beagles, 19-year old pianist of Newberg, gave a most brilliant performance in his rendering of the piano part of "Concerto No. 2, Opus 22 in G Minor" by Saint Saens. The audience was so pleased with his presentation that Mr. Beagles was called back to the stage several times.

"The Peasant Chorus" from "Prince Igor" by Borodine and transcribed by Fabien Sevitsky was more subdued in tone.

The last selection, "Polovetsian Dances," by Borodine was more colorful and dashing, and was played in a most vivacious manner by the group.

The ovation given Mr. Gershkovitch and his orchestra portrayed in a small manner the enjoyment the audience had received.

This program was sponsored by the Oregon City-West Linn Rotary club for the benefit of the Boy Scouts of Clackamas county.

NEWS-TELEGRAM FEB. 21, 1938

Concerts of Symphonies Thrill Many

By EMIL ENNA

Willen van Hoogstraten conducted the last of the season's matinees for the Portland symphony orchestra at the auditorium Sunday afternoon.

The program was resplendent with colorful and attractive compositions by Wolf-Ferrari, Mozart, Mendelssohn, Beethoven, Bach, Massenet, Deems Taylor and Wagner. Van Hoogstraten's resourceful, delightful and artistic readings of every number made the concert one of the most arresting of the season.

The Portland junior symphony, under the direction of Jacques Gershkovitch, was heard in the second concert of the 14th season at the auditorium Saturday night.

Warren Signor, violinist, was the soloist. The orchestral performance included works by Rossini, Borodine, Dukas, Handel, White and Rimsky-Korsakoff.

Number Repeated

The large audience enjoyed splendid and colorful interpretations of the orchestral numbers.

White's "Mosquito Dance" made such a splendid impression with the audience that it was repeated.

Signor played the Bruch violin concerto Op. 26 in a brilliant manner. Few violinists could have performed this concerto with such execution, rythmatic feeling, and above all, a sonorous tone.

His performance reflected great credit upon his teacher of a number of years standing, Franck Eichenlaub.

NEWS-TELEGRAM APR. 25, 1938

Junior Symphony Praised Over "Carmen"

By EMIL ENNA

The Portland junior symphony orchestra, under the direction of Jacques Gershkovitch, presented Bizet's opera, "Carmen," in concert form at the auditorium Saturday night, sustaining the brilliancy and reputation of the past seasons and gaining new laurels and distinction at this particular performance, presented before a large and enthusiastic audience.

With the director's reading and wielding of the baton the opera was given a most mature performance. The splendid selected soloists and choruses responded with earnest enthusiasm.

Members of the cast included Anne Ruth Toreson, Harry Steele jr., Michael Gulen, Ruth Horne Laird, Neil Pairan, William Elliott, Marion Munger, Crystalee Pelay and William Savage.

Vocal soloists in "Eugene Onegin": Gladys Berg Vickery, Olga Stolie, Betty Starr, Kathryn Porter.

The SPECTATOR FEB. 26, 1938

By HILMAR GRONDAHL

THE second concert of the Portland Junior Symphony orchestra's fourteenth season at the Auditorium on last Saturday evening would indicate that Jacques Gershkovitch, with his uncanny ability for winning discipline and cooperation from these young players, is likely to make this the brightest season in the orchestra's history.

The earlier program acquainted people with the remarkable piano abilities of George Beagles of Newberg. Last week there was orchestral playing of sterling quality as well as a guest soloist: Warren Signor, onetime head of the second violin section.

We have been listening to the Junior Symphony for lo, these many years, and we find ourselves just as susceptible now to the thrill of a passage neatly turned as we were in the beginning.

It was a vital band of 100 young players that Mr. Gershkovitch handed the prime joke in French musical idiom; "The Sorcerer's Apprentice" by Dukas. What they, in turn, did with the score was the salient ensemble experience of the evening.

Something of their youth and imaginative extravagance went into the crackling instrumentation; the brasses in that frantic call for the sorcerer, the bassoons in their hollow imitation of the pestle going about its enchanted business. It was a performance to remember.

Another humorous section called "Mosquito Dance" delighted the audience to the point that a repeat was necessary.

When Warren Signor came onto the stage to play the solo part of the Bruch violin concerto, the orchestra had played enough to be in good coordinative condition. This was reflected in the accompaniment through security and balance. The Bruch concerto is one of the favorites in this field.

In the soloist's hands it did not seem difficult at all.

OREGON JOURNAL FEB. 21, 1938

Junior Group Wins Praise For Artistry

By Susie Aubrey Smith

The Portland Junior Symphony orchestra provided enjoyable entertainment for a large audience Saturday evening at The Auditorium in its second concert of the season.

After listening to the opening number, the overture to "The Barber of Seville," one was struck particularly by Mr. Gershkovitch's skill in bringing out all the essential melodies and by his inspiring the orchestra members with a feeling for the brilliance and the theatrical style of Rossini's music. Dukas' much-played "The Sorcerer's Apprentice" seemed to acquire new vitality and interest as rendered by the Junior symphony. Mr. Gershkovitch took the work at an unusually fast tempo, and kept his listeners almost literally on the edge of their chairs from the first note to the last. In the excerpt from "Prince Igor," the orchestra achieved and sustained successfully the exotic quality of Borodine's music.

The orchestra introduced as its soloist a gifted young violinist, Warren Signor, who played the Max Bruch concerto in G minor. The excellent style of Warren's playing revealed exceptionally fine training. He drew a resonant tone from his instrument and, overcoming the technical difficulties of the concerto without undue emphasis, contrived to give a musicianly and artistic interpretation of the piece. The audience gave him warm and unstinted applause, recalling him to the stage several times.

Following its usual custom, the Junior symphony included a work by an American composer on its program. This was a clever and amusing musical trifle, "Mosquito Dance," in modernistic mood by Paul White. In Handel's classic "Fireworks" suite the youthful artists succeeded in recreating for their auditors the quiet beauty of this great composer's music. Climaxing their program, Mr. Gershkovitch and his orchestra gave a dramatic and thrilling reading of Rimsky-Korsakoff's "Capriccio-Espagnol." In this Robert Mann, the concert master, exhibited his skill in the solo violin passages.

OREGON JOURNAL APR. 24, 1938

YOUNG MUSICIANS WIND UP SEASON

BY HILMAR GRONDAHL
Music Editor, The Oregonian

It was the responsibility last night of Jacques Gershkovitch and about 250 young singers and instrumentalists to provide the musical sustenance for the final regular concert program of the year by the Portland Junior Symphony Orchestra association in the public auditorium.

The program consisted of a concert version of Bizet's "Carmen."

Big Chorus Presented

A chorus of approximately 140 and an orchestra of 90 pieces completed the array of musical forces on the stage.

Last season the Junior Symphony association gave an evening of operatic excerpts, using vocal soloists. Last night was the first opportunity this reviewer had of judging the effect of this new line of endeavor.

The most effective musical moments last night were those purely orchestral sections such as the prelude and entr'acts: and some of the more spacious accompaniments.

Opera Unsuited to Concert

It just happens that a concert version of an opera is neither fish nor fowl.

Illusion is one of the prime requisites of opera, and Essamillio in a tuxedo has a difficult time bringing his audience the picture of "blood upon the sand."

The choruses last night were sung with the pleasing quality of tone characteristic of of young voices singing in unison on pitch. A few of the soloists had a fair grasp of their parts, but in order to find voices of even moderate training, it is apparently necessary to accept an age scale which threatens the juvenile standing of the entire group.

The choruses of a few seasons ago seemed better in line with the educational aims of the junior group than last night's operatic performance.

OREGON JOURNAL APR. 24, 1938

Symphony Jr. And Chorus Make Big Hit

By Susie Aubrey Smith

The Portland Junior Symphony orchestra and chorus appeared Saturday evening in the annual opera-concert sponsored by the Portland Junior Symphony Orchestra association at The Auditorium with Jacques Gershkovitch, conductor of the orchestra, directing the program.

The opera was Bizet's "Carmen" and, judging by the spontaneous applause, the program was as enjoyable to the audience as it seemed to be to the performers.

Well-Defined Rhythms

Mr. Gershkovitch's reading of the stirring prelude and, indeed, of all the music, had sharply defined rhythms and rich tonal colorings. The reviewer has never heard the prelude played with more dash and assurance. The orchestra excelled also in the difficult business of accompanying the singers.

Naturally, these youthful soloists cannot be judged or written of as if they were operatic artists in a professional company. Their voices are of lighter caliber; their experience in interpreting operatic music is small. One can say, however, that each had a pleasing and easy stage presence and sang in a manner that showed excellent training and much natural ability.

Songsters Expert

Ruth Laird, mezzo-soprano, sang the "Habanera," "Seguidilla" and other music of the title role delightfully and with good diction. Anne Torreson's pretty soprano voice was well suited to the music of Micaela. Neil Pairan, tenor, won much well deserved applause for his rendition of the "Air de la Fleur," and his duets with Miss Laird and Miss Torreson. The popular Toreador song gave William Elliott a chance to exhibit his baritone voice to good advantage. The music of minor roles was pleasingly sung by Harry Steele Jr., Michael Gulan, Marion Munger, Crystalee Pelay and William Savage.

The chorus work also showed that careful preparation evident in renditions of all the young musicians under Mr. Gershkovitch's guidance, the girls' voices sounding especially fresh and pretty.

15th Season

Jacques Gershkovitch, Conductor

November 19, 1938

Raymond Overture	Thomas
Unfinished Symphony	Schubert
Dance of the Buffoons	Rimsky-Korsakoff
Serenade No. 1, in D major	Brahms
Christmas Tree – For Strings	Rebikoff
Prelude to "Die Meistersinger"	Wagner

February 18, 1939

Oberon Overture	Weber
Scherzo-Midsummer Night's Dream	Mendelssohn
Concerto for Piano	Grieg
Kyoko Matsui, *Soloist*	
Sinfonia in Bb	J. C. Bach
Funeral Music – "Siegfried"	Wagner
Parade of the Ponderous Pachyderms	Enna & Buck
Rhumba, from Second Symphony	Harl Mc Donald

April 22, 1939

Overture, "Marriage of Figaro"	Mozart
Symphony No. 92, "Oxford"	Haydn
Le Coq d'Or	Rimsky-Korsakoff
Introduction & Cortege	
Prelude, Chorale & Fugue	Bach/Abert
Danse Americaine	Dent Mowrey
La Grande Paque Russe	Rimsky-Korsakoff

June 6, 1939 "Pop" Concert

Merry Wives of Windsor Overture	Nicolai
Eine Kleine Nachtmusik	Mozart
Violin Concerto in D, "Adelaide"	Mozart
Elliot Rapaport, *Guest Soloist*	
Overture, "Gypsy Baron"	J. Strauss
Praeludium	Jarnefelt
Introduction to "Khovanshchina"	Moussorgsky
Polovetsian Dances	Borodin

THE OREGONIAN

JUNIOR SYMPHONY OPENS NEW YEAR

Admirers Pack Auditorium for First Concert

BY HILMAR GRONDAHL
Music Editor, the Oregonian

The Portland Junior Symphony orchestra, now in its 15th year under the direction of Jacques Gershkovitch, played the first concert of its new season Saturday night at the public auditorium. Several thousand admiring spectators and auditors were in the hall enjoying the sight and sound of nearly 100 young players on their mettle.

We cannot recall a year's opening concert by this unique organization which offered as much proof to the public of the efficacy of its purpose and the soundness of its practice. The demonstration came through the overture to Ambroise Thomas' opera "Raymond."

Overture Well Played

It was the Junior Symphony's careful attention to details, unanimity of attack, accuracy of intonations, fluency of rhythm and responsiveness to dynamic directions which made Thomas sound like a better composer than we usually think he is.

Now this is an accomplishment which you do not expect to come from an ensemble of amateur musicians averaging something like 15 years in age. Particularly does it surprise you in an orchestra of this size and age.

In a city of Portland's population it would seem possible to assemble, by the right method of selection, some dozen or 18 players of marked interest, talent and capacity who could work into a compact and efficient ensemble. But when the ages of individual members vary from 6 to 20 or thereabouts, the problem of molding the whole membership into a workable mass is much, much greater.

Musicians Work Finished

It was the realization of these factors in the relationship to the finished performance of the "Raymond" overture, which re-emphasized the aim of the junior symphony organization, and gave some immediate measure of its current success.

Another composition of the pre-intermission period which received a musically affectionate collaboration from the orchestra was the Dance of the Buffoons from Rimsky-Korsakoff's opera "The Snow Maiden."

The last half of the program included a performance of Brahms' early serenade in D major, the waltz from Rebikoff's "Christmas Tree" suite and the prelude to "Die Meistersinger."

Kyoko Matsui, piano soloist.

THE OREGONIAN FEB. 19, 1939

BIG OVATION GIVEN JUNIOR ORCHESTRA

Thousands Attend Event on 14th Anniversary

To Jacques Gershkovitch and the Portland Junior Symphony orchestra came well-earned reward Saturday night for the 14 years they have labored to enrich the music life of Portland. The applause of an audience of several thousand persons that heard them at the public auditorium celebrating the 15th anniversary of the orchestra amounted to an ovation.

The eager enthusiasm of the orchestra's admirers was a triumphant event for Mr. Gershkovitch, who has directed the junior symphony since its founding in 1924. It was no less of a triumph for a charming little Japanese girl, 20-year-old Kyoko Matsui, who made her debut as piano soloist with the symphony.

Pianist Shows Artistry

The three movements of Grieg's concerto for piano and orchestra gave Miss Matsui full opportunity to display the youthful vigor of her artistry. This she undertook with graceful assurance and completed with enthusiastic approval of her appreciative listeners.

Through the sparkling overture to Von Weber's opera, "Oberon," the delicate fantasy of the scherzo from "Midsummer Night's Dream," by Mendelssohn, Bach's "Sinfonia in B Major" and the stately "Funeral March at the Death of Siegfried," by Wagner, the youthful musicians appeared at their very best.

They stirred quick response in the audience with the modern "Parade of the Ponderous Pachyderms," by the Portland composers, Emil Enna and Ronald Buck, and brought the concert to stirring conclusion with Harl McDonald's "Rumba from the Second Symphony."

Many Calls Made

Aisles were vacant, marked by not a single departing listener as the audience recalled Mr. Gershkovitch time after time to pay its tribute.

OREGON JOURNAL FEB. 19, 1939.

Junior Symphony Concert Celebrates 15th Year

By Susie Aubrey Smith

The Portland Junior Symphony concert Saturday evening, second of its season, was a fitting celebration of the orchestra's 15th anniversary year. An exceptionally interesting program arranged by the conductor, Jacques Gershkovitch, a most gifted soloist and unusually fine work by the 90 or more young musicians in the orchestra made the occasion a notable one in the history of the organization.

Opening with a fanfare and "The Star Spangled Banner," directed by James Eoff, assistant conductor, the first programmed number was von Weber's lilting overture to "Oberon." Next came the gay Scherzo from Mendelssohn's "Midsummer Night's Dream" music. Under Mr. Gershkovitch's eloquent baton the young musicians produced splendid volume and color of tone and clear-cut and definite rhythms. Their rendition of the "Siegfried's Death" music from Wagner's "Gotterdammerung" was among the most surprisingly effective work of the evening. A popular number with players and audience was "Parade of the Ponderous Pachyderms," from "Circus Suite" by Dr. Emil Enna, composer-pianist and critic, and Ronald Buck, both Portland musicians.

Kyoko Matsui, Portland Japanese girl, was the soloist, playing the Grieg A minor concerto with the orchestra. The petite pianist managed a brilliant tone that soared over the orchestra and her interpretation was at all times interesting. The excellence of her technique was especially evident in the difficult cadenza. It was superlative playing for a girl of 20.

The program closed with the stirring "Rhumba" movement from Harl McDonald's "Rhumba" symphony.

Preceding the concert proper, Dorothy Hutchison, concertmaster, presented a scroll signed by the orchestra members to Charles A. Hart, Junior Symphony association president, in appreciation of the board's efforts for the orchestra. Mr. Hart spoke briefly in response.

A reception in the south wing followed the concert.

OREGON JOURNAL APR. 23, 1939.

Audience Enjoys Junior Symphony

By Susie Aubrey Smith

A diversified program ranging from Mozart and Haydn to modern American music was offered by the Portland Junior Symphony orchestra Saturday evening at The Auditorium as its third concert of the season.

Mr. Gershkovitch opened with the gay and sparkling overture to Mozart's "Marriage of Figaro" and its performance was marked by the excellent attack and spontaneous response to the conductor's indications that is typical of the Junior symphony members. Haydn's "Oxford" symphony, which was played next, drew more heavily on the artistic resources of the orchestra, and excerpts from Rimsky-Korsakoff's "Le Coq d'Or," with its Oriental imagery, gave Mr. Gershkovitch a chance to show of the proficiency of his youthful musicians in an even more colorful manner.

Following the intermission, the program continued with the Bach-Abert "Prelude, Chorale and Fugue." The brilliant measures of the "great fugue" and the pretty chorale of Abert's own composition were admirably played. Next in order came "Danse Americaine" by Dent Mowrey, Portland composer, with its intriguing rhythms given in spirited style. The climactic place was allotted to Rimsky-Korsakoff's "The Great Russian Easter," one of the most thrilling overtures in symphonic literature. The Junior symphony "men" and their Russian conductor transmitted all the color and drama of the Russian music and ended their program in the grand manner.

THE OREGONIAN APR. 23, 1939

MUSIC'S WIZARDRY FILLS AUDITORIUM

Vibrant 'Golden Cockerel' Thrills Big Audience

BY HILMAR GRONDAHL
Music Editor, The Oregonian

For one thrilling moment Saturday night the people, the chairs and even the concrete floors at the public auditorium were alive with the vibrant tonal splendor of the final measures of the wedding procession from Rimsky-Korsakoff's "Golden Cockerel." Spaces actually shook as Jacques Gershkovitch guided the Portland Junior Symphony orchestra through the most stirring period of the association's third regular concert in the current season.

The concert began with the familiar and merry overture to "The Marriage of Figaro," then heard Haydn's "Oxford" symphony, another brilliant composition by Rimsky-Korsakoff, the Bach-Abert prelude, choral and fugue, and the "Danse Americaine," by the resident composer, Dent Mowrey.

Neglected Passages Shine

Rimsky-Korsakoff, master orchestrator, served admirably to bring generally neglected sections of the orchestra out in strong relief. That some of the wood winds, and particularly the horns, trombones and trumpets sounded to advantage is a fitting commentary upon the growing interest among the youth in these instruments.

Musically rewarding in equal force, but, in opposite mood, was the effectively restrained handling of the slow movement from the symphony in G now called "Oxford."

Mowrey Dance Heard

Pursuing its policy of presenting at least one work by an American composer on each of its public programs, the Portland Junior Symphony orchestra gave its first performance of the dance which Mr. Mowrey conceived and completed in Paris.

The players, evidently enjoying its melodic and rhythmic virtues and well as the fact that they know something about the resident composer, set the music forth in commendable fashion.

OREGON DAILY JOURNAL JUN. 7, 1939

Violin Prodigy Is Soloist With Junior Symphony

By Susie Aubrey Smith

The Portland Junior Symphony orchestra gave the fourth concert of its present season, an extra "pop" program, Tuesday evening at The Auditorium to a good-sized and most appreciative audience.

In the opening number, the overture to Nicolai's "Merry Wives of Windsor," and, in fact, all through the program, the young musicians demonstrated again the qualities which make their performances so satisfying to the music lover—their fine attack and effective dynamics and their enthusiastic response to the baton of their conductor, Jacques Gershkovitch. Mozart's charming "Eine Kleine Nachtmusik" led up quite appropriately to his "Adelaide" violin concerto, which was played by the soloist of the evening, Elliot Rapaport of Los Angeles.

This 14-year-old boy is a young artist from whom interesting things may be expected. He has the beautiful individual tone and the artistic unselfconsciousness of a great talent, and through excellent training he has acquired a facile and fluent technique and a well-controlled bow. Elliot invested the Adagio movement with poetic charm and the final Allegro, which he took at a fast tempo, was played in splendid style by both soloist and orchestra. Insistent applause brought the soloist back to the stage to give three encores.

After the intermission, Mr. Gershkovitch offered four popular numbers from lighter symphonic literature, ending with the colorful "Polovetsian Dances," from Borodin's "Prince Igor." The young musicians took a final bow with Mr. Gershkovitch.

THE OREGONIAN JUN. 7, 1939

VIOLINIST DRAWS PRAISE OF CROWD

BY HILMAR GRONDAHL
Music Editor, The Oregonian

The Portland Junior Symphony orchestra's special "Pop" concert at the public auditorium Tuesday night was of special and two-fold service in bringing Portland its first hearing not only of Elliot Rapaport, a California violinist of 14 summers, but also of the "Adelaide" concerto which Mozart wrote during his tenth year.

Audience Absorbs Music

It was this score, disarmingly ingenious and quietly engaging, which Elliot Rapaport and the orchestra, under Jacques Gershkovitch's direction, set before an absorbed and appreciative audience Tuesday night.

The visiting violinist was more than equal to the technical requirements of the solo lines. He has a fluency of style, a vitality of instrumental engagement which attests his youth and buoyant enthusiasm.

The tumult of resounding hands which fell upon the heels of the young violinist as he quitted the stage brought him, a piano and an accompanist, Robert Gerretson, on the scene for a series of encores. These pleased the crowd and convincingly showed the sensitive and resourceful stuff of which the young Portland pianist is made.

16th Season

Jacques Gershkovitch, Conductor

November 18, 1939

Overture, "The Magic Flute"	MOZART
Symphony NO. 4, Bb	BEETHOVEN
Russian Sailor's Dance from "The Red Poppy"	GLIERE
The Last Spring–arr. Gershkovitch	GRIEG
Festivals, from Nocturnes	DEBUSSY
Symphonic Poem NO. 3 "Les Preludes"	LISZT

February 10, 1940

Symphony NO. 7	SCHUBERT
Concerto NO. 22, for Piano Majolaine Le Beck, *Soloist*	MOZART
Moldau	SMETANA
The Summit Temple Prelude to the Opera, "Yang Kwei Fei"	*A. AVSHALOMOFF
Caucasian Sketches	IPPOLITOV-IVANOV

April 6, 1940

Overture, "Fingal's Cave," op. 26	MENDELSSOHN
Suite from The Water Music	HANDEL/HARTY
Scherzo-Midsummer Night's Dream	MENDELSSOHN
Concerto for 2 Violins, in D minor Elizabeth Zwerenz & Phillis Falkoff, *Soloists*	BACH
Baba Jaga	LIADOW
Menuetto in Bb	BOLZONI
Romeo & Juliet	TCHAIKOVSKY

June 9, 1940

Concert for Rotary Conference District NO. 101

Retrospective Program from the Season

THE OREGONIAN FEB. 11, 1940

Players Give Rich Program

BY HILMAR GRONDAHL
Music Editor, The Oregonian

When the Portland Junior Symphony orchestra came to its mid-season concert Saturday night at the public auditorium, it was with a program rich in notable music.

Jacques Gershkovitch had drilled the players in the great, difficult and singularly beautiful C major symphony of Schubert. He had prepared them for collaboration with Majolaine le Beck, the young pianist, in Mozart's E-flat major concerto. And in company with his cherished Ippolitov-Ivanov, he accomplished his first American performance of a composition by his friend, A. Avshalomoff of Shanghai. This last brought the audience attention to Jack Avshalomoff, son of the composer, who played the piano part.

It should be said of Saturday's soloist that she did not obtrude herself between the composer and his intention. She sat in the directive shadow of the conductor's baton, a very attractive picture, indeed, prompting the charming phrases and melodies from the ebony instrument with graceful assurance and a musical demeanor.

Reading Held Fresh

The young players preceded their success in Mozart with a reading of the C major symphony that was fresh and spontaneous in its spirit. Schubert, especially, should be that way, one feels. There were places in the score in which the brasses had chances to shine; chances which they accepted with a certain admirable relish. Flute and bassoon likewise gave distinguished service.

The operatic prelude by Avshalomoff, attractively fashioned, was enjoyed by the audience, which seemed to express its appreciation to the composer through his son.

OREGON JOURNAL APR. 7, 1940

Junior Symphony Closes Season In Fine Concert

By Susie Aubrey Smith

One of the most delightful programs the orchestra has given in several seasons was chosen for the Portland Junior symphony's last concert of the season Saturday evening by it conductor, Jacques Gershkovitch. The usual large and enthusiastic audience at The Auditorium applauded the artistic efforts of the young musicians in their fine presentation of such selections as Mendelssohn's "Fingal's Cave Overture" and the suite from Handel's "Water Music."

The orchestra's rendition of this latter piece was exceptionally smooth and finished with lovely tone and good contrast in the six parts. Mr. Gershkovitch offered as the main feature Tschaikowsky's beautiful "Romeo and Juliet" overture and , in his reading and the orchestra's playing, proved that the music was not beyond the abilities of his youthful musicians.

Two of the orchestra's first violin section, Elizabeth Zwerenz and Phyllis Falkoff, appeared as soloists in the Bach D minor double concerto and, under Mr. Gershkovitch's directing baton, played the melodiously rhythmic measures in commendable style. The girls were recalled several times by the spontaneous applause of the music patrons present.

Lighter numbers which were enjoyed by the audience included Laidow's amusing "Baba Jaga": the lilting "Scherzo" from Mendolssohn's "Midsummer Night's Dream" and the Bolzoni minuet in which the strings distinguished themselves.

THE OREGONIAN APR. 7, 1940

Players End Music Year

Junior Symphony Gives Finale

BY HILMAR GRONDAHL
Music Editor, The Oregonian

Another season of the Portland Junior Symphony orchestra's year-by-year course of accomplishment came to a close Saturday night at the public auditorium. Jacques Gershkovitch had prepared a program appealing to various tastes.

To at least one of the audience Bach's D minor concerto for two violins turned out to be more than a work of genius serving as a vehicle for the talents of two of the orchestra's leading instrumentalists. It became, as one listened, the symbol of one of the organization's most valuable contributions—the development of co-operation.

So in the close musical association of Phyllis Falkoff and Elizabeth Zwerenz with one another and with the orchestra under Mr. Gershkovitch . . . the focus of applause fell naturally and strongly upon the two soloists for their skillful management of the difficult lines of the concerto. The grateful slow movement was warmly and persuasively handled.

Love Theme Liked

Tchaikowsky's fantasy-overture "Romeo and Juliet," was another admired section of the program. Its romantic context was apparently congenial to the ensemble, for they became enthusiastic participants in its dramatic spirit, and the emotional intensity of the haunting love theme. The brasses sounded to advantage here as in the Handel "Water Music."

The concert was the fitting summary of another year; the orchestra responding to its conductor competently and bringing music to its audience in a way that was highly pleasurable.

THE OREGONIAN NOV. 19, 1939

Junior Symphony Concert Heard at Auditorium

BY HILMAR GRONDAHL
Music Editor, The Oregonian

For 15 years the Portland Junior Symphony orchestra has been making music in its own unique way and Saturday night at the public auditorium it set forth upon another season with the good wishes of a fair-sized audience.

Fourth Symphony Heard

Saturday night there was a complete performance of Beethoven's Fourth symphony. There was, besides, such solid orchestral fare as Liszt's"Les Preludes," one of the Debussey nocturnes, the Russian sailor's dance by Gliere and a special arrangement by Conductor Jacques Gershkovitch of Grieg's "The Last Spring."

The opening concert of each Junior Symphony season is one of the most conjectural undertakings of their musical history for a reason aptly stated by William Lamont, principal oboist, at the head of his program notes on the concert:

"If you have a memory for faces, you will note that the personnel of the Junior Symphony changes from year to year. Some members leave to go to college. Young students enter for the first time. The orchestra must be recreated every year."

Players On Alert

But seldom, if ever, has a brand new assemblage of players responded so alertly and with such a fair share of assurance to the conductoral indications as this young blending of neophyte and briefly-seasoned musician did on Saturday night.

Especially in the Beethoven music their strings were unified, coordinative, the wood winds exact, definitive. The meandering wood wind line of the third movement was as appealing as it was illusive. Mr. Gershkovitch directed the applause to favored instruments and then motioned the entire orchestra to stand for the approval of its work.

OREGON JOURNAL NOV. 19, 1939

Junior Symphony Opens Season In Fine Program

By Susie Aubrey Smith

The Portland Junior Symphony orchestra opened its 16th season Saturday evening at The Auditorium with a program that did credit to everyone concerned with it—the young musicians, their conductor, Jacques Gershkovitch, their assistant conductor, James Eoff, and the officers and directors of the Portland Junior Symphony.

For this opening concert, Mr. Gershkovitch offered an entire symphony, Beethoven's Fourth in B Flat. It is remarkable, of course, that children are able to play a symphony at all. These children played Beethoven's music in a manner to delight their audience. From beginning to end, their response to their leader's baton was spontaneous. Mr. Gershkovitch took the final allegro at an effective tempo and at its end came much applause which he shared with his young musicians.

In the second half of the program the orchestra gave that favorite of symphonic poems, "Les Preludes," by Liszt, in which the youthful musicians again emphasized their splendid musical training under the guidance of Mr. Gershkovitch.

OREGON JOURNAL FEB. 11, 1940

Junior Symphony In Successful Second Concert

By Susie Aubrey Smith

In the second concert of its 16th season the Portland Junior Symphony orchestra delighted a large audience Saturday evening at The Auditorium. Jacques Gershkovitch, the conductor, and his young musicians were in excellent form and the program boasted a first American performance.

This was "The Summit Temple," an atmospheric operatic prelude by A. Avshalomoff, Russian composer and resident in China, who made Portland his home for several years. Mr. Gershkovitch gave the work a masterly interpretation and, for its performance, the composer's son, Jack Avshalomoff, was at the piano which augmented the orchestra.

The orchestra presented as soloist its principal double-bass player, Majolaine LeBeck, 18-year-old pianist, in the Mozart concerto No. 22 in E flat major. Miss LeBeck gave a surprising mature performance marked by clearcut phrasing and a feeling for the grace and delicacy of Mozart's music. Her playing is sure and effortless. She was recalled to the stage several times by enthusiastic applause.

The junior musicians also offered on their program three movements from Schubert's Seventh symphony which called for all their musical prowess, and the hauntingly beautiful "River Moldau" by the Czech composer, Smetana, which Mr. Gershkovitch took at the most effective tempos.

The first of Ippolitow-Ivanow's "Caucasian Sketches" gave interesting solo passages to the viola, and Janee Gilbert should be commended for lovely tone and artistic playing. The second sketch, "Procession of the Sardar," brought the concert to a conclusion in a riot of musical color.

17th Season

Jacques Gershkovitch, Conductor

November 16, 1940

Phedre Overture	MASSENET
Adagio for Strings	*BARBER
Piano Concerto NO. 3, C minor	BEETHOVEN
Russell Palmer, *Soloist*	
Petite Suite	DEBUSSY
Symphony, "Rustic Wedding"	GOLDMARK
In the Garden; Finale	

February 15, 1941

Merry Wives of Windsor Overture	NICOLAI
William Lamont, *Student Conductor*	
Concerto Grosso, C minor, op.6 NO.3	CORELLI
Invitation to the Dance	WEBER
Music Box	LIADOW
Italian Caprice	TCHAIKOVSKY

April 19, 1941

Roman Carnival Overture, op.9	BERLIOZ
New World Symphony	DVORAK
Adagio: Allegro Molto	
Largo	
Concerto for Viola, B minor	HANDEL/CASADESUS
Janee Gilbert, *Soloist*	
Peter and the Wolf, op. 67	*PROKOFIEFF
Don Marye, *Narrator*	
Cradle Song	LIADOW
Dance of the Buffoons	RIMSKY-KORSAKOFF

* *Portland Premiere*

OREGON JOURNAL NOV.17, 1940

Junior Symphony Scores Success At First Concert

By Susie Aubrey Smith

The Portland Junior Symphony orchestra opened its 17th season Saturday evening at The Auditorium with a program varied and interesting which served to display to the best advantage the talents of the 100 young musicians. A large and enthusiastic audience applauded the orchestra and its conductor, Jacques Gershkovitch.

There are new faces among the "orchestra men," as well as those familiar to the audience. This happens each year, but the excellence of the ensemble remains up to standard.

A real artistic achievement was the performance of Beethoven's Concerto No. 3 in C minor with Russell Palmer, 19-year-old pianist, as soloist. Russell showed a mature understanding of the music, his technique was fluent, his interpretation was unmarred by mannerisms. Here was a serious young musician playing with other serious young musicians to the evident delight of their listeners. Under the baton of Mr. Gershkovitch, the orchestra gave the soloist splendid support.

The "American" number, Barber's "Adagio," gave the string sections an opportunity to prove their artistic merit. Massenet's "Phedre" overture was a colorful opening number and the selections played after the intermission, Debussy's "Petite Suite" and "In the Garden" and the Finale to Goldmark's "Rustic Wedding" symphony were given delightful readings by the conductor.

The orchestra gave part of its program on Saturday morning at The Auditorium as the opening event of the children's Saturday morning series.

THE OREGONIAN FEB. 16, 1941

Baton Handled By Students

Orchestra Podium Filled by Youths

BY HILMAR GRONDAHL
Music Editor, The Oregonian

The Portland Junior Symphony orchestra did play a concert at the public auditorium Saturday night; but that performance does not give the whole story of its musical activities for the day.

In some ways the young people's concert at 11 o'clock in the morning was more specifically the expression of the orchestra's basic purpose.

Hall Like Convention

There is an aliveness about this morning crowd that cannot last till night. The hall buzzes with energy on unnatural leash. Children are everywhere, assailing the orderly space of the aisles with running and bright colors. On the stage 100 musicians sit somewhat quietly with instruments at rest. It looks like a political convention; placards on sticks indicate the location of certain instrumental choirs; blue for strings, etc.

Presently the commentator, David Campbell, brings the restless audience to order with a few well-chosen comments upon the music to follow. It is the overture to Nicolai's "Merry Wives of Windsor," and the conductor is to be, not Jacques Gershkovitch, but one who has studied in his conducting class—William Lamont. The young man has forsaken his oboe and English horn for the siren call of "the stick." On the stand, he leads with energy and purpose, the players respond with care and skill.

Conductor Aged 11

The next number brings another conductor. It is Arthur Edmonds, age 11. He bows reservedly and steps upon the stand to conduct "Ase's Death."

Needless to say, the audience was very favorably disposed toward the two student conductors and their way of doing things. And the occasion showed another facet of the educative function of the symphony association and a favorable reflection upon the teaching ability of Mr. Gershkovitch.

Saturday night he was given attention in plenty for his handling of the orchestra in such scores as Mendelssohn's "Italian" symphony, Corelli's concerto grosso and Tchaikowsky's "Italian Caprice."

OREGON JOURNAL FEB. 16, 1941

Junior Symphony Concert Honored

By Susie Aubrey Smith

Saturday was a busy day for the 100 musicians of the Portland Junior Symphony orchestra and their conductor, Jacques Gershkovitch. In the morning they gave their regular program on the Saturday series for children and, in the evening, they played their second concert of the present season at The Auditorium.

Mr. Gershkovitch offered an unusually ambitious program at the evening concert, including Mendelssohn's melodious "Italian Symphony," Corelli's "Concerto Grosso" in C minor, opus 6, No. 3; von Weber's "Invitation to the Waltz," Laidlow's "Music Box" and Tschaikowsky's "Italian Caprice." William Lamont, student conductor, led the orchestra in the opening number, the overture to "The Merry Wives of Windsor" by Nicolai.

The young musicians were quite equal to the symphony, in which they gave fine response to their conductor's baton. Their most delightful presentation was, however, the Corelli "concerto." Featured in this number were Elizabeth Zwerenz and Gladys Stevenson, violins; Marie Eddy, viola, and Beverly LeBeck, cello, and the string section.

Played at the morning concert was "Parade of the Ponderous Pachyderms" by Dr. Emil Enna and Ronald Buck. Arthur Edmunds, youngest member of Mr. Gershkovitch's conducting class, led the orchestra in "Ase's Death" by Grieg and Clarence Faris directed the audience, made up mostly of children, in singing.

THE OREGONIAN APR. 21, 1941

Young Audiences Thrilled At 'Peter Wolf' Concerts

BY HILMAR GRONDAHL
Music Editor, The Oregonian

Jacques Gershkovitch directed both Saturday performances of the Portland Junior Symphony orchestra at the public auditorium before record crowds. There was fun and good music morning and night, but it was with the earlier audience that one felt the contagious enthusiasm and inspiring purpose of youth most sharply.

When Don Marye, director of the Portland Civic theater, gave the several thousand youths the narrative line, and Mr. Gershkovitch built the musical setting and atmosphere for Prokofieff's "Peter and the Wolf," it was an extraordinary projection of fanciful music through young musicians to listeners of their own age. The point and humor of the story readily reached home. And the groundswell of applause which ensued was deserved by all participants.

Audience Well Pleased

It was a signal service that Mr. Gershkovitch and the junior symphony association did for the players under their wing, and for the local concertgoers, in effecting the first performance of this new and highly enjoyable score.

Equally valuable was the first performance of the Henri Casadesus arrangement of a Handel concerto for viola and orchestra. This is one of the most significant contributions to the undernourished solo desires of a lovable member of the string choir.

Janee Gilbert was the viola soloist; a very attractive girl of 17 who looks very much like Alice about to grow up. She had her musical materials very well in mind and hand, defining the melodic lines with excellent taste, style and intonation. She was an engaging soloist even to depth of her curtsy.

OREGON JOURNAL APR. 20, 1941

Junior Symphony Third Concert Best of Season

By Susie Aubrey Smith

The Junior symphony programs have been increasingly interesting this season and Saturday evening's concert at The Auditorium was the best of all. It featured an entertaining modern composition—Prokofieff's "Peter and the Wolf" and introduced as soloist the orchestra's 17-year-old first viola player, Janee Gilbert.

Jacques Gershkovitch, the conductor, had chosen a program rich in color, rhythm and melody, opening with the stirring "Roman Carnival Overture" by Berlioz. The two movements from Dvorak's "From the New World" symphony seemed more interesting than usual as played by the Junior musicians. William Lamont gave the English horn solo in the Largo.

Handel's Concerto in B minor was played by Janee Gilbert in the true Handelian tradition; with her sure technique and fine musicianship, it proved a most satisfying solo instrument. Her tone in the Andante was exceptionally beautiful.

Prokofieff's orchestral fairy tale was entertaining from everybody's point of view as narrated by Don Marye and played by the young musicians under Mr. Gershkovitch's capable baton.

18th Season

Jacques Gershkovitch, Conductor

November 8, 1941

Rosamunde Overture	Schubert
Symphony No. 1, Op. 21	Beethoven
Concerto for Piano, Eb major	Liszt
Geneva Ide, *Soloist*	
Variations on a Theme by Tchaikowsky	Arensky
Le Coq d'Or	Rimsky-Korsakoff

February 28, 1942

Overture, "Marriage of Figaro"	Mozart
Violin Concerto, D major, Op. 61	Beethoven
Elizabeth Zwerenz, *Soloist*	
Dream Pantomime from "Hansel & Gretel"	Humperdinck
Sinfonia in Bb major	J. C. Bach
Overture, "1812," Op. 49	Tchaikovský

April 25, 1942

Egmont Overture	Beethoven
Concerto for Violoncello, in D	Haydn
Beverly LeBeck, *Soloist*	
Symphony No. 8, B minor, "Unfinished"	Schubert
First Roumanian Rhapsody	Enesco

THE OREGONIAN NOV. 4, 1941

Group of 100 Gives Concert

BY HILMAR GRONDAHL
Music Editor, The Oregonian

Those qualities which for 17 years have been regarded as characteristic of the Portland Junior Symphony orchestra were dominant again Saturday night when these 100 young musicians, at the behest of Jacques Gershkovitch, coursed through a program of substantial masterworks at the public auditorium. It was the first concert of the new season.

The healthy enthusiasm and purpose of which the young are so capable showed itself at practically all stages of the concert. It was at hand for the selections of Schubert's music to "Rosamunde."

Geneva Ide Soloist

It was evident in Beethoven's youthful C major symphony. And it was abundantly noticeable when, with Geneva Ide as soloist, the ensemble poured itself into the colorful measures of the Liszt E flat major concerto.

Miss Ide showed herself sufficiently adept of technic and interpretive skill to surpass any other young pianist who appeared before three judges in the Junior Symphony's regular yearly competition.

Together the soloist, conductor, and instrumentalists lifted this time-honored musical showpiece up so that its most sentimental sonorities and glittering technical essays could be vividly felt.

Despite a large proportion of new members, the orchestra did some of its finest ensemble playing in the concerto. And young Miss Ide received salvos of applause.

Those attending will long remember the restrained beauty of the second movement of the Beethoven. This is a high artistic point in junior symphony history.

OREGON JOURNAL NOV. 9, 1941

Junior Symphony Opens Season In Fine Concert

By Susie Aubrey Smith

The Portland Junior symphony opened its 18th season Saturday evening at The Auditorium with as fine a concert as any music lover could wish to hear.

Under the expressive baton of Jacques Gershkovitch, the orchestra's conductor, the 100 young musicians played with spirit and spontaneity. They gave an entire symphony—Beethoven's No. 1 in C major—in a manner to rival many adult orchestras; but it was, perhaps, in the excerpts from Rimsky-Korsakoff's "Coq d'Or" that they did their finest work.

The soloist was Geneva Ide, 19-year-old Gresham pianist, who was presented in the Liszt E-flat concerto with the orchestra. Miss Ide has a lovely singing tone and a brilliant technique well suited to the florid Liszt music. She played with assurance and with musical intelligence. Both soloist and orchestra should be commended on their excellent co-ordination of artistic effort in the concerto.

Mr. Gershkovitch opened with Schubert's "Rosamunde" overture, a melodious and favorite piece which he and his young musicians gave a most creditable reading. The string players had an opportunity to prove their artistic worth in the Arensky "Variations on a theme by Tschaikowsky."

The Junior symphony with Mr. Gershkovitch conducting and David Campbell as commentator gave the first musical program of the Junior League's Saturday Morning Series at 11 a.m. at The Auditorium. The program was opened with a stirring rendition of the national anthem. A demonstration of instruments was a feature.

THE OREGONIAN MAR. 2, 1942

Junior Group Goes Over Big

Second Concert Of Season Liked

BY HILMAR GRONDAHL
Music Editor, The Oregonian

Jacques Gershkovitch put the Portland junior symphony orchestra through its paces Saturday night at the public auditorium. It was the second concert of season No. 18.

If it was not the finest performance of the organization's history it had here and there those periods of striking excellence that find their way into practically every program these 100 eager young players put forth.

Long Practice Shows

Brass and woodwind players practice week after week in the informal spaces of Holladay school until they are apparently letter perfect. But at the concert conditions have changed; they are excited, the hall is warmer and intonation sometimes veers away from the straight and narrow. But again the breath comes, the lips function and the elusive beauty that they have practiced for comes to pass. And the audience gets another thrill.

Saturday night there was a soloist. Elizabeth Zwerenz, for seven years a member of the orchestra, rose to that eminence by dint of native violinistic ability, application and competitive examination. She played the noble lines of Beethoven's concerto against a well-molded counterpart prepared by Mr. Gershkovitch and her fellow musicians. She handled the difficult assignment with simple assurance and a tone of quite agreeable proportions. Her best work came in the less ornate portions of the larghetto and in the second theme of the rondo.

The concert wound up with a swirl of martial sound as the orchestra, assisted by the Franklin high school band, offered Tschaikowsky's historical zombie, the "1812 Overture."

THE OREGONIAN APR. 26, 1942

Young Cellist Held 'Comer'

Soloist Provides Brilliant Music

BY HILMAR GRONDAHL
Music Editor, The Oregonian

After hearing her brilliant performance with the Portland Junior Symphony orchestra Saturday night you can write yourself a note to look for Beverly LeBeck among the important musical headlines not so many years from now.

To appear as soloist with the junior symphony under the baton of Jacques Gershkovitch is something of a debut. But Miss LeBeck made it an event. It was not anything that she did self-conciously, for she appears to be the most unaffected youngster alive. She simply set her intelligence, temperament, technical skill and cello at the service of the Haydn concerto in a manner so disarming and artistically illuminating that one felt something of the fascination which emanates from genius.

Orchestra's Pace Fast

Remarkable as her reading was, it would have more nearly reflected the appealing substance of the score had external factors been somewhat altered. The orchestra took off at a pace no cellist would choose. And while the soloist held nobly to the tempo suggested, it was too hurried to permit the warmth of interpretive impulse that should govern this section. It would have been more of a musical entity, too, if the accompanying orchestra had been held to perhaps two dozen for the public occasions.

The program opened with one of Mr. Gershkovitch's most vivid readings, the "Egmont" overture by Beethoven. After intermission there was the "Unfinished" symphony, and Enesco's first Rumanian rhapsody.

OREGON JOURNAL APR. 26, 1942

Junior Symphony Closes Season In Fine Program

By Susie Aubrey Smith

The Portland Junior Symphony orchestra closed its 18th season Saturday evening with its third concert played to a large and exceptionally demonstrative audience at The Auditorium.

Two special features made the program unusually interesting. The Junior symphony presented its leading cellist, Beverly Le Beck, as soloist in the Haydn concerto and offered as its closing number Georges Enesco's rhythmically difficult, "Rumanian Rhapsody," one of the most ambitious performances the orchestra has ever attempted.

It was Miss LeBeck's first solo appearance with any orchestra. She is 16 years of age—one of the youngest soloists ever presented by the orchestra. She played with that absorption in the music which marks the true artist. Her technique was brilliant and at the same time without visible effort and there was just the right touch of drama in her virtuosity to keep her performance interesting.

Mr. Gershkovitch opened with Beethoven's "Egmont" overture. He offered the Schubert "Unfinished," which was the first symphony the young musicians ever attempted. At that former concert it was an ambitious attempt. Last night it was a mature and artistic performance with the added vitality Mr. Gershkovitch and his orchestra always manage to put into a symphonic work.

The program ended in a blaze of orchestral color that is Enesco's Rhapsody.

OREGON JOURNAL MAY 1, 1942

Junior Symphony Treats Audience To Big Thrills

By Susie Aubrey Smith

The large audience at the second Junior symphony concert of the season Saturday night at The Auditorium was treated to three big thrills, unusual even in a program given by this group of excellent musicians under the able baton of their conductor, Jacques Gershkovitch.

The Junior symphony's arrangement and rendition of the American national anthem is one of the most stirring the reviewer has heard to date. The young musicians' performance of Tschaikowsky's "1812 Overture" was particularly appropriate as this work celebrated an earlier century's victory of the Russians over an invading army. Augmented by members of Franklin high school band, Vern Wilson, director, the Junior orchestra played the dramatic music better than any ensemble has played it here since the visit of the Mexican police band some years ago.

The third feature of the evening that impressed both musicians and music lovers was the playing of the Beethoven concerto in D major by Elizabeth Zwerenz, who is the orchestra's concert-master. Beethoven's difficult and delightful music found the young artist equal to its many technical obstacles and its interpretative nuances. Miss Zwerenz displayed musicianship of a high order and established herself as one of Portland's most promising violinists.

OREGON JOURNAL MAY 1, 1942

Junior Concert Great Success

The second concert of the eighteenth season of the Portland Junior Symphony Orchestra held Saturday night, February 28, 1942 was a colossal success. The concert was opened by the entire orchestra standing and playing the "Star Spangled Banner." The program opened with the Overture to the "Marriage of Figaro," by Mozart. The second number of the evening was the "Concerto in D. Major for violin and orchestra," by Beethoven. The soloist was Elizabeth Zwerenz. After intermission the orchestra opened the second half of the program with the Dream Pantomone from "Hansel and Gretel", by Humperdinck. Next was played the "Sinfonia in B flat major," by Bach. The grand finale was the playing of the Overture, 1812, by Tschaikovsky. In this selection the orchestra was assisted by members of the Franklin High School Band. Roosevelt High school was well represented in the second violin section. Gladys Stevenson, concert master, second violin, and Eileen Hanks and Gale Dick.

19th Season

Jacques Gershkovitch, Conductor

November 7, 1942

Overture, "Russlan & Ludmilla"	GLINKA
Persian Dances from "Khovanschina"	MOUSSORGSKY
Piano Concerto NO. 1, op. 25	MENDELSSOHN
Polka from "The Golden Age"	SHOSTAKOVITCH
Valse, from Serenade for Strings	TCHAIKOVSKY
Symphonic Poem, "Moldau"	SMETANA

February 20, 1943

Overture, "The Gypsy Baron"	J. STRAUSS
Classical Symphony, op. 25	PROKOFIEFF
Violin Concerto, E minor, op. 64	MENDELSSOHN
Elinore Sharpe, *Soloist*	
Nutcracker Suite	TCHAIKOVSKY
Intermezzo II "Jewels of the Madonna"	WOLF-FERRARI
Rhumba, from Symphony NO. 2	MCDONALD

April 24, 1943

Symphony op. 5 in C minor	BEETHOVEN
Concerto for Flute & Harp	MOZART
Betty Abbett & Verda Mae Griesinger, *Soloists*	
Adagio for Strings, op. 11	BARBER
Overture, La Grande Paque Russe	RIMSKY-KORSAKOFF

THE OREGONIAN NOV. 8, 1942

Boy Pianist, 13, Featured At Opening of Symphony

BY HILMAR GRONDAHL
Music Editor, The Oregonian

With Barry McClymont, age 13, as soloist in Mendelssohn's G minor piano concerto, and with a varied group of Russian scores on his stand, Jacques Gershkovitch, conductor of the Portland Junior Symphony orchestra, swung his ensemble into a new season Saturday night to the appreciative attention of a warm gathering at the public auditorium.

There was one exception to the diet of Russian music, Smetana's "Moldau." Otherwise there was a polka by the now famous civilian defender of Leningrad, Dmitri Shostakovitch; the overture to Glinka's "Russlan and Ludmilla," the serenade for strings by Tschaikowsky, and some Persian dances by Moussorgsky.

This pleasant assortment of music was vitalized with the gusto for which this young organization is now known. Well stocked with strings, it gave an uncommon richness of texture to the sweeping lines of the Tschaikowsky serenade.

Artist Shows Assurance

Barry McClymont looks like a real American boy; one who would be as much at home in a game of marbles as he is at the keyboard. With his shirt collar open and an easy gait, he strode to the piano and took possession. He probably didn't feel it, but he looked as nonchalant as a veteran. And he played with a calm assurance that made his brilliant assignment knit accurately and effectively into the score. He is an able young musician, for whom the audience showed an unrestrained liking.

One's ears told one that the orchestra had spent a good share of its rehearsal time on this concerto. It was one of the best played scores, and even one of the best concerto offerings in several seasons. Mr. Gershkovitch deserves much credit for the result.

OREGON JOURNAL FEB. 21 1943

Junior Symphony Thrills Audience

By Susie Aubrey Smith

Pleasant and stimulating musical fare was offered by the Portland Junior Symphony orchestra at its second concert of the season Saturday evening at The Auditorium. It was one of Mr. Gershkovitch's most successful program arrangements. A gifted young soloist added interest to the occasion.

The young musicians opened with the lilting "Gypsy Baron" overture of Johann Strauss in which their precise attack and fine feeling for rhythm was evident. Prokofieff's "Classical Symphony," which came next, was an interesting contrast.

Elinore Sharp, 15-year-old member of the orchestra, was the violin soloist, playing the Mendelssohn concerto like a veteran concert artist. Elinore's assurance of manner and execution was backed by well-grounded technique and sound musicianship, vibrant tone and excellent artistry.

After the intermission, came a charming interpretation of Tschaikowsky's "Nut-cracker Suite." In the "Dance of the Sugarplum Fairy," the symphony's first bass player, George Hurst, proved equally good on the celesta.

OREGON JOURNAL NOV. 8, 1942

Junior Symphony Gives Season's Opening Concert

By Susie Aubrey Smith

The Portland Junior symphony opened its 19th season Saturday evening with a concert that drew a large and appreciative audience to The Auditorium. A program in which Russian music predominated and one of the youngest soloists ever presented made the event of special interest.

Mr. Gershkovitch and his young musicians opened with the spirited overture to "Russlan and Ludmilla" by Glinka which the conductor took at a fast and effective tempo. Next came the dramatic music of the Persian dances from Moussorgsky's "Khovantchina" and, last before the intermission, the Mendelssohn concerto for piano with Barry McClymont, 13-year-old pianist, as soloist.

The Junior symphony has never presented a more satisfactory soloist. Barry has a fine command of tone and a clear and fluent technique. He has also an unusually sensitive feeling for the lyric which made his playing particularly well suited to the Mendelssohn work. The orchestra gave him excellent support.

The modern number of the program was the amusingly dissonant "Polka" from the satirical ballet, "The Golden Age," by Shostakovitch. The other number for strings was the lilting waltz from Tschaikovsky's "Serenade."

To end with, Mr. Gershkovitch gave a brilliant and moving reading of Smetana's "The Moldau."

Among the 83 young musicians in the Junior orchestra one noted many new faces, but the quality of their playing retained the high standard which they have set in the last few years.

In the morning, the orchestra gave part of the program as a young people's concert, also at The Auditorium. David Campbell, Portland pianist, was the commentator.

THE OREGONIAN FEB. 21, 1943

Concert Rates High Praise

BY HILMAR GRONDAHL
Music Editor, The Oregonian

The Portland Junior Symphony orchestra appears to be one playing body not seriously affected by the war. Saturday night at the public auditorium it faced a crowd that seemed average in size; the audience, in turn, faced an ensemble that sounded well up to the standard in performance.

Violin Soloist Lauded

There were two ways, however, in which the concert was not average. First was the quality of the soloist: in this case Elinore Sharp, a 15-year-old violinist, who was featured in Mendelssohn's concerto. Miss Sharp was definitely above par in appearance, ease, musicianship and appeal. There have been other soloists in the past who may have excelled in one or another of these several virtues, but not one who held them all to an equal degree.

The second way in which this concert was above average was in the use of Prokofieff's "Classical" symphony as the program novelty.

Rewards Many

Prokofieff created something in his brief symphony which is at once ingratiating music and stimulating satire. It is a kind of music that is not often available, and the performance by Mr. Gershkovitch and his young musicians was rewarding on both sides of the footlights.

THE OREGONIAN APR. 25, 1943

Final Concert of Season Pleases Symphony Crowd

BY HILMAR GRONDAHL
Music Editor, The Oregonian

In the concluding concert of its 19th season, given Saturday night at the public auditorium, the Portland Junior Symphony orchestra presented two of its veteran members in solo roles. These two were Betty Abbett, flutist, and Vedra Mae Griesinger, harpist, whose vehicle was the Mozart concerto for these two instruments and orchestra.

Their feeling for the score impelled them to dispense music beautifully and have a good time while they were doing it. Miss Abbett, who is one of the best flutist, hereabouts, displayed a purling cantabile that was wholly delightful. Miss Griesinger, who has already appeared a good deal in public for one of 14 years, played with a decided flair for the style of the concerto, and a remarkable mastery of the tone coloring possible in her instrument.

The orchestra, under the baton of Jacques Gershkovitch, imbued the complementary assignments with their proper balance and relationship. It was a performance that pleased the listeners visibly.

Mozart was preceded by intermission and a reading of Beethoven's now-called "Victory" symphony. The young musicians attacked this assignment with relish, with vigor, and much musical sense. Being the best known of the Beethoven nine, it was probably familiar, phrase by phrase, to everyone in the house. But the young musicians brought to it an enthusiasm that amounted to freshness.

Samuel Barber, a young composer of Philadelphia, was represented by an Adagio for Strings which sounded well, and very much like Bach.

OREGON JOURNAL APR. 25, 1943

Junior Symphony Concert Pleases

By Susie Aubrey Smith

Concluding its 19th season, the Portland Junior Symphony orchestra on Saturday evening gave one of the finest concerts in its history. The young musicians, under their conductor, Jacques Gershkovitch, did certainly their best playing of the year.

The opening number was the Fifth Symphony of Beethoven, which has been called unofficially the "Victory" symphony and the boys and girls of the orchestra brought to its performance that spontaneity and zest which make their concerts something out of the ordinary.

Featured as soloists were the orchestra's first flutist, Betty Abbett, and its first harpist, Verda Mae Griesinger, who gave the Mozart concerto for flute and harp with all the aplomb of veterans and a charm all their own. Their technical skill and evidently excellent training were matched by a feeling for the delicacy and elegance of Mozart's music.

Samuel Barber's intriguing "Adagio for Strings" was the American number. As a climax appropriate to the Easter season, Mr. Gershkovitch and his musicians gave a thrilling reading of that most impressive Easter overture, Rimsky-Korsakoff's "La Grande Paque Russe."

20th Anniversary Season

Jacques Gershkovitch, Conductor

November 20, 1943

Symphony NO. 5, E minor, Op. 95	DVORAK
Piano Concerto, C major, K.467	MOZART
Roslyn Frantz, *Soloist*	
Russian Folk Songs	LIADOW
Romeo & Juliet Overture	TCHAIKOVSKY

February 12, 1944

Twentieth Anniversary Concert

Overture, "Die Fledermaus"	J. STRAUSS
Organ Concerto, A minor	BACH/GLASS
Symphony NO. 8, B minor "Unfinished"	SCHUBERT
Concerto for Violoncello NO. 1	SAINT-SAENS
Allan Herndobler, *Soloist*	
A Night on Bald Mountain	MOUSSORGSKY
Dance of the Buffoons	RIMSKY-KORSAKOFF

April 29, 1944

Oberon Overture	WEBER
Symphony in F minor, Allegro	*GERRITSEN
Violin Concerto NO. 4, D major	MOZART
Helen Claire Hodgkins, *Soloist*	
"Fetes" from Nocturnes	DEBUSSY
"On the Trail," from Grand Canyon Suite	FERDE GROFE
Emperor Waltz	STRAUSS
Russian Sailor's Dance from "The Red Poppy"	GLIERE

* *Portland Premiere*

OREGON JOURNAL NOV. 22,1943

Junior Symphony Opens New Season With Fine Concert

By SUSIE AUBREY SMITH

The Portland Junior Symphony orchestra opened its 20th anniversary season Saturday evening at The Auditorium with one of the finest concerts it has ever given. The special celebration of the anniversary will be a part of the February 12 program.

Roslyn Frantz, winner of the Junior Symphony piano contest, was presented as soloist and at 12 is the youngest soloist ever to appear with the orchestra. The Mozart Concerto in C major was selected for her appearance and, through the work's three movements, Roslyn maintained an artistic assurance amply justified by her fluent technique and sensitive musicianship.

The first half of the program was made up of Dvorak's "From the New World" symphony. Under the eloquent baton of their conductor, Jacques Gershkovitch, the young musicians made this much-played music seem brighter and more vivid than in many professional orchestras' reading.

Four Russian folk songs by Liadow in an orchestral arrangement provided a melodious interlude before the closing number, Tschaikowsky's "Romeo and Juliet" overture. This favorite and beautiful selection gave Mr. Gershkovitch and the orchestra an opportunity to display to the fullest advantage their technical co-ordination and musical affinity.

A large audience applauded the youthful musicians' efforts.

Saturday morning the orchestra gave part of the same program at the first of its young peoples' concerts, also at The Auditorium.

OREGON JOURNAL FEB. 13, 1944

Anniversary Concert Given By Juniors

By SUSIE AUBREY SMITH

An exceptionally fine program and gifted soloist made the 20th anniversary concert of the Portland Junior symphony Saturday evening a notable event of the music season. Jacques Gershkovitch, the conductor since the orchestra's founding, directed his young musicians before a large audience at The Auditorium.

The major work was Schubert's Symphony No. 8 (the "Unfinished") which the Junior orchestra had played at its first concert February 14, 1925. Under Mr. Gershkovitch's baton, the musicians gave it a splendid reading.

Allan Herndobler of the cello section, was the soloist, playing the Saint-Saens Concerto in A minor. His tone was smooth and beautiful, his intonation sure and his technique excellent. The orchestra gave him good support, occasionally in its exuberance too much support, the volume of orchestral tone overpowering the solo voice of the cello.

Mr. Gershkovitch opened with the sparkling overture to "The Bat" by Johann Strauss, played with zest and charm. The strings were pleasantly featured in the Glass arrangement of Bach's Organ Concerto in A minor. To end with, Moussorgsky's thrilling fantasy, "A Night on Bald Mountain" and Rimsky-Korsakoff's stirring "Dance of the Buffoons" from "The Snow-maiden" were given effective renditions.

After the intermission, W. P. Stalnaker, president, presented to Mr. Gershkovitch on behalf of the Junior Symphony association, a charcoal sketch of the conductor by the well known artist, Sidney Bell.

THE OREGONIAN FEB. 13, 1944

Young Artists Celebrate

Junior Symphony Now 20 Years Old

BY HILMAR GRONDAHL
Music Editor, The Oregonian

For its 20th anniversary program Saturday night at the public auditorium, the Portland Junior Symphony Orchestra association had a sheaf of items of both musical and educational interest.

There was the presentation of a token of appreciation to Jacques Gershkovitch, who presided at that first concert as he has at 75 concerts and innumerable rehearsals since. And there was a performance of the Saint-Saens cello concerto in A minor with Allan Herndobler as soloist.

Contrast Termed Notable

Some in Saturday night's audience heard the Schubert "Unfinished" symphony when it was played in the Lincoln high school auditorium on Valentine's day in 1925. They will recall a smaller orchestra made up mainly of boys. The contrast with today's orchestra was notable, not only in size, but because a war at hand has shifted the ratio of boys to girls to the latter.

Young Mr. Herndobler's performance of the solo lines of the difficult Saint-Saens concerto was a a welcome surprise. One doesn't expect the technical grasp, the interpretive discipline and the poise needed to effectively trace this music in one so young.

But he put himself into this score with a sense of its effective features which was in every way pleasing to his hearers.

THE OREGONIAN MAY 1, 1944

Final Concert Wins Praise

Junior Symphony Season 'Curtains'

BY HILMAR GRONDAHL
Music Editor, The Oregonian

The world premiere of a Portland-born symphonic work and a sterling solo essay of Mozart's D-major violin concerto by one of the orchestra members were features of the final concert of the Portland Junior Symphony orchestra's 20th season which drew a near-capacity house to the public auditorium Saturday night.

The orchestral premier was of the first movement of a symphony in F minor by Gerard Gerritsen, a resident composer. Now in his 70s, Mr. Gerritsen completed the music in 1941. Under the careful guidance of conductor Jacques Gershkovitch, the young musicians divulged the spirit, form and harmonic texture of the work in a manner that was patently pleasing to the audience and obviously agreeable to the composer, who was called repeatedly to the stage to acknowledge the applause.

Girl Proves Hit

Mozart's violin concerto brought a very young, very attractive and very capable violinist to the stage, a 15-year-old girl named Claire Hodgkins. She met the demands of the solo assignment with well-considered musicianship: she understood and preserved the graceful dignity of the second movement, she knew and projected the charming gaiety of the past.

Ensemble Wins Praise

And what made the occasion worth remembering in addition to the sight and sound of a serious young musician playing so ably, was the truly superior ensemble that Mr. Gershkovitch and the youthful confreres provided for this concerto. It was one of the best pieces of accompanying that the group has given a soloist in a long while.

THE OREGONIAN MAY 12, 1944

New Symphony Given By Juniors Season Hit

A locally composed symphony, Gerard Gerritsen's "Symphony No. 1 in F Minor: Allegro," presented for the first time in a formal public performance was the highlight of the closing concert of the Portland Junior Symphony Orchestra under the brilliant conductorship of Jacques Gershkovitch, at the Municipal Auditorium last Saturday. This third symphonic concert was the climax of the twentieth season of spectacular musical achievements, symbolic of the new west and unique in America in its outset.

This achievement has been wrought almost single-handed by the concert master and conductor, Jacques Gershkovitch, using as raw material the annual flow of naturally talented and rigorously trained youngsters whose capabilities are fired by the brilliant light of Gershkovitch's burning devotion. Gerritsen, a native born Hollander, who finished his symphony as he neared seventy, was given an ovation.

The opening "Overture to the Opera 'Oberon'" was an exciting event both tantalizing and deeply satisfying.

Tall Claire Hodgkins, fifteen-year-old violin soloist, played with vibrant delicacy.

Nothing surpasses the notable musical events of the Junior Symphony Orchestra concerts locally, and they are the climax of the musical and cultural season for both juveniles and adults.

OREGON JOURNAL MAY 1, 1944

Junior Symphony In Final Concert

By SUSIE AUBREY SMITH

A first performance of music by a Portland composer, a gifted young soloist and a large and responsive audience contributed to the success of the Portland Junior symphony's final concert of its 20th anniversary season Saturday night at The Auditorium.

Under the expert baton of their conductor, Jacques Gershkovitch, the youthful musicians played the Allegro of the Symphony in F minor by Gerard Gerritsen in splendid style. Mr. Gerritsen's music is interesting and colorful and shows a sure knowledge of the resources of the various instruments. The composer took a curtain call with the orchestra and conductor.

Claire Hodgkins is one of the most delightful soloists ever presented by the Junior symphony. The 15-year-old violinist played the Mozart Concerto No. 4 in D major with the orchestra and played like a veteran concert artist. Her musicianship matched her technical facility and her performance of the Mozart music was altogether enjoyable.

Mr. Gershkovitch opened with the tuneful overture to Weber's opera, "Oberon." After the intermission, the orchestra gave DeBussy's "Fetes"; Grofe's "On the Trail" and the "Emperor Waltz" of Strauss, ending with the "Russian Sailor's Dance" from "The Red Poppy." Seldom has the orchestra played better and the audience responded with approving applause.

21th Season

Jacques Gershkovitch, Conductor

November 18, 1944

National Anthems of the Allied Nations

The United States of America, England, China, Union of Soviet Socialist Republics

Overture, "Barber of Seville"	ROSSINI
Symphony NO. 8, F major	BEETHOVEN
Piano Concerto in A minor,	SCHUMANN
Betty Barnard, *Soloist*	
Coppelia Ballet	DELIBES
Dance of the Automatons & Valse	
March Slav	TCHAIKOVSKY

February 24, 1945

Overture, "The Gypsy Baron"	STRAUSS
Dream Pantomime from "Hansel & Gretel"	HUMPERDINCK
Sinfonia Concertante, K. 364, for Violin & Viola	MOZART
Elinore Sharpe & Arthur Edmunds, *Soloists*	
Berceuse & Praeludium	JARNEFELT
"L'Arlesienne," Suite NO. 2	BIZET
Roumanian Rhapsody NO. 1	ENESCO

April 21, 1945

Rosamunde Overture	SCHUBERT
The Last Spring, Arr. Gershkovitch	GRIEG
Symphony NO. 1, C major, OP. 21	BEETHOVEN
Concerto for Violin, G minor	BRUCH
Margaret Say, *Soloist*	
Tales from the Vienna Woods	STRAUSS
Mosquito Dance from "Five Miniatures"	WHITE
Le Coq d'Or	RIMSKY-KORSAKOFF

OREGON JOURNAL NOV. 18, 1944

Allied Hymns Open Concert

Junior Symphony Pleases Hearers

Under the flags of the allied nations, Portland's junior symphony orchestra opened its 1944 season Saturday night in the public auditorium with arrangements of the allied national anthems under the baton of Jacques Gershkovitch. The opening revealed not only that the eagerness of youth which the junior symphony still has always has characterized it, but also that Portland is learning to sing "The Star Spangled Banner" with some conviction.

The clear brilliance and good balance of Rossini's "Barber of Seville" overture gained a bow for the whole orchestra.

The Beethoven eighth symphony, which followed, though it seemed more labored, had moments of delicate phrasing.

The Schumann concerto with Betty Barnard at the piano was more generally satisfying. Here the orchestra achieved better tonal ensemble, paced by the sound musicianship of Miss Barnard. The effect was particularly lovely in the dreamy moments of the first movement where the players could stay well within their limits. Betty Barnard plays with dependable rhythm and phrasing and is always clear and musically reasonable, the deserving winner of the 15th annual piano contest.

The thunders of "Marche Slav" rounded off a successful first concert, and Mr. Gershkovitch responded to the hearty applause from the large audience.

THE OREGONIAN FEB. 25, 1945

Music Thrills Concert Goers

Junior Symphony Soloists Acclaimed

BY HILMAR GRONDAHL
Music Editor, The Oregonian

Elinore Sharp, violinist, and Arthur Edmunds, violist, shared honors with Jacques Gershkovitch, conductor, and the personnel of the Portland Junior Symphony orchestra Saturday night st the public auditorium when the second concert of the association's 21st season was released to an audience of nearly 3000 persons.

The overture to the "Gypsy Baron," which opened the concert, was dynamically alive and accurately integrated as anything we have heard these young people do in a long while.

After a go at the dream pantomime from "Hansel and Gretel," the starring vehicle arrived. This was Mozart's sinfonia concertante for violin, viola and orchestra, with the aforementioned girl and boy as soloists.

Work Handled Well

This is not to suggest that Miss Sharp and Mr. Edmunds did not address themselves to their lines with enthusiasm and to good purpose. But they were unequal, not so much because the violinist played with better definition as because the viola resists definition more.

The seldom programmed Mozart score deserved its place on the program, both for its educative value to the playing group and the pleasure it brought the audience.

THE OREGONIAN APR. 22,1945

Symphony Concert Master Is Soloist

Saturday evening at The Auditorium, the Portland Junior symphony presented its concert-master, Margaret Say, as soloist. Although her ankle had been injured in an automobile-bus accident Friday night, Miss Say, true to stage tradition, made her programmed appearance with most commendable courage and good sportsmanship. She also made her scheduled appearance at the young peoples concert Saturday.

The violinist gave the Max Bruch concerto, playing with poise, assurance, a lovely tone and a brilliant technique. The orchestra gave her excellent support. She was recalled to the stage several times by spontaneous applause.

The program opened auspiciously with the beautiful "Rosamunde" overture of Schubert. The symphony was Beethoven's First and, under the eloquent baton of the conductor, Jacques Gershkovitch, the young musicians displayed in its performance a brisk attack, a fine volume of tone and good musical teamwork.

The amusing "Mosquito Dance," by White, Johann Strauss' "Tales From the Vienna Woods," and the introduction and "Cortege de Noces," from "Le Coq d'Or," brilliantly played, concluded the Junior symphony's third concert of its 21st anniversary season.

Soloists Elinore Sharpe and Arthur Edmunds with their teacher, Frank Eichenlaub, and Jacques Gershkovitch.

22nd Season

Jacques Gershkovitch, Conductor

November 17, 1945

Overture, Russlan & Ludmilla	GLINKA
Waltz from Serenade for Strings	TCHAIKOVSKY
Piano Concerto NO. 2, Bb major	BEETHOVEN
Tana Bawden, *Soloist*	
Symphony NO. 5, Bb major	SCHUBERT
Norwegian Dances, op. 35, 1 & 2	GRIEG
Symphonic Poem, The Moldau	SMETANA

February 16, 1946

Overture, "The Merry Wives of Windsor"	NICOLAI
Symphony, "Rustic Wedding"	GOLDMARK
Brandenburg Concerto NO. 3 Allegro Moderato; Allegro	BACH
Adagio for Strings	BARBER
Polovetsian Dances, from "Prince Igor"	BORODIN

April 27, 1946

Overture, "Die Fledermaus"	J. STRAUSS
St. Paul's Suite for Strings	HOLST
Classical Symphony, op. 25	PROKOFIEFF
Violin Concerto NO. 2, D minor	WIENIAWSKI
Einard LeBeck, *Soloist*	
Invitation to the Dance, op. 65	BERLIOZ/WEBER
Rhumba, from Symphony NO. 2	MCDONALD

Juniors Show Fine Advance

Orchestra Reveals New Qualities

BY HILMAR GRONDAHL
Music Editor, The Oregonian

The Portland Junior Symphony orchestra has now arrived.

Two circumstances in particular came out of the latest concert which give evidence of what may develop in little more than a score of years. The first is the emergence as soloist of a young man who, perhaps nine years ago, sat at the last stand of violins, his short legs dangling well off the floor. Saturday night, 17 years of age, as athletic appearing as a coming quarterback, Einard LeBeck performed the Wieniawski D-minor concerto very creditably with Jacques Gershkovitch and his young confreres.

Reading of High Order

The other circumstance is the skill and musicianship which made of the Gustav Holst "St. Paul's Suite" the most professional reading these young players have ever offered.

Getting back to the soloist—his was a well-schooled, assured, and graceful performance with technic in admirable control. His tone is clean and nicely proportioned.

Junior Symphony Closes Season

By SUSIE AUBREY SMITH

In their third and final concert of the season Saturday night, the young musicians of the Portland Junior symphony gave one of their best performances in several years. There was a fine fervor, a youthful exuberance in their playing that added enjoyment to their music. The large audience at The Auditorium gave them spontaneous and approving applause.

The Junior symphony conductor, Jacques Gershkovitch, chose a particularly interesting program ranging from Weber and Johann Strauss to Prokofieff and Harl McDonald. He opened with the popular overture to "Die Fledermaus" and offered as the major work Prokofieff's "Classical" Symphony. His "orchestra men" entered completely into the spirit of Prokofieff's clever and mocking music which Mr. Gershkovitch gave an expert reading.

The solist was Einard LeBeck, 17-year-old violinist, who played the familiar Second Concerto of Wieniawski with dash and assurance. Einard is equipped with a technique both facile and brilliant which showed to the best advantage in the finale. One might suggest that he work for a more sustained legato as, in the slow movement as he played it, this would have established a more assured melodic line.

A feature number, believed to have been a first performance in Portland, was "St. Paul's Suite" for strings by the English composer Holst, which won deserved applause for the symphony's string section. Next came Weber's lilting "Invitation to the Dance" and Mr. Gershkovitch ended with the brilliant "Rhumba" from the McDonald Symphony No. 2.

Board meeting, January 1943, M & F Tea Room.

THE OREGONIAN NOV. 18, 1945

Artist, 11, Piano Prodigy

Junior's Concert Exciting Event

BY HILMAR GRONDAHL
Music Editor, The Oregonian

Saturday night's concert by the Portland Junior Symphony orchestra was one of the most exciting in this organization's 22 seasons, principally because of the piano playing of 11-year-old Tana Bawden. She was soloist with the ensemble in Beethoven's second concerto.

Child prodigies are young musicians who do not play like children. This was no performance in which sympathy took the place of admiration. Tana is a genuine musician.

Playing Credit to Adult

One thought, as this little wisp of youth in pink sat at the huge black Steinway rolling off Beethoven sonorities, of how many serious musicians older by half would have counted themselves fortunate to have rounded out a comparable reading.

The lack of volume was very effectively minimized by the little pianist's balance and disposition of tone. Her range was from the merest whisper to not so loud, a lead in which the conductor, Jacques Gershkovitch, skillfully persuaded the orchestra to follow her.

3000 Attend Concert

Nearly 3000 persons were on hand to approve the tiny soloist, the ensemble and their seasoned leader.

The orchestra offered the waltz from Tschaikowsky's string serenade as one of its choicest pre-intermission readings. The texture and pacing of this music was uncommonly good.

OREGON JOURNAL NOV. 18, 1945

Youngest Soloist Thrills Audience

By SUSIE AUBREY SMITH

At the opening concert of its 22nd season Saturday night, the Portland Junior symphony presented the youngest soloist in its history. And Tana Bawden, 11-year-old pianist, with her fine playing thrilled the large audience assembled at The Auditorium.

Seated before the big grand piano, Tana, with her curls and her short pink frock looked even younger than her 11 years. Her concerto was the Beethoven No. 2 in B flat major and the orchestra was diminished in numbers to fit the orchestration demanded by the work.

Tana has everything that goes to the making of a fine pianist—sensitiveness, poise, a surprisingly big tone, a sure technique, a sense of style, rightness of rhythm and complete absorption in the music she is playing. To her collection of cups for wining contests she now may add a fine performance of a major concerto with symphony orchestra, a performance that was technically brilliant and artistically sophisticated. The audience was spontaneously enthusiastic and recalled her to the stage several times.

The well-arranged and melodious program chosen by Jacques Gershkovitch, Junior Symphony conductor, opened with the overture to "Ruslan and Ludmilla," which Mr. Gershkovitch gave a spirited reading. His young musicians responded admirably to his eloquent baton in the entire program. A charming waltz by Tschaikowsky, played before the concerto, gave the string sections a chance to display their excellent artistic co-ordination.

As its major offering the orchestra programmed the Schubert Symphony No. 5. The concert ended with Smetana's tuneful tone poem, "The Moldau."

OREGON JOURNAL FEB. 17, 1946

Concert Goers Enjoy Program

By SUSIE AUBREY SMITH

An increasingly large number of Portland music lovers are enjoying the Portland Junior symphony concerts this season.

Under the expert direction of its conductor, Jacques Gershkovitch, the orchestra played first the sparkling overture to Nicolai's "Merry Wives of Windsor." Next the young musicians offered Goldmark's "Rustic Wedding" symphony and it is doubtful whether they have ever played a major symphonic work better. In its rendition the orchestra members displayed not only their customary enthusiasm and technical facility, but also a really mature musicianship and style. The audience recalled Mr. Gershkovitch to the stage several times and he shared the applause with his "orchestra men."

An unusual feature and one much enjoyed to judge from the spontaneity of applause it evoked was the Bach "Brandenburg Concerto No. 3" in G major performed by a small group of string players. James Eoff, for a number of years assistant conductor of the orchestra and recently returned to Portland after war service, headed the violas.

THE OREGONIAN FEB. 17, 1946

Juniors Play 'Best Ever'

Crowd Delighted By Symphony

BY HILMAR GRONDAHL
Music Editor, The Oregonian

What sounded like the most effective group of musicians the Portland Junior Symphony orchestra has ever assembled played at the public auditorium Saturday night to a large and demonstrative crowd. Jacques Gershkovitch was obviously delighted with an ensemble complete in virtually every department.

Symphony Flows Freely

Mr. Gershkovitch proved this point Saturday night by offering Goldmark's "Rustic Wedding" symphony. From the opening at which the horns are put glaringly on their own until the dance ends five movements later, the score is filled with tricky ensemble relationships or salient melodic assignments. With ten cellos, five basses and his reliable quartet of horns to set the tone the music moved with assurance into more complex areas.

The richness of the orchestral texture and the general accuracy of intonation were the best yet. And Mr. Gershkovitch, undoubtedly realizing the comparative quality of his material, didn't strain at manipulating every measure with the result that the music ran more freely and naturally than it is apt to when forced. This seemed by far the finest performance of a romantic work yet done by this group.

Of equal interest, but on a smaller scale, was the playing of the third Brandenburg concerto, in its original style with three violins, three violas, and three cellos, with a string bass serving as continuo. For its educational value as well as for the opportunity it gave some of the orchestra's best string players to work in close association it was an interesting and worthwhile feature.

The program also included the overture to "The Merry Wives of Windsor," Samuel Barber's adagio for strings, and the dances from "Prince Igor."

23rd Season

Jacques Gershkovitch, Conductor

November 23, 1946

Symphony No. 5, E minor, op. 64	TCHAIKOVSKY
Piano Concerto No. 1, C major	BEETHOVEN
Robert Vance, *Soloist*	
Air, from Suite No. 3, D major	BACH
Quick-Step from Symphony No. 2	GOULD

February 15, 1947

Overture, "William Tell"	ROSSINI
Suite from "The Water Music"	HANDEL/HARTY
Waltz from "Eugene Onegin"	TCHAIKOVSKY
On the Steppes of Central Asia	BORODIN
Variations on a Theme by Tchaikovsky	ARENSKY
Polka & Dance of the Comedians from "The Bartered Bride"	SMETANA

April 26, 1947

Symphony No. 5, E minor "From the New World"	DVORAK
Concerto for Two Pianos, K. 365	MOZART
Tana Bawden & Wayne DeMott, *Soloists*	
Suite No. 3, D major	BACH
My Country, A Scenic Fantasy	*M. WILSON

* *Portland Premiere*

THE OREGONIAN NOV. 25, 1946

Juniors Give Fine Program

BY HILMAR GRONDAHL
Music Editor, The Oregonian

An exciting performance of Tschaikovsky's E-minor symphony and the introduction of an outstanding piano talent in Beethoven's C-major concerto were conspicuous features of the Portland Junior Symphony orchestra's autumn program Saturday night at the public auditorium.

A conductor less successful in enforcing his design than Jacques Gershkovitch could still bring out some pretty exciting effects, particularly in a score as teeming with sentiment as the Tschaikovsky fifth, when he has 50 strings and five French horns. Add to this stands of trumpets, trombones and tubas behind which are eager young beavers.

Horn Solo Liked

It is Mr. Gershkovitch's particular talent to be able to impose implicit obedience without arousing the slightest ill will. His hundred-odd charges will go with him along the most torturous musical paths with a sense of direction and an interpretive surefootedness which is often beyond their normal capacities in care and artistry.

The tough solo assignment for French horn in the second movement of the Tschaikovsky was one example; the brilliant staccato work of the brasses in the first and final movements were others; and the work of the entire group in the andante cantabile was yet another.

From the full, colorful and frenetic Tschaikovsky symphony to the classically circumscribed and restrained concerto of Beethoven they gave some notion of the adaptability of this earnest host of instrumentalists.

Piano Work Notable

This section of the program turned the spotlight on Robert Vance, an uncommonly talented young pianist who after a tentative beginning apparently found his ease in his solo position and proceeded to remind one and all that the C-major concerto is both a delightful and unduly neglect work of art.

Mr. Vance's grasp of the spirit of the three movements was admirable. But to us the poetry, the unhurried beauty, the significant understatement in the slow movement produced the most inspiriting period of his performance.

OREGON JOURNAL NOV. 24, 1948

Juniors Play Tschaikowsky Symphony

By SUSIE AUBREY SMITH

Opening its 23rd annual season the Portland Junior symphony gave an exceptionally fine concert Saturday evening at The Auditorium. The quality of musicianship does not change very much from year to year, although at this concert the orchestra seemed to be in especially fine form.

For the first time the Junior symphony essayed Tschaikowsky's Fifth symphony. Under the skillful guidance of their conductor, Jacques Gershkovitch, the youthful musicians gave an amazingly good performance of this major symphonic work. The brass and woodwinds deserve special commendation. The strings and percussion sections were excellent as always.

The Beethoven Concerto No. 1 served to introduce as the soloist a gifted 18-year-old pianist, Robert Vance, who won the right to appear with the orchestra at its annual piano contest last spring. The young soloist's finger work was sure and exceptionally clear and his rhythm and phrasing were almost incredibly right. He played the difficult cadenza like a veteran concert artist, which he certainly is not. His entire performance, in fact, revealed an assurance and understanding of the concerto far beyond his years.

THE OREGONIAN FEB. 16, 1947

'Wilhelm Tell' In New Guise

Junior Symphony Gives Pleasure

BY HILMAR GRONDAHL
Music Editor, The Oregonian

Some of the listeners at the Portland Junior Symphony orchestra concert at the public auditorium Saturday night were surprised to find that there is much worthwhile music in the "Wilhelm Tell" overture besides that used by the Lone Ranger. They also found that a program can have plenty of substance without containing a symphony or a concerto.

Cello Section Noteworthy

Even before the Rossini overture reached the area of flying hooves, listeners were aware that the junior orchestra has a cello section worth hearing, and that the whole ensemble, through the generalship of Jacques Gershkovitch, can whip up a storm and the ensuing calm with an uncommon blending of realism and musicianship.

To our ears the most delightful and artistically rewarding excursions on Saturday night were two: the Handel "Water Music" in Hamilton Harty's arrangement, and Arensky's variations on a theme by Tschaikowsky, whose appeal to the audience was in the discipline and richness of the string choir.

Woodwinds, Brasses Good

It was in the "Water Music" that some of the brasses and woodwinds ran their colors up to a glorious height. The French horns and trumpets, and the oboes dispensed artistic thrills in one section of the Handel score to a degree that is rare even among professional groups.

The balance of the program included dances from two operas and Borodin's "On the Steppes of Central Asia." The "Bartered Bride" dances whipped up an enthusiasm which for Portlanders was equivalent to standing in a chair and tossing your neighbor's hat in the air.

OREGON JOURNAL APR. 27, 1947

Junior Symphony Presents Two Fine Young Soloists

By SUSIE AUBREY SMITH
Journal Music Editor

Portlanders who attended the concert of the Portland Junior symphony Saturday night at The Auditorium received an additional esthetic thrill to those usually experienced by Junior Symphony audiences.

Two 12-year-old pianists, Tana Bawden and Wayne DeMott, appeared as guest soloists with the orchestra and gave an amazingly fine performance of the Mozart "Concerto for Two Pianos in E flat major." There was no "child prodigy" stuffiness about the proceedings. Here were two gifted young musicians playing a beautiful and difficult work they had prepared carefully and well.

Their musical endowments, while blending successfully, are different. Tana has exceptional assurance and brilliant technique. In addition to a facile technique, Wayne showed sensitive musicianship most unusual in a boy of his age. In the playing of both there was correct phrasing and evident understanding of Mozart's style.

The orchestral part of the program opened with the Dvorak "From the New World" symphony. With excellent response from the orchestra, Jacques Gershkovitch, the conductor, gave the work an interesting reading with effective tempos. In the famous "Largo," Dale Kugel, the orchestra's first oboist, played the English horn solo.

The Bach "Suite No. 3 in D major," which contains the familiar "Air for the G string," was given an unusually good performance. The concluding number was "My Country," a fantasy by the contemporary American composer, Mortimer Wilson, which gave heads of several sections a chance for incidental solo work.

THE OREGONIAN APR. 27, 1947

Junior Group Real Triumph

BY FRED M. WHITE
Assistant City Editor, The Oregonian

Portland's Junior Symphony orchestra lived up to its splendid tradition again Saturday night at the public auditorium giving not only a skillful, highly enjoyed performance but also reassurance in a larger sense that the culture of the community, despite some apprehension to the contrary, is safe in the hands of its 10–21 age group.

Under the good-natured direction of Jacques Gershkovitch, in the third concert of its 23rd season, the young musicians wove works of Dvorak, Mozart and Bach into a smooth fabric of sound, in which the designs of the composers were clearly and meaningfully drawn.

Mozart Work Feature

The high point of the program, was Mozart's Concerto in E Flat for two pianos and orchestra, with two remarkable 12-year-olds, Tana Bawden and Wayne DeMott, at the grand pianos. The young pianists' co-ordination, precision, musicianly skill and understanding were all worthy of a two piano team that had been working together as many years as these two are old. Loud and prolonged applause showed appreciation on the part of the audience of the result.

Also inspiringly played and warmly enjoyed was the familiar Dvorak "New World" symphony which opened the program—a work admirably suited to such an orchestra because it affords opportunities for many instruments to show what they can do, while employing to advantage the vigor and enthusiasm of junior musicians.

A concert by the Portland Junior Symphony orchestra is always an uplifting experience.

24th Season

Jacques Gershkovitch, Conductor

November 29, 1947

Overture, "Barber of Seville"	ROSSINI
Symphony NO. 4, Bb major, op.60	BEETHOVEN
Piano Concerto NO. 24, C minor Lamar Crowson, *Soloist*	MOZART
Suite in D minor	CORELLI
Prelude to "Die Meistersinger"	WAGNER

February 28, 1948

Concert Dedicated to the National Federation of Music Clubs at their Fiftieth Anniversary

Overture, "Die Freischutz"	WEBER
"A Midsummer Night's Dream" Scherzo	MENDELSSOHN
Concerto for Two Violins Nancy Schmitt & Shirley Barnard, *Soloists*	BACH
Peter & the Wolf Don Marye, *Narrator*	PROKOFIEFF
Berceuse & Praeludium	JARNEFELT
Symphonic Poem, "The Moldau"	SMETANA

April 24, 1948

Eugene Linden, *Guest Conductor*

Eine Kleine Nachtmusik	MOZART
Concertante Quartet Dale Kugel, *Oboe;* Muriel Bermel, *Clarinet;* Raymond Schaer, *Bassoon;* Douglas Van Fleet, *Horn*	MOZART
Dream Pantomime from "Hansel & Gretel"	HUMPERDINCK
Organ Fugue in G minor	BACH/ABERT
Emperor Waltz	STRAUSS

THE OREGONIAN NOV. 30, 1947

Junior Group Makes Debut

Crowson Soloist In Mozart Work

BY HILMAR GRONDAHL
Music Editor, The Oregonian

Jacques Gershkovitch brought the 24th edition of his Portland Junior Symphony orchestra to the stage of the public auditorium Saturday night, and with it a performance of Mozart's C-minor piano concerto featuring Lamar Crowson as soloist which disclosed some extremely sensitive pianism. On the purely orchestral side were readings of the overture to "The Barber of Seville," Beethoven's Fourth symphony, part of Corelli's D-minor suite and the prelude to "Die Meistersinger."

As far as we are concerned Mozart never wrote a more imaginative, inspired or fascinating concerto for piano than the one in C-minor.

Grace, Spirit Invoked

Young Mr. Crowson has had plenty of technic for a long time, but with the Mozartian subtleties of grace, phrasing humor and spirit what he now has sounds very fine indeed.

Mr. Gershkovitch managed well with more resources than he needed for this concerto. He might have reduced his orchestra for the occasion and undoubtedly had an easier time holding to a simulation of scope. But that would have denied nearly half the orchestra the educative value of participation, and the conductor is the last person who wants to neglect the original purpose of the organization.

Early Diversion Overcome

Whatever headaches the conductor is subject to because of new or shifting personnel are most apt to show up at this first concert of the season. That is why it was so exciting to this listener, after hearing a new set of winds run into one snag after another in the early part to find them coming together at the second theme of the finale and playing like troupers through some difficult areas from there on.

The Beethoven Fourth was gratefully worked out in the Gershkovitch planning, some broad effects being accomplished especially in the strings.

OREGON JOURNAL NOV. 30, 1947

Portland Junior Symphony Heard in Fine Program

By SUSIE AUBREY SMITH
Journal Music Editor

The Portland Junior Symphony orchestra opened its 24th season with one of the fine programs Portland music lovers have come to expect of this ensemble of youthful musicians. Jacques Gershkovitch enters his 24th season as conductor.

Each season new faces are seen in the orchestra, as some go on to college or pass the age limit. Their places are taken by equally gifted young people and it is inspiring to adult concert goers to hear great music so excellently played by such young musicians.

Saturday night the soloist was Lamar Crowson, a pianist who has had all his training in Portland and is now a student at Reed college after service in the navy. In the Mozart Concerto in C minor, he displayed not only a facile and brilliant technique, but an understanding of and a feeling for the Mozartean style with all its finesse and artistic nuances. He won a deserved ovation from the audience.

The symphony was the Beethoven Fourth and this gay rather than grand music proved particularly well suited to a junior orchestra. Mr. Gershkovitch's readings of the symphony, of the opening overture to "The Barber of Seville" and the concluding prelude to "Die Meistersinger" were all marked by effective rhythms and the best musical taste. The string sections were featured in a well-played number by Corelli.

All in all it was an auspicious beginning to the 1947-48 Junior Symphony season.

OREGON JOURNAL FEB. 29, 1948

Fine Soloists, Fairy Tale Music Liked

By SUSIE AUBREY SMITH
Journal Music Editor

Two features of the Portland Junior Symphony orchestra's concert Saturday night at The Auditorium made it particularly interesting, the Bach double concerto and Prokofieff's musical fairy tale, "Peter and the Wolf."

For the second time in Junior symphony history, Jacques Gershkovitch, the conductor, presented two gifted girls of the violin section in the beautiful Bach concerto for two violins. At last night's concert the soloists were Nancy Schmitt and Shirley Barnard, and they blended their tones and their talents most effectively in the noble Bach music. The orchestra gave them splendid support.

Narrator in the Prokofieff work was again Don Marye, director of the Portland Civic Theatre and he read the story with that balance of humor and dramatic zest the piece calls for. The young musicians who had the themes for the various characters and animals in the fairy tale did fine playing in their performance of this charming fantasy.

The concluding selection was Smetana's charming "The Moldau," a work well suited to the young players and which they gave a delightful reading under their conductor's eloquent baton.

THE OREGONIAN APR. 25, 1948

Batonist Back In Guest Role

Juniors Play Under Eugene Linden

BY HILMAR GRONDAHL
Music Editor, The Oregonian

Eugene Linden, onetime assistant conductor of the Portland Junior Symphony orchestra, returned as guest conductor Saturday night to a crowd in the public auditorium eager to witness the extent of his interim progress.

With one possible exception there was not a player in the orchestra who had been a member when Linden was flutist and assistant to Jacques Gershkovitch. But there were many in the hall who knew him and his work then, have followed his career since and have evidence now of his remarkable musical growth.

Mozart Scores Chosen

We were able to hear little more than the two Mozart scores which came before intermission. But we can't imagine a better basis for evaluating the skill of a conductor, especially in guiding an orchestra of the age and make-up of this one, than the serenade "Eine Kleine Nachtmusik" and the concertante quartet for oboe, clarinet, bassoon and French horn.

What was amazing about Mr. Linden's handling of "Eine Kleine Nachtmusik" was the nearness of his approximation to the Mozartian ideal for which ably guided professional ensembles strive; the clarity and texture, a dispassionately reserved range of dynamics, a restrained pace that never lacks propulsion, grace of phrase and clean articulation.

It was a beautifully proportioned performance.

The concertante quartet was almost unbelievable. The woodwinds were excellently played for the most part, and were, what's more, almost always in tune thus licking one of the most vexing problems in an amateur band. Dale Kugel played the oboe, Muriel Bermel the clarinet, Raymond Schaer the bassoon and Douglas Van Fleet the French horn.

THE OREGONIAN FEB. 29, 1948

Junior Symphony's Concert Interlaces Music With Fun

BY HILMAR GRONDAHL
Music Editor, The Oregonian

There was plenty of musical meat and an uncommon amount of fun in the second concert of Portland Junior Symphony orchestra's 24th season which Jacques Gershkovitch arranged and directed Saturday night at the public auditorium. No less than three persons, beside the conductor, were featured: Nancy Schmitt and Shirley Barnard as duo-artists in the Bach concerto for two solo violins and string orchestra, and Don Marye, narrator, in the orchestral fairy tale, "Peter and the Wolf."

Narration Provides Fun

This latter was the source of the fun, a diversion shared freely both sides of the footlights. Prokofieff has done his level best, which is substantial, to combine shrewd irony and childish wonder in the interlacing of work and tone. The humor of the story is pointed up by some of Prokofieff's most colorful instrumental assignments.

The house was comfortably laced with children, who appeared to be having an even better time than their parents. It was a child who set the tone of general appreciation. When the kettledrum tattoo which heralded the entrance of the hunters from the woods came to an abrupt stop the response from the eager listener was a gurgle that could be heard through the entire house. This touched off a gale of laughter which reached even to members of the orchestra.

Mr. Marye conveyed the excited wonder of the child's story. The whole performance was in the spirit.

OREGON JOURNAL APR. 25, 1948

Portland Junior Symphony Plays Under Eugene Linden

By SUSIE AUBREY SMITH
Journal Music Editor

For the first time in its 24 years of existence, the Portland Junior Symphony orchestra appeared in concert Saturday night without its permanent conductor, Jacques Gershkovitch, on the podium. Mr. Gershkovitch was unable to lead his young musicians because of illness.

In his place, Eugene Linden, young associate conductor of the Pacific Northwest symphony, came down from Seattle to rehearse the junior orchestra and to conduct its final concert of the season. Mr. Linden was assistant conductor of the Portland junior symphony when he was only 17 and since then he has gone on to a most successful career in music.

Saturday evening under his expert guidance the young musicians played two Mozart numbers in fine style, "Eine Kleine Nachtmusik" and the "Concertante Quartet," the second a difficult piece in which orchestra members Ray Schaer, bassoon; Douglas Van Fleet, French horn; Dale Kugel, oboe and Muriel Bermel, clarinet, distinguished themselves as soloists.

Mr. Linden gave a delightful reading of the "Dream Pantomime" from "Hansel and Gretel" and led his orchestra successfully through the majestic measures of the Bach "Fugue in G minor." As a finale to the concert, he programmed the "Emperor Waltz" by Johann Strauss II, and, under his eloquent baton, the orchestra played it with the true Viennese lilt.

A young people's concert was given Saturday morning, also at The Auditorium, by the Junior symphony with a somewhat shortened program.

25th Season

SILVER ANNIVERSARY CONCERT

Jacques Gershkovitch, Conductor

November 20, 1948

Oberon Overture	WEBER
Symphony NO. 1, C major, op. 21	BEETHOVEN
Piano Concerto, A minor, op. 16	GRIEG
Madelon Adler, *Soloist*	
St. Paul's Suite for Strings	HOLST
Polka & Fugue from "Schwanda"	WEINBERGER

February 26, 1949

Raymond Overture*	THOMAS
Symphony NO. 8, B minor*	SCHUBERT
"Lieutenant Kije" Suite, op. 60	PROKOFIEFF
Concerto for 2 Pianos, C minor	BACH
Lois Randolph & Helen Randolph, *Soloists*	
Baba Jaga, op. 56	LIADOV
Polovetsian Dances from "Prince Igor"	BORODIN

* Performed at the Portland Junior Symphony's First Concert Twenty-five Years Ago This Month

---

April 30, 1949

Overture, "Marriage of Figaro"	MOZART
Symphony, "Rustic Wedding"	GOLDMARK
Bassoon Concerto NO. 2, B♭ Romance	MOZART
Raymond Schaer, *Soloist*	
Petite Suite	DEBUSSY
Polka & Dance of the Comedians from "The Bartered Bride"	SMETANA

THE OREGONIAN NOV. 21, 1948

Juniors Score With Concert

Silver Anniversary Program Success

BY HILMAR GRONDAHL
Music Editor, The Oregonian

The Portland Junior Symphony orchestra played the first of its Silver Anniversary programs Saturday night at the public auditorium with the silver-haired Jacques Gershkovitch directing vigorously and to the point as he has during these 25 seasons since the orchestra was conceived in necessity and dedicated to the proposition that everyone under the age of 20 who could and wanted to should have a chance to make symphonic music in an ensemble of his equals.

It was an occasion for celebration, and we are informed that at the morning children's concert there was a cake with the required number of candles plus enough cupcakes to assure an ample supply for those who listened as well as those who listened as well as those who played.

At the night concert there was a speech by the association's president, L. R. Hussa, and a presentation by him to Conductor Gershkovitch of a box containing gifts appropriate to the occasion and his years of devotion to the cause.

All "Musts" Included

Saturday night's program contained much of that standard repertory which every young player should learn along with his several Rs, namely the overture to "Oberon," Beethoven's First symphony, the Grieg piano concerto and the polka and fugue from "Schwanda." There was, in addition, a composition which is good enough to grace the standard repertory, the St. Paul suite by Gustav Holst.

Even the featured soloist who appeared in the Grieg concerto would not have been on hand but for the ever-widening reputation and influence of the orchestra, for Madelon Adler, aged 17, is from Klamath Falls. Soloists in earlier years have come from nearer home.

OREGON JOURNAL NOV. 20 1948

Portland Junior Symphony Opens Anniversary Season

By SUSIE AUBREY SMITH
Journal Music Editor

Starting off their 25th annual season, the Portland Junior Symphony and its conductor, Jacques Gershkovitch, gave a concert Saturday evening at the Auditorium that was certainly one of the best they have ever given.

This season the boys and girls of the orchestra seem to be playing unusually well. Their response to Mr. Gershkovitch in the difficult music programmed did credit to their native talents, their serious musicianship and their fine training. The symphony was Beethoven's First, a particularly happy choice for an orchestra made up of youthful players. Under their conductor's eloquent baton, they gave an excellent performance of the work.

The soloist was 17-year-old Madelon Adler of Klamath Falls, who won the honor of appearing with the Junior symphony in the annual piano contest. She played the Grieg concerto with the orchestra with a sureness of style, a distinction of phrasing, an individual singing tone and a brilliance of technique that made the concerto a delight from the first note to the last. The orchestra gave her splendid support.

Young Miss Adler is an alert performer. Furthermore she has a grasp of brilliance in her hands and a feeling for lyricism in her heart which are of equal importance in the Grieg music. Much of the first movement's cadenza was thrilling to hear and virtually everything she did was musical.

The second movement of the concerto provided for our ears the finest playing the orchestra did during the evening, too. Mr. Gershkovitch had a stunning control here of dynamics, phrasing, and total balance. It was available, likewise in parts of each movement of the Beethoven symphony but not so consistently as in the middle section of the Grieg.

To open their anniversary season, Mr. Gershkovitch led his young musicians in the sparkling music of Weber's overture to "Oberon." The strings—and very fine strings they are—were featured in "St. Paul's Suite" by Holst. The gay "Polka and Fugue" from Weinberger's "Schwanda" brought the program to a stirring close.

THE OREGONIAN MAY 1, 1949

Bassoonist, 19, Scores in Solo

BY HERB PENNY
Staff Writer, The Oregonian

Highlight of the Portland Junior symphony orchestra's third concert of the season Saturday night at the auditorium was the short Romance from Mozart's newly-discovered Second Bassoon Concerto in B Flat with 19-year-old Raymond Schaer as soloist. Continued applause greeted Schaer's rendition.

The program conducted by Jacques Gershkovitch opened with a presentation of the delicate overture to the Marriage of Figaro, a familiar piece featuring the stringed instruments. This was followed by Carl Goldmark's Symphony No. 1 in E Flat, known as the Rustic Wedding symphony.

After the Mozart concerto the orchestra began the Petite Suite by Debussy, an orchestral version by Henri Busser of Debussy's Suite composed for piano.

The program was concluded with dances from the opera "The Bartered Bride" by Friedrich Smetana, which was strongly presented by the drums and cymbals and was well received by the audience.

Junior Symphony Concert Closes Anniversary Season

By SUSIE AUBREY SMITH
Journal Music Editor

The Junior Symphony orchestra closed its 25th anniversary season Saturday evening at The Auditorium with one of the best concerts in its history. Jacques Gershkovitch, the conductor who has guided the youthful musicians of the orchestra since their first concert, was on the podium.

The program was made up of sparkling and cheerful music. It opened with the overture to Mozart's "The Marriage of Figaro," in which the young orchestra players displayed their customary zest and serious musicianship. Next came Goldmark's "Rustic Wedding" symphony, a work depicting in music pleasant pastoral scenes. Mr. Gershkovitch gave the symphony a reading that held the interest of his audience from the first note to the last.

After the intermission, Ray Schaer, principal bassoonist of orchestra, was presented as soloist in the "Romance" from Mozart's bassoon concerto No. 2. He played with technical sureness and artistic integrity and won much applause.

Debussy's charming "Petite Suite" displayed the young musicians' versatility in interpretation. The program ended with the gay and colorful dances from Smetana's opera, "The Bartered Bride."

Rehearsal at Holladay School, 1951.

26th Season

Jacques Gershkovitch, Conductor

November 12, 1949

Coriolanus Overture, op. 62	BEETHOVEN
Symphony NO. 3, E♭, "Rhenish"	SCHUMANN
Piano Concerto, A major, K 488	MOZART
Louanne Laird, *Soloist*	
Last Spring (arr. Gershkovitch)	GRIEG
Nutcracker Suite	TCHAIKOVSKY

February 25, 1950

Roman Carnival Overture	BERLIOZ
Symphony NO. 5, B♭ major	SCHUBERT
Horn Concerto NO. 2, E♭, K. 417	MOZART
"On the Trail" from Grand Canyon Suite	GROFE
Emperor Waltz, op. 437	STRAUSS
"L'Arlesienne" Suite NO. 2	BIZET

April 22, 1950

Overture, "Russlan & Ludmilla"	GLINKA
Sinfonia in B♭ major	J. C. BACH
Violin Concerto NO. 4, D major	MOZART
Catherine de Moss, *Soloist*	
Concerto Grosso NO. 1	BLOCH
Alden Gilchrist, *Piano Obbligato*	
Prelude to "Khovanschina"	MOUSSORGSKY
Caucasian Sketches: In the Village; March of the Sardars	IPPOLITOV-IVANOV

THE OREGONIAN NOV. 13, 1949

Young Pianist Wins Acclaim

BY HILMAR GRONDAHL
Music Editor, The Oregonian

A 17-year-old girl named Louanne Laird gave listeners at the public auditorium Saturday night a musical experience of high order. She was soloist in Mozart's A-major concerto (K.488) with the Portland Junior Symphony orchestra under Jacques Gershkovitch. One could hear that what she had in her hands and her mind and her emotions had become completely her own. She had acquired an understanding of a score which was vivid and convincing and alive enough to her that she could give it back through the keyboard in that same crystalline manner.

Interpretive Gifts Displayed

The dark and haunting beauty of the andante is not the kind of thing one tosses off lightly for an extra curtain call. And as it is the central jewel of Mozart's contriving, so it was the most impressive evidence of Miss Laird's considerable interpretive gifts.

Here she caught all the grace, delicacy and warm sentiment without once sacrificing substance, nor the significance of her part in relationship to that of the orchestra. It became integrated through the conductor into one of the most musicianly concerto performances this enterprising ensemble has given.

Symphony Proves Ambitious

Another feature of the orchestra's first program in season number 26 was a first performance by the group of Schumann's "Rhenish" symphony.

It is something of a venture for an orchestra, functioning as this one does, to undertake a symphony of this magnitude at the beginning of a season.

The majestic fourth movement came off with an amazing simulation of the huge cathedral organ, thanks in large measure to the remarkable brass choir.

OREGON JOURNAL NOV. 13, 1949

Junior Symphony Orchestra Gives Fine Opening Concert

By SUSIE AUBREY SMITH
Journal Music Editor

The Portland Junior symphony opened its 26th annual season Saturday night at The Auditorium with an exceptionally fine concert. Jacques Gershkovitch, the orchestra's conductor, also began his 26th year with the junior musicians.

The program opened with one of the favorite Beethoven overtures, that to "Coriolanus." Under the skillful guidance of their conductor, the young musicians played this music like veterans. The major work was Schumann's "Rhenish Symphony." Mr. Gershkovitch led his players with sure effectiveness from the opening Allegro to the final brilliant Allegro.

Soloist was the 17-year-old Portland pianist, Louanne Laird, who won the honor of appearing with the Junior symphony at its annual spring contest. Louanne proved to be a sensitive musician and an excellent technician. Her phrasing and expressive tone shading were meticulous and her pedaling was unusually good. Her entire performance was really on a professional level.

After the concerto, the strings had a chance to show their artistic prowess in Grieg's lovely "Last Spring." The concert ended with the sparkling ballet music which makes up the Tschaikowsky "Nutcracker Suite."

A capacity audience, 1951.

27th Season

Jacques Gershkovitch, Conductor

November 18, 1950

"Merry Wives of Windsor" Overture	NICOLAI
Symphony NO. 7, C major	SCHUBERT
Piano Concerto NO. 3, C minor	BEETHOVEN
Arnold Cohen, *Soloist*	
Suite NO. 2 from "Carmen"	BIZET

February 17, 1951

Overture, "The Bat"	STRAUSS
Water Music Suite	HANDEL/HARTY
Concerto for Viola, B minor	HANDEL/CASADESUS
Fred Cone, *Soloist*	
Dream Pantomime from "Hansel & Gretel"	HUMPERDINCK
Suite in D minor, for Strings	CORELLI
Hungarian Dance NO. 1	BRAHMS
Rhumba from Second Symphony	MCDONALD

April 21, 1951

Overture, "Marriage of Figaro"	MOZART
Symphony NO. 4, A major	MENDELSSOHN
Carnival of the Animals	SAINT-SAENS
Janet Schille & Tana Bawden, *Soloists*	
Concerto for 2 Pianos, Eb, K. 365	MOZART
Diane de Mott & Raymond Graap, *Pianists*	
Berceuse & Praeludium	JARNEFELT
Russian Easter Overture	RIMSKY-KORSAKOV

THE OREGONIAN NOV. 19, 1950

Junior Symphony Performs Notably

BY HILMAR GRONDAHL
Music Editor, The Oregonian

Jacques Gershkovitch certainly put a difficult score up to his young charges when he selected the Schubert C-major for the opening program of a new season. Especially with the composer's reputed innocence in the matter of effective orchestration, plus the fact that a large number of the boys and girls of the ensemble have been members for only a few months. So we sat there as these 100 young musicians accepted the summoning horn call that opens this Schubert symphony, and thereafter went, through succeeding surprises throughout the entire glorious work.

The first surprise after this opening was the section which asks for unison playing by the woodwind choir. It is not enough that woodwinds play in tune, per se; they must play in tune with one another, which amounts to a balancing of timbre as well as pitch. It is one of the hardest things to accomplish, especially among players of limited experience and technic. Well, this the young musicians accomplished at this point, and at almost every other required spot from there on.

Beside the smooth-functioning woodwinds there was a fine trombone section, excellent trumpets, well-disciplined and responsive strings, all of whom combined, under Gershkovitch's direction, to make the C-major symphony sound great and essentially Schubertian. It was one of the best performances in Junior Symphony history.

The other major program item was the Beethoven C-minor piano concerto which brought Arnold Cohen to the platform as soloist. He is a gifted young man who has power and fleetness in his fingers and sensibility in his musical thought. He seemed rather nervous and got into some difficulty with his part, but on the whole it was an acceptable demonstration of youthful pianism. His solo statement at the opening of the slow movement was poetic.

It happened, too, that the slow movement was the best realization of the score from the standpoint of solo and instrumental collaboration. There was some pulling and hauling in the first and final movements, but the total effect was a pleasurable rehearing of a great piece of music.

OREGON JOURNAL NOV. 19, 1950

Portland Junior Symphony Opened 27th Season Saturday

By SUSIE AUBREY SMITH
Journal Music Editor

The Portland Junior symphony opened its 27th consecutive season Saturday night with a fine concert at The Auditorium. It was the start of a 27th season also for the orchestra's popular conductor, Jacques Gershkovitch.

As is customary in its first concert of each season, the Junior symphony presented as soloist the winner of its piano contest held the previous spring. Saturday it was the 20-year-old pianist, Arnold Cohen, a former New Yorker, who played the Beethoven Concerto No. 3 in C minor with the orchestra.

ARNOLD PROVED to be a serious young artist with a fluent technique and rhythmical assurance. He displayed also a real sense of style in his interpretation. The orchestra gave him excellent support.

Mr. Gershkovitch opened with the overture to Nicolai's "The Merry Wives of Windsor," which his young orchestra men and women gave an admirable performance.

The major work was the Seventh Symphony of Schubert. This composer is rewarding alike for performers and listeners and, in his reading, Mr. Gershkovitch made the most of the melodious beauty of the score.

* * *

THE CONCERT closed with a brilliant performance of a favorite in the Junior symphony repertoire, the "Carmen Suite No. 2" by Bizet.

Saturday morning, also at The Auditorium, the orchestra gave a shortened program for young people and music students with David Campbell as commentator.

OREGON JOURNAL FEB. 18, 1951

Junior Symphony Orchestra In Season's Second Concert

By SUSIE AUBREY SMITH
Journal Music Editor

Favorite music from the symphonic repertoire was offered by the Portland Junior symphony Saturday evening in the second concert of its 27th season. A large audience was on hand at The Auditorium to applaud the fine program given by the orchestra under the able baton of its conductor, Jacques Gershkovitch.

Opening with a stirring performance of the overture to "Die Fledermaus" by Johann Strauss, Mr. Gershkovitch programmed next Handel's "Water Music Suite" in Sir Hamilton Harty's arrangement.

FRED CONE, who heads the Junior symphony viola section, was presented as soloist in the Handel-Casadesus "Concerto in B minor" for viola and orchestra. This melodious work displays to advantage all the resources of the solo instrument. The youthful violist drew a resonant tone from his instrument and played the work's three movements in excellent style.

Portland Junior Symphony Called Lasting 'Monument'

BY HILMAR GRONDAHL
Music Editor, The Oregonian

Jacques Gershkovitch and I had been seated only a moment at our table in the hotel dining room when a man came over who had been president of the Portland Junior Symphony association for several years.

"I didn't know a thing about music," he said, "But I was interested in the educational worth of the enterprise; keeping children occupied, and giving them a purpose, an objective."

Before quitting our table, he turned to Dr. Gershkovitch and said, "You have built your own imperishable monument in this community."

Gershkovitch gifts are particularly appreciated by teachers in the public schools. It is a source of undying amazement among those who have attended a Junior Symphony rehearsal to notice that there may be some small quotient of fear that is heightened by the force and mingled syntax of the director. But there is more of love and respect. Each player in the course of his membership in the orchestra is apt to acquire a pretty durable fondness for much of the literature of the traditional repertory.

Under Gershkovitch, he has also become acquainted with works enjoying their local premiers. Those who have followed the doings of this organization will recall the first Portland performance of Prokofieff's "Peter and the Wolf" with Donald Marye as narrator. The same composer's amusing suite, "Lieutenant Kije" was first played here under these auspices, as was the Kalinnikov First Symphony. Gershkovitch's girls and boys also introduced Atterburg's symphony, two Chinese pieces by Avshalomoff, the petite suite by Debussy, Barber's adagio for strings, Harl McDonald's rhumba, and a pair of witty brevities entitled "The Mosquito" by White and "The Ponderous Pachyderm" by Emil Enna.

Even before Reed College signalized the Gershkovitch achievements by an honorary doctorate, there were young musicians the country over who had enjoyed his ministrations with profit. As for example, Robert Mann, first violinist of the Juillard String quartet, which is to be heard here Wednesday night. Or Jacob Avshalomoff, composer, and teacher at Columbia university in New York. Or Geraldine Peterson, who toured with Stokowski's Youth orchestra and is now playing with the Los Angeles Philharmonic. Today's Portland Symphony has a Junior Symphony graduate in first violist Elizabeth Zwerenz Bell. It used to have a husband-wife team of Mary and Sam Fischer.

But above and beyond the demonstrable results as shown by such outstanding talent, is the general cultural benefit for a thousand unnamed participants who will never go into music professionally, and for their parents and friends, who, in many cases, would not have attended a symphony concert except out of interest for these young players.

It was no simple decision for a graduate of the Petrograd conservatory to devote himself to working with children when the more challenging work of the professional orchestra was raising its siren voice. But the Gershkovitch decision was a fortunate one for the development of music interest in Portland.

THE OREGONIAN FEB. 18, 1951

Strauss, Handel Selections Top Program By Portland Junior Symphony Orchestra

BY HILMAR GRONDAHL
Music Editor, The Oregonian

Taking a cue from the ascendant popularity of Johann Strauss' "Fledermaus," Jacques Gershkovitch used the sparkling overture to that lively opera to open the Saturday night concert of the Portland Junior Symphony orchestra in the public auditorium.

Its immediate fellows were the Harty selection from Handel's "Water Music" and the Casadesus reworking of Handel's viola concerto. This latter featured Fred Cone as soloist.

This score didn't have its most effective performance Saturday night. Perhaps the fact that most of the compositions this group essays come off with surprising felicity leads one into the error of expecting everything to.

This was probably one of Saturday night's problems. Fred Cone, who is a substantial player, with a strong bow arm, and technical facility, was so concerned with his own solo that he hadn't ears for the rest of the concerto.

It is not enough for the soloist to play very well, as he did. He would, as a matter of fact, have played even better had he felt reassured by an orchestral complement. But he hadn't the experience and the patience to wait for and associate himself with this larger body of tone.

The young players were back in their surprisingly felicitous role for much of the Handel "Water Music" and the Dream Pantomime from "Hansel and Gretel."

THE OREGONIAN APR. 22, 1951

Junior Symphony Delivers Buoyant Fanciful Concert

BY HILMAR GRONDAHL
Market Editor, The Oregonian

A program that was gay and fanciful in about nine-tenths of its content was what Jacques Gershkovitch and the young personnel of the Portland Junior Symphony orchestra delivered to their patrons at the public auditorium Saturday night. Except for Rimsky-Korsakov's "Russian Easter" overture, which concluded the concert, there was an endless string of music animated by buoyancy and good humor.

Saturday night's excursions through the overture to "The Marriage of Figaro," Mendelssohn's "Italian" symphony, the Saint-Saens "Carnival of the Animals" and Mozart's two-piano concerto in E-flat (K.365), emphasized the fact that musicians of this age are a plastic lot who can sustain the bright spirit and drive of scores dominated by wit, invention, technical brilliance and emotional restraint.

Musicianly Command Shown

The two-piano work which Mozart wrote for his sister Nannerl and himself brought Diane DeMott and Raymond Graap to the stage as soloists. Dr. Gershkovitch had reduced the orchestra for the occasion, achieving a balance between the twin keyboards and instrumental complement which was serviceable to the spirit of the music.

The young soloists showed a musicianly command of their individual roles and an admirable understanding of their dual responsibilities. It would be understandable and twice as easy at this age and with this score to play with technical proficiency and a mechanical gaiety. But this pair had something to say, and a way of saying it that went beyond the metronomic. It was sensitive, considered playing which caught the composer's spirit with a cogency not generally found in a girl of 14 and a boy of 15.

There was some fine playing in the Mendelssohn symphony, but the real fun came when the whole orchestra put on its mardi-gras a la Saint-Saens. Janet Schille and Tana Bawden occupied the carnival cage where the two pianists were kept and made a substantial contribution to the occasion. Catherine Halverson made a hit as the cuckoo in the woods, and Jane Taylor had the seriously eloquent theme of the swan.

Jarnefeldt's Berceuse and Praeludium came between the Mozart concerto and the final number.

28th Season

Jacques Gershkovitch, Conductor

November 17, 1951

Eugene Fuerst, Guest Conductor

Overture, "Donna Diana"	REZNICEK
Roumanian Folk Dances	BARTOK
Piano Concerto NO. 1, G minor	MENDELSSOHN
Symphony NO. 8, F major	BEETHOVEN
Le Coq d'Or Prologue & Processional	RIMSKY-KORSAKOV

February 23, 1952

Leonore Overture NO. 3	BEETHOVEN
Violin Concerto, E minor, op. 64 Walter Maddox, *Soloist*	MENDELSSOHN
Symphony NO. 5, E minor, op. 64	TCHAIKOVSKY

April 26, 1952

Jacques Gershkovitch, *Conductor*

Overture, "Barber of Seville"	ROSSINI
Adagio from Toccata & Fugue in C Fugue in G minor (The Shorter)	BACH/STOKOWSKI
Piano Concerto NO. 1, Bb minor First Movement David Campbell, *Soloist*	TCHAIKOVSKY
Sinfonie Concertante, Bb major Catherine De Moss, *Violin;* Lucille Grabovac, *Oboe;* Jane Taylor, *Violoncello;* Wayne De Mott, *Bassoon*	HAYDN
Valse de Concert	GLAZOUNOW
Symphonic Poem, The Moldau	SMETANA

THE OREGONIAN NOV. 18, 1951

Juniors Win High Praise

Music Program Boosts Variety

BY HILMAR GRONDAHL
Music Editor, The Oregonian

Patrons of the Portland Junior Symphony orchestra association's concert at the public auditorium Saturday night had an assortment of related musical interests.

In Eugene Fuerst they saw an experienced conductor with a clear baton technic and admirable musical intelligence. It was evident that he had worked painstakingly with the orchestra as, for instance, the elaborate ritardandos and bravura passages of the Bartok music or the clear, details and pacing of the Beethoven symphony.

Eighth Steals Show

In Larry Smith the audience saw and heard a remarkable young keyboard talent who knew not only the brilliant solo passages given him by the composer, but was aware of what was in the orchestra score as well, and what was expected of him in relating his part to that of instrumental complement.

Young Smith had self reliance, the preparation, the technical knowhow and the innate musicianship to see himself through the headlong passages of the finale as ably as through the somberly poised beauties of the andante.

The sheaf of Romanian folk dances were of wonderful educative worth to the members of the orchestra, while their nostalgic tunes and exciting rhythms were excellent program variety for the listeners.

But it was the Beethoven Eighth which proved to be the finest example of ensemble musicianship. This "little" symphony was delightfully stylish and properly paced. Not the least eloquent moment of the concert was the playing of the horns in the trio of the third movement. Considering the average technical capacity of these young players and the general quality of their instruments, the entire symphony was remarkably precise and agreeable to the ear.

OREGON JOURNAL NOV. 18, 1951

Junior Symphony Presents Fine Program, Fine Soloist

By SUSIE AUBREY SMITH
Journal Music Editor

The Portland Junior Symphony orchestra opened its 28th season Saturday evening at The Auditorium with a fine program and a fine soloist. The symphony was the bright and lively Beethoven Eighth and the soloist was the 15-year-old pianist, Larry Smith.

For the second time in its history the Junior symphony gave an entire program under, the baton of a guest conductor. Jacques Gershkovitch, its leader since its beginning, is on leave in California because of ill health. Guiding the young musicians last night was Eugene Fuerst, internationally known conductor, who now makes Portland his home.

THE YOUNG musicians responded splendidly to Mr. Fuerst's expert direction both in the lilting overture to "Donna Diana," by Von Reznicek, which came first and in Bartok's "Roumanian Dances."

A concert by the Junior symphony is always a thrilling experience. Last night it was doubly so because of the soloist, who played the Mendelssohn G minor concerto with the assurance of a veteran concert pianist. Larry has brilliant technique and youthful ardor and he has something more—that sensitive musicianship which made his performance not only dazzling virtuosity, but also artistically secure interpretation. His playing of the Andante was beautiful. After the final Presto, which he took at a very fast tempo, the audience gave him a storm of applause.

THE OREGONIAN FEB. 24, 1952

Junior Symphony Proves Adept at Difficult Works

BY HILMAR GRONDAHL
Music Editor, The Oregonian

If the Portland Junior Symphony society's music committee had gone into a huddle to plan a program that would put its young musicians on their mettle, it could hardly have chosen more adroitly than it did in the list which Eugene Fuerst conducted at the public auditorium Saturday night. The selection was Beethoven's Third "Leonore" overture, Mendelssohn's violin concerto, and Tchaikovsky's Fifth symphony. Walter Maddox, a 17-year-old musician, was soloist in the Mendelssohn work.

This would be a challenging string of pieces for many a professional orchestra.

Considering the problems involved, Saturday night's concert was a notable accomplishment. The scores used were presented with style, a high level of technical competence, and an uncommon felicity of expressive means.

Interestingly enough, the most challenging of the compositions, the Tchaikovsky symphony, was the finest reading of them all. It was an interpretive endeavor that had moments of incandescence that flamed and flowered with the lush and heady emotional excesses native to its spirit without ever getting beyond the acceptable. Much of the success was in the proper use of dynamic range stresses, and well-built climaxes.

If there was a deficiency of strength in the winds there was unusual strength in the brasses. From the moment Shirley Roeckel began the horn solo in the andante cantabile one was free from concern over bloops.

Good Teaching Revealed

The solo lines of the Mendelssohn violin concerto are taxing for violinists of 17 not in the prodigy class. Walter Maddox is a serious student of more than common capacity. He played his assignments in a straightforward and businesslike way, which gave evidence of good teaching and a fair grasp of the musical ideas involved. If his tone acquire more body with his development, as it probably will, he will make a more properly telling thing of the heavenly slow movement. His technic is good, but he is not yet assured enough in some of the most intricate passages to carry them off with the ease they require.

One was impressed with his bowing, the steadiness of his tone and his general musicianship.

The orchestral complement was nicely proportioned and the entire concerto warmly received.

THE OREGONIAN APR. 27, 1952

Juniors Give Notable Bill

Orchestra Batonist Back on Podium

BY HILMAR GRONDAHL
Music Editor, The Oregonian

Had there been no affairs of memory and sentiment associated with Saturday night's concert by the Portland Junior Symphony orchestra at the public auditorium, there would still have been plenty to engage the crowd's interest on purely musical grounds. It was an evening bursting with matters of the spirit and first performances.

On the sentimental side there was the return of Conductor Jacques Gershkovitch to the podium after a "health" vacation that kept him away from the season's two earlier concerts.

Then as an event combining both sentiment and musical interest was the performance of the first movement of the Tchaikovsky piano concerto with David Campbell as soloists.

The first performances were of two Stokowski transcriptions of organ works by Sebastian Bach, Haydn's sinfonie concertante in B-flat, Opus 84, and Glazounow's concert waltz.

Mr. Gershkovitch's appearance for the final program of his 28th season was the occasion for an especially warm display of welcome. While the conductor appeared to use his gestures with a more circumscribed sweep than heretofore, there was no lack of clarity in their intent and the vitality of their purpose was conveyed to player and music alike. Prior to the Tchaikovsky section, he achieved an affective contrast between the bounding overture to "The Barber of Seville" and the "Little" fugue in G-minor.

Hussa Makes Presentation

The appearance of Mr. Campbell as guest soloist, was something of a historical occasion, for the association has never before welcomed to this position one of its directors. But Mr. Campbell is unique not only in that he has been an active board member for 25 years and as such has been instrumental in determining policies of the music committee and telling the story of music to the children's audiences: what is really unique is that he was qualified to accept an invitation to appear as guest artist.

The Tchaikovsky music was played with cautious tempos, but the soloist's own statements were given in clear, ringing tones, and the favorite themes expressed with engaging lyricism.

The real novelty of the evening was the charming Haydn concertante which brought four of the orchestra's principals to the forefront.

It was a notable addition to the orchestra's repertory. The solo players were Catherine De Moss, violin; Jane Taylor, cello; Lucille Grabovac, oboe, and Wayne De Mott, bassoon.

OREGON JOURNAL APR. 27, 1952

Portland Junior Symphony Concert Proved Gala Affair

By SUSIE AUBREY SMITH
Journal Music Editor

The Portland Junior symphony's third concert of the season Saturday night at The Auditorium was a gala affair for both orchestra and audience.

Jacques Gershkovitch, its conductor, returned to the podium after a several-months absence and the soloist was David Campbell, well known concert artist, who is celebrating his 25th anniversary as member of the board and commentator for the morning concerts.

Mr. Campbell played the first movement of the Tschaikowski piano concerto in B flat minor with the orchestra. He gave a superb performance of this difficult and thrilling work with excellent support from conductor and players. At his final curtain call he was presented with a silver cigarette box, gift of his fellow board members. And closing with the ever-popular "The Moldau."

After the concert, a reception honoring Mr. Campbell was held in the South wing.

Birthday Celebration at Public Auditorium Attracts 2000 Children, Some From Afar

Jacques Gershkovitch at the Orchestra's 25th Anniversary.

Two thousand delighted youngsters joined in a birthday party Saturday morning at the auditorium.

The party, which followed the final Portland Junior symphony young people's concert of the season, was in honor of David Campbell, who has narrated the junior concerts for 25 years.

It also welcomed back Jacques Gershkovitch, veteran conductor of the junior symphony. Illness had curtailed many of Gershkovitch's activities during the past season.

The party was highlighted by the cutting of an elaborate cake, baked in the shape of an assembled orchestra.

Present at the event were children from various communities outside Portland. Two hundred youngsters from Prineville journeyed to Portland by bus for the concert and party.

After the brief cake-cutting ceremony, members of the Portland Junior league passed out cup cakes to the youngsters.

The day's festivities ended with an evening concert at 8:30 featuring the works of Rossini, Bach, Glazounow, Haydn and Smetana. Campbell was soloist on the first movement of Tschaikowsky's B flat minor piano concerto.

A reception followed in Campbell's honor in the south wing of the auditorium. An engraved cigaret case was presented him by the junior symphony board in appreciation of his work with the group.

29th Season

Jacques Gershkovitch, Conductor

November 22, 1952

Oberon Overture	WEBER
Symphony No. 4, Bb major, op.62	BEETHOVEN
Piano Concerto No. 12, A major	MOZART
Patricia Ann Taylor, *Soloist*	
Adagio for Strings	BARBER
Prelude to "Die Meistersinger"	WAGNER

February 21, 1953

Eugene Fuerst, Guest Conductor

Overture, "Magic Flute"	MOZART
"From Heaven Above," Chorale	BACH/ORMANDY
Symphony in G major, "Surprise"	HAYDN
"Francesca da Rimini" op. 32	TCHAIKOVSKY
Good Friday Spell from "Parsifal"	WAGNER
Tales from the Vienna Woods	STRAUSS

April 25, 1953

Roman Carnival Overture	BERLIOZ
Petite Suite	DEBUSSY
Concerto for 2 Violins, D minor	BACH
Eleanor Wolfe & Ann Bogard, *Soloists*	
The Sorcerer's Apprentice	DUKAS
"The Love for Three Oranges" March	PROKOFIEFF
Suite No. 1 from "Carmen"	BIZET

THE OREGONIAN NOV. 23, 1952

Young Pianist Concert Star

Junior Symphony Earns Applause

BY HILMAR GRONDAHL
Music Editor, The Oregonian

At a Portland Junior Symphony orchestra concert it is sometimes difficult to tell whether the applause from the audience to conductor and ensemble, the orchestra's response to the conductor, or the conductor's approval of his players is the most heartening consequence of a performance.

It was that way Saturday night when the players had completed Beethoven's Fourth symphony before an animated crowd at the public auditorium. Jacques Gershkovitch was called back several times before people were willing to agree to an intermission, and while he indicated with pride his 80 young musicians they joined with those beyond the footlights in approving his direction.

'Oberon' Opens Bill

This is the way sentiment flows back and forth at these concerts. You will not find it the same at professional concerts, for here the relationship between listener and performer is at some point the relationship of parent and child.

Saturday's program opened with one of the Junior Symphony's standard works; the overture to Weber's "Oberon." No one passes through the membership of this organization without getting a firm grasp on this fanciful curtain raiser. It is a composite of those elements which appeal to the young both in idea and effect, and on this occasion Mr. Gershkovitch turned both idea and effect out with more than his customary zip.

The highlight in this first concert of the orchestra's 29th season was the performance of Mozart's Piano concerto in A (K. 414) which featured Patricia Ann Taylor as soloist. It proved to be one of the most sensitive associations of solo and ensemble that these programs have furnished.

Pianist's Talent Notable

Miss Taylor is a pianist of remarkable talent who has obviously studied this music with discerning intelligence. Technical matters were no problem to her as she dealt with interpretive factors of style. There were no passages too fleet to reflect the coloration of her thought and such lyric opportunities as the andante she put to artistic good use.

She treated the solo instrument too lightly in the opening movement, rather like a salon piece with small accompanying orchestra. The balance was good through all of the second movement and nearly all of the finale.

OREGON JOURNAL APR. 26, 1953

Gershkovitch Leads Junior Symphony, Third Concert

By SUSIE AUBREY SMITH
Journal Music Editor

Home from a winter vacation in California, Jacques Gershkovitch conducted his Portland Junior symphony in its third concert of the season Saturday evening in The Auditorium. A demonstrative but not overlarge audience was on hand to welcome him and hear the fine program offered by the youthful musicians.

Mr. Gershkovitch opened with Berlioz' colorful "Roman Carnival" overture, which the orchestra played brilliantly under his inspired leadership. Next came Debussy's "Petite Suite," four captivating musical miniatures, which the young players gave a pleasing performance.

As on several previous occasions, Mr. Gershkovitch presented two of his best violinists in the Bach D minor Concerto for Two Violins. The soloists were Eleanor Wolfe, concertmaster, and Ann Bogard, assistant concertmaster of the orchestra. They played the beautiful Bach music with beautiful tone and in the most felicitous style and were recalled to the stage several times by applause.

Another special feature was the march from "Love of Three Oranges," which Mr. Gershkovitch played in memory of the composer, Serge Prokofieff, once his classmate in student days in Old Russia.

The Junior Symphony's interpretation of Dukas' "Sorcerer's Apprentice," played after the intermission Saturday, is always gay and zestful. Its program and its 29th season closed with the sparkling "Carmen Suite No. 1" by Bizet.

OREGON JOURNAL FEB. 22, 1953

Juniors Play Under Guest Conductor

By SUSIE AUBREY SMITH
Journal Music Editor

The Portland Junior symphony gave the second concert in its 29th consecutive season Saturday night in The Auditorium under the baton of a guest conductor, Eugene Fuerst. Its permanent conductor, Jacques Gershkovitch, is in California on sick leave.

Mr. Fuerst conducted with precise and effective tempos and the suave authority of experienced musicianship. The youthful musicians responded splendidly and gave a performance quite up to the high standard they have set over the years.

* * *

THE PROGRAM opened with the overture to "The Magic Flute," one of the most charming Mozart overtures. Under Mr. Fuerst's skillful guidance, the orchestra interpreted it with all the grace and elegance of the Mozartean tradition. The Bach Chorale, as the junior musicians gave it, is a real orchestral gem.

The conductor's reading of the Haydn "Surprise" symphony was a bit more dramatic than is customary. It is, however, always pleasant music and was well received by the audience.

Featured was Tschaikowsky's beautiful fantasy, "Francesca da Rimini," which brought much well deserved applause. Appropriate to the Lenten season, the "Good Friday Spell" from "Parsifal" was given a reverent rendition.

Portland Junior Symphony Audience Receptive

BY HILMAR GRONDAHL
Music Editor, The Oregonian

Under the baton of Jacques Gershkovitch at the public auditorium Saturday night, the Portland Junior Symphony orchestra rounded out 29 seasons of exceptionally valuable service to music lovers of all ages in this area.

The first most interested group is, of course, the performers themselves; the youngsters who year after year gather training and musical experience at rehearsal and concert. The second most interested group is made up of the relatives of performers: fathers, mothers, brothers, sisters, aunts, uncles, cousins, etc., by the dozens.

And finally, the largest group of all, the crowd of listeners untouched by ties of kinship or training who are interested at some degree between quiet curiosity and passionate admiration in the music these 80 young people prepare and deliver three time each year.

Dr. Gershkovitch was back on the podium after his second rest in California, conducting with somewhat less vigor, but with no less precision than before. In fact, this new-found restraint was, if anything, easier for the players to follow, and consequently at the service of the performance.

Among the varied program items was Sebastian Bach's concerto in D minor for two violins and string orchestra. This featured the two girls who normally occupy the first stand of violins: Eleanor Wolfe, concertmaster, and Ann Bogard, assistant concertmaster.

This is one of the most difficult concerto works in the repertory. It asks for, but seldom receives, a pair of perfectly matched violinists.

While each of these young musicians is gifted and capable, they are not matched in tone or temperament. The one is a stronger player; the consequence of this was that secondary material often sounds as strong as primary. They were individually too concerned with their own parts to be able to observe the niceties of ensemble balance, and the first movement was taken at such a pace that they couldn't attain the repose imperative for the proper blending of Bach's entwined tendrils of melody. The largo was better, and the finale had some very attractive moments.

The "Roman Carnival" overture was the genuinely effective piece in the first half, with some brilliant work by trumpets, trombones and bassoons.

Fuerst Leads Junior Symphony Group Through Program of Tension, Delight

BY HILMAR GRONDAHL
Music Editor, The Oregonian

When the 80 Portland Junior Symphony musicians had finished playing the first half of their program under Eugene Fuerst's direction at the public auditorium Saturday night, they knew that they had been on a musical trip of some tension and palpable delight. They had followed some precipitous thematic contours at a lively rhythmic pace in the Haydn "Surprise" symphony, pierced the colorful panorama of Bach's chorale "From Heaven Above" and peered among the mysterious symbols of Mozart's "Magic Flute" overture.

One of the observations frequently made by this orchestra's sustaining society is that these young musicians play nothing but original scores; they shun simplified arrangements as they shun sin. But it is not enough for the listener to hear that instrumentalists are playing from the original score. To him it is much more of significance that the score be played as the composer intended, with each measure respectful in shape and sound and spirit, with the proper pulse and with the integrity of design that he had in his own mind and heart.

Genuine Style Achieved

It was amazing with what respect these 80 juniors brought their instruments and technics and scores into consonance on this occasion. In the Haydn they were up to tempo even in the liveliest of sections. There was articulation by sections and an uncommon sounding together of the entire ensemble. There was genuine style and an astonishing breadth of dynamics and orchestral coloring. It was a fine example, from the listener's standpoint, of giving a respectful and properly musical salute to a score unsimplified in content or intent.

The post intermission pieces were Tchaikowsky's "Francesca da Rimini." the Good Friday Spell from "Parsifal," and "Tales from the Vienna Woods."

Here again Mr. Fuerst gave an astonishing demonstration of this junior ensemble as a musical body. The Tchaikowsky work is one which gives headaches even to professional orchestras.

It was not to be expected that everything Tchaikowsky wished to convey by tone would have its full measure of felicity from musicians whose capabilities are not yet fully developed, and yet there were moments of suspense and tension, excitement, organic beauty such as we have seldom previously heard at one of these concerts. It was a score beyond their present grasp yet from their very striving they have shown remarkable musical growth. And knowing this music in this practiced way has certainly been worth their time and attention.

Salutes at Earlier Anniversaries

Salutes

AT THE 35TH ANNIVERSARY

New York, March, 1958

THE CELEBRATION of the work of the Portland Junior Symphony draws attention to a cultural movement which is exactly the same age as this young orchestra itself. I have in mind the movement of the western democracies toward the unaffected enjoyment and practice of the arts, particularly music.

Since the late 1920s, certainly, the American people was passed from the age of the isolated connoisseur and collector of art to that of the ubiquitous devotee and participant. No longer is it thought sissified for the healthy and cheerful child to play an instrument, no longer does the citizen find it odd if his friends play chamber music every week or if his wife joins a choral society: he himself buys records and tinkers at high-fidelity equipment.

Similarly, people in increasing numbers paint, carve, dance, and put on plays, for their own pleasure and that of the community. The museum, the library, the college, have become art centers.

Any addiction to art must be linked to the strongest part of us—to our will, our mind, our muscles. And this is why I find the purpose of the Portland Junior Symphony admirable. "Young musicians in the orchestra are expected to strive for the disciplined performance of the true artist."

Greatness, it is true, is not attained by mere effort; it comes as a gift—but only to those who have worked themselves up to the heights where greatness strikes.

Besides, greatness is not the point. The point is to grapple with the difficulty the moment brings, whether to the mind, the breath, or the fingers. For the beholder, the difficulty is to understand with heart and brain what is put before him; which is why new art, contemporary work, is the true test of the devotee. It is easy to love the familiar, in an absent-minded way; it takes effort—often wasted effort— to find one's proper meat in the jungle of the contemporary. Yet without the joint striving of disciplined performer and disciplined audience, there is no likelihood of notable creation—that ultimate strength by which a culture professing to be artistic must be judged.

For all these reasons and what they imply, the Portland Junior Symphony commands our respect: it requires discipline and has imparted it to thousands of talented youths; it produces contemporary works and does not baby its audience; and in the person of its conductor, the composer Jacob Avshalomov, it has shown that out of a small army of disciplined amateurs comes the creative mind. Let the forces that have fashioned and sustained this institution continue on the same path and they will fulfill the poet's ideal of social effort: "to make the gift of life more valuable, and the men more worthy of the gift."

JACQUES BARZUN

New York, December 3,

To my future fellow-alumni,

A whole week has gone by since Lucy I made music with you and we shall remember this for a very long time. I am sure you must know that there is no organization in this country, nor most likely anywhere in the work, to compare with Portland Junior Symphony, I say this without excess subjectivity or pointless loyalty. There is simply no other place which offers such an immediate opportunity to develope keen musical discipline, a professional aplomb, and well of strength to nourish growing love of music.

If this is not clear to you now, you will sense it in retrospect as I do. How grateful I am that people such as Mrs. Noyes and many others have dedicated their efforts to continue this tradition with each new group of youthful music lovers. How grateful I am that Portland has not let up its support and continuance of the Junior Symphony concerts. How glad I am that Jacob Avshalomov, like Mr. G., has continued to mand and obtain the most that members the Junior Symphony have in them.

And last, how happy and refreshing for me to return and experience your particular brand of warm, wholehearted commitment of the act of making music.

Even at the risk of sounding fatherly, I plead with you not to lose the quality musicians do in the passing of time

You were magnificent and we thank you for the pleasure you have given us. Wishing you all a wonderful future, whether you end up in music or not,

Sincerely
BOB MANN

(Robert Mann had just performed the Mozart Violin Concerto no. 3 and conducted his composition "The Terrible Tempered Conductor." with his wife as narrator initiating the 35th Anniversary.)

Salutes

AT EARLIER ANNIVERSARIES

Munich, November 3, 1963

An institution that has reached its fortieth year has virtually achieved immortality, as human things go. At such a time one can dare to say that the Junior Symphony has a future because it has such a past.

There are other orchestras of this sort. As a former member and assistant to Jacques Gershkovitch I have tried to keep an eye on them. Few have so truly become institutions in their communities.

That orchestras tend to be identified with their conductors is no accident. We have heard of *charisma* in recent years, the attraction of a magical personality. This indeed Jacques Gershkovitch possessed for us. He was from a far country, and the clouds of legend readily settled over him. The Russian Revolution, which he had lived through, was then not very far behind us. It was the era before which was remote to us. But the storied musical names of that age, Rimsky-Korsakov, Glazunov, Chaliapin, Leopold Auer, were suddenly endowed with reality when we heard them spoken of as living persons.

Exotic tradition and musical lineage will not by themselves explain the secret of the continuance of the Orchestra even through years of depression and war. The answer lies in the man and the community behind him.

Alumni of Jacques Gershkovitch's orchestra learned that the only reply to his "you must" was "I can." With that, children learned maturity from what, it turned out, was the gentlest possible master for so earnest a lesson. Joining to the love of the amateur a real measure of the authenticity of the professional we learned how music is made.

To equal such good fortune in a founder one can only hope for an equally genial successor. In Jacob Avshalomov the Orchestra has such a man. In him more and more of the promise that the Orchestra perpetually holds is being realized. One can entrust developing young musicians to no better hands than those of a man who is not only a scholar and a conductor but a creative artist as well.

KARL ASCHENBRENNER

(Dr. Aschenbrenner, professor of philosophy at the University of California at Berkeley, and his wife Marie, are both alumni of the PJS.)

Cincinnati, Ohio, April 7, 1964

When I look back, it is with unreserved joy that I remember my days in the Portland Junior Symphony Orchestra. Although it was thirty years ago, the memory of the experience is sometimes so vivid that many incidents seem to have occurred either yesterday or very recently. We as individuals didn't look upon the Orchestra as a community venture or as an institution. To us it was a living, vital organism that became as important as life itself.

The conductor, Jacques Gershkovitch, was a stern father to us; he prodded, cajoled, chided us as his children. And we obeyed. With this obedience came the understanding and, more important, the love of the music we played. While the concert was the crowning act, it was the rehearsals that gave us the will. First readings, sectional rehearsals, and polishing were all part of the total which the public saw and heard. They appreciated the final act; we appreciated and loved the formulation that we saw grow to excellence from the shapeless beginnings.

I remember too the repertoire. We played not only standard symphonic works, but opera, ballet and oratorio. Each concert was an adventure. And each adventure led us to know and to appreciate music at a time when concerts were a rarity and the phonograph was a luxury which only few enjoyed.

Now when I think back I realize what caused this wonderful institution to grow and prosper. Not only we who made the music: it *was* the community which fostered our interest. It was Jacques Gershkovitch who had a dream that was unique, and he had the vitality and the tenacity to see it manifest.

I knew the present conductor, Jacob Avshalomov, first as a colleague in the percussion section. We became good friends, and one of my biggest thrills was to be asked to play percussion for his music to the Hindu play, *The Little Clay Cart,* given at Reed College. I know that he has carried on in the tradition of our beloved Jacques Gershkovitch, extending the same inspiring musical experience to this generation. And I am sure that "Mr. A" evokes the same love and devotion in his Orchestra that "Mr. G" did in ours.

JOSEPH E. KARASICK

(The late Rabbi Karasick was Academic Coordinator at Hebrew University College, Cincinnati. He played in the Junior symphony 1934–38. During that period he frequently wrote Notes for PJS programs, as he later did for the Honolulu Symphony.)

At this 50th Anniversary of the Orchestra and the 20th of Jacob Avshalomov as Conductor, our feelings cannot be more truly expressed than they were when he was conferred an honorary doctorate of Humane Letters by Reed College last September.

"Jacob Avshalomov, gifted composer, eminent conductor, skilled and patient teacher, it is our privilege to acknowledge in this formal way your achievement in the world of music.

"When your crossed the China seas to begin a new life in this country you had been thoroughly schooled in music by your father, Aaron Avshalomov, himself a composer of great merit. You attended Reed and the Eastman School of Music. Your teachers, Jacques Gershkovitch and Bernard Rogers, made further contributions to your developing talents, and in your years as a teacher at Columbia University you achieved national recognition: the Alice M. Ditson Fellowship in composition, a Guggenheim Fellowship, and the New York Music Critics Circle Award, to name only a few of your many awards.

"It was Portland's good fortune that you returned in 1954 as conductor of the Portland Junior Symphony. Under your direction this orchestra achieved international acclaim. Many of its alumni—a very special group—are highly placed in professional positions throughout the country. Words simply cannot express the depth of gratitude that Portlanders, who care about the culture of their city, feel toward you for your successful leadership of this unique orchestra.

"Reed's special pride is that your career exemplifies an ideal blend of creativity and the liberal arts. Your programs and you compositions reflect a broad knowledge and a scholarly approach that is indeed rare in professional conductors and composers. You rehearsals and coaching sessions combine professional discipline with the patience of a devoted teacher. The ultimate attestation to this is the esprit of your players, and their attitude toward you that is manifest in every performance."

All who have been privileged to share the unique talents of this gifted man join tonight in our appreciation of what he has given of himself to our community.

EDWARD H. LOOK, *President*
Portland Junior Symphony Association
May 18, 1974

The Avshalomov Era

The Joyful Workings of America's First Youth Orchestra

1939

1954

1968

1958

1960

1964

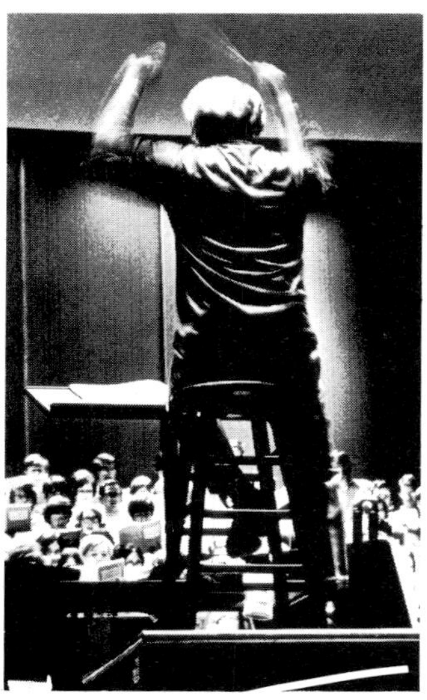
1969

1988

1970

1975

1979

1989

Opposite. Jacob Avshalomov.

GATHERING THE ORCHESTRAS

Come into the auditorium of Glencoe School in southeast Portland any Wednesday of the school year and you will see one hundred or more students playing as if their lives depended on it. It could be the Brahms *Third Symphony,* the Stravinsky *Firebird Suite,* or Bergsma's *Chameleon Variations.* Dressed in jeans or whatevers, the young people look like your kids and mine. Who are they? Where do they come from? Why are they here?

They are here because it is inherently gratifying to play this great music—to practice and rehearse it with the prospect of being able to perform it well, in short, to work hard at it and *realize* it.

They come from all over northwest Oregon and southwest Washington, within a radius of 80 miles of Portland. Most young musicians know of the Orchestra, either by its reputation, or through siblings or teachers. They come to it as moths to light or bees to flowers.

The Orchestra has always been open to anyone within the age limit: 22 is the top; the lower limit for the Prep Orchestra has hovered around 10. The policy is to rotate students out of the Orchestra at a certain point to give others a turn. Acceptance depends on musical ability and vacancies in the Orchestras. All irrelevant distinctions are ignored, including chronological age, and it is wonderful to see the respect accorded a grade-school violinist by high-schoolers sitting farther down the ranks.

The players are chosen by audition, generally held in early September, when the school year begins, but in recent seasons also in May. All members are expected to be taking private lessons on their instrument.

Portland has been a magnet for young musicians for many years. Its population is about 400,000, with the metropolitan area holding nearly one million. I have always felt there to be a relationship between the success of the Orchestra and the size of the city. It is large enough to have a good pool of talent, but not so large as to have several civic centers. In Portland, artistic endeavors tend to focus on one main center, so there is a healthy concentration of energy and patronage on the primary cultural organizations.

The 200-plus players in the two orchestras come from over 90 different schools and colleges. About 20% of the young musicians are grade-schoolers, 65% are in high school, while 13% are enrolled in local colleges. Most of the area schools are represented by only one or two students, so one can imagine what it means to these isolates to participate in a large group of capable peers. A handful in any given season are not in school but hold a job while pondering their next step, cleaving to the Orchestra for tonic to the spirit.

The students thus gathered are a very special group. For one thing, they are self-motivated; and they are often gifted in many ways. Requests for excused absence from rehearsals come throughout the season: for speech tournaments, athletic meets, dramatic performances, religious and academic conferences, outdoor school. The proportion of honor students has always been high. The members of such an orchestra might be called an elite.

We need not shy away from the term if we define *elite* as "any corps of working talent." That would include the skilled craftsmen in any field, an elite not of pedigree but of accomplishment.

This belief is nicely confirmed by the cross-section of citizenry shown in the occupations of our players' parents. Although historically there was some justification for the view that the high arts, and serious music in particular, were the special preserve of the privileged, in a social or financial sense, we can see that this is no longer so. The intriguing list of parents' occupations, compiled from our recent rosters, shows that symphonic music can be fulfilling to people of widely differing backgrounds.

Accountant
Architect
Advertising
Artist
Attorney
Banker
Bondsman
Carpenter
Cartographer
Contractor
Customs Official
Designer
Doctor
Draftsman
Electrician
Engineer
Estimator
Florist
Forester
Graduate Student
Inspector, BPA
I.R.S. Agent
Lab Technician
Lineman
Lumberman
Machine Operator
Management
Mathematician
Meat Cutter
Mechanic
Millwright
Minister
Musician
Nurse
Orchestra Conductor
Pharmacist
Piano Tuner
Plumber
Printer
Private Investigator
Professor
Public Affairs
Real Estate Broker
Salesman
Scientist
Sheetmetal Worker
Social Worker
Speech Pathologist
State Fiscal Officer
Stock Broker
Switchman
Teacher
Television
Travel Agent
Trout Farmer
Truck Driver
Veterinarian
Welder

THE PUBLIC PROGRAMS

An amateur performing group lives mainly in its rehearsals. With young people especially, like those in PYP, the chief purpose of rehearsals is to develop their skill, insight, and rich enjoyment of the music they play. To run the full course, however, they need to perform as well as prepare. In any endeavor performance is a prime test and measure of achievement. Learning to cook well is surely related to having a guest at your table. When we declare the purpose of an activity to be educational, it should be remembered that the ability to perform—to deliver the goods—is one of the chief aims of that training.

The PYP programs embrace the full range of orchestral music, and closely resemble the offerings of major orchestras. We have always used the composer's authentic version, never an abridgement or simplification.

The Evening Concert programs are designed for an adult audience—a serious one, with the middle-aged majority nicely balanced by students and the elderly. They are reviewed in the local press, the major substance of this book, and, on occasion, in journals of national circulation. Between 1,500 and 2,500 people attend our performances regularly. A PYP concert is always an *event*, not only for the public, but more especially for the Orchestra members. They prepare themselves for it, musically and in their spirit, and come ready to give their all—which is often more than anyone knew they had in them.

Programming has been progressive rather than radical, playing as we do for the general public and not a university or contemporary-music audience. But almost every concert has a modern, if not avant-garde work. A soloist is presented at two concerts a season, and a major choral work every year or two.

In devising programs for a youth orchestra there are many considerations which do not figure in the planning of a program for professionals. Each season the changing strength and weakness of the various sections must be taken into account: if the English-horn player is excellent, one thinks of Dvorák's *Symphony from the New World* or Franck's *D. minor;* whereas a weak section of French horns may be too tame to work up a good fright in Prokofiev's *Peter and the Wolf.* And many a work, which sounds innocent enough to the audience, has to be checked for difficulties that may be hazardous to the health of second-violins.

Not only must each concert present a balanced bill-of-fare—appetizer, soup, salad, entree, dessert—but it must also make sense within the whole season. Where only four or five programs are prepared each year, it is imperative to maintain a healthy variety in the styles, composers, and periods of music. In fact the programs are viewed over a longer range than the single season. On the average, students remain in the Orchestra for four years, a span comparable to high school or college. Over this period we try to give them as broad a musical experience as possible.

The Children's Concerts were originally an outgrowth of the dress rehearsal held on the morning of the adult concerts. Selected movements from large works and shorter pieces (5–8 minutes) are best suited to the attention span of children. Audiences of 2,000 to 3,000 youngsters converge on the Municipal Auditorium, and in recent years, the Arlene Schnitzer Concert Hall, from many points—a cheery sight as they come—in small groups and in busloads, some from as far off as the coastal towns of Tillamook and Seaside, over 80 miles to the west.

For 25 years David Campbell, much respected teacher and pianist, served as the commentator for these Children's Concerts with charm and distinction. His role had a special importance in the early days, since Jacques Gershkovitch never gained a command of English sufficient for public use.

From the beginning, both the Conductors and the Board realized the potential inspiration to children in the audience of seeing performers their own age take such pleasure in excelling. Until the Auditorium was renovated in 1968, the Children's Concerts were followed by a sort of jamboree in the south wing, where the audience could throng to meet the members of the Orchestra as they demonstrated their instruments, individually and in small groups; the greater the uproar, the greater the delight.

And then there is always some sort of audience participation: singing, clapping, interjecting; and projects such as drawing their own imagined *Pictures at an Exhibition,* and scenes from *Babar the Little Elephant.*

Interspersed with the main concerts downtown, the Orchestra has always presented assorted performances for special occasions. These, perhaps more than anything else, reveal the range of the Orchestra's involvement and appreciation in the City. In addition to visits to schools and colleges, programs have been given for the dedication of new halls at the Art Museum and Mt. Angel Abbey, for trade missions, and for national and international conferences—scientific and religious and academic. The Orchestra learns a great deal from playing their programs a second and third time. It is one thing to present the program in the white heat of preparation, and quite another, having come through the fire creditably, to repeat it. The gained assurance makes for greater flexibility, variety, and subtlety, and the very act of performance is placed in a different light. The students come to realize that each performance is a unique expression, that musical events in a composition are very much affected by the way they are approached and projected, and that no two performances of a work need, or can, be exactly alike. We are careful, however, not to exceed three repeats of any program, since doing that would approach a "run" which is the business of professionals and not students.

We have found that comments given from the podium can give the audience a way of entering into sympathy with unfamiliar works. Encouraged by the response to this practice, we continued them during the seasons at the Oriental Theatre where the lighting was inadequate for reading program notes. The public seemed so pleased by this reaching out across the footlights, and this relaxation of concert formality, that we have forsaken printed notes about the music altogether in favor of the verbal introduction.

INNER WORKINGS*

Our working methods were established in almost every detail by Jacques Gershkovitch. This means not only the schedule, but more especially the *tone* of the rehearsals. Gershkovitch's legacy was a sense of serious devotion to making music which he imparted to all who came within his orbit. His influence was felt by parents and visitors as well as by the Orchestra. It was always *quiet* at rehearsal; there was no conversation, no coming in and out, no commotion—all was attention. Mr. Gershkovitch made it clear that, unlike school, no one was required to be present; they were there to make music; if not, they were free, nay urged, to leave. They *earned* and kept their place in the group by their commitment and application. This basic philosophy prevailed throughout the nearly 30 years of his tenure, and continues to the present day.

The truth is that young people prefer to be serious about what they are doing; they need only to be in a climate where seriousness is not an embarrassment, and is not made synonymous with *solemnity.* It is a beautiful thing to see the group of 100 and more players so absorbed in their work that the intermission comes as an interruption and the end of the rehearsal as a surprise. They are there ready to begin exactly on time; if someone is late, an explanation is given afterward; if anyone is ill, or absent for some other reason, his folder of music is brought in—so that no one will be without. Altogether they comport themselves with a wonderful sense of responsibility, and it is clear to all that the strict regimen is kept in the name of *music,*—not of the Conductor—and that to comply is to respect one another, as well as the whole undertaking.

To be a member of such a group is to take up a way of life.

SOLOISTS*

From ancient times people have admired those who could perform feats—of daring, strength, skill, dexterity, memory—any extraordinary concentration of the abilities possessed by the average person in modest measure. Witness the perennial popularity of the circus, athletics, marksmanship, storytelling, and the arts in all lands. Music, especially, holds the promise of touching the feelings, the highest virtue of virtuosity.

For these reasons, soloists have always been an attractive feature at concerts. Outstanding students need and deserve opportunities to be heard in public, and the PYP has offered a dignified platform to a great many of them. Perhaps pianists have found this a greater boon than other young musicians: it is not easy for them to get within sparring distance of a full orchestra. For nearly 60 years the Association has held a contest for pianists in May, the winner of which appearing as soloist the following November.

Every season we also provide a chance for members of the Orchestra to appear as soloists. They too are chosen by audition. The Orchestra, which always takes pride in playing a sensitive accompaniment, seems to have a special measure of responsiveness in supporting its own members.

All soloists are carefully coached by the Conductor before they appear in public, or even at rehearsals. This not only saves time; it also supports the soloist's confidence if he or she is not called into question before the whole group but can be treated as the respected protagonist.

Vocal soloists are presented principally when called for in choral works. For this repertoire our practice has been to invite artists suitable to the part who are known by virtue of their work in local circles. The 22-year age limit is waived because, the person being the instrument, voices are seldom mature enough before this age to undertake a major role. Thus our vocal soloists tend to be young adults rather than undergraduates.

Young adult instrumentalists also appear with us under a special program that brings guest artists to Portland from elsewhere. Sympathizing with the difficulties faced by musicians of great skill and high integrity as they wander the no-man's-land between national contest winner and professional artist, it seems fitting for us to invite them to perform with our group of equally dedicated, if less developed players. We offer them a thorough preparation, a dignified occasion in a major hall, and publicity in the press and other media.

SCHOLARSHIPS*

Virtually the entire program of the PYP is maintained on a scholarship basis. There is no charge to Orchestra members for the training they receive; we ask only a small registration fee and that parents attend the concerts.

The scholarship program has two auxiliary elements: tuition-aid for private lessons during the season, and awards for study at well-known summer schools. The tuition-aid is granted to deserving students—for private lessons on their instrument—with the teacher of their choice. It is given on a noncompetitive basis in recognition of inherent talent and proven commitment to the work of the Orchestra. In addition to these individual considerations, there is the overriding necessity of ensuring a complete instrumentation; thus the tuition-aid is directed toward the development of those sections of the Orchestra which most need it. In the large view, this policy benefits all the members since the music cannot be seriously played unless the Orchestra is complete.

The summer awards, unlike the aid for lessons, *are* competitive and send the students to such places as Tanglewood and the Aspen School of Music.

JOINING HANDS*

From its earliest days the Junior Symphony has worked with kindred elements in Portland, although in the 1920s and '30s collaborative groups such as chorus and ballet sometimes had to be formed by the PJS itself. Over the years many cultural activities have developed, and in recent times it has been an integral part of our program to invite the participation of existing groups.

Choruses have been our most frequent companions, and perhaps the most joyful. The waves of emotion that surge over an assemblage of 300 people singing and playing their hearts out over some exalted humanistic theme are irresistible. Everyone involved is transported beyond himself to another spiritual plane, or as they used to say, "out of this world."

As described earlier, dance groups had a part in our programs as early as the 1930s when the PJS Ballet was formed. Jacques Gershkovitch, with his background as conductor for the great ballerina Anna Pavlova, naturally moved in this direction. In later years when the Portland Ballet School, the Portland Dance Theatre, and the Jefferson Dancers came into being, they were invited to join us from time to time.

Diversions of a lighter weight have included puppeteers from the Junior League, television creatures "in person," bellringers, jugglers, even a unicyclist!

Art students have been involved over the entire span of the Orchestra's life, beginning with the design of a program cover in 1928. This idea was developed into an ongoing project that lasted over 20 years, beginning in 1954 when students from the Art Museum designed such covers. They worked under the guidance of Douglas Lynch who himself designed the elegant cartouche which has been the PYP's logo ever since. Many of those designs appear, miniaturized, on these pages, and several of those student artists have become established professionals in the City.

Educative projects of various sorts have been offered. Program notes have been written by students, beginning with those in the Orchestra and moving out to involve nearly every college in the area, and sometimes as far as the Ivy League universities and conservatories—the New England, Peabody, et al.

One particularly successful project involved four high schools, whose choirs were singing the Brahms *Schicksalslied* with us. Their language classes were invited to provide modern, laconic translations of the Hölderlin text, and several were printed in the concert program beside the original.

Out-of-town concerts were given as early as 1916, and have continued intermittently ever since. During the Oregon Centennial in 1959, we took three trips around the State. In 1977, a safari to eastern Oregon proved highly successful when, in addition to playing concerts, the Orchestra was divided up into several teams and invaded the schools of La Grande with demonstrations and workshops.

Fraternity among musicians can be warm enough simply in conversation, but nothing matches the camaraderie of rolling up the sleeves, rehearsing, and performing together. The satisfactions of our visits to neighboring regions inspired thoughts of more distant horizons; sometimes dreams do come true.

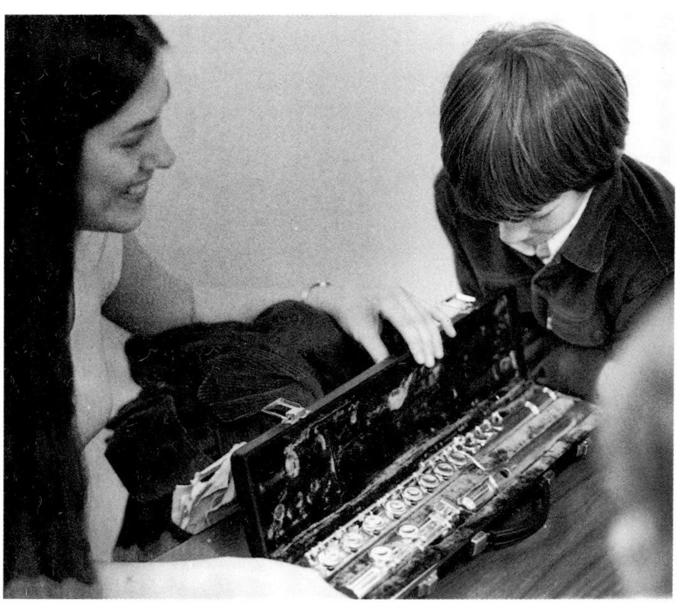

Safari to eastern Oregon, 1977.

St.-Martin-in-the-Fields, London rehearsal, 1970 tour.

FIRST INTERNATIONAL TOUR, 1970

Hopes of traveling abroad had been hovering around the Orchestra for some years, but they remained a dream because the costs seemed unthinkable. Why *does* anyone take a symphony orchestra to Europe? Not just because "travel is broadening"; it would be much handier without all that baggage of instruments; nor because there is any lack of music in the Old World. The yearning has to do with the fact that most of our repertoire originated there, that the tradition of performing it is known as a mother tongue, and that the public's response to serious music rests on centuries of understanding and respect for the art and for artists. Here in America we are still missionaries in our own land, swimming in the fresh waters of musical innocence, as contrasted with the buoyant salt water of European experience.

In the orchestral field Europeans are amazed by the quality of our leading ensembles. Still, the Boston, the New York, the Philadelphia, the Chicago, the Los Angeles, and even the Utah symphonies all make trips abroad, at great cost and loss; partly to bring credit to their cities, but just at much, I declare, to receive the kind of "accreditation" which a good European press and public response bring. We all appreciate favorable "outside, independent review."

Whatever the mix of reasons, a chance invitation to us made the unthinkable thinkable. A full account of the 1970 Tour is given in *Music Is Where You Make It/II.* so it does not appear here. The memories of it are still vivid 20 years later.

RADIO, TELEVISION, AND OTHER BLESSINGS*

The media, as they are termed, are mixed blessings. While we are learning how to use these marvels, their productions proliferate, unchecked, at a great rate; everything, almost anything, is grist to their mills. Entertainment is available, almost unavoidable, at any hour of the day or night. The lines separating what is educative or elevating from what is merely amusing become fuzzy. The real world and that portrayed in the media are apt to be mistaken for one another; they interpenetrate and sometimes fuse.

But the basis of real events is the interaction of live beings; and in the arts, as in most other facets of human society, *participation* is the prime source of self-realization and fulfillment. The arenas of participation need to be protected, and so does the distinction between firsthand activities and their replication.

Still, it is true that radio and television make it possible to reach vast audiences not otherwise accessible. There is a reciprocity in sharing what we produce and receiving appreciation for it. This was realized early in our history when the Orchestra was first heard on the NBC radio network, over local KGW, in April 1931. Later network broadcasts have been described above. My own first nationwide program went out over NBC in 1956. The Voice of America has broadcast our concerts overseas many times, beginning in 1960 with the Symphony No. 3 by Carl Nielsen.

Our television debut came shortly after my appointment, in 1955, when KPTV did a concert preview, bringing the whole Orchestra into the studio. Since then every local station has done public service programs of one sort or another with us.

In November 1972 the Corporation for Public Broadcasting made plans to film a show live at a concert, with segments taken at rehearsal together with interviews with players and Conductor. Despite the discomfort of the bright lights, both the Orchestra and the audience survived, and a good program was put together. It was first shown on the network in March 1974, and 12 more times during the next two seasons. Letters again came in from all over the country. When the prospect of a documentary on Ernest Bloch appeared two years later, we were already geared up to do our part.

COMMISSIONS AND RECORDINGS*

Enterprising performers are interested in having new music to present. Soloists can always write music for themselves—as countless of them have done over the centuries—from Bach to Mozart to Liszt and Rachmaninov, as well as the pop-rock folk, who are like medieval minstrels born again. Orchestras, however, can hardly create their own new music.

Within the past century, as the great orchestras of the world became firmly established, they have besought the noted composers of their day to write works for them. There is always a certain glamor that comes with having a work especially created for us. There are good reasons for this: one is the obvious public notice; then there is the direct contact with the creative mind and personality, particularly if the composer comes to town for the rehearsals and premiere; and there is the elation of having brought a work into being which might take its place in the world repertoire and redound to the credit of the patron.

In any case, commissioning presupposes an interest in contemporary music. Such an interest was evident early in the PJS/PYP programs that presented new works with some frequency. In 1955 the American Composers Alliance invited the orchestra to present a program of new works. In the course of selecting the music it became clear that a good deal of contemporary music is too difficult for students to play well. This was regrettable since young musicians, having fewer (or different) prejudices than their elders, are potentially the best advocates of new music. Although contemporary composers, from time to time, have written works which are technically easier to play, it seemed to me worthwhile to stimulate them to produce such works, rather than to leave it to chance.

That same year we submitted a proposal to the Rockefeller Foundation to help provide an incentive for composers of stature to write works which were within the reach of student players. These were not to be children's pieces, but music as serious, exalted, or whimsical as the composer wished; the only limitation being that the facility required of the individual player be less than professional.

The proposal was approved, and we received a grant of $10,000 to commission six works over a period of three years. All were published and five of them were recorded by the PYP for Composer's Recordings, Inc. (CRI) of New York. The records are still in print and are sold worldwide.

BLOCH AND THE BICENTENNIAL*

With the approach of 1976, for all of us who were ready to wave our Bicentennial banners and review the nation's achievements, it was clearly a time to honor Ernest Bloch, giant among 20th-century composers. Oregonians especially could rejoice as he wrote some of his most substantial works while living among

Filming for National Educational Television.

us. With the hearty endorsement of our Board, a calendar of events was designed that was ambitious for any organization, but especially for a youth orchestra.

Among them was a nationwide competition to select a young soloist for Bloch's *Symphony for Trombone and Orchestra.* As judges, we invited the first-chair trombone players of the Boston, Los Angeles, and San Francisco orchestras. Tapes were received from many quarters and listened to anonymously by our Music Committee and the guest judges. Howard Prince, a senior at Juilliard School of Music, was chosen winner; our own principal, Randall Malmstrom, was runner-up.

The Bloch festival called for some daring, too: on February 27, at the dress rehearsal for the concert, in which we performed both the *Suite Symphonique* and the *Symphony for Trombone,* we made an audio recording (again for CRI) while simultaneously filming the concert for television.

Our Association took special pleasure in coordinating that tribute to Bloch. He had often expressed his enthusiasm for the Orchestra, and we felt privileged to show our respect for him in this way.

SECOND INTERNATIONAL TOUR, JAPAN, 1979

Following the publication of *Music Is Where You Make It/II* in 1979, the 56th Season began with a bang. We had been dreaming of a second trip abroad ever since the joyous 1970 European Tour which had made us many friends and admirers and was such a wonderful experience for the players.

Situated as we are on the West Coast, it was only natural for us to contemplate the Orient. During a visit to Japan in 1978 en route to China for the first time in 40 years, I met and instantly became friends with Setsuo Tsukahara, the gifted composer and conductor of the Tokyo Junior Philharmonic. He invited me to bring our Orchestra to join them in their National Music Camp during the summer of 1979. Sadly, his untimely death deflected those plans.

Our Board and Orchestra, however, were in the grip of tour-fever, and word was spreading around the City that we were hoping to travel again. At the same time City Hall was thinking about the 20th Anniversary of the sister-city relationship with Sapporo, Japan, and of ways to celebrate it. When the Japanese side suggested we send our Orchestra, the Tour was triggered. Our then mayor, now Governor Neil Goldschmidt, raised funds sufficient for half the airfare to Japan for 100 players; the students' families promptly agreed to provide, or earn, the matching half, which was $350 per student. The City of Sapporo offered, insisted, on providing lodging for the Orchestra members, and our Board proceeded energetically to raise the remaining funds necessary for the trip.

Central to my aims was the musical contact between our young musicians and those in the host cities. We had successfully joined hands with others in

Europe in 1970 so I spared no effort to achieve this again. We wanted to do a substantial work with several Japanese university choruses; to have our chamber groups visit schools for musical encounters; and to offer a Children's Concert. I was also determined to have a joint performance with Tsukahara's orchestra in Tokyo and to play some of his music in his memory.

To cap it all, we were able to interest NHK, the prestigious Japan National Broadcasting Corporation, in televising the main anniversary concert.

With these aims in view our Board and Staff went into a frenzy of preparations, including many transpacific phone calls. As usual, to our national chagrin, we had to rely on the ability of the Japanese to speak English.

We were cheered by the willingness of three notables to be our Honorary Sponsors—Seiji Ozawa, Conductor of the Boston Symphony; Mike Mansfield, then our Ambassador to Japan; and Neil Goldschmidt.

On November 3rd we enplaned with an entourage of 134, which included the Orchestra of 102, adult escorts, staff, and a small fan club. November was certainly not the most convenient period for our students to be away from their studies, but the Tour had been set to coincide with an Oregon trade mission that was going to Sapporo for the Sister-City Anniversary.

Upon our arrival we were met at the airport by three Misses Sapporo and the media. Our first taste of Sapporo hospitality was a fabulous lunch given in a country lodge at Lake Chitose. The entire group was accommodated in one large room with floor-to-ceiling windows facing the lake. Seated on cushions on the floor, we were treated to steaming cauldrons of a delicious, hearty salmon soup, cooked before us, with hosts from the City and the Department of Education helping with chopsticks and explaining the mysteries of ripe persimmons.

After lunch we were taken to City Hall for the homestay assignments. The host families were seated at the back of the room while we took our seats down front. After speeches of greeting and welcome, the names of our players and their host families were read off, bows exchanged, and off they went. Our plans made in Portland had been meticulous and had included a family profile of each student, lectures on Japanese culture, food, and bathing routine, and a survival vocabulary. We had also planned to phone every student at his or her "home" that evening to make sure no one was forlorn. Far from it—all were happy.

The musical schedule included six concerts during the 11-day trip, plus school visits and rehearsals. We began with a Children's Concert in Sapporo for an audience of 1,600 grade schoolers, which was carried on Hokkaido Broadcasting Corporation (HBC) television. The program opened with a welcoming performance by the HBC Junior Orchestra while our offerings included the *Story of Babar the Little Elephant* (Poulenc) with a Japanese narrator. Be sure, I had taken the precaution of asking for a tape of the narration ahead of time!

On the second day a runout had been arranged to the neighboring town of Ebetsu, sister-city to our neighbor Gresham, with a visit en route to the Sapporo

Centennial Museum and another festive lunch at Asahi Beer Garden. Ebetsu has a new hall (1,400) in which we were the first performers from abroad. Our major work was the Respighi *Roman Festivals* for which we used Japanese trumpeters on the external *buccine* parts. This was their first time with us. Our section very much enjoyed rehearsing with them, and they did well. It was also the first performance of Tsukahara's music—two movements of his First Symphony. But what brought tears to the eyes of the audience were the Japanese folk songs given as encores by one of our leading artists, Alyce Rogers, who had come with us as an escort and who had two children in the Orchestra. Finally the "Stars and Stripes Forever" had the audience clapping in rhythm.

Preceded by the Mayor's greetings and followed by another of those fabulous receptions, it was an evening to be remembered. The performances were splendid and the Japanese chorus members were as convivial after the concert as they had been reticent at the rehearsals.

The musical experiences were gratifying, but I think it no exaggeration to say that for our students the warmth of the homestays were at least as moving. Genuine bonds of affection developed in those few days, and at parting, in the lobby of City Hall, many tears were shed and promises to write and visit were made. After five days in Sapporo we moved on to Tokyo. The Secretary General of the Tokyo Junior Philharmonic, Michiko Kobayashi, was able to get the very handsome Memorial Hall at Gakushuin University, where the Emperor and his family had studied. It was there that we were able to join two halves of our orchestras in playing Tsukahara's music. The composer's widow had come up to Sapporo for that concert; now in Tokyo she had been most helpful with the arrangements, and on both occasions was touched by our tribute.

The U.S. Embassy, at the instance of our Ambassador, had arranged a Serenade Reception for an invited audience of musicians and educators. We presented a program of chamber music. Earlier in the day we had made a pilgrimage to the historic shrine city of Kamakura, where the gigantic statue of Buddha awed us all.

Some of our group opted for a different kind of pilgrimage: a visit to the Suzuki Institute at Matsumoto. Led by an alumna escort who was a public school music teacher, about a dozen of our players visited a teacher-training session, attended an afternoon recital by pupils of various ages, and, as luck would have it, the Master, Suzuki himself, generously spent three hours with them. They came away inspired and laden with brochures and tapes of the Institute's working methods.

Our way was smoothed all along the way by a Japanese student, Hiroko Fukabori, who had spent a year in Portland in 1975, spoke excellent English, and played in our Orchestra that season, which she rejoined for the Tour. For free-time sightseeing we enlisted a number of English-speaking students, friends of another former member, Carolyn Wasser, who were training as interpreters.

A visit to the Great Buddha at Kamaura, Jappan Tour, 1979.

One of the most interesting visits was to the labyrinthine studios of NHK. Our students were enormously impressed by the extent and complexity of the facilities, all the more because they knew that their program would be going out on those very airways in a month.

The final concert was given in Iruma-shi, a suburb of Tokyo. Only 25 miles away, it took over two hours by bus to get there, so congested was the traffic. The joint sponsors of that event were the local Junior Chamber of Commerce and Esso Standard Oil. This concert was led by the Assistant Conductor for the Tour, my son David, who was also in charge of logistics. It was one of the most exciting performances of all, the Orchestra having by then been well played in, and they responded with enthusiasm to a fresh baton.

In a letter from Miss Kobayashi, received after our return home, she said, "We were very glad to be able to have your Orchestra in our country. Your splendid performances gave great pleasure to us, the Tokyo Junior Philharmonic, and to all the people who heard you....Your success in Japan gave me great courage and hope."

Japan Tour, 1979.

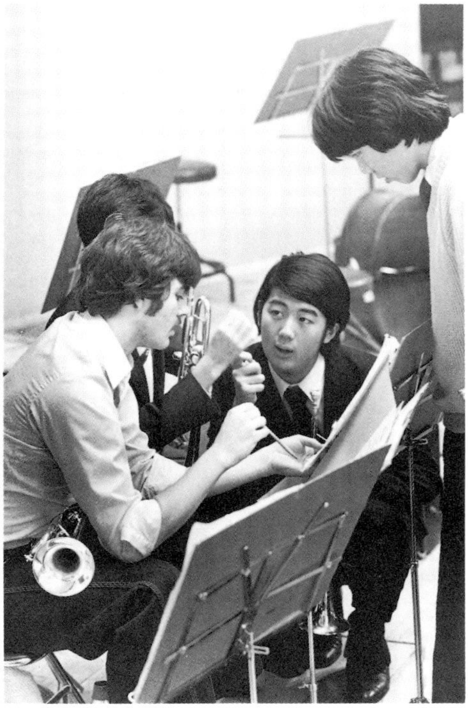

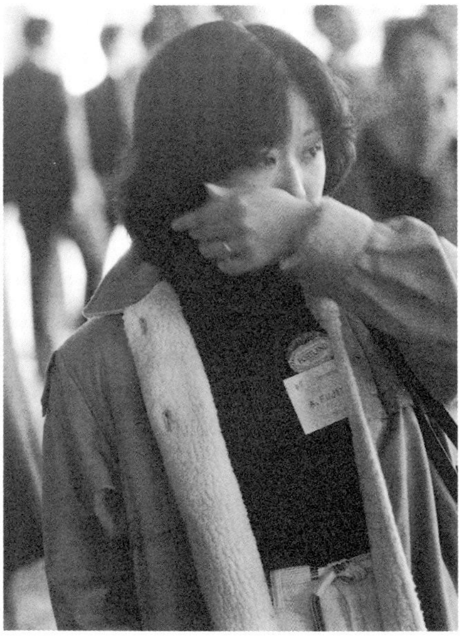

The Tour was documented by Hank Kranzler, who took hundreds of photos, many of which were shown at our gala homecoming concert. Giving the whole undertaking a special feeling of glamour was a television crew of three from Portland's Channel 8, KGW. This friendly, dedicated, and thoroughly professional team recorded the trip from many angles, the human, cultural, and historic, as well as the musical. Upon their return home they produced two hour-long programs from the footage they had taped with the cordial help of Japanese television studios.

A Tour such as this obviously depends on a great many more people for its success than just the performers. At the center of our efforts were a most dedicated and resourceful Board of Directors and Staff, led by President Elise Rosenfeld, Tour Manager Robert Knoll, and Orchestra Committee Chairman Ernestine Oringdulph. Assistance from the City of Portland was not only financial but also facilitative; throughout the community, many friends helped with goods, services, time, and affection. It was all done with the conviction that good relations between different peoples of the world are developed by meaningful exchanges in the realm of the spirit. Our young people were both the bearers and the beneficiaries of the goodwill generated by us all.

56th SEASON, 1979–80

Upon our return home from Japan, the November Concert included my report on the Tour, given from the podium—much like the one you have just read.

The Christmas Concert brought Willa Dorsey, the well-known gospel singer, to our stage. An unusual ceremony took place at that event: the presentation of a new viola to the Orchestra. It was the gift of Sidney Ray Stukelman, a custodial worker in the schools, and an ardent fan of the PYP. He commissioned it from Mark Moreland, an alumnus of the Orchestra who trained with, and was working for, violin master Paul Schubach. Stukelman knew that we liked to have a few violas on hand to lend to students daring enough to switch from violin to viola; buying a second instrument was a deterrent to many of them, but having our loaner eased the way.

COMMUNITY RELATIONS*

A cultural organization does not establish good relations with its community merely by publicity. Good community relations are developed, over a long period, by dedication to high ideals and high standards manifested in programs which benefit the citizenry. A good press, of course, is helpful, and the

Orchestra has enjoyed this since its beginnings. Notices of coming events have been regularly published, concerts reviewed enthusiastically—as this book attests. News of auditions, anecdotes of human interest, the needs of the fund drive—everything that makes an institution tick has been supported by the papers, their reporters, photographers, columnists, and editors. All told, we have been well handled.

Until recently, that is. Within the past decade the trend in the press has shifted its attention away from the more serious levels of art—despite great public attendance and interest in cultural events. The amount of press space given to preconcert notices has shrunk dramatically. The reason offered is that papers focus on what the public is interested in reading. The PYP is learning to live with this situation and to compensate for it through the use of more direct mail and the placing of articles about our work in the house organs of business and professional organizations.

We also use radio for spot announcements of auditions, concerts, and special events, many written by Board volunteers. Preconcert broadcasts of our program items serve to familiarize the public with the music; postconcert airings show how the Orchestra has acquitted itself.

Our relations with Local 99 of the American Federation of Musicians have always been excellent. This is partly due to the enlightened attitude of our union officials. But just as important has been the Association's belief that the function of our Orchestra is primarily educational; and we have always been careful not to perform any service that would properly be the employment of professional musicians.

Relations between youth orchestras and schools and colleges in their vicinity can, at their best, be mutually beneficial; at their worst, thorny. During our history of 65 years we have run the gamut. When there are collisions of dates the students are often caught in the bind of conflicting obligations. As a general rule I feel that one group's performance takes precedence over another's rehearsal, and I excuse students on that basis, provided they ask for permission in advance, so that I can adjust my rehearsal order when necessary.

During my years as Conductor I have held to this policy. But the irreconcilable cases—dress rehearsals head to head, or concert versus concert—do occur and upset school directors if the students opt for the PYP despite peril to their grades.

The private instrumental teachers have almost unanimously been supportive of our program. They help prepare students for auditions and for solo appearances, and realize that, save for the rare potential virtuoso, most of their pupils will become yeomen in the service of music, whose greatest fulfillment will be as a member of some group, large or small.

The State and local governments have always been proud of the Orchestra, and from its earliest years mayors and governors have been glad to issue proclamations honoring the young musicians at appropriate times. Financial support from City and State, however, has only begun to come in the past few years—since they formed their own arts agencies. The Association has been generously dealt with by the Metropolitan Arts Commission and modestly by the Oregon Art Commission.

ALUMNI*

Of the 4,000 and more young people who have passed through the ranks of the PJS/PYP and the Prep Orchestra since 1924, all but the 200 on the roster of any current year *are* alumni.

Enough of our players have gone on to the Oregon Symphony to have filled it more than once. In any given year they comprise about one-third of that orchestra's roster. But this is not always the next step for our alumni. Many of them have gone on to study at professional schools, such as the New England Conservatory, the Eastman School of Music, the Peabody Conservatory, the Curtis Institute of Music, and others. Many of them have made a fine career in music; more are on their way.

However, they are only a minority of our former members. The majority will excel in various walks of life. Excel, because we know the able ones are apt to be gifted in many ways, and the habit of serious endeavor fostered by the PYP extends to their work in other fields. From our rosters have come philosophers and rabbis, doctors and scientists, composers, artists, poets and folk-singers, mathematicians, fencing champions, and beauty queens. Whatever their life work may be, these devotees of music will have acquired training and insights into the structure and performance of music which are first-hand and penetrating. They know that an evening at pops is not an evening with Bach. Their intimacy with the master works provides them with a touchstone for the assessment of new works as well as a gauge for the performance of professionals. In all the fuss and fad of hi-fi or sci-fi, quadri-phonic or hydro-ponic, they will be among those who can judge how high fidelity is, and to what it is faithful.

The main purpose of a youth orchestra is not to produce professional musicians—although one of our alums said, "Everything I needed to know to become a member of the Boston Symphony I learned in this room [Holladay School]." The purpose is to inspire young people to function like *artists* even while they are amateurs. The continuance of our musical culture may well depend on such enlightened, practicing citizens.

Opposite. Set of timpani, gift from PYP Women's Committee.

PROPERTIES*

A building of our own is not among our properties. Some of us have taken pride in being "a school without walls," almost. We have worked in borrowed premises ever since the day we started. But we have acquired many of the necessities. The repertory list in *Music Is Where You Make It/II* shows the music we own. The collection has come from various sources: Jacques Gershkovitch brought a number of full sets of score and parts from Russia—how he got them here is a marvel. We have had a budget for the purchase of music for over 50 years; local music stores have often made us gifts; the John Sails Higgins Memorial Library was established in 1958.

A student librarian keeps the Orchestra furnished. This is tricky because, unlike professional orchestras, we insist that the players take their parts home to practice. There is some loss and a lot of wear and tear on the material, but that is what it's there for.

The Association owns a number of instruments, some received as gifts. In the early days instruments of all kinds were offered to us and accepted—to loan to the students who lacked one. As the decades rolled by, virtually all the students

who came to us had an instrument, so in recent years we have limited our holdings to those items which a student would not be apt to own: bass clarinet, English-horn, contra-bassoon, or those difficult to transport—string bass, harp, large percussion.

We received a fine set of timpani from the Women's Committee on the occasion of our 50th Anniversary. We have a kitchen full of percussion. Half a dozen violas are kept on hand to encourage the "converts" from the violin.

The Archives include tape recordings of virtually all concerts given since 1954 and a few before that.

THE PORTLAND YOUTH PHILHARMONIC ORCHESTRA ASSOCIATION*

From the beginning, the Association has been blessed with many dedicated Directors, and its Board was long known as one of the happiest and most effective in Oregon. Among those who have served are doctors, lawyers, bankers, musicians, merchants, architects, printers, professors, public-relations and real estate men, ship builders, housewives and househusbands—many of them civic leaders. Their range of professional ability is wide, and their combined store of enlightened goodwill prodigious. Both Conductors have found it an inspiration to work with these wonderful people and to have their guidance and energetic support.

The Board has performed many of the functions which, in a larger organization, would be handled by a business manager. In recent years, paid staff has consisted of a Manager of Support Services, the matchless Janet Fry, a secretarial assistant, plus a part-time bookkeeper and other help as needed at peak times.

The Board is made up of 40 Directors, most of whom are elected for a three-year term, on a staggered basis, with a limit of two consecutive terms. After a year off many have returned for additional terms, one for the astonishing total of 26 years.

All Directors are expected to help with the fund-raising efforts of the Association. They serve on two or more of the twenty committees, each of which reports to one of the three Vice-Presidents.

Every aspect of the Orchestra's educational and artistic program is planned by the Conductor in collaboration with the committee named to its supervision—Music, Scholarship, Orchestra, Public Relations. The committees for developing the support of the Association work with the head of Staff who, with her assistants, carries out the myriad duties of running the Office and coordinating all efforts.

Volunteer help is welcome in most arts institutions. It takes good leadership to use it to advantage. We have been fortunate in this regard. It would be hard to describe the affectionate care with which the good people on the Board consider every aspect of the Orchestra's activities; and it is heartwarming to see how consistently the welfare of our students is kept as the central concern.

Board members visiting a rehearsal include four past Music Committee Chairmen.

Programs & Reviews

30th Through 56th Season

30th Anniversary Season

Guest Conductors

November 21, 1953

Eugene Fuerst, Guest Conductor

Komm, Susser Tod	BACH
In Memory of Dr. Jacques Gershkovitch	
Symphony NO. 38, D major, K. 504	MOZART
Symphonic Variations for Piano & Orchestra	FRANCK
James Bastien, *Soloist*	
"Lieutenant Kije" Suite	PROKOFIEFF
Overture, "Flying Dutchman"	WAGNER

February 27, 1954

Thirtieth Anniversary Concert

Jacob Avshalomov, Conductor

Overture, "Marriage of Figaro"	MOZART
Violin Concerto, D major, OP. 61	BEETHOVEN
Robert Mann, *Soloist*	
Fanfare to "La Peri"	DUKAS
Symphony NO. 8, B minor	SCHUBERT
The Taking of T'ung Kuan	*J. AVSHALOMOV

April 24, 1954

Eugene Linden, Conductor

Overture, "Iphigenia in Aulis"	GLUCK
Wind Serenade NO. 10, Bb	MOZART
Nocturnes 1 & 2	DEBUSSY
Fantasy on a Theme of Tallis	VAUGHN-WILLIAMS
Firebird Suite	STRAVINSKY

* *Portland Premiere*

Concert by Junior Symphony Tribute To Memory of Jacques Gershkovitch

BY HILMAR GRONDAHL
Music Editor, The Oregonian

The memory of the late Dr. Jacques Gershkovitch who directed the destinies of the Portland Junior Symphony orchestra throughout 29 years was very much in evidence at the first concert of this unique organization's 13th season at the public auditorium Saturday night.

The program opened with a performance of Sebastian Bach's chorale, "Komm, Susser Tod" as a memorial offering. And during intermission a long-play record was releasing its music to patrons in the corridors; a record on which four performance numbers and a rehearsal session under Gershkovitch was being demonstrated for those interested in contributing through its purchase to the Gershkovitch Memorial Scholarship fund.

But the immediate business of demonstration the continuing force of this musical enterprise for young performers was very much in the keeping of Eugene Fuerst who was guest conducting this concert.

It was an amazing concert during the first half for two special reasons; a beautifully integrated and nicely styled playing of Mozart's "Prague" symphony, and a stunning collaboration between Pianist James Bastien and the orchestra in Cesar Franck's symphonic variations.

So all the players who could be accommodated played, and played so much in the way their conductor wished that they produced a very remarkable performance of Mozart's famous symphony without a minuet. There was a pretty clear revelation of detail, excellent style, and an admirable balance. The concluding rondo contained some of the neatest playing this young group has done.

James Bastien turned out to be a lad of musical depth with an evident affinity for the keyboard. There was feeling, a secure and fluent technic and a good idea of how the music ought to sound. The orchestra was with him, and he with it in virtually every important instant, and the conversation between solo instrument and ensemble was precise and expressive.

We heard the opening sections of Prokofieff's "Lt. Kije" suite after intermission, and that was going on at a perky pace with some bright playing by the solo trumpet, woodwinds, and even a spate of celesta.

THE OREGONIAN MAR. 1, 1954

Juniors Note 30th Birthday

BY HILMAR GRONDAHL
Music Editor, The Oregonian

The experience of being in on the Portland Junior Symphony orchestra's 30th birthday celebration at the public auditorium Saturday night was one which few present are likely to forget. There was a spirit of festivity about the event as exemplified by the large cut-out letters over the proscenium which read:

HAPPY BIRTHDAY TO US

But there was, through and beyond this spirit of celebration, the deeper and more sobering sense of achievement; of history made and goals won. This latter spirit was exemplified by the presence and performance of two of the organization's distinguished alumni, Jacob Avshalomov, who conducted, and Robert Mann, who was solo violinist in the Beethoven concerto.

Two Attain Fame

It was a touching site, to find these two young men on the stage, musicians who have gone on to make names for themselves out of the talents which this orchestral institution helped to nourish; Avshalomov to become known and honored in the triple fields of composing, conducting and teaching; Mann to organize one of the foremost string quartets, to teach at one of the finest schools of music, and be a solo performer. Only 16 years ago Mann was concertmaster of the orchestra before which he stood and played Saturday night.

But this joint appearance was more than a heart-warming sight. It was musically rewarding, and a glowing testimonial to the purposes and accomplishments of the Portland Junior Symphony orchestra under its late conductor, Jacques Gershkovitch.

We are wondering if the junior musicians ever played so well together as they did Saturday night.

The players were carefully guided, for Avshalomov is both an intelligent musician and an informed conductor. But they are neither driven nor coerced, and the resulting participation appears to be their eagerly given best.

Brass Salute Notable

Of what we heard the most satisfying ensemble musicianship came in the Dukas fanfare for brass, which served as a salute to the 30th anniversary, the Schubert C-minor symphony and the second movement of the Beethoven concerto.

It was this last named section which showed "Bobby" Mann as practically a spell-binder of a string beauty. His tone had sounded small in the opening statement of the allegro, but as the music moved on his command of it grew, and in the lovely andante his tone was as romantic as Beethoven's idea. He is a richly endowed musician, fully matured, and the evident master of every technical need.

He demonstrated by providing his own cadenzas that he is a violinist in the creative tradition. These were not ordinary exercises, he made but brilliant and imaginative use of thematic materials from the score. It sounds to us as though he had made a genuine contribution to future performers of this concerto.

OREGON JOURNAL FEB. 28, 1954

Youngsters In Gala

Junior Symphony Has Anniversary

By FREDERIC ROTHCHILD
Journal Music Editor

What a tremendous thing is the talent of young people, and what a rare thing is its use, encouragement and guidance by competent and dedicated older people.

For 30 years Portland has had one place, at least, where young people were encouraged to make the most rather than the least of their talents. The Junior Symphony is one of perhaps a half dozen institutions which have set and maintained the cultural strength and tone of this community.

AT AN anniversary concert at The Auditorium on Saturday night these 30 years of accomplishment were celebrated by what may be the 20th or 21st or 22d group of a hundred youngsters who have succeeded one another as the Portland Junior Symphony orchestra.

That Dr. Jacques Gershkovitch could not have lived for the occasion is a cause for sorrow. That the orchestra lives on without him, and that it will live on, is a cause for joy, for us as it would be for him.

Jacob Avshalomov conducted the concert on Saturday. He is an alumnus of the orchestra, and he is a composer of talent and a conductor of skill and vitality. He led the players in a brilliantly orchestrated and vigorously conceived work of his own, "The Taking of T'ung Kuan," which, because of a deadline, I missed, a Dukas fanfare for brass and the Schubert "Unfinished," but I did hear a performance of the Mozart "Marriage of Figaro" overture which was remarkable for its fleetness and clarity.

THE PRECISION of the Juniors as Mr. Avshalomov has trained them and led them was impressive. He achieved a group understanding on the players' part which resulted in performances both musical and convincing.

The soloist, Robert Mann, is another alumnus of the orchestra. He flew from New York for this one concert. As the founder and first violin of the Julliard Quartet he is known to concert audiences and record collectors everywhere. As one of the most serious and penetrating soloists on his instrument he is known much less, because he plays very few solos.

IT WAS an act of graciousness and a recognition of what the Junior Symphony has meant in his life for his to travel so far to play. His performance of the Beethoven concerto and of the really monumental cadenzas which he has composed for it was a moving experience and a demonstration that he is one of the most musical of all violinists.

During the intermission of the concert there was a kind of auction in which the person contributing the most to the orchestra received a baton presented for this purpose by Arturo Toscanini.

Thirtieth Anniversary

CONCERT

Jacob Avshalomov, *Guest Conductor*

Robert Mann, *Guest Artist*

MUNICIPAL AUDITORIUM

Saturday, February 27, 1954

OREGON JOURNAL APR. 25, 1954

Juniors End 30th Year

By FREDERICK ROTHCHILD
Journal Music Editor

The Portland Junior Symphony orchestra ended its 30th year Saturday evening at The Auditorium. Eugene Linden, director of the Northwest Grand opera and an alumnus of the orchestra, was the conductor.

The program included a Gluck overture, a Mozart serenade for winds, two Debussy nocturnes and the Vaughan Williams "Fantasia." I heard these works, but was obliged to miss the Stravinsky "Firebird" suite, which concluded the evening.

It is unquestionably difficult to choose music for these programs. A just balance between the facility of the players, the amount to be gained in improvement of that facility, the interest to the listeners and the setting off of the elan which young people possess is not easy to achieve.

I BELIEVE that the works played Saturday were not an entirely happy choice. The Mozart is of great value pedagogically, but too difficult to have been played with the point and style which it needs. The Gluck, Debussy and Williams are all sophisticated music, needing the kind of maturity which is a special quality of adults.

There was, these limitations aside, excellent playing and a demonstration of solid training. Several players, among them the concert master, Walter Maddox, and the first oboe, Joan Baker, played remarkably beautiful solo passages.

My quibbles, if they are that, do not imply any but a high regard for this wonderful organization and for Mr. Linden. They both have my respect. I hope they will accept that—and also, critics being fond of having their own way, a little bit of my counsel.

Oregon Journal — MAY 17, 1954

His Talents Will Enrich Our City

The Junior Symphony seems to be well on its way to another 30 years of fine music-making with the appointment of Jacob Avshalomov as conductor of the orchestra.

Avshalomov (former Reed college student and member of the Junior Symphony association) will bring enthusiasm and great gifts to our nationally known junior orchestra. When he guest-conducted the orchestra's 30th anniversary concert in February, he displayed his talent to lead and inspire young people, and to conduct great music with a sure and spirited touch.

In addition to conducting, he is a teacher and a composer of great merit. He has been on the faculty of Columbia university for six years, and during the last year he was chosen as one of the exceptional younger faculty members by the bicentennial office. His composition won him this year one of the highest tributes given composers: An award by the New York Music Critics circle.

The Junior Symphony association is to be congratulated on its new conductor, and the city of Portland is also to be congratulated, for Avshalomov's talents are sure to enrich our entire cultural life.

THE OREGONIAN — MAY 16, 1954

Back Home

For nearly 30 years, until his death in August of last year, Jacques Gershkovitch was the conductor of the Portland Symphony orchestra, the remarkably successful organization of which he was the founder. It is a tribute to Mr. Gershkovitch that one of his proteges, a former member of the orchestra, Jacob Avshalomov, has been recalled to Portland as junior symphony conductor.

Mr. Avshalomov need not depend on reflected glory. Since the late 1930s, when he lived with Mr. Gershkovitch and played in the orchestra, he has fashioned a solid reputation of his own in music. He received the Alice M. Ditson and Guggenheim awards for composition, and earlier this year was announced as one of three winners of the top awards of the Music Critics Circle of New York. The critics honored him for his 1953 composition, "Tom O'Bedlam," a choral work.

But, quite apart from his talent, Mr. Avshalomov is a young man with enthusiasm for civic responsibility and a variety of cultural interests. We join his many friends in welcoming him back to Portland.

May 8, 195
Portland, Or

Dear Mr. Avshalomov,
On behalf of the entire Junio
Symphony, I wish to welcome you
our new conductor, back again for
our coming season. We all look
forward to seeing you very muc
You can't imagine how excited
we were last Wednesday night w
Marilynn's father told us that y
were to be our new conductor.
I guess the impossible things stil
happen!

Your concertmaster
Walter Maddo

31st Season

Jacob Avshalomov, Musical Director

	November 13, 1954
Berlioz	Corsair Overture, op. 21
Schumann	Piano Concerto, A minor, op. 54 Diane De Mott, *Soloist*
Haydn	Symphony No. 92, Oxford
Monteverdi	Music for Brass
Dukas	Fanfare to "La Peri"
Weinberger	Polka & Fugue, "Schwanda"

	February 19, 1955
Beethoven	Egmont Overture, op. 24
Handel/Beecham	"The Great Elopement" Suite
Saint-Saens	Violin Concerto No. 3, op. 61 Marilynn Nudelman, *Soloist*
Offenbach	Waltz from "La Belle Helene"
Moussorgsky/ Ravel	Pictures at an Exhibition

	April 23, 1955
Brahms	Serenade in D, op. 11
Delius	On Hearing the First Cuckoo in Spring
Toch	*Circus Overture
Mozart	Requiem, K. 626 in D minor

Bonnie Newberg, *Soprano*; Marybelle Bunnett, *Alto*
Dean Lieber, *Tenor;* Andre Kurmins, *Bass*
Guest Choirs: Portland High Schools, Lewis & Clark College, Portland State, Reed College & University of Portland

* *Portland Premiere*

THE OREGONIAN NOV. 14, 1954

Guest Soloist Wins Acclaim

Junior Symphony Also Applauded

By HILMAR GRONDAHL
Music Editor, The Oregonian

The Portland Junior Symphony orchestra concert at the public auditorium Saturday night, which featured Jacob Avshalomov as the new permanent conductor and Diane de Mott as guest artist, was a stimulating occasion in more ways than one.

It is really stimulating to an auditor who is aware of the complexities involved in performing a score such as the Schumann piano concerto, to find that work being made pleasurably clear and tangible. While it is too difficult in its orchestral relationships to yield wholly to the attentions available for a junior first concert there were things about its reading Saturday night that were above and beyond the educational aims of the society.

Confidence Abets Skill

The focal point of interest, by the nature of the piece and its performance was, of course, the young pianist Diane de Mott.

She was one of the most self-possessed young artists we have had the pleasure of hearing. She behaved like a true veteran, and in addition imbued her own playing with a spirit that was admirably romantic. Her fingerwork was cleanly articulated, her phrasing was delightfully expressive; in fact, her entire concept was the product of sensitive and informed musicianship.

The concert's curtain raiser was one of the rousing overtures by that master of brilliant scores, Hector Berlioz. This was "The Corsair," which in its course showed off the orchestra's remarkable staff of brass players.

Demands of Discipline Met

But if the Berlioz gave some hint of a freewheeling discipline where precision was effective in a brilliant way, the score of Haydn's "Oxford" symphony showed how well the new conductor can achieve that tight precision that brings polish and expressive verities to a score in which disciplines are rigidly prescribed.

The opening adagio was a perfectly handsome unfoldment, an artistic preparation for the bounding allegro that followed. And the second movement was one of those difficult projects, of carrying melody of great breadth and fragile beauty in such a secure way that no hint of wavering or weakness results. It is hard to achieve, but delightful if and when achieved. The Juniors did it, and it was lovely. Bravo!

OREGON JOURNAL NOV. 14, 1954

Concert Success

Juniors Opener

By FREDERIC ROTHCHILD
Journal Music Editor

We have wonderful kids in these parts. No doubt of it—

This is the opening Junior Symphony concert of the season I'm talking about—the first with Jacob Avshalomov as permanent conductor. It was at the Auditorium on Saturday evening, and it starred Diane De Mott as soloist in the Schumann piano concerto.

TO SEE and hear a young lady who combines the poise and confidence of an old hand at the concert business with the freshness and charm of the pretty 17-year-old which she is, gave me, as it must have given everyone there, a good deal of pleasure. Her performance was solid and musical, and the orchestra accompanied her well.

The program which Mr. Avshalomov conducted began with the Berlioz "Corsair" overture, played because this is the 150th anniversary of the composer's birth. It's a difficult work, and it was played clearly and vigorously.

After the intermission the kids—who deserve to be called artists, this time—played the Haydn "Oxford" symphony. It was so good, so right, so live, so musical, that it was a real struggle to have to leave the hall before the program was finished. However, this Saturday deadline didn't prevent my hearing the Haydn, and for that I'm really grateful.

Oregon Journal FEB. 20, 1955

Violinist Found Tops

Junior Symphony Plays Saturday

A performance by a young person can show many things, or the lack of them. The most important are: musicality, or a natural aptitude for music; musicianship, or a mastery of the traditions and craft of music; intelligence, poise, temperament, technical accomplishment, and the hard work necessary to put all these into effect.

That paragraph is a background for telling you that on Saturday night at the Auditorium I heard Marilynn Nudelmann as soloist with Portland Junior Symphony in their second concert of the season. Jacob Avshalomov conducted, and Miss Nudelmann played the Saint-Saens third violin concerto.

THE YOUNG violinist, to refer to the long list above, has, in good share, each of the qualities and accomplishments mentioned. I've seldom heard a more professional job done by a young person.

Her accompaniment was expertly played by her colleagues—she is principle second violin of the orchestra. Since her tone, while of extraordinary sweetness and purity, is not large, this accompaniment was the more difficult and the more commendable.

THE BEETHOVEN "Egmont" overture and an Offenbach waltz were both satisfactory.

I could hear only the first five parts of the Moussorgsky-Ravel "Pictures." Whether some good purpose is served by having the orchestra play music so much too difficult for it is open to question.

Joan Baker, the first oboe, gave an altogether remarkable performance throughout the evening, on both oboe and English horn. She is a real artist in the making.—**F. R.**

THE OREGONIAN FEB. 20, 1955

Concert Rich With Variety

By **HILMAR GRONDAHL**
Music Editor, The Oregonian

A program of attractive balance and variety was offered by Jacob Avshalomov and the Portland Junior Symphony orchestra Saturday night in the public auditorium. It included such seldom heard scores as the Handel-Beecham "Great Elopement," the Third violin concerto of Saint-Saens (with Marilynn Nudelman as soloist) and such durable favorites as Beethoven's "Egmont" overture and the Ravel orchestration of Moussorgsky's "Pictures at an Exhibition."

It was abundantly observable in these compositions, as well as the pretty piece of fluff from Offenbach's "La Belle Helene," that the members of the orchestra are advancing their proficiencies at an accelerated rate. There is in brief, a refinement of performance developing that speaks well for teachability of the players and the conductorial teaching of Mr. Avshalomov.

Mature Task Assigned to Girl

As to the Saint-Saens concerto it was the case of sending a girl violinist to do the work of a burly gypsy fiddler. We would hesitate a long while before making a debut, even with an amateur orchestra, in a Saint-Saens concerto; especially the Third in B-minor.

Vote of Thanks Bestowed

Miss Nudelman was an alert and resourceful protagonist of this difficult part. She played cleanly and with a good, if modified, concept of what the music should convey. For a while in the finale she came close to the size of tone this music requires. But if she did not accomplish what she hoped to, interpretively, she deserves a vote of thanks (and gets ours) for bringing her part of the production near enough to the composer's notations to suggest the full effectiveness of the original.

We could stay for only one movement of the Moussorgsky suite, but in that little bit we heard some excellent work by the brasses, and the fine feeling of space which the conductor was assigning to the composition as a whole.

THE OREGONIAN APR. 24, 1955

Junior Symphony Concert Gives Variety in Concert

By **HILMAR GRONDAHL**
Music Editor, The Oregonian

The concert of the Portland Junior Symphony orchestra at the public auditorium Saturday night touched the ludicrous and the sacred with equally sincere regard.

The audience and the playing body, especially the brasses, had a real round of fun with one of Ernest Toch's latest compositions, the "Circus" overture. The audience, the orchestra, and a special chorus participated in the stirring solemnity of Mozart's Requiem, which drew its choral strength from the local high schools and four local colleges, with Bonnie Newburgh, Marybelle Bunnett, Dean Lieber and Andre Kurmins as the solo quartet.

Other scores used were the Brahms serenade in D, and Delius' "On Hearing the First Cuckoo in Spring."

Group Gets Education

It was apparent in this concert, as it has been in earlier ones during his first season as permanent conductor, that Jacob Avshalomov gives major consideration to the premise that the Junior Symphony is first of all an educative endeavor.

If he were thinking only in terms of find sounding performances, Avshalomov wouldn't program a work with the technical pitfalls of the Brahms serenade.

Mozart Work Feature

Of course, the most important area of the evening from the standpoint of significant musical literature, and its dramatic impact, was that masterpiece of choral writing, the Mozart Requiem.

The pictorial effect of two hundred young singers massed above and beyond the large youth orchestra was impressive. And when the surge of their fresh voices filled the huge hall with well modulated tones, scrupulously balanced sound and understandable diction, there was a beauty that tightened the throats of some auditors. It was a well-drilled ensemble. And the four solo voices were admirable in themselves and nicely blended in their several ensemble sections.

We had known of Mr. Avshalomov's skill as a choral leader before we became acquainted with his ability to lead an orchestra, so we were not surprised to hear how handsomely the two branches of this directorial art joined in bringing the choral and instrumental into a smooth flowing and dramatically affecting performance. It was a striking finale to Mr. Avshalomov's first season as the orchestra's leader.

OREGON JOURNAL APR. 25, 1955

Juniors' Form Good

Youngsters Play Big Mozart Work

By **FREDERIC ROTHCHILD**
Journal Music Editor

The Portland Junior Symphony, when I had to leave The Auditorium Saturday evening, was well into an impressive performance of the Mozart Requiem. Jacob Avshalomov was conducting, and the first four sections of the work had showed an admirable preparation of chorus, orchestra and soloists.

Of the quartet of these—Bonnie Newburgh, Marybelle Bunnett, Dean Lieber and Andre Kurmins—all sang well. Miss Newburgh was particularly impressive for both voice and style. The excellent choruses were from Portland high schools and colleges.

THE JUNIORS, In the first part of their concert, played a "Circus" overture, by Ernest Toch. They played this difficult, noisy and very witty piece expertly with an absolute sobriety of manner. Maybe it's too hard to treat otherwise, but even at its conclusion scarcely a youngster smiled.

The Brahms opus 11 serenade and Delius' "On Hearing the First Cuckoo in Spring" were the other works played. In both of them, the impressionistic Delius and the youthful, moonstruck Brahms, the players showed well the polish which they are acquiring under Mr. Avshalomov's guidance.

32nd Season

Jacob Avshalomov, Conductor

November 19, 1955

BRAHMS	Academic Festival Overture
CHOPIN	Piano Concerto NO. 1, E minor Margaret Kochendorfer, *Soloist*
GABRIELI	Sonata Pian e Forte
WEBER	Invitation to the Dance, op. 65
BLOCH	*Suite Symphonique

February 18, 1956

GLINKA	Overture: "Russlan & Ludmilla"
DEBUSSY	Clarinet Rhapsody NO. 1 Robert Lauinger, *Soloist*
AARON AVSHALOMOV	*Hutungs of Peking
BEETHOVEN	Symphony NO. 3, Eb major "Eroica"

April 21, 1956

HANDEL	Concerto Grosso, D minor, op. 6 NO. 10
STRAVINSKY	Symphony of Psalms
VERDI	Overture: "King for a Day"
VIVALDI	Gloria Bonnie Newberg, *Soprano*

Guest Choirs: Klamath Falls High School, Willamette University, University of Portland

* *Portland Premiere*

Junior Symphony Succeeds In 'Tough' Brahms Concert

By Frederick Rothchild
Journal Music Editor

Portlanders are so used to reading about our "world-famed" Junior Symphony orchestra that they tend to forget that the description is not a publicity trick but a reality.

The Junior Symphony is, and deserves to be, world-famed. It's unlikely that many such organizations exist, and again unlikely that those which do are of the quality of this one.

I COULD hear only the first half of Saturday night's concert at The Auditorium, because on Saturdays my reviews have to be in earlier than on week nights. What I heard was a really clear, musical and convincing playing of the Brahms' "Academic Festival overture and a playing of the first Chopin concerto which featured one of the finest young piano talents to appear in a very long time.

The Brahms overture is not kid stuff—certainly not technically. Even a passable performance of it by young people would be remarkable. But Junior Symphony Conductor Jacob Avshalomov and his orchestra achieved not just a passable but a vigorous and persuasive one. The piece, in short, was played.

MARGARET Kochendorfer is 15. She played, and extremely well, the solo part of the Chopin F minor concerto. I have written before that I thought this wasn't an ideal choice of works for a Junior Symphony piano contest. I still feel that way about it, but I must confess that this young pianist is a talent of higher caliber than I knew was available for the solo part. She and her teacher, Nellie Tholen, have my most sincere admiration.

The concert included a suite by Ernest Bloch, played in honor of his 75th birthday, and pieces by Weber and Gabrieli, but these I was unable to hear.

Girl Pianist Precocious

Junior Symphony Program Lauded

By HILMAR GRONDAHL
Music Editor, The Oregonian

A young pianistic wonder, a tribute to a great resident composer, and a good deal of handsome ensemble playing characterized the concert of the Portland Junior Symphony orchestra under Jacob Avshalomov's direction Saturday night in the public auditorium.

Margaret Kochendorfer, a mere wisp of a girl, who was a soloist in the *Chopin E-minor* concerto, provided the pianism to wonder at. The homage implied in programming Ernest Bloch's "Suite Symphonique" was a testimonial to 75 years and the continuing creative vigor of this world-famous composer who has elected to live in Oregon. And the handsome playing was to be heard in each section of the program—an audible enhancement in precision over what was to be heard one concert ago.

Small Groups Pay Off

Part of the reason for this increased technical efficiency, observable in the strings particularly in the opening "Academic Festival" overture of Brahms, was undoubtedly induced by the conductor's policy of forming numerous small ensembles within the orchestra. In these groups of four and five, organized ostensibly for reading and study, the need for unison performance and the justifiable tyranny of the precise beat are magnified boldly. After these sessions the young players go back to the full orchestra with a clearer understanding of the necessity, the possibility and the beauty of precise playing. The entire ensemble was there with controlled enthusiasm and appropriate vigor for the "Gaudeamus Igitur" section of the Brahms overture.

Young Pianist Precocious

The piano concerto was a particularly fine piece of playing by the interdependent forces of solo and orchestral complement. One doesn't expect a girl of 15 to be fully aware of all the emotional implications of a Chopin score, such as this but Miss Kochendorfer appears to be as precocious in her musical comprehension as she is in her technical development. This was not a performance in the so-called "grand" manner, but between the materials in her control and those in the conductor's there was a balancing style and scale that brought everything to the listen's ear clearly and in proper proportion.

Soloist Shows Composure

There was more than a little bit of delight in visual aspects of this performance; the composure of the soloist, her assured assignment of finger and force, and the continuous unspoken understanding between soloist and conductor.

The first postintermission feature was a tour de force for brasses with two bassoons added, a Gabrieli sonata arranged by Theodore Thomas. This essay in echo, alternately soft and loud playing, is more than an effective study. It is attractive music and showed effectively how the wind players perform.

After Weber's "Invitation to the Dance," and last on the program came the Bloch composition, which, because of the lateness, we were forced to miss.

Juniors Tackle 'Hutungs' With Surprising Success

By **HILMAR GRONDAHL**
Music Editor, The Oregonian

If we ever saw a busy quartet of tympanists, it was at the Saturday night concert of the Portland Junior Symphony orchestra when that ensemble under the direction of Jacob Avshalomov, was playing a composition entitled "Peiping Hutungs" by Aaron Avshalomov, father of the orchestra's conductor.

"Hutungs," according to the program notes, is North Chinese for "street," and the piece turned out to be an atmospheric impression of an awakening town, followed by a kaleidoscopic account of the doings in busy thoroughfares as well as the lazy byways of Peiping.

It is in keeping up with the myriad sounds of the city; the cries of the vendors, the cobbler at his last, the scissors-grinder at work, and the other evidences of the massive toil of humanity in a huge tone painting that kept the four young lads at the back of the stage hopping.

There was another instrument more singly featured in Saturday night's concert, and that was the clarinet of Robert Lauinger, who was soloist in Debussy's Rhapsody for that instrument with orchestra. Young Lauinger not only played the notes in their ordained places with their explicit values, but he lent them an expressiveness with a firm support of breath that was a recognition and projection of their musical worth. The orchestral accompaniment was handsomely set forth by the ensemble.

Other works on the program were the "Russian and Ludmilla" overture which opened the program and Beethoven's "Eroica" symphony which closed it.

This last is one of the heroic scores for orchestra, and although the Juniors were in trouble more often among its difficult ramifications than they have been with anything in several concerts, we are prepared to joust with anyone who says they should not have attempted it.

Organization Ambitious

True, it is an ambitious work, but the Junior Symphony is an ambitious organization. If it ever ceases to glorify the opportunity of playing music that is sometimes over its collective head, it should close up shop.

These young musicians are to be envied for their chances to participate in great music. And even when everything is not going as smoothly as it might, something comes up like Joan Baker's playing of the oboe theme in the Funeral march that is a genuine delight.

Best Music Weak Draw, Junior Concert Shows

By **Frederic Rothchild**
Journal Music Editor

Contrasts can be painful—and instructive.

Friday The Auditorium was full, to and including the wings. The offering was an evening of "pops" music, well played by a touring orchestra under Arthur Fiedler. It was entertaining, but not intended to stick to the ribs.

SATURDAY The Auditorium was, to a shameful degree empty. The offering was an evening of the finest and most serious music, played by the Portland Junior Symphony under Jacob Avshalomov. It was another startling demonstration of excellence by the group of young people whose accomplishment surpasses that of any other group of young people in this part of the world.

Those who were there heard the Portlanders play Glinka, Debussy, Beethoven and a work by Aaron Avshalomov, father of the conductor.

The Glinka "Russian" overture, an old standby in the Juniors' programs, got a clear, crisp reading. It was followed by the Debussy rhapsody for clarinet and orchestra.

ROBERT LAUINGER was the soloist. First clarinetist of the orchestra and a pupil of Owen Sanders, this young artist gave so beautiful, so persuasive, so musical, so professional a performance of Debussy's music that it seemed, sometimes, that the music and the instrument played him rather than he them.

The accompaniment he received was the best done here since the Portland Symphony's Serkin concert.

The music of Aaron Avshalomov was a tone picture of the streets of Peiping. It puts Peiping not far from the Rome of Respighi—a comment not disparaging, since Avshalomov's music is every bit as agreeable as Respighi's. The percussion section did a fine job here. The piece was impressively played and well received.

OREGON JOURNAL APR. 22, 1956

Youngsters Excellent

By Frederic Rothchild
Journal Music Editor

Sometimes miracles are shrugged off—taken for commonplace and ignored.

This is what happens too often when the Portland Junior Symphony plays one of its three annual concerts, as it did Saturday night at The Auditorium with Jacob Avshalomov conducting.

The "sophisticated" music public says "only kids!" and stays away. Those who believe nothing good unless it's imported say "just a local outfit" and stay away, too.

PARENTS, people interested in the projects of youth and those music lovers who trust their ears and only their ears go and hear again and again the durable miracle which is the Junior Symphony. The pity is that they never come near to filling the hall. The miracle, for most Portlanders, is simply shrugged off.

Saturday nights I can hear only half of a program. The half I heard this time included a Handel D minor concerto grosso and the Stravinsky "Symphony of Psalms." The Handel was as fine as any playing I have heard from the Juniors. In respect of both clarity and style it was practically without a flaw.

The Stravinsky, in which choruses from the University of Portland, Klamath Falls high school and Willamette university joined the players, was as fine as any choral singing we have had here. It was a better performance of this music—difficult as it is technically and exhalted spiritually—than any I have heard by anybody, including those with the composer conducting.

HARD TO believe? You'd have to have been there to disagree, but if you were there, it's more likely you would have found, as I did, that this was, indeed, a nearly miraculous performance.

Prep violin sectional rehearsal.

Prep music theory class.

33rd Season

Jacob Avshalomov, Musical Director

November 17, 1956

GOLDMARK	"Rustic Wedding" Symphony
HAYDN	Piano Concerto, D major
	Ruth Myrick, *Soloist*
GUARNIERI	Dansa Brasiliera
TCHAIKOVSKY	Romeo & Juliet

February 16, 1957

WEBER	"Euranthe" Overture, op. 81
WARD	Fantasia for Brass & Timpani
BACH	Concerto for Violin & Oboe

Marlene Majowski, *Violin;* Joan Baker, *Oboe*

STRAUSS	Symphony for Winds, op. posth.
	Allegro
MENDELSSOHN	Symphony NO. 4, A major, "*Italian*"

February 23, 1957

R. A. Long High School, Longview, Washington

Selections from the Season

April 27, 1957

MOZART	Overture: "Don Giovanni"
MOZART	Symphonie Concertante, Eb, K. 364

Elinore Sharp, *Violin*; Catherine Petersen, *Viola*

RAVEL	Bolero
DVORAK	Symphony NO. 5, E minor, op. 95
	"From the New World"

May 12, 1957

Special Free Concert of

NEW MUSIC

Supported by a Grant from the Music Performance
Trust Fund of the Recording Industries

Crowd Enthusiastic at Opening Concert of Junior Symphony

By Martin Clark
Journal Music Editor

The Portland Junior Symphony opened its 33d season Saturday night with an enthusiastic reception which portends a happy future for concerts to come. Under the brilliant leadership of Conductor Jacob Avshalomov, a varied program was presented highlighted by Goldmark's "Rustic Wedding" symphony and the Haydn Concerto for Piano and Orchestra in D with Ruth Myrick as soloist.

OBTAINING a performance which far surpasses what is usually termed "adequate" from a youthful group as large as this is a genuine feat. Conductors who can work satisfactorily with young people are not particularly rare, but when such a one is found who also brings to his work the background of an internationally recognized composer, the effect is an emphasis on interpretation which is rarely found in youthful orchestras of this size.

Goldmark's popular, if unconventional, "Rustic Symphony" opened the concert, receiving a reading which underlined the graceful lilting melodies abounding in the composer's works. This composer has never been ranked with the giants of music, yet his works probably have accounted for a disproportionate number of young and older individuals deciding that serious music did offer something truly enjoyable.

PIANIST Ruth Myrick displayed a sound technic in the Haydn concerto. The 16-year-old artist possesses a flexible approach which prevented a work such as this from becoming purely mechanical. In the accompanying passages, the orchestra offered a full-bodied but sufficiently soft accompaniment to enhance the elegant phrases of Haydn.

The balance of the printed program consisted of "Dansa Brasileira" by the Brazilian composer, Camargo Guarnieri, and Tchaikovsky's "Romeo and Juliet" overture which concluded the program.

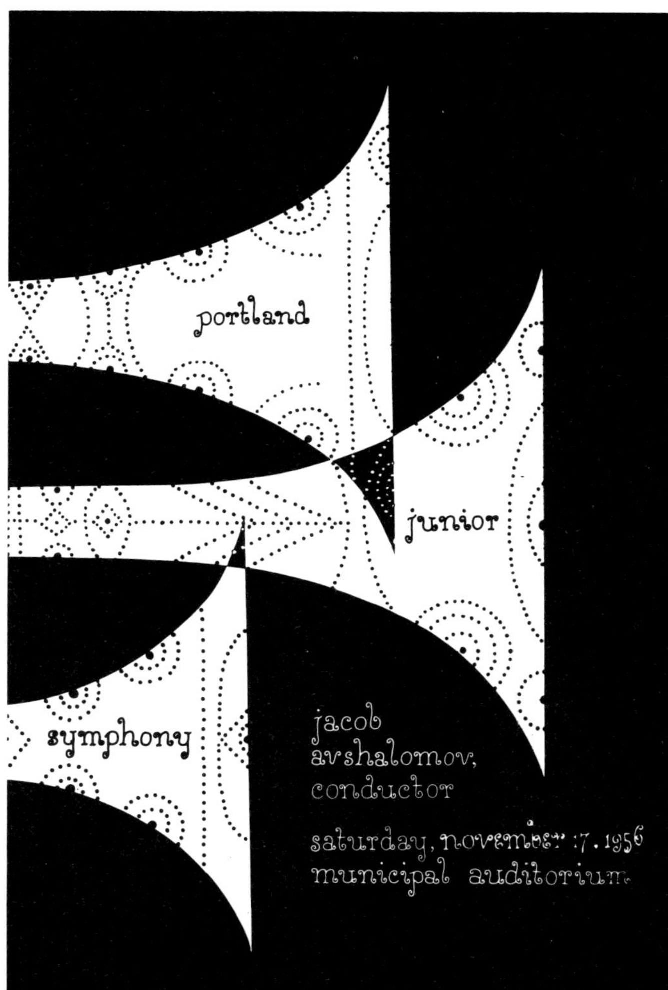

THE OREGONIAN FEB. 17, 1957

Junior Group Shows Skill

Conductor Picks Diversified Scores

By HILMAR GRONDAHL
Music Editor, The Oregonian

Another evening of musical adventure was available to those who heard the Portland Junior Symphony orchestra in concert at the public auditorium Saturday night.

Again Conductor Jacob Avshalomov had scheduled scores of wide diversity in type and style, and again his earnest young charges brought them off with a will and a skill that gave a fine view of their musical outlines and a good idea of their expressive content.

Among the unusual pieces was a brand new fantasy for brass choir and tympany by Robert Ward, and the opening movement of the Richard Strauss symphony for winds. Novel only because of the infrequency of its performance was the C-minor concerto for violin and oboe by Sebastian Bach which featured Marlene Majovski and Joan Baker as soloists.

Problems Resolved

To frame this program with the traditional there was the "Euryanthe" overture of Weber and Mendelssohn's "Italian" symphony. . . .

. . . When Mr. Avshalomov puts his brasses into the elaborate statements of the Robert Ward fantasy, one hears that there is a refinement among these instruments and a precision for they had been drilled and coaxed and persuaded to play with uncommon uniformity. In fact, for at least one listener, the Strauss music was not in itself half so interesting as the demonstration it gave of young musicians being better than expected.

Skills Demonstrated

But the most exciting demonstration of individual skills came in the Bach concerto when Miss Majovski left her place as concertmaster, and Miss Baker her place as principal oboe to blend their talents in one of the loveliest works in old style. Both girls are highly gifted and well trained. Perhaps the most appealing solo utterance was that of the oboist in the middle movement where one of Bach's melodies of heavenly length and contour was taken with a steady tone and very musicianly phrasing. The violinist also had a handsome tone and a very good feeling for the style.

The Mendelssohn symphony, a standard work in everybody's repertory, served to show how continuously these young musicians improve in tone, texture, ensemble values under Mr. Avshalomov's guidance.

Oregon Journal JAN. 11, 1957

Junior Symphony Gets Grant for Compositions

The Portland Junior Symphony association has received news from the Rockefeller foundation in New York confirming a grant of $10,000 that will open a new phase of activity for the orchestra. The specific purpose of the grant is to make possible the "commissioning of orchestral works suitable for performance by junior orchestral groups."

The grant is one of the few ever given by a major foundation to an orchestra society for a commissioning series, and is possibly the only one ever given to a youth orchestra. L. B. Staver, president of the orchestra association, reported that the grant was made in response to a proprosal submitted by the board's music committee, Dr. R. F. Arragon, chairman.

MAJOR composers will be invited to write works expressly for the Junior Symphony. The compositions then will be introduced to the music world in Portland premier performances by Jacob Avshalomov, conductor of this city's nationally famous youth symphony.

A nation-wide committee of composers, critics, conductors and musicologists will join with the Portland orchestra's music committee to select the composers who will be offered commissions.

The grant is for a three-year period and allows for the commissioning of six new works.

The request for a grant was made because of the scarcity of contemporary compositions suitable to the technical advancement of young players.

The first performance of a new work in all likelihood will be held in the spring of 1958.

Junior Symphony Tribute to Alumni

By Martin Clark
Journal Music Editor

A popular program, but with substance, was presented by the Portland Junior Symphony Saturday night in The Auditorium as a tribute to the more than 2000 former members of the orchestra who have played in it since it was founded 33 years ago by the late Jacques Gershkovitch.

Conductor Jacob Avshalomov opened with an incisive, provocative reading of Mozart's overture to "Don Giovanni." This was followed by the same composer's Symphonie Concertante in E Flat for Violin and Viola.

SOLOISTS in the latter were Elinore Sharp, violinist, and Catherine Petersen, viola. The two were well balanced in their solo passages. Under Avshalomov's direction the Mozartean style emerged in a satisfying manner. Soloists and conductor were called back by an appreciative audience of about 2000.

Both Miss Sharp and Miss Petersen are former Junior Symphony concertmasters who went on to advanced study and returned to open studios in Portland and become members of the Portland Symphony.

A DRAMATIC performance of Ravel's "Bolero" concluded the first half of the concert. Second half of the program was devoted to the "New World" Symphony No. 5 in E Minor by Dvorak.

Guests Shine In Symphony

Junior Orchestra Pleases Audience

By HILMAR GRONDAHL
Music Editor, The Oregonian

The Portland Junior Symphony orchestra, under Jacob Avshalomov's guidance, welcomed two of its former concertmasters to the stage of the public auditorium Saturday night to participate as guest artists in a performance of the Mozart Symphonie Concertante.

The two stars were Elinore Sharp, violinist, and Catherine Petersen, violist, both of whom are now professionals and mainstays in their respective sections in the Portland Symphony orchestra.

We can think of no one whom this particular kind of homecoming would not please. Certainly it was a pleasure for the audience to hear a pair of the city's finest resident instrumentalists joined in a masterpiece of rare and beautiful fashioning.

It would not be just simply to suggest, as we have above, that the two solo participants were uncommonly able in their individual roles. The conscientious care with which their instruments were blended bespoke their sensitive musicianship.

Discipline, Skill Shown

The concert opened with another Mozart work, the "Don Giovanni" overture. This is a tough score to bring off even by widely experienced players, and it was satisfying to realize how well Mr. Avshalomov pointed up its dramatic content.

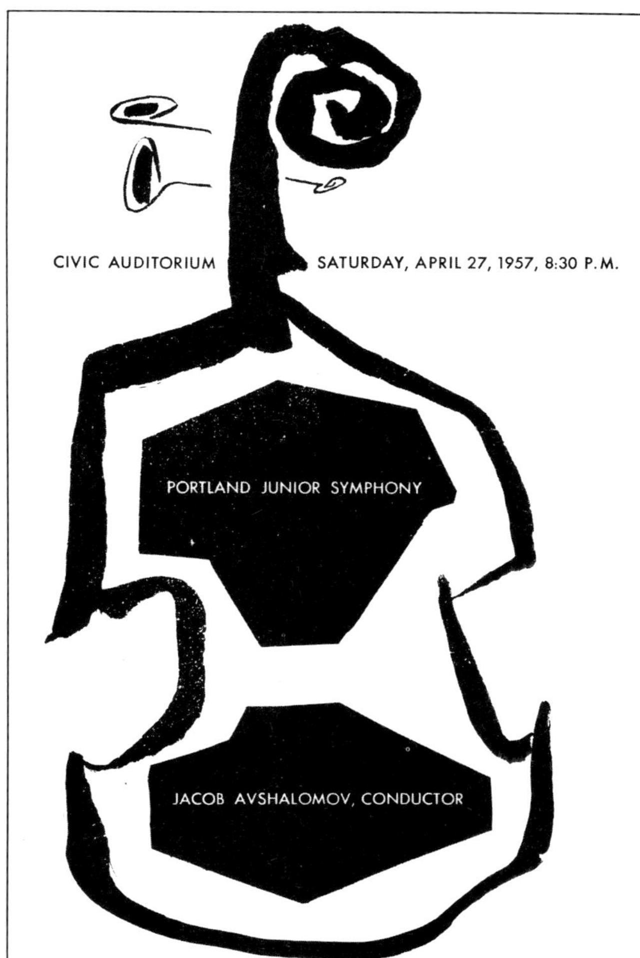

Junior Symphony, Brass Join in Music Experiment

BY HILMAR GRONDAHL
Music Editor, The Oregonian

How serious contemporary composers are finding their musical materials and the sort of use to which they are putting them was the basis for discussion and performance at the public auditorium Sunday night when the Portland Junior Symphony orchestra plus the brass section of the Portland Symphony joined in the educational venture of giving sound to the diverse ideas of Wallingford Riegger, James Beale and the team of Ussachevsky and Luening.

Jacob Avshalomov, conductor of the Junior Symphony directed the instrumental forces, and set the stage by informative comment for each successive offering. Being himself a composer much in the today's creative current, he was a sympathetic proponent of the scores programmed.

8 French Horns Enlisted

So that none of the 800 auditors present might become wholly lost in the sea of strange sounds, the ensemble provided an anchor to windward first in a rousing Sousa march, and later in a suite for strings by Arthur Foote, as well-behaved a practitioner in tone as New England produced in the early 20th century.

To present the Riegger "Music for Brass Choir" it was necessary to enlist eight French horns, eight trumpets, eight trombones and a pair of tubas.

He Knows When to Stop

There was little of tangible tune after the original statement by the French horn, but there were many subtlties of texture and some very expert grading of volume. There were inner climaxes, and much that was impressive as an investigation of sounds suggesting strange worlds; the industrial rings of metals, the vague intangibles of outer space.

The composer asked for special skills from his interpreters, and if, as Mr. Avshalomov said, this is hardly "lovely" music, it was absorbing in its interest and often compelling in its expressive resource.

"Divertimento" by James Beale, a professor at the University of Washington's school of music, was a piece not needing a repetition for complete understanding, supposing, that is, that the listener has some familiarity with the school of composition associated with Paul Hindemith. In the five short movements of this score the composer makes it crystal clear that he has something to say, in a friendly way, that he knows expertly how to say it, and that when his piece is spoken he is willing to stop; which is a virtue not all contemporary composers possess.

The score called "Poem in Bells and Cycles" which Ussachevsky and Luening contrived to piece together is a strange bit. In the process of making this music they gathered scraps of sound on a tape recorder. These they blew into whatever shape or volume or tempo they wanted and subsequently related them to some scoring for orchestra.

Grant Credited for Concert

There is little coming from the tape machine that could not have been created by live players in the concert hall, unless these players would feel ashamed of what they were producing.

Mr. Avshalomov and his ensemble performed the Riegger and Ussachevsky-Luening scores both before and after intermission. Aaron Copland's "El Salon Mexico" wound up the evening.

NEW MUSIC

special concert free to the public

PORTLAND JUNIOR SYMPHONY

Jacob Avshalomov, conductor

MAY 12, 1957

PUBLIC AUDITORIUM, 8:30 pm

PROGRAM

Wallingford Riegger	Music for Brass Choir (1950)
James Beale	Divertimento (1954)
Ussachevsky-Luening	Poem in Bells and Cycles (1954) Tape Recorder Solo with Orchestra

INTERMISSION

Wallingford Riegger	Music for Brass Choir (*repeat*)
Arthur Foote	Suite for Strings in E (1908)
Ussachevsky-Luening	Poem in Bells and Cycles (*repeat*)
Aaron Copland	El Salon Mexico (1936)

The concert is made possible by a grant from the Music Performance Trust Fund of the Recording Industries obtained with the cooperation of Local 99 American Federation of Musicians.

(*An additional contribution has been made by the American Composers Alliance for the performance of contemporary music*).

The 83-piece Portland Junior Symphony Orchestra has been augmented by the 17 members of the Portland Symphony brass choir for the program.

Appreciation is extended to the girls from Catlin School who are serving as usher-hostesses this evening.

Ampex Tape Deck and Wharfdale Speaker System courtesy Burke-Arenz Music Co.

The concert is being given in cooperation with the Reed College Pacific Coast Arts Festival.

OREGON JOURNAL APR. 23, 1957

GUEST EDITORIAL

Junior Symphony Ranks Above All Like Institutions

By Frederic Rothchild

THE PORTLAND in which I grew up was a small city, yet it had in it everything which is of value in the Portland of today.

Our city has grown in numbers, but its unique institutions and accomplishments date from its earlier days.

And the unique institutions? My own list would include in the first rank our superb library, the Portland Junior Symphony orchestra and that glory of an often unseeing community, Reed college. Of great value, but more likely to be rivaled elsewhere, are the medical school, the art museum and, in some periods, the Portland Symphony. Together with the natural beauty of this area, these seem to me the things which make Portland worth living in.

OF OUR INSTITUTIONS, the Junior Symphony is closest to being without a parallel anywhere. There are no other orchestras of a hundred youngsters which do a comparable job of playing the serious symphonic repertoire. A combination of dedicated hard work on the part of many generations of players and of dedicated leadership by the late Jacques Gershkovitch, the orchestra's first and long-time conductor, and by Jacob Avshalomov, its current leader, have produced results in music-making which have, at the best, been unbelievably good. Anyone who has heard other orchestras of young people, including those gathered from all over the nation in summer music camps or those made up of the pick of a whole city school system, may well have found the Juniors different not only in degree but in kind. This group plays great music usually well and sometimes unforgettably. Other youth orchestras are likely only to emphasize the limitations which the Juniors regularly transcend.

What the Junior Symphony does and has done is to demonstrate the nobility of musical art and the potential for accomplishment and expression in this field of great numbers of young people. Anyone who believes in youth, in music or in Portland should listen to and concern himself with the Junior Symphony as with one of our community's greatest treasures.

34th Season

Jacob Avshalomov, Conductor

November 23, 1957

SMETANA	Overture to "The Bartered Bride"
MOZART	Divertimento in Bb, K. 287
BACH	Piano Concerto, G minor
	Barbara Hinshaw, *Soloist*
PROKOFIEV	"Peter & the Wolf"
	William L. Alderson, *Narrator*
BIZET	"Carmen" Suite

February 15, 1958

HANDEL	Gavotte & Bouree from "The Faithful Shepherd" Suite
FRANCK	Symphony in D minor
DIAMOND	**The World of Paul Klee
COMMISSIONED BY	THE PORTLAND JUNIOR SYMPHONY
VIVALDI	Concerto for Two Flutes, C major
STRAUSS	Chit-Chat & Furioso Polkas
	Emperor Waltz

April 19, 1958

BEETHOVEN	Coriolanus Overture, op. 62
J. C. BACH	Sinfonia for Double Orchestra, Eb
HARRIS	**Revery & Dance
	Mr. Harris *Conducting*
COMMISSIONED BY	THE PORTLAND JUNIOR SYMPHONY
SIBELIUS	Third Symphony, op. 52
BOCCHERINI	Minuet
RIMSKY-KORSAKOV	Dance of the Tumblers

September 28, 1958

Free Family Pops Concert–3:p.m.

Peninsula Park

A Short Program of Light Classics

Bring a balloon for the 'pops' feature

** *World Premiere*

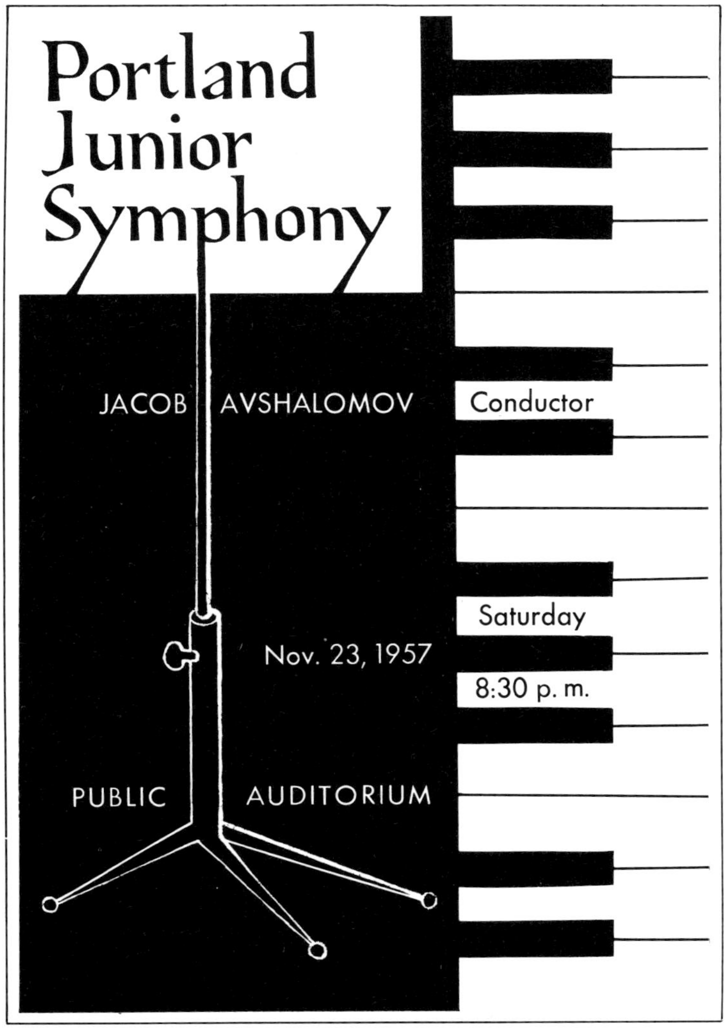

OREGON JOURNAL NOV. 25, 1957

Birds Fail to Dim Success of Juniors

By Martin Clark
Journal Music Editor

If he had only known earlier, Jacob Avshalomov could have presented one of the most realistic performances of Wagner's "Forest Murmurs" or Beethoven's "Pastoral Symphony" ever heard anywhere. But we doubt if anyone thought to inform the talented young maestro in advance that the annual pet fair and competitive parakeet judging show would be housed in the south wing of The Auditorium Saturday night when the Junior Symphony gave the opening concert of its 34th season.

The result was some rather chirpy competition for the orchestra during the first half of the program. Actually, it would have made an effective background for Prokofiev's "Peter and the Wolf," but that came after intermission and by that time someone apparently had either removed them or managed to shut them up with covers.

SOLOIST for the evening was Barbara Hinshaw, who appeared in the Bach Concerto for Piano and Orchestra in G Minor. An appreciative audience recalled Miss Hinshaw repeatedly for a performance marked by a high degree of technical fidelity to the intent of Bach.

Smetana's bouncy overture to "The Bartered Bride" opened the program with suitable verve and enthusiasm.

AVSHALOMOV has accustomed us to such a near-professional standard of performance from the Juniors, that when any section delivers less than excellence we are acutely aware of it. We refer to a hard tone in the violin section we don't recall hearing last year. It was evident through the Mozart and Bach, but dissolved in the Prokofiev; nor could it be attributed to classic restraint.

Prokofiev's "Peter and the Wolf" received a thorough musicianly treatment. With William L. Anderson, professor of literature at Reed college, as a capable narrator, the popular composition received fine support from soloists in the orchestra. Avshalomov's reading captured the true spirit of a piece that has become a classic for young and adult alike.

Bizet's "Carmen" Suite was the concluding number of the evening. One of the largest audiences we've seen for a Junior concert (upwards of 2500) was present for the highly successful opening concert.

Oregon Journal FEB. 16, 1958

This Is Paul Klee?

Junior Symphony Plays New Work

By Martin Clark
Journal Music Editor

"The World of Paul Klee" is a mighty busy one. At least, the "World" is which David Diamond portrays in his composition by that name inspired by four paintings of the noted Swiss artist, Paul Klee (pronounced "Clay").

Saturday night at The Auditorium Jacob Avshalomov conducted the Portland Junior Symphony in the premier of the Diamond work, commissioned by the Juniors under a grant from the Rockefeller Foundation. The concert drew an audience of about 2000.

We don't want to be unkind, but with the exception of the last of the four "frames," the "Twittering Machine," a great to-do is made about getting started but nothing comes of the effort.

In spite of an anxious moment or two, the Juniors extracted the essence of what Diamond had to offer, and in a professional manner at that.

Carol Fogdall and Marilyn Winslow gave an enchanting performance as soloists in the Vivaldi Concerto for Two Flutes and Orchestra in C Major, with good balance and support by the orchestra.

HANDEL'S Bouree and Gavotte from "The Faithful Shepherd" received deft handling as an opener, followed by a warmly applauded performance of the popular Franck Symphony in D Minor.

THE OREGONIAN FEB. 16, 1958

'Klee World' Memorable

By HILMAR GRONDAHL
Music Editor, The Oregonian

The Portland Junior Symphony Orchestra's concert Saturday night in the public auditorium under Jacob Avshalomov's baton, will be remembered for several different features, of which the most significant historically will be the world premier of David Diamond's composition, "The World of Paul Klee."

The Klee score was composed especially for the Portland Junior Symphony Orchestra Assn. as the first of six commissioned works by contemporary composers through a grant of the Rockefeller Foundation. It was the composer's understanding that the premier would be directed by Mr. Avshalomov.

Concert patrons were uncommonly fortunate in their introduction to the Diamond music, in that of the four Klee pictures which served as the inspiration for his composing, three were available for inspection Saturday night. The original water color of "The Twittering Machine" stood impressively in its glass case in the lobby, on loan for the evening from the Portland Art Museum, to whom it was on loan from its owner, New York's Museum of Modern Art.

Program Attractive

Two other pictures, "Dance of the Grieving Child" and "The Black Prince" were observable in quite good color reproduction on the center spread of the concert program. Furthermore, there was a very perceptive word picture of the composer and his work as a special article in the program over the modest initials of J.A.

Actually there is a close and subtle kinship between what one sees in the Klee pictures and what one hears in the Diamond. And it is hoped that these four handsome tonal portraits will not be turned to the wall after a single showing, for it will take more than one glance to bring a full awareness of their remarkable craftsmanship, their distinctive colorations and their sly humor.

This is the first time the Juniors have become involved with a score of such involved and modern technnics. What they did with it in the short time they had it before them is eloquent testimony to their seriousness, their teachability and the pedagogic skill of their conductor.

Flutists Perform

Miss Fogdall, principal flutist, and her companion, Miss Winslow, were busy enough in the Diamond, but immediately thereafter they stepped up ahead of the conductor's podium to show their sprightly art in the Vivaldi. They are an uncommonly skillful pair with fleet fingers and a steady breath, both of which are necessary for good flute playing, especially along the classical lines of their chosen piece.

THE OREGONIAN SUNDAY, APR. 20, 1958

Harris Leads World Premiers

By HILMAR GRONDAHL
Music Editor, The Oregonian

For members of the Portland Junior Symphony Orchestra, as well as patrons across the footlights, Saturday night's concert in the Public Auditorium must stand as a historical event. On that occasion they played and heard the world premier of two pieces by Roy Harris with the composer himself conducting. This was a highly stimulating occasion.

A second event for which the ensemble and its regular conductor, Jacob Avshalomov, should properly take pride was a singularly affecting performance of the Third symphony by Sibelius.

The two Harris scores, as is well known by now, were composed especially for the Junior Symphony on a commission made possible by a grant from the Rockefeller Foundation.

Own Youth Scanned

The composer had in mind certain specifics for this composition, such as the age and technical capability of the ensemble for which he was writing. But what occurred to him, additionally, was that he would take his inspiration from thoughts and motivations he could recall from when he was the approximate age of the older members of the junior orchestra.

As a consequence there is a fresh youthfulness, a dewy-eyed idealism about the "Reverie," and the lovely lonely theme in the various winds that must be listened for over and beyond the general texture of the orchestra as though one were trying to recollect the melody from a dream.

But all of the "Dance" is directly before you. It has the quality of free animal spirits. These dance rhythms are not those of a city ballroom; they are more spacious, more suggestive of the open, more rustic in their swing.

Dance Could Be Popular

Roy Harris is a master of his materials. His scores derive logically, almost inevitably, out of their sources. His harmonic treatment is colorful, varied, and always in support of his strong sense of formal structure.

The Sibelius Third, freighted throughout with the composer's special 'creative devices, was an ideal work to assign these young musicians as a training course in the special problems of a particular composer. But these alert and musical youths under Avshalomov's guidance absorbed these technical problems in stride and went on to convey in full measure the artistic and emotional content of this score. It is difficult, it is tricky, but it is musically effective, and the effects, in first rate musical style, were passed on to the audience Saturday night.

Oregon Journal SUNDAY, APR. 20, 1958

Roy Harris Premiere Season's High Point

By Martin Clark
Journal Music Editor

What was easily the high point of the Portland Junior Symphony's season took place at The Auditorium Saturday night when Roy Harris conducted the world premiere of his "Reverie and Dance." It was the orchestra's final subscription concert of the season.

AS THE title indicates, the work is in two movements. Harris' treatment is as unpretentious and genuine as the two themes chosen. The first is "Black Is the Color of My True Love's Hair." The dance movement is based on another southern mountain air, "The Bird's Courtin' Song."

His variations on the two folk tunes consistently retain the characteristic simplicity of the songs. The "Reverie" depicts the dream world of the young while the dance movement describes their world of action. In refreshing contrast to much of contemporary composition, Harris' approach is of the earthy type with a discernible pattern, and not of the abstract variety which so often tends to leave the listener hanging in space along with the composer's bodiless creation.

NATURALLY enough, the variations of the first movement emphasize strings and woodwinds while the dance portion leans heavily on brass and percussion.

PROLONGED applause by an audience of about 2000 followed presentation of the new work, the second composition commissioned by the Junior Symphony association with its Rockefeller grant.

Jacob Avshalomov, the Juniors' talented young regular conductor, conducted the balance of the program.

Roy Harris conducts premiere of his "Reverie & Dance", April 1958.

CLASS OF SERVICE
This is a fast message unless its deferred character is indicated by the proper symbol.

WESTERN UNION
TELEGRAM
W. P. MARSHALL, PRESIDENT

SYMBOLS
DL = Day Letter
NL = Night Letter
LT = International Letter Telegram

(56) 1201

The filing time shown in the date line on domestic telegrams is STANDARD TIME at point of origin. Time of receipt is STANDARD TIME at point of destination

LLD054 SYA031 1958 APR 18 AM 6 20

SY PGA109 DL PD=PITTSBURGH PENN 8 801AME=

JACOB ASHALEMOV=

DIRECTOR PORTLAND JUNIOR SYMPHONY

618 PARK BLDG PORTLAND ORG=

WILL ARRIVE NORTH WESTERN 615 AM APRIL 14 WOULD APPRECIATE SEPARATE EXTRA STRING REHEARSAL LOOKING FORWARD TO A WONDERFUL EXPERIENCE WITH DISCIPLINED TALENTED YOUTH

PLEASE PUT THESE CUTS IN THE PARTS OF THE DANCE MEASURES ONE TO TWENTY ALSO MEASURES 217 TO 223 GREETINGS=

ROY HARRIS==

THE COMPANY WILL APPRECIATE SUGGESTIONS FROM ITS PATRONS CONCERNING ITS SERVICE

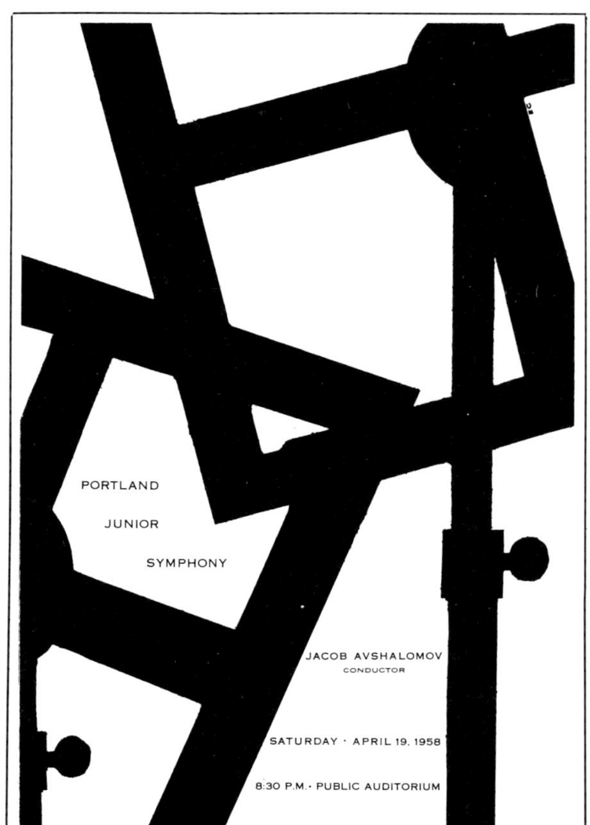

35th Season

Jacob Avshalomov, Conductor

November 22, 1958

SCHUMANN	Symphony NO. 1, Bb, Op. 38
AVSHALOMOV	Phases of the Great Land
BEETHOVEN	Piano Concerto NO. 2, Bb, Op. 19 Linda MacNaughton, *Soloist*
GRAINGER	Tune from County Derry Irish Reel: "Molly on the Shore"

February 21, 1959

CIMAROSA	Overture to "The Impressario"
NIELSEN	*Symphony NO. 3, "Espansiva"
MENDELSSOHN	Violin Concerto, E minor, Op. 64 Adell Hansen, *Soloist*
ENESCO	Roumanian Rhapsody NO. 1

April 18, 1959

HAYDN	*Symphony NO. 95, C minor
ORFF	*Carmina Burana

Maria Rogndahl Peake, *Soprano;* William Miller, *Tenor;* Neil Wilson, *Baritone*

Guest Choirs: Oregon State College, Oregon College of Education, Pacific University, Portland Junior Symphony, Powellhurst Public School

May 16, 1959

FANCIES & ENCORES

HANDEL	Suite from the Water Music
VILLA-LOBOS	Bachianas Brasilieras NO. 5 Jean Burlingame, *Soprano & Cello Octet*
LEES	*Prologue, Capriccio & Epilogue

COMMISSIONED BY THE PORTLAND JUNIOR SYMPHONY

DEBUSSY	"L'Apres-midi d'un Faune"
LOCKWOOD	*Concerto for Organ & Brass Valerian Fox, *Organist*
ENESCO	Roumanian Rhapsody NO. 1

Nielsen Third Symphony, Hansen Solo Features of Junior Group Concert

By HILMAR GRONDAHL
Music Editor, The Oregonian

The concert by Portland Junior Symphony Orchestra in the Public Auditorium Saturday night was remarkable for two factors in particular; the introduction of Carl Nielsen's Third symphony and the solo appearance of Adell Hansen in the Mendelssohn violin concerto.

It was wonderful thing for Jacob Avshalomov and his ensemble to bring Portlanders their first hearing of a Carl Nielsen symphony. One doesn't expect an organization such as the Junior Symphony to blaze a trail of first performances in a community such as this; they are generally busy acquainting their members with materials from the standard repertory. For this reason they deserve all the more credit for giving a fresh experience to their participants and a fresh experience to the audience.

Music Has Substance

A first hearing of Nielsen is a fresh experience and one which communicates something of substance at once. He was one of the great composers of the century and his relative neglect by the British and American conductors for the 20 years following his death is largely due to the singular devotion they were giving at that time to the music of Sibelius. Nielsen has a more free-ranging musical imagination, a sure hand with instrumental resources and a lyric impulse that suggests Mahler more than any other symphonist. Like Mahler his symphonic ideas sometimes incorporate the human voice as an instrument of the orchestra. This was the case in his Third Symphony which brought Janet David Day, soprano, and Earl Winchester, baritone, into the web of tone in the second movement.

Young Violinist Precise

The demonstration young Miss Hansen gave of her capacities as a violinist were quite impressive. She is a strong player, obviously well schooled, and almost invariably a strict adherent of precise intonation.

The conductor and orchestra made a beautiful thing of that transitional chord which ties the first and second movements together and thus prepared the way for some of her most attractive playing, the lush slow movement theme and the finely articulated section with which it closes. There was an animated stir of applause when the concerto ended.

Concert Held Surprises

There were two surprises at this concert. The first was the discovery that the germs of Centennial hirsutitis have affected several of the young male musicians. The second was the post-intermission crash of a jazz band, mysteriously out of sight, which came to light when the elevator came up disclosing what the Society's president, Waldo B.Taylor called the "Roaring Twenties" combo. This was the cue for Taylor to recall the history of the orchestra from its beginning in the twenties, and to cite some of the individuals who contributed to its growth. Among these were the widow of the original conductor, Jacques Gershkovitch, David Campbell, Mrs. Robert H. Noyes, and some of the citizens who were members of the original orchestra that night of February 14th, 1925 when the first public concert was given with Gershkovitch on the podium.

Junior Symphony's Open Air Concert Lures Hundreds to Peninsula Park

Bright sun Sunday brought hundreds of Portlanders and their families to Peninsula Park, where in shirt-sleeve weather, they enjoyed the first open-air concert given by the Portland Junior Symphony Orchestra.

The free pop concert is the first ever presented in Portland parks by the Symphony, but the conductor said he hoped it would not be the last time.

Although it was late September, it seemed like mid-summer as the orchestra assembled in the bandstand and the audience sat on the grass or benches to hear the program.

Led by Conductor Jacob Avshalomov, the "come as you are concert" included a number in which children participated by popping balloons. The concert-goers were asked to bring balloons for this special number, the Chit Chat polka by Strauss.

Avshalomov told the children, "Now when I point my baton at you, pop your balloon," and the number proceeded with great success until every balloon in the park was popped.

Other numbers presented by the orchestra included the Furioso Polka and Emperor Waltz, by Strauss, a minuet by Boccherini and the "Dance of the Tumblers" by Rimsky-Korsakov.

OREGON JOURNAL APR. 19, 1959

Juniors Play Orff's Work

By Martin Clark
Journal Music Editor

Jacob Avshalomov and the Portland Junior Symphony gave the most exciting concert Saturday night this reviewer has heard from them to date.

They had a lot of help, but made the most of it. The help was in the form of Carl Orff and his fabulously colorful "Carmina Burana," three soloists and a chorus of about 200 drawn from colleges in the Portland area.

In "Carmina Burana," the contemporary German composer Orff, has created a musical sensation that brings the listener to the edge of his seat with the opening chorus and keeps him there until that chorus rolls around again well over an hour later. It's the sort of thing to renew faith in contemporary composers.

Avshalomov welded orchestra, chorus and soloists into one working unit. The result was an inspired performance.

NEIL WILSON had the biggest share of the soloists' lines and sang them with knowing interpretation and a keen insight into musical and dramatic phrasing.

Portland's well-known soprano, Marie Rogndahl Peake, achieved some exquisite effects in her difficult assignment in spite of a fast tremolo.

Tenor William Miller supplied one of the most offbeat moments of the evening with his one solo opportunity. His use of head tones is the sort of thing usually associated with a Swiss yodeler or a first tenor in a Don Cossack chorus. However, the way Orff uses the tenor solo (as a roasted swan—that's right, a roasted swan) it's most effective.

As if "Carmina" wasn't enough, the Juniors opened with a superb reading of Haydn's Symphony No. 95 in C Minor. It's hard to believe, but the program said so, this symphony was receiving its Portland premiere. Of course, "Carmina" was a "first."

About 2000 enthusiastic listeners were present for the Saturday night performance.

Testing "musical chains" at a Children's Concert.

THE OREGONIAN APR. 15, 1959

'Carmina' and Juniors Score Top Success

By HILMAR GRONDAHL
Music Editor, The Oregonian

One of the most notable first performances to take place hereabouts in years was the Portland Junior Symphony Orchestra's offering of Carl Orff's "Carmina Burana" with a chorus of 200 recruited from schools and colleges nearby. To say that the crowd in the Public Auditorium Saturday night enjoyed it is to use pitifully modest language. Approval was as vociferous as it was extended. The fact that Conductor Jacob Avshalomov brought another first performance in Haydn's Symphony No. 95 was all but lost in the stir for Orff.

"Carmina Burana" is an exciting orchestral setting by a contemporary composer of selections from an anthology of 13th century poems found in a Bavarian monastery. The verses are evidently the work of wandering scholars who mingled their thoughts of Christianity with more worldly matters; who in their conviviality evidently ate a little, drank a lot, made love and exaggerated the beauty about them in a way, as someone suggested, "that recalls those ages when Pan and Jove were not considered incompatible deities.

In these fancifully colored vocal narratives Orff creates a gusto and a lust for living that is exhilarating.

Soloists Offer Bits

This direct and appealing material, its vast resources and its complex means, is not an easy thing to produce. But Avshalomov and his helpers made it an unforgettable occasion. The major protagonist in Orff's plan is the chorus and these 200 members responded in admirable style. Their membership came from Oregon State College, Oregon College of Education, Pacific University, the University of Portland, the Portland Junior Symphony Choir and the Powelhurst Public School.

The Haydn symphony was played with commendable taste and proficiency. But it was apparent Saturday night that all ears were on "Carmina Burana."

OREGON JOURNAL MAY 14, 1959

Junior Symphony's High Standards

For nearly 30 years in Portland the name of Jacques Gershkovitch was synonymous with dedication to youth and fine music.

Under his baton, the Portland Junior Symphony orchestra achieved a nation-wide reputation for the quality of its music and for the high places which its "graduates" won in the musical world.

When death removed him in 1953, it was not an easy thing to find a suitable successor, nor was it a certainty that the orchestra could be continued at the same high level.

But now, as this musical organization concludes its 35th season, it is pleasant to record that it has continued to perform, under Gershkovitch's successor, Jacob Avshalomov, at the same high level. It is still earning national recognition. It is still sending out well-trained young men and women into positions of high achievement. It is making a double contribution to Portland's cultural level through its own performances and by feeding into the senior symphony players with the training and ability to keep its standards higher than they could otherwise be.

Saturday night at The Auditorium the junior symphony will present a free concert made possible by a grant from the music performance trust fund of the recording industries, with the cooperation of local 99, American Federation of Musicians. This will be an excellent opportunity for lovers of fine music to celebrate the 35-year record of this unique organization.

The Journal has sought from time to time to recognize the achievements of young people in particular fields, to counteract the often distressing news of outrageous acts committed by a relatively few teenagers. Those who play in the junior symphony would be a credit to any generation. It is fitting now that tribute be paid to them, to conductor Avshalomov and to the dedicated board which makes the continuance of this organization possible.

OREGON JOURNAL MAY 18, 1959

Contemporaries Prove Top Fare in Concert

By Martin Clark
Journal Music Editor

Saturday night's "bonus" concert of the Portland Junior Symphony under Jacob Avshalomov's direction was precisely that.

Topping a program filled with choice selections were Villa-Lobos' "Bachianas Brasileiras No. 5" with San Francisco Opera soprano Jean Burlingham as soloist with an augmented cello section from the orchestra; and a first performance in Portland of the "Concerto for Organ and Brass" by Norman Lockwood, with organist Valerian Fox and the orchestra's brass players.

THE VILLA-LOBOS work is the sort of thing that proves again that contemporary music can be radically different from " the usual" in music, and still be not only interesting but beautiful. Miss Burlingham captured the warm sensuous quality of the text and fully conveyed its haunting beauty. This is a thrilling voice of true operatic timbre, one we hope to hear more of locally in the future.

Avshalomov's introductions to each work not only proved interesting and enlightening to the audience but gave an informal touch that the adults Saturday night enjoyed as much as the children at the regular Saturday morning concerts earlier in the season.

TITLED "Fancies and Encores," one of the "fancies" which proved fortunate to choose was the Lockwood concerto. Valerian Fox demonstrated that in the Lockwood, and with the aid of the brass players and Avshalomov provided one of the most exciting interpretations of the evening.

Another Portland first performance was a work commissioned by the Junior Symphony under its grant from the Rockefeller foundation, Benjamin Lees' "Prologue, Capriccio and Epilogue." In this composition Lees demonstrates a wonderful grasp of provocative orchestration. It has a charming pixyish quality. It's the type of work that leaves the listener with no concept of the composer's actual capacity but with a definite desire to hear more from him.

HANDEL'S suite from the "Water Music," the Enesco Roumanian Rhapsody No. 1, and Debussy's "Afternoon of a Faun" were the other numbers. Carol Fogdall supplied a thoroughly professional flute in the Debussy.

36th Season

Jacob Avshalomov, Conductor

	November 28, 1959
BEETHOVEN	Symphony NO. 5, C minor
MOZART	Violin Concerto, G major
	Robert Mann, *Soloist*
MANN	**The Terrible Tempered Conductor
	Lucy Rowan, *Narrator*
DVORAK	Slavonic Dances, op. 46, NOS. 5, 7, 8

	February 20, 1960
ROSSINI	Sonata for Strings NO. 6
DOHNANYI	Variations on a Nursery Song, op. 25
	Darlene Barnes, *Soloist*
SHOSTAKOVITCH	Symphony NO. 5

	April 23, 1960
BRAHMS	Symphony NO. 2, D major, op. 73
VIVALDI	Winter (Concerti of the Seasons)
	Delmar Pettys, *Violin Soloist*
SAINT-SAENS	Cello Concerto, op. 33
	Paul Speaker, *Soloist*
BERGSMA	**Chameleon Variations

COMMISSIONED BY THE PORTLAND JUNIOR SYMPHONY

May 21, 1960

FANCIES & ENCORES

Retrospective program of commissioned works by
Diamond – Harris – Lees – Bergsma

** *World Premiere*

OREGON JOURNAL NOV. 29, 1959

Juniors Open 36th Season

Robert Mann Heard In Own Work

Portland Junior Symphony opened its 36th season Saturday night with a program that will be hard to match for entertainment value in the concerts ahead.

Jacob Avshalomov, the orchestra's regular conductor, has outdone himself from one season to the next in the imaginative programming of concerts of high audience appeal (without resorting to mere popular appeal). If Saturday night's performance is any indication, this season is well on its way to outstripping its predecessors.

Robert Mann—violinist, composer and conductor—was featured, in those capacities, by Avshalomov in the orchestra's opening concert. Mann is first violinist of the Julliard String Quartet, well known here from appearances on the Friends of Chamber Music series, and a former member of the Junior Symphony when he was a student in Portland in the 1930s.

Mann Composition Featured

Center of attraction Saturday night was Mann's composition for orchestra and narrator, "The Terrible Tempered Conductor," which the composer conducted with his wife, Lucy Rowan, as narrator. Mann is a persuasive storyteller in words and music. The fantasy concerns a hot tempered conductor who is finally called to conduct his own orchestra and eventually succeeds in winning over the orchestra, making great music, and eliminating his terrible temper with the aid of a good fairy's magic wand in place of his baton.

The program notes included this sentence by the composer; "Any resemblance of any conductor, orchestra, or audience to the characters in this story is perfectly understandable."

Husband and wife received enthusiastic applause from an audience of nearly 2,500. It was a beautifully written and well performed work.

Mozart Concerto Played

Earlier, the former Portlander was featured as soloist in Mozart's Concerto in G for Violin and Orchestra. Like some other virile violinists of high talent, Mann is tempted to demand more from his instrument than a violin can give, but there were many telling passages by soloist and orchestra.

Avshalomov opened the evening with a straightforward reading of Beethoven's Fifth Symphony and concluded with a spirited performance of three Slavonic Dances by Dvorak.

A public reception was held following the concert in the south wing of The Auditorium honoring the guest artists and conductor.—M.C.

THE OREGONIAN FEB. 22, 1959

Young Pianist Highlights Fine Jr. Symphony Event

By HILMAR GRONDAHL

We have been listening to the Portland Junior Symphony Orchestra ever since it began functioning here 30-odd years ago, and in that time have heard many beautiful and striking performances. But nothing we recall could surpass Saturday night's concert in the Public Auditorium for style, polish and excitement.

The program included the Sixth Sonata for Strings by Rossini, Dohnanyi's "Variations on a Nursery Song," and the Shostakovich "Fifth Symphony." Darlene Barnes, a 15-year-old girl, was piano soloist in the Dohnanyi.

This is a program of joyful and stirring variety, which Conductor Jacob Avshalomov and his skilled charges set forth with disciplined zest.

It was the vehicle which brought the highly gifted young Miss Barnes to the piano where she participated like a veteran with all the self-assurance and positive command one could wish for. She was so well prepared in mind and technical means that she was less than a worry to the conductor; he knew she would be with him and Dohnanyi whenever and however the two of them required.

The Shostakovich Fifth is a big symphony for a big orchestra. It is the means by which Bernstein and the New York Philharmonic overwhelmed the Russians at Moscow. It is a great symphony by any measurement and certainly the finest work to come from the mind of Shostakovich and one of his most difficult.

We mention its stature and difficulty only to indicate why some of us were surprised that it should have been selected by Mr. Avshalomov for performance by his young musicians. But when we heard with what competence they projected the "exposed" texture of the Rossini Sonata and the vast complexity of the introduction to the Dohnanyi variations, our fears fell away.

It was this performance of the Shostakovich symphony which provided the tension and excitement of the evening. Musicians of broad experience were amazed at the score so tough and terrifying, so beautiful and yet so bellicose, should yield both its toughness and its beauty to those young players. It was a triumph in justification of this educative—musical organization, its objectives and its directors.

Junior Symphony Offers Impressive Surprises In Demanding Program

By HILMAR GRONDAHL

The Portland Junior Symphony Orchestra has had a way over the years of exerting one surprise after another on its patrons, and the concert Saturday night in the Public Auditorium was one of the most impressive of the lot.

The program included a first performance by this group of a Brahms symphony, a Vivaldi violin concerto and a Saint-Saens cello concerto in which the solo positions were occupied by the members of those two sections, and the world premier of William Bergsma's "Chameleon" variations.

The event coincided with the ending of the 36th season for the orchestra and the sixth for Conductor Jacob Avshalomov. It was a testimonial, without being so heralded, to the good works of the conductor, the validity of the idea the organization stands for, and the quality of performer it attracts to its ranks.

Both the soloists, violinist Delmar Pettys, and cellist, Paul Speaker, have in common an assurance and instrumental command which sets their hearers immediately at ease. They have in common, also, an immaculate sense of intonation; something more rare in cellists, but strikingly evident in Mr. Speaker's case.

Young Pettys addressed himself to the severely classical concerto called "Winter" in which the second movement "by the fireside" offers a slow movement of tranquility and contentment which is expressed in a melody of delightful breadth; delightful in the score, delightful in the soloist's assured handling.

Young Speaker had the colorful and fleet statements of a romantic vehicle to deal with, and gave a completely satisfying account of his assignments with a trueness of tone and color and a facility of technique which were enjoyable to eye and ear as well.

Works Difficult

The performance of the Brahms Second Symphony is a story in itself. There has been some worry or concern among even the staunchest supporters of the Junior Symphony as to whether or not certain works in the standard repertory were not too difficult for an ensemble under legal age to tackle.

Stimulating Experience

These concerts and these worries have evidently been in Mr. Avshalomov's consciousness during these past six seasons while he has been teaching, coaching, and drilling his young musicians. And after trying his charges out on the Beethoven "Eroica", the Carl Nielsen "Espansiva" and the Franck D-minor he was ready to let them try one of the Brahms symphonies.

When any youth orchestra can play an item out of the standard symphonic repertory with the assurance, the zest, and the general competency which the Juniors displayed the Brahms D-major Saturday night, the question of whether or not it should be done is pointless. Such a performance becomes more than an educational benefit for the players themselves. It becomes a stimulating experience for the audience as well.

As for Mr. Bergsma's variations, we would like to hear them again, for surely they must contain more substance than we detected at first hearing. To our ears there appeared to be a good deal of instrumental attention to ideas which were fundamentally simple, attention which was more of duplication than enrichment in sound or vitalizing the rhythmic interest.

CLASS OF SERVICE
This is a fast message unless its deferred character is indicated by the proper symbol.

WESTERN UNION
TELEGRAM
W. P. MARSHALL, PRESIDENT

SF-1201

SYMBOLS
DL = Day Letter
NL = Night Letter
LT = International Letter Telegram

The filing time shown in the date line on domestic telegrams is STANDARD TIME at point of origin. Time of receipt is STANDARD TIME at point of destination

(1157 AMP APR23 60) LLD163
SYA078 SY NZA056 PD GRANDVIEW NY 23 248PME 1960 APR 23 PM 12 26
JACOB AVSHALOMOV, DLR 745PMP CONDUCTOR PORTLAND JUNIOR SYMPHONY
CIVIC AUDITORIUM
PORTLAND ORG
GOOD LUCK WITH MY PIECE THANKS AND ALL BEST WISHES TO YOU AND THE ORCHESTRA
BILL BERGSMA.

37th Season

Jacob Avshalomov, Musical Director
Donald Thulean, Guest Conductor Sabbatical Term

November 26, 1960

BEETHOVEN	Overture: Consecration of the House
MENDELSSOHN	Symphony NO. 5, "Reformation"
MOZART	Piano Concerto, Bb, K. 450 Patricia O'Banion, *Soloist*
BARTOK	Hungarian Peasant Songs

February 4, 1961

CIMAROSA	Overture: "The Three Brothers"
MILHAUD	Concerto for Percussion Louis Wildman, *Soloist*
HAYDN	Symphony NO. 88, G major
BRITTEN	Young Person's Guide to the Orchestra: David Campbell, *Narrator*
WAGNER	Die Meistersinger–Exerpts

PROGRAM REPEATED at MT. ANGEL COLLEGE–FEBRUARY 11

April 22, 1961

HANDEL	Concerto Grosso, B mi., op. 6 NO. 12
DELIUS	Walk to the Paradise Garden
WARD	**Divertimento for Orchestra

COMMISSIONED BY THE PORTLAND JUNIOR SYMPHONY

BRAHMS	Song of Destiny
KODALY	Te Deum

Evelyn Caldwell Phillips, *Soprano;* Frank Holman, *Tenor;*
Carolyn Faulkner Foos, *Contralto;* Stanton Choate, *Bass*

Guest Choirs: Lewis & Clark College, Linfield College, Oregon College of Education, Pacific University, & University of Portland

May 13, 1961

FANCIES & ENCORES

Free Concert Sponsored by the Music Performance Trust Fund of the Recording Industries

** *World Premiere*

Guests, Young Orchestra Delight

By **HILMAR GRONDAHL**
Music Editor, The Oregonian

The Portland Junior Symphony offered two special attractions at its concert in the Public Auditorium Saturday night. One was the guest conductor, Donald Thulean. The other was a guest soloist, Patricia O'Banion, pianist.

The large audience was entitled to wonder how Mr. Thulean would do directing this youth ensemble in the first of his three concerts during the season of Jacob Avshalomov's sabbatical, and also how little Miss O'Banion would do as soloist in the Mozart B-flat concerto K 450.

This is no hesitation from this department in saying that both special musicians deserved their success. Furthermore, the event was another high point for members of the orchestra.

It was delightful to hear from these young musicians performances in which the sectional balances were justly observed, where there was clarity of attack and unity of speech even when all strings were playing as in the opening of the first Bartok setting of the Hungarian Peasant Songs. There was a stylish grace and piquancy in the way they played the orchestral complement for the Mozart concerto.

Balance Evident

It was apparent at the outset of the concert that in the rehearsal periods since this season began, the musicians of the orchestra have adjusted themselves to a conducting technique quite different from that of their regular leader. Mr. Thulean conducts without baton, and his right hand does not convey simply the beat; it is a partner in expressive direction as well. He also dispensed with the score (except for the concerto) and it was obvious that he knew the musical material with which he was dealing.

Certainly the acclaim Mr. Thulean and his young charges won was not through any simple programming. The scheduled works were Beethoven's overture "Consecration of the House", Mendelssohn's "Reformation" symphony, the aforementioned concerto Hungarian Peasant Songs.

Pianist Impressive

It would be impossible for one not to be captivated by Patricia O'Banion and her playing. She came onto the stage looking like the fetching figure on a valentine. And a colleen with the name Patricia O'Banion suggests Mozart and his friend Michael Kelly. Miss O'Banion was friendly and faithful to Mozart's B-flat concerto, and if, as it sometimes does to professionals, it taxed her memory, she made a brave recovery and finished to the soaring approval of the house.

She plays with taste, sensibility, and good style. The way she brought out the sly byplay on the main theme of the slow movement was charming, and if there were moments in which her tone seemed small, there were those other moments in which it came through with remarkable vitality.

OREGON JOURNAL NOV. 27, 1960

New Conductor Debuts With Junior Symphony

By **MARTIN CLARK**
Journal Music Editor

Enthusiasm is a quality that permeates the work of Donald Thulean, conductor of the 1960–61 season of the Portland Junior Symphony. Thulean made his debut Saturday night at The Auditorium in the opening concert of the season for the orchestra.

The juniors are indeed fortunate to have a young man of such perceptive musicianship during the year their musical director, Jacob Avshalomov, is in Europe to study and compose.

Soloist of the evening was Patricia O'Banion, 15, a student of Nellie Tholen.

She was heard in the Mozart Piano Concerto in B flat major. The young lady disclosed a nice feeling for what might best be described as the Mozartean elegant hesitation or pause, an elusive characteristic of the composer, but one which runs throughout all his work.

An audience of about 2,600—one of the best on record for the juniors—gave a warm reception to the concert which opened with the Beethoven overture, "Consecration of the House."

Mendelssohn's Symphony No. 5 (Reformation), with its familiar but ever stirring themes—the "Dresden Amen" and "A Mighty Fortress Is Our God"—concluded the first half of the performance.

A public reception honoring Mr. and Mrs. Thulean was scheduled in the south wing of The Auditorium after the program.

THE OREGONIAN FEB. 5, 1961

Symphony Throng Big

A record crowd of 5,000 youngsters was on hand Saturday morning to hear a performance of the Portland Junior Symphony Orchestra at the Municipal Auditorium. Forty-four buses brought elementary and high school children from all over Oregon and Washington, Mrs. Doris H. Johnston said.

One of the largest groups present was from the Beaverton schools: 650 youngsters who came in ten buses. There was also a considerable number of children from Washington. Camas was represented by about 270, Kelso about 170, and Longview Community Church about 30.

Groups came from as far off as Garibaldi on the Oregon coast. Tucker-Maxon Oral School, in Portland, sent about 10 children

According to all officials present the children were exceptionally well behaved. Mrs. Claude Farrow Jr., one of the directors of the Junior Symphony Association and co-chairman for this concert said she was "thrilled both with the response and the conduct."

There were a few small groups that could only look bewildered and hope some one would aim them in the right direction. One little girl was heard warning a little boy, "Eddie, you're gettin' lost."

THE OREGONIAN FEB. 5, 1961

Junior Symphony Gives Crowd-Pleasing Concert

By HILMAR GRONDAHL
Music Editor, The Oregonian

Some sparkling playing was done Saturday night in the Public Auditorium as the Portland Junior Symphony Orchestra under Donald Thulean addressed itself to music by Cimarosa, Milhaud, Haydn, Britten and Wagner.

Humor was a concomitant ingredient in the "Three Brothers" overture by Cimarosa and the Haydn symphony No. 88 in G, as well as the Milhaud concerto for percussion and small orchestra which featured Louis Wildman as soloist.

This Haydn symphony is hard to play if one wants to reproduce anything but the bare notes; and even a literal reading is difficult. But these young musicians were aware of and in command of the subtleties which make the music delightful rather than simply pleasant. The perky decorations which embellish the lovely theme of the largo were as enchanting as they are meant to be.

While there was little humor invested in the music of Milhaud's concerto as such, there was amusement in the outward aspects of this piece performed by Louis Wildman within and among his battery of percussion which came riding up out of the pit in a quantity to fill the entire elevator.

Simply watching this talented young musician encompassing the effects the composer had written into the solo part amused at least one of his auditors as well as exciting that same listener's admiration.

It was a pleasing piece of music in Milhaud's free and easy style which young Wildman and his associates appeared to enjoy to the fullest.

Following intermission Thulean and the orchestra exposed the large audience to a piece of music which exposes each of the sections of the ensemble to the aural scrutiny of the audience. This was Benjamin Britten's clever set of variations and fugue on a theme by Henry Purcell, called "The Young Person's Guide to the Orchestra" for which David Campbell, an honorary director of the orchestra, was the narrator.

The last section of the concert consisted of three sections from Wagner's "Die Meistersinger"; the introduction to Act 3, the dance of the apprentices, and the procession of the Mastersingers.

Here again was scrupulous playing, well prepared and in excellent style. It was a concert of more than passing pleasure.

World Premiere Feature Of Symphony's Concert

By HILMAR GRONDAHL
Music Editor, The Oregonian

The world premiere of Robert Ward's Divertimento for Orchestra was only one of the highlights of the Portland Junior Symphony Orchestra concert which Donald Thulean conducted Saturday night in the Public Auditorium.

There were also choral works by Brahms and Kodaly of size and substance engaging singers for a massed chorus of several hundred from five local and nearby schools; Lewis and Clark, Linfield Oregon College of Education, University of Portland and Pacific University.

And not least significant insofar as interpretive skill was concerned were the performances of Handel's Twelfth Concerto Grosso and "The Walk to the Paradise Garden" by Delius.

Ward's divertimento was made to order for the Junior Symphony as another of the six commissions granted to the Portland ensemble by the Rockefeller Foundation. One of the specifications for composing these scores is that they shall be within the technical grasp of the ensemble for which they are composed. It must be said that in this regard Mr. Ward was flattering to the local ensemble, for there are areas in his score which would bother a professional orchestra.

But difficulties didn't bother the local performers, in fact, the difficulties hardly showed. For one reason the players had a composition done in a vein of contemporary means and American style which they could grasp regardless of its tough sections. There were syncopations of the foot-tapping kind and melodies which had a strong folk flavor. The writing is technically adroit, making effective use of the entire ensemble from the striking fanfare which opened the proceedings to the rousing roundup at the end.

There was no doubt from the way it was played that the orchestra liked what it and Conductor Thulean found in the divertimento. And it appeared to be immediately diverting to the audience as well.

Music Impressive

But if you were present Saturday night, and emotional impact is what you remember about a piece of music, you are undoubtedly going to think of this as the concert that provided a singularly thrilling performance of Kodaly's Te Deum. Here is a sacred composition which differs from the traditional by reason of an almost barbaric fervor and a flamboyancy of instrumental and vocal coloring.

The choral statements were magnificently intoned by the large and well trained chorus, and the solo quartet composed of Evelyn Caldwell Phillips, Carolyn Faulkner Foos, Frank Holman and Stanton Choate gave refined tonal highlights to the total effect. This is a complex piece to direct, and Mr. Thulean gave it a vivid and persuasive reading.

The Kodaly was preceded by the Brahms "Shicksalslied" for chorus and orchestra. This is a handsome piece. Typical Brahms, it was performed with taste and good effect.

38th Season

Jacob Avshalomov, Conductor

	November 18, 1961
BOCCHERINI	*La Musica Notturna di Madrid
BARTOK	*Piano Concerto NO. 3 Katherine Anne Fischer, *Soloist*
BERLIOZ	Symphonie Fantastique, OP. 14

	February 17, 1962
TCHAIKOVSKY	Symphony NO. 4, F minor
BACH	Brandenburg Concerto NO. 2
DEBUSSY	Nocturnes 1 & 2
HONEGGER	Pacific 231

	April 14, 1962
DONIZETTI	Overture: "Don Pasquale"
MOZART	Symphony NO. 40, G minor
CHAUSSON	Poeme for Violin, OP. 25 Gilda Muhlbauer, *Soloist*
CHAVEZ	Toccata for Percussion
BRUCKNER	Symphony NO. 4, Eb, Allegro

April 28, 1962

Seattle World's Fair

Selections from the Season

* *Portland Premier*

Progress In Musicianship Praised

By HILMAR GRONDAHL
Music Editor, The Oregonian

When Jacob Avshalomov conductor of the Portland Junior Symphony Orchestra returned from his sabbatical year in Europe he brought with him a charming suite by Boccherini which served as the opening number on this ensemble's program Saturday night in the Public Auditorium. The other features were Bartok's Third Piano Concerto starring Katherine Ann Fischer at the solo instrument, and the Symphonie Fantastique by Berlioz.

There was fun and a lot of solid musicianship displayed at this affair which attracted a large audience, and showed the members of the orchestra to be in extra fine fettle for their season's first concert.

The Boccherini suite is a nocturne, and one gathers that the evening is warm, since the musicians seldom play very hard, and there appear to be zephyrs which carry off some of the instrumental sound from time to time.

It is fun for the players, especially in that movement which permits the string players to treat their instruments like guitars. It's a refreshing score which the orchestra played with engaging spirit. Also it was a first local performance.

Little Miss Fischer proved to be an amazing keyboard soloist. Petite to the degree that one would have questioned her ability to manage a concerto of this magnitude.

But no difficulties beset Miss Fischer, as, with complete assurance and obviously complete comprehension, she related the solo portions of the concerto to the entire concept.

Together the musical director and the soloist were bringing, by way of this second local premier, an entirely new field of sound to the orchestra and, in actual performance, to the audience.

Concerto 'Adventure'

So the Bartok Third Concerto was an educational adventure for the ensemble and soloist; it was communion with a tonal creation which rates among the masterpieces of this century. Those who know this score cannot applaud too highly the care and artistry which Miss Fischer, Mr. Avshalomov and the Junior Symphony brought to bear on its realization.

As a concluding work the conductor let his charges see what they could do with an old warhorse such as the Berlioz Symphonie Fantastique. He must have been pleased with the result for they responded to the impetuous sentiment with an alertness and general skill which was perceptive and enjoyable.

The regular Saturday morning concert for school children brought about 2,500 youngsters from 20 schools in Oregon and Washington.

Junior Symphony's Season Opener Said Credit to Professional Group

By DONALD DIERKS

The Portland Junior Symphony's first concert of the season was performed with such skill and musicianship that it is difficult to imagine a finer organization of young people in this country—or anywhere.

Civic pride in the Junior Symphony is highly justified.

The compositions this orchestra performs are always of the highest musical quality and Saturday night's program included two masterworks which would do credit to the repertoire of professional orchestras. They were the Symphony Fantastique, Op. 14, of Hector Berlioz and the Third Concerto for Piano and Orchestra by Bela Bartok, the latter being a first performance in Portland.

The soloist in the Bartok was Katherine Ann Fischer, a young pianist of exceptional talent. Were it not so, she would not have been equal to the myriad difficulties of this concerto. One never had the impression that her technical abilities were taxed to the limit, and therefore there was an ease about her playing which invited confidence and enjoyment. Equally gratifying was the young artist's apparent understanding of the musical implications of this demanding composition.

The playing required of the orchestra in the Bartok is no less demanding or taxing. The various problems of balance, rhythm, ensemble, and rapport with the soloist were handled with a collective talent equal to the pianist's and, therefore, equally praiseworthy.

The romantic and enjoyable Symphony Fantastique requires a large and varied instrumentation and is a fine display piece. Soloists and the various sections of the orchestra were heard in bold relief and performed commendably.

Mr. Avshalomov's tight rein on the orchestra during the Berlioz resulted in admirable precision and accuracy, but at the same time limited some of the delightful excitement which this work possesses.

La Musica Notturna di Madrid by Luigi Boccherini, a suite for string orchestra, contributed to the program as a conversation piece and as a vehicle for the string section. Special commendation is due the violins who performed in this and throughout the evening with great tonal beauty and nearly flawless intonation.

Juniors Rated Best In Debussy Nocturnes

By MARTIN CLARK
Journal Music Editor

Saturday night at the Auditorium Jacob Avshalomov conducted the Portland Junior Symphony in as pleasantly varied a program as he has presented during his years at the helm of the orchestra.

Tchaikovsky's Fourth Symphony took care of the first half of the concert, followed after intermission by the Bach Brandenburg Concerto No. 2, two Debussy nocturnes, "Nuages" and "Fetes," and Arthur Honegger's "Pacific 231."

THE ORCHESTRA was at its technical best in the Debussy works, though it was more than equal to the tricky stylistic mannerisms Honegger has incorporated in his engine piece. However, contrary to what the composer himself has said about the work, it does give a highly realistic picture of the locomotive itself. And there's nothing wrong in that.

The Brandenburg No. 2 has always posed a problem with its excessively high part for the trumpet.

AVSHALOMOV'S solution was to split the part between an E-flat clarinet and trumpet. While I can't say this is THE solution, it must be conceded it comes as close as any other approach to solving what I'm afraid is an insoluble dilemma. Able soloists were Marylou Speaker, violin; Mary Bovey, flute; Martin Friedman, oboe; Sharon Wills, E-flat clarinet; and Don Riley, trumpet.

The best performed movement in the Tchaikovsky was the third, in which the strings get a workout a la pizzicato. Familiar though the Fourth may be, familiarity should not be confused with simplicity. This is a difficult and challenging work for any orchestra, junior or otherwise.

AN AUDIENCE approaching 2,000 expressed great enthusiasm for what, in many ways, was one of the most ambitious programs of the Juniors.

Again, I never cease to marvel at the individual musicianship of these young people and Avshalomov's ability to get a maximum of really musical readings from them.

Junior Symphony Music Admirable

By DONALD DIERKS

The Portland Junior Symphony presented its second program of the season Saturday evening at the Civic auditorium. As has come to be expected, the young performers played an ambitious program with admirable musicianship.

Two of Claude Debussy's three nocturnes for orchestra furnished the musical high point of the evening. This music was exceedingly well chosen and suited to the orchestra. The impressionistic style, with its muted sonorities and languid, melancholy solos, is one which the Junior Symphony readily grasped and performed with grace and subtlety.

This is music which lies well within the emotional realm of young people; and although there are many technical difficulties to be found in the score, each section of the orchestra distinguished itself.

Perhaps not so aptly programmed was the Symphony No. 4 in F minor of Tchaikovsky. This symphony is difficult for a young orchestra because of its heady emotionalism, and because its appeal relies so heavily upon sentimentality, overstatement, and the bravura style. These considerations, together with its formidable technical problems, make the symphony best suited to a mature orchestra.

Nevertheless, it was enjoyable to see the Junior Symphony address itself so intently and earnestly to music of this kind, and in the scherzo some really fine ensemble work was achieved

Such a work definitely has a place in the training repertoire, but perhaps is not for putting the orchestra's best public foot forward.

Five very able musicians formed the concertino group for the Second Brandenburg Concerto of J. S. Bach.

In the slow movement, especially, did these young performers display their abilities. Their balance was good and they were generally responsive to one another.

Without the high trumpet in the first and third movements the whole character of this concerto is changed. These parts, which add the stately jubilation and exhilaration surely intended by Bach, are excessively difficult to be sure. However, when this performer is not available there are five other Brandenburgs from which to choose.

Arthur Honegger's Pacific 231 is a tone poem describing a locomotive starting, accelerating and stopping. This was an excellent final selection and one which the orchestra played very well and with obvious relish and enthusiasm.

American Way Develops Violinists

By HILMAR GRONDAHL
Music Editor, The Oregonian

(Ed. Note: This is the second part of an interview with Jacob Avshalomov, conductor of the Portland Junior Symphony, on his doings in Europe on a sabbatical, and with his orchestra members here. We had been talking about the development of solo violinists in Europe, notably in Russia.)

"While our American system doesn't resemble either the Russian or German, we have been able to develop some fine violinists, such as Ricci, Menuhin and Isaac Stern. You have known Stern for some time, haven't you?" we asked.

"Yes, I've know Stern ever since I showed him my father's violin concerto twenty-one years ago in New York," said Jacob Avshalomov, conductor of the Portland Junior Symphony Orchestra.

"He invited me to attend a chamber music session at his apartment at the Henry Hudson Hotel, and to bring along any quartet music I had written. I had none at that time that I cared to show, but I went anyhow. It was an event to remember; the quartet was made up of Stern, Bob Mann, William Primrose and Leonard Rose."

Players Responsive

We had heard some rhapsodic accounts of the reactions of Junior Symphony members to the rehearsal session they had with Stern, so we asked Avshalomov how he had arranged this great experience.

'It started last summer when I was teaching at Northwestern University. I went to hear Stern play at Ravinia. Afterwards I asked him if he'd play through a concerto with the Junior Symphony in private when he came to Portland in March. He said, 'can do.' He had known of the JS for some time, and is a member of the advisory committee in the selection of composers commissioned under our Rockefeller grant. But his willingness to play with us is part of a larger generous concern for music-making in the world.

"Before the session here, I asked him whether he would prefer to play straight through the Beethoven concerto, knowing we had a concert with the Portland Symphony that same evening in Salem, or whether he would like to stop and work with the orchestra. He said, characteristically, that the students might get more out of the session if he worked with them. I was delighted, because we had prepared for this meeting with great care and I knew the players were in fine fettle to respond to whatever he might do.

"We arrived at the rehearsal hall to find the orchestra and a goodly assemblage of parents and board members, each in his own way attuned to the moment. We played through to the first tutti after the solo enters, and Stern flagged us down to a stop; 'Before we go any farther, he said, I want to say Bravo, all of you.'

"He then suggested that we might learn something by analyzing what we were doing. Addressing the oboist he asked him how he would sing the first phrase. Would all notes be equally weighted? No. Where would the stress be? Ah, good! Now play it just that way.

Hints Valuable

'In this manner Stern stopped every so often. His remarks to the strings included valuable hints on fingering, bowing and the relativity of dynamic markings. At structural points in the music he stopped to note the problems of setting a new tempo, a problem faced jointly by soloist and conductor. When the French horn missed a note in the adagio, Stern remarked that this was a famous, or infamous note. And when, later in the movement, it was played perfectly he sang out "good boy" over his own playing.

"At one point, glancing at the clock, Stern asked me how much time we had. I told him as much as he could spare. We continued for another half hour, taking the rondo through to its delightful end. And while he packed up his fiddle to the general applause of the orchestra, he quieted us all, and said he'd love to stay on and on, but he had a paid job that evening. However he hoped that he could make music with the orchestra another time.

"As we walked out he said to me, 'I must say that is a responsive group.' I couldn't disagree with him. They certainly had been."

We can imagine that no one at that rehearsal, parent or child, will ever forget the thrill of that experience. Can't you imagine the players saying years from now, "Remember the day Isaac Stern rehearsed with us?"

Isaac Stern Inspires the PJS

SUNDAY OREGONIAN FEB. 18, 1962

Portland Junior Symphony Produces Exciting Moments

By HILMAR GRONDAHL
Music Editor, The Oregonian

The Portland Junior Symphony Orchestra produced some really exciting moments in its concert under the direction of Jacob Avshalomov in the Public Auditorium Saturday night. Excitement as a musical ingredient came primarily in their performance of Tchaikovsky's Fourth symphony.

There was vividly colorful spirit in Honegger's "Pacific 231" which concluded the concert. Between these two scores there was a performance of the Second Brandenburg concerto and two movements from Debussy's suite of nocturnes.

The Bach Concerto had as its featured players Marylou Speaker, violin; Mary Bovey, flute; Martin Friedman, oboe; Sharon Wills, clarinet; and Don Riley, trumpet. The problem of the high trumpet passages was shared in this performance by a regular trumpet and an E-flat clarinet, this latter being a small high pitched instrument generally used in bands.

'Shocks' Suggested

The program notes frankly suggested that "purists will be shocked." If they were, they remained quiet about it for there was no whistling, hissing, or sudden gallops toward the exits that we noticed. Actually, it seemed a reasonable compromise with the almost impossible requirements of the trumpet of Bach's day, and a musical accommodation which both gave the spirit and an agreeable set of sonorities suitable to the ideas in the original. At least suitable enough.

Mr. Avshalomov had his small orchestra with cello and harpsichord continue moving in the proper pace and style. What was especially delightful was the andante in which the violin, flute and oboe handed a lovely theme around with the support of Barbara Hinshaw at the harpsichord and Paul Speaker, cellist.

We don't recall hearing the Junior Symphony play the Tchaikovsky Fourth before, so our assumption is that it is brand new to their repertory. It is fine score for this and successive personnel to sharpen their instrumental and musical skills on for it is challenging in both these ways.

Mr. Avshalomov kept the work moving in true Tchaikovskian spirit with rather spectacular help from his brass and a little less than satisfactory balance from the woodwinds, particularly in those areas in which an instrument or two was posed against the total body of strings.

The two Debussy nocturnes, "Nuages" and "Fetes" were done with a fine feeling for the texture and atmosphere inherent in these pieces.

THE REPORTER APR. 16, 1962

Junior Symphony's 3rd Concert Maintains Highest Standards

By DONALD DIERKS

Conductor Jacob Avshalomov chose an interesting and varied program for the concert and the orchestra performed it earnestly, with a number of rewarding high points.

Donizetti's infrequently heard overture to "Don Pasquale" opened the program. This light, melodious work, so typical of its genre, was performed with ease and an obvious understanding of the style.

The same assured playing was heard again when the orchestra accompanied the evening's soloist in the beautiful "Poeme op. 25" for violin and orchestra by Chausson.

Gilda Muhlebauer, a young violinist from New York City, has won many awards in this country and abroad.

Her tone, while not large, was warm and clear and her sense of pitch was highly developed. Beyond this, she ably apprehended the musical ideas contained in this beautiful score.

The orchestra, for its part, unfolded an accompaniment which was mobile in terms of tempi and always well regulated in dynamics.

After the intermission, the percussion section of the orchestra returned to perform the "Toccata for Percussion" by Carlos Chavez. This is a virtuoso work for these instruments and it was performed with near-virtuoso skill.

Intricate rhythms rumble from the low to the high drums, and sounds requiring split-second timing rebound like echoes from one instrument to another. These percussionists deserve high praise, indeed, for their excellent playing.

It is very wise to take percussion instruments seriously; one reason is their importance to the full orchestra, and another is that they comprise an art medium in their own right.

The allegro of the "Symphony No. 4" of Bruckner contained its highest levels of musical attainment reached this season.

In the solo passages very fine work was done by various members of the ensemble. In the tuttis there were sonorities which result only when there is excellent balance among sections and a general trueness of pitch throughout the orchestra. The tempi were well chosen and the dynamic contrasts were arresting.

It was just the kind of playing with which to end a concert.

Junior Symphony Offers Mozart

By **HILMAR GRONDAHL**
Music Editor, The Oregonian

The Portland Junior Symphony Orchestra, under Jacob Avshalomov's direction, gave one of its most delightful concerts Saturday night in the Public Auditorium when it presented Gilda Muhlbauer in the Chausson Poeme and a list of orchestral works by Donizetti, Mozart, Chavez and Bruckner.

It was the rollicking overture to "Don Pasquale" which opened the concert and the first movement of Bruckner's "Romantic" Symphony which brought it to a close. Each served to give scope to the playful and affecting aspects of the two pieces, but it was the Mozart G-minor symphony which gave significant measure of the artistic awareness and persuasive performance of these young musicians.

The G-minor is one of the two most challenging as well as most beautiful of the Mozart symphonies. The 80 players who were directing their attention to this music Saturday night do not consider themselves as professionals, but they had had a professional revealing to them over a period of several weeks those interpretive problems which must be solved before Mozart permits himself to be heard as the incomparable genius he was.

The perfect structure of the four movements, the need for purity of intonation and simultaneous attack, the spirit of simplicity amidst effects of utmost subtlety; these are some of the challenges which are imposed, and which were met under Mr. Avshalomov's knowledgeable direction.

It is all very well and very appropriate to make large and even spectacular effects as this ensemble often does, but as an indication of the effectiveness of teaching they get and the effect it has on their musicianship, nothing they have done in years has carried such a strong testimonial of their emergence as student musicians who know what is worthwhile and how to express it. The first three movements were admirable, the winds in the trio of the minuet quite remarkable. Older heads and nimbler fingers than these have found the opening statement of the finale a hard thing to keep in clear unison, but this too was bettered as the movement went on.

Violinist Engaging

The appearance of Miss Muhlbauer as violin soloist with the orchestra was a happy occasion which seems to inaugurate a new policy of welcoming young musicians from out of town to its concert platform. Was it nervousness which gave her opening statement such a rapid vibrato? Her tone is clear, and pure, her intonation exact, her musicianship of engaging sensibility. Her solo assignments were nicely related to the whole fabric of sound, the occasions of prominence being delightfully stylish, the concourse of the full ensemble being in character and well played.

The Chavez toccata for percussion was, as we recall it, performed here once when the composer was guest conducting the Portland Symphony. A sophisticated virtuoso piece built upon certain primitive rhythms and employing instruments the ancient Mexican Indians never dreamed of, it is a fascinating piece which the six percussionists on stage managed with notable precision.

OREGON JOURNAL APR. 16, 1962

Violinist Prevails Over Percussionists

By **MARTIN CLARK**
Journal Music Editor

Sometime when you have absolutely nothing to do, and don't feel like doing that, listen to Carlos Chavez' "Toccata for Percussion."

I'm not suggesting that was the situation of Jacob Avshalomov and the Portland Junior Symphony when they chose this classic (in a class by itself) for their program Saturday night at The Auditorium, but this was the impression made on at least one listener.

IN CASE you're wondering what this 1942 composition by one of Mexico's foremost composers sounded like, it sounded just like you would suspect six percussionists would sound like let loose for three movements without any melodic interference from strings, violins, or brass. Africa would love it.

Other than that, it was a delightful evening—and maybe the Chavez bit was Avshalomov's sly way of making us appreciate the rest of the evening that much more.

SATURDAY night Gilda Muhlbauer appeared as soloist with the Junior Symphony in a performance of Ernest Chausson's "Poeme." In this brief appearance Miss Muhlbauer revealed an unmistakable excitement in her playing, the sort of thing a violinist either has or doesn't have. While the Chausson may not plumb the full range of a violinist's virtuosity, it demands qualities of a more subtle, expressive nature than the stock-in-trade pyrotechnics of any first-rate concert violinist. Her lush, sensuous tone was ideally suited to the Chausson.

DONIZETTI'S Overture to "Don Pasquale" and Mozart's popular Symphony No. 40 in G Minor received positively exhilarating readings. First movement of Bruckner's Fourth Symphony didn't fare as well, but, then, there's not as much to work with there, either.

An audience of about 2,000 responded to the performance with hearty applause, particularly when Miss Muhlbauer was presented with a lovely bouquet of roses by handsome Harry Hanson, Auditorium manager.

The Oregonian APR. 28, 1962

Century 21 Overture

Youth will characterize Portland's representation on the official program of the Seattle World's Fair on Portland Day, Sunday, when Seattle hopes residents of the Rose City will take opportunity to see the sights before the big rush is underway. Portland's delegation to the fair, headed by Mayor Terry Schrunk, will feature the Portland Junior Symphony, which will perform during the day in the new World's Fair Opera House.

Portland can be proud of its representation at an event which, during the next six months, will feature some of the world's most celebrated artists. The Portland Junior Symphony, which has one of the longest histories of such organizations in this country, is also, under the direction of Jacob Avshalomov, one of the best by consensus of the critics. And the superlative may as well be world-wide in application; for the Opera House will be the setting for performances by the best of orchestras, soloists, and ballet and dance troupes from a dozen or more nations.

Although the fair promoters may not know it, the Portland Junior Symphony has more than talent and precision to recommend it to the Opera House stage. There are just 100 members, all under 21, an appropriate company to play what amounts to the overture to Century 21.

OREGON JOURNAL APR. 1962

Major and Minor

By MARTIN CLARK
Journal Music Editor

Familiarity may not always breed contempt, but there is a tendency to take the familiar for granted.

So it is with the Portland Junior Symphony. Although Portland music critics have, over the years, sung the praises of the Juniors and their conductor, Jacob Avshalomov, I still have the feeling a huge number of music-loving individuals in the Portland metropolitan area are not aware of the importance of the remarkable organization in our midst.

SINCE ITS founding in 1924 under the guiding hand of Jacques Gershkovitch, the Juniors have grown to become probably the outstanding youth orchestra in the United States.

This is not an organization for youngsters to get together just to "express themselves." Self-expression is well and good, but without professional discipline and instruction it remains merely an outlet, and not a channel of growth and development into something young people carry over into their adult life.

The past season gives a slight idea of the caliber of this orchestra.

IN ADDITION to the usual three concerts, this season in Portland concluded with "A Triskelion of the Arts," including reading of poetry by young northwest writers with interludes of chamber music. In the evening of the same day, May 12, two new works for soprano and orchestra by Seattle composers Michael White and John David Lamb were presented.

Climaxing years of successes by the orchestra was this year's concert in the Seattle World's Fair Opera House April 29. The Seattle critics were unanimous in singing the praises of Avshalomov and his enthusiastic, young orchestra.

Although critics may differ on the value of some of the new works selected for performance by the Juniors, there is no disagreement on the value of including new works in practically every concert.

NO LESS IMPORTANT is the great work the orchestra has done in giving young talent an opportunity to perform with a fine symphony orchestra—not an opportunity readily available.

This past season the solo spot was extended to a gifted New York violinist, Gilda Muhlbauer, and the orchestra's board has indicated young prize-winning soloists from other parts of the country will be given an opportunity in the future to display their talents to Portland audiences.

Parents of musically talented children should be doubly grateful they live in a city that offers such opportunities as those available in the Portland Junior Symphony.

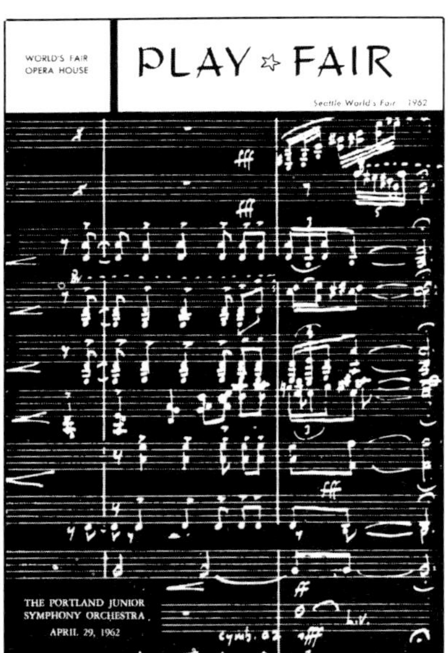

Seattle Post-Intelligencer APR. 30, 1962

Portland Junior Symphony Scores

BY JOHN VOORHEES

In some ways the second concert in Seattle's new Opera House was even more exciting than the first.

For the free concert by the very fine Portland Junior Symphony Orchestra yesterday afternoon in the Opera House allowed one to roam about between selections since there were no reserved seats.

And listening to the Portland group corroborated what seemed apparent at the gala opening concert—that the acoustics in the new Opera House are fantastically good.

THE PORTLANDERS did themselves proud in their ambitious concert—Donizetti's "Don Pasquale" Overture, Bartok's Third Piano Concerto, Tchaikovsky's Symphony No. 4 and Chavez' Toccata for Percussion.

Composer Jacob Avshalomov is the orchestra's conductor and he has welded it into a very fine unit that plays with professional polish and musicianship. It is, undoubtedly, a marvelous training ground for players that move up to Portland's Symphony Orchestra.

The Donizetti was given a polished, lively reading and the Tchaikovsky was rendered with an emphasis on the drama in that popular symphony.

The Bartok concerto was the least successful. Although there were notable moments by both the orchestra and the pianist, Katherine Ann Fischer, the work never fell thoroughly into focus, in terms of form. Still, it was a noble attempt at performing a most challenging work.

AT FIRST glance the Chavez Toccata for percussion seemed a strange choice for it uses no players except those in the percussion section. But as the work progressed under Avshalomov's dynamic direction, it emerged as not only a tour de force for percussionists but in terms of composition as well. The six young musicians played it brilliantly and earned not only enthusiastic audience applause but applause from their fellow musicians.

Several notables, including Fair president Joseph Gandy, the respective mayors of Seattle and Portland, and Vilem Sokol, conductor of the Seattle Youth Symphony spoke briefly during intermission. All of them praised Avshalomov for the work he has done with the Portland Junior Symphony Orchestra. It was praise well deserved.

Seattle Post-Intelligencer APR. 30, 1962

By LOUIS R. GUZZO

TALENT FROM PORTLAND: Fairgoers who walked into the Opera House yesterday afternoon by accident or design must have marveled at the high quality of the 90 or so young musicians on stage.

They were members of the Portland Junior Symphony, as gifted a collection of 21-and-under musicians as exists anywhere in America. Much of the credit for the high rating the orchestra has achieved (which includes foundation grants for the introduction of new music) must go to its fine conductor and musical director, Jacob Avshalomov.

Known to many Seattleites as a composer and former member of the University of Washington music faculty, Avshalomov drew two hours of expert music-making from his inspired Oregonians.

The program indicated the conductor is unusually fond of percussive music. It included Bartok's Third Piano Concerto, a feast of percussive color and compelling sounds in the solo instrument, as well as in the orchestra, and Chavez's tantalizing, ingenious Toccata for Percussion.

Katherine Ann Fischer, a pianist from Lewis and Clark College, was the soloist in the Bartok and brought it off creditably, although her interpretation lacked the sheer power and incisive brilliance the concerto demands.

Other works on the program included the overture to Donizetti's "Don Pasquale" and Tchaikovsky's Fourth Symphony.

The Portland Junior Symphony is blessed with riches in many choirs, notable French horns and brass. Such wealth of material enables Avshalomov to essay virtually any work in the traditional or contemporary repertoire.

It is a well disciplined orchestra and a great credit to Portland.

39th Season

Jacob Avshalomov, Conductor

November 17, 1962

BEETHOVEN	Symphony NO. 8, F major
PETRASSI	»Prologue & Five Inventions
	Commissioned by the Portland Junior Symphony
BRUCKNER	Symphony NO. 4, Eb, Allegro
RIMSKY-KORSAKOV	Capriccio Espagnol

March 9, 1963

CHERUBINI	*Overture: "Ali Baba"
RAMEAU	"Les Indes Galante" - Suite NO. 1
IBERT	*Concerto for Flute
	Victoria Poullette, *Soloist*
DUKAS	Symphony in C major

April 25, 1963

Endowment Fund Benefit Concert

Portland Art Museum

Portland Junior Symphony Chamber Orchestra

With Doriot Anthony Dwyer, *Flute*, & Joseph Hearne, *Bass*, of the Boston Symphony Orchestra

HANDEL—ECCLES—MOZART—DRAGONETTI AVSHALOMOV

May 12, 1963

BOYCE	Symphony NO. 5
TIPPETT	*A Child of Our Time

Gloria Cutsforth, *Soprano;* Helen Bolton, *Contralto;* William Hazelbauer, *Tenor;* Neil Wilson, *Bass*

Guest Choirs: Lewis & Clark, Portland State, Warner-Pacific Colleges and Oregon State University

---

May 12, 1963

Triskelion of the Arts

Poetry Reading - Chamber Music - Art Exhibition

Portland Art Museum

* *Portland Premier*

» *World Premier*

OREGON JOURNAL NOV. 19, 1962

Juniors Play 'Joke' In Opening Concert

By MARTIN CLARK
Journal Music Editor

I can take a joke as well as anyone—I thought.

But my Scotch blood draws the line at jokes that cost money, even if it's someone else's money.

This is the only explanation I can think of for the Portland Junior Symphony's sixth commissioned work under its grant from the Rockefeller Foundation, "Prologue & Five Inventions" by Goffredo Petrassi. It received its world premiere Saturday night at The Auditorium in the opening concert of the Juniors' 39th session.

IT WAS AN expensive joke. I think they pay something like $1,200 or $1,500 for these commissioned works. Granted the Rockefellers may have plenty of money, I still don't think it should be thrown away.

On second thought, maybe this sort of commissioned work is not a joke. Maybe it's group self-hypnosis. After 50 years of grinding out this stuff, maybe these composers sincerely think this is music. Could be, you know.

Sure, you have to have the background, the developed technique, the self-discipline to work long and hard hours to be any kind of composer; but all this and a modicum of talent may still produce nothing. It takes all this and one little ingredient we seem to have forgotten today: inspiration.

The Juniors wrapped the Petrassi (he's probably a very nice man, too) with Beethoven (his Eighth Symphony was the opener) and Bruckner (the Allegro movement of his Symphony No. 4) and washed the whole thing down with Rimsky-Korsakov's "Capriccio Espagnol."

THE OREGONIAN NOV. 18, 1962

Junior Symphony Adds Controversy To Program

By HILMAR GRONDAHL
Music Editor, The Oregonian

Without the "Prologue and Five Inventions" of Goffredo Petrussi on the program which the Portland Junior Symphony Orchestra played Saturday night in the Public Auditorium, it would have been a concert of good, but very staple items.

Certainly the Beethoven Eighth Symphony, a movement from the Bruckner "Romantic" Symphony and Rimsky-Korsakov's "Capriccio Espagnol" are not novelties. But in having the world premiere of the contemporary Italian composer's avant garde score to dispense, Jacob Avshalomov had a collection of sound materials which would keep any concert from seeming merely good; it was at once controversial.

The conductor explained before commencing the Petrassi work, which is the sixth in the series of works commissioned for the Junior Symphony through a grant from the Rockefeller Foundation, that the composer was seeking in this piece to do away with a beat basic to body rhythms.

This, in itself, is not a new idea, even among the "far out" composers. But is was the thing, Mr. Avshalomov said, which might make his indications to the orchestra seem meaningless; so much so that he had considered conducting from behind a screen, being anxious not to confuse the audience.

Sounds Pleasing

Soundwise there was a good deal to recommend the Petrassi score. The writing for all instruments is shrewd and knowledgeable; in many instances giving some melodic satisfaction to those who might have thought the pauses too long. Even the pauses were eloquent at times, providing as they did a sense of tension between instrumental statements.

We found the work quite agreeable. Perhaps because of its many silences, and despite its occasional tonal eruptions, it is a score of surprising serenity. It is a credit to the players that they "counted" their entrances precisely and helped with the general cohesion of music which might conceivably have fallen apart.

'Staples' Delightful

The staple items of the program were a delight, the Beethoven symphony with its charming humor, orderly and beautiful invention went smoothly and in excellent style despite a bit of horn trouble in the trio.

The Bruckner allegro was a showpiece for the size and quality of the brass section which from the tuba upwards produced a rich sound. However, it wasn't all for the brasses. This ensemble has more first and second violins than larger orchestras, and these were providing a richness to the texture of this music.

The Rimsky-Korsakov caprice has been a staple item of this orchestra from its beginnings, but it is doubtful if the score has ever been given a more colorful and exciting reading that Mr. Avshalomov managed Saturday night.

THE REPORTER NOV. 19, 1962

Junior Symphonists Off to Great Start

By DAVID CAMPBELL

THE OREGONIAN MAR. 1963

Junior Symphony Flutist Said 'Something Special'

By HILMAR GRONDAHL
Music Editor, The Oregonian

Jacob Avshalomov, conductor of the Portland Junior Symphony Orchestra, is not lacking in ingenuity when it comes to planning programs through which to show the public what and how well his young charges are doing. Saturday night the concert was all French, an arrangement which brought three local premiers to those in the Public Auditorium.

The first performances were the overture to "Ali Baba" by Cherubini, Ibert's concerto for flute, and the one and only symphony by Paul Dukas. Victoria Poullette was soloist in the concerto.

Miss Poullette may not be as French as her name suggests nor as the music she addressed, but nationalities aside, she was a delight visually as well as musically. She was a winning sight what with her classical features, her lovely flaxen hair, her electric blue gown and her reassuring assurance.

Flutist 'Special'

As a flutist Miss Poullette is something special. Here is a real musician, one admirably prepared and exhibiting qualities which are native and inherent as well as those carefully learned.

The Cherubini overture which opened the concert was a rousing mass of joyful sound, more mellow and ample in this populous ensemble than any its composer ever heard.

The Dukas symphony, the score of which Mr. Avshalomov found on his European sabbatical, was composed in 1896 and dedicated to his friend, Paul Vidal. That Dukas was a superlative orchestrator everyone knows who is familiar with his best known piece "The Sorcerer's Apprentice."

The score is typical of French treatment of romantic materials.

The entire concert was evidence of the quickening process in the orchestra's dealing with new materials.

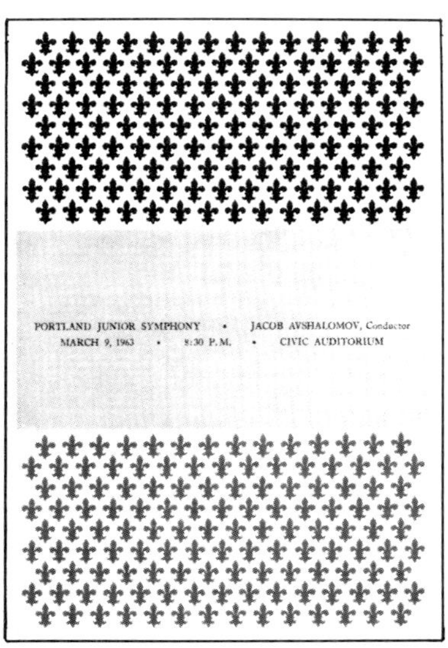

4,000 Children Attend Concert

Attendance at the Portland Junior Symphony's afternoon children's concert Saturday was about 4,000, greatest in the history of the 39 year series, Mrs. Claude Farrow, children's concert chairman announced.

In addition to the children from the Portland area, 58 buses conveyed young music lovers from points as distant as Newport and Oceanlake, Mrs. Farrow said.

Reloading the school buses after a Children's Concert.

OREGON JOURNAL MAR. 11, 1963

Juniors' All French Program Impressive

By MARTIN CLARK
Journal Music Editor

The Portland Junior Symphony's all French program Saturday night at the Auditorium underscored the fact there is a quantity of excellent French composition not dependent on impressionism, which is probably one reason why I was tremendously impressed by the concert.

Jacob Avshalomov conducted his juniors in an unusually polished performance. Outstanding in a thoughtfully chosen program were the Flute Concerto of Jacques Ibert and the Symphony in C Major by Paul Dukas.

Victoria Poullette, an 18-year-old student at Portland State College, was the soloist in Ibert's Concerto for Flute and Orchestra. The work is filled with scintillating cadenzas and instrumental acrobatics to which Miss Poullette was more than equal; but it was in the slow movement the distinctive charm of the composition was most in evidence. The soloist sustained the legato of the lyric line with moving effect.

FOUR DANCES by the 18th century composer Jean-Philippe Rameau, "Les Indes Galantes" Suite No. 1, filled out the first half of the program. They added a graceful, expressive touch to the evening. With the exception of these dances by Rameau, everything on the program was receiving its Portland premiere.

Most pleasant surprise of the evening was Dukas' Symphony in C Major, which took up the final half of the concert. Like nearly everyone else, I've been familiar with his programmatic "The Sorcerer's Apprentice" and paid little attention to anything else he wrote.

HIS SYMPHONY and the sorcerer piece both received their first performances the same year, 1897. The symphony reveals the painstaking workmanship of Dukas the teacher. Although filled with romantic warmth, the work never departs from an individual elegance of style and refinement of expression. It's a work that should be in the standard symphonic repertoire.

Sunday Oregonian OCT. 7, 1962

Juniors Here To Stay

Announcement by officers of the Portland Junior Symphony Assn. of the establishment of a Junior Symphony Endowment Fund is of special significance, for it symbolizes both the maturity and the permanence of this youngsters' orchestra as a major Oregon institution.

The announcement does not signalize a fund drive, but it does serve as an invitation for gifts or bequests to build an income from which the orchestra can enrich and expand its program. Revenue from the endowment will initially go to presentation of young soloists, scholarships for summer study at such music centers as Tanglewood and Aspen, recordings of commissioned works, and trips by the orchestra such as that this summer to the Seattle's World's Fair, among other things.

Portland's is one of the very few junior symphonies in the nation receiving the serious attention of the critics. Such organizations often have a precarious existence because of lack of a financial base. Portland's Junior Symphony has made the first move to make it's base secure.

THE OREGONIAN APR. 26, 1963

Musicians From Boston Spice Benefit Concert

By HILMAR GRONDAHL
Music Editor, The Oregonian

TV "creatures" come to visit a Children's Concert.

It isn't often that we review benefit concerts, but the endowment fund benefit concert of the Portland Junior Symphony Orchestra in the Art Museum Thursday night was irresistible.

It wasn't alone the fact that flutist Doriot Anthony Dwyer and bassist Joseph Hearne, both members of the Boston Symphony Orchestra which played here Tuesday night were guests artists, although that fact was certainly compelling. It was also the fact that endowment fund concerts, which are a commonplace in some musical centers, are practically unheard of here, and dual purpose of music and the support of music seemed, in this instance at least, worth reporting.

To hear either of the guests in his capacity as soloist would be a great treat; to hear them both was to create an event of rare and memorable beauty.

Conductor Jacob Avshalomov had gathered twenty-five of his best players under the collective title of "Soloisti di Portland Junior Symphony" and they proved to be far less awkward than their title. In fact, they served a very tasteful reading of the tenth concerto grosso of Handel's Opus 6 collection. They were a good complement as well in those works featuring the guest artists.

One does not recall the playing of either soloist without a vaunting admiration both for the technical resource and the persuasive musicality. Probably Mr. Hearne, being a product of this city and its Junior Symphony, had the deeper claim to an emotional contact with his audience. Last fall he became the youngest member of the Boston Symphony and its latest addition to the string bass section.

There are perhaps other bass players who are just as agile and accurate in racing over the huge strings of that vast fingerboard, but we have never seen one such.

What Mr. Hearne did with the materials of the Eccles sonata and the Dragonetti concerto showed what a fine musician who is master of his huge viol can convey eloquently to his audience.

Mrs. Dwyer was better served by creative concern, having as her vehicle the Mozart flute concerto in G. This is a very attractive young musician with a wistful face and a very impressive command of her instrument.

The concert was concluded with some of the music Mr. Avshalomov wrote as incidental to "The Little Clay Cart."

THE REPORTER MAY 13, 1963

Collegians Join Final Symphony

By DONALD DIERKS

The Portland Junior symphony gave its final concert of the season Sunday evening at the Civic Auditorium. Jacob Avshalomov, Junior symphony conductor, programmed the Michael Tippett "A Child of Our Time," a sober and serious composition with a very important message concerning the staggering persecutions and pogroms of World War II. Though the text is based upon one particular incident, it deals broadly with the evils of war and violence.

The musical style which sets this text is one with some mildly enriched harmonies, but nevertheless is direct, simple and traditionally understandable. The form employed is one similar to a cantata or oratorio of the 18th century and for that matter is much like a cantata of J. S. Bach.

Within its three parts there are solos, duets and quartets, as well as sections for chorus and orchestra, and the use of Negro spirituals, which are heard five times, is much like the function of the chorale in Bach cantatas.

The orchestral playing during the evening was quite distinguished and notable for its security and fine accompaniments to the choir and soloists. In the Symphony No. 5 of William Boyce, which opened the program, the strings sounded especially rich and performed with excellent intonation.

The four college groups sang very much as if they had been singing as one chorus for some time, and this is a credit to the members as well as the directors who trained them. One might have wished for more volume from this large body of singers at times, but they sang very accurately and with sureness.

Northwest premiere of Tippett's "A Child of Our Time".

THE OREGONIAN MAY 13, 1963

Oratorio Said Excellent In 1st City Performance

By HILMAR GRONDAHL
Music Editor, The Oregonian

Michael Tippett's oratorio "A Child of Our Time" had its first local performance Sunday night in the Public Auditorium as final part of the Portland Junior Symphony Orchestra's triskelion of the arts for this season. Jacob Avshalomov conducted with a large chorus made up of singers from Oregon State University, Portland State, Lewis and Clark and Warner Pacific colleges and a quartet of talented local soloists; Gloria Cutsforth, Helen Bolton, William Hazelbauer and Neil Wilson.

Tippett, an English composer now nearing his sixties, composed this contemporary oratorio in 1939 on a tragic historical incident which occurred in Paris the year before. A young Jewish refugee, frustrated by his inability to obtain the proper official papers from the German officials, and worried for the safety of his mother, shot a German diplomat. The consequence was one of the most ruthless pogroms in history.

The historical, political and philosophical implications of this event are readily imaginable and the composer made a starkly realistic thing of his musical setting. Gruesome orchestral sounds lead into gruesome statements such as "the living god consumes within and turns the flesh to cancer." The tenor sings, "I have not money for my bread; I have no gift for my love." The soprano sings, "How can I . . . become a mother in a world of destruction?" Often there is a gentle ending to a violent sentiment; a severe understatement in the orchestra of a compelling situation.

Message Evident

Tippett has great instrumental knowledge, a gift of melody and a sense of organization and climax. He has composed a score for voices and orchestra that, while it carries a strong and deliberate "message" is striking and beautiful in its own right.

The writing for massed voices is excellent, and the 200 or so who sang these sections on this premiere occasion did a memorable thing. Not that everything sounded as dramatically as it might have, for the problem of having crisp ejaculations such as "Curse them!" "Kill Them!" penetrate an instrumental web equally intent upon being articulate is not always easy.

The soloists carried their individual assignments with generally good results. The bass had a rather deliberate clarity of enunciation which was good since he was the narrator as well. Miss Cutsforth and Miss Bolton sang well, as did Mr. Hazelbauer, although his singing would profit from a clearer diction in a work such as this where words are important.

Mr. Avshalomov managed the oratorio's large forces with admirable dexterity and point.

The concert opened with the playing of the Boyce Fifth symphony, which went well once the brasses got the bubbles out of their instruments.

40th Season

Jacob Avshalomov, Conductor

November 23, 1963

DUKAS	Fanfare: "La Peri"
BEETHOVEN	Triple Concerto, op.56

Jacqueline Anderson, *Violin;* Beverley LeBeck, *Cello;*
Lawrence Smith, *Piano*

DEDICATION OF
JACQUES GERSHKOVITCH COMMEMORATIVE PLAQUE

ROGERS	*Three Japanese Dances
TCHAIKOVSKY	Caprice Italien

March 7, 1964
Aaron Copland, Guest Conductor

SCHUBERT	Symphony NO. 8, B minor
COPLAND	*The Red Pony Suite Mr. Copland conducting
WIENIAWSKI	Violin Concerto NO. 2, D minor Marylou Speaker, *Soloist*
CHOU WEN-CHUNG	*All in the Spring Wind
SURINACH	*Feria Magica

April 25, 1964

CHABRIER	Espana Rhapsody
BARATI	*The Dragon & The Phoenix
SAINT-SAENS	Carnival of the Animals

Barbara May & Robert Arenz, *Duo Pianists*
Joseph Libonati, *Narrator*

MOZART	Concerto NO. 2 for Horn Patrick Fay, *Soloist*
DOHNANYI	Suite in F sharp minor, op. 19

* *Portland Premier*

Sadness, Triumph Mark Junior Open

By MARTIN CLARK
Journal Music Editor

Portland Junior Symphony's opening concert of its 40th anniversary season at The Auditorium Saturday night was a sad, but triumphant, occasion; sad, naturally, because of the death of President Kennedy the preceding day; triumphant, because the selections and performance justified all high hopes held for the nationally recognized youth orchestra for so many years.

A plaque honoring the orchestra's founder and conductor for 30 years, Jacques Gershkovitch, was unveiled by his widow and presented to the city of Portland by Mrs. Harold S. Hirsch, association president, on behalf of the Junior Symphony. Mayor Terry Schrunk received the plaque, which will be mounted in The Auditorium for the city. Frederick Littman, sculptor of the plaque, was also on stage.

IN PLACE OF the opening work scheduled, Paul Dukas' "Fanfare" from his ballet, "La Peri," a selection from the second half of the program was substituted. It was "Mourning Dance," one of three Japanese dances by the American composer, Bernard Rogers. Following this, the audience and orchestra stood for a moment of silence in tribute to President Kennedy.

This was followed by Hadyn's "Mourning Symphony" (Symphony No. 44 in E Minor), a first performance for Portland and judging from what we heard Saturday night, a performance long overdue. The orchestra's attention to minute detail reflected the meticulous concentration of numerous hours of rehearsal by their dedicated teacher and conductor, Avshalomov.

THEN CAME the evening's big work, the Beethoven Triple Concerto, also, incredible as it may seem, receiving its Portland premiere. Three of the orchestra's alumni were featured: Jacqueline Anderson, violin, and Beverly LeBeck, cello, both members of the Portland Symphony; and Larry Smith, one of Portland's leading pianistic lights before he went East several years ago where he is now musical assistant to Eric Leinsdorf, conductor of the Boston Symphony.

It must have been an inspiring experience for the youngsters in the orchestra to have the opportunity of playing with three artists who, not too many seasons ago, were playing in that same orchestra (Smith was piano soloist). Their performances were smooth and professional. The orchestra, in its complementary role, played better than anyone had any right to expect. It was a competent performance.

THE REMAINING two Japanese dances, "Dance of Pennons" and "Dance with Swords," were performed following intermission. These dances also received their Portland premiere. Rogers has captured in music the charm of the woodblock prints of the Japanese masters. It's unfortunate that Rogers, who composed these dances in 1933, could not have been commissioned to compose a work for the Juniors instead of some of the composers who were chosen. This was delightful music.

A wonderful topper for the evening was Tchaikovsky's "Capriccio Italien." It was a well selected program.

Mourning Dance Subs For Symphony Opener

By DONALD DIERKS

The Portland Junior symphony opened its 40th season Saturday night at the Public auditorium, and what was to have been an especially gala occasion was, of course, subdued by the prevailing sadness of these times.

The program which was to have opened with a brilliant fanfare by Dukas, was re-ordered and the second of the "Three Japanese Dances" (mourning dance) of Bernard Rogers was performed in its place. After this work the audience and orchestra stood for several silent moments of tribute to our late president.

Not frequently heard, in fact this performance was the first in Portland, is the Haydn Symphony No. 44 in E Minor. One can justly ask why this engaging symphony is not more often performed because it has so much to recommend it; and certainly no less admirable than the composition itself is the way in which it was played.

The really fine string players of the orchestra performed with great earnestness and produced large amounts of string tone, so much at times that the few winds which Haydn's score calls for had occasional difficulty in projecting their parts; but it was a generally fine performance.

As yet another way of bringing attention to its anniversary year, conductor Jacob Avshalomov invited three alumni members of the orchestra to return to perform Beethoven's "Triple Concerto, opus 56" for violin (Jacqueline Anderson), cello (Beverly LeBeck) and piano (Lawrence Smith).

The performance of these three superior musicians, and the kind of accompaniment which was provided for them, is further testimony to the force for excellence exerted by this orchestra upon its former members as well as its present players.

Just after the intermission there was a ceremony honoring the founding conductor of the Junior Symphony, Jacques Gershkovitch. A likeness of Mr. Gershkovitch in the form of a bronze plaque, which the Junior Symphony Assn. caused to be created by the Portland artist Frederic Littman, was unveiled by the founder's widow.

This presentation was made by Mrs. Harold S. Hirsch, president of the Junior Symphony Assn., and accepted for the community by Mayor Terry D. Schrunk. The plaque will be placed in the Public auditorium.

The intriguing "Dance with Pennons" and "Dance with Swords" (the remaining two of the Rogers "Three Japanese Dances") and a long-time favorite of the orchestra's, the "Capriccio Italien," completed the second half of an evening's program which was enjoyable and highly reassuring to the many who are interested in the Junior Symphony and its future.

Junior Symphony Alumni Join In Local Premieres

By **HILMAR GRONDAHL**
Music Editor, The Oregonian

The Portland Junior Symphony Orchestra began the celebration of its 40th anniversary Saturday night in the Public Auditorium with a concert that brought several local premiers as well as several distinguished alumni into the performances.

Coming, as this concert did, in a period of national mourning, the program was altered so that the opening work was Bernard Rogers' "Mourning Dance," after which the audience and orchestra stood for a moment of silent prayer.

The first local performances were the Haydn Symphony No. 44, the Beethoven Triple Concerto and the Three Japanese Dances by Rogers, of which the aforementioned "Mourning Dance" was one.

The distinguished alumni brought together for the occasion were violinist Jacqueline Anderson, cellist Beverly LeBeck and pianist Lawrence Smith. The two string players are regular members of the Portland Symphony Orchestra. The pianist is musical assistant to Erich Leinsdorf, conductor of the Boston Symphony Orchestra. These three were soloists in the Beethoven concerto.

It was a fine thing for Jacob Avshalomov to program and play this score, not only for its value for his ensemble, but also for the rare opportunity it provides the rest of us to become acquainted with its many interesting aspects. While the balance of the three instruments was not always precise, and this is a difficult feat, their individual playing was generally good, and occasionally superb.

One has an idea that the orchestra itself had more fun in Haydn with its sudden starts and stops, its sharp dynamic contrasts. It had a very creditable performance, and one hopes it will show up on future programs with some regularity. It's an excellent piece.

First Conductor Honored

During intermission a plaque was unveiled honoring the orchestra's founding conductor, Jacques Gershkovitch. Participating in the service were the Orchestra Association's president, Mrs. Harold Hirsch, who introduced Frederick Littman, the sculptor who executed the commission. Mrs. Gershkovitch, widow of the founding conductor, who unveiled the plaque, and Mayor Terry D. Schrunk, who accepted the bas relief on behalf of the city.

The program notes were written by a former Junior Symphony alumnus, Dr. Karl Aschenbrenner, now professor of philosophy at the University of California at Berkeley.

The concluding work on Saturday night's program, Tchaikovsky's "Capriccio Italien," was an old favorite of Mr. Gershkovitch's, and was another attractive obeisance to the memory of the founding conductor.

Copland Work Performed For Enthusiastic Crowd

By **DAVID CAMPBELL**

Aaron Copland, famous composer, conductor, savant and protagonist of American music—is much in the limelight here this weekend. He has come as honored guest of the Portland Junior Symphony Orchestra Assn. on the occasion of the 40th anniversary of its founding.

In addition to conducting his "Red Pony" suite scheduled for the morning and evening concerts of the youth orchestra on Saturday, a concert of his chamber and choral works was given to an enthusiastic and capacity audience Friday evening at Evans auditorium, Lewis and Clark college.

Jacob Avshalomov, conductor of the Junior Symphony, introduced Copland warmly, stressing his importance as a cultural force and a good will ambassador to South America and Russia. However, he said, it is due to Copland's enormous pedagogical influence that he is especially welcome to the Junior Symphony in this, its anniversary year.

Copland spoke briefly and tellingly of the numbers included in this "one-man show," explaining their genesis and something of his intention in writing them. He is a felicitous speaker. The pertinent remarks, delivered with a casual manner and mild humor, were illuminating.

Mary Lou Speaker, concertmaster of the Junior Symphony, and Linda Morgan, alumna of Lewis and Clark, played the sonata for violin and piano. Copland had spoken of the work as melodic, cyclic, and mentioned the sparse notes of the slow movement as being typical of his style. The bristling difficulties of the final movement were easily handled, and the performers gave an excellent account of themselves.

Gloria Cutsforth, with the composer at the piano, sang 7 from a cycle of 12 songs, settings of poems by Emily Dickinson.

"Danzon Cubano" for two pianos, souvenir of a visit to Havana in pre-Castro days, was given a brilliant, swinging performance by two exceptionally gifted boys, John Reitz and Michael Songer. It elicited rounds of applause.

At the close Copland led the Lewis and Clark choir in two choruses: "Lark," a serious work in elevated mood, and the infectious, comic "I Bought Me a Cat," the latter made famous by the inimitable interpretation of the great Negro bass, William Warfield.

Copland's engagement was made possible through the generous fund donated by the Portland Junior League.

Jr. Symphony Concert Is Resounding Success

By DONALD DIERKS

There were a number of admirable ingredients which went into making the Portland Junior Symphony's Saturday night concert the resounding success it was; but most important was the individual preparation made by members of the orchestra for this concert. Without it, the collective beauty of the orchestra under the eminent composer and guest conductor, Aaron Copland, would not have been possible, nor could the orchestra have presented repertoire of such uniformly find quality.

"The Red Pony" suite by Aaron Copland is derived from an earlier film score, and it was this popular work that the composer chose to conduct.

He knew exactly what he wanted and expected to hear, and the players sensed this and responded to him in a highly pleasing way.

Forty years ago, on the first program ever given by the Junior Symphony, the Schubert Symphony No. 8 was heard. For this reason, and because it is an exceedingly lovely masterwork, Jacob Avshalomov conducted it on Saturday's anniversary program. It was well conceived Schubert too—calm, serene, moderate in its contrasts, and lyrically beautiful.

The soloist of the evening was the orchestra's concert-mistress, Marylou Speaker, who performed the Wieniawski Concerto No. 2 in D minor. There were occasional technical imperfections, but these did not detract from the total effect in any important way. The really admirable part of her performance was the apparent understanding of style and the intensity and insight of her interpretation.

Aaron Copland conducts the PJS at its 40th Anniversary.

THE OREGONIAN MAR. 9, 1964

Composer Scores Hit

Aaron Copland Aided By Soloist

By JOAN RIGGS
Special Writer, The Oregonian

Famous composer-conductor Aaron Copland and 18-year-old Portland violinist Marylou Speaker highlighted a Junior Symphony concert Saturday night that was probably the most exciting musical event of the year in Portland.

Copland conducted the orchestra in his suite from "The Red Pony." He had said in rehearsal that the Junior Symphony interpretation was the best he had ever heard, and the performance Saturday did not disappoint expectations. It was spirited and youthful, and rendered with vigor and freshness.

Marylou Speaker followed with a virtuoso performance of the familiar Wieniawski Violin Concerto. The young concert mistress of the orchestra played the difficult concerto with a notable combination of feeling and control. Particularly in the final movement, it was a performance that alone would have made the evening a success.

Two other, more esoteric selections, a Chinese "All in the Spring Wind," by Chou Wen Chung, and "Feria Magica," by Surinach.

As usual, Avshalomov conducted the orchestra skillfully. The performance marked the 40th anniversary of the Junior Symphony, and the 10th anniversary of the concert conducted by Avshalomov which led to his appointment as permanent conductor.

It was a diverse and complicated program, but every piece was expertly played.

For exuberance and freshness, as well as feeling and skill, it was a performance that will not easily be equalled.

OREGON JOURNAL MAR. 9, 1964

Violinist Acclaimed By Critic

By MARTIN CLARK
Journal Music Editor

Portland Junior Symphony continued the celebration of its 40th anniversary season Saturday night at The Auditorium with a star-studded concert that drew an audience of nearly 3,000. (The morning children's concert packed in a capacity house of 3,400.)

The stars were Aaron Copland, this country's most famous living composer; Marylou Speaker, violin soloist; Jacob Avshalomov, celebrating his 10th anniversary as conductor of the orchestra; and, of course, the Juniors themselves.

AS SOLOIST in Henri Wieniawski's Concerto No. 2 for Violin and Orchestra, Marylou Speaker, the 18-year-old concertmaster of the Junior Symphony, gave one of the most moving performances of that popular work I have heard. Not only was Miss Speaker more than equal to the virtuoso demands made upon her technique, but she has something not to be found in more than one leading concert violinist of the day—and that is a sweet, warm, singing tone. It is no wonder the young lady has walked away with practically all the honors available to her here, and many elsewhere. She provoked an ovation climaxed by presentation of a huge bouquet of roses.

After a polished performance of the Schubert "Unfinished" Symphony (No. 8 in B Minor), Copland mounted the podium to conduct his "Red Pony" Suite. The orchestra responded remarkably well to the brilliant and stimulating, but far from simple score.

TWO PORTLAND premieres concluded the evening: Chou Wen-Chung's "All in the Spring Wind" and Surinach's "Feria Magica," followed by a standing ovation for Avshalomov and the orchestra.

Mrs. Harold Hirsch, president of the Junior Symphony Association, opened the program with a tribute to Avshalomov from the Association, saying: "It is rare enough to be worthy of note when a man and his work are so harmoniously matched that one wonders which was created for the other . . ."

OREGON JOURNAL MAR. 9, 1964

Jr. Symphony Reputation 'Lure' for Copland Visit

By DONALD DIERKS

Aaron Copland, the composer, is quite well known to musicians and music lovers through his musical works. Not so well known, but also highly agreeable, is Aaron Copland, the man.

At an interview Friday he proved to be a natural and friendly person, not at all formidable as his reputation as one of the foremost American composers might lead one to expect. There is about him a warmly human quality.

He is in Portland for rehearsals with the Portland Junior Symphony for its concert Saturday evening at the Public auditorium, when he will conduct the orchestra in one of his own compositions, a suite from his film score, "The Red Pony."

As to what had helped him decide to accept the Junior Symphony's invitation to come to Portland, Copland said his long-time friendship with the orchestra's conductor, Jacob Avshalomov, had been a factor; and "I also was curious to see if the Junior Symphony could live up to the reputation it has in the East."

As he talked on about his rehearsals and the possibility of his composing a work especially for the PJS, his enthusiasm made it clear he thinks it does, indeed, live up to its reputation.

The importance of this visit to the Northwest to Copland is nicely pointed out by the events which surround it in his busy schedule. Just before coming to Portland he video-taped a "Young People's Concert" with Leonard Bernstein and the New York Philharmonic, in which he played the solo part to his Concerto for Piano and Orchestra.

Mr. Copland Pays a Birthday Tribute To Junior Musicians With Senior Skills

PORTLAND, ORE.

Composer-conductor Aaron Copland dropped the baton on the last chord of a suite from his *The Red Pony* film score and remarked that the orchestra's interpretation was "the best I have ever heard."

High praise, indeed, from the dean of American composers. But Mr. Copland's comment here March 21 was the more remarkable because it concerned no ordinary orchestra: The object of his enthusiasm was a group whose members range in age from 12 to 21.

The group is the Portland Junior Symphony, celebrating its 40th anniversary this year. Mr. Copland's visit was part of the anniversary celebration; a former pupil of his, composer-conductor Jacob Avshalomov, is conductor of the orchestra.

The Tough Works They Try

A number of cities and towns have youth orchestras in their midst, of course—some independent, some associated with public schools or music schools. But Portland's is the nation's oldest independent one, and it may well be the best. Said Mr. Copland: "It compares favorably with the best college orchestras in the country."

There is nothing childish about the orchestra except its make-up. Members play from the same musical scores as adult professionals. The balance of the program at which Mr. Copland conducted was made up of such demanding works as Schubert's *Unfinished Symphony*, Wieniawski's *Concerto No. 2 for Violin and Orchestra* (with the group's 18-year-old concertmaster, Marylou Speaker, as soloist), Chou Wen-chung's *All in the Spring Wind*, and Surinach's *Feria Magica*.

Few consider the orchestra a "training ground" though some members go on to professional careers. (Among them: bassist Joseph Hearne, one of the youngest men ever to join the Boston Symphony; and violinist Robert Mann of the Juilliard Quartet.) Most performers, however, enter other fields.

The orchestra was founded by conductor Jacques Gerskovitch, a graduate of the Imperial Conservatory in St. Petersburg, Russia, to accommodate some of his students who wanted to make music together. Mr. Avshalomov, now marking his 10th year with the group, once was a percussionist in the Junior Symphony under Gerskovitch. He went on to study with Mr. Copland at the Berkshire Music Festival in Massachusetts and to the Eastman School of Music, then taught at Columbia before returning to Portland.

Anecdotal Sessions

Mr. Avshalomov, 44, has flowing gray hair and laces his rehearsals with anecdotes of composers, conductors, and other orchestras. He's been known to halt at the end of a work and remark, "Well, that was a heroic attempt at the real thing." The orchestra loves him.

As is evident from its program during the Copland visit, the orchestra does more than simply play "old standards." Among other things, it has commissioned six works from professional composers (five of them American) under a grant from the Ford Foundation. An example is Goffredo Petrassi's *Prologue and Five Inventions*, a far-out composition that attempts to do away with a beat entirely. Said Portland music critic Hilmar Grondahl after the world premiere: "The Portland Junior Symphony . . . in all ways kept the music from falling apart"—a considerable feat with much contemporary music.

Musicians for the orchestra come from a 50-mile radius. There are nearly 100 in the regular orchestra and another 95 in a preparatory group, which seldom performs publicly but acts as a "farm system" for its parent. Some 150 young musicians audition for the two groups every year.

The current president of the symphony, Mrs. Harold S. Hirsch, says the orchestra produces a "magic that comes of eager students and an exacting teacher working together." And that is probably as good a summation as any.

—DOUGLAS MCCONNELL

Junior Symphony Offers Fine Music, Much Fun

By HILMAR GRONDAHL
Music Editor, The Oregonian

There was fun as well as fine music at the last of the Portland Junior Symphony Orchestra's fortieth anniversary concerts, which took place Saturday night in the Public Auditorium.

The "Carnival of the Animals" by Saint-Saens brought one of the Symphony's alumni, Robert Arenz, to the stage with Barbara May as the starring two-piano team. Joseph Libonati was narrator of the witty Ogden Nash verses.

Filling out the program Conductor Jacob Avshalomov gave a first performance of George Barati's "The Dragon and the Phoenix" plus Chabrier's Rhapsody Espana, the Dohnanyi F-sharp minor suite and the second horn concerto by Mozart. Patrick Fay, the orchestra's principal French horn, was guest soloist in this score.

Comments Delightful

The pace and spirit of the evening was set by the bright and brassy Chabrier rhapsody which opened the concert. The hall rang with the exuberance of this playing. The brasses were precise in their brilliance and the intonation of the massed strings has never sounded better.

Mr. Nash added a new dimension of enjoyment to the Saint-Saens "Carnival" when he concocted his set of zany comments in rhyme about the various animals involved.

Libonati read his lines with a pacing that gave the punch word its full measure of impact, and the two keyboard artists embellished such simple means as a Czerny scale with zest. But these three were not the only stars of this event. Hats off to George L. Derry principal bassist for his sterling endeavor to depict the elephant dance, to principal cellist, Louise Byers for portraying the Swan which, as Nash says, "swims sitting down," and to flutist Barbara Bernhard and clarinetist Susan Anderson for speaking of birds fluttering and cuckoo.

The musical area which struck this reviewer as the highlight of music and its reflection of outstanding talent was the Mozart concerto and the remarkable young Patrick Fay.

Solo Enchanting

Mr. Avshalomov gave this lovely score its proper setting in instrumental size, and provided a handsome opening for the solo horn. Young Mr. Fay occupied his role with admirable ease and a fine command of his instrument and its dynamics.

Another delightful section of the concert was the Dohnanyi suite.

Junior Symphony Ends Musical Year With Notable Artistic Performance

By DONALD DIERKS

The Portland Junior symphony presented the last concert of its 40th anniversary season Saturday evening at the Public auditorium. This performance was a fine one, and it ended the musical year for the orchestra and its conductor in just the right way. It was an artistic success when heard, and to see the size of the orchestra and its extreme youth gives every reassuring indication of a healthy future and many more anniversary celebrations.

The program opened with the exuberant Espana Rhapsody by Chabrier and proceeded to a composition heard in Portland for the first time. This was George Barati's "The Dragon and the Phoenix." Barati, who is the conductor of the Honolulu symphony and a friend and admirer of the Junior symphony, has composed a work which is pleasant and readily understood and enjoyed. Perhaps its most notable feature is its perceptive use of orchestral color.

Saint-Saens' "Carnival of the Animals" is the kind of composition which is always sure to please an audience, and this is exactly what it did on this occasion. Although it really doesn't need to be well played to be highly appealing, this performance was especially enjoyable because of its musical quality.

The duo-pianists, Barbara May and Robert Arenz, with the narrator Joseph Libonati, turned in performances which were musically and technically secure, and all the more admirable because of their full-time pursuits outside of the world of musical performance.

The various incidental soloists from the orchestra distinguished themselves, and the level of the orchestral accompaniment deserves praise, as well.

After the intermission the orchestra's first hornist, Patrick Fay, performed the Mozart Concerto No. 2 in E flat, K. 417. This young player displays facility and great ease of execution with moderate accuracy; and his conception of Mozart's style is well taken—a somewhat more elegant interpretation than forceful, but nevertheless a reasonable choice. By any standard it was an enjoyable performance.

The final work was the Suite in F Sharp Minor, Op. 19, by Dohnanyi. This is an interesting composition and one in which the woodwinds play a role of greater than average importance. These players deserve special commendation for the generally high quality of their performance.

In enthusiasm for the work of these young musicians, it is well not to overlook the excellence of their teacher and conductor, Jacob Avshalomov, who always displays his knowledge of the intricacies of the scores he conducts. Looking beyond the beauty of the performance at hand, it is easy to imagine the excellence of the training the young musicians receive.

41st Season

Jacob Avshalomov, Conductor

November 21, 1964

WAGNER	Overture: "The Flying Dutchman"
BEETHOVEN	Piano Concerto NO. 3, C minor Mark Westcott, *Soloist*
FAURE	*Pelleas et Melisande Suite, op. 80
KAY	*Of New Horizons
GLAZOUNOV	Concert Waltz NO. 1

March 6, 1965

NIELSEN	*Overture: "Maskarade"
TCHAIKOVSKY	Variations on a Rococo Theme Toby Saks, *Violoncello Soloist*
J. C. BACH	Sinfonia in E♭, op. 18 NO. 1 for Double Orchestra
CASELLA	*Paganiniana

April 24, 1965

BERNSTEIN	*Jeremiah Symphony Georgia Davis, *Contralto*
MOZART	Recitative & Rondo, K. 505 "Ch'io mi scordi di te?"

Miss Davis & Mark Westcott, *Piano Obbligato*

PRESENTATION OF THE DITSON CONDUCTOR'S AWARD TO JACOB AVSHALOMOV BY JACK HAMILTON BEESON OF COLUMBIA UNIVERSITY

BACH	Cantata: Christ Lag in Todesbanden
BRUCKNER	*Te Deum

Maria Novak, *Soprano;* Georgia Davis, *Contralto;*
Donald Koponen, *Tenor:* David Jimerson, *Bass*
Guest Choirs: Marylhurst, Cascade & Clark Colleges,
Beaverton & Centennial High Schools

* *Portland Premier*

April 10, 1965,
Preparatory Orchestra Debut
Children's Concert, 11: a.m.
Civic Auditorium

Everybody Sing	America the Beautiful
BEETHOVEN	Six Contradances
SCHUMANN	Scherzo, Symphony NO. 1
MOUSSORGSKY	Night on Bald Mountain
Demonstration of Instruments–Strings	
GRAINGER	Tune from County Derry
	Molly on the Shore

THE OREGONIAN APR. 11, 1965

Symphony's '2nd Team' Scores Highly On Own

By HILMAR GRONDAHL
Music Editor, The Oregonian

The Portland Junior Symphony Association made a special thing of its Saturday morning children's concert in the Public Auditorium by devoting the entire affair to its preparatory orchestra which is drawn from 30 schools in the metropolitan area.

In the past this group, which is the training body for the regular ensemble, has been allowed a portion of one of the season's programs, but never the whole program.

So Saturday the 94 youngsters (average age 14) who comprise the preparatory orchestra were featured in a full program.

The hall was packed to the roof with eager youngsters, plus some parents. Whether this special occasion engendered some special enthusiasm from the young fry, one doesn't know for sure, but every situation which would support some additional applause had it. Even as the young players came in to their stands there was a fresh burst of clapping for each new entrant.

The orchestra itself contains some interesting elements; more cellos than the majority of professional orchestras could afford, five French horns, six flutes, four trumpets, three trombones and a tuba plus the full complements of strings in all but the bass section, and a harp.

The program consisted of six contradances by Beethoven, the scherzo from Schumann's "Spring" Symphony, "A Night on Bald Mountain" and a pair of Grainger settings of English folk tunes.

Training Impresses

Added was the singing by all of one verse of "America, the Beautiful" and the learning and singing as a round of a new set of words to "Freres Jacques," the verses having to do with good behavior at a concert.

One could be no less than strongly impressed by the training and performance of this junior youth orchestra under the guidance of Jacob Avshalomov. Not only did they play the notes as written, but they were free to observe significant accents, to move effectively with the signs of expression and to participate in sudden dynamic changes.

In advance of each number Mr. Avshalomov told something about the music. In the case of the Schumann Scherzo he made an analysis of sections which the orchestra demonstrated.

OREGON JOURNAL APR. 22, 1956

THE OREGONIAN NOV. 22, 1964

Pianist Star Of Symphony

Youth Performs With Aplomb

By HILMAR GRONDAHL
Music Editor, The Oregonian

The concert by the Portland Junior Symphony Orchestra in the Public Auditorium Saturday night was rich in present pleasure and future promise.

It was the first concert of the organization's 41st season, and conductor Jacob Avshalomov gave two local premieres by Faure and Kay along with established works by Wagner and Beethoven. The Beethoven work was the Third Piano Concerto, which featured Mark Westcott as soloist.

The Beethoven C-minor concerto is a tough assignment to put before a lad of 16; it is difficult for a seasoned performer.

An Astonishing Feat

What young Mr. Westcott accomplishment was an astonishing feat, and all the more so because he had to make his way through and over an initial nervousness. He has talent, a strong, clean and highly serviceable technique, and musicality which encompasses qualities intuitive as well as learned.

The concerto was a total delight. There had apparently been thorough preparation by both soloist and ensemble. The beauties that were shared had a persuasive mutuality and the orchestral statements were deeply expressive.

The program opened with the overture to "The Flying Dutchman," one of the few times, we gather, a Wagner number has been programmed. The young musicians took to it with a relish, making much of the opportunities in the brasses, and getting a strong effect from the strings.

Strings Expressive

It was in the Faure suite from "Pelleas and Melisande" that the strings had their golden opportunity. Here their presence is controlling, and it was good to hear how disciplined and expressive this part of the orchestra is after only the pre-season rehearsals. It was this we had in mind when we mentioned "future promise." If the youngsters play this well at their first concert, what might the effect not be by the third.

The other first performance of "Of New Horizons" by Ulysses Kay, a piece which is said to reflect the composer's hopes for a post-war world.

Guest Cello Soloist Stars With Junior Symphony

By HILMAR GRONDAHL
Music Editor, The Oregonian

Toby Saks was guest cello soloist with Jacob Avshalomov and the Portland Junior Symphony Orchestra Saturday night in the Public Auditorium. Their vehicle was the Tchaikovsky Variations on a Rococo Theme for Cello and Orchestra.

It was a realization of this sparkling music which did credit to everyone concerned: composer, conductor, soloist; and complementary ensemble.

Miss Saks is a small woman with extraordinary musical gifts which are impressively developed and disciplined. Her instrument is a pure extension of these large talents; her temperament and musical intelligence shining through the beautiful phraseology and detailed articulation of her art.

She is a strikingly balanced musical entity, having singularly effective technical resource and sure command of expressive means.

The difficulties of the score are obvious, the spirited discourse between solo and orchestra being one of the most critical. While the Juniors didn't make a perfect mark here, they were very good.

The exercise in which they achieved a perfect grade was the Sibelius Valse Triste, done to honor the centennial anniversary of that Finnish master. The pacing Mr. Avshalomov took was exactly right to express the somber nature of the piece, and his strings supplied a uniform legato of warm and vibrant texture.

It was, in fact, a concert of several high points of interest. Two of these were first performances in Portland. One was the festive overture by Carl Neilsen to his opera "Maskarade." The other was Alfredo Casella's "Paganiniana."

This latter, as its title suggests, is a composition drawing its melodic nourishment from pieces by the fabulous violinist, Nicola Paganini. The contemporary Italian created a vigorous display piece from this material, one which had the young instrumentalists on their mettle.

For us one of the most delightful items was the Sinfonia in E-flat for Double Orchestra by Christian Bach. Here the orchestra was divided into two relatively equal forces to play an unpretentious and wholly engaging score in three movements. The visual and aural experience of these two nicely balanced ensembles joining in common action or doing imitative sections was a distinct pleasure.

The PJS cello section awaits guest artist Toby Sax.

THE OREGONIAN APR. 25, 1965

Junior Symphony Conductor Receives $1,000 Prize To Climax Performance

By CHARLIE HANNA
Staff Writer, The Oregonian

The Portland Junior Symphony's third and final concert of the season was performed before a packed house at the Public Auditorium Saturday night.

The Portland Junior Symphony, under direction of the able Jacob Avshalomov proved that there is very little about the orchestra that is junior.

A sweeping, sad, slow, stately, gay, exhilarating and rich "Jeremiah Symphony" by Leonard Bernstein set the caliber of the evening at high immediately.

The voice of guest contralto Georgia Davis was introduced in the third movement of the colorful and moving symphony. The voice of Miss Davis, who wore a strikingly attractive saari-style white formal and white gloves, was rewardingly warm, rich and mobile.

Emotion Conveyed

The ability of Bernstein to convey vivid emotionality, as he did in this work of 1942, was well illustrated by the performance of the orchestra.

Miss Davis was featured again, this time with pianist Mark Westcott, in Mozart's "Recitative & Rondo," which was perhaps more pleasing to the traditionalists. After the Bernstein work, however, it proved an exercise of markedly less excitement.

Bach's Cantata No. 4, first performed on Easter Sunday, 1794, is indeed a massive work. Saturday night it was performed by a massive chorus of 250 voices from Cascade, Marylhurst and Clark Colleges, and Centennial and Beaverton High Schools.

Uniformity of attack and clarity of words were exceptional in this work and in the one that followed Anton Bruckner's "Te Deum."

Featured in the latter work with the orchestra and chorus were Maria Novak, soprano; Miss Davis, contralto; Donald Koponen, tenor; and David Jimerson, bass. Their presentation combined to make the Bruckner composition an exciting and worthwhile close to the program.

Midway in the evening, Conductor Avshalomov was presented Columbia University's "Conductor Award" for 1965.

The $1,000 prize is given annually by Columbia's Alice M. Ditson Fund to an American conductor for his encouragement of contemporary American music.

The presentation was made by Jack Beeson, associate professor of music at Columbia. This year's award is the first given to a conductor of a junior symphony in the 21 years of the Ditson prizes.

In past years the prize has gone to such musical notables as Alfred Wallenstein (1947), Leopold Stokowski (1952), Robert Shaw (1955), and Leonard Bernstein (1958).

Beeson was introduced by Mrs. Leslie Sherman, president of the Portland Junior Symphony Orchestra Association.

A reception for the orchestra members, board and families was held in the auditorium south wing following the concert. It was sponsored by the National Conference of Christians and Jews.

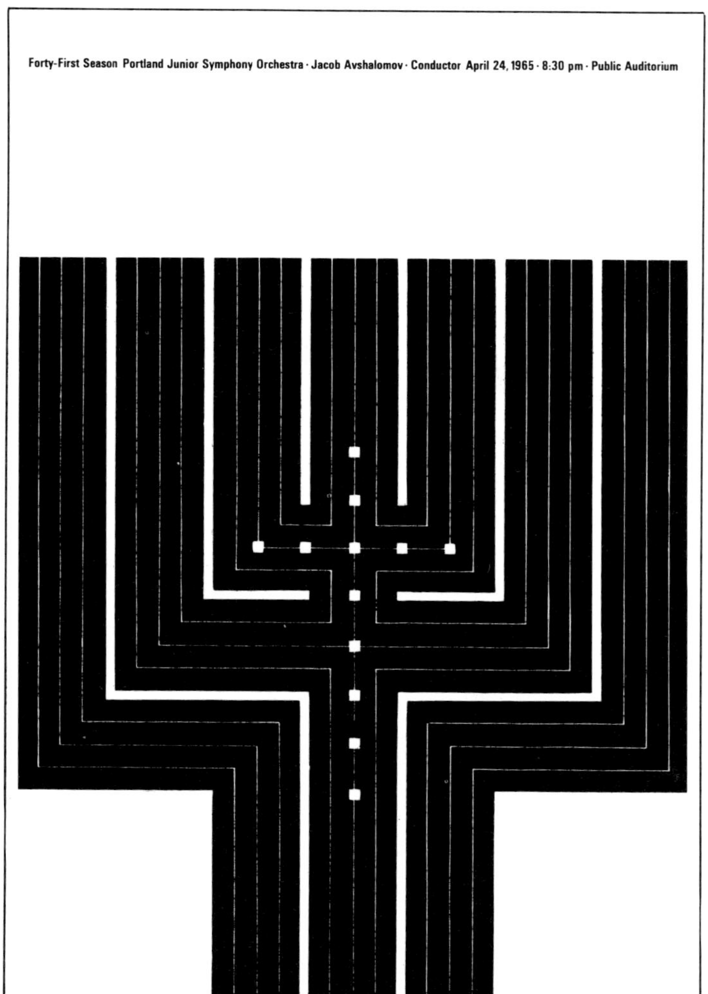

42nd Season

Jacob Avshalomov, Conductor

November 20, 1965

GLUCK	Overture: "Iphigenia in Aulis"
	Dance of the Furies: "Orpheus"
CHERUBINI	• Symphony in D
STRAVINSKY	• Capriccio for Piano & Orchestra
	Michael Songer, *Soloist*
BORODIN	In the Steppes of Central Asia
	IN MEMORIAM AARON AVSHALOMOV
	Polovetsian Dances

March 5 1966

REZNICEK	Overture: "Donna Diana"
BRAHMS	Variations on a Theme of Haydn
READ	• Night Flight
GLAZOUNOV	• Concerto for Saxophone & Strings
	Karin Rascher, *Soloist*
KOCH	• Concerto Piccolo
	Karin & Sigurd Rascher, *Soloists*
HOLST	• The Planets

April 30, 1966

WEBER	Overture: "Oberon"
CHAUSSON	• Symphony in Bb, op. 20
STUCHEVSKY	• Concertino for Clarinet & Strings
	Madelon Bose, *Soloist*
MENDELSSOHN	"Midsummer Night's Dream"

May 18, 1966

Recording Preview–Oriental Theater

AARON AVSHALOMOV	Hutungs of Peking
	• Piano Concerto, G major
	Margaret Moore, *Soloist*
JACOB AVSHALOMOV	• Cantata: "How Long, O Lord"

Neil Wilson, *Baritone;* Portland Symphonic Choir

Issued by Composers Recording, Inc. CRI210

• *Portland Premier*

THE SUNDAY OREGONIAN NOV. 21, 1965

Junior Symphony Opens 42nd Season On High Note At Oriental Theater

By HILMAR GRONDAHL
Music Editor, The Oregonian

The Portland Junior Symphony Orchestra opened its 42nd season Saturday night in the Oriental Theater with a program two principal items of which were local first performances. These were the Cherubini Symphony in D, and the Stravinsky Capriccio for Piano and Orchestra—with Michael Songer as guest soloist.

To put the 106 members of this ensemble on the stage of this theater it was necessary to occupy the entire apron. Seventy of these players are in the string family.

A string section of these dimensions, if only partly compatible and skillful, promises a richness of sound and the opportunity for impressive effects. These young musicians are carefully drilled and conductor Jacob Avshalomov used this drilling and indications of the moment to effect some of the best playing we can recall originating in these concerts.

Woodwinds, Brass Talented

It is not that there is less purposeful skill and musicianship in the other sections; in fact some of the most talented people are among the woodwinds and brass. It is that in works such as the two pieces by Gluck which opened the concert and the Cherubini symphony, the principal musical ideas involve the strings, and it was with these players that the conductor achieved those remarkable musical effects.

Especially lovely in the Cherubini was the way the conductor shaped the figures of the opening largo. Another delight was the solo flute playing in the trio of the third movement.

Score Tricky

The Stravinsky Capriccio is a tricky score, which hardly exposed to the fullest extent the remarkable talent of young Michael Songer. In any concerto up to and including those of Saint-Saens the pianist would have some long and pleasing melodic lines with which to display his gifts of pianism and lyricism. With the Capriccio these opportunities are bits and patches; the call is more for rhythmic urgency than tune in the traditional sense. The piano is brought closer into the orchestra and its most engaging moments are when it is teamed up with a small ensemble. The writing for woodwinds is superlative.

If the Stravinsky piece is less than grateful for the solo instrument, there was still ample evidence that Mr. Songer, who did his role without a hitch, is one of the truly exceptional pianistic talents hereabouts.

The concert concluded with two pieces by Borodin which used to be staples in the Gershkovitch regime; "In the Steppes of Central Asia" and the Polovetsian Dances. The former piece was played in memory of the conductor's father, Aaron Avshalomov, himself a distinguished composer.

OREGON JOURNAL NOV. 22, 1965

Junior Symphony Opens With Ambitious Program

By MARTIN CLARK
Journal Music Editor

It happens every year and every year I never cease to be amazed. I'm referring to the near-professional sound produced by the Portland Junior Symphony under the direction of Jacob Avshalomov.

Saturday evening at the Oriental Theater the Juniors opened their 1965-66 season for a 1,500-plus audience. The youngsters' programs are always ambitious, but this one seemed to be particularly so. The most noticeable work of the evening was Stravinsky's "Capriccio for Piano and Orchestra," with Michael Songer, 17, a senior at Jesuit High School, as soloist. A student of Marjorie Trotter, Songer won the annual piano contest held by the Juniors last spring.

IF THE STRAVINSKY was the most noticeable, Borodin's "In the Steppes of Central Asia" was unquestionably the most touchingly beautiful selection of the evening—as a composition and as performed by the youngsters. Appropriately enough, it was programmed in memory of the conductor's father, Aaron Avshalomov, who passed away earlier this year.

Excellent readings were given in the first half of the concert to Gluck's "Iphigenia in Aulis" Overture and his "Dance of the Furies" from "Orpheus," and Cherubini's occasionally ponderous Symphony in D.

MICHAEL SONGER gave a brilliant account of himself in the difficult, demanding, intricate Stravinsky score. He was called back repeatedly to acknowledge the applause. But there was little doubt the audience was applauding him and Avshalomov's highly competent members of the orchestra rather than the composition.

Saxophone Soloists Featured By Juniors

By MARTIN CLARK
Journal Music Editor

Portland Junior Symphony's program Saturday night at the Oriental Theater was one of the best chosen programs the Juniors have performed in the last 10 seasons.

It included four compositions receiving Portland premieres (one of these is hard to believe), and every one of the four was more than worthy of a public hearing. I will assume the juniors' program was accurate in labeling the performance of Gustav Holst's "The Planets" as a Portland premiere, but I must confess this is astonishing.

CONDUCTOR Jacob Avshalomov and the Junior Symphony gave a near-professional reading of five movements of the seven-movement work, with the Marylhurst College Choir, rehearsed by Maria DeRungs, supplying the eerie effect in the final pages of the concluding movement "Neptune."

Soloists for the evening were Sigurd Rascher and his daughter, Karin. Rascher is considered by many as today's foremost saxophone virtuoso. Miss Rascher was soloist with the International Youth Orchestra in Berlin last August, playing the Glazounov Concerto for Saxophone and String Orchestra, which she performed Saturday night with the Juniors. Father and daughter were soloists after intermission in the Concerto Piccolo for Two Saxophones. If the saxophone is ever to be accepted as a concert instrument, it will be through brilliant performances such as those heard from the Raschers Saturday night.

THE OVERTURE to "Donna Diana" by the Austrian composer, Emil Nikolaus von Reznicek, opened the concert, followed by a thoroughly creditable reading of Brahms' "Variations on a Theme of Haydn." Next was "Night Flight" by Gardner Read, another Portland premiere (as were the Koch and Glazounov). Anyone who has done much private flying at night will agree Read has captured "the loneliness and mysterious beauty" of any isolated area encountered in night flying.

Junior Concert Features Chausson and Stuchevsky

By Martin Clark
Journal Music Editor

In keeping with its progressive policy of presenting music either new or new to Portland, the Portland Junior Symphony Saturday at the Oriental Theater performed Portland premieres of two significant works.

Under the direction of its regular conductor, Jacob Avshalomov, the orchestra played Ernst Chausson's Symphony in B Flat and Stuchevsky's Concertino for Clarinet and Strings, with Madelon Bose as clarinet soloist.

Miss Bose, completing her third season with the Junior Symphony after four years in the Preparatory Orchestra, gave an assured performance which produced thunderous applause and a bouquet of roses, presented by Harry Hanson, Oriental manager. The Stuchevsky concertino is a work in the contemporary idiom but not without design. The solo line explored the considerable technical resources of the clarinetist while conveying a mood of plaintive sadness.

The Chausson symphony received a well prepared performance from the Juniors.

Two popular favorites opened and closed the concert: Weber's "Oberon" overture and Mendelssohn's incidental music to "A Midsummer Night's Dream." An audience of more than 1,500 gave enthusiastic response throughout the program.

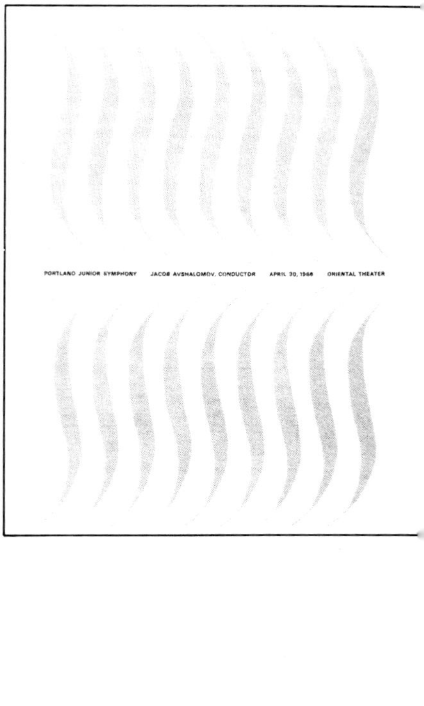

Junior Symphony Performs Avshalomov

By HILMAR GRONDAHL
Music Editor, The Oregonian

What was billed as a Recording Preview Concert by the Portland Junior Symphony Orchestra in the Oriental Theater Wednesday night was preceded by a spectacular surprise.

The printed program listed two compositions by Aaron Avshalomov and one by his son Jacob, conductor of the Junior Symphony. But the first phrase the orchestra played was the introduction to the overture to "Oberon" by Weber.

This was surprise enough. But when the piece got under way, Jacob Avshalomov did what some conductors would fear to do. He laid down his baton and took a seat on the piano bench a few paces from the podium.

The young musicians played on with as much assurance as if their mentor were still guiding them, observing the tempi, the dynamics and all other expressive details right up to the final chord.

It was a moving sight, as well as being a surprising feat, and indicated in no small way the security of means which these young players have been able to achieve through the rehearsals.

Recordings Noted

From this point on the program was concerned with the works of the two Avshalomovs which had been recorded in three sessions, the last of which had transpired only an hour earlier in the same hall.

Jacob Avshalomov explained his late father's preoccupation with the dialect of Oriental music through his thirty-year residence in China, and how he has sought in all his compositions to convey eastern speech through western means.

The first piece played was "Peiping Hutungs" which is, apparently, a leisurely stroll through one of the many byways of the big city in the course of which the listener hears various street cries as well as the hubbub of traffic and overhears household music and that of a long funeral procession.

The second piece was a cantata "How Long, O Lord?" by the Junior Symphony conductor which was dedicated to his father. This was sung by the Portland Symphonic Choir with baritone Neil Wilson of Eugene in the very important solo role. This is a moving work, usually congenial in its vocal lines as a means of conveying the dramatic impact of the text. In a few places the weight of the orchestral sound obscured the strong solo voice.

Concerto Played

The final piece was what Jacob Avshalomov described as perhaps the evening's major work; his father's piano concerto in G. This is a large score in three movements which handsomely explores the sounds and rhythms of Chinese musical speech. It is a colorful work, vital in its momentum and consistently interesting as music.

The soloist in this concerto was Margaret Moore, a highly accomplished young pianist, who had memorized her role in short order and played it with an assured spirit and flawless musicianship.

These three Avshalomov scores were recorded for the firm called Composers Recordings, Incorporated, and will be available in record stores this fall.

OREGON JOURNAL MAY 19, 1966

Avshalomov Works Praised

By MARTIN CLARK
Journal Music Editor

It would be no exaggeration to say the Portland Junior Symphony's Wednesday night free concert in many ways was the best concert of the orchestra's 1965-66 season.

Unfortunately, the Oriental Theater was only about half filled for the occasion (about 1,000), but that was the loss of the other 1,000 who weren't there.

Billed as a "Recording Preview," the concert featured two works by the late Aaron Avshalomov and one by his son, Jacob Avshalomov, conductor of the Junior Symphony.

AND THERE was "a surprise," as described by conductor Avshalomov. This consisted of the Weber "Oberon" overture, with which the orchestra opened the concert. It was not listed on the program and was performed without announcement. A few measures after the opening of the overture, Avshalomov stepped down from the podium and sat on the piano bench, arms folded. The kids played on without him in great style. (It was a nice touch of showmanship but let's hope it didn't give the kids any ideas.)

With the exception of the Weber, the entire program was recorded earlier for commercial release this fall. The primary aim is to preserve the works of Aaron Avshalomov, according to this son's running commentary throughout the concert.

IT'S DIFFICULT to understand why we have not heard more of Aaron Avshalomov's "Peiping Hutungs" and his Piano Concerto in G. Margaret Moore, a young pianist who debuted with the Juniors some years ago under her maiden name of Kochendorfer, gave a brilliant performance as soloist in the concerto. She completely captured the delicate enchantment of the Oriental atmosphere and the contrasting saucy syncopation. Some of the most charming moments of the evening were supplied by the "Peiping Hutungs" which included a vast variety of Chinese street sounds.

Between these two works was Jacob Avshalomov's cantata, "How Long O Lord?", with the Portland Symphonic Choir, prepared by its director, Frank Holman, and baritone Neil Wilson as soloist. Wilson gave a consistently able performance matched by the choir and orchestra.

The performance was aided by a grant from the Recording Industries.

43th Season

Jacob Avshalomov, Conductor

	December 3, 1966
MASON	*"Chanticleer" Overture
MACDOWELL	Piano Concerto NO. 2, D minor
	John Reitz, *Soloist*
SESSIONS	"The Black Maskers" Suite
GOTTSCHALK	Night in the Tropics

	December 26, 1966
5th Annual	Family Christmas Concert
BALAKIREV	Overture on Three Russian Songs.
BEETHOVEN	Symphony NO. 3, Allegro
BACH	Cantata NO. 142
BERLIOZ	Trio from L'Enfance du Christ
JUNE PIMENT	Relatives for Christmas
	Mrs. James Cameron, *Story Teller*
LIADOV	Music Box
BOCCHERINI	La Musica Notturna di Madrid
Seasonal	Music & Carol Singing

	February 25, 1967
BALAKIREV	Overture on Three Russian Songs
SIBELIUS	Symphony NO. 5, op. 82
BARTOK	*Viola Concerto
	Samuel Rhodes, *Soloist*
GRIEG	Music for "Peer Gynt"

	April 22, 1967
LULLY	*Suite from "Psyche"
BIZET	Symphony in C
CRESTON	*Fantasy for Trombone & Orchestra
	Linda Small, *Soloist*
RESPIGHI	*Rossiniana

* *Portland Premiere*

THE OREGONIAN FEB. 26, 1967

Bartok Viola Concerto Has Portland Premiere

By HILMAR GRONDAHL
Music Editor, The Oregonian

Except for the Bartok Viola Concerto, the scores used by Jacob Avshalomov for the Portland Junior Symphony concert in the Oriental Theater Saturday night were by North European composers.

The Bartok Concerto, in which Samuel Rhodes of Princeton was guest soloist, was enjoying a local premiere and the Sibelius symphony #5 was making its initial entry into the repertory of this youth ensemble.

This symphony is a welcome addition to the orchestra's literature for other reasons than its titanic sweep, although the epic style in itself constitutes an educative factor of significance. The power and elemental pulsation are uniquely expressed and offer an additional challenge in the growing sophistication of these young players.

The ensemble had obviously made good use of rehearsal time for the music flowed into the house with disciplined vigor and in a style essentially right. It was well received.

The Bartok, too, was something fresh in the repertory and likewise a stimulating exercise in another style. It is pure Bartok, despite the fact that its final measures were filled in by the composer's friend, Tibor Serly.

The solo playing of Mr. Rhodes was an impressive realization of the Bartok writing and a joy to hear. The technical complexities were no problem to him. Measure by measure, phrase by phrase, the sense of the music built up to an impregnable structure, lyrically persuasive and emotionally compelling. It was string playing of the most admirable sort.

Impressive, too, was the total performance which the conductor and his players coordinated with that of the soloist.

OREGON JOURNAL APR. 24, 1967

Juniors Please With Last Concert

By MARTIN CLARK
Journal Music Editor

Someone will probably say right off "He's said that before!" but the fact remains that Saturday night's performance by the Portland Junior Symphony was one of the most satisfying in the past several seasons.

It was the final concert of the regular series, the 43rd season for an organization which seems each year to produce a more incredible bunch of youngsters than the season before.

THE CONCERT was fairly typical of the skillful programming provided by the Juniors' conductor, Jacob Avshalomov—a sampling of orchestral styles from the Baroque to the contemporary. Lully's suite from "Psyche" was the Baroque opener for the program, followed by Bizet's Symphony in C. Here is music appreciated on a first hearing but whose delights never dim with repetition. I never hear it without marveling that a 17-year-old boy could have written it.

Paul Creston's "Fantasy for Trombone and Orchestra" supplied the contemporary ingredient of the program, with Linda Small as soloist.

Miss Small negotiated the intricate solo path laid down by Creston with a sound technique more than equal to the heavy demands made by Creston. It was tricky work, and the orchestra deserves real credit for a well played difficult accompaniment.

An ideal final work for any concert was the one chosen for Saturday night, Respighi's "Rossiniana," a suite based on melodies from Rossini's "Les Riens." The composition makes use of an unusual variety of instruments, concluding with a tarantella which brought down the near-capacity house.

THE OREGONIAN DEC. 5, 1966

Junior Symphony Displays Pianistic Talent

By HILMAR GRONDAHL
Music Editor, The Oregonian

The Portland Junior Symphony's all-American concert in the Oriental Theater Saturday night was not only a demonstration that there are native composers with something to say, but also that all-American pianistic talent of stellar quality exists. This quality was personified in John Reitz, the 17-year-old Portlander, who was soloist under Conductor Jacob Avshalomov in the MacDowell D-minor concerto.

Orchestral programs limited to American composers have generally been all-Gershwin programs, but here was a listing spanning a century of men and styles from Louis Moreau Gottschalk to Roger Sessions.

John Reitz would have been a substantial success on a professional program. With this ensemble of juniors he was a sensation.

Other items on the program were the "Chanticleer" overture of Daniel Gregory Mason, "The Black Masters" by Sessions and Gottschalk's "Night in the Tropics." This last was having its first Portland performance, as was the Mason score.

Music Demands Skills

The Sessions music played is one of the composer's most successful scores, being music written forty odd years ago for a performance at Smith College of the Andreyev play.

It is music that asks expressive skills, especially from the wood winds and brasses. Mr. Avshalomov's forces acquitted themselves handsomely in these areas.

"Night in the Tropics" is an orchestral piece of Cuban flavor and infectious gusto.

THE OREGONIAN APR. 20, 1967

Juniors Still Excel

It has been remarked here before that the Portland Junior Symphony Orchestra has no superior in its class in American music. Its continuing excellence is confirmed in the national distribution of a recording by the orchestra of compositions by its conductor, Jacob Avshalomov, and his late father, Aaron.

Those who attended an audition of the recording the other afternoon at the Portland Art Museum noted its reflection of the Oriental backgrounds of both composers. Jacob Avshalomov was born in China, where his father achieved fame as a composer of many works, including the symbolically named "The Great Wall." Aaron Avshalomov continued his career as a composer in America after China fell to the Communists.

This is the Junior Symphony's third recording, once again making widely available the evidence of the orchestra's extraordinary merits. These will also be on public display this Saturday night at the Oriental Theater when the orchestra appears in its last concert of the 1966-67 season.

OREGON JOURNAL APR. 20, 1967

Another Way A City Grows

The Portland Junior Symphony had a little party at the Portland Art Museum the other night to introduce a new nationally distributed recording made by the Junior Symphony and the Portland Symphonic Choir.

The record is worth noting outside of the music critics' columns because big-league cities are not measured by their ball parks alone. It's a fortunate place where the people can take it for granted that their city will be a producer as well as a consumer of culture. The recording, the third in which the Junior Symphony has been involved, moves Portland a little further in that direction.

The music performed consists of a cantata, "How Long, Oh Lord," composed by the Junior Symphony's conductor, Jacob Avshalomov, and sung by the Portland Symphonic Choir, and two orchestral works on Chinese themes written by Jacob Avshalomov's late father, Aaron Avshalomov.

It's a happy combination of talents. Aaron Avshalomov, born in Siberia but living for 30 years in China, wove the music and street sounds of that country into compositions which are both Oriental and Western at once, and which seem likely to be continually interesting as the day comes closer when more than 1 out of every 3 persons in the world is Chinese. His son, Jacob, the loved and respected conductor of the Junior Symphony for the past 13 years, has had the rare satisfaction of recording his father's works and his own with two first-rate musical organizations, the Junior Symphony and Symphonic Choir.

It's a good kind of thing to be going on in our town.

44th Season

Jacob Avshalomov, Conductor

November 18, 1967

MOZART Piano Concerto, Eb, K. 271
Brigida Ritmanis, *Soloist*

SCHUBERT Overture: "Rosamunde"

MARTIN *Petite Symphonie Concertante
Jennifer Hoesly, *Harp;* Brigita Ritmanis, *Piano;*
Julane Anderson, *Harpsichord*

NIELSEN *The Four Temperaments
Symphony NO. 2, op. 16

December 26, 1967

6th Annual Family Concert at Christmas

VIVALDI Concerto Grosso, D minor

BERWALD *Sinfonie Singuliere

ENGLEMAN *Quandary

GABRIELI O Magnum Mysterium
Sonata Pian' e Forte

& Carol Singing by All

March 2, 1968

BEETHOVEN Overture: Leonore, NO. 2

KABALEVSKY *Concerto for Violoncello, op. 94
Nathaniel Rosen, *Soloist*

MAHLER *Symphony NO. 4, G major
Marilyn Kinkaid, *Soprano*

STRAUSS Perpetuum Mobile

May 4, 1968

CIVIC AUDITORIUM DEDICATION CONCERT

BERLIOZ Corsair Overture
Alumni join the Orchestra

HANSON *Serenade for Flute
David Bryant, *Soloist*

WEBER Concertino for Clarinet
Catherine Moore, *Alumna Soloist*

VAUGHAN-WILLIAMS Fantasia on a Theme of Tallis
Alumni join the Orchestra

AVSHALOMOV *Inscriptions at the City of Brass
Mara Stahl as Sheherezade

Guest Choirs: Lewis & Clark and Portland State Colleges
and Oregon State University

* *Portland Premier*

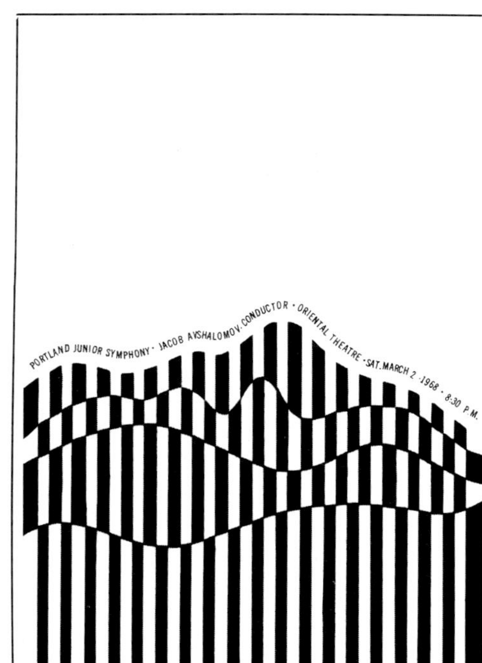

THE OREGONIAN MAR. 3, 1968

Junior Symphony Soloist Makes Concerto Exciting

By HILMAR GRONDAHL
Music Editor, The Oregonian

Two items in the Portland Junior Symphony program at the Oriental Theater Saturday night which expanded the compass of the youth ensemble were the Kabalevsky Cello Concerto and the Mahler Fourth Symphony. Both were having their Portland premieres.

The performance of the Kabalevsky concerto was an exciting experience. Kabalevsky writes exciting music, and that's part of it. But the participation of Nathaniel Rosen as soloist in this score was stunning evidence of remarkable talent headed in the right direction.

The Kabalevsky was a fine score for the orchestra to take part in also; a bouncy piece, spendthrift in energy like the youngsters who played it. Under Jacob Avshalomov's assured control it was a handsome presentation all around.

The theory books would hardly suggest that one assign the Mahler Fourth to an ensemble of 100 players averaging 17 years in age. It is one of the repertory's "large" works not only in orchestral size but in interpretive dimension. Even so, the Fourth is perhaps the best of the Mahlers for first acquaintance since it is lighter in spirit than the other nine and presents a delightful child's eye view of heaven in the final movement. This is a folk-song from the collection "Des Knaben Wunderhorn."

Here Marilyn Kinkaid was the soloist, singing with engaging style and delightful voice these winningly innocent sentiments.

One imagines that parents of the performers, and even the conductor himself might have been popping with pride that these charges could bring off this taxing score with such a high degree of musical competence. It was thoroughly enjoyable with some ensemble touches and some solo playing that were more than impressive.

THE OREGONIAN NOV. 19, 1967

Junior Symphony Proves Delightful In Concert

By HILMAR GRONDAHL
Music Editor, The Oregonian

OREGON JOURNAL MAR. 4, 1968

Imaginative Concerts By Juniors Praised

By MARTIN CLARK
Journal Music Editor

OREGON JOURNAL NOV. 20, 1967

Junior Symphony Scores In Opener

By MARTIN CLARK
Journal Music Editor

When a program is well chosen, highly qualified soloists are scheduled, and the ensemble is competent, well rehearsed and conducted with inspiration, the results can only be a resounding success.

Such was the case Saturday night at the Oriental Theater when the Portland Junior Symphony under the direction of Jacob Avshalomov, presented its opening concert of the 44th season. Brigita Ritmanis of Portland, was the soloist in the opening work, Mozart's Piano Concerto in E Flat. K271.

A DELIGHTFUL reading of Schubert's ever scintillating "Rosamunde" Overture was programmed between the Mozart opener and the Martin work, which featured a quality performance by Jennifer Hoesly, harp, Julane Anderson, harpsichord, and Miss Ritmanis at the piano, with a double string orchestra.

To find two contemporary works on a program, both receiving their Portland premieres eminently worthy of performance, is little short of phenomenal. The second work was the second symphony of the great Dane, Carl Nielson, based on four temperaments—choleric, phlegmatic, melancholic, and sanguine. Neilsen not only portrays the four accurately, he gives us some deeply moving music in the process thereof.

THE OREGONIAN MAY 5, 1968

Reinforced Orchestra Performs Splendidly

By HILMAR GRONDAHL
Music Editor, The Oregonian

The Portland Junior Symphony's Dedication Concert in the new Civic Auditorium Saturday night was an event of large and significant elements.

The regular orchestra of 100 was enlarged by an additional 60 former members of the ensemble. There were pieces engaging instrumental soloists from both current and former members. And finally there was the first performance here of conductor Jacob Avshalomov's composition, "Inscriptions at the City of Brass," which requires narrator, orchestra and a large mixed chorus.

The concert opened with the Berlioz overture, "The Corsair," which would have delighted the composer. He had a particular yen for large effects, and here was an orchestra of 160 completely filling the huge shell with 11 string basses deployed across the top at the back. There were acres of strings and flutes and French horns by the half dozen. It was an impressive sight!

Response Accurate

But the Berlioz was much more than a show to the composer's liking. It was a fine demonstration of highly synthesized and coordinated playing in which the response of the sections was remarkably clear and accurate and the scaling of dynamics was uniform and highly expressive. The lively response of the new hall was a distinct factor in the pleasure this music offered.

OREGON JOURNAL MAY 6, 1968

Jacob Avshalomov's 'Brass City' Praised

By MARTIN CLARK
Journal Music Editor

Such an impression was made Saturday night at the auditorium by "Inscriptions at the City of Brass" by Jacob Avshalomov, conductor of the Portland Junior Symphony, who was on the podium for the performance! This was the Portland premiere of the work although Avshalomov was teaching at Columbia University, and finished it in 1958.

Avshalomov comes honestly by the oriental atmosphere of the music, having spent his early years in China. The narrator was well chosen. Mara Stahl, wearing a provocative gown of gold, was curled up at stage right. A standing ovation followed the performance.

The Saturday night concert by the Portland Junior Symphony drew a capacity house. Interesting programming is a hallmark of these concerts, and Saturday night was no exception. The program opened with an exciting reading of the all-too-seldom-heard "Corsair" Overture by Hector Berlioz, for which alumni of the orchestra swelled its ranks. The orchestra's principal flute, a tall young man named David Bryant, gave a good accounting of himself in Howard Hanson's Serenade for Flute, another Portland premiere. Catherine Moore, alumna soloist, gave a truly virtuosic performance of Carl Maria von Weber's Concertino for clarinet with the orchestra. Vaughan-Williams' "Fantasia on a Theme by Tallis" concluded the first half of the concert, for which the alumni rejoined the orchestra.

The second soloist was an alumna, Catherine Moore, principal clarinetist of the Oregon Symphony, who was heard in the Weber Concertino, another virtuoso show piece which she placed with technical ease and artistry.

Tone Effective

The last pre-intermission piece was the Vaughan-Williams Fantasy on a Theme by Tallis. Here there was wealth of string tone effectively marshaled.

The Avshalomov score is an impressive work that solicits one's attention from the moment the narrator comes on-stage. In this performance it was Mara Stahl, beautifully garbed as the seductive Scheherezade who carries the narrative of the 339th of the 1001 nights. The poetic setting is Oriental and the fascinating music set to it is eloquently in the same character; full of evocative sounds made up from a remarkably diverse and inclusive range of instruments from gongs to banjos. It's a masterly orchestration.

45th Season

Jacob Avshalomov, Musical Director
Norman Leyden, Guest Conductor Sabbatical Term

December 7, 1968

WAGNER	Prelude to "Die Meistersinger"
MOZART	Concertante and Rondo, K. 320
LISZT	Piano Concerto No. 1, Eb Garrick Ohlsson, *Soloist*
SILVERMAN	*Tenso (Afternoon Music)
DVORAK	Symphony No. 8, G major, op. 88

December 21, 1968

7th Annual Family Christmas Concert

STRAUSS	Overture: "Die Fledermaus"
BACH	Concerto for Two Violins Valerie Poulette & Anne Cramer, *Soloists*
BIZET	Farandole, L'Arlesienne Suite
VAUGHN-WILLIAMS	Fantasy on Greensleeves
KAY	Deck the Halls–*Preparatory Orchestra*
SMETANA	Dance of the Comedians
HUMPERDINCK	Prayer & Dream Pantomime

March 2, 1969–4:p.m.

MOZART	Symphony No. 36, C minor (Linz)
BRUCH	"Kol Nidrei" Robert Kindler, *Violoncello Soloist*
BERLIOZ	Rakoczy March
BRAHMS	Tragic Overture, op. 81
BEETHOVEN	Romance in F, op. 50 Regan Crowley, *Violin Soloist*
PISTON	"The Incredible Flutist" Suite

April 26, 1969

GRETRY	"Cephale et Procris" Ballet Suite
BRUCH	Violin Concerto, G minor Nancy Mathis, *Soloist*
VAUGHN-WILLIAMS	A London Symphony

* *Portland Premiere*

THE OREGONIAN DEC. 7, 1969

Youth Fine In Concert

Junior Symphony

Meets Challenges

By SALLY LANDAUER
Special Writer, The Oregonian

Portland Junior Symphony musicians justified interim conductor Norman Leyden's pride in their artistry during a fine concert Saturday night at the Civic Auditorium.

Wagner's Prelude to "Die Meistersinger von Nurnberg" was tonally rich and many hued, an excellent demonstration of the increasing maturity of the tonal qualities and dynamic capabilities of this young orchestra.

In Mozart's Concertante and Rondo from Serenade No. 9 in D (K. 320), Leyden reduced the size of the 106-man orchestra to approximately 40, as is fitting. This is a work which requires crystalline clarity of expression. Fortunately, the eight soloists (flutes, oboes, bassoons, and horns) were equal to the demand for clarity, and Leyden achieved a lovely balance between soloists and strings.

Guest Proficient

Guest pianist Garrick Ohlsson exhibited technical proficiency and an astonishing dynamic range in Liszt's Piano Concerto No. 1 in E flat. In a virtuoso work noted for its difficulty as well as its musical bombast, the 6-foot 4-inch, 20-year-old student at Julliard School of Music dominated the piano with sheer strength as well as talent. His force and power are extraordinary, almost overwhelming, while his gentleness and lightness of touch are unexpected and welcome in a work whose lyricism is a necessary relief from the more flamboyant passages.

The supportive role of the orchestra was a little ragged in the first and third movements. However, Ohlsson and the ensemble suitably caught fire in the pyrotechnic fourth movement and performed in bravura style.

The fourth work on the well-balanced program, Stanley Silverman's Tenso (Afternoon Music for Orchestra), was commissioned in 1962 by the Greater Boston Youth Symphony Orchestra. It is appropriate that another youth orchestra plays it here. Silverman builds on three basic notes by means of unusual sounds and rhythms, assisted by the activities of six percussionists. This is a delightful work played with the verve and enthusiasm one expects from this excellent group of young musicians.

The preceding works showed what the Junior Symphony can achieve. Dvorak's Symphony No. 8 in G Major (Opus 88) showed what they are.

Leyden asks them to reach in this more difficult work, and it reveals an occasional weakness.

The violins have a tendency to sharp in the higher registers. A lack of unison in some entrances and attacks is noticeable, but this is quickly corrected in three or four measures.

Dvorak's symphony was a challenge for the orchestra. It fittingly concluded the program with a good indication of the direction in which the Junior Symphony is growing.

THE OREGONIAN FEB. 6, 1969

'Continuing Wonder' Revealed In Junior Symphony Concert

By HILMAR GRONDAHL
Music Editor, The Oregonian

The concert by the Portland Junior Symphony Orchestra in the Civic Auditorium Sunday afternoon revealed the continuing wonder of this operation as evidenced in its general musicianship as well as by the uncommon talent of two of its members. Norman Leyden was the conductor, and the soloists were principal cellist, Robert Kindler, and assistant concertmaster, Regan Crowley. His solo was Bloch's "Kol Nidrei," and hers the Beethoven "Romance in F."

It was a program, nearly two hours long, which provided wide leaps of musical impulse and style, from Mozart's "Linz" Symphony to the Rokoczy March by Berlioz, from the Brahms "Tragic" Overture to Walter Piston's ballet suite, "The Incredible Flutist." Out of this amalgam of young performers a pair are picked to declare their special talents.

Quite substantial talents they proved to be. Once young Kindler got settled and into the spirit of Ernest Bloch's haunting adagio for cello and orchestra, his shyness vanished and he became the eloquent champion of a Hebrew melody, strong and songful. And Miss Crowley dealt with the solo lines of the Beethoven romance in a remarkable purity of tone and persuasive musicianship.

This was the first occasion on which we have had to witness Norman Leyden conducting this ensemble. The occasion bespoke a community of purpose based on mutual respect. The players responded alertly to his clear indications.

Leyden had a microphone handy and made comments at several points. The one which most of the audience will recall had to do with the "Incredible Flutist." In explaining and demonstrating its several sections, he invited those present to join in welcoming the band which is due to arrive midway through the ballet. The crowd accepted the invitation, many rising to their feet shouting and clapping as the brasses in the rear stands blasted out the circus band's arrival.

'London Symphony' Played By Juniors

By MARTIN CLARK
Journal Music Editor

One of the most musically rewarding seasons of the Portland Junior Symphony came to a close Saturday evening at the Civic Auditorium. An audience of more than 2,000 received the final concert with great enthusiasm.

The concert reflected the imaginative type of programming characteristic of Junior Symphony performances. This was the final concert for Norman Leyden as a conductor of the Juniors. He has conducted this season during the absence of Jacob Avshalomov who returns this fall to resume his duties as musical director of the orchestra after a sabbatical in Europe.

Andre Gretry's ballet Suite from "Cephale et Procris" was the opener. Although the suite contains some of the most ingratiating music in the orchestral literature.

Max Bruch's Violin Concerto in G Minor features as soloist Nancy Mathis, the Junior Symphony's concertmaster. In one of the most popular concertos for violin she demonstrated a high degree of musicianship and reflected fine training. Miss Mathis, who is completing six seasons with the orchestra, is a good example of what the invaluable routining of orchestral participation does for a performer.

The "big number" of the evening was Ralph Vaughan Williams' second symphony, better known as "A London Symphony," written in 1913. This is an ambitious composition for a youth orchestra, but Leyden extracted a noble performance from his young players.

1st International Tour preview concert from the KGW studio, March 1970.

46th Season

Jacob Avshalomov, Conductor

November 22, 1969

BEETHOVEN Overture: Leonore NO. 2

DIAMOND The World of Paul Klee

Commissioned by the Portland Junior Symphony

RAVEL Concerto for Piano

Lena-Liis Kiesel, *Soloist*

DOHNANYI Suite in F sharp minor, op. 19

February 15, 1970

Ft. Vancouver High School Auditorium

Vancouver, Washington

Selections from the Season

March 7, 1970

AVSHALOMOV The Glistening City

from Symphony: The Oregon

BEETHOVEN Triple Concerto, op. 56

Marylou Speaker, *Violin;* Robert Kindler, *Cello;*
Margaret Moore, *Piano*

BRAHMS Symphony NO. 2, op. 73

March 12-29, 1970

First International Tour

London—Croydon—Lisbon—Milan—Florence—Parma

New York—Washington, D.C.

Honorary Sponsors: Leonard Bernstein, Aaron Copland,
Robert Mann, Isaac Stern, Sir Michael Tippett

April 26, 1970

MOZART Symphony NO. 40, G minor

STRAVINSKY Firebird Suite

REPORT ON THE EUROPEAN TOUR

BRUCKNER Te Deum

Judy Page, *Soprano;* Alyce Rogers, *Alto:*
Guy Aydelott, *Tenor;* Donald Newman, *Bass*

Guest Choirs: University of Oregon Singers, Chorale, Chamber Chorus;
Clark College Chorus

September 21, 1970

Endowment Fund Benefit Concert

CAROLINE BERG SWANN AUDITORIUM DEDICATION

Portland Art Museum

MOZART	Symphony NO. 40, G minor
MAHLER	*Kindertotenlieder
	Alyce Rogers, *Mezzo-Soprano*
RESPIGHI	*Gli Uccelli

Portland Junior Symphony Chamber Orchestra

Portland Premier

**Portland Premier*

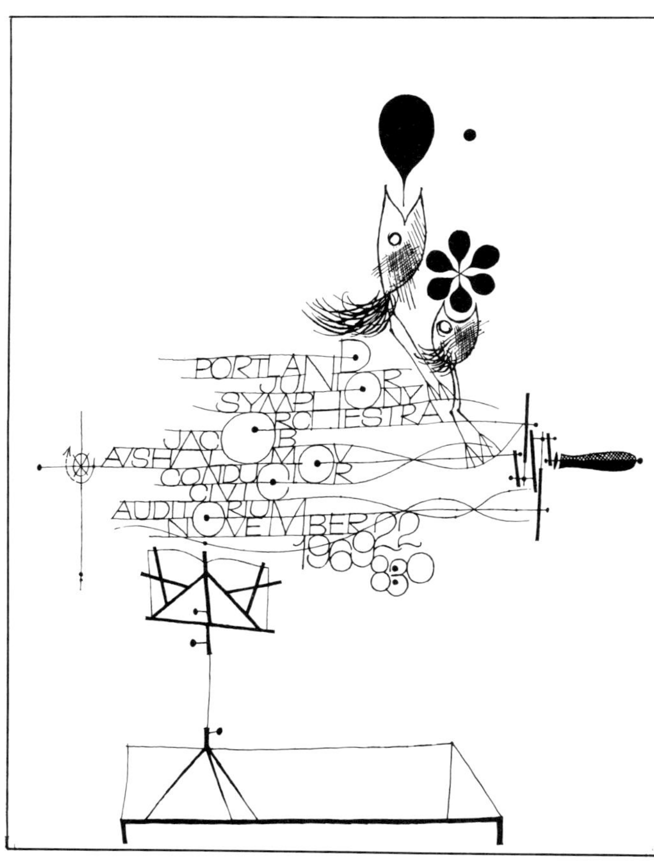

THE OREGONIAN NOV. 22, 1969

Junior Symphony Gives Uniformly Bright Concert

By HILMAR GRONDAHL
Music Editor, The Oregonian

The Portland Junior symphony opened its 46th season in the Civic Auditorium Saturday night with its hundred players addressing themselves to a program almost uniformly bright in character. Jacob Avshalomov, back from his sabbatical in Europe, was again directing his eager charges.

The entire concert was an unmixed pleasure, one of its highlights being a stunning performance of the Ravel Piano Concerto in G with Lena-Liis Kiesel, a talented 17-year-old, as soloist. Other items were Beethoven's Leonore Overture No. 2, Diamond's "The World of Paul Klee," and the Dohnanyi F-sharp Minor Suite.

The Leonore Overture opened the concert, and it was played with fitting skill and dramatic thrust.

Appearance Delightful

Miss Kiesel's appearance in the Ravel concerto was a delightful affair.

It is almost incredible that a pianist of her youth could come so near to expressing the total wit and sophistication of a work as urbane and mature as this one. She had the style with its jazzy inflections, brittle accents, infection themes and perky spirit in the outer movements. The middle movement is reverie of Gallic piquance from which she might have drawn more expressivity, but in the main it was a performance of uncommon technical assurance and palpable artistry. The orchestra joined knowledgeably in the spirit.

"The World of Paul Klee" is a score commissioned by the Junior Symphony a decade ago, in which Diamond takes his inspiration from four paintings by Klee. It's an engaging work, worthy of its repetition.

The concert was concluded with Dohnanyi's highly romantic suite which is so widely orchestrated that it shows off the entire orchestra as well as individual sections. The six variations of the first movement went beautifully, as did the lively scherzo. The romance was a sentimental ball.

A post-intermission ceremony was the presentation of the Oregon State Flag to the orchestra by Clay Meyrs, secretary of state.

OREGON JOURNAL MAR. 9, 1970

Juniors' Send-Off Concert Lauded

By MARTIN CLARK
Journal Music Editor

Portland Junior Symphony, under the direction of Jacques Avshalomov, presented its "gala commencement" concert of its "First International Tour" Saturday night at the Civic Auditorium.

If audiences abroad are half as enthusiastic as Saturday night's 1,500-plus-audience was, there's no question about the success of the tour.

HIGH POINT of the concert was the performance of the Beethoven Triple Concerto, Op. 56. Soloists were Marylou Speaker, former concertmaster of the Junior Symphony; Margaret Moore, piano soloist with the orchestra in her student days; and Robert Kindler, current principal cellist with the orchestra.

Orchestra and soloists exhibited a high degree of musicianship in the Beethoven. The young cellist had occasional difficulty with intonation, but on the whole gave a remarkably adept performance. Miss Moore proved to be a skilled technician at the keyboard, and Miss Speaker revealed that she has long since passed over that fine line between the gifted amateur and the inspired professional . . . a fine line but a huge difference.

A PART OF that difference is that the artist literally "plays" on the instrument, being able to give all thought to the essence of interpretation, subtle shading and phrasing, "thinking" the music. Miss Speaker unveiled a depth of insight and a musical maturity genuinely impressive in one of her tender years.

Scheduled for the second half of the concert was the Brahms Symphony No. 2, "the" symphony on the orchestra's tour. Opening the program was an excerpt from Avshalomov's own "Symphony: The Oregon," commissioned by the state for Oregon's centennial celebration in 1959. This is a good selection for performance abroad, demonstrating as it does the inventive originality and orchestration of one of this country's leading composers.

The concert was a resounding "send-off" success for the Juniors. They will leave Wednesday morning on the three-week tour which will include concerts in London, Milan, Florence, New York City, and Washington, D.C.

THE OREGONIAN SEP. 22, 1970

First Concert Heard In New Auditorium

By HILMAR GRONDAHL
Music Editor, The Oregonian

The premiere concert in the Portland Art Museum's new Caroline Berg Swann Auditorium was given Monday night by a chamber ensemble of the Portland Junior Symphony under Jacob Avshalomov's direction.

In introducing the acoustics of the hall, the program selection was made, not on the basis of lively and festive pieces full of sonorous brasses, but through a collection of works, the majority of which are notable for their somber beauty.

They were the Mozart Symphony No. 40 in G-minor, the Mahler "KinderTotenlieder" with Alyce Rogers as the soloist, and Respighi's suite "Gli Uccelli" (The Birds).

Singer Praised

The acoustics of the 500-capacity hall are on the very lively side. Single instruments and small ensembles come forth with striking clarity, and even the 40 players onstage disclosed a remarkable articulation in moderate volume. The second movement of the Mozart Symphony was a model of clear and integrated sound.

The Mahler song cycle had not been performed locally before, it seems, and what the audience heard was a superb performance of one of the composer's most intimate and moving creations: symphonic melodies of nobility dealing with the tragic aspects of the death of children.

Miss Rogers is a singer of remarkable vocal gifts and a musician capable of expressing the most subtle aspects of mood and melody. Her production is so secure that she has all the breath she needs for the long lyrical lines frequently required in these five songs. Her tone is always responsive to the poetic imagery.

Mr. Avshalomov not only had the Mahler score intimately in hand and well rehearsed, but he had the advantage of some extraordinarily gifted horn and oboe players; instruments of which this music makes such elegant and effective use.

All elements thus combined to provide a wholly artistic association between soloist and instrumental ensemble in a truly great musical creation.

Respighi's "Birds" is a bright suite created as incidental music to the Aristophones play by the same name. The composer makes direct imitation of bird sounds, a practice that seems to have come into use through the French composer, Daquin a couple of centuries earlier. It's a joyful imitation of nature, cleverly done by Respighi and enjoyed by audience and performers.

OREGON JOURNAL SEP. 22, 1970

'Juniors' Help Open Swann Hall

By PHIL HUNT
Journal Staff Writer

There was a fullness of sound at the premiere concert in the new Caroline Berg Swann Auditorium of the Portland Art Museum Monday night, an indication and an expectation that this will become the appropriate setting for numerous chamber style musical offerings in the years ahead.

With the Chamber Orchestra of the Portland Junior Symphony performing under the baton of Conductor Jacob Avshalomov, it was the right orchestra in the right place at the right time, and playing the right style of music.

THE MUCH-TRAVELLED Juniors were the right orchestra because they have had a long and close association with the museum, and with the Museum Art School in particular. Since 1955 classes in commercial design, under the direction of Douglas Lynch, have been creating cover designs for the PJS programs.

The "right music" included Mozart's Symphony No. 40 in G Minor and Portland premiers of Mahler's Kindertotenlieder sung by mezzo-soprano Alyce Rogers, and Respighi's Gli Uccelli (The Birds).

The 40-member Chamber Orchestra was about the maximum, both for the stage and the size of the sound that could be comfortably presented in the new brick-walled theater with its seating capacity of slightly less than 500 persons.

WARM APPLAUSE greeted the efforts of Miss Rogers in her rendition of the Mahler "Songs on the Death of Infants," based on Friedrich Ruckert poems. The music calls for a rich, full-bodied voice. The orchestral accompaniment, was subdued, with frequent duet style passages featuring the French horn of Dirk Hillyer.

The Respighi suite was full of delightful surprises such as a sudden trumpet blast at the end of the third section, the piccolo chirpings of the nightingale in the fourth, and the distinct tik-tok of the cuckoo in the finale. It left one wondering why this work is not performed more often, unless possibly in a larger concert hall some of the effects might sound lost.

IN THIS EARLY season appearance, with school vacations barely over, and with several new principals occupying their lead positions for the first time, including Concertmaster Robin Obrien, the orchestra opened with the familiar Mozart, a happy choice for the premiere concert in the acoustically near-perfect auditorium.

The strings in the G Minor sounded extra bright in the modest-sized hall. Woodwind statements and echoes, runs and trills, a mark of most Mozart but often lost in more cavernous surroundings, came through with extra clarity.

1924-1970
FORTY-SIXTH SEASON

Portland Junior Symphony Orchestra

JACOB AVSHALOMOV
Conductor

HONORARY SPONSORS

Leonard Bernstein

Aaron Copland

Robert Mann,
JUILLIARD QUARTET

Isaac Stern

Sir Michael Tippett

Norbert Brainin,
AMADEUS QUARTET

First International Tour March 12·29 1970

GALA COMMENCEMENT

PORTLAND, OREGON
Civic Auditorium

LONDON
Camden School for Girls
BBC Maida Vale Studios
St. Martin-in-the-Fields

CROYDON
The Fairfield Hall

LISBON
Tivoli Theater

MILAN
Sala Grande,
Conservatorio Giuseppe Verdi

FLORENCE
Sala del Cinquencento,
Palazzo Vecchio

NEW YORK
Alice Tully Hall,
Lincoln Center

WASHINGTON, D.C.
Washington Cathedral

NOTES

Planning the repertoire for a concert tour is an exhilarating task, and in reviewing the great wealth of music available clear objectives are needed to guide and limit choices. The wish to join hands with fellow-musicians abroad led to the idea of a choral work, and with the approach of Beethoven's bi-centennial came the suggestion of his concertos, presented with guest soloists. These would naturally be balanced by soloists from the Orchestra, which in turn led to inviting former members, now professional artists, to celebrate the tour in the same role.

Then, it seemed fitting to complement the standard repertoire with works which were associated with the Orchestra and its home. These considerations brought the problem to a manageable scope, and from the following list the tour programs have been devised.

BEETHOVEN'S *Triple Concerto*, a product of his ripe middle years, was written out of friendship for the Archduke Rudolph of Austria, who was also his piano pupil. Concertos for multiple instruments were more common before Beethoven's time than after it and his work has stood practically alone despite the fact that the solo combination is the usual trio of violin, cello and piano. Two movements of grand scale contrast with a short Largo, an interlude really, of great tenderness. The solo parts are written not so much as virtuoso oratory as chamber-music dialogue in an orchestral setting.

The Portland performance brings the return of MARYLOU SPEAKER, former concertmaster of the Orchestra, a winner of many awards, on the threshold of her professional career; and MARGARET MOORE, who was piano soloist with the Orchestra in her 'teens and later as recording artist, is now established as teacher, composer and reviewer; ROBERT KINDLER, the current principal, is the cellist. Last year, he was the Association's scholarship student at "Tanglewood," the Boston Symphony's summer school which has invited him to return this season.

The two works of symphonic proportions in the repertoire are both highly romantic. BRAHMS' *Second Symphony* seemed the most appropriate of his major works for

PORTLAND, OREGON
Civic Auditorium
Saturday, March 7 at 8:30 p.m.

Assisting Artists:
Marylou Speaker, *violin*
Robert Kindler, *cello*
Margaret Moore, *piano*

PROGRAM

Avshalomov
The Glistening City

Beethoven
Triple Concerto, Op. 56
ALLEGRO
LARGO
RONDO ALLA POLACCA

INTERMISSION

Brahms
Symphony No. 2, Op. 73
ALLEGRO NON TROPPO
ADAGIO NON TROPPO
ALLEGRETTO GRAZIOSO
ALLEGRO CON SPIRITO

LONDON
St. Martin-in-the-Fields
Sunday, March 15 at 3:30 p.m.

PROGRAM

Beethoven
Violin Concerto, Op. 61
ALLEGRO MA NON TROPPO
LARGHETTO
RONDO
Rolf Wilson, *Guest Soloist*

INTERMISSION

Brahms
Symphony No. 2, Op. 73
ALLEGRO NON TROPPO
ADAGIO NON TROPPO
ALLEGRETTO GRAZIOSO
ALLEGRO CON SPIRITO

LONDON
Camden School for Girls
Friday, March 13 at 2:30 p.m.

PROGRAM

Beethoven, *Leonore Overture No. 2*
Debussy, *1st Clarinet Rhapsody*
Diamond, *Twittering Machine*
Ravel, *Introduction and Allegro*
Dohnanyi, *Suite in F♯ minor*

LONDON
BBC Maida Vale Studios
Sunday, March 15 at 10:00 a.m.

PROGRAM

Diamond, *The World of Paul Klee*
Avshalomov, *The Rose;*
The Glistening City
Dohnanyi, *Suite in F♯ minor*

SPONSOR: Youth and Music
Sir Robert Mayer,
Founder and Chairman
David Chesterman, *Manager*

CROYDON
The Fairfield Hall
Monday, March 16 at 8:00 p.m.

With the participation of
The Choir of the Royal Academy of Music*
Conductor, Frederic Jackson, F.R.A.M.

PROGRAM

Beethoven
Leonore Overture No. 2

Albinoni
Oboe Concerto, Op. 9, No. 2
ALLEGRO E NON PRESTO
ADAGIO
ALLEGRO
Kathie Egbers, *soloist*

Bruckner
Te Deum
Margaret Adams, *soprano*
Susan Lees, *contralto*
Gareth Roberts, *tenor*
Ian Caddy, *bass*
Mr. Jackson conducting

INTERMISSION

Diamond
The World of Paul Klee
FRAME, Dance of the Grieving Child
FRAME, The Black Prince
FRAME, Twittering Machine

Ravel
Introduction and Allegro
Jennifer Hoesly, *harp*

Avshalomov
The Rose
The Glistening City

*By kind permission of the Principal, Anthony Lewis, C.B.E.

young musicians to present, and it hardly needs an introduction. DOHNANYI'S *Suite F# minor* is one of the most inexplicably neglected orchestral works. Written in 1911, a time when Schoenberg and others were so discouraged by the staleness of tonal music that they postulated "atonality," Dohnanyi produced this exuberant piece, as melodious as Brahms or Dvorak, as witty as Strauss and as crafty in orchestration as the master of one's choice. Hungarian by birth, Viennese in training, Dohnanyi's career as pianist, conductor and composer cast a brilliant light over all of Europe. Curiously the last decade of his life was spent in Florida where he died only a few years ago, in his mid-eighties.

The Orchestra's London concert in St. Martin-in-the-Fields will be preceded by a performance at the Camden School for Girls and a recording session at the BBC. All three of these events have analogies in the Orchestra's activities at home. For the BEETHOVEN *Violin Concerto* the guest soloist is ROLF WILSON, presented under the auspices of Youth & Music. This brilliant young English artist is the winner of many awards and a member of the Royal Philharmonic Orchestra.

The concert in Croydon welcomes the participation of the chorus and soloists from the Royal Academy of Music and their conductor, FREDERIC JACKSON. (Choral works are programmed every other year or so in Portland, and by now practically every college group within reach has sung with the Orchestra.) The BRUCKNER *Te Deum* provides a splendid sampling of this master's fervent sacred music on a scale which allows other works on the program.

At home soloists from within the Orchestra appear each season and are chosen at auditions before the Music Committee. For the tour three of the principals, KATHIE EGBERS, GARY MCGEE and JENNIFER HOESLY were invited to represent their fellow members in the spotlight. All of them have played in the Orchestra at least five years.

The ALBINONI *Concerto for Oboe,* Op. 9, No. 2, is the work of a prolific composer from a country and a time which was prolific in composers. Among those voices of the Italian Baroque Albinoni is considered a minor poet, but Bach held him

LISBON
Tivoli Theater
Wednesday, March 18 at 6:30 p.m.

PROGRAM

Beethoven
Leonore Overture No. 2

Albinoni
Oboe Concerto, Op. 9, No. 2
ALLEGRO E NON PRESTO
ADAGIO
ALLEGRO
Kathie Egbers, *soloist*

Diamond
The World of Paul Klee
FRAME, Dance of the Grieving Child
FRAME, The Black Prince
FRAME, Twittering Machine

Debussy
First Clarinet Rhapsody
Gary McGee, *soloist*

INTERMISSION

Brahms
Symphony No. 2, Op. 73
ALLEGRO NON TROPPO
ADAGIO NON TROPPO
ALLEGRETTO GRAZIOSO
ALLEGRO CON SPIRITO

SPONSOR: Juventude Musical Portuguesa
Joao de Freitas Branco, *President*

MILAN
Sala Grande,
Conservatorio Giuseppe Verdi
Saturday, March 21 at 3:30 p.m.

PROGRAM

Brahms
Symphony No. 2, Op. 73
ALLEGRO NON TROPPO
ADAGIO NON TROPPO
ALLEGRETTO GRAZIOSO
ALLEGRO CON SPIRITO

INTERMISSION

Beethoven
Triple Concerto, Op. 56
ALLEGRO
LARGO
RONDO ALLA POLACCA

Avshalomov
The Rose
The Glistening City

MILAN
Children's Concert
Friday, March 20 at 3:30 p.m.

Albinoni, *Oboe Concerto, Op. 9, No. 2*
Diamond, *Twittering Machine*
Dohnanyi, *Suite in F# minor*

SPONSOR: Gioventu Musicale d'Italia
Baroness Dorothy Lanni della Quara,
President and Founder

FLORENCE
Sala del Cinquecento, Palazzo Vecchio
Monday, March 23 at 6:00 p.m.

PROGRAM

Beethoven
Leonore Overture No. 2

Albinoni
Oboe Concerto, Op. 9, No. 2
ALLEGRO E NON PRESTO
ADAGIO
ALLEGRO
Kathie Egbers, *soloist*

Diamond
The World of Paul Klee
FRAME, Dance of the Grieving Child
FRAME, The Black Prince
FRAME, Twittering Machine

Debussy
First Clarinet Rhapsody
Gary McGee, *soloist*

INTERMISSION

Dohnanyi
Suite in F# minor, Op. 19
ANDANTE CON VARIAZIONI
SCHERZO
ROMANZA
RONDO

SPONSOR: American Society of Florence
Mrs. Merritt N. Cootes,
Chairman, Music Committee

in high enough esteem to borrow his themes more than once.

The RAVEL *Introduction and Allegro* is a unique gem, an ecstatic statement for harp accompanied by strings, flute and clarinet. It breathes the same scented air as the DEBUSSY *Clarinet Rhapsody*. Both rise from a mood exquisitely pensive to a climax which is animated but without urgency; both stop without really ending, as if the implication of a full close should suffice.

Some aspects of the impressionistic manner are to be found in DIAMOND'S *The World of Paul Klee*, based on paintings by the Swiss abstractionist: a gauzy texture produced by pointillist technique, the rarity of dense sonorities and throbbing climax, and the preference of suggestion to statement. The melodic lines and counterpoints have an angularity that come of a free use of serial methods. Diamond is the first of six composers commissioned by the Association to write works especially for young players. In the decade since that project was begun all of the works have been published and five of them recorded by the Orchestra.

A second work being taken abroad from home is AVSHALOMOV'S *Symphony: The Oregon*. This was commissioned by the State for Oregon's centennial celebration in 1959. *The Rose* is Portland's flower, and an inscription in the score speaks of it as a "warm, intimate emblem of beauty; lasting, fragrant, convolute; its tenderness protected by its thorns."

The Glistening City is Portland, where "after rain the sun and the gleaming air make countless jewels in the teeming city." The omitted movements are entitled *"The Fog Serpent* (an early settler's allusion to mist in the Columbia River Gorge) and *The Mountain* (Mt. Hood, Mt. Adams, Mt. St. Helens, choose one).

The concerts in Lisbon and Florence do not include guest artists, regrettably, but in Milan the three gifted soloists are presented under the auspices of Gioventu Musicale d'Italia.

Children's concerts are an integral part of the Orchestra's season at home and the Association takes a particular pleasure in having it play to audiences of children in London and Milan.

Returning to the United States the Orchestra will be joined by old friends in the brand-new Alice Tully Hall of Lincoln Center. LAWRENCE SMITH was piano soloist in his student days and again at the 40th anniversary concert when he played the Triple Concerto with a different pair of alumni. In 1964 he won the Mitropoulos International Conductor's Competition and has recently joined the faculty of the Curtis Institute at the invitation of its new director Rudolf Serkin.

GERALD APPLEMAN has been principal cellist of the Cleveland Orchestra and is now a member of the New York Philharmonic. He studied at the Juilliard School when it was uptown on Claremont Avenue. Now, with the Juilliard at Lincoln Center, the current members of the Orchestra will tour the new building after a rehearsal, wondering which of them will follow his path. Coming in from the West Coast, Marylou Speaker will again be the violinist in the solo trio.

Among the old friends will be some of the Honorary Sponsors and, it is hoped, DAVID DIAMOND. He knows the Orchestra from its recordings, but the personnel has turned over completely since his composition was recorded.

The final stop on the tour's itinerary is the nation's Capitol. All along the route rehearsals and concerts will have been interlaced with sight-seeing and friend-making with new-found colleagues. Among the accumulated impressions of beautiful, strange and historic sights the Washington Cathedral will have a special place. Here the Orchestra presents the Evensong program on Easter Sunday with the Cathedral Choral Society, PAUL CALLAWAY its conductor.

Justly rounding out the tour, Bruckner's *Te Deum*, given earlier in England, will serve as the resplendent finale. Its concluding text, "In Te, Domine, speravi"—"In Thee, Lord, do we hope," sung aloud in this vaulted sanctuary, will echo in the ears of the hundred young artists and their shepherding elders long after the return home.

NEW YORK

Alice Tully Hall, Lincoln Center
Thursday, March 26 at 8:30 p.m.

Assisting Artists:
Marylou Speaker, *violin*
Gerald Appleman, *violoncello*
Lawrence Smith, *piano*

PROGRAM

Dohnanyi
Suite in F♯ minor, Op. 19
ANDANTE CON VARIAZIONI
SCHERZO
ROMANZA
RONDO

Diamond
The World of Paul Klee
FRAME, Dance of the Grieving Child
FRAME, The Black Prince
FRAME, Pastorale
FRAME, Twittering Machine

INTERMISSION

Beethoven
Triple Concerto, Op. 56
ALLEGRO
LARGO
RONDO ALLA POLACCA

Avshalomov
The Rose
The Glistening City

WASHINGTON, D.C.

The Washington Cathedral
Easter Sunday, March 29 at 4:00 p.m.

With the participation of
The Cathedral Choral Society
Conductor, Paul Callaway

EVENSONG PROGRAM

Beethoven
Leonore Overture No. 2

Albinoni
Oboe Concerto, Op. 9, No. 2
ALLEGRO E NON PRESTO
ADAGIO
ALLEGRO
Kathie Egbers, *soloist*

Ravel
Introduction and Allegro
Jennifer Hoesly, *harp*

Avshalomov
The Rose

Bruckner
Te Deum
Carol Cramer, *soprano*
Margery Clifford, *alto*
Edward Jackson, *tenor*
James Johnson, *bass*

Portland Junior Symphony Association

222 S.W. Harrison, Portland, Oregon 97201

Jacques Gershkovitch, *Founding Conductor*
Jacob Avshalomov, *Conductor*

OFFICERS:
Mrs. A. Gordon Russell, *President*
Mrs. Walter C. Lobitz, Jr., *Vice-President*
Mrs. Marcus Leupold, *Vice-President*
Henry T. Stanley, *Vice-President*
Mrs. Dean Vincent, *Secretary*
Alfred O. Stromquist, *Treasurer*
Mrs. Ralph C. Angell, *Executive Secretary*

DIRECTORS:
Ben L. Bernhard
Worth W. Caldwell
Mrs. Robert G. Cameron
Mrs. Adolph Carr
Mrs. John F. Cramer, Jr.
Victor Critchlow
C. P. Davenport
Mrs. Donald Drake
Mrs. Jan de Graaff
Walter A. Durham
James Eklem
Maurice Engleman
Mrs. Donald Hering
Mrs. Jason A. Hervin
Thomas J. Holce
William H. Holm
Kenneth C. Hume
Phil Hunt
Dr. Richard H. Kosterlitz
Dr. Daniel H. Labby
Mrs. Verner Lindgren
Malcolm J. Montague
Mrs. Clay Myers
Mrs. Thomas J. Niedermeyer
Dr. Reinhard Pauly
Mrs. J. Richard Raines
George C. Reinmiller
Mrs. Morris Schnitzer
Andrew V. Smith
Mrs. J. C. Stevens
Mrs. David K. Taylor
Mrs. Harold F. Wendel

HONORARY DIRECTORS:
Mrs. Jacques Gershkovitch
Eugene R. Nudelman
Mrs. Percy Smith
Mrs. Estes Snedecor
Mrs. Robert H. Strong

A. Verne Wilson, *Liaison with the Public Schools*

Orchestra Personnel 1969-1970

James Eoff, *Assistant to the Conductor*

FIRST VIOLIN:
Valerie Poulette, *Concertmaster*
Robin O'Brien, *Asst. Concertmaster*
Anne Cramer
Diane Debrisay
Monica Stelter
Paula Sisson
Teresa Schuster
Lorely Petrasso
John Weller
David Swanson
Bruce Ruben
Dale Herigstad
Bernice Bush
Jolan Friedhoff
Steven Critchlow
Mary Ann Rees
Wende Wetzel
Andrius Faruolo
David Newman

SECOND VIOLIN:
Janet Eoff, *Principal*
Edith Bennett, *Asst. Principal*
Susan Vorm
Bruce Sweetman
Susan Hardie
Gary Hurst
Steve Kindler
Van Vinikow
Kathy Dewoina
Kathy Carrol
Valerie James
Karen Verbout
Ann Corkum
Dinah Ward
Michael Hansen
Wanda Wayrenen
Roberta Pieters
Lawrence Kee

VIOLAS:
Daniel Avshalomov, *Principal*
Sharon Eng, *Asst. Principal*
Brad London
Debbie Drysdale
Maren Rispler
Dick Nicholson
Kathy Simmons
Margaret Baker
Terese Stahl
Margaret Leeb
Patrick Kroboth

CELLOS:
Bob Kindler, *Principal*
Jane Sanborn, *Asst. Principal*
Lynn Nowels
Ruth Walker
Carla Saiger
Mike Shaw
Jim Washington
Mary Ruth Storer
Mary Ann Campbell
Fred Nussbaum
Martin Hansen

BASS:
Bill Balch, *Principal*
Jim Cole, *Asst. Principal*
Stashia Colby
Margaret Storer
David Koehler
Stephanie Smith

FLUTE:
Carol Lange (picc.)
Kathy Bauer
Mary Petralli (picc.)
Karen Stromquist
Sue Borgensgard

OBOE:
Kathie Egbers
Michael Cory (Eng. Horn)
Nan Nowels
Pam Smith
Peter Dietz (Eng. Horn)

CLARINET:
Gary McGee
Phil Baldino (B. Cl.)
Patty Vinikow
Scott Swope (Eb Cl.)
Nancy Johnson

BASSOON:
Rae Louise Kalk
Janet Robinson (Contra)
Priscilla Jester
Debbie Johns

HORN:
Dirk Hillyer
Roger Kaza
Harry Bell
Kent Fisk
Carolyn Klaner
Steven Estep
James Bates

TRUMPET:
Rex Smith
Christy Dana
Jess Smith
Gary Guthman

TROMBONE:
Jeff Craig
Gary Powers
Michael Lotz
Michael Powers

TUBA:
Tim McCarthy

PERCUSSION:
Dwight Gruber (timp.)
Casey Wamble
Dan Fiebiger
Ron Dobbin

HARP:
Jennifer Hoesly

PIANO:
Nan Nowels

LIBRARIAN:
Scott Swope

TOUR STAFF AND ESCORTS:
Henry T. Stanley, *Tour Chairman*
Mrs. Richard L. Rosenberg, *Asst. Tour Chairman*
Alfred O. Stromquist, *Finance and Logistics*
Dr. Daniel H. Labby, *Physician*
Mrs. John F. Cramer, Jr., *Orchestra Chairman*
Wes Taft, *Photo Journalist*
Mrs. Jacob Avshalomov
Mr. and Mrs. Ben Bernhard
Mr. and Mrs. Victor Critchlow
Eugene Kaza
Mrs. Clay Myers
Mrs. Guy Nowels
Mrs. A. Gordon Russell
Mr. and Mrs. William B. Webber

ACKNOWLEDGMENTS:
Lynch & Van Cleve, art direction
Irwin Hodson-Arcady Press
Pacific Color Plate Co.
Schlegel Typesetting Co.

LA NAZIONE

NEL SALONE DEI CINQUECENTO DI PALAZZO VECCHIO

Un commovente esempio dai giovani di Portland

Il concerto dei ragazzi della Portland Junior Symphony Orchestra
Pochi di loro faranno della musica la loro professione—Caloroso successo

MOVING EXAMPLE GIVEN BY THE YOUNG PLAYERS OF PORTLAND

"The concert of the boys and girls of the Portland Junior Symphony Orchestra. Few of them will make music their profession. Extremely warm success."

Facing, with youthful exuberance, the chilly and ancient walls of Palazzo Vecchio, the Portland Junior Symphony Orchestra gave yesterday afternoon a concert in the Hall of the 500. The ensemble left Portland, Oregon on March 7th, and has played in London, Croydon, Lisbon and Milan. After its Florentine concert, it will return to the United States, where it will perform in New York and Washington as a conclusion to its first International Tour. The orchestra will probably not arouse there the same emotions that it has been able to spark in Italy and especially in Florence.

An orchestra composed of boys and girls between 12 and 22 years of age (but the average is 15 to 16) is already an exceptional achievement. The fact that in this country of ours—a country of musicians, saints, navigators, poets, etc., etc.—a great symphonic ensemble made up of nonprofessionals can give full-fledged concerts, is something which fills one, first with amazement and then with unconditioned admiration and wonder.

In this blessed country of ours, where much fuss is made over "structural reforms," "regional theatres" and "diffusion of music at all levels," we still have to resolve the problem of an education which can make us not only a country of "great ones of the past" but indeed a civilized country for what concerns musical education today.

Piero Bellugi, who briefly introduced the Portland Junior Symphony Orchestra, did well in hinting politely at the example which comes from these young people. Most of them will not make music their profession, and yet they will be able to play an instrument well no matter what their future profession will be, whether he will be a milkman, engineer or a physics professor.

The guidance of Jacob Avshalomov has above all the merit of having made the huge ensemble compact and flexible at the same time. He conducted with extreme clarity. The young Americans gave yesterday a concert of high technical level, far from giving the impression of an occasional getting together of non-professionals. The mistakes in the Leonora no. 2, probably due to emotion, did not prevent the quality of the young trumpet players from shining through. When Kathie Egbers was the oboe soloist in the concerto No. 2 Opus 9 by Albinoni, we admired not only her extremely musical tranquility but also the gifts she has with the timbre and expression with her instrument. Indeed extraordinary was also the young solo clarinetist Gary McGee, in the first Rhapsody by Debussy.

One might think that these soloists are exceptions, but what can we say then of the quality of the brass players, who are worthy to stand comparison with our best professionals, and of the excellence of the whole string ensemble headed by a 19-year-old girl as concertmaster, who only next year will study at a conservatory? Yesterday afternoon, it was really to be amazed and moved. Therefore, the gifts of David Diamond became secondary in this first performance of his suite "The World of Paul Klee" which he composed a couple of years ago in Florence. Perhaps even the merits of the conductor himself (as a composer) become less important as well.

The success of the concert was overwhelming, calling for an encore. However, if we should make in Florence a census of non-professionals capable of playing in an orchestra, would we be able to count them on the fingers on our two hands? We better think on it.

The New York Times

MAR. 27, 1970

PORTLAND GROUP IN DEBUT CONCERT

Junior Symphony Presents 'The World of Paul Klee'

By Donal Henahan

The Portland Junior Symphony, a 46-year-old orchestra that was one of the first such youth ensembles in America, played its first New York concert last night at Alice Tully Hall. Fresh from a European tour—its first—the group presented works by Dohnanyi, Diamond, Beethoven and its conductor, Jacob Avshalomov, and sent the listener away persuaded he had heard a serious, conscientiously trained band of young musicians.

David Diamond's "The World of Paul Klee,," which the Portland group commissioned under a Rockefeller Foundation grant in 1959, proved an excellent piece to display the orchestra's capacities . . .

Of course, these are youngsters, most of them apparently in their late teens. But, like most such training orchestras, the Portlanders could pull matters together well and at times approach surprisingly professional levels. In the Romanza of Dohnanyi's work, there were excellent contributions from the solo oboe, cello, English horn, harp, violin and viola.

The Washington Post

MAR. 30, 1970

EASTER CONCERT

By Paul Hume

The Portland Junior Symphony of Oregon joined forces with the Cathedral Choral Society yesterday afternoon to give Washington Cathedral an unusual memorable concert for Easter afternoon.

Just back from a two-week tour of Europe, the orchestra was in top form as it played the second Leonore Overture of Beethoven, an Albinoni Oboe Concerto, Ravel's Introduction and Allegro, and a short work by its composer-conductor, Jacob Avshalomov, The Rose. The choral work for which the Orchestra provided a smooth and proficient accompaniment was the Bruckner Te Deum.

When this orchestra's top form appears, it comes with excellent strings, handsomely balanced, fine winds both brass and wood, and able percussion. Its soloists, from an outstanding concert mistress to a notable first cello, include Kathie Egbers, who made the oboe concerto a real joy, and Jennifer Hoesly, whose harp was distintive in Ravel.

Portland is proud of its Junior Symphony with good reason. The music making of this ensemble of 100 players—47 young men and 53 young women—between the ages of 12 and 21 is quite special. Their playing in Europe, obviously of the caliber of yesterday's concert, was a great credit to this country.

The Oregonian

DEC. 7, 1962

IDEAL ENVOYS

All of the Pacific Northwest would bust its buttons with pride should Secretary of State Dean Rusk adopt the recommendation of Portland's Mayor Terry Schrunk that the Portland Junior Symphony Orchestra be chosen as one of the units to be sent abroad by the President's Fund for travel abroad by the Performing arts.

The local orchestra has been one of Oregon's most valued institutions in its 40 years of existence. It earned regional sponsorship in the critical and popular success of its appearance at this year's World's Fair in Seattle.

Few performing groups dispatched to win friends for America in other lands could do such a comprehensive job as could the youngsters of the Junior Symphony. Not only are their professional qualifications worthy of the highest respect, they are also representative of the very best of American youth. In 40 years, not one of the hundreds of youngsters who have performed with the Junior Symphony has been in trouble with the law. In the homes and salons of other countries, as well as on the concert stages, they would be a credit to their country, whose youth is viewed in some quarters of the globe as existing only in the black-jacketed duck-trailed gangs of the big city sidewalks.

Corriere d'informazione
Milan, March 23-24, 1970
"Orchestra Giovane Che Incanta"

A Young and Enchanting Orchestra

It is a proud achievement for a country to have an orchestra formed by young people. The Gioventu Musicale had as its guests at the Conservatory about 100 Americans of the Portland Junior Symphony, an organization which is 46 years old. It was founded by a Siberian exile, Gershkovitch, and is now directed by Mr. Avshalomov, who was born in China. These men have known how to educate. The young "professors" played with passion and bravura. They are not afraid to enter the difficult spirals of Beethoven and Brahms and they give due homage to the music of their leader. Strengthened in the Beethoven triple concerto by adult soloists such as our Pocaterra and Marengoni, the young players of Portland and their conductor obtained an overwhelming success.

M. P.

London, 31st March 1970

In a letter received today from the Vicar of St. Martin-in-the-Fields he writes: "The Concert at St. Martin's was received with more acclamation and pleasure than almost any Concert I can remember in the Church."

No doubt you would like to add this to the many trophies which you and your splendid Orchestra collected during your European tour.

SIR ROBERT MAYER,
Founder & Chairman
Youth and Music

DIARIO DE NOTICIAS,
LISBON MAR. 19, 1970

SYMPHONIC CONCERT AT THE TIVOLI BY A GREAT ORCHESTRA OF YOUNG PEOPLE

The Juventude Musical Portuguesa presented to our public last night in the hall of the Tivoli, the "Portland Junior Symphony Orchestra," under the direction of Maestro Jacob Avshalomov.

In every way, it was a positive affirmation never to be forgotten. For this reason, it does not surprise or amaze us that from the stage of the Tivoli came something like a breath of fresh air. With it came the carefully balanced enthusiasm, the sincerity and a deeply felt and vivid penetration . . . all that can be expressed by suggestive power and exemplary performance.

The young symphonic orchestra of Portland presented the following program: the Leonore Overture no. 2 of Beethoven, a Concerto by Albinoni for oboe and orchestra, for which the soloist was Kathie Egbers, the Orchestral Triptych "The World of Paul Klee" by the North American composer Diamond, a Rhapsody for Clarinet by Debussy with Gary McGee as a soloist and the Second Symphony of Brahms.

With this program, maestro Jacob Avshalomov and the orchestra gave an ample and convincing demonstration of what they can do in the field of technical execution and even beyond that, their musicality and interpretation. It is an "instrument" of great quality, giving consideration to the age factor and to the composition of the orchestra, which the maestro "plays" with proficiency, affection, stimulating vigor and interpretative feeling and style.

All of the pieces were excellently performed, the brilliancy of the soloists was remarkable, but the performance and interpretation of the Symphony of Brahms remained in our memory as an example of ability, musicianship and art. It was a success in all aspects.

The Maestro and his little-great collaborators were given an ovation. As an encore, they offered a witty and brilliant performance of a page of Johann Strauss. The name of the Portland Junior Symphony should be long remembered for the life it brought us and for the fine example it gave.

London, March 27, 1970

I trust that the rest of your tour went as happily and successfully as the London part of it. The Choir send their greeting and their very warm praise of the Orchestra's very high standard.

My congratulations on your training and conducting of them, not only for their fine technical accomplishments but for their very sensitive musical response. This was evident both in the Beethoven Violin Concerto which I heard, and in their complete willingness to give me their *musical* cooperation in the Bruckner.

We all enjoyed the Fairfield Hall concert very much . . . and I send my great gratitude to you for giving me such a delightful and accomplished band of players to work with.

FREDERIC JACKSON
Royal Academy of Music

Lisbon, March 1970

A large audience at the leading theater of this capital gave the group a rousing ovation, insisting on five encores. Ambassador Ridgeway Knight was present and congratulated conductor Avshalomov for the performance and the distinct contribution to better U.S. relations abroad. Congratulations to you, to Portland citizens for their support of this Orchestra.

Letter to Mayor Shrunk from the Director of the U.S. Information Agency

Concertmaster Valerie Poullette, cited in Florence review.

Copenhagen, May 27, 1959

At last I brought together the two daughters of Carl Nielsen so we could enjoy the recording of your splendid rendition of Nielsen's *Symphony no. 3* . . . we were all taken by the musicality of your approach, the conviction of your tempi and your wonderful grasp of the style and atmosphere of Neilsen. Personally I felt that you have even more drive and energy than most people conducting Nielsen in his own part of the world.

And your orchestra! One could wish to be only sixteen, a resident of Portland, and member of your group. What an experience for young people. You ought to make a European tour. . . . It might make people think over the old phrase about cultural heritage of the Old World. Most certainly we don't have anything like your Junior Symphony.

With best wishes for the glorious future of your great undertaking in music.

ROBERT NAUR, *Music Critic*
Politiken

THE OREGONIAN APR. 26, 1970

Europe Training Shown By Junior Symphony

by HILMAR GRONDAHL
Music Editor, The Oregonian

The presence of the Portland Junior Symphony in the Civic Auditorium Saturday night was more than a concert appearance; it was a celebration. It was the homecoming of 100 young players and their conductor, Jacob Avshalomov, who had together made a palpable hit in Europe.

There was a difference even in appearance, the girl musicians in their festive full-length concert gowns of deep blue. There was a difference, to be heard in the playing, too, the consequence, obviously, of their concentrated regimen of rehearsals and performances while on tour.

It was a grand concert in many respects. Even the forces engaged were large. In addition to the 100 orchestral musicians, there were 140 choral singers from three ensembles at the University of Oregon plus 60 from Clark College, in the concluding work, Bruckner's Te Deum. This was a score presented several times during the tour, and its inclusion here as the program's concluding work was gauged to be the climax to the excellent playing done by the orchestra earlier in the Mozart G-minor Symphony and the Stravinsky suite from "The Firebird."

Unfortunately we were able to hear only a very small bit of the Bruckner score, only enough to recognize its tremendous sonic resources and choral magnificence.

Back to the orchestra. It was delightful to hear with what technical assurance and interpretive zeal the young musicians responded to their conductor's indications throughout the concert. The Mozart Symphony is a pretty familiar piece, yet there were fresh pleasures and infectious subtleties to stimulate one's deeper enjoyment. The frenetic, yet controlled outburst of brasses in Kastchei's dance in the ballet bit, was a demonstration at the other extreme of appropriate musical exposition.

The audience response, too, was in the nature of a celebration; the Juniors were back, and playing beautifully.

Bruckner's "Te Deum" at the National Cathedral, Washington, D.C.

OREGON JOURNAL APR. 27, 1970

Bruckner Tops Music By Juniors

By MARTIN CLARK
Journal Music Editor

Anton Bruckner's mighty "Te Deum" topped the Portland Junior Symphony's homecoming and final subscription concert of the season Saturday evening at the Civic Auditorium.

The program drew a near-capacity house (about 2,700), one of the largest—if not the largest—audience I've seen for a subscription evening concert by the Juniors.

THERE MUST have been nearly 250 performers on stage for the "Te Deum." It was a well balanced performance, no small feat with so many involved. The four soloists gave an even performance. They were soprano Judy Page, mezzo Alyce Rogers, tenor Guy Aydelott, and bass Donald Newman.

Bruckner's symphonies tend to be uneven in quality, and this characteristic carries over somewhat into the "Te Deum," but the overall effect of the work is deeply moving. Avshalomov seemed to underscore the composition's strength and minimize its weaknesses.

Preceding the Bruckner, the final work of the evening, Avshalomov gave an entertaining verbal sketch of the Juniors' recent tour abroad and the warm reception they encountered everywhere they went.

THE TWO selections on the opening half of the program demonstrated the remarkable versatility of musicians of such youth. Mozart's Symphony No. 40 (G Minor) revealed crisp attacks, clean releases, and a grasp of Mozartean nuances rarely encountered in youth orchestras. Stravinsky's "Firebird Suite" gave the youngsters an opportunity to demonstrate the high degree of virtuosity of individuals and individual sections of the orchestra.

It was a most gratifying evening.

47th Season

Jacob Avshalomov, Conductor

November 6, 1970

TELEMANN	*Overture for Horns & Strings
MENDELSSOHN	Piano Concerto NO. 1, G minor Nan Nowels, *Soloist*
DUKAS	Sorcerer's Apprentice
SHOSTAKOVITCH	Symphony NO. 5

December 26, 1970

9th Annual Family Concert at Christmas

Seasonal Music & Carol Singing

BACH	Cantata NO. 63 "Christen, atzet diesen Tag" *Guest Choir:* Vancouver Brahms Singers
BARBER	Die Natali
BRUCKNER	Symphony NO. 4–Allegro

February 26, 1971

BERLIOZ	Symphonie Fantastique, op. 14
J. C. BACH	Viola Concerto, C minor Daniel Avshalomov, *Soloist*
GINASTERA	*Pampeanas NO. 3
GOULD	Latin-American Symphonette

April 23, 1971

HAYDN	Symphony NO. 92, Oxford
BEETHOVEN	*Equali* for Trombones
DEBUSSY	Afternoon of a Faun
WALTON	Belshazzar's Feast Neil Wilson, *Baritone*

Guest Choirs: Clark College, George Fox College, Linfield College, Warner-Pacific College

---

**Portland Premier*

OREGON JOURNAL

'Professional Attitude' Characterizes Juniors

By MARTIN CLARK
Journal Music Editor

Friday night at the Civic Auditorium under the direction of its regular conductor, Jacob Avshalomov, the Portland Junior Symphony opened its 47th season with one of its most remarkable concerts to date.

Remarkable not because the playing was so much better than other concerts of other seasons, but because never have I heard a season opener of the group approached with such professional concern. In some ways the playing was not up to that of previous years, but even with an abnormally large turnover this year the ensemble has retained—and even seemed to add—a professional consciousness which sets it apart from the best of "youth orchestras" across the country.

THE PROGRAM was one to tax the resources of any symphony orchestra. To say that the juniors sound like a first rate professional symphony orchestra would be not to overstate the case so much as to misstate it. The point is that I was acutely aware of the collective seriousness of the players' approach to music making . . . that is, to me they seemed to be reflecting an attitude of: "Of course, we love music and we know that making music can be a lot of fun; but there is no real satisfaction to be gained unless performing is approached as a serious, demanding job."

THAT IS a professional approach even if the instruments and individual players are not yet of professional caliber. The Shostakovitch Fifth Symphony, which was the second half of the program, is not only a great work but one which makes exhaustive demands upon the resources of an orchestra. The manner in which the youngsters rose to the challenge was impressive.

Not so impressive was the performance of Telemann's Overture for Horns and Strings, billed as a first performance for Portland. The horns (admittedly a most difficult piece of metal to play) were simply not up to the level of playing in the other sections.

NAN NOWELS, soloist in the Mendelssohn Piano Concerto No. 1 in G Minor, revealed a great quantity of that quality expounded on above—professionalism. She is enormously competent and technically precise, but also managed to extract the ineffable sweetness of Mendelssohn.

The Dukas "Sorcerer's Apprentice" received the sort of spritely reading a popular favorite requires to strip off the patina of familiarity and expose the factors which made it such a favorite in the first place.

An audience of more than 1,500 responded to the performance with the sort of warm enthusiasm which has come to typify Junior Symphony audiences.

OREGON JOURNAL FEB. 28, 1971

Juniors Feature Berlioz

Portland Junior Symphony presented its second subscription concert of the orchestra's 47th season Friday evening at the Civic Auditorium.

Jacob Avshalomov conducted the ensemble in a program which featured the Berlioz "Symphonie Fantastique" as the first half of the program. Although the Junior Symphony is, as the name obviously indicates, a youth orchestra, its repertoire has never been characterized by any youthful limitations.

Friday night's program was no exception. The Berlioz "Fantastique," when played as it should be, is a challenge to any orchestra—youth or otherwise. The Juniors rose to the Berlioz challenge remarkably well.

—Martin Clark

THE OREGONIAN FEB. 27, 1971

Conductor's Son Soloist With Junior Orchestra

By JANET GOETZE
Staff Writer, The Oregonian

The Portland premiere of Ginastera's "Pampeana No. 3" was a work of grand feeling with hot and primitive, cool and poetic sounds Friday when Jacob Avshalomov directed the Portland Junior Symphony in Civic Auditorium.

In his verbal "program notes," the maestro pointed out Alberto Ginastera regards the work as a pastorale, evoking the wide open spaces of the pampas of his native Argentina, as well as the primitive rhythms and natural sounds of the region.

As played by the Junior Symphony, the work has a feeling of fettered civilization reaching out for the freedom of nature in a big, colorful land.

Daniel Avshalomov, 17, principal violist and son of the conductor, was soloist in the Bach "Viola Concerto in C Minor," exhibiting a singing, flowing sound that took all the bow he had.

The angular, handsome youth plays with the seemingly effortless grace of a seasoned soloist.

Berlioz' "Symphonie Fantastique," recounting experiences of a young artist seemed a good major work for the musicians, with its variety of feelings, tempos and moods.

Latin Tempos New

Avshalomov said the "Guaracha" and "Conga" tempos of Gould's "Latin American Symphonette" were new to the symphony members, but they sounded as though they were able to get into the old fashioned swing of things.

Portions of the Friday concert will be repeated Saturday in the children's concert beginning at 11 a.m. in Civic Auditorium.

The second program also will include 500 Beaverton school district children participating.

OREGON JOURNAL APR. 24, 1971

'Belshazzar' Triumph For Junior Symphony

By MARTIN CLARK
Journal Music Editor

"Thou art weighed in the balance and found wanting," wrote the hand on the wall for Belshazzar's benefit, but "Belshazzar's Feast" was anything but wanting in the Portland Junior Symphony's performance of it Friday night at the Civic Auditorium.

Under Jacob Avshalomov's direction, the juniors were joined by choruses from Clark, George Fox, Warner-Pacific, and Linfield Colleges, which were prepared by their directors — Marion van Dyk, Josoph Gilmore, Lauren Sykes, and George Bell.

IT WAS SOMETHING of a triumph for the juniors and the colleges involved. "Belshazzar's Feast" by William Walton is an ambitious cantata in every sense of the word. It takes not only a mammoth chorus but an outsized orchestra (shades of Berlioz) as well. The additional brass required, stationed in the downstage niches on either side of the stage, came from alumni of the orchestra and members of the Preparatory Orchestra.

Neil Wilson, the baritone soloist, was equal to the heavy dramatic demands Walton makes upon his soloist. The composition took about half an hour to perform but never does Walton's work sag and neither did Avshalomov's performers of it Friday night.

It was a tremendous undertaking which came off with great dramatic impact.

THE FIRST HALF of the program was, apparently, deliberately chosen for its subdued atmosphere to contrast with the unmitigated drama of the Walton. Opening with the melodic, ingratiating Haydn "Oxford" Symphony, the tranquility deepened with "Three Equali for Trombones" by Beethoven, and was totally established with the ever-popular "Afternoon of a Faun" by Debussy.

The eight trombones, who performed without a burble, were Gary Powers, Michael Lotz, Erik Olsen, Michael Powers, George Reinmiller, Jeff Craig, Alan Pierce, and Randy Malmstrom. Some of these were part of the additional brass bands drawn from alumni and the preparatory orchestra.

The performance was received with what has almost become stereotyped enthusiasm for Junior Symphony audiences.

THE OREGONIAN APR. 24, 1971

Portland Jr. Symphony Ends Season In Style

By HILMAR GRONDAHL
Music Editor, The Oregonian

It is always stimulating to watch the hundred or more young players of the Portland Junior Symphony as they fill the stage of the Civic Auditorium and give their alert responses to their conductor, Jacob Avshalomov as they customarily do, and did again at the final concert of the season Friday night.

But on this occasion they were joined by 250 singers from six colleges to perform William Walton's grand oratorio, "Belshazzar's Feast" which proved to be one of the magnificent offerings of the season.

Beside the massive effects of the Walton works, there were the more moderate assertions of Haydn's "Oxford" Symphony and the quite modest beauties of Debussy's "The Afternoon of a Faun." There were, as well, the special sonorities of eight trombones in Three Equali by Beethoven.

"Belshazzar's Feast" is one of this century's notable oratorios; bright, flashy and irresistibly exciting.

Not since Handel and Mendelssohn brought episodes from the Bible to vital presence has there been another score of such passionate eloquence, unless it be Ernest Bloch's Sacred Service.

The impact of instruments and voices on the word "slain" is cataclysmic, and the rhapsodies of the trumpets in the phrase "blow up the trumpet in Zion" are a masterful association of spirit and sound. Mr. Wilson's assignments, especially the one relating to the handwriting on the wall were musically impressive.

Well, these 350 musicians under Avshalomov's guiding hand made us all witnesses to the glory and drama of this music.

Problem Noted

The printed page didn't specify which young flutist carried the solo in the Debussy tone poem, but it was beautifully stated, even a bit modestly, as becomes this music.

One recognizes a problem this orchestra's conductor has in programing a work such as the Haydn symphony when he uses the wind and brass complements of the composer's own choosing and yet sets them against a body of strings more than twice that of the original score.

The sticky decision is this; whether to deprive 60 per cent of the strings from the learning and playing experience simply to guarantee a balance of parts as indicated by the composer. From the educative standpoint the conductor's decision is indisputable.

48th Season

Jacob Avshalomov, Conductor

October 28, 1971
The New Greater Portland Jewish Community Center
Dedication Concert

TELEMANN	Don Quixote Suite—Moderato
A. AVSHALOMOV	Four Biblical Tableaux
TELEMANN	—Allegretto
RAVEL	Sheherazade
	Emilie Berendsen-Bloch, *Mezzo*
TELEMANN	—Allegro Moderato
BLOCH	Schelomo
	Roman Dukson, *Cello Soloist*
COPLAND	Fanfare for the Common Man

November 14, 1971

COPLAND	Fanfare for the Common Man
TELEMANN	*Don Quixote Suite
SCHUMANN	Piano Concerto, A minor, op. 54
	Linda Lorati, *Soloist*
MOUSSORSKY/ RAVEL	Pictures at an Exhibition

December 26, 1971
10th Annual Family Concert at Christmas
Seasonal Music & Carol Singing

BALAKIREV	Overture on Three Russian Songs
TELEMANN	Don Quixote-Moderato
MOZART	Wind Serenade No. 10-Rondo
MOORE	Balletude
DELLO JOIO	Sonata No. 3
Portland Ballet School, Jacqueline Schumacher, *Director*	
HOLST	Uranus, Venus, Jupiter

February 27, 1972

ROSSINI	Overture: "Barber of Seville"
MOZART	Horn Concerto NO. 3, Eb, K. 447
	Harry Bell, *Soloist*
HANDEL	Zadok the Priest
BRAHMS	Song of Destiny, op. 54
Guest Choirs: Aloha, Catlin-Gabel, Centennial, & Madison High Schools	
RESPIGHI	*Roman Festivals

April 30, 1972

RIMSKY-KORSAKOV	"Russian Easter" Overture

IN MEMORIAM LUCIA GERSHKOVITCH

DELIUS	On Hearing the First Cuckoo In Spring
KHATCHATURIAN	*Violin Concerto Paula Sisson, *Soloist*
MOZART	Wind Serenade, c minor, Allegro
HINDEMITH	*Concert Music: Strings & Brass

May 7, 1972

Reed College

Selections from the Season

**Portland Premier*

Our typical audience at the Civic Auditorium.

THE OREGONIAN NOV. 15, 1971

Junior Symphony 'paints pictures' for audience

By KATHLEEN PIPER
of The Oregonian Staff

Jacob Avshalomov and 105 young musicians painted pictures Sunday night, dazzling a full auditorium with an inspiring "Pictures at an Exhibition" by Moussorgsky.

Performing with strength and finesse the entire Portland Junior Symphony orchestra came together under the baton of Maestro Avshalomov for its season premiere to render musically the scenes that Moussorgsky's friend, architect Victor Hartmann, had drawn.

Seventeen-year-old Linda Lorati impressed the audience with her skill at the keyboard in Schumann's romantic "Piano Concerto in A Minor."

Miss Lorati, as guest soloist, won the Junior Symphony's annual auditions last spring. The Sunset High School senior earned a standing ovation Sunday night.

Telemann's "Don Quixote Suite" had the distinction of being a premiere performance for the city. In it, the orchestra aptly illustrated the seven-part story, in Baroque fashion.

OREGON JOURNAL FEB. 28, 1972

Juniors, Choir Score With Brahms

By MARTIN CLARK
Journal Music Editor

Surely some kind of record was set Sunday night at the Civic Auditorium for sheer numbers on stage. Choirs from four Portland area high schools joined the Portland Junior Symphony for a performance of Brahms' "Schicksalslied" (Song of Destiny or Fate).

With 250 from the four high schools and 100-plus in the Junior Symphony, that made a grand total on stage of about 350!... plus chairs... and Jacob Avshalomov, conductor of the Junior Symphony. An audience of more than 1,500 was on hand for the event.

BUT THE important point was that they sounded so well. There's a particular thrilling impact which can be made only by a huge mass of voices.

This impact was made Sunday night in the Brahms. But it would not have been possible without the thoughtful training of the directors at the four high schools represented—G. Richard Muhle, Centennial; B. Fred Hammack, Madison; David G. Schauffler, Catlin Gabel; and Stephen L. Stone, Aloha High School... and Avshalomov's sure control of the massed situation.

THE CONCERT opened with a glittering performance of Rossini's Overture to "The Barber of Seville," which never ceases to amaze me with its sparkling gaiety, and the Mozart Horn Concerto No. 3 in E Flat, K447. Harry Bell, 19, a student at Lewis and Clark College and principal horn of the PJS, was the able soloist.

But the surprising note of the evening was the PJS information that Respighi's "Roman Festivals" was receiving its Portland premiere! The last of the three symphonic poems in which he recorded three different facets of Rome—its fountains, pines, and festivals—"Roman Festivals" (1928) may not be the absolute equal of the first two, but the difference is not that much. And when you consider the drivel performed here occasionally in the past 15 years, it's incredible that a work of such great worth could have been bypassed all this time. The PJS was thoroughly involved in it.

THE OREGONIAN FEB. 28, 1972

Concert by Juniors brilliant

By HILMAR GRONDAHL
of The Oregonian staff

A stimulating concert was given by the Portland Junior Symphony under Jacob Avshalomov's baton Sunday night in the Civic Auditorium, with singers from four area high schools: Aloha, Madison, Catlin Gabel and Centennial. Their materials were the Coronation Anthem, "Zadok the Priest" by Handel and the "Song of Destiny" by Brahms.

The 250 singers plus 100 instrumentalists on stage was an eye-filling sight and the sound of this vast ensemble was ear-filling as well. It was a lovely, well controlled sound, exuding a freshness of quality that was particularly satisfying in the sentiment of the Holderlin verses.

The score offered as a local premiere was Respighi's "Roman Festivals." This is a work of vivid contrasts and exciting coloristic instrumentation. It is the musical language of circuses, festivals, carousals. Its brassiness was a marvelous opportunity for the excellent section the Juniors have, and the hall range with its brilliant sound.

THE OREGONIAN MAY 11, 1972

Junior Symphony's concert stimulating, skillful program

By HILMAR GRONDAHL
of The Oregonian staff

The Portland Junior Symphony, after nearly a half century, is still creating stimulating events for its performers and audiences.

The concluding concert of the season Sunday night in the Civic Auditorium was additionally stimulating, for its conductor, Jacob Avshalomov, had several heartwarming items to offer.

One was the memorial tribute to the late Lucia Gershkovitch, wife of the orchestra's founding conductor, and a foster mother to Avshalomov for a few years of his youth in Portland. A memento in this tribute was the playing of the "Russian Easter" Overture by Rimsky-Korsakov (a conservatory teacher of Gershkovitch in Russia).

The concert contained two local premiers, one the Khachaturian Violin Concerto, which featured concertmaster Paula Sisson as soloist, the other Paul Hindemith's Concert Music for Strings and Brass, Op. 50.

Parts of this concerto are more muscle than music, but the attractive young violinist was equally ready for the technical flourishes and the areas in which sentiment had its sway. Her performance was an admirable one and had the whole hearted approval of the house.

One of the most delightful manifestations of what the conductor and his operations are all about came after intermission when he entrusted the first movement of the Mozart Serenade in C-minor, K. 388 to eight of his wind players; a pair each of oboes, clarinets, horns and bassoons. This was an artistic exposure of members not often allowed this prominence and they came through like pros, tonally clean and clear, with beautiful unanimity and articulation. It was artistically a special spot in the concert.

This is the second concert in eight days in which Delius' "On Hearing the First Cuckoo in Spring" has been played, but it doesn't seem to advance the season much.

The premiere performance here of the Hindemith music for strings and brass was an unusual treatment of these two forces, sometimes in conflict sometimes in consonance. In his verbal annotation Avshalomov spoke of the massive "musculature" of the work, but the strengths here were more congenial than they were in the Khachaturian. In fact, it was a thrilling disposition of material and some brilliant work came from the orchestra's brasses.

OREGON JOURNAL MAY 1, 1972

Khachaturian Concerto Highlights Junior Concert

By MARTIN CLARK
Journal Music Editor

That was quite a season-closing concert the Portland Junior Symphony gave Sunday night at the Civic Auditorium under the direction of Jacob Avshalomov and dedicated to the late Howard Leib, a generous supporter of the orchestra.

As an opener they performed the "Russian Easter" Overture by Rimsky-Korsakov, in memory of the late Lucia Gershkovitch, widow of the founder-conductor of the Junior Symphony. As one who played in the orchestra under Gershkovitch during those earlier years, Avshalomov was particularly well qualified to make some touching comments on the great contribution which Mrs. Gershkovitch made to his own personal music career and to the orchestra.

In total contrast, the second work of the evening was Frederick Delius' charming "On Hearing the First Cuckoo in Spring," which received some perspective touches from conductor and orchestra.

Soloist of the evening was Paula Sisson, the orchestra's concertmaster, in a performance of the Khachaturian Violin Concerto. It's hard to believe that something was comparatively familiar as this was receiving its Portland premiere, but that's the way it was announced. It's not only a technically demanding piece, it makes exhaustive physical demands on the performer. The slim girl who played it tossed it off with a technical mastery not often encountered in a 21-year-old violinist of either sex, receiving a standing ovation for her efforts.

49th Season

Jacob Avshalomov, Conductor

November 19, 1972

BEETHOVEN	Symphony NO. 7, A major, op. 92
SCHOENBERG	*Five Pieces for Orchestra, op. 16 Premonitions, Yesteryears, Peripetia
MOZART	Piano Concerto, NO. 17 G major Theodore Sawyer, *Soloist*
COPLAND	El Salon Mexico

December 26, 1972

11th Annual Concert at Christmas

BEETHOVEN	Symphony NO. 7—Allegro con brio
BACH	Violin Concerto, E major Delmar Pettys, *Soloist*
VAN DELDEN	Intrada e Danza, *Harp Ensemble*
VAUGHAN-WILLIAMS	*Hodie—Christmas Cantata

Alyce Rogers, *Mezzo-Soprano;* James Kempster, *Tenor;*
Barry Spencer, *Baritone;* Marquam Krantz, N*arrator*

Guest Choirs: Franklin, Lake Oswego & Roosevelt High Schools
& Saint Mary's Acadamy

February 25, 1973

BRAHMS	Symphony NO. 3, F major, op. 90
WEBERN	Six Pieces for Orchestra, op. 6
SPOHR	Quartet-Concerto, op. 131 *The Fine Arts Quartet*
ENESCO	Rumanian Rhapsody NO. 1

April 29, 1973

SULLIVAN	Overture: "H.M.S. Pinafore"
BACH	Ricercar a 6, Musical Offering
BACH/WEBERN	Ricercar a 6
DESENCLOS	*Incantation, Threne, et Danse Gary Guthman, *Trumpet Soloist*
TCHAIKOVSKY	Symphony NO. 5, E minor, op. 65

May 12, 1973

Medford High School Auditorium

Selections from the Season

**Portland Premier*

OREGON JOURNAL NOV. 21, 1972

Juniors Taped In Campaign For Excellence

By MARTIN CLARK
Journal Music Editor

Sunday night's opening concert of the season by the Portland Junior Symphony could very possibly be the beginning of a bright new chapter in the history of the internationally famous youth orchestra.

Oregon's educational station videotaped the program as part of its "Campaign for Excellence" In addition to being shown on television in Oregon (on a date to be announced), the program will be submitted to the national Public Broadcasting Service in Washington, D.C. for possible presentation over the national network.

For Sunday night's momentous occasion, Jacob Avshalomov, the Junior Symphony's conductor, chose a program as representative as any I can recall of the orchestra's programming: Beethoven's Seventh Symphony, three selections from Schoenberg's "Five Pieces for Orchestra," and, after intermission, the Mozart Piano Concerto No. 17 in G, with Theodore Sawyer as soloist, and Copland's "El Salon Mexico."

IT WAS A demanding program for any concert of the season, but especially so for the season's opener.

It was well done, but it was not quite up to the high level of performance with which the Juniors have spoiled us, particularly in the Beethoven.

THE OREGONIAN DEC. 27, 1972

Audience responds to 'mixed' concert

By JOHN WENDEBORN
of The Oregonian staff

The free concert was relaxed, informal and was met with general enthusiasm, from the opening Beethoven finale from his Seventh Symphony to the final work on the bill, the Vaughan-Williams Christmas Cantata, "Hodie," or "This Day."

And in between, the crowd of youngsters and adults was treated to a spirited and delightful violin solo by former PJS violinist Delmar Pettys, now a member of the Lenox String Quartet in New York.

It was a conglomeration of styles that gave the capacity audience in the Civic Auditorium plenty of reason to applaud performers through three curtain calls.

Major works

The two major works of the evening were the Bach Violin Concerto in E Major, played by Pettys, and the choral piece. Pettys is an accomplished, inspired violinist and his treatment of the Bach was coupled in kind by the orchestra, which was diminished in size from the large PJS to a chamber orchestra, more in keeping with Bach's orchestration.

While vocal soloists Alyce Rogers, James Kempster and Barney Spencer were the most visible in the Vaughan Williams cantata, it was the work of the massive chorus, made up of choirs from Franklin, Lake Oswego, Roosevelt and St. Mary's high schools, that brought the 45-minute composition to its full fruition.

THE OREGONIAN FEB. 26, 1973

Junior Symphony offering attractive

BY HILMAR GRONDAHL
of The Oregonian staff

One of the best assorted concert programs offered by director Jacob Avshalomov and the Portland Junior Symphony contained four indisputable attractions Sunday in Civic Auditorium.

The appearance of the Fine Arts Quartet and the first hearing of the Spohr concerto were the highlights of the evening.

The wonders of the youth orchestra's training program were plentifully evident in the Brahms symphony.

OREGON JOURNAL APR. 31, 1973

Junior Symphony Closes With Triumphant Fifth

By MARTIN CLARK
Journal Music Editor

It was an auspicious opener, the bright, bouncy overture to Gilbert and Sullivan's "H.M.S. Pinafore." And the Portland Junior Symphony's final subscription concert of the season was a handsome season finale. This was the Sunday night concert in the Civic Auditorium for an audience of nearly 2,000.

Gary Guthman, the 20-year-old trumpet soloist in the Desenclos. Here's a performer with a commanding technique who plays with a panache which gave the Desenclos an interest it was otherwise lacking.

The ambitious closing selection for the concert was Tschaikovsky's sublime Symphony No. 5 in E Minor. Conductor Jacob Avshalomov mentioned in his introductory remarks that the current members of the orchestra were playing the symphony for the first time and he felt we would feel that enthusiasm. It was there, and much of the original excitement of one of the most popular of all symphonies was there.

When I hear something like this, I must again marvel at Avshalomov's patience and exactitude, as conductor and teacher. Because the orchestra has an amazingly good sound, and the response to his baton is remarkably accurate.

A standing ovation followed the Fifth, lending just the right touch to the closing concert of the season.

50th Anniversary Season

Jacob Avshalomov, Conductor

December 1, 1973

BACH/RESPIGHI	Passacaglia & Fugue, C minor
BENJAMIN LEES	Prologue, Capriccio & Epilogue

Commissioned by the Portland Junior Symphony

RACHMANINOV	Rhapsody on a Theme of Paganini

Tana Bawden, *Soloist*

PROCLAMATION BY THE HON. NEIL E. GOLDSCHMIDT, MAYOR

DUKAS	Fanfare: "La Peri"
MENDELSSOHN	Symphony NO. 1, OP. 11

December 26, 1973

12th Annual Concert at Christmas

Seasonal Music with Carol Singing &
The Preparatory Orchestra, Alexander Ghillany Conducting,
Alumni Orchestra, Jerome D. Cohen, James White, &
David Avshalomov Conducting

APPRECIATION OF JAMES EOFF,
Assistant to the Conductors, 1923–1973

February 16, 1974

MOZART	Sinfonia Concertante, K. 364

Robert Mann, *Violin*; Samuel Rhodes, *Viola*

AVSHALOMOV	»The Thirteen Clocks

DEDICATED TO THE PORTLAND JUNIOR SYMPHONY AT 50

Marilyn Krowartz & Richard Hurst, *Storytellers*

FANFARE: SALUTE FROM THE GOVERNOR,
THE HON. TOM LAWSON MCCALL

NIELSON	*Symphony NO. 1, G minor

Joined by International Youth Orchestra Delegates

» *World Premier*

* *Portland Premier*

April 13, 1974

HAYDN	Symphony No. 96, "Miracle" *Portland Ballet School*
VAUGHAN-WILLIAMS	Tuba Concerto (2 movements) Robert Spellman, *Soloist*
GRIEG	Piano Concerto (1st movement) Clair Olsen, *Soloist*
BACH	Brandenburg Concerto No. 3 "Backgammon to Bach" *Portland Dance Theater*
RAVEL	Tzigane Stephen Kindler, *Soloist*
MILHAUD	Creation of the World "The Seventh Day" *Portland Dance Theater*
BACH	Contrapunctus II *Brass Ensemble*

May 18, 1974

Fanfares in the Forecourt

BERLIOZ	Requiem John Gilbertson, *Tenor*

Guest Choirs: Oregon State University, Portland State University, Vancouver Brahms Singers

Presentation of the "14th Clock" at the 50th Anniversary Concert.

OREGON JOURNAL DEC. 3, 1973

Juniors Open Golden Anniversary Season With Shining Performance

By MARTIN CLARK
Journal Music Editor

Portland Junior Symphony opened its golden anniversary season in the Civic Auditorium Saturday night with a shining performance for a house that looked nearly sold out for the occasion.

There was all the excitement that an "opening night" should have. Anticipation of something extraordinary was in the air before conductor Jacob Avshalomov walked on stage. The performance that followed lived up to the anticipation.

The internationally acclaimed youth orchestra, hailed by critics far beyond the boundaries of Oregon as the most outstanding one of its kind, opened with the Bach Passacaglia and Fugue in C Minor as arranged for orchestra by Ottorino Respighi. It was an auspicious opener, the ensemble producing a tone and sensitivity of response I cannot recall hearing on a first concert of a season.

This was followed by the Benjamin Lees Prologue, Capriccio and Epilogue commissioned by the PJS Association 15 years ago under a Rockefeller grant especially for the Junior Symphony.

Of course, the highlight of the evening was the appearance of pianist Tana Bawden in the Rachmaninoff Rhapsody on a Theme of Paganini. Miss Bawden made her debut with the Junior Symphony at the ripe age of 11 when she was a student of Nellie Tholen.

Miss Bawden brought a freshness and vitality to her playing of the Rachmaninoff that was genuinely moving. She draws upon great power, when needed, but employs it with the selective sensitivity of a first rate artist.

Following intermission Edward H. Look, PJS Association president, read a proclamation by Major Neil Goldschmidt proclaiming Dec. 1-3 as PJS Week in recognition of its 50 anniversary season.

This was followed by the Paul Dukas Fanfare to the dance-poem, "La Peri," performed at the 30th anniversary concert of the orchestra.

Closing the concert was a Portland premiere of Mendelssohn's Symphony No. 1, written when the composer was only 16 years old. The young performers captured the youthful genius of Mendelssohn.

No wonder Portland is so proud of its Junior Symphony.

THE SUNDAY OREGONIAN DEC. 2, 1973

Junior Symphony opening indicates astonishing ability

By HILMAR GRONDAHL
of The Oregonian staff

The opening of the Portland Junior Symphony's 50th anniversary season in the Civic Auditorium Saturday night was one of those events that have the spectators blinking in disbelief.

Can you imagine an ensemble of 100 players averaging 16 years of age, and not members of a conservatory of music, doing a creditable job with the orchestral complement of Rachmaninoff's Rhapsody on a Theme of Paganini? Well, they did, and one was astonished at the proceedings.

This was not the only astonishing item on the program; there was the Bach Passacaglia and Fugue in C-minor as orchestrated by Respighi, and only less complex and demanding than the Rhapsody because there was no guest soloist to accommodate to.

Tana Bawden, a former Portlander, who is now justly famous for her remarkable capabilities, was soloist in the Rachmaninoff rhapsody. She is a sensitive artist, whose felicity of feeling for the piano as a musical extension of her personality communicates well.

While her tone doesn't have the plangency we recall in Rachmaninoff's playing, the scale of her operation does justice to the spirit and substance of that composer's score. Her technique is clear, strong and responsive to a concept that is informed and affecting.

For the orchestra to accommodate to her playing was no problem for she has her solo lines so well in hand that she can relate pliantly to those areas of interdependence.

Even so, it was amazing to see these young players responding with as much assurance as they did to Conductor Jacob Avshalomov's way of relating the printed details to sound and sense.

It is obvious that there is an ever increasing standard of excellence required of those who come into this youth orchestra, and a more serious demand on their time and talents, for no previous season has begun with playing of this quality.

As the final item on Saturday night's concert, Avshalomov introduced Mendelssohn's First Symphony to the local audience. This piece, at an earlier time, would have been considered a satisfactory challenge to the capabilities of the young players.

And if their natural affinity was closer to the 16-year-old Mendelssohn than the 60-year-old Rachmaninoff, their teaching and discipline let them understand the older composer; not totally, but to an admirable degree.

Junior Symphony marks 50th year

By HILMAR GRONDAHL
of The Oregonian staff

The Portland Junior Symphony's 50th anniversary concert in the Civic Auditorium Saturday night was replete with delectable items.

First, there was the event itself, the celebration of a half century of developing music and humanism in more than 3,000 girls and boys.

Second, there was a world premiere of a musical score by Jacob Avshalomov, created especially for this occasion which observed both the ensemble's anniversary and the composer's 20th year as the orchestra's conductor.

This composition, entitled "The Thirteen Clocks," had its inspiration in James Thurber's fantastic fairy tale and employed two narrators, Marilyn Krowarts and Richard Hurst.

Third, there was the participation in the orchestra of 32 of the finest players from as youth orchestras the country over, itself a tribute to the local ensemble at a special point in time.

Guest artist

Fourth, there was the appearance with the ensemble as guest artist, one of its most famous alumni, Robert Mann, as solo violinist in the Mozart Sinfonia Concertante. Mann is first violinist of the Juillard String Quartet, and the violist of that noble body, Samuel Rhodes, was his associate in the Mozart score.

Fifth, there was the first local performance of the First Symphony by Carl Nielsen.

Sixth, there was Gov. Tom McCall, a protagonist of cultural values, to express in his eloquent English what this enterprise means and has meant to Oregon youth and those in areas far beyond our borders. Incidentally, while on stage, the governor was spokesman for a presentation to Avshalomov of a clock, which must be numbered as No. 14 in the composer's list.

What Avshalomov created in his "Thirteen Clocks" is a work of delightful humor and fancy. He has made fascinating use of atmospheric tunes; the echoes of Gilbert and Sullivan's "Mikado" when the narrator described the price as a "wandering minstrel of rags and tatters" and when a martial mood is called for there are hints from Sousa.

It's a musically sound score and a delightful composition. It was introduced by a large orchestra, but there ought to be a reduction so it can be widely performed.

The appearance of Mann and Rhodes in the Mozart duo concerto was proof that these roles are best served by chamber players whose major concern is this close musical association. Splendid musicians each, they were wonderfully expressive as a duo whether in imitation or unison and parallel playing.

The entire score was handsomely set forth, in gracious style, and luminous sound.

The Nielsen Symphony in G-minor is a work deserving to be heard and this ensemble, enlarged by its visiting players, was opulent in sound, handsomely disciplined and a delight to the ears.

OREGON JOURNAL THURSDAY, DEC. 27, 1973

'. . . Grand Time Was Had By All'

By MARTIN CLARK
Journal Music Editor

Wednesday night at the Civic Auditorium was an "Ingathering of the Clan" (the clan being the Portland Junior Symphony), and certainly a grand time was had by all.

And by "all" is meant the Preparatory Orchestra, the Alumni Orchestra, and the Junior Symphony proper. Appearing in that order, there must have been a total of nigh on to 300 instrumentalists onstage during the evening.

This was the annual "Christmas Concert" of the Juniors, often held on Sundays. But this being the 50th Anniversary Season of the Portland Junior Symphony, alumni of the orchestra from all over the country were invited back to celebrate the anniversary and perform in the Alumni Orchestra.

An audience literally overflowing was on hand for the free concert, made possible by a grant from the Music Performance Trust Fund of the American Federation of Musicians.

Presiding over the "in-gathering" of the Junior Symphony "family" like the Grand Guru himself, was Avshalomov attired in a striking, purple tunic. Obviously, he was proud of his players, and well he might be. He was such a natural choice to carry on the work of the orchestra's founding conductor Jacques Gershkovitch. He has every right to be proud of leading what is generally conceded to be the foremost youth orchestra in the country—and probably beyond.

A special tribute was paid to James Eoff, assistant conductor of the PJS, who played in the original orchestra of 1923-24. He has been assistant to both Gershkovitch and Avshalomov.

OREGON JOURNAL FEB. 17, 1974

Junior Symphony Concert Tops All

By MARTIN CLARK
Journal Music Editor

I would like to make a flat prediction; I predict that Jacob Avshalomov's "The Thirteen Clocks," based on the hilarious fairy tale of James Thurber, will receive in this country and abroad ten times the performances all his other compositions combined have received to date.

Saturday night in the Civic Auditorium the Portland Junior Symphony presented its 50th anniversary concert for a near capacity audience. The evening was one outstanding feature after another.

"The Thirteen Clocks" captures in music the delightful humor of Thurber, including orchestral parodies of everything from "A Wandering Minstrel" to "Yankee Doodle." It's imaginative and it's commercial.

Opening the concert was the Mozart Sinfonia Concertante K364 featuring as soloists violinist Robert Mann and violist Samuel Rhodes. Mann is a former member of the Junior Symphony. Both he and Rhodes are members of the Julliard String Quartet. It was inspired chamber music all the way through, the orchestra seeming to catch the soloists' Mozartean elegance, with strong emphasis on the flowing legato of the second movement.

The second half of the program was the Portland premiere of the Nielson Symphony No. 1 in G Minor. The Juniors turned in the sort of professional, meticulous performance their listeners have come to take for granted.

Ned Look, president of the Junior Symphony Association, presented Gov. Tom McCall after an impressive fanfare from the orchestra following intermission.

The governor paid tribute to the orchestra on its 50th anniversary, the delegates from 32 youth orchestras around the country participating in the performance, and presented conductor Avshalomov with a mantelpiece clock.

OREGON JOURNAL APR. 15, 1974

PJS Integrates Dance In Highly Varied Fare

By MARTIN CLARK
Journal Music Editor

Innovative and imaginative programming has been something of a hallmark of the Portland Junior Symphony, but in a program in the Civic Auditorium Saturday night the members surpassed themselves (and also drew a sold out house).

In fact, they got so carried away with such inspired, creative programming that the final curtain was almost half an hour past the usual two-hour concert. The big thing Saturday night was the skillful, professionally arranged inclusion of the Portland Ballet School and Portland Dance Theater.

The program opened with the orchestra seated on the upstage half of the stage, framed by the curtains. After a bright rendition of the opening movement of the Haydn "Miracle" Symphony No. 96, a scrim was lowered in front of conductor Jacob Avshalomov and the orchestra and members of the Portland Ballet School danced the remaining movements on the downstage half of the stage.

An ingenious blend was achieved by the tuned-in choreography of director Jacqueline Schumacher, the dreamy, pastel costumes of Margaret Appleton, with the incisive Haydn rhythms provided by the Junior Symphony.

The downstage curtain was lowered, and when raised the orchestra was seated downstage for the balance of the first half of the program. Robert Spellman, the PJS tuba player, was then featured in the Vaughan-Williams "Tuba Concerto." Young Spellman did a magnificent job of capturing the elusive lyricism the composer rather wickedly wove into a score for an instrument most famous for three or four notes in its bass range.

After intermission the orchestra was in the pit for Portland Dance Theater's "Backgammon to Bach" (Brandenburg Concerto No. 3), which had some hilarious touches, and the highly original "The Seventh Day" (Milhaud's "La Creation du Monde"). Bonnie Merrill choreographed the Bach and Jann McCauley and Judy Patton, the Milhaud.

In between these two works was concertmaster Stephen Kindler, attired somewhat a la Gypsy, spotlighted downstage center for Ravel's "Tzigane."

OREGON JOURNAL MAY 20, 1974

PJS Triumphs With Berlioz

By MARTIN CLARK

With fantastic consistency, the Portland Junior Symphony has been topping itself with each concert of this 50th season anniversary celebration.

Saturday night at the Civic Auditorium they did it again, this time with the Hector Berlioz "Requiem Mass." It's a massive Mass in every way.

It was a signal occasion. At the conclusion conductor Jacob Avshalomov was presented a plaque by Edward H. Look, president of the PJS Association, in appreciation of the conductor's 20th anniversary at the helm of the orchestra.

The Requiem drew a standing ovation, and Avshalomov drew another one on his acceptance.

For this momentous event a chorus of 300 participated, well drilled singers from Oregon State and Portland State Universities and the Brahms Singers from Vancouver, Wash. That is an enormous choir, but naturally Berlioz called for 400 (I don't know where another 100 could have been put).

Even without meeting the incredible numbers prescribed by the composer, a huge number of musicians were involved, including brass choirs totalling 32 players, arranged so as to give a live, and very loud, stereo effect.

Two pairs were positioned in recesses extending out from the stage on either side, plus four players in each of the boxes closest to either side of the stage. When they all cut loose in the "Dies Irae" surely the most fanatic rock fan would have been delighted with the deafening din. It was thrilling.

Granted, Berlioz' skill is often greater than his inspiration this is a great work deserving of more frequent performances (in spite of the enormous demands made). However, I do wish he had included four vocal soloists. Jon Gilbertson's brief tenor solo in the "Sanctus" (brief, but killing tessatura) pointed up beautifully what an asset the contrasts would have supplied.

The 125-piece orchestra was remarkably responsive to the baton of Maestro Avshalomov, as was the massed choir. He deserves all the tributes paid to him—and they were many.

THE OREGONIAN MAY 19, 1974

Orchestra offers impressive work

By HILMAR GRONDAHL
of The Oregonian staff

In Civic Auditorium Saturday night, the Portland Junior Symphony under Jacob Avshalomov's direction offered one of the most impressive works—The Hector Berlioz Requiem Mass.

Moreover, it was another highlight in the orchestra's 50th anniversary celebration, and at the conclusion of the concert Avshalomov was presented a scroll from the association honoring his 20th year with the ensemble.

The Berlioz Requiem, which the composer himself seemed to cherish above all his other works, is a grandiose score built on the formal Catholic Mass, and contains some of the most noble and sublime music, which in places amounts to overwhelming grandeur. Nothing is quite so expressive musically as a multitude of voices, fresh, well balanced and alert to the moods and inflections of score such as this.

The singers were well disciplined, as was the youth symphony; it was a cohesive whole which Avshalomov related specifically and eloquently to the music.

Each of its 10 sections had its special appeal, but for this listener two of the most satisfying sections were the Lachrymosa and Offertorium. The former was virtually a tonal spectacle, made particularly exciting by the entrance of the brasses. The latter was treated with the utmost delicacy, the prayers gathering strength in a pulsating accompaniment and diminishing in sound to a mere pianissimo. Chorus and orchestra were responsive to this need.

51st Season

Jacob Avshalomov, Musical Director

George Barati, Guest Conductor, Sabbatical Term

October 26, 1974

Central Oregon Community College

Preview of Season's Programs

Guest Choruses: Bend High School, Crook County, Madras High School, Central Oregon Community College

November 9, 1974

REVUELTAS	*Sensemaya
RAMEAU	Dance of the Savages
BEETHOVEN	Piano Concerto NO. 1, C major Mitchell Vines, *Soloist*
DVORAK	Symphony NO. 6, D major

December 26, 1974

13th Annual Concert at Christmas

Jacob Avshalomov, Conductor

Seasonal Music, with Carol Singing, The Preparatory Orchestra, & Two Past Presidents of the Board, Victor Critchlow & Maurice Engleman as Soloists in the Bach Concerto for Two Violins

February 22, 1975

SCHUMANN	Symphony NO. 1, Bb, op. 38
BARATI	*Configuration
VITALI	Ciaconna for Cello & Strings Martin Hanson, *Soloist*
MOZART	Horn Concerto in Eb, K. 417 Robin Merriman, *Soloist*
RAVEL	Bolero

April 26, 1975

MOZART	Symphony NO. 38, D major, "Prague"
BRUCH	Violin Concerto NO. 1, G major
DEBUSSY	Printemps—Symphonic Suite
STRAVINSKY	Firebird Suite

**Portland Premier*

THE OREGONIAN NOV. 10, 1974

Junior symphony competent, poised

By HILMAR GRONDAHL
of The Oregonian staff

The concert of the Portland Junior Symphony under Jacob Avshalomov's baton in the Civic Auditorium Saturday night was a refreshing experience generated, in part, by the wonder of hearing this aggregation of young musicians playing the masterworks with such competence and aplomb; particularly with the regenerative beauty they brought to the Dvorak Sixth Symphony.

The most piquant moment of the evening came in the Dvorak Symphony which Avshalomov and his charges had honed to a brilliant polish without losing any of its tender lyricism or compulsive dynamic surge.

The juniors have never played with more musical knowledge and skill than they did in this score. They responded with balanced dynamics, from whispers to roars. Of course, it was no handicap to have the orchestral dimension that this group has with four clarinets, flutes, trumpets and trombones, and ten doublebasses. It adds up to a great sound.

"Sensemaya" was having its first performance. The Mexican composer in this work has sought to recall through his sophisticated orchestral means those sounds of primitive music which he attributes to the Mayas. He had worked wonders in suggesting through this complex orchestral fabric, the simple and repetitive sounds of the ancient peoples, persistently using the hypnotic monotony of the persistent drums as the basic rhythmic pattern and the wind sounds that might come from a conch horn or a simple whistle.

The Rameau piece was the composer's notion of how the music to accompany a dance by savages in the Indies might sound. He used his instrumental skills in a way that was no more savage than the sound of a song Swallow.

JOURNAL NOV. 11, 1974

Martin Clark's
MUSIC

PORTLAND JUNIOR SYMPHONY under the direction of Jacob Avshalomov opened its 51st season Saturday night at the Civic Auditorium to an audience of 2,600.

I never cease to be amazed at the ambitious programming planned by Maestro Avshalomov for these youngsters . . . and even more amazed at the style with which they carry it off.

THE OREGONIAN DEC. 16, 1974

Junior Symphony outstanding in Family Christmas Concert

By JOHN WENDEBORN
of The Oregonian staff

Jacob Avshalomov may wish to count the number 13 as his lucky one after Thursday night's Portland Junior Symphony Orchestra concert in Civic Auditorium. The concert, witnessed by a capacity audience of 3,000, was the orchestra's 13th annual Family Christmas Concert.

His two orchestras, the PJS and the Preparatory Orchestra, performed what Avshalomov referred to as "Christmas ornaments," which numbered 10 compositions. The connection between the concert and Christmas was slim but the music was beautiful throughout, including the audience participation in three carols, which turned out to be the only actual Christmas music.

The Bach piece featured the talents of two adult members of the Music Committee of the PJS, Maurice Engleman and Victor Critchlow, and Avshalomov's genius in keeping the PJS an orchestra that continually comes up with something new was again recognized here. He not only has a supertalented orchestra of young musicians, he keeps concerts from becoming mired in boredom by his outward geniality and obvious efforts to communicate.

But the tour de force Thursday night came from the talents of French hornist Roger Kaza. From the technique and the command and control he has, young Kaza will be a much in-demand player before too long.

He played the long Horn Concerto No. 1, by Strauss, flawlessly, reaching his high notes from the low register as easily as he might pick them materially from the air. Slow or fast, he played with feeling and played in tune. And Kaza was greeted with an instant standing ovation, which he thoroughly deserved.

OREGON JOURNAL FEB. 23, 1975

Barati Lucky Find For Juniors

By MARTIN CLARK
Journal Music Editor

Finding someone of the caliber of George Barati to act as interim conductor during Jacob Avshalomov's sabbatical was one of the luckiest things to happen to the Portland Junior Symphony since Avshalomov was signed as conductor and music director of the youth orchestra more than 20 years ago.

Here's a man, Barati, that is, who was responsible for bringing the Honolulu Symphony to maturity during his 18 years as its music director, and now tours regularly conducting such orchestras as the London Philharmonic and the Vienna Opera Orchestra. He has the obvious patience needed for any kind of youth orchestra, but, like Avshalomov, will settle for nothing less than first rate musicianship from his players, regardless of age.

Saturday night's performance by the Juniors under Barati's direction was a delight. The Schumann Symphony No. 1 was a special pleasure, since I had not heard it for a while. Barati extracted the full quota of bursting enthusiasm that runs throughout the work.

Barati's own composition, "Configuration," which closed the first half of the concert, is not to my taste. However, in all fairness, considering it among works of like genre it's practically a masterpiece. That is to say, it is an ingeniously constructed work which exploits the orchestra's resources in an intriguing manner.

Martin Hanson was the able soloist in the Vitali Ciaccono for Cello and Strings, and Robin Merriman was featured in the Mozart Horn Concerto in E Flat, the latter a work so appealing it makes the horn seem like an instrument of lyricism. The bouncy, rollicking rondo never fails to lift the listener—and Merriman did it justice.

Ravel's "Bolero" was the crowd-pleasing finale.

THE OREGONIAN FEB. 23, 1975

Symphony responsive to leader

By HILMAR GRONDAHL
of The Oregonian staff

George Barati, a widely regarded conductor, led the Portland Junior Symphony Orchestra in the Civic Auditorium Friday night, the first interim leader in six or seven seasons.

It is indicative of the quality of training these young players receive and their attitude toward concert performance that they responded with as scrupulous care under the guest conductor as they do under their regular mentor, Jacob Avshalomov, who is on sabbatical leave. What difference there was to be heard was simply in the differing style of the two conductors. This testifies to the musical precepts which enliven the behavior of the 100 or more young players.

From what I heard it seemed pertinent that the "Spring" Symphony, the freshest and brightest of Schumann's large pieces, should be realized through an aggregation of vital musicians in the springtime of life and musical enthusiasm. They played with verve and were directed with a persuasive concern for the romantic inflections that dominate its themes and ensemble statements.

One of the brightest spots of the evening was the performance of the Mozart Horn Concerto. Barati and the orchestral complement set the mood of the piece at once and young Merriman came on with an assured and musicianly delineation of the solo lines that was true to the spirit and the style of the work.

Barati's "Configuration" is a very handsome piece.

Prep violin sectional.

THE OREGONIAN APR. 28, 1975

Stanford man's solo highlight of concert

By HILMAR GRONDAHL
of The Oregonian staff

The second and final concert by the Portland Junior Symphony under its interim conductor, George Barati, in the Civic Auditorium Saturday night was a credit to this astonishing band of young musicians and to the various scores through which they displayed their collective talents.

The evening was additionally enlivened by the presence and solo performance of Mark Volkert in the Bruch Violin Concerto in G-minor. Volkert is concertmaster of the Stanford Symphony Orchestra and a member of the San Francisco Symphony.

The concert opened with Mozart's "Prague" Symphony, one of his most beautiful and one in which he uses the largest complement of instruments. Barati and his young charges gave voice to this rich mixture of sonorities, serious and aggressive spirit. The strings particularly were admirable in their modified tone and the propulsion they animated.

Volkert is a tall lad of dark complexion who plays with sufficient zest and musicality to fulfill the appealing beauties of Bruch's melody-laden concerto. His technical equipment is substantial, but not infallible, and one was concerned here and there with intonation in single and multiple stops that was impure.

These were minor defections in a performance that searched for and found the impressive impact of glowing themes and thrilling cadences. Particularly in the finale, the orchestra created a glorious setting of sound in which he could spend those luxurious melodies. The joint product was absorbing beauty.

The concert was concluded with the 1919 version of Stravinsky's suite from the "Firebird" Ballet. It is full of Russian coloring, and the opportunities for some fancy solo work abound. Barati and the many brasses, winds and strings had a great time with these multifaceted and richly hued themes.

OREGON JOURNAL APR. 28, 1975

Brilliant Concert Marks Barati Finale

By MARTIN CLARK
Journal Music Editor

Two thoughts predominated as I listened to the concert by the Portland Junior Symphony Saturday night in the Civic Auditorium for an audience of about 2,500.

The first was that it was obvious we were witnessing a performance with a major conductor on the podium. The other thought was, "Isn't the Junior Symphony (and Portland) fortunate to have a music director of sufficient musical stature and security as an individual that he goes out of his way to find a conductor of extraordinary talent to take the podium during his sabbatical?"

Saturday night was the final concert with the Junior Symphony for George Barati, interim conductor during the absence of Jacob Avshalomov on sabbatical. It was a brilliant finale for a farewell.

And this is what Barati provided in the Symphony No. 38, the "Prague," Saturday night—with a youth orchestra, yet.

The same quantity of inspiration was apparent in the Bruch Violin Concerto No. 1, with young Mark Volkert of San Francisco as soloist revealing a rich tone of distinctive individuality and great appeal.

Also programmed was the Debussy "Printemps" and the demanding "Firebird Suite" by Stravinsky.

52nd Season

Jacob Avshalomov, Conductor

November 15, 1975

SOUSA	The Stars & Stripes Forever
MASON	Chanticleer Overture
SAINT-SAENS	Piano Concerto NO. 2 Neal Goren, *Soloist*
HONEGGER	Pacific 231
DVORAK	Symphony NO. 9, "New World"

December 26, 1975

14th Annual Concert at Christmas

HONORING MR. & MRS. ROBERT H. NOYES

Seasonal Music with Carol Singing &
The Preparatory Orchestra, Warren Dalby, Conducting

February 28, 1976

IVES/SCHUMANN	Variations on "America"
BLOCH	Suite Symphonique
JOPLIN	Maple Leaf Rag; The Entertainer
STRAVINSKY	Ragtime
BLOCH	*Symphony for Trombone & Orchestra, Howard Prince, *Soloist*
BLOCH	America Anthem—*All Sing*

April 11 & 17, 1976

Beall Hall—University of Oregon
& Portland Civic Auditorium

ANTES	Four Anthems Myra Brand, *Soprano*
JACOB AVSHALOMOV	*City Upon a Hill Tom Lawson McCall, *Reader*

Guest Choirs: University of Oregon Chamber Choir, Chorale & Singers, Thurston Area Children's Choir, & The Children's Choir of The First Presbyterian Church of Portland

SIBELIUS	Violin Concerto Michael Hansen, *Soloist*
GOTTSCHALK	Night in the Tropics

---

*Portland Premier

THE OREGONIAN DEC. 27, 1975

Family concert offers another seasonal treat

By BOB MICHELET
of The Oregonian staff

Just when you thought all the holiday gift-giving was over, the Portland Junior Symphony came up with another seasonal treat Friday night—its annual Family Christmas Concert.

As in the past, the program was an entertaining blend of lighter fare with serious compositions, and during the evening every section had its moment in the limelight.

Even the young Preparatory Orchestra had a part, turning in a very commendable rendition of Britten's pleasing "Courtly Dances" under intern conductor Warren Dalby.

The string section of the Junior Symphony was put to the test twice, most impressively with Barber's beautiful "Adagio for Strings." This moving work received a performance rich in feeling and ability, producing the maximum emotional effect.

Less successful was its earlier "Cannon and Gigue in D" by Pachelbel, which suffered somewhat from unequal pacing and playing weaknesses.

The first movement of Mozart's wind serenade No. 12 was an appropriate showcase for the talents of eight wind players. The well-balanced octet executed the piece with spirit and accuracy.

Conductor Jacob Avshalomov's talent for programming was evident, as he led the orchestra through a pair of interesting and little-known works. One was a set of three movements of hymns and dances from "The Sweet Bye and Bye," an opera by the contemporary American Jack Beeson.

Eclectic in style—and trying to say more things than Avshalomov was able to describe in his commentary—the music is nonetheless interesting and was an effective challenge for the versatility and talent of the orchestra.

Tibor Serly's "Quodlibet on American Songs" followed the Barber "Adagio," and its lighthearted nature was an effective contrast.

"Quodlibet" is a Latin phrase roughly meaning as many as you'd like, and in it Serly has taken several well-known American tunes and woven them into an intricate and intriguing quilt of musical delight. More than a few feet were seen tapping during its lively performance.

The evening's encore was the first movement of Dvorak's "New World" symphony. Quite a number for an "encore," and its faithful performance provided an appropriate bow for the entertaining musical package.

THE OREGONIAN NOV. 16, 1975

Patriotic kickoff concert stirring

By HILMAR GRONDAHL
of The Oregonian staff

The performance of Sousa's "The Stars and Stripes Forever" which opened the Portland Junior Symphony concert in the Civic Auditorium Saturday night was a spring-tingling affair full of high spirits and compelling march steps animated by conductor Jacob Avshalomov.

It was the introduction to a season which will generally feature some American composer and/or a composer who drew musical inspiration from some phase of this country that can be used as part of the celebration of the Bicentennial.

The American composer who followed on the program, while less famous than the March King, was a genuine leader in developing the country's musical heritage: Daniel Gregory Mason, whose overture, "Chanticleer" proved to be a delightful and often pastoral score suggesting the period of Thoreau and his love of nature.

One of the features of the concert was the performance by 17-year-old Neal Goren of the solo lines of the Saint-Saens Piano Concerto No. 2. That the lad is remarkably gifted was evidenced from the first as he stated the solo theme which brings the orchestra into the action. His technical grasp is extraordinary as the brilliant concerto proved.

There was a spirited performance of Honegger's tonal account of the huge locomotive "Pacific 231" before the evening's musical treat was reached. This was a heartfelt and incessantly beautiful performance of Dvorak's Symphony "From the New World." Undoubtedly the familiar and incessant warmth and sensuous charm of this music impelled these 100 talented young musicians to follow their conductor's concept of the composer's score with devoted spirit.

Each movement had its own particular delights, all sections played as though inspired; the woodwinds and brasses creating some particularly affecting ensemble work. There was an amazing range of dynamics, handsome balance of the sections, admirable space for solo voices and stimulating climaxes.

It was one of the top performances by this amazing band of young musicians, a fascinating account of a musical message sent to the world from America.

THE OREGONIAN FEB. 29, 1976

Trombonist, ensemble combine in powerful evening of Bloch

By HILMAR GRONDAHL
of The Oregonian staff

The Portland Junior Symphony presented the local premiere Saturday night of Ernest Bloch's Concerto for Trombone and Orchestra, with Howard Prince as guest soloist.

Jacob Avshalomov directed.

The event could well have been designated "Ernest Bloch Night," for Bloch, who came to live in Oregon 30 years ago, and while dwelling at Agate Beach produced some of the great music of the century.

Suite Symphonique is a work of compelling power, impeccable craftsmanship, and taste with even a touch of humor. Its middle movement is a passacaglia containing 22 variations with a climax of lyrical character, leading to an exuberant finale into which he incorporates a grotesquely sardonic fugue. The passacaglia, in particular, is an inspired contrapuntal work, grand in design and gripping both intellectually and in its precisely ordered sound.

The so-called concerto for trombone and orchestra has the rhapsodic overtones and some of the epic mysticism of his "Schelomo." Some of its climaxes are overwhelming in their size and emotional effect. The intense feeling and dramatic impact are offset by passages of touching lyricism.

Howard Prince, the New York trombonist, was an admirable champion of the solo lines.

Seldom has the ensemble responded so precisely and effectively to the demands of the score.

The educative purpose of the Junior Symphony is to teach its members the significant musical literature. On this occasion the learning process extended to the audience to whom they were introducing a score of unquestionable merit.

OREGON JOURNAL MAR. 1, 1976

Bloch Works Top Concert By PJS

By MARTIN CLARK
Journal Music Editor

Half of the works and more than half of the playing time of the Saturday night program by the Portland Junior Symphony were devoted to the compositions of the late great composer, Ernest Bloch. If their applause was any indication, members of the audience seemed to agree with me that the Bloch works were well chosen and well played.

The most publicized selection of the evening was the Bloch Symphony for Trombone and Orchestra which received its Portland premiere Saturday night in the Civic Auditorium for a near-capacity house. Trombone soloist in the work was Howard Prince, a student at Juilliard School of Music who won the nationwide competition held for the assignment. The 21-year-old Prince was equal to its considerable technical demands.

The other Bloch works were the Suite Symphonique, whose grand sweep was captured by the PJS under the direction of Jacob Avshalomov, and his genuinely inspired Anthem from his symphony, "America," which the audience sang as the closing work.

HIGH FIDELITY DECEMBER 1976
and musical america

BLOCH: Symphony for Trombone and Orchestra*; Suite symphonique. Howard Prince, trombone*; Portland Junior Symphony Orchestra, Jacob Avshalomov, cond. [Carter Harman, prod.] COMPOSERS RECORDINGS SD 351, $6.95.

Here's a substantial entry in the discography of one of twentieth-century music's splendid isolates. Both works stem from Bloch's years in Oregon, whose half-century-old Portland Junior Symphony Orchestra plays with enormous affection and no little skill.

The 1944 *Suite symphonique* is very attractive music, well scored and lively, but its three movements could perhaps be mistaken for one another. There is a powerful Overture in grave-allegro sequence, then a Passacaglia that changes gears abruptly like the preceding movement. Fewer neo-baroquisms are found in the riotous finale. The 1954 *Trombone Symphony* is probably the more significant of the two works. There is a dazzling panoply of Oriental color in much of the orchestral writing and a few meditative interludes, but most of the time the trombone snaps and harangues angrily at the pulsating and agitated orchestra like some hoary Old Testament prophet. It is the most vigorous concerted work for this instrument I've run across, and it also has much to say.

Howard Prince, who was a senior at Juilliard when this was made, handles his solo role with great aplomb. Jacob Avshalomov, in addition to his podium duties, also contributes some warmly personal, if unabashedly partisan, liner notes.

The engineering is an example of what is sometimes regarded as honest amateur recording—just plunk down a couple of good mikes in a tolerable-sounding hall, set your levels, and let the music play. Considering some of the "professional" excesses of the big labels nowadays, this approach sounds positively refreshing. A.C.

Oregon Honors Ernest Bloch

IN THE BICENTENNIAL SEASON

CALENDAR OF EVENTS 1975-76

Nov. 30 Chamber Music and Exhibition of Photographs by Bloch at Portland Art Museum

Dec. 8 KOAP - TV repeats November 30th Program

Jan. 18 Portland Junior Symphony holds nationwide competition for young trombone soloist

Jan. 23 Concertino for Flute and Viola with Piano performed by PJS Trio for Multnomah County Intermediate Education District's Conference on Gifted and Able Students

Feb. 27 Suite Symphonique and Symphony for Trombone and Orchestra recorded by PJS for Composers Recordings, I

Recording session filmed by OEPBS in cooperation with WNET as part of a 90 minute TV Special on Bloch. Performances by the Cleveland Orchestra, Lorin Maazel, Conductor, and the PJS, Jacob Avshalomov, Conductor

Feb. 28 Suite Symphonique and Symphony for Trombone & Orchest performed at Civic Auditorium. Howard Prince, solois

Mar. 15 16 Proclamation for Trumpet & Orchestra performed by Ore Symphony, Fred Sautter, soloist; Lawrence Smith, cond

Apr. 10 Dedication of Commemorative Plaque near Bloch residen at Agate Beach, Oregon

The Portland Junior Symphony Association takes special pleasure in coordinating this season-long tribute to Ernest Bloch. He expressed his enthusiasm for our Orchestra in the letter quoted here. It is a privilege for us to share our enthusiasm for him in all the ways listed above, and we wish to offer our thanks to the Oregon Arts Commission, the Bicentennial Commission of Oregon, and the Metropolitan Arts Commission for their support of the several projects.

In the course of Bloch's years in our state it became natural to speak of him as an Oregon composer. The spirit of neighborly pride which prompted this, is one we all share; but no one need be reminded that he belongs to the world, and that his works and his name are honored wherever music, as we know it, is played.

THE OREGONIAN APR. 18, 1976

Symphony year ends in stimulating concert

By HILMAR GRONDAHL
of The Oregonian staff

The Portland Junior Symphony Orchestra concluded its 52nd season Saturday night with a stimulating concert in Civic Auditorium.

Jacob Avshalomov's choral work, "City Upon a Hill," was having its Portland Premiere with former Gov. Tom McCall as the speaker; concertmaster Michael Hansen was soloist in the Sibelius Violin Concerto, and there were two pieces by Louis Gottschalk.

In his "City Upon a Hill," the ensemble's conductor has composed a work of moving beauty. He has set a text that "captures the enterprise and hope of the land, and sets these words with a grace and scintillating to music of specific suitability."

Being a singularly literate and articulate man, a poet with words, he was by nature equipped to synthesize these words with a musical line and structure which would insure their imperatives of force and harmony.

There are climaxes of language and climaxes of music. One of these was the passage, "Let your light shine before all men." It virtually glowed with significance, and filled the mind with images of hope.

McCall was a splendid protagonist of the lines that John F. Kennedy spoke in the Massachusetts capital that are the poetic and inspiring verbal skein that runs through the entire work and holds it in consistent and logical form.

The combined vocal forces of the University of Oregon Chamber Choir, Chorale and Singers, plus the Thurston Area Student Choir and the Children's Choir of the First Presbyterian Church participated in the Avshalomov score.

But the culminating and climactic beauty came with the flowing ode by James Russell Lowell, which sped with the force and sparkle of a mountain stream—lovely in sound, compelling in sense and a thrilling finale to a work of absorbing beauty.

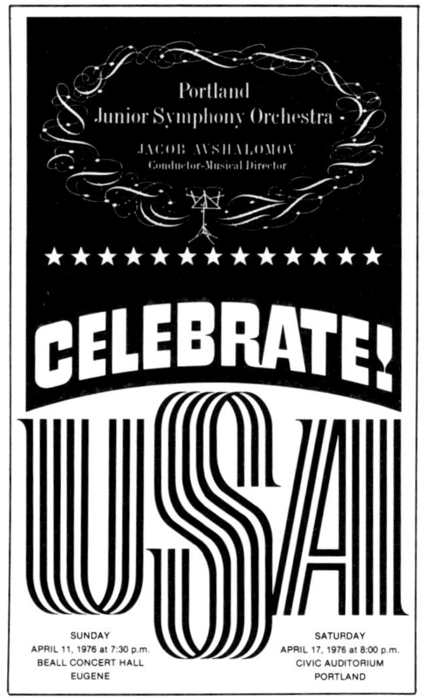

OREGON JOURNAL APR. 19, 1976

PJS Ends Season On High Note

By MARTIN CLARK
Journal Music Editor

Portland Junior Symphony, under Jacob Avshalomov's direction, ended the season on a high note in its concert Saturday night in the Civic Auditorium for a near capacity audience.

The two highlights of the evening were the Portland premiere of Avshalomov's "City Upon A Hill" and the Sibelius Violin Concerto with concertmaster Michael Hanson as soloist.

The Avshalomov work was quite a production, including former Oregon Governor Tom McCall as narrator, the Junior Symphony, University of Oregon Chamber Choir, Chorale and Singers, Thurston area student choir, and the Children's Choir of First Presbyterian Church in Portland.

McCall was impressive and moving in the lines of the late President John F. Kennedy delivered to the Massachusetts legislature before leaving to become President.

"City Upon A Hill" holds the attention throughout and his generous portions of sustained inspiration. The composer's lifelong love of literature results in a superb match of words and music.

The 17-year-old Hanson received a standing ovation for his performance of the demanding Sibelius concerto, passing from the turbulent first movement to the romance of the second and the strong-fibered rondo of the finale with absolute authority.

A certificate of appreciation was presented to Raphael Spiro, the teacher of young Hanson and many other able string players who have performed with the Junior Symphony.

Tom McCall of Oregon

April 18

Dear Jack: Enclosed is my first "major" contribution to the Portland Junior Symphony. I'd have to be pretty hard up to accept an honorarium from this beloved institution, even if I had talent. It was terrifying being so close to greatness in perfectionist form -- and if this durned virus hadn't persisted I would have made a more effective complementer of your truly momentous work. My best to you and your great team of youngsters and helping parents.

Admiringly

Tom

4/19/76

United States Senate

WASHINGTON, D.C. 20510

June 15, 1976

Mr. Jacob Avshalomov
Conductor-Musical Director
Portland Junior Symphony Orchestra
Portland, Oregon

Dear Mr. Avshalomov:

Congresswoman Edith Green has very kindly sent to me the tape of the Portland Junior Symphony Orchestra's "City Upon a Hill" program. She told me how enthusiastically this work was received, and I only wish I could have been present to hear this performance.

I am looking forward to playing the tape for my family, and I just wanted you to know how much we all appreciate this meaningful tribute to the President. It is a source of continuing comfort and inspiration to us all to know he is remembered with such affection.

Please accept my personal congratulations on the fine job you are doing directing the Portland Junior Symphony Orchestra, and my thanks for your remembrance of my brother.

Sincerely,

Edward M. Kennedy

53rd Season

Jacob Avshalomov, Conductor

November 20, 1976

WAGNER	Lohengrin: Prelude to Act III
MACDOWELL	Piano Concerto NO. 2
	Ann Smith, *Soloist*
CHAVEZ	Sinfonia India
HARRIS	Third Symphony

December 26, 1976

15th Annual Concert at Christmas

The Oregon Repertory Singers, Gil Seeley, Director &
The Preparatory Orchestra, Mark Weinsoft Intern Conductor

Seasonal Music Carol Singing

MENDELSSOHN	Reformation Symphony

February 26, 1977

WEBER	Overture: "Oberon"
POULENC	*Sinfonietta
MOZART	Concerto for Bassoon, K. 191
	Ron Wirt, *Soloist*
STRAUSS	Rosenkavalier Waltz
SCHOENBERG	*Theme & Variations, op.43b

April 23, 1977

TCHAIKOVSKY	Caprice Italien
IBERT	Concerto for Flute
	Victoria Johnston, *Soloist*
SHOSTAKOVITCH	Symphony NO. 6

May 8, 1977

Masonic Temple - 4: PM

FANCIES & ENCORES

Retrospective Program from the Season

A Free Concert Sponsored by
The Music Performance Trust Fund

**Portland Premier*

THE OREGONIAN NOV. 21, 1976

Symphony strikes brassy note

By HILMAR GRONDAHL
of The Oregonian staff

If conductor Jacob Avshalomov wished to justify the title "Gala Concert" for the opening event of the Portland Junior Symphony season, he could do no better than to mark the occasion with the brassy and sparkling Prelude to Act III of "Lohengrin."

This Wagnerian score crackles with ceremony and jubilation, delighting Saturday night's audience at Civic Auditorium.

And there were other matters to glorify the evening, notably the performance of the MacDowell Second Piano Concerto with Ann Smith as soloist. Here was playing to delight the spirit, a handsome concerto deeply observed in its musical and stylistic essence by the 17-year-old pianist.

The piece was set forth with a beguiling assurance that confirmed the proficiency of a firm and fleet technique and the depth of interpretive comprehension to assure fulfillment of the score's substance.

It was a pleasure, as well, to watch the interdependence of conductor and soloist in creating the ensemble fluency, which, with the alert responsiveness of the orchestra, achieved an admirable faithfulness throughout, from the Grieg-like opening to the final chord.

OREGON JOURNAL NOV. 22, 1976

PJS Opener Dominated By MacDowell Concerto

By MARTIN CLARK
Journal Music Editor

It never ceases to amaze me the quantity of quality talent produced in this area. Saturday night the Portland Junior Symphony (PJS) opened its 53rd season with three American works and Wagner's Prelude to Act III of "Lohengrin." In the latter, the brass section outdid itself with stirring results.

An example of the talent referred to above is Ann Smith, 17, a pupil of Nellie Tholen (and a violin pupil of Raphael Spiro) who was soloist in the MacDowell Second Piano Concerto. Miss Smith displayed a high level of musicianship and technical precision, receiving a standing ovation for her efforts. Her performance was the result of winning the PJS's 47th annual piano solo contest last May.

Carlos Chavez' "Sinfonia India," which followed intermission, received meticulous treatment from the PJS under the direction of Jacob Avshalomov, conductor and music director, but although its primitive rhythmic force has impressive moments, Chavez tends to monotony in repetition.

The Roy Harris Symphony No. 3, composed in 1938, contains a considerable measure of dramatic intensity and concentration, but I don't feel that it reflects his best salient characteristics as a composer. However, it received a compelling reading from Avshalomov and the PJS.

OREGON JOURNAL DEC. 28, 1976

Juniors Bring Christmas Cheer

By MARTIN CLARK
Journal Music Editor

Portland Junior Symphony, under the direction of Jacob Avshalomov, its conductor-music director, presented a program filled with variety Saturday night in the Civic Auditorium for a capacity audience.

Billed as a "Family Concert at Christmas," the concert opened with three selections by the PJS Preparatory Orchestra. Listening to the caliber of music making by these youngsters, most or many of whom go on to the PJS, it can be more readily understood why the performance level of the PJS is as high as it is.

Jr. Symphony shows vitality in annual family concert

THE OREGONIAN FEB. 27, 1977

Bassoonist plays Mozart with skill

By HILMAR GRONDAHL
of The Oregonian staff

The rarely-heard bassoon concerto by Mozart was a central point of interest in the Portland Junior Symphony's Winter Concert in Civic Auditorium Saturday night.

Conductor Jacob Avshalomov and his music committee chose the score to spotlight the uncommon talent of soloist Ron Wirt, a five-year member of the Junior Symphony.

Wirt exhibited assurance throughout the bassoon's wide range, sounding the popping staccato notes with the same felicity as the long, unbroken theme, melding his role easily into that of the ensemble.

Other compositions on the program included Weber's Oberon Overture, Francis Poulenc's Sinfonietta, Arnold Schoenberg's Variations for Orchestra. The ensemble played these variations with appropriate vigor and tonal beauty.

Oberon's horn call was not the purest heard from this orchestra, but the sight of the dozens of string players bowing in unison and creating the dynamic nuances implicit in the Weber score and the robust sonic surge of the four trombones were admirable. Nor could one miss the neatly phrased solo theme of the clarinet.

The Poulenc Sinfonietta was a welcome addition to the repertory. Gallic wit as well as symphonic expertise are here, the first movement being a solid symphony in brief. But throughout the succeeding three movements were witty excursions into musical fun-making—good natured and snappy surprises without being trite or banal. There was the suggestion of music hall music in a few places and portions full of sprightly dances and songs.

The ensemble played under Avshalomov's direction with verve and palpable spirit, but I had the feeling the humor might have been a little brighter if the work had been played by a smaller ensemble.

OREGON JOURNAL FEB. 28, 1977

By MARTIN CLARK
Journal Music Editor

A near-capacity audience of all ages was present for what was actually a rather sophisticated program that might have been played by any major symphony orchestra in the country. After all Schoenberg and Poulenc (Sinfonietta) are not exactly staples in symphonic programming—youth orchestras or major symphony orchestras. And whereas the Weber "Oberon" Overture and the Strauss waltz might be considered as frosting, Mozart's Concerto for Bassoon K191 is substantial fare, indeed, when served up with the Poulenc and Schoenberg.

The point is, although there were numerous little kids as well as teenagers present, it was as attentive as any subscription concert audience of the Oregon Symphony.

Ron Wirt, the Junior Symphony's principal bassoonist, was the highly competent soloist in the Mozart concerto. . . .Wirt wrote the cadenzas which he played Saturday night. They were clearly articulated and blended well with the style of the concerto. He received something of an ovation for his performance.

If Poulenc and Schoenberg were going to be programmed, it would be difficult to come up with any composition by either of them with as much appeal as the two chosen by Avshalomov.

As usual, the orchestra reflected meticulous preparation and sensitive response to their conductor.

OREGON JOURNAL MAY 9, 1977

By MARTIN CLARK
Journal Music Editor

Highlight of the PJS concert was the appearance of Lawrence Smith, conductor of the Oregon Symphony, as soloist in the Beethoven Piano Concerto No. 2 in B Flat. It was local history-making when you consider that Smith appeared with the PJS as piano soloist when he was a kid in his teens. With Jacob Avshalomov on the podium, orchestra and soloist romped through this delightful concerto drawing out the flowing legato of the middle movement and the never-failing excitement of the rondo. One of those spontaneous ovations erupted in the audience of about 1,200 that involved more than just an excellent performance.

KBPS broadcast the performance live.

54th Season

Jacob Avshalomov, Conductor

October 22-25, 1977
Safari to Eastern Oregon
& Whitman College, Walla Walla, Washington

November 12, 1977

BRAHMS	Symphony NO. 3, F major, op. 90
DOTSON	Rondo Scherzando for Percussion
MOZART	Piano Concerto, D minor, K. 466
	Jill Niizawa, *Soloist*
WEINBERGER	Polka & Fugue from "Schwanda"

December 26, 1977
16th Annual Concert at Christmas
Seasonal Music, Carol Singing,
The Preparatory Orchestra
& The Brahms Singers of Vancouver

BACH/STRAVINSKY	Variations on "Von Himmel Hoch"
BACH	Cantata: "Sehet, welch' eine Liebe"
HINDEMITH	*Nobilissima Visione

February 25, 1978

BEETHOVEN	Symphony NO. 4, Bb, op. 60
STERN	*Carom - Orchestra & Magnetic Tape
BERLIOZ	*The Death of Cleopatra
	Alyce Rogers, *Mezzo-soprano*
GABRIELI	Canzon Noni Toni
SIBELIUS	Lemminkainen's Return

April 22, 1978

STRAVINSKY	Scherzo a la Russe
RACHMANINOV	*The Bells

Bonnie Hensley, *Soprano;* Ron Jeffers, *Tenor;* David Berger, *Baritone*
Guest Choirs: Lewis & Clark College, Oregon State University

OFFENBACH	Waltz, "La Belle Helene"
FRANCK	Symphony in D minor

Portland Premier

OREGON JOURNAL NOV. 13, 1977

Pianist, Junior Symphony excel at Auditorium

By MARTIN CLARK
Journal Music Editor

Petite Jill Niizawa was soloist in the Mozart Concerto for Piano and Orchestra in D Minor, K466 with the Portland Junior Symphony under the direction of Jacob Avshalomov Saturday night. There were few empty seats for this opening concert of the season for the PJS.

It's a profound challenge for any pianist, let alone a very young one. But the 19-year-old Reed college sophomore seemed to relish the opportunity of dealing with the somber moods and emotional turmoil of the D Minor with its dramatic conflicts. The ovation that followed was richly deserved.

Ms. Niizawa is a student of Frederic Rothchild, former Journal music editor, who played the same concerto with the Junior Symphony when he, too, was a sophomore at Reed College.

Before intermission, Hilmar Grondahl, music editor of The Oregonian for 45 years who recently retired, was presented with a citation of appreciation for his support of music in Portland.

After intermission came the Mozart concerto, and the program concluded with the polka and fugue from the Czech composer Jaromir Weinberger's opera, "Schwanda der Dudelsackpfeifer," which is based on Czechoslovakian folk legends. The excerpts received a lilting performance by Avshalomov and the orchestra.

"We would play an encore," Avshalomov said at the completion of the excerpts, "but we are leaving in 35 minutes to hear our son perform in Lincoln Center."

THE OREGONIAN NOV. 12, 1977

PJS opening concert pianist praised

By ROBERT LINDSTROM
of The Oregonian staff

Piano soloist Jill Niizawa, winner of the Portland Junior Symphony Association's 50th annual soloist contest, gave a poetic performance of Mozart's concerto for Piano, K. 466, with the Portland Junior Symphony at Civic Auditorium Saturday night.

Even at the relatively young age of 19, Miss Niizawa seems a self-confident performer who doesn't have to rely upon showy musical theatrics to make an effect. Instead, her playing was fluid and gently polished, which allowed Mozart's music to sing naturally of its own accord.

Throughout the concerto, Miss Niizawa received the firm but responsive support of the Junior Symphony under the baton of Conductor Jacob Avshalomov.

Brahms' Symphony No. 3 was an ambitious choice of repertoire for the Junior Symphony to tackle. The work is one of Brahms' most intense compositions and presents many problems for the string players—wide melodic leaps, lengthy sustained passages and extensive work in the high ranges of the instruments.

The orchestra met all these challenges admirably. Avshalomov led a moderate, lilting version of the work and the youthful players responded enthusiastically. The Germanic fullness of the score was matched by the rich tone of the orchestra which was occasionally dominated by the brass section.

Principal french horn player Greg Gadeholt made a fine impression in his third movement solo.

THE OREGONIAN APR. 24, 1977

Russian music spices concert

By HILMAR GRONDAHL
of The Oregonian staff

The Portland Junior Symphony's "mostly Russian" concert in the Civic Auditorium Saturday night was a rousing and singularly attractive event.

The major orchestral item was the Shostakovitch Sixth Symphony, but there were also the U.S.S.R. National Anthem and the Tchaikovsky Capriccio Italien.

The Sixth Symphony is a work of great depth, a powerful and consistently inspired composition. The first movement is spacious and serious. The scherzo turns again to the perky and satirical grotesqueries of earlier works and the concluding presto is a buoyant and virile statement.

The young musicians, at Avshalomov's urging, made a moving experience of this music. It was remarkable playing, disciplined in its technical and expressive needs.

The performance of the Ibert concerto was a delight from first to last. Vicki Johnston has a winning stage presence and commanding talent. She was totally assured in her proficient and perceptive playing. Her fluency in the peppery speed of some of Ibert's statements was charming and right in the spirit. She expends her breath in a controlled and steady stream and is equally in charge whether in rapid staccato or legato phrasing.

The Capriccio Italien reflected its innate color and Latin verve as it was paced by Avshalomov and his remarkable ensemble.

The Junior Symphony is one group of which Portland can be proud

elaine cogan

The street lights cast long shadows as the young people move hurriedly in the nippy air. Some have light burdens: others carry more bulky items. After a full day of school they have gulped down a hasty dinner and rushed off, knowing they face several hours of school work when they return home. But never mind that now. Greeting their friends, tuning up and looking at their conductor expectantly, they settle down to two hours of serious testing of their musical skills.

Dressed in typical teen-age casual attire, the 110 members of the Portland Junior Symphony rehearse their craft twice a week at Glencoe School in Southeast Portland. Though each rehearsal is charged with seriousness, it is not solemn, a careful distinction made by Jacob Avshalomov, conductor and musical director of this outstanding youth ensemble. There young people work hard and a gentle but firm reprimand or correction usually brings about positive results. After two months of rehearsals, they presented their first concert at the Civic Auditorium last week and are busy preparing for their next one in December. There will be two others next year.

At 54 years of age, the Junior Symphony is a special Portland institution. When some groups reach that venerable age there is a tendency to atrophy, or at least to lose some vitality. That is not so with the Junior Symphony, perhaps because it is constantly infused with new youthful enthusiasm; in some measure because of an exceptionally dedicated board of directors; certainly in large part because of the high standards and exultant spirit of its conductor. It is a dynamic organization seeking new ways to fulfill its mission of helping infuse young people with a love of music.

Each fall, everyone, from the anxious novice to the seasoned performer, auditions before Avshalomov, who chooses approximately 100 young people for the symphony and the same number for the less experienced preparatory orchestra. Advancement is based upon musical progress, seniority and proven commitment. Age is not a factor. There is one young member of 11 and several 21-year-olds, which is the maximum. The most distinguished alumnus of the orchestra is Robert Mann, leader of an acclaimed string quartet, who was concertmaster of the Junior Symphony from 1937 to 1939. The majority has gone on to other careers in which music is an important avocation.

While the orchestra is indeed elitist in its adherence to high musical standards, it is not a socially rigid institution.

Unlike the members of some youth orchestras in other parts of the country, the young people in Portland pay no fee for participating, though their families are expected to pay for a $24 annual membership, which entitles to two tickets for each concert. Scholarships are available to those unable to afford the costs of private lessons. A promising college music student assists as intern educator and this is the second year that Mark Weinsoft has had the position.

In 1970 the symphony took its sound and spirit to Europe in a series of widely-acclaimed concerts. This fall it embarked upon a less ambitious but much appreciated trip to Eastern Oregon and Washington; the orchestra not only performed for the communities of La Grande, Enterprise and Walla Walla, but also gave musical lessons in the local schools. Here at home they present daytime concerts in the Civic Auditorium for thousands of enthusiastic grade school children from the metropolitan area.

In its more than half a century of musical excellence, the orchestra has been fortunate in having the guidance of only two conductors, its exacting founder, Jacques Gershkovitch, and his pupil, Jacob Avshalomov, an accomplished composer as well as a fine musician. It is lucky, too, in having people like James Eoff and Ruth Leupold, who played in the orchestra's early years and continue their dedicated interest: Eoff as assistant conductor and Mrs. Leupold still as willing volunteer board member.

THE OREGONIAN DEC. 27, 1977

Jr. Symphony shines light on suite

By ROBERT LINDSTROM
of The Oregonian staff

Jacob Avshalomov and the Portland Junior Symphony have consistently provided some of Portland's most imaginative symphonic programming. In a concert Monday night at Civic Auditorium, the orchestra presented welcome performances of three infrequently heard works by Hindemith, Bruckner and J. S. Bach in a performing edition by Igor Stravinsky.

The printed program said this was the first Portland performance of Paul Hindemith's "Nobilissima Visione," an orchestral suite extracted from his ballet based on the life of St. Francis of Assisi.

It is difficult to understand how such an inspired score, one of the composer's most exalted and melodically accessible, could have been so overlooked.

How fortunate that the first local presentation of this great work was so well done. Under conductor Avshalomov, the Junior Symphony gave its best in a performance of mounting intensity which culminated in a rapturous reading of the final movement—St. Francis' canticle to the sun.

One wouldn't expect young musicians to respond perceptively to the religious profundities of Bruckner, but the ensemble gave an expansive and warmly colored account of this energetic and massively proportioned work.

Performing Rachmaninov's "The Bells".

Oregon Journal

WHERE HAS CLASSIC 'BELLS' BEEN?

By Martin Clark, *Music Editor*

Incredible. When a major work of obvious genius is permitted to languish without performance for well over half a century—it is to wonder.

Anyway, thanks to Jacob Avshalomov and the PJS, Rachmaninoff's "The Bells" received handsome treatment in its premiere for a near-capacity audience in the Civic Auditorium which gave it the sort of enthusiastic reception it richly deserved.

It was a thrilling performance of a magnificent work. It's certainly worth an encore next season.

THE OREGONIAN FEB 26, 1978

Symphony wins with 5 pieces

By MARK MANDEL
Special writer, The Oregonian

Five utterly dissimilar compositions, each stunning in its own way, helped make Saturday night's Portland Junior symphony concert in Civic Auditorium a knockout.

Robert Stern's "Carom," a 1972 composition for orchestra and magnetic tape, was performed with the composer in attendance. It was a brief but fascinating glimpse into the huge range of sonority available to the composer who combines live and taped sounds.

Members of the orchestra under Jacob Avshalomov obviously enjoyed playing it, and the tremendous crescendo with which "Carom" concludes touched off an enthusiastic response from the audience.

A similar reaction was accorded mezzo-soprano Alyce Rogers after her performance of Berlioz' "The Death of Cleopatra."

Miss Rogers fused passion with nobility befitting that Queen of the Nile to create a moving performance. Her acting ability (Cleopatra takes the asp and dies) was no small ingredient in her success.

The large Junior Symphony made for a beefy Beethoven Symphony No. 4. Under Avshalomov, however, the symphony's inner voices were always intelligible and the buoyancy of the outer movements never bogged. The Fourth is one work that can sound right whether played by 30 or 90 musicians, and it was a treat to hear the massive approach for a change.

Sibelius' "Lemminkainen's Return," a portrayal of the Finnish folk hero galloping home through the forests of the Northland, gave the bassoonists an opportunity for virtuoso display and brought the concert to a rousing conclusion.

THE SUNDAY OREGONIAN APR. 23, 1978

'Bells' given impressive Portland premiere

By ROBERT LINDSTROM
of The Oregonian staff

Rachmaninoff's symphonic choral work, "The Bells," received an impressive Portland premiere Saturday night by the Portland Junior Symphony in Civic Auditorium.

The Portland Junior Symphony was joined by the choirs of Lewis and Clark College and the Oregon State Civic-University Chorus. The massed singers were well-drilled and presented a sonorous and frequently powerful tone.

Baritone David Berger demonstrated that he is one of Portland's finest concert singers with a musically rich and verbally incisive interpretation of "The Iron Mourning Bells."

The orchestra was in superb form and gave one of its most polished performances. Although the entire ensemble played well, the cello section deserves special praise for its mellow tone and technical control. The young musicians negotiated even the high passages of the final movement confidently.

Jacob Avshalomov gave one of his finest conducting performances in an interpretation of Cesar Franck's Symphony in D Minor.

Franck's massive orchestration and heart-on-sleeve emotionalism make it relatively easy for a conductor to produce a dynamic effect with this music. However, the many emotional gear changes throughout the work make a coherent and comprehensible performance much more difficult.

This was where Avshalomov excelled. His detailed attention to phrasing and his grasp of the work's long lines held the many changes of mood firmly together.

The ensemble responded in kind to Avshalomov's leadership and gave a performance that fully realized Franck's extroverted emotionalism. The brass section came through forcefully in the huge climaxes and, again, the cello section captured the mysterious atmosphere of the opening phrase perfectly.

OREGON JOURNAL JUN. 8, 1978

PJS is Youth Philharmonic

By MARTIN CLARK
Journal Music Editor

Say goodby to "Portland Junior Symphony" and welcome the "Portland Youth Philharmonic."

This was the official announcement made at the annual meeting of the Junior Symphony Association at which board members were elected and plans made for the upcoming 55th anniversary season of the internationally acclaimed youth orchestra.

William Webber, outgoing president of the association, gave the following report of the committee assigned to study the subject of changing the name of the Junior Symphony:

"When the orchestra was organized in 1924," said Webber, "the name Junior Symphony seemed an appropriate parallel to the Journal Juniors, Junior Rose Festival Court, and other activities primarily involving grade school and junior high school children.

"In the past 35 years, however, the average age of the orchestra members has been 17, with the top age 21. About 65 percent of the players are in high school, 30 percent in college, and 5 percent in grade school.

"During the same period of time," Webber continued, the independent student orchestra movement, pioneered by the Portland group, spread across the country. Of the nearly 300 such groups now in existence, more than 90 percent are called their city's Youth Orchestra, Youth Symphony, or Youth Symphony Orchestra.

"The name review committee was chaired by PJS alumnus George Reinmiller. Reinmiller was one of the orchestra's first scholarship recipients to Tanglewood, is a former member of the Portland Symphony, and is a well known jazz band leader who is also a practicing attorney.

"The committee decided unanimously to recommend to the board that Portland Junior Symphony Association be retained as the name of the organization which maintains the youth orchestras and programs, and the name of the first orchestra be changed to Portland Youth Philharmonic, with the younger orchestra retaining the name of Preparatory Orchestra.

"The Greek roots being "philos" (loving) and "harmonia" (harmony), the association felt that philharmonic not only refers to music but also describes the relationship between the young musicians, the conductors and the board over the past half century and more."

On a motion from the floor, the name change was approved unanimously by the membership.

William Webber was thanked for his service to the association and presented with a travel book as a token of appreciation from the board.

James Eoff, assistant to conductor Jacob Avshalomov, was presented with a gift of crystal upon his retirement after more than 40 years of service to the orchestra.

55th Season

Jacob Avshalomov, Conductor

November 25, 1978

BEETHOVEN Leonore Overture NO. 2

CHAVEZ Toccata for Percussion

BARTOK Piano Concerto NO. 3

Mark Westcott, *Soloist*

TCHAIKOVSKY Symphony NO. 4

December 26, 1979

17th Annual Concert at Christmas

Seasonal Music, Carol Singing,
The Preparatory Orchestra
& An Alumni Orchestra

February 17, 1979

JACOB AVSHALOMOV 25th ANNIVERSARY CONCERT

MAHLER Symphony NO. 4

Susan Burns, *Soprano*

BARTOK Viola Concerto

Daniel Avshalomov, *Soloist*

AARON AVSHALOMOV Hutungs of Peking

JACOB AVSHALOMOV The Taking of T'ung Kuan

David Avshalomov, *Conductor*

April 21, 1979

RAMEAU Rondeau & Chaconne

DEBUSSY First Clarinet Rhapsody

Todd Kuhns, *Soloist*

RESPIGHI Roman Festivals

MOZART Requiem

Bonnie Hensley, *Soprano;* Lori Karvandi, *Alto*
Ron Jeffers, *Tenor;* Peter Lovely, *Bass*

Guest Choirs: Oregon College of Education,
Oregon State University, Portland State University

THE OREGONIAN DEC. 27, 1978

Youth orchestra homecoming proves delight

By ROBERT LINDSTROM
of The Oregonian staff

It was old home night at the Civic Auditorium Tuesday as the Portland Youth Philharmonic invited some 65 former members of the Portland Junior Symphony to participate in the orchestra's 17th annual Christmas concert.

For most people homecoming means football games, sock hops and sticky spaghetti dinners but the Portland Youth Philharmonic, formerly the Portland Junior Symphony, presented an evening of Mendelssohn, Martin and Elgar to celebrate the return of old friends.

The alumni joined together for a performance of Mendelssohn's Symphony No. 4 "Italian" which evoked the sprightly energy of the composer's brilliant score.

As in all Portland Youth Philharmonic concerts, this one presented some unfamiliar musical treats. Sir Edward Elgar's seldom-performed "The Wand of Youth" Suite No. 1 was presented in excerpt by the youth orchestra.

The swaggering overture brimmed with Elgar's robust British geniality and conductor Jacob Avshalomov effectively characterized the contrasts of the movement "Fairies and Giants."

A highlight of the evening was the first movement of Haydn's Symphonie Concertante played by alumni soloists Nancy Mathis, violin; Elizabeth LeGuin, cello; Pablo Izquierdo, oboe; and Ron Wirt, bassoon.

OREGON JOURNAL DEC. 27, 1978

Alumni join Youth Phil

By MARTIN CLARK
Journal Music Editor

It was really "Homecoming" Tuesday evening at the Civic Auditorium, when the Portland Youth Philharmonic family gathered for a concert featuring the Preparatory Orchestra, the Portland Youth Philharmonic (formerly Portland Junior Symphony) and alumni of the Youth Philharmonic.

Jacob Avshalomov, conductor and music director of the Youth Philharmonic, was as obviously proud as any proud papa could possibly be of his "family."

A surprise pleasure of the evening was hearing movements of Edward Elgar's "Wand of Youth" Suite No. 1 which, I must agree with Avshalomov, has a title which does put one off a bit.

Another pleasant surprise was Frank Martin's "Petite Symphonie concertante" featuring as soloists Diane Demott Spencer, harpsichord; Jenny Lindner, harp; and Neal Goren, piano.

THE OREGONIAN NOV. 26, 1978

Student, teacher honored

By ROBERT LINDSTROM

During the Saturday night concert in Civic Auditorium, the Portland Junior Symphony Association presented Miss Tholen with a certificate of recognition for her musical contributions to the community.

Preceding the award was a fine performance of Bela Bartok's Concerto No. 3 for piano and orchestra with soloist Westcott.

The orchestra, under Jacob Avshalomov, gave an admirable performance, a large share of which brought out Bartok's energy and orchestral virtuosity.

The major work of the evening was Tchaikovsky's Symphony No. 4, one of the cornerstones of the symphonic repertoire.

While this was a far from ideal interpretation, conductor and orchestra captured the volatile emotions of the music.

The six percussionists of the Portland Youth Philharmonic gave a precise and vivacious performance of Chavez's "Toccata for Percussion."

OREGON JOURNAL FEB. 28, 1978

By MARTIN CLARK
Journal Music Editor

Portland Youth Philharmonic opened its 55th season Saturday evening in the Civic Auditorium with a sampling of works played on tour the last several years by the noted youth orchestra.

It has changed its name, but the same high quality of this country's first youth orchestra continues as before.

Westcott, a native Portlander who made his first appearance with the PYP (at that time Portland Junior Symphony) in 1964, distinguished himself in the Bartok.

At the beginning of the second half of the concert a certificate of appreciation was presented to Nellie Tholen of the piano faculty of Lewis and Clark College for her contributions to the music life of Oregon.

Usually, attempts at composition for percussion alone result in more novelty than genuine interest. A true exception is the Carlos Chavez toccata, which the percussion section of the orchestra delivered with intriguing results in response to Avshalomov's crisp direction. It was an ideal interlude between the Beethoven and the Bartok.

The "big" work of the evening was the Tschaikowsky Fourth, which the internationally famous youth orchestra performed with a musicality that always comes as a revealing surprise to those hearing it for the first time.

'Avshalomov Night' at the Auditorium

By MARTIN CLARK
Journal Music Editor

To anyone who pays even the most casual attention to the activities of the Portland Youth Philharmonic, it came as no surprise that the concert by the orchestra Saturday evening in the Civic Auditorium developed into "Avshalomov Night." As my late mother would say, it was "a regular love feast."

"Avshalomov Night" included not just Jacob Avshalomov celebrating his 25th anniversary as conductor and music director of the famed youth orchestra, but the entire gifted family. The orchestra is marking its 55th anniversary.

It was a sophisticated bit of programming any symphony orchestra in the country would consider well off the beaten track of programing. Opening the concert was the Mahler Symphony No. 4 in G Major (written in 1900). In the final movement, soprano Susan Burns gave a satisfying account of herself in an old Bavarian folk song and a lyric found in "Des Knaben Wunderhorn."

The parade of the rest of the family talent began after intermission with son Daniel, 25, as soloist in the Bartok Viola Concerto. This is one of that composer's more ingratiating works, providing a wide-ranging vehicle for Daniel A. to demonstrate that the viola is fully deserving of treatment from composers approaching equality with the concerto repertoire available to violin and cello.

Attention then turned to Aaron Avshalomov, father of Jacob, and his "The Hutungs of Peking." This is a fascinating composition describing Peking coming to life in the early hours of the morning ("hutungs" are the winding, narrow Chinese streets). The elder Avshalomov spent most of his adult life in China, and son Jacob grew up there. This work was played by the Philadelphia Orchestra directed by Leopold Stokowski in 1935.

Concluding the evening was Jacob's 'The Taking of Tung Kuan," conducted by son David, 32. This is an intriguing work with great color contrast, effectively outlined by the guest conductor. Some genuinely moving poetry by Doris (Mrs. Jacob) Avshalomov was included in the printed program.

A citation of appreciation and proclamation of Saturday as "Avshalomov Day in Oregon" was read at intermission. A standing ovation followed that, and another came after the concluding work.

THE CITY OF
PORTLAND
OREGON

OFFICE OF
THE MAYOR
NEIL GOLDSCHMIDT
MAYOR

1220 S. W. FIFTH AVE
PORTLAND, OR 97204
503 248-4120

P R O C L A M A T I O N

WHEREAS, Jacob Avshalomov has in the twenty-five years in Portland contributed a lifetime of musical and cultural enrichment to the people of Portland, and

WHEREAS, these contributions as conductor, composer, teacher, lecturer, and involved and active citizen are so numerous that we conclude that Jacob Avshalomov is our "Renaissance Man," and

WHEREAS, his personal involvement with the young musicians of the Youth Philharmonic (formerly the Junior Symphony) has given us a generation and a heritage of fine musicianship, and

WHEREAS, his commitment to consistent excellence has provided both orchestras of the Youth Philharmonic with a model of maestro, musicianship, and man;

NOW, THEREFORE, I, Neil Goldschmidt, Mayor of the City of Portland, Oregon, the "City of Roses," do hereby proclaim this day and night of February 17, 1979, to be

JACOB AVSHALOMOV
DAY AND NIGHT

and I join his many admirers with gratitude for the maestro's great energy, exceptional intelligence, and unique talent which we acknowledge as gifts to our City.

Neil Goldschmidt
M A Y O R

Avshalomov's silver anniversary a family affair

By ROBERT LINDSTROM
of The Oregonian staff

Portland Youth Philharmonic conductor Jacob Avshalomov received a citation signed by Gov. Vic Atiyeh Saturday night as the Portland Junior Symphony Association celebrated the musician's 25th anniversary with the orchestra at a concert in Civic Auditorium.

The citation proclaimed Feb. 17 "Avshalomov Day" and an enthusiastic audience gave Avshalomov a lengthy standing ovation.

The concert was not only a significant event for Portland music lovers and musicians, almost all of whom Avshalomov has touched in some way in his quarter-century here, but also an important event for the Avshalomov family. in the program. Father and son composers, Aaron and Jacob, were represented by Aaron's "Peking Hutungs" and Jacob's "The Taking of T'ung Kuan."

Jacob's two sons, Daniel and David, were talented participants with Daniel as soloist in Bartok's Viola Concerto and David conducting Jacob's Oriental-flavored tone poem.

Aaron Avshalomov's Peking Hutungs" ("Alleyways of Peking") is an extraordinary work rich with musky exoticism and sensual orchestral colors of a Chinese shade.

Jacob conducted a vibrant and throbbing performance of this music which blends eastern harmonies with thick post-Romantic symphonics. The orchestra was in top form, and one could scarcely ask for a more satisfying performance of this fine work.

Jacob's "The Taking of T'ung Kuan" was written when the composer was a mere 24-year-old. The complex modern harmonies, effectively controlled, and the bold use of the orchestra betray a precocious musical understanding.

David Avshalomov, conducted cleanly with a distinctly young man's interpretation of this distinctly young man's composition. The music is broad in effect and dynamically exciting, as was David's propulsive leadership.

The orchestra's performance was excellent, wringing every bit of drama from the score.

Daniel Avshalomov, after fulfilling engagements with the Tanglewood and Spoleto Festivals, became violist of the American String Quartet two years ago.

In Bartok's difficult Viola Concerto, the 25-year-old Avshalomov displayed a supple tone which had an easy, unforced fullness. If the early sections of the score lacked atmosphere, Avshalomov warmed to the lyrical central section and extracted lively folk idioms from the gypsy-styled final section.

The orchestra had problems throughout but, with the soloist, came alive during the final section to bring the work to a brilliant close, under Jacob's baton.

Mahler's Symphony No. 4, the major work on the program, was performed as the first piece in the concert. The orchestral players showed a technical command seemingly beyond their years in the work but, though surprisingly mature, the performance was not altogether convincing.

Soprano Susan Burns, however, gave a poised and incisive performance of the last movement vocal part.

VICTOR ATIYEH
GOVERNOR

OFFICE OF THE GOVERNOR
STATE CAPITOL
SALEM 97310

February 16, 1979

STATEMENT BY GOVERNOR VIC ATIYEH

Through 25 years of dedicated leadership of the Portland Youth Philharmonic, formerly the Portland Junior Symphony Orchestra, Jacob Avshalomov has shown his creative ability in composition, programs and conducting and been a leader in the culture of our state.

He has received musical recognition for publications and recordings, awards for conducting, and appointments to national councils and foundations.

The youth of Oregon have benefitted from his finest creative talents. He has been a guide for young people striving for the disciplined performances in life that lead to greatness.

For this perceiving, loving kindness in leading the young, the state is grateful.

For his future plans with the Portland Youth Philharmonic, the state is joyful.

Therefore, as Governor of Oregon, I am pleased to proclaim Saturday, February 17, 1979, as "Avshalomov Day in Oregon."

Vic Atiyeh
Governor of Oregon

Photo credit: Sepanik

IN APPRECIATION OF JACOB AVSHALOMOV

It is perhaps a little unusual that one conductor should write an article about another. However, in this particular case, it is a very pleasureable thing to do, since the existence of the Portland Youth Philharmonic and Doctor Avshalomov runs through my life-experience like a brightly-colored ribbon.

My first experience with the organization goes back to 1952 and the annual Concerto competition. Very shortly thereafter, Doctor Avshalomov (permit me to call him Jack) was appointed music director. A few years later, I remember how honored I felt when Jack asked me to proof-read through some of his choral works on the piano just prior to their being sent to the publisher. I was struck by the beauty of the compositions and the thorough knowledge of composition and craftsmanship of Avshalomov the composer. And I'll *never* forget the experience of hearing his *Tom O'Bedlam* performed by the touring Robert Shaw Chorale when I was a student at Oregon State University. The emotional message of this beautiful piece remains strikingly vivid in my memory to this day.

Avshalomov the composer has continued to play in important part in my life. A few years ago, when I was conducting in Austin, Texas, I heard a tape of a piece of his called *Praises from the Corners of the Earth* for Chorus, organ, and percussion. I suggested that it might sound well with symphony orchestra instead of organ and asked him to set it, with my promise that I would perform it with my orchestra in Austin. As fate would have it, I moved to Portland at that time, and we did a very successful first performance here in January of 1976.

We are all fortunate to see Avshalomov the conductor many times each season. I am always impressed by his dignified and magistral presence on the podium and the marvelous response he obtains from his orchestra. We were all pleased to hear him conduct *Messiah* with the Portland Symphony Choir and the Oregon Symphony Chamber Orchestra last December. Of course, Jack's influence on the Oregon Symphony is readily seen with many of the present symphony personnel being ex-members of the Youth Philharmonic.

I'm sure that every one in the Portland musical community will join me in congratulating Jack for twenty-five years of wonderful music-making and wishing him continued success for many scores of years to come!!

Lawrence Smith
Music Director and Conductor
The Oregon Symphony

Few persons are more identified with their occupations than Jacob Avshalomov. His work and his pleasure are synonymous. He rejoices in his daily life as his blitheness of spirit elevates all tasks. His seriousness is not solemn. And his enjoyment of exercising his full potential inspires others to stretch toward theirs.

This rare quality of full-aliveness is combined with practicality, flexibility, sound judgement, warmth, humor, and a fine sense of fitness.

Add to this fortunate personality his great talents as musician, composer, and teacher, and it becomes inevitable that the Boards of Directors, the students in the Orchestras, and his colleagues everywhere feel privileged and inspirited in working with him. And so they have always felt, over these twenty-five years. The present Board is confident in speaking for them all.

1978-79 Board of Directors
Portland Junior Symphony Association

When we walk through the doors of Glencoe School for a rehearsal, we enter as ones occupied with our own existence. Whether it be school, a job, or any of a number of things, all have our own private thoughts and worries. Once the rehearsal begins, however, the extra-musical aspects of each player's personality are "left outside." Over one-hundred young people join together, not only to make music, but to learn and live it as well. Mr. A. has been dealing with and directing this phenomenon for twenty-five years, but each year it is a fresh experience. The real tribute to Mr. A. is the legacy of these rehearsals, which will stay with each one of us for the rest of our lives. We enter and leave the rehearsals as individuals, but inside we are an orchestra.

An Orchestra Member
Portland Youth Philharmonic

Youth orchestra ends season vibrantly

By ROBERT LINDSTROM
of The Oregonian staff

The Portland Youth Philharmonic, under Jacob Avshalomov, gave a vibrant reading of Italian composer Ottorino Respighi's extravagant "Roman Festivals" in its final series concert of the season.

Also on the program Saturday night in Civic Auditorium, principal clarinetist Todd Kuhns appeared as an accomplished soloist in Debussy's First Rhapsody for clarinet and orchestra.

Respighi was a student of Russian orchestral master Rimsky-Korsakov and became one of the greatest orchestral magicians of the early part of this century. In "Roman Festivals," he achieved effects that are remarkably pictorial—from the growling of hungry lions to the swaggering of wine-soaked celebrants.

One can only recreate the composer's specific effects, however, with musicians of high caliber, and the youth orchestra rose to the occasion with superb playing. Avshalomov extracted most of the raw excitement from the music, although his brisk pacing flagged a bit in the third and fourth movements.

The major work of the evening was a solid version of Mozart's Requiem featuring the choirs of Oregon College of Education, Oregon State University and Portland State University.

Given such massive performing forces, Avshalomov's interpretation concentrated on the epic qualities of this great work. He was aided by a fine quartet of soloists—soprano Bonnie Hensley, alto Lori Karvandi, basso Peter Lovely and tenor Bruce Browne, a last-minute replacement for an indisposed Ron Jeffers.

Although details might have been more carefully treated, this was a performance of breadth and sweep with outstanding contributions from soloists, choirs and orchestra.

OREGON JOURNAL APR. 23, 1979

'Repeat' concert tops

By MARTIN CLARK
Journal Music Editor

Portland Youth Symphony departed from a practice of 15 years in its final subscription program of the season Saturday evening in Portland Civic Auditorium.

For the last 15 years, music Director-Conductor Jacob Avshalomov has made a point of not repeating works played at previous concerts. For Saturday night's concert, Avshalomov devoted the entire program to works previously performed by the orchestra.

To anyone hearing the orchestra for the first time, the concert quickly would have made it clear why this oldest of youth orchestras in the United States is also the most famous and the best, according to a consensus of critics who have heard the other leading youth orchestras.

The program was one any major symphony orchestra anywhere might have scheduled as one of its weightiest concerts of the season.

Opening with the rondeau and chaconne from Rameau's "Les Indes Galantes," the next selection was Debussy's "First Clarinet Rhapsody" with Todd Kuhns, principal clarinet with the youth orchestra since 1977.

The facility revealed by the Portland State University junior music major is one of numerous examples of individual talent inspired by performance with the orchestra.

Any program containing both Ottorino Respighi's "Roman Festivals" and the Mozart "Requiem" is bound to be considered a highlight of any orchestra's season.

The rest enjoyed by the brass section in the early portion of the program was more than made up for in the Respighi, which poses an enormous challenge to any orchestra—a challenge that the thoroughly rehearsed youth orchestra met.

Impressive guest choirs were: Oregon College of Education Choir, Duane Kuenzi, director; Civic and Oregon State University Choir, Ron Jeffers, director; and Portland State University Choir, Bruce Browne (the tenor soloist) director.

The huge massed choirs threatened to overwhelm orchestra and soloists, but Avshalomov succeeded in balancing the disparate elements under his baton.

56th Season

Jacob Avshalomov, Conductor

November 5-14, 1979

SECOND INTERNATIONAL TOUR

Sapporo Ebetsu Tokyo Iruma

November 24, 1979

The State Song of Oregon

National Anthem of Japan

TSUKAHARA *Symphony No. 1, "The Myth"
1st and 3rd movements

FRANCK Symphonic Variations
Mike Vukelich, *Piano Soloist*

JAPAN TOUR REPORT

GERSHWIN Suite from Porgy & Bess

RESPIGHI Roman Festivals

December 26, 1979

18th Annual Concert at Christmas

Seasonal Music, Carol Singing,
The Preparatory Orchestra
& Gospel Songs with Willa Dorsey

February 23, 1980

BEETHOVEN Prometheus Overture

FRANZ STRAUSS Horn Concerto
Greg Gadeholt, *Soloist*

SCULTHORPE *Sun Music II

WILLIAMS Star War Themes

HOLST The Planets

---

* *Portland Premier*

April 13, 1980

Reed College

BEETHOVEN	Prometheus Overture
VIVALDI	Concerto for Two Violins, op. 3
	Barbara Litt & Katrin Talbot, *Soloists*
HAYDN	Symphony NO. 94, G major
STRAVINSKY	Octet for Strings
BLOCH	Concerto Grosso NO. 1
	Ann Smith, *Piano Obbligato*

April 26, 1980

HAYDN	Symphony NO. 94, G major
BRAHMS	Song of Destiny
STRAVINSKY	Symphony of Psalms

Guest Choirs: Lewis & Clark College, Oregon State University, Portland State University, Reed College, University of Portland

RIMSKY-KORSAKOV	Capriccio Espagnol

OREGON JOURNAL DEC. 27, 1979

Gift of viola brightens PYP concert

By MARTIN CLARK
Journal Music Editor

One of the wonderful features of the Portland Youth Philharmonic concerts is their unpredictability. Jacob Avshalomov, conductor and musical director, is bound by no sense of hidebound orthodoxy or rigid traditionalism. His programming is inspired as is his teaching.

Nor is that inspiration restricted to program selections. Friday night's 19th Annual Concert at Christmas is a case in point. A certificate of appreciation was presented to Sidney Ray Stukelman for his gift of a viola to the orchestra.

But the presentation ceremony did not end there. Much to the delight of the audience, Avshalomov presented his son Daniel, recently returned from the Orient, to demonstrate the beautiful tone of the instrument.

Stukelman was a custodial helper for the Portland School District for eight years. When he left his job earlier this year, he withdrew his pension fund and used it to pay for the viola which was made by Mark D. Moreland, an apprentice to master violin maker Paul Schuback, Moreland is a former member of the Portland Youth Philharmonic.

This annual "Concert at Christmas" by the Portland Youth Philharmonic is something of "a love feast". Orchestra alumni from all over the United States return to perform with the orchestra at this time. They represent some of the major symphony orchestras of this country.

This also is the time of the season when the Preparatory Orchestra of the PYP performs on the same program with the PYP. Their selection Friday night was Johann Strauss' "Chit Chat Polka."

OREGON JOURNAL DEC. 21, 1979

Avshalomov makes it with 'Music Is Where You Make It'

By MARTIN CLARK
Journal Music Editor

Once more Jacob Avshalomov has made it to some kind of music hall of fame, this time with a truly colorful, inclusive, detailed history of the Portland Youth Philharmonic (better known to one-track minds as Portland Junior Symphony).

"Music Is Where You Make It/II" is a must for anyone who has had any contact with the famous youth orchestra, which has seen more than 4,000 students play their way through its professionally routined rehearsals and performances over 51 years.

It's only fitting that the "most famous youth orchestra in the U.S." (the opinion of musicians who've heard them all), the oldest such ensemble in this country, and the one used as a model for all the others in the United States, should have its deeds chronicled by one who knows his subject intimately—and has the literary ability to reflect it.

Avshalomov is one of those rare conductors who writes as well as he conducts. He is a learned man, one who can discourse on a variety of subjects.

Copies are available at the PYP office, 922 SW Main St., phone 223-5939. They aren't cheap. The soft cover goes for $20, the hard cover for $35. But it's the sort of thing those who have been connected with the orchestra in any way (which certainly includes the audiences) will treasure for the rest of their lives.

It's 168 pages in what is almost a 10-inch-by-10-inch size, abounding in pictures covering the half century of its existence. Among the better photos are those of Maurice Engleman, a past president of the association.

My favorite is the one of the laureates of the Petersburg Conservatory graduation of 1913, which includes Jacques Gershkovitch (founder-conductor of PYP) in a group of 11 with Glazounov, who was director.

Other highlights are perceptive profiles by the late David Campbell of Gershkovitch and Avshalomov.

It's all there—the complete story of Portland Youth Philharmonic by Jacob Avshalomov, conductor and music director of the orchestra.

OREGON JOURNAL NOV. 26, 1979

Triumph!
Youth orchestra shares tour joys

The Portland Youth Philharmonic's concert Saturday night in the Civic Auditorium served two purposes: It was the orchestra's opening concert of its 1979–80 season and it served as a triumphant homecoming concert for the young musicians.

The Youth Philharmonic returned last week from a trip to Japan primarily to visit Portland's sister city, Sapporo, in honor of the 20th anniversary of the relationship between the two cities.

However, in addition to performances in Sapporo, the tour also included concerts in Ebetsu, the sister city of Gresham, Iruma and in Tokyo in the U.S. Embassy Auditorium.

Jacob Avshalomov, conductor and music director of the orchestra for 25 years (the second director of the orchestra in its 54-year history), then gave a report on the ensemble's tour. No doubt about it, if Avshalomov ever wearies of conducting (highly unlikely) he can always make it with travelogues.

After intermission the orchestra was heard in the George Gershwin Suite from his opera, "Porgy and Bess," followed by Ottorino Respighi's "Roman Festivals."

I was getting up to leave (the printed program was completed) when Alyce Rogers, Portland's widely known mezzo soprano, was brought on stage to sing a song of Sapporo.

With all due respect to the splendid performance preceding her appearance, I must say the song and her singing of it were totally enchanting.

Mike Vukelich's performance in the Franck variations drew the sort of enthusiastic response from his peers in the audience which they might have given a quarterback scoring the winning touchdown in the final minute of play. And it was richly deserved. Young Vukelich provided a musicianly performance of a difficult work which is the closest that Franck came to writing a piano concerto (after an adolescent experiment in that form by the composer).

Saturday's concert was a reminder of why the famous youth orchestra, the oldest of its kind in the United States (founded in 1924), still serves as a model for such orchestras throughout the country.

Martin Clark

■指揮　ジャコフ・アブショルモフ
■演奏　ポートランド・ユース・フィルハーモニー

曲目

●小象ババールのお話(1945年)

現代フランスの代表的作曲家フランシス・プーランクの音楽には動物の躍動する姿や心の動きを音楽に表現する作品が多くみられます。

小象のババールを主人公としたジャンド・ブリュノフの児童むけ絵本をもとに、プーランクが作曲したもので、作曲に取り組んだ時代背景は第一次大戦勃発と前後しており、醜い人間の世界に絶望したプーランクが動物の世界をこまかく観察し、はじけるようなアレグロと甘美なメロディによって、彼の音楽の本質を表現したものである。

物語は……初めて人間の街にやって来た象のババールは何もかもが珍しくビックリ、やがて森に帰り象の国の王さまに……

ジャコフ・アブショルモフ　プロフィール

1919年●中国のチンタオに生まれる
●父親はシベリア生まれの作曲家、母親はサンフランシスコ生まれ
1937年●父親か指揮する上海交響楽団の活動に参加
1946年●渡米し、コロンビア大学の音楽教員及び指揮者となる
1954年●ポートランド・ジュニア・シンフォニーの指揮をとり作曲家として知られる一方Guggenheim Fellowship賞をはじめ各賞と名声を得る
1959年●リード大学、ワシントン大学、ノースウエスト大学の客員教授となる
1973年●リード大学の人文学博士号を受ける

●テレビ放送
HBCテレビ11月16日(金)16：00～16：50

FIFTY-SIXTH SEASON

Portland Youth Philharmonic

JACOB AVSHALOMOV
Conductor Musical Director

SAPPORO
Sister - City
20th Anniversary Concerts

EBETSU
Civic Auditorium

TOKYO
Gakushuin Memorial Hall
U.S. Embassy Auditorium

IRUMA
City Auditorium

PORTLAND
Gala Homecoming Concert
Civic Auditorium

SECOND INTERNATIONAL TOUR : JAPAN NOVEMBER 3-14 1979

Honorary Sponsors

Maestro
Seiji Ozawa

The Honorable
Mike Mansfeld
U.S. Ambassador to Japan

The Honorable
Neil Goldschmidt
U.S. Secretary of Transportation

NOTES

Our State of Oregon stands at the western shore of the United States, from which we can look directly across the Pacific Ocean toward Japan. Most of us have seen it only in the mind's eye and therefore look forward with great eagerness to this visit.

Ever since our joyous European Tour in 1970 — when we made many friends among young musicians and adult audiences — we have hoped to share similar experiences in Japan, and to learn something of a culture new to us.

Now, it is a special pleasure and an honor to represent the City of Portland for the celebration of the 20th Anniversary of our Sister-City relationship with Sapporo.

The program of activities has been planned with much attention to the ways in which we can join hands with our Japanese hosts - to begin with, a Children's Concert, which we frequently give at home. We have welcomed HBC's invitation to do such a concert for TV–taping and broadcast. We look forward to the 'greeting performance' by the HBC Junior Orchestra, and to the new experience of performing with a narrator speaking Japanese. POULENC's charming musical fable about **Babar the Little Elephant** makes some nice points—about human behavior and our relationship to the animal world—which are universal; and the music can accept the story told in any and every language.

The presentation of the Children's Concert will be aided by a Japanese student who played with the Orchestra in Portland several seasons ago and has been invited to re-join us during this Tour.

We are glad to have the invitation to perform in Ebetsu, the Sister-City of Gresham, which is our neighbor. Almost every year we have some players from there. For this concert some music with a special American flavor has been added: a Jazz Interlude prepared by the students themselves, and our most famous band March, arranged for orchestra by Stokowski.

For the main Anniversary Concert in Sapporo we particularly wanted to have Japanese students join us, so two choral works have been programmed. The BRAHMS **Song of Destiny** has a brooding and philosophical text which speaks of the troubles we face on earth and the promise of peace in heaven; and HANDEL's coronation anthem, **Zadok the Priest,** is both solemn and joyful. We very much appreciate the work of the Directors of the three Choruses which are singing with us.

We are also very grateful to Mayor Itagaki and his staff for making the arrangements for all the events of our visit, and give particular thanks and compliments to Miss Akiko Sugioka.

Symphony #1, "The Myth" is one of the strongest works written by the well-known composer Setsuo TSUKAHARA. When we met for the first time in Tokyo, nearly two years ago, we became 'old friends' almost instantly. His untimely death last

SAPPORO
Civic Auditorium
Tuesday, November 6 at 2:00 p.m.

Children's Program

Welcome performance by HBC
Junior Orchestra
National Anthem of Japan: Kimigayo
The State Song of Oregon

POULENC
The Story of Babar the Little Elephant
Miss Obara, Narrator
Meet the Players and their Instruments

GERSHWIN
Suite from Porgy and Bess

GRANDJANY
The Children's Hour—*Harp Solo*

SOUSA
The Stars and Stripes March

SPONSOR: Hokkaido Broadcasting Corporation.
TV-taped by HBC

SAPPORO
Thursday, November 8

Musical exchange at Kashiwagaoka Junior High, Asahigaoka Senior High and other Schools

EBETSU
Civic Auditorium
Wednesday, November 7, at 6:00 p.m.

Program

National Anthem of Japan: Kimigayo
The State Song of Oregon

TSUKAHARA
Symphony #1 "The Myth"
1st and 3rd movements

HANDEL
Sinfonia: Zadok the Priest

RESPIGHI
Roman Festivals

Intermission

Harp Interlude

AVSHALOMOV
The Taking T'ung Kuan

GERSHWIN
Suite from Porgy and Bess
Favorite Songs
Alyce Rogers, *mezzo-soprano*

Jazz Interlude

SOUSA
The Stars and Stripes March

SPONSOR: Ebetsu-Gresham Sister City Association

SAPPORO
Civic Auditorium
Friday, November 9 at 6:00 p.m.

With the participation of the Hokkaido University Chorus, Otani Junior College Chorus, Hokkai-gakuen College Chorus

Program

AVSHALOMOV
The Taking of T'ung Kuan

BRAHMS
Schicksalslied

HANDEL
Zadok the Priest

TSUKAHARA
Symphony #1, "The Myth"
1st and 3rd movements

Intermission

GERSHWIN
Suite from Porgy and Bess
Favorite Songs
Alyce Rogers, *mezzo-soprano*

RESPIGHI
Roman Festivals

SPONSOR: Sapporo-Portland Sister City Association

TV-taped by Japan Broadcasting Corporation, NHK

December was a loss to the world of music; and our performance of his composition is in tribute to this fine artist.

GERSHWIN is one of the best-loved American composers, and his opera Porgy & Bess has some of his most enchanting music. We are fortunate to be able to present some of his other favorite songs because one of Oregon's leading singers has come with us on the Tour as an Escort, and also is the mother of two players. ALYCE ROGERS sings with the Portland, the Seattle and the Vancouver, B.C. Opera companies; she is a frequent soloist with the symphony orchestras of these cities; she has recorded Bach contatas with Helmuth Rilling in Germany and was the only American to be soloist with his Gaechinger Kantorei on tour from Stuttgart.

RESPIGHI's **Roman Festivals** is one of the most dramatic, colorful and melodious works in the international repertoire. The Orchestra performed it last season as part of a world-wide celebration of the composer's 100th anniversary; and his widow, Mme. Elsa Respighi, has sent us her best wishes for our performances in Japan. Each of the four movements reflects a particular episode or festival in Christian religious life as it has been celebrated at different periods in history.

In Tokyo we are fulfilling, in a small way, a dream of Mr. Tsukahara's, to have our two Orchestras join in performance; we are very happy to have this musical meeting now.

The fine reputation of the Suginami Juvenile Chorus has come to us and we also welcome the chance to join them in the November 11th program. Almost every year young singers join us in our programs in Oregon.

With Ambassador Mansfield as one of our Honorary Sponsors, it is very appropriate that we present a program of chamber music at the U.S. Embassy in Tokyo. We remember with nostalgia the warm welcome we had at the London and Florence embassies in 1970, and appreciate this new forum for our musical goodwill offerings.

The final concert of the Tour is in Iruma-shi. We are most grateful to Miss Michiko Kobayashi, Secretary General of the Tokyo Junior Philharmonic, for making the arrangements and securing instruments for the concerts of November 11th & 13th.

Our Assistant Conductor, DAVID AVSHALOMOV, has been conductor of the Missoula Symphony, in Montana, and studied under Leonard Bernstein last summer at Tanglewood. In August he had the pleasure of conducting at the National Music Camp in Tokyo, and now will be conducting the concert at Iruma-shi.

Our last performance of this program will be at the Gala Homecoming in Portland, where the audience will hear a report on the tour as part of the concert.

TOKYO
Gakushuin Memorial Hall
Sunday, November 11 at 2:00 p.m.

With the participation of the Suginami Juvenile Chorus and the Tokyo Junior Philharmonic Orchestra

Program

AVSHALOMOV
The Taking of T'ung Kuan

TSUKAHARA
Scherzo *from* Symphony #1

GERSHWIN
Suite from Porgy and Bess

RESPIGHI
Games at the Circus Maximus
The October Festival
from Roman Festivals

SOUSA
The Stars and Stripes March

SPONSOR: Takechi Music Office and Tokyo Junior Philharmonic Orchestra

TOKYO
U.S. Embassy Auditorium
Monday, November 12 at 5:30 p.m.

Serenade—Reception

Varied Chamber Groups from the Orchestra perform for the Embassy's invited audience

TOKYO
Monday, November 12
Tuesday, November 13

Entourage divides up for visits to:

Kamakura historic shrines

Kyoto historic monuments

Suzuki Institute classes and concert in Matsumoto

Studios of Japan Broadcasting Corporation (NHK)

IRUMA
City Hall
Tuesday, November 13 at 6:00 p.m.

David Avshalomov, Conducting

Program

National Anthem of Japan: Kimigayo
The State Song of Oregon

POULENC
Episodes from Babar

HANDEL
Sinfonia: Zadok the Priest

REICHA
Wind Quintet: Allegro

RESPIGHI
Roman Festivals

Intermission

GERSHWIN
Suite from Porgy and Bess
Favorite Songs
Alyce Rogers, *mezzo-soprano*
Percussion Interlude

TSUKAHARA
Scherzo from Symphony #1

Jazz Interlude

SOUSA
The Stars and Stripes March

SPONSOR: Iruma-shi Junior Chamber of Commerce
Esso Standard Oil

A Tour such as this depends on a great many more people for its success than just the performers. At the center of our effort, has been a most dedicated and resourceful Board of Directors and Staff, led by President Elise Rosenfeld. Major financial assistance came from the Portland City Council at the insistence of former Mayor Neil Goldschmidt. At City Hall Shirley Tanzer has been a staunch ally. In the program we have listed friends who have assisted in many ways — with goods, services, time, thought and love.

This has all been done with the conviction that good relations between different peoples of the world are developed by meaningful exchanges in the realm of the spirit. Our young people are both the emissaries and the beneficiaries of the good will which we have all generated.

J.A.

JACOB AVSHALOMOV

Born in Tsingtao, China, 1919; son of composer Aaron A.; educated in American and British schools in China, Reed College, Eastman School of Music (B.M. & M.A.), Honorary Doctorates from U. of Portland, Reed College, Linfield College.

Recipient Ditson Conductor's Award; member National Council for the Humanities; Co-Chairman, National Arts Endowment, Planning Section.

Music faculty Columbia University, U. of Washington, Northwestern U., Berkshire Music Center, Aspen Music School.

Composer of more than 40 works for orchestra, chorus, voice and chamber-groups; Guggenheim Fellow; recipient N.Y. Music Critics Award, Naumburg Recording Award; works performed in Oslo, Leningrad, Moscow, Amsterdam, London, Paris, Munich, Paris, Milan and over 125 cities in the U.S.A.

Conducted his own works for Columbia Records and Composers Recordings, Inc.

Conductor of Portland Youth Philharmonic since 1954.

PORTLAND
Civic Auditorium
Saturday, November 24 at 8:00 p.m.

Program

The State Song of Oregon
National Anthem of Japan

TSUKAHARA
Symphony #1, "The Myth"
1st and 3rd movements

FRANCK
Symphonic Variations
Mike Vukelich, *Piano Soloist*

JAPAN TOUR REPORT
Jacob Avshalomov

Intermission

GERSHWIN
Suite from Porgy and Bess

RESPIGHI
Roman Festivals
Games at the Circus Maximus
The Jubilee
The October Festival
The Epiphany

Orchestra Personnel 1979/80

FIRST VIOLIN
Irene DeLessert
Janet Groh
Co-Concertmasters
Tina Alexander
Karen Hilley
Luther Stohs
Barbara Litt
Linda Ackley
Denise Smesrud
Phil Richardson
Ruth Sadilek
Pam Holcomb
Kathy Cook
Judy Oringdulph
Jeff Fillis
Wendell McRae
Louise Moore
Deda Gillespie
Jonathan Dubay
Lennie Wong
†Craig Mosbaek

SECOND VIOLIN
Ann Smith
Principal
Robin Cook
Asst. Principal
Tammy Chambers
*Theresa Gatto
Hiroko Fukabori
Cynthia Rogers
Shannon Wick
Maria Schleuning
Danette Warren
Trina Vahsholtz
Jim Toussaint
Kari Keiser
Sarah Borowiak
Gail Vore
Nadine Moore
Chip Whitesides
Russell Graham
Robin Oge
†David Gerber
†Drue Fergison
†Janet Fogle
†Pam Gilmore
†George Shiolas

VIOLA
Lisa Perry
Principal
Jerry Couture
Asst. Principal
David Litt
Aloysius Joseph
Karl Blume
Kim Lorati
Melinda Benson
Sarah Willner
Kim Wick
Leonard Cogan
Linda Davies
Louise Sermal

CELLO
Kathy Rust
Principal
Linda Groh
Asst. Principal
Sue Oleksak
Robert Schlichting
Drew Eckhard
Karen Anderson
Mary Ann Oringdulph
Jeff Edens
Carrie Hooten
Greg Dubay
Jennie Starr
Ann Dinsmore
†Bruce Anderson
†Brenda Ewing

BASS
Vernon Vasey
Principal
Todd Seeber
Asst. Principal
David Powloski
Julie Halladin
Christy Boehr
Sue Roth
David Captein
†Robert Durych

FLUTE
Myra Becraft
Pamela Matthews
Co-Principals
Jane Rupert
Cindy Mitch (Picc.)
*Karla Takasumi

OBOE
Paul Sadilek
Principal
Pablo Izquierdo (E.H.)
Alan Juza
Anne Sansregret

CLARINET
Todd Kuhns
Principal
Brad Butterfield (E♭)
Mark Rogers
Marc Eklof (Bass)
*Ron Hayward

BASSOON
Jan Richardson
Principal
Rosalie Brown
Vic Walton (Contra)
Wanda Ford
*Edward Grohnke

HORN
Greg Gadeholt
Principal
Larry Johnson
Marilyn Olsen
Anthony Hardt
David McDade
Terry White
*Tim Crisp

TRUMPET
Stephen Smith
Principal
Shaindell Goldhaber
Steve Conrow
Michael Stodd

Assistant to the Conductor — Cline Otey

Assistant Conductor on Tour — David Avshalomov

TROMBONE
David Bryan
Principal
Mark Sellman
Carl Mazzio
Jim Miller (B.)

TUBA
Michael Grose

PERCUSSION
Clayton Smith
Principal
Christopher Lee
Timpani
Kevin Follis
Bill Ohle

HARP
Maria Casale
*Sarah Poulsen

PIANO & CELESTE
Mary Ann Oringdulph

LIBRARIAN
Anthony Hardt

STAGE MANAGERS
Vernon Vasey
Aloysius Joseph

†Non-touring member
*Alternate for tour

Portland Junior Symphony Association
922 S. W. Main St., Portland, OR 97201

Jacob Avshalomov
Conductor/Musical Director

OFFICERS

Mrs. Edward Rosenfeld
President
William B. Webber
Vice President
Mrs. Robert Oringdulph
Vice President
Mrs. Alexander Schleuning
Vice President
Mrs. Thomas L. Miller
Secretary
John E. Huisman
Corporate Secretary
Frank H. Eiseman
Treasurer

DIRECTORS

Mrs. John A. Baines
Mrs. Howard C. Burnett
Mrs. John Cook, Jr.
Mrs. Betty Cramer
David S. Davies
William R. deWeese
Mrs. Robert F. Dwyer, Jr.
Maurice Engleman
Dr. James Fenwick
Peter Friedman
John W. Harris
Mrs. Robert L. Harrison
Mrs. Harold S. Hirsch
Mrs. J. Michael Keane
Mrs. W. Dean Kendall
Dr. Harvey Klevit
Robert F. Knoll
Mrs. James L. McAlpin
Mrs. Arthur McArthur
Mrs. Robert H. McCall
B. A. McPhillips, Jr.
Mrs. Monford Orloff
Mrs. Robert Rogers
Jess A. Rogerson
Dr. Ottomar Rudolf
Mrs. Bruce Senders
Ralph Shaw
Mrs. William Swindells, Jr.
Mrs. Vance Taylor
Tom Wheeler
Don Wilner
Robert Zwald

TOUR STAFF

Robert F. Knoll
Tour Manager
Mrs. Robert Oringdulph
Asst. Tour Manager
Kay Young
Asst. to the Tour Manager
Dr. Harvey Klevit
Physician
David Avshalomov
Asst. Conductor
Edie Eisele
Sapporo Liaison & Escort
Hank Kranzler
Photographer

NON-VOTING MEMBERS

Mrs. George Crisp
Mrs. Paul Eckard
John E. Huisman

STAFF

Mrs. Kay Young
Executive Secretary
Mrs. Marilyn Couture
Assistant

ESCORTS

Mr. & Mrs. Harry Benson
Mrs. Paul Eckhard
Mrs. Harvey Klevit
Mrs. Robert Knoll
Mrs. Richard Rogers
Mr. & Mrs. Edward Rosenfeld
Mrs. Alexander Schleuning
Mr. & Mrs. Bruce Senders
Mr. & Mrs. Ray Steed

KGW-TV STAFF

George Bieber
John Haney
Patricia Joy

The Association gratefully acknowledges significant gifts toward the Japan Tour from the following:

Alpine Veneers
Anzen Imports
Associated Press
Autzen Foundation
Azumano Travel Service,
  Scott Wakasugi
Bingham Willamette
Boise Cascade
Canadian Bank
William Carver,
  U.S. National Bank of Oregon
Churchill Tours
Clark Foundation
Commercial Investments
Cronin and Caplan
First National Bank of Oregon
Fred Meyer
Eccles & Funatake, Advertising
Pamela Glen, Catlin-Gable School
Senator Mark O. Hatfield and staff
Fred Hammack, Madison High School
Curtis Holloway, Aloha High School
Hyster Company
Irwin-Hodson Company
Tom Iverson, Centennial High School
Japan Air Lines,
  Peter Ohtaki, M. Kodama
Japan Travel Bureau
Japanese Consulate General
Johnson Acoustical
Richard Jones,
  Lincoln High Int'l Studies Center
Kaiser Foundation
KGW-TV
  George Beiber
  John Haney
  Patricia Joy
Laventhal and Horwath
Norman Leyden
Lindsay Nahstoll
Magic Pan Creperie
Meier and Frank
Mitsubishi International
Mt. Hood Chemical
Murdock Trust
North Pacific Canners
Guy Nowels, U.S. Customs
Office of the Mayer
  Shirley Tanzer
The Oregon Journal
Oregon Mutual Savings Bank
The Oregonian
Pendleton Woolen Mills
City of Portland
  Mayor Connie McCreadie
  Commissioners:
    Charles R. Jordan
    Francis J. Ivancie
    Mike Lindberg
    Mildred A. Schwab
Portland Luggage
Promotion Products, Inc.
  Bob Tobias
Schuback Violin
Gil Seeley Lewis and Clark College
Dick Scott's ARCO
Kanematsu-Gosho U.S.A., Inc.
Robert W. Sheets
  Portland Branch Manager
  Japanese Consulate General
Sister City Committee
Standard Insurance Company
Tektronix Group
Templeton Foundation
Thuemmel, Marx and Associates, Inc.
Secretary of Transportation
  Neil Goldschmidt
Tucker Trust
United Air Lines
United Press International
Weight Watchers
Weyerhouser Foundation
White Stag, Inc.
Arthur Young and Co.
Pacific Power & Light
Purdy Brush

And a number of anonymous gifts from friends of the Orchestra toward individual student travel costs.

This list is incomplete; names of additional Tour benefactors will be listed in our December program.

PORTLAND
YOUTH PHILHARMONIC

THE OREGONIAN FEB. 24, 1980

Youth Philharmonic

Soloist impressive in concerto

By ROBERT LINDSTROM
of The Oregonian staff

Franz Strauss' Concerto for Horn and Orchestra received a rare performance Saturday in Civic Auditorium featuring soloist Greg Gadeholt and the Portland Youth Philharmonic. Soloist Gadeholt, the philharmonic's principal horn player, effectively played the warm themes of the work and negotiated the fast passages with aplomb.

The orchestra, under Jacob Avshalomov, gave an idiomatic, Germanic account of the music, experiencing some rhythmic problems in the second movement.

A fat, rounded Teutonic sound also characterized the orchestra's boisterous interpretation of Beethoven's Overture to the ballet "The Creatures of Prometheus."

Conductor Avshalomov all but apologized for the programming of Australian contemporary composer Peter Sculthorp's "Sun Music II," calling it "the ugliest piece of music we've played in 25 years."

In the event, the Sculthorpe work proved to be a fascinating, if progressive, work.

The orchestra groaned and exploded, by turns, stamping feet, croaking through mouthpieces, searing the strings with high notes, all of it made relentless by primitive percussion.

The orchestra bit into the aboriginal, avant-garde "Rite of Spring" lustily, giving one of the most rhythmically inspired performances of the evening.

OREGON JOURNAL FEB. 25, 1980

PYP concert 'astronomical'

By MARTIN CLARK

So what does astronomy have to do with the Portland Youth Philharmonic concert Saturday night in the Civic Auditorium?

Well, the final half of the program was devoted to six of the seven "movements" of Holst's "The Planets" (only Neptune was ignored). And the Williams' "Star Wars" Themes concluded the first half of the concert, preceded by the Australian composer Peter Sculthorp's "Sun Music II."

The program deviated somewhat from celestial subjects with the opening Beethoven "Prometheus" Overture, followed by the Horn Concerto by Franz Strauss, the papa of the slightly better-known Richard Strauss, with Greg Gadeholt as soloist. But, all in all, it was a heavenly evening.

Not only did Gadeholt acquit himself with honors as soloist in the Strauss concerto, but I'm happy to report that his peers in the audience greeted his superb performance with the sort of uninhibited cheers usually reserved for unadulterated garbage in Memorial Coliseum presented by con artists labeling themselves as combos of one sort or another. It was most refreshing.

There's really no such thing as *avant-garde* music any more, but if there were, Sculthorp's "Sun Music II," mostly rhythmic, percussive sound lasting (mercifully) about five minutes, might qualify. Jacob Avshalomov, conductor and music director of the Philharmonic, kindly and graciously resisted the temptation to repeat it for our edification.

THE OREGONIAN DEC. 27, 1979

Philharmonic offers 'un-Christmas' concert

By ROBERT LINDSTROM
of The Oregonian staff

The Portland Youth Philharmonic carefully entitled its 18th annual yuletide performance a "Concert at Christmas," presumably so audiences wouldn't expect a Christmas concert.

Instead, the Philharmonic and its companion Preparatory Orchestra offered a smorgasbord of romantic and baroque works with a nod toward the festive season in the form of a carol sing-along and four gospel songs by Portland's Willa Dorsey.

On the classical side, the centerpiece of the concert was the Portland premiere of the scherzo and finale from Anton Bruckner's Symphony No. 0.

The symphony was given its unique number by Bruckner's publisher, who resurrected the youthful and unnumbered work after the composer's death.

The orchestra under Avshalomov coped well, generally, with this uneven piece, but painfully loud trombones and minor rhythmic inaccuracies tempered the success of the interpretation.

More impressive was a colorful performance of Maurice Ravel's sparkling "Alborada del Gracioso" and a virile version of Franz Liszt's tone poem "Les Preludes."

Youth chorus, orchestra end season well

By ROBERT LINDSTROM
of The Oregonian staff

A fine performance of Igor Stravinsky's "Symphony of Psalms" highlighted the final concert of the Portland Youth Philharmonic's 50th anniversary of the Boston Symphony, this setting of three excerpts from the Vulgate Psalms represents one of Stravinsky's most spiritual scores and one of the most deeply felt.

However, the religious sincerity which inspired the work did not draw from the composer an imitation of conventional religious music. Here is all of the dissonance, rhythmic jolt and extraordinary instrumentation of those earlier works but brilliantly put to a moving, liturgical purpose.

As he often does when presenting 20th century scores, conductor Jacob Avshalomov offered a gentle apology (by way of explanation) for performing the work. But this was not a compromising performance. Avshalomov launched into the opening section with intensity and, when called for, massive sonic impact.

The impressive sound was largely due to an incisive interpretation from a chorus of over 200 voices.

Members of the orchestra coped admirably with the unusual orchestration of woodwinds, brass, percussion and low strings. The woodwind and brass sections made valiant contributions.

Brahms' "Schicksalslied" ("Song of Destiny") was effective, though somewhat less successful due to a performance which gave short measure to Brahms' long phrases. Both orchestra and chorus produced a vibrant, muscular tone.

The orchestra found few technical obstacles in a lively version of Haydn's "Surprise" Symphony, No. 94. This was a precocious interpretation bothered only by a few tempo disagreements in the middle movements.

The program closed with Rimsky-Korsakov's Irresistible warhorse "Capriccio Espagnol."

PYP season finale features choruses

By MARTIN CLARK
Journal Music Editor

As one who has spent most of a lifetime in the study (and worship) of beautiful tone, I must say there not only is safety in numbers—but beauty, as well.

Unless we are speaking of a professional chorus of about two dozen voices, each of whom is an excellent soloist, the bigger the chorus the better. An amalgamation of tone takes place in huge numbers that simply does not occur with choruses of 50 or 60 voices—or even 80 to 100.

Saturday evening in the Civic Auditorium the Portland Youth Philharmonic presented its final concert of the season, featuring the choruses of five Oregon colleges: Lewis & Clark College, Gilbert Seeley, director; Oregon State University, Ron Jeffers, director; Portland State University, Bruce Browne, director; Reed College, Virginia Hancock, director; and University of Portland, Roger O. Doyle, director.

They performed with the PYP under the direction of Jacob Avshalomov in the Brahms "Schicksalslied" and Stravinsky's Symphony of Psalms. Opening the program was the Haydn "Surprise" Symphony No. 94 in G Major. Closing it was scheduled the Rimsky-Korsakov "Capriccio Espagnol."

I heard the Haydn and Brahms (before departing to hear pianist Steven De Groote). It was in the Brahms that my observation on choral tone was proven once again. More than 200 voices made up the combined chorus and the tone—and response—was truly impressive . . . genuinely moving.

Avshalomov and the PYP presented an incisive reading of both works, making one wonder again if there is any youth orchestra in the country to compare with what we have in Portland.

Percussion demonstration after a Children's Concert.

Music As We've Made It Since The 56th Season

The **57th Season,** 1980–81, brought the Orchestra to one of its pinnacles of achievement. Ever since the 50th Anniversary in 1974, when the Orchestra was especially good, I had the nagging feeling that we might never reach that standard again. But here we were at the Winter Concert with the Brahms *First Symphony,* the Mozart *Clarinet Concerto,* and the Stravinsky *Rite of Spring* all sounding like gangbusters. This was the program we took to Charleston, South Carolina, in June when we were invited to play at the Spoleto/USA Festival by its founder-composer, Giancarlo Menotti. The invitation had been set up through alumna Ellen Dietz Dressler, who was the organizer of the Piccolo Spoleto events for the City of Charleston. After our performance Menotti came backstage and said to the Orchestra, "When I read your program I couldn't believe my eyes; now after hearing you I can hardly believe my ears!"

Composer Giancarlo Menotti congratulating the Orchestra at the Spoleto/USA Festival.

At the Spring Concert we did the Verdi *Requiem* for the first time in our history. This required fully professional soloists, whom we invited, and an intrepid chorus, which we usually have.

In the **58th Season,** 1981–82, I took my first mini-sabbatical. So for the Spring Concert we invited another composer-conductor to take over, Tomas Svoboda, Czech-born and Paris-trained, now on the faculty of Portland State University. He was encouraged to present a work of his own, and chose *Sinfonietta à la Renaissance.* His musicianly approach was much appreciated both by the Orchestra and our audience.

The **59th Season,** 1982–83, revived a project whose time had clearly come, the Sing-Your-Own Messiah. I had tried such an event a decade earlier, once at the Auditorium and once at the secularized Old Church. Neither drew more than a few hundred people, so I put the idea aside. By 1982, this ultimate in singalongs had been successfully done in many cities in the East, but it was from San Fran-

Sing-Your-Own Messiah.

cisco that some of our Board members caught the spark. Thanks to the prompting of Jacqueline LeBeck and the planning of Marjorie Wilson and Ernestine Oringdulph it became an instant tradition in Portland. Over 2,000 singers and friends showed up. Channel 8, KGW-TV, agreed to film it for broadcast and we were off the ground.

The test run of the first chorus, "And the glory of the Lord," was a scary moment, not knowing what kind of sound or response we would get. But it was reassuringly plausible and we plunged in. After the event KGW aired it twice, once on Christmas Eve and again on Christmas Day. We received enthusiastic letters from all over the region, making it clear that the PYP had established a new form of outreach.

At the Winter Concert in February we revived a practice from Gershkovitch's day, presenting opera in concert form. I had come across Tchaikovsky's neglected *Maid of Orleans* which, while dull on stage, has marvelous music. We were able to borrow the scores from the Opera Company of Toronto, had a fine time doing it, and a good success in the hall. But some flaws in the performance were mentioned in the review and magnified by the headline (which see). Now, after the shock has long since worn off, I rather cherish that notice because it breaks the nearly perfect record of favorable, not to say glowing, reviews we've had over the decades.

An already eventful season was brought to a rousing close by the arrival in Portland of 32 delegates from youth orchestras around the world. They had been invited to join the Orchestra to herald our forthcoming anniversary. We sent them their parts for the Berlioz *Symphonie Fantastique*; the players came for a week, rehearsed with us, enjoyed homestays, played chamber music in private and on the air, took scenic trips, and finally, greeted by Governor Tom McCall, joined us in a terrific performance of the Berlioz masterpiece at the Civic Auditorium. Everyone should hear it once with an orchestra of 140!

That program was intended as a warm-up for the **60th Anniversary** celebration in 1982–83. We began the new season by bringing back former concertmaster May Lou Speaker Churchill, to do the Brahms Violin Concerto. She was by then a fixture in the Boston Symphony Orchestra, principal of the second violins. Coming into the PJS at age 10, she had moved steadily up; becoming soloist at 16, concertmaster the next year, going to Tanglewood as our scholarship student, continuing to the New England Conservatory, and, almost inevitably, to the Boston Symphony Orchestra. At the November concert we paid tribute to the 30 years which Jacques Gershkovitch had devoted to the PJS by performing one of his favorite works, Borodin's *Polovetsian Dances.*

The Concert at Christmas brought several alumni into the spotlight. The Winter Concert celebrated the 60th Anniversary of our very first concert in 1925. And on March 11, we embarked on our Third International Tour to Yugoslavia and Austria.

En route to Europe we stopped to join the New York Philharmonic in a concert at Avery Fisher Hall. By coincidence they were due to celebrate their 60th year of giving children's concerts.

I arranged this event with Albert K. Webster, Executive Director of the New York Philharmonic. He and I had served as co-chairmen of the National Arts Endowment Music Planning Section, and he was very enthusiastic about my suggestion of a joint performance. Indeed, he was able to get Leonard Bernstein to participate and conduct the combined PYP and NYP—totaling 208 players—in Tchaikovsky's *Romeo and Juliet.*

Accounts of the concert are included among the reviews, but a couple of sidelights must be recounted. The New York Philharmonic's famous English-horn player, Thomas Stacy, was so taken with our Rick Olsen that after the morning rehearsal he invited him to lunch and brought him back for a two-hour lesson. And our youngest bass player, coping with a poor rented instrument, was offered the use of a fine Italian bass by her "stand partner," the New York principal.

In every way the event was a touching tribute to Portland's creation and sustenance of the nation's first-founded youth orchestra. Our students were already high before lifting off from Kennedy airport for Belgrade.

Joint Concert with the New York Philharmonic and Leonard Bernstein.

THIRD INTERNATIONAL TOUR, 1984

This Tour certainly had its origins in serendipity. The very first meeting of the 60th Anniversary Committee, early in 1983, was interrupted by a phone call from New York. A Mr. Elliott Ritter, Director of Cultural Omnibus, Inc., was calling on the recommendation of critic Paul Turok to ask whether we might be interested in making a tour with the Orchestra to Europe. We were all pleasantly astonished, and the Committee, after only a moment's discussion, said to give him a tentative "yes."

Such projects take an inordinate amount of planning—which can only be hinted at here. Ritter had been organizing a tour of student and amateur groups to Europe for some 15 years and had a good network of contacts. We signed on with him to visit Yugoslavia and Austria. In Yugoslavia the coordinator of Jeunesses Musicales activities was a pale, moon-faced, red-headed young man named Zoran Damnjanovic. It was through him that most of the arrangements were made in Graz, Austria, as well.

The evening departure from JFK on Yugoslav Airlines was a scramble, and the plane was cramped for space and smoke-filled. In Belgrade, we were met at the gate by a crew of guides from Mercator Tours who greeted us in good English and led us to baggage claim and out to a waiting reception group which included officials from Muzichke Omladine (Jeunesses Musicales), players from the Belgrade Youth Orchestra, and the cultural attaché from the U.S. Embassy. This was a serious reception, complete with trays of glasses filled with zubrovka (vodka-like) and crusts of dry bread and salt—the traditional welcome. Our innocents from Portland were hardly prepared for such festivities, especially so early in the day; but it certainly did wake everyone up.

We were all piled into buses and to our quarters. Some adults stayed at a hotel, while the students went to hostel-style cabins at an out-of-season camp. I hardly had time to set down my bags and change into city clothes before being whisked away to a press conference. In downtown Belgrade, at the International Press Club, were gathered some 25 news people from the dailies, radio, television, and educational circles, together with interpreters. Along with my wife Doris and me were our tour managers, and Zoran with his beatific smile and his beauteous bride, Marina—a musicologist.

Before the question period began there were welcoming remarks, during which I noticed that copies of our advance publicity had been distributed. We had a lively exchange. Near the end of the session a young woman came from the other end of the table to my place, mike in hand, to ask if I would tell them about the most gifted member of the Orchestra—remarking that surely among so many talented young people there would be an outstanding member. I smiled and replied that yes, I could, but would not. Before she could register surprise or disappointment, I began my credo that this Orchestra is something more than the sum of its talented

Third International Tour, Yugoslavia, 1984.

Sava Center, Belgrade.

parts, that cooperatively they produce something greater than any one or few of them could, that we had never depended on prodigies. To the contrary, it was our special tradition of careful, intensive work that enabled thousands of young people, over the decades, to achieve wonderful things in music. Before I was done the gathering sighed their approval of what clearly seemed to them to be an enlightened attitude, and we parted with the warmest expressions of appreciation. A hearty meal awaited us in a side room.

The next day we were all taken to the venue of the first concert—the Sava Center. On the way into town from the airport the day before, we had passed three huge banners, across major streets, heralding, "PORTLAND YOUTH PHILHARMONIC PRVO PUT U JUGOSLAVJA, SC/3/18/84," giving the code for the place, date, and hour of our concert. Now we saw that it was really a convention hall, with adaptable spaces. For our purpose it was opened all the way. I walked in and gasped to see seating for 4,000 people! I wondered what they would do with all those empty places. There was no proscenium to the stage area, only a back wall which must have been 150 feet across. There were chairs and stands enough for two orchestras—the "Borislav Poscan" Youth Orchestra of Belgrade were to join us in one number.

After completing our sound check they came on and we shared the stands—with one of our players and one of theirs at each. We had agreed to do the Dvorák *Slavonic Dance No. 8*; but somewhere along the way they had added the Ravel *Bolero*—which had gained renewed popularity at the Olympics. We had not prepared it, but about half of our Orchestra knew it from having performed it the previous season. I advised our players to use their discretion and play what they could—the Yugoslav conductor was to lead—but before the rehearsal was over, virtually all our people were playing without qualms.

In the scale of those spatial arrangements the orchestral piano had been set on a high dais over 50 feet away! I asked to have it brought closer but nothing I could say was of any avail. It was Sunday, no movers were available, it was not permitted for amateurs to move it. I was concerned because our major work was the Shostakovitch *Fifth Symphony,* in which the piano has a very important and exposed part. But our pianist, Mimi Irlandez, proved to be unshakable and didn't miss a beat.

At the concert that evening we entered to find every seat occupied with many people sitting in the aisles; even our escorts had to hunt for places. Astonished as I was to see those acres of people, I was even more impressed by the hush that prevailed in the hall throughout the 44 minutes of the Shostakovitch Symphony. The ovation that followed sounded all the louder for it.

The following day the U.S. Ambassador, David Anderson, gave a reception for us, to which many of the leading artists, educators, and composers were invited. The handsome embassy villa, on spacious grounds, was filled to bursting, and there was a festive air that everyone sensed. We later received a lovely letter from Ambassador Anderson which is reprinted here among the reviews.

On the third day we played Novisad, about a two-hour runout from Belgrade. The hall is really a theatre, not a concert room, seating 1,100, with black drapes everywhere; but the acoustics were not bad and the performance went well.

Zagreb proved to be a much more interesting city—its antiquities preserved. And the hall, Lisinski Theater, was a wonderful, newish building with lots of wood and a beautiful sound. Before we got to it, though, we were beset by vicissitudes. The accommodations for the Orchestra and escorts were poor. In the late afternoon we were taken to a charming restaurant at the edge of town; the service was slow and I was edgy about getting to the hall on time. When we finally swept everybody out, the bus drivers, who were from Belgrade, didn't know the way to the Lisinsky. We arrived, breathless, just 10 minutes before concert time. Furious, I called for the manager of the hall and insisted that he announce that, due to transportation problems, the concert would start 20 minutes late. After getting everyone calmed down, including myself, we went on to a most satisfying performance.

Here, too, the concert was followed by a reception; a most lavish affair in a lovely room at the theatre. Many local musicians and artists were there, including composer Bruno Bjelinski—a hearty 72-year-old with excellent English who said to me, "Everyone speaks to you as the conductor of this wonderful orchestra, but let us speak as composers," which we did.

Congresshale, Graz, Austria.

The next afternoon, following the Ambassador's lead, the U.S. Consul in Zagreb also held a fine reception in the Orchestra's honor. Evidently we were among the first American ensembles to appear in Yugoslavia and as such were especially welcome—both to the citizenry and to our government officials.

The fourth concert was given in Graz, Austria, at the Congresshalle. This modern evocation of a historic building also has a wonderful sound. However, the stage is very small. Rolling with the punches, I decided to send the Orchestra on in shifts—about half for each half of the program. It worked out very well—they were able to listen to each other, and no one was left out. Playing the Schubert *Eighth Symphony* I felt as though we were returning this music to its home. The audience included a large contingent of students bused in from all around Graz, many of them in their school uniforms.

As fine as things were in Graz they were mirrored by disaster in Linz. This historic city, close to the Monastery of St. Florian, where Bruckner had been organist, has a gem among modern concert halls, the Brucknerhaus. We arrived to murmurs of a "poor house," and as the hour of the concert approached it became clear that nothing had been done to promote our event, and that only nine tickets had been sold! The only thing to do was to scrub the concert; but not wanting the Orchestra to miss a chance to play in that beautiful hall, I sent them on for a "rehearsal." We ended with our co-concertmaster playing some unaccompanied

Bach for her relatives who had driven from Salzburg. The nine ticket holders were refunded their money, and invited to listen to our rehearsal. We then cleared the stage before 8:00 P.M. and were able to avoid paying rent for the hall. Can't win 'em all!

The last concert of the Tour was in Rijeka, formerly an Italian city called Fiume. Set in the northern arc of the Adriatic Sea, it is a city of palm trees and Italianate architecture, the most typical example of which is the Opera House, where we played. Essentially cylindrical, with five tiers of boxes, that jewelled house almost seemed as though *it* were the stage set.

The Beethoven *Fifth Symphony* had been scheduled for this concert, but the Orchestra, having been deprived of its final go at the Shostakovitch *Fifth* in Linz, asked to do it here. This change from the printed program had to be announced. I counted on Zoran to do this, but he had come in casual clothes and pressed me to do it myself. As I pondered backstage, one of our guides passed by, and in a trice I had him coach me in a few sentences of Serbo-Croatian, which I did not find too hard since it resembles Russian, which I know in a homespun way. When I faced the audience and began, *"Dobar vecha,"* they practically cheered, and when I went on with my four sentences, the Orchestra almost slid off their chairs in astonishment. Needless to say, the concert went on to succeed splendidly, a great finale to the Tour. It was topped off by a party where we were entertained by folk dancing, in which we all joined.

Opera House, Rijeka, Yugoslavia.

The reviews of the concerts given on this Tour are included this collection: they testify to the warmth of our reception and show how the Orchestra rates on an international standard.

Back home, we returned to the idea of a double orchestra and organized our alumni into a group of 100, and with the PYP, 200 strong, we presented the grand Bruckner *Seventh Symphony* in a performance that was remarkable not just for its power, to be expected, but also for the nimble lightness where needed.

The 1983–84 season seemed impossible to top, but each year has a way of bringing something special, and the **61st Season,** 1984–85, started with a dedication of the rebuilt Paramount Theatre as the Arlene Schnitzer Concert Hall. This renewal was done by the architectural firm of Broome, Oringdulph, O'Toole, Rudolph and Associates. As it happened, they were celebrating *their* 25th year and invited us to do a concert for them and their constituency in the remodeled hall. The Orchestra, still exhilarated by their Tour of the previous spring, rose to new heights with the Sibelius *Second Symphony* in November and the Ravel *Daphnis and Chloe* in May.

Between those events came another form of community outreach. We joined the Choir of Trinity Episcopal Church, directed by John Strege, and gave the beautiful Dvořák *Mass in D,* seldom heard in Portland. For this we selected an orchestra of 40, to balance the Choir, and our players had the meaningful experience of presenting a religious work in a house of worship to its own congregation—quite different from doing it in a concert hall.

This collaboration with Trinity's Choir continued in 1985–86, the **62nd Season,** when we did the Haydn *Mass in Time of War.* Another choral piece, given at the Winter Concert, with full orchestra, was the Berlioz *Lelio.* The three major choruses, rarely heard, are full of vigor and fantasy, especially the one based on *The Tempest.*

That August brought us our widest outreach of all: The Waterfront Classics concert at Tom McCall Riverside Park. This series, sponsored by KOIN-TV, U.S. Bank, and other corporations in other years, draws a light-hearted audience of thousands (10,000 was the estimate that year). While the electronic sound amplification leaves much to be desired, the event nonetheless brings many citizens, often for the first time, within earshot of classical music in the casual setting of their picnics.

The **63rd Season,** 1986–87, opened with a heartfelt gesture to an 82-year-old benefactress of the Orchestra, Ludmilla Schlesinger. We played the overture to Glinka's *Russian and Ludmilla* to this modest lady who had been so generous to our scholarship fund; and a commemorative scroll was presented to her at her seat in the Hall.

The Season's programs introduced Portlanders to two unfamiliar works: the Bartok *Suite No. 1,* in anticipation of a tour to Hungary (postponed because of heightened terrorist activity worldwide), and the *Symphony No. 4* by Franz

Schmidt. Until 1984 I had not only never seen this wonderful piece, I had never known of the composer. During a short sabbatical the previous spring I did a little research in Vienna, where my way was smoothed by musicologist and longtime Portland friend, Reinhard Pauly. The preparation and performance of this masterpiece proved to be one of the most gratifying experiences of my career.

One of our initiatives for the canceled tour was to contact the U.S. Information Service. To get their endorsement we had to submit recordings to the National Arts Endowment's orchestral panel for their evaluation of our work. Their letter of review, which is most gratifying to us all, is printed in the following section.

The **64th Season,** 1987–88, was preceded by our second Waterfront Classics Concert. Having learned that the spring sign-up for the Orchestra worked, we had much less concern about bringing off this event. The crowd was estimated this time at 22,000. It's hard to know how accurate such figures are, but from the podium I did see acres of people—happily settled on their blankets and cheering us on.

A second pre-season event was the premiere of my suite, *Up At Timberline,* written to celebrate the 50th Anniversary of the famous Lodge which had been dedicated by Franklin D. Roosevelt in 1935. I wrote the piece for 16 players—wind, brass, percussion, and string bass—who performed antiphonally at the Lodge under hair-raising conditions, but with good success.

The season proper brought back to our platform the Florestan Trio, whom we had helped introduce to Portland a decade earlier when they came to Portland State University. They played, naturally, the Beethoven *Triple Concerto.* Now fully established here, the members of the Trio—Carol Swindell, Hamilton Cheiftez, and Harold Gray—have proven themselves not only as performers but also as dedicated and effective teachers with whom a number of the Orchestra members study.

The Winter Concert was eventful in more than one way. The previous spring at our Baroque Ball, the auction included a chance to conduct a piece at a concert. As luck had it, the winner was the father of an alumna, Danette Warren, who had played first violin and was now studying conducting in Houston. Danette came home to conduct the Alfven *Midsommarvaka,* and did it very deftly. Later in the program, Jonathon Talbott, playing the Ravel *Tzigane,* and doing splendidly, broke a string, swapped violins with the concertmaster in the classic manner, and then went on to break a second string! I was able to "vamp" two extra bars until he could continue, and we concluded without a break in step.

Finally, in April we did the Portland premiere of the Delius *Appalachia.* For this we invited the Trinity Choir to our premises; we concluded with a blazing performance of the Dvorák *Symphony from the New World* which we carried to the Old World the following season.

Thus we are brought back to the point at which this book began—the 65th Anniversary Season.

Sharing appreciation with the Orchestra in Graz.

A Waterfront Classics concert.

Programs
&
Reviews

57th Through 64th Season

57th Season

Jacob Avshalomov, Conductor

November 22, 1980

BEETHOVEN	Symphony NO.3, OP.55, "Eroica"
SHOSTAKOVITCH	Piano Concerto NO.1, OP.35
	Christina Haan, *Soloist*
	Steve Conrow, *Trumpet Obbligato*
BRITTEN	Young Person's Guide to the Orchestra

December 26, 1980

19th Annual Concert at Christmas

Seasonal Music, Carol Singing,
& The Preparatory Orchestra

February 28, 1981

BRAHMS	Symphony NO.1, C minor, OP.68
MOZART	Clarinet Concerto, A major, K.622
	Brad Butterfield, *Soloist*
STRAVINSKY	The Rite of Spring

April 18, 1981

VERDI Requiem

JoAnn Ottley, *Soprano;* Alyce Rogers, *Mezzo-Soprano;*
Bruce Browne, *Tenor;* Jon Enloe, *Bass*

Guest Choirs: Oregon College of Education, Pacific University, Portland State University, & Reed College

---

June 6, 1981

SPOLETO/U.S.A. FESTIVAL

Charleston, South Carolina

BRAHMS	Symphony NO.1, C minor, OP.168
STRAVINSKY	The Rite of Spring

OREGON JOURNAL NOV. 24, 1980

Youth ensemble opens season

By MARTIN CLARK
Journal Music Editor

The Portland Youth Philharmonic opened its 57th season with an impressive program in the Civic Auditorium Saturday evening under the direction of the orchestra's music director, Jacob Avshalomov.

At the conclusion of the first movement of Beethoven's ("Eroica") Symphony No. 3, Avshalomov stepped to the microphone and announced that the second movement of the symphony would be dedicated to the memory of Robert Blanchard, former Portland school superintendent, who died recently.

The famous youth orchestra—under the gentle but persistent persuasion of Avshalomov—captured the majestic nature of the lament, the violins introducing the death theme against throbbing surges of anguish in the basses.

Christina Haan, winner of the 52nd annual contest held by the Portland Junior Symphony Association, was featured as soloist in the Shostakovich Concerto for Piano, Trumpet and String Orchestra. She is a student of Darlene Cusick, herself a winner and soloist with the orchestra in her student days.

It's a tricky piece for piano and trumpet, but Christina Haan had the accuracy and sparkling vitality to carry it off superbly, technically and interpretively. Happily, trumpeter Steve Conrow proved an able collaborator. The concerto drew a rousing ovation.

THE OREGONIAN NOV. 23 1980

Philharmonic features winner

By ROBERT LINDSTROM
of The Oregonian staff

The winner of the Portland Junior Symphony Association's 52nd annual soloist competition appeared at the season premier of the Portland Youth Philharmonic, Jacob Avshalomov conducting, Saturday in Civic Auditorium.

Christina Hahn, 20, performed Shostakovich's Piano Concerto No. 1. The pianist is a junior studying music at Portland State University. A former resident of The Dalles, Miss Hahn is presently a piano student of Darlene Cusick who was, herself, winner of the association's competition in 1960.

The work requires pinpoint technical accuracy from the piano soloist and from the solo trumpet player who is given a challenging but rewarding obligato part.

Miss Hahn provided the expected degree of precision as well as an unexpected understanding of the charm of the score.

Steve Conrow was the accomplished trumpet soloist. The strings of the orchestra provided solid accompaniment.

THE OREGONIAN FEB. 29, 1981

Young musicians excel in Brahms, Stravinsky

By ROBERT LINDSTROM
of The Oregonian staff

Even a professional orchestra might reasonably shy away from a concert which included Brahms' Symphony No. 1, a musical monument of the 19th century, and Stravinsky's "The Rite of Spring," a pinnacle of the 20th-century repertoire.

The Portland Youth Philharmonic under the baton of Jacob Avshalomov courageously tackled just such a program Saturday in Civic Auditorium. Though each of the two scores is fraught with profound technical and interpretive challenges, the ensemble turned the difficulties into a show of strength.

The orchestra was in form for this concert. Obvious careful preparation and the anticipation of visits to the Spoleto USA Festival in Charleston, S.C., and concerts in Washington, D.C., inspired precociously accomplished performances.

A musical tether between theses two creative peaks was Mozart's Clarinet Concerto. Brad Butterfield, principal clarinetist of the orchestra, was the first-rate soloist.

But it was in the two major works that the 100-plus membership of the orchestra excelled.

While the young musicians could bring only limited maturity to Brahms' First Symphony, they brought a wealth of enthusiasm and musical skill. The timbre had an authentic Brahmsian sound and climaxes were built with power.

Breadth is not an issue in Stravinsky's "The Rite of Spring," and in this work the orchestra provided a full measure of precision and clarity.

Hearing such a performance from primarily teen-age players, one marveled at the progress which instrumental virtuosity has made in this century. At one time professional musicians considered Stravinsky's daring ballet virtually unplayable.

Now musicians seem to begin lisp its tunes from the cradle and proba with more understanding and accur than was possible a mere 68 years a at its riotous Paris premier.

The artwork of Portland St University students depicting vari scenes of the ballet was attractive a added decoration, but nothing mo The Portland Youth Philharmo covered virtually all the signific points in its musical performance.

OREGON JOURNAL MAR. 1, 1981

Youth orchestra plays 'big' ones

They played a couple of the big ones Saturday night in the Civic Auditorium. According to Jacob Avshalomov, conductor and music director of the Portland Youth Philharmonic, the concert presented "the pinnacle of the orchestra's 57-year history."

That sounds like an accurate summation when you consider that the program included the Brahms First Symphony and the Stravinsky "Rite of Spring," never before performed by the ensemble,plus the Mozart Clarinet Concerto in A Major, K622, which was played by the orchestra more than 30 years ago.

To end the suspense: Yes, they brought it off. And no mean feat that is.

Brad Butterfield, principal clarinet in the orchestra, was the soloist in the Mozart concerto. You would have thought he played concertos in the Auditorium every week of the year. It takes a confidence born of a sure technique and a thoroughly grooved in performance to come up with this kind of playing. Not only did he have excellent intonation throughout, but he had that—marvel of marvels—a genuine legato. To top it off, he captured most of the subtle nuances of the interpretation.

YOUNG BUTTERFIELD WAS CALLED back repeatedly by a wildly enthusiastic audience.

It's one of those musical ironies that compositions which demand the most in technique often reveal the least in the way of faulty execution. Igor Stravinsky's "Le Sacre du Printemps" (The Rite of Spring) is a prime example. Mind you: Just getting the right notes at the right time with some sort of approximation of the observance of correct tempi and dynamics is a triumph for any youth orchestra.

THE PORTLAND YOUTH PHILHARMONIC, under Avshalomov's guidance, did this—which is a formidable accomplishment in itself. What is remarkable, however, is that it was sufficiently routined so that the drama of the piece was captured.

The irony referred to above is that the Brahms First, although technically not as demanding as the Stravinsky (or some other symphonies, including some other Brahms), because it is not nearly a work of such heavy texture it betrays the slightest flaw in performance. With this in mind, it is all the more impressive that the youth orchestra succeeded—with only minute flaws—in protecting the famed "soaring" qualities of the symphony and probing the justly vaunted soulful depths of one of the milestones in 19th century symphonic literature.

Lou Ocepek's summer class in illustration at Portland State University was asked to produce paintings to illustrate the action of the music. About 50 of the paintings were projected on a screen suspended above and slightly in front of the orchestra.

It was an interesting touch, but the performance would have been sufficient by itself to paint the pictures.

MARTIN CLARK

Young musicians master Requiem

By ROBERT LINDSTROM
of The Oregonian staff

The young age of most of the performers offered no reason for critical compromise Saturday in Civic Auditorium. The Portland Youth Philharmonic's version of Verdi's Requiem was a creditable performance by any standards.

Conductor Jacob Avshalomov led a comfortably paced interpretation that involved not only the members of the Youth Philharmonic but massed choirs from Oregon College of Education, Portland State University, Pacific University and Reed College.

Avshalomov mustered his performing forces with a minimum of fuss, garnering musical excitement with little physical strain.

Here as elsewhere the orchestra was dedicated and effective giving one of its most polished performances within memory.

In addition to the skillful contribution of the choristers, the presentation profited from the work of a quartet of talented soloists: soprano JoAnn Ottley, mezzo-soprano Alyce Rogers, tenor Bruce Browne and basso Jon Enloe.

All told, it was an interpretation that communicated the essential vigor and awe of Verdi's score and one that brought a fulfilling close to the Portland Youth Philharmonic's 57th season.

'Requiem' receives good treatment

By MARTIN CLARK
Journal Music Editor

Today we have such reverence for Verdi's "Manzoni Requiem" that many flinch at the mention of a performance of the great work by any organization less than a leading symphony with soloists drawn from the top of the roster of La Scala.

I had to admit Saturday night's performance by the Portland Youth Philharmonic came off in highly creditable fashion. Under Jacob Avshalomov's able direction the three components—chorus, soloists and orchestra—merged to provide good treatment for one of the most powerful compositions ever written.

It was a balanced quartet of soloists—soprano JoAnn Ottley, mezzo soprano Alyce Rogers, tenor Bruce Browne and bass Jon Enloe.

Ms. Rogers handling of the low tessitura was beautifully done, and the Ottley high pianissimi were just what Verdi ordered. Jon Enloe is that rarity in vocal quartets—one singing the bass line who has REAL bass notes in the nether region of the singer's range. He was a potent addition to the quartet. Having heard Bruce Browne only in some songs of a non-operatic nature, I was delighted when he met the Verdi demands, especially in the challenging "Ingemisco." That final high B Flat has been the downfall of many a tenor. Browne arrived in steely fashion—a little tight, perhaps, but absolutely secure.

The chorus for the occasion was drawn from the Oregon College of Education, Portland State University, Pacific University and Reed College. The members caught the Verdi Italian spirit with enthusiasm. The Verdi "Requiem" may not be as technically difficult as the "Rite of Spring," but believe me it's much more difficult musically. To resort to a cliche, "most orchestras can play it but few can play it well." The Portland Youth Philharmonic responded to Avshalomov's direction not only with accuracy but, equally if not more important, with musical perception and Italianate style.

The News and Courier
THE EVENING POST CHARLESTON, S.C., JUN. 7, 1981

Portland Youth Philharmonic Mature, And Accomplished

By
ELSA F.
McDOWELL

It's tempting to compare Jacob Avshalomov and the Portland Youth Philharmonic to a father leading adoring children, but the metaphor just doesn't work.

First, although the orchestra members are from 12 to 22 years of age, they play with the virtuosity of mature, accomplished musicians.

Second, no father has ever had such control over his children as Avshalomov had over the orchestra Saturday for the 5 p.m. performance at the Cathedral of St. Luke and St. Paul.

The orchestra gave an inspired performance of the Brahms First Symphony and a stirring performance of Stravinsky's "The Rite of Spring" that won them a standing ovation from the audience, and a personal salute from Spoleto Festival Founder Gian Carlo Menotti.

Those who might have been deterred by the orchestra's name, anticipating an amateurish program, missed a fine chance to see the embodiment of one of the Spoleto Festival' objectives—the discovery and encouragement of young musicians.

The Brahms, a familiar favorite, was played with passion and precision. The program notes explain that the work is technically not the most difficult of Brahms' symphonies, but "emotionally very demanding." The orchestra met the challenge with great success.

Throughout, the strings were smooth and unified, and the winds clear and clean. In the first movement, the brass section had a few ragged spots, however.

The entire work was taken a bit slower than expected, but was beautifully executed and didn't drag despite the slower tempo.

Janet Groh, concertmaster, gave a lovely, poignant solo performance during the Brahms second movement, and handled the high notes with ease and assurance.

Her performance proved the orchestra's stringent membership requirements—re-auditioning each season; weekly classes in music theory; weekly sectional and full rehearsals; and private lessons.

The Stravinsky, written by the composer when he was in his 30s, was bold and dramatic. The work, which caused a huge scandal when it premiered in Paris in 1913, was dynamic and moving. The orchestra handled the complex rhythms with competence.

THE OREGONIAN JUN. 1, 1981

Portland ensemble chosen for festival

By ROBERT LINDSTROM
of The Oregonian staff

It will be a memorable summer for four members of the Portland Youth Philharmonic and one former member who comprise the Portland Youth Philharmonic Brass Ensemble, who played last season during the orchestra's visit to the Spoleto Festival USA in Charleston, S.C.

Michael Stodd and Steven Conrow, trumpet; David Bryan, trombone; Dorothy Rusk, french horn; and Indiana University student and tuba player Michael Grose have been named the official brass quintet for the 17-day international festival.

The choice was personally approved by festival founder Gian Carlo Menotti, who was greatly impressed by the group's playing.

This is the first year that a student quintet has been chosen to represent Spoleto USA.

58th Season

Jacob Avshalomov, Conductor & Musical Director

November 21, 1981

WEBER	Overture: "Euryanthe"
BEETHOVEN	Piano Concerto NO.4, G major
	Maria Choban, *Soloist*
DUKAS	The Sorcerer's Apprentice
DEBUSSY	Afternoon of a Faun
RAVEL	Bolero

December 26, 1981

20th Annual Concert at Christmas

Seasonal Music, Carol Singing,

The Preparatory Orchestra,

P.S.U. Dancers: *The Company We Keep*

February 20, 1982

MARTIN	*Ballade for Flute, Strings & Piano
	Adrienne Inglis, *Soloist*
SCHUMANN	Symphony NO.2, C major, op.61
PROKOFIEV	"Alexander Nevsky" Cantata
	Christine Ross, *Mezzo-Soprano*

Guest Choirs: Oregon Repertory Singers, George Fox College Chorale

April 17, 1982

Tomas Svoboda, Guest Conductor Sabbatical Term

HAYDN	Symphony NO. 102, Bb major
SVOBODA	Sinfonietta alla Renaissance, op.60
ARUTUNIAN	Concerto for Trumpet
	Michael Stodd, *Soloist*
DVORAK	Slavonic Dances, NOS. 1, 5, 10, 8

* *Portland Premier*

Piano soloist exhibits artistic poise, clarity

By **ROBERT LINDSTROM**
of The Oregonian staff

A classical poise prevailed in the performances of Miss Choban, Avshalomov and the orchestra. Rather than dwelling on the dynamic potential of the score, the artists concentrated on the balance and craftsmanship of the work.

The controlled attitude toward the music did not dictate a retiring interpretation. Miss Choban had the digital clarity and strength to hold her own against Beethoven's ambitious orchestration and Avshalomov, and a reduced orchestra provided an unaffected view of the accompaniment.

Brass dominated a brisk version of the overture to Carl Maria von Weber's forgotten opera "Euryanthe." The string section was sometimes covered within the group texture. In the lighter moments of the piece, the strings produced a full, warm tone.

For the second half of the program, Avshalomov chose an ambitious trio of French orchestral showpiece: Claude Debussy's Prelude to "The Afternoon of A Faun," Maurice Ravel's "Bolero" and Paul Dukas' pictorial "The Sorcerer's Apprentice."

The student players aptly captured the pastel shades of these multicolored scores. At the same time, the well-known climactic moments of the Ravel and Dukas pieces were presented with the full measure of orchestral weight.

OREGON JOURNAL NOV. 23, 1981

Choban in Beethoven rated high

By **MARTIN CLARK**
Journal Music Editor

Portland Youth Philharmonic opened its 58th season Saturday evening at the Civic Auditorium with one of the most beautifully balanced programs it's presented in many seasons.

As has become a delightful custom of these concerts, we were treated to the pithy and humorous commentary of Maestro Avshalomov.

The orchestra was unusually well prepared for a first concert of the season.

While serving as a judge on a number of occasions, it's been my privilege to hear Maria Choban. Saturday night was a gratifying culmination of those auditions. She has the precision and technique of a real professional. The 20-year-old pianist, a junior at Reed College, is a pupil of Nellie Tholen.

59th Season

Jacob Avshalomov, Conductor

November 20, 1982

WAGNER	Prelude: "Die Meistersinger"
MOZART	Piano Concerto NO. 9, Eb, K.271
	Shaun Irelan, *Soloist*
BERGSMA	Chameleon Variations
DOHNANYI	Suite in F sharp minor

December 9, 1982

First Annual

SING-YOUR-OWN-MESSIAH

Civic Auditorium

December 26, 1982

21st Annual Concert at Christmas

Seasonal Music with Carol Singing

Preparatory Orchestra, Cline Otey *Conducting*

February 26, 1983

TCHAIKOVSKY *"The Maid of Orleans"

Alyce Rogers, *Mezzo-soprano;*

Bruce Brown, *Tenor;* James Terrell, *Baritone*

Guest Choirs: Portland State University & Western Oregon State College

---

April 23, 1983

COPLAND	El Salon Mexico
BARBER	Adagio for Strings
DIAMOND	Twittering Machine
REVUELTAS	Sensemaya
BERLIOZ	Symphonie Fantastique

With International Youth Orchestra Delegates

---

* *Portland Premier*

THE OREGONIAN APR. 24, 1983

International cast shades orchestra

By ROBERT LINDSTROM
of The Oregonian staff

The Portland Youth Philharmonic featured an all-star international cast for its final subscription concert of its 59th season Saturday in Civic Auditorium.

The orchestra and Jacob Avshalomov, conductor-musical director, were hosts to 29 delegates from youth orchestras around the world. The young musicians, who played as members of the Youth Philharmonic in Saturday's concert, came from locales as near as Berkeley, Calif., and as distant as Belgium.

Avshalomov assembled the first half of the program as a tribute to American composers, including the music of Aaron Copland, Samuel Barber, David Diamond and Silvestre Revueltas.

Copland's "El Salon Mexico" was composed in 1934 in of all places, Bemidji, Minn. The composition was inspired by a visit to Mexico in the early 1930s and was not completed until another trip to Mexico in 1936, when Copland finally undertook the orchestration of the work.

Copland captured the rhythms and slangs of Mexico in a work that constitutes a kind of drug store post card of Mexican folk music. The Youth Philharmonic bounced through the music in authentic style.

With Barber's sublime Adagio for Strings, Avshalomov and the orchestra gave one of their finest performances. The string sections produced a mature, rich sound, and Avshalomov moved the music along gracefully.

Professional orchestras can be intimidated by the problems of Hector Berlioz's Symphonie Fantastique. The Portland Youth Philharmonic's performance was a precocious wonder.

THE OREGONIAN NOV. 21, 1982

Review

By ROBERT LINDSTROM
of The Oregonian staff

Avshalomov is one of the few conductors to champion the music of Ernst von Dohnanyi, particularly his Suite in F-sharp Minor. The Portland Junior Symphony performed the score throughout Europe under Avshalomov some 12 years ago and repeated the forgotten masterwork at Saturday's concert.

Avshalomov treated the suite with affection and received a rich-sounding, expressive performance from the orchestra.

THE OREGONIAN FEB. 27, 1983

'Maid' wrecked by immature performances

By ROBERT LINDSTROM
of The Oregonian staff

The Portland Youth Philharmonic made a pyre out of Tchaikovsky's opera "The Maid of Orleans" and the composer burned Saturday in Civic Auditorium.

As always, Conductor-Musical Director Jacob Avshalomov and his young musicians reached beyond themselves to achieve a precocious success with the forgotten Joan of Arc opera. In this case, however, the difficulties of the score remained just outside their grasp.

The vocalists were all excellent, led by mezzo-soprano Alyce Rogers in the title role. The best pages of the opera are Joan's duets with the love interest, Lionel. Rogers and bass-baritone James Terrell sang nobly but were frequently inaudible beneath the overzealous orchestral accompaniment.

Like Terrell, tenor Bruce Brown doubled in several male roles and was in fine voice throughout the concert, projecting a full sound into the auditorium.

Avshalomov took a chance with this obscure opera. All involved made a serious effort, but Tchaikovsky's "Maid of Orleans" simply required more mature recruits.

THE OREGONIAN APR. 18, 1982

Trumpeter shines with Philharmonic

By ROBERT LINDSTROM
of The Oregonian staff

Trumpet soloist Michael R. Stodd was a crowd-pleaser in Soviet composer Alexander Arutunian's Concerto for Trumpet and Orchestra with the Portland Youth Philharmonic Saturday.

Interim Conductor Thomas Svoboda, filling in for Jacob Avshalomov while the musical director is on sabbatical, led the ensemble in the Civic Auditorium concert.

Supporting Stodd's excellence was a lively accompaniment by Svoboda and the orchestra. The musicians were totally committed to the neo-romantic excesses of the music, and the general enthusiasm of soloist and orchestra resulted in one of the youth orchestra's most appealing performances.

Svoboda, who is also a professor of music at Portland State University, opened the concert with a bracing, extroverted interpretation of Haydn's Symphony No. 102 in B-flat Major.

Sabbatical-term guest conductor Tomas Svoboda conducts his "Child's Dream".

THE OREGONIAN FEB. 12, 1982

Youth Philharmonic squeezes out drama

By ROBERT LINDSTROM
of The Oregonian staff

The Portland Youth Philharmonic wrung the drama from Sergei Prokofiev's film score cantata "Alexander Nevsky" Saturday in Civic Auditorium.

Prokoflev culled this symphonic cantata from his score to Einstein's 1938 film "Alexander Nevsky." Like most film music, this work makes few pretensions toward depth or substance. As impact is purely visceral. However, with the composer's garishly brilliant orchestration and sincere evocation of Russian folk music, "Nevsky" is a stunning orchestral and choral showpiece.

The term showpiece could also describe what the performers made of the cantata under the baton of Musical Director Jacob Avshalomov. The score called for large forces: a sizable mixed chorus, mezzo-soprano soloist and a huge orchestra, including the full brute force of the philharmonic's brass section.

Former Portland mezzo-soprano Christine Meadows Ross gave a good account of the brooding sixth movement "The Field of the Dead."

Prokofiev's glittering instrumentation suited the young players perfectly. As usual, the musicians surpassed expectations with a dedicated and ambitious performance.

In fact, the technically excellent student performance was surpassed by the excitement of "The Battle on the Ice." In the graphic musical depiction of a 13th century skirmish on a frozen lake, the young instrumentalists reached toward a level of intensity that would have done a professional orchestra proud.

OREGON JOURNAL FEB. 22, 1982

PYP's 'Nevsky'

By MARTIN CLARK
Journal Music Editor

THE PORTLAND YOUTH Philharmonic, under the direction of Jacob Avshalomov, opened its Saturday evening concert with the Swiss composer Frank Martin's Ballade for Flute, Strings & Piano, with Adrienne Inglis, PYP principal flutist, as soloist. It's a brief work, but tedious. However, it does require a first-rate soloist and Adrienne Inglis demonstrated she not only had the requisite technique but the musical insight to extract what little of value was there.

The Schumann Symphony No. 2 in C, Opus 61, which concluded the first half of the program, drew yeoman's service from the orchestra, but the entire first half was really only a preface for the big attraction of the evening, the Prokoflev "Alexander Nevsky" Cantata.

Actually, the cantata was one of the most thrilling performances ever given by the Portland Youth Philharmonic with choral participation.

60th Anniversary Season

Jacob Avshalomov, Conductor

November 19, 1983

BRAHMS Violin Concerto in D, op. 77
Marylou Speaker Churchill, *Soloist*

BORODIN Polovetsian Dances

CELEBRATING JACQUES GERSHKOVITCH'S
30 YEARS AS CONDUCTOR, 1924–1953

BEETHOVEN Symphony NO. 5

December 6, 1983

SING-YOUR-OWN-MESSIAH
Civic Auditorium

December 26, 1983
22nd Annual Concert at Christmas

ANDERSON Christmas Festival

HANDEL Overture: Messiah

VIVALDI Concerto for Four Violins
Delmar Pettys, John Weller, Valerie Poullette, Paula Sisson Francis

WEBER Concertino for Horn
Roger Kaza, *Soloist*

RAVEL Introduction & Allegro
Maria Casale, *Harp;* Carol Perala, *Flute;* Brad Butterfield, *Clarinet,*
Irene Gadeholt & Lynne Finch, *Violins;* Daniel Avshalomov, *Viola*
Martin Hanson, *Cello*

CHAVEZ Toccata for Percussion
In Memoriam John Markham

SCHEIDT Three Carols for Brass

All Sing: Angels We Have Heard On High

February 25, 1984

DUKAS Fanfare: "La Peri"

SCHUBERT Symphony NO. 8, B minor

AVSHALOMOV Praises from the Corners of the Earth
Lewis & Clark College Chorus, Oregon State University Chorus,
Portland State University Chamber Choir

March 11-26, 1984

THIRD INTERNATIONAL TOUR

Portland New York Belgrade

Novisad Zagreb Graz Rijeka

May 12, 1984

TCHAIKOVSKY	Romeo & Juliet
MILHAUD	Creation of the World *Combined Ensemble with Alumni*
BRUCKNER	Symphony NO. 7 *Current and Alumni Orchestras*

PORTLAND YOUTH PHILHARMONIC

FIRST VIOLIN

Ruth Sadilek
Concertmaster
Maria Schleuning
Associate
Shannon Wick
Marty Jennings
Cathy Girardeau
Leslie Gray
Dan McCormick
Paul Cheng
Ann Warton
Veronica Li
Mary Dakin
Patti Fry
Yin Kan Hwee
Andy Laird
Kristen Lee
Amy Ratzlaff
Todd Roy
Andrew Foley
Richard Fordyce
Shane Artis

SECOND VIOLIN

Judy Oringdulph
Principal
Suzie Segerstrom
Assistant
Rochelle Pearson
Julie Issac
Renee Hague
Karla Kan
Mike Lauderdale
Dorothy Blankenship
Jeff Muller
Jonathan Talbott
Margaret Richen
Ann Smith
Mimi Irlandez
Jean Cheng
Creagh Breuner
Pekio Vergotis
Ted Jossy
Jennifer Covert
Yukiko Simmons

VIOLA

Kim Lorati
Principal
Carol Mulder
Assistant
Linda Davies
John Leuthauser
Mary Li
Meghan Peddicord
Heidi Johnson
Elizabeth Casale
Christopher Naze
Janice Richards
Lisa Lee
Heather Johnson
Melinda Benson

CELLO

Robert Schlichting
Principal
Jeff Edens
Assistant
Lena Bonhorst
Lane Dahlke
Anne Neace
Leslie Jones
Christopher Hardt
Jason McComb
Kim Waitt
Laura Richardson
Julie Dunne
Drew Eckhard

BASS

Todd Larsen
Principal
Bill Mankin
John Landstrom
Alan Regnier
Vance Selover
Joy Hackett
Eric Johnson
Denise Dawson
Barry Newton

LIBRARIAN

David McDade

FLUTE

Alisa Cross (Picc.)
Principal
Hilari Allred
Kristen Gygi
Margaret Warton (Picc.)
Cathy Nichols

OBOE

Richard Olsen (E.H.)
Principal
Michelle Nelson (E.H.)
Ron Solomon
Helen Shin

CLARINET

Theresa Schumacher
Principal
Glenn Eppick
Dale Ryan (B. Cl.)
Richard Spece

BASSOON

Mary Ellen Harris
Principal
Sarah Peniston (C.F.)
John Flanery

HORN

David McDade
Principal
Doug Riggs
Laura VanFleet
Jay Sanders
Erik Peterson
Kevin Walczyk
Laura Smith

TRUMPET

Jeff Hornick
Michael Stodd
Principals
Ken Aikin
Doug Smith
Matt Swafford

TROMBONE

Peter Ellefson
Principal
Martha Brenneman
David Otey (B.)

TUBA

Mike Ferries

PERCUSSION

Fred Morgenstern
Principal
Jeffrey Peyton
Karl Blume
Scott Wallace

HARP

Leigh Stevens

PIANO & CELESTE

Mimi Irlandez

STAGE MANAGERS

Fred Morgenstern
Vance Selover
Richard Olsen

STAFF & ESCORTS

Patricia O. Schleuning
President
Elise Rosenfeld
60th Anniv. Chairman
Cline Otey
Asst. to the Conductor
Dr. Harvey Klevit
Tour Physician
Marilyn Couture
Tour Manager
Harriet Bonhorst
Orchestra Chairman
John Huisman
Mary Huisman
Ernestine Oringdulph
Edward Rosenfeld
Carol Shoemaker
Richard Talbott
William Webber
Maggie Webber
Jerry Baker
Photographer

60th Anniversary Season

Portland Youth Philharmonic

JACOB AVSHALOMOV
Conductor-Musical Director

Third International Tour

Honorary Sponsor – Leonard Bernstein

Gala Commencement
PORTLAND
Civic Auditorium

With New York Philharmonic
NEW YORK
Avery Fisher Hall

BELGRADE
Sava Center

GRAZ
Congress Hall

NOVISAD
Grand Serbian Theater

LINZ
Bruckner Hall

ZAGREB
Lisinski Theater

RIJEKA
Opera House

March 11-26, 1984

NOTES

The Portland Youth Philharmonic celebrates its history of sixty years with a full season of festive events, the most ambitious of which is its 3rd International Tour. Earlier trips, to Europe in 1970, to Japan in 1979 and to the Spoleto/USA Festival in Charleston, S.C. in 1981, convinced us that the educational benefits to our young players and the credit brought to our City, State and Nation make these Tours worth the considerable effort they require.

To begin the 3rd Tour in New York — at Avery Fisher Hall, playing together with the N.Y. Philharmonic, and under Leonard Bernstein — is a three-stage dream come true. The honor this betokens to our Orchestra and Association is thrilling to us all. The kindness and generosity shown by the N.Y. Philharmonic has been far beyond the bounds of reasonable hospitality coming from the good offices of Albert K. Webster and Daniel Windham and their staff. The effect of all this on our Orchestra can only be described as inspiring. We hope, for our part, to bring a measure of inspiration to the young people in the New York audience, and to their parents, by our zeal in making music.

We are delighted that the N.Y. Philharmonic would celebrate their sixtieth year of Youth-Concert-giving with us at the same anniversary of our founding by producing this evening's concert.

APPRECIATIONS

A Tour such as this depends on a great many people besides the performers. At the center of our efforts has been our dedicated Board of Directors, led by Patti Schleuning, President, and Elise Rosenfeld, Chairman of the 60th Anniversary Committee. Tour Manager, Marilyn Couture has done an outstanding job coordinating with the N.Y. Philharmonic and Cultural Omnibus, Inc.

In addition we wish to thank our hosts and sponsors in Yugoslavia and Austria for their enthusiastic support of our visits.

At home, friends of the Orchestra have assisted in many ways — with goods, services, time, thought and love.

This has all been done with the conviction that good relations between different peoples of the world are developed by meaningful exchanges in the realm of the spirit. Our young musicians are both the emissaries and the beneficiaries of the good will which we have all generated.

J.A.

NEW YORK
Avery Fisher Hall
Wednesday, March 14, 7:30 p.m.

60th Anniversary Celebration
with New York Philharmonic

Program

TCHAIKOVSKY
Dance of the Clowns

SCHUBERT
Symphony #8, Allegro moderato

AVSHALOMOV
The Glistening City

Portland Youth Philharmonic

MAHLER
Symphony #2, Andante al moto

New York Philharmonic

TCHAIKOVSKY
Romeo & Juliet

Both Orchestras conducted
by Leonard Bernstein

Sponsor: N.Y. Philharmonic
Educational Activities

BELGRADE
Sava Center
Saturday, March 18,

ZAGREB
Lisinski Theater
Tuesday, March 20

With Belgrade Youth Philharmonic
& Ivo Lola Riber Chorale

Program

COPLAND
El Salon Mexico

GERSHWIN
Porgy & Bess Suite

AVSHALOMOV
Praises from the
Corners of the Earth

SHOSTAKOVITCH
Symphony #5
Moderato
Allegretto
Largo
Allegro non troppo

Sponsor: Muzichke Omladina
Zoran Damnjanovic, Coordinator

NOVISAD
Grand Serbian Theater
Sunday, March 19

GRAZ
Congress Hall
Wednesday, March 21

RIJEKA
Opera House
Saturday, March 24

Program

DUKAS
Fanfare from 'La Peri'

SCHUBERT
Symphony #8

TCHAIKOVSKY
Romeo & Juliet

COPLAND
El Salon Mexico

BARBER
Adagio for Strings

DIAMOND
Twittering Machine

AVSHALOMOV
Glistening City

GERSHWIN
Porgy & Bess Suite

Sponsor: Muzichke Omladina
Sponsor: Institute for Music of Graz

Enthusiastic crowd stamps passport of Europe-bound youth orchestra

By ROBERT LINDSTROM
of The Oregonian staff

The Europe-bound Portland Youth Philharmonic gave a hometown preview Saturday of what they'll be taking to Austria and Yugoslavia next month. With performances as good as the ones heard in Civic Auditorium, Europe won't be disappointed.

Saturday's concert commemorated 60 years of the orchestra as the Portland Junior Symphony and the Portland Youth Philharmonic and paid tribute to Conductor-Musical Director Jacob Avshalomov's 30th anniversary with the ensemble.

Avshalomov's three-decade achievement suggests that, in addition to being the United States' oldest youth orchestra, the philharmonic also may hold a record for conductor tenures. In six decades, it has had only two conductors: Avshalomov, 64, and founder Jacques Gershkovich.

Several honors have accompanied the anniversary celebrations. On Feb. 14, Avshalomov and the orchestra were given a Governor's Arts Award. On Saturday, Portland Mayor Frank Ivancie declared Feb. 25 Portland Youth Philharmonic Day.

The reason for the accolades was evident during the concert. This was one of the orchestra's best. Obviously eager about their European tour, the musicians had prepared the scores with extraordinary care.

Following Paul Dukas' brief Fanfare from the ballet "La Peri," Avshalomov led the orchestra in a sturdy and thoughtful performance of Schubert's Symphony No. 8 "Unfinished."

Intonation, phrasing, instrumental balance—the fundamentals of this interpretation were solidly in place. Avshalomov's conducted with grace and momentum, sensitively shaping Schubert's extended melodies.

The rich tones in the Schubert and the precision displayed in Shostakovich's Symphony No. 5 revealed that the string sections were in top form. The opening movement of the Shostakovich Fifth is a prolonged tightwire act for the strings. Violins, violas, cellos and basses were sharply balanced on the composer's high notes and sudden climaxes.

The brass section, occasionally the over-loud bullies of the philharmonic, were submissive as needed, yet powerful when driving a grand climax to its conclusion.

The woodwinds tiptoed lightly through the rapid passages of second movement allegretto and brought pointed accuracy throughout the symphony.

Joining the philharmonic for Avshalomov's own "Praises from the Corners of the Earth" were the Lewis and Clark College Choir, the Portland State University Chamber Choir and the Oregon State University Chorus.

With those scores in their repertoire, Avshalomov and the Portland Youth Philharmonic will be first-class cultural ambassadors.

THE OREGONIAN NOV. 19, 1983

Youth orchestra offers homecoming

By ROBERT LINDSTROM
of The Oregonian staff

Former Portland Junior Symphony Concertmaster Marylou Speaker Churchill came home Saturday to open the Portland Youth Philharmonic's 60th anniversary season in Civic Auditorium.

Churchill, principal second violin with the Boston Symphony, was soloist in Brahms' Violin Concerto in D Major.

Churchill performed with the Junior Symphony for several years before leaving Portland to study at the New England Conservatory of Music under Joseph Silverstein. She is now a member of the faculty of the New England Conservatory Extension Division and a summer faculty member at the Berkshire Music Center at Tanglewood.

Supported by the sure conducting of Jacob Avshalomov, Churchill gave a mainstream interpretation of this cornerstone of the solo violin repertoire. After a few moments of unsettled intonation in the opening movement, her playing became secure.

The second movement, ably underscored by the orchestra, was confident and evenly phrased. Churchill molded the music with precision. Avshalomov's conducting reflected Churchill's traditional approach, and the musicians played with maturity.

This introduction to the orchestra's 60th season could have had no more familiar conclusion than Beethoven's Symphony No. 5.

Aside from a few uncertain rhythms in the first and third movements, the Youth Philharmonic and Avshalomov created a brisk, dynamic account of the symphony.

The second movement moved forward lightly and surely. The lively interpretation of the final movement brought the concert to an impressive close.

The Portland Youth Philharmonic Association announced Saturday a certificate that was to have been presented to the late Martin Clark, long-time music critic of the Portland Journal at this concert.

Presented by the board of directors and conductor of the philharmonic, the certificate saluted Clark, who died in August, and noted "His perennial enthusiasm, joined to his sympathetic understanding . . . have had a considerable effect on the appreciation which the orchestra has enjoyed in the community over the past two decades."

Music: 2 Anniversaries And Leonard Bernstein

SOMEBODY at the New York Philharmonic had a bright idea to celebrate the 60th anniversary of the orchestra's Young People's Concerts. The Portland Youth Philharmonic is the oldest youth orchestra in the country, and it, too, is celebrating its 60th anniversary this year. So the Oregon ensemble, on its way to a European tour, was invited to Avery Fisher Hall for a joint concert with the local Philharmonic Wednesday night.

First the Portland ensemble played three pieces on its own under its regular conductor, Jacob Avshalomov. Then Leonard Bernstein led the New Yorkers in the second movement of Mahler's "Resurrection" Symphony, and finally the two orchestras together, 210 musicians strong, charged through Tchaikovsky's "Romeo and Juliet" under Mr. Bernstein's enthusiastic leadership. It was a grand night, and the audience, full of parents and youngsters, seemed to enjoy it all.

No one better than Mr. Bernstein could have been chosen to officiate over this combination of young people playing and young people listening. Now white-haired with age, he seems rapidly on his way to becoming a revered grand master of the baton. But he still has that ebullient, youthful energy that distinguished his tenure as music director of the Philharmonic.

The Portland Youth Philharmonic consists of 100 musicians between the ages of 12 and 22. It made a big, bold, slightly coarse sound and delivered playing more notable for generalized vigor than special refinement. Still, the music-making was adept enough, and Mr. Avshalomov's interpretations were clear-cut and sensible.

After the "Dance of the Clowns" from Tchaikovsky's opera "The Maid of Orleans" and the first movement of Schubert's "Unfinished" Symphony, the Portland orchestra offered the fourth movement of Mr. Avshalomov's own symphony, "The Oregon" subtitled "The Glistening City." This proved to be an earnest, rather dated exercise in splashy orchestral display peppered with mild dissonance. Toward the end, appropriately enough, it worked in the "Happy Birthday" tune.

Mr. Bernstein, who had maintained a suitably avuncular demeanor for the Mahler, reverted excitingly to his foot-stamping youth for "Romeo and Juliet." The two orchestras were mixed together on a stage that extended six rows out over the regular seats. The sheer weight of orchestral tone, and the sheer volume of the combined forces (augmented, of course, by Fisher Hall's brilliant acoustics) made for as rousing a conclusion as one could have wished.

John Rockwell

Portland Youth Philharmonic. . . .

By ROBERT LINDSTROM
of The Oregonian staff

NEW YORK CITY—With one more encouragement to practice, an assurance that the performance would go well and a round of vigorous applause from the players, the conductor stepped off the podium and quickly disappeared backstage. The 100 musicians stole looks at one another as 90 minutes of tension turned to elation. Tuesday in Lincoln Center, the Portland Youth Philharmonic had met and rehearsed with Leonard Bernstein.

PYP Musical Director Jacob Avshalomov, a man with a gift for putting his young colleagues in prestigious places, brought off his biggest coup yet in arranging a joint concert with Bernstein and the New York Philharmonic, which took place Wednesday in Lincoln Center's Avery Fisher Hall.

By a fortunate coincidence, the PYP, the nation's oldest youth orchestra, was celebrating its 60th anniversary at the same time the NYP commemorated the 60th anniversary of its Young People's Concerts.

It was a perfect combination. At Wednesday's anniversary concert, both orchestras played separately and then joined for a massive account of Tchaikovsky's "Romeo and Juliet" Overture-Fantasy conducted by Bernstein.

The 100 members of the Youth Philharmonic, accompanied by several adult chaperones, left Portland Sunday and after one day to rest and see the sights, prepared for their first rehearsal with Bernstein Tuesday afternoon.

As the bundled instrumentalists found their way to the rehearsal, even a casual observer could see they were unaware of the snow and sleet that was making an unpleasant March in the city. Their minds were on other things. Would Bernstein be demanding? Would he like their playing? Would the tempos be too fast?

A few of the orchestra members had attended Bernstein's morning rehearsal with the New York Philharmonic. What they saw couldn't have been soothing.

"That's just stupid and lazy," barked Bernstein as the NYP's second violin section missed a simple entrance. "How many decades has it been since you've played this piece?" he asked rhetorically when "Romeo and Juliet" required more rehearsal than Bernstein had anticipated.

Discouraging words travel fast. Ten minutes

masters its lesson from the master

before the PYP's rehearsal was scheduled to begin, the young players were in their seats with Avshalomov waiting on the podium, anxiously glancing backstage. The instrumentalists stayed cool and expectant.

The serious nerves seemed to be concentrated among the chaperone-observers in the auditorium who were perched on the edge of their box seats.

Precisely at 1:30 p.m., Bernstein strode onstage to a round of spontaneous orchestral applause. Avshalomov put out his hand. Bernstein grabbed Avshalomov in a bear hug, spun him around and finished off the maneuver by planting a kiss on the top of Avshalomov's balding head.

Dressed in slacks and khaki jacket, Bernstein was ready for serious work, and after a short self-introduction ("You might have seen me on T.V."), he began rehearsing the PYP with the same dedication that he had shown the NYP that morning.

"Bassoon," he said, interrupting the introduction to "Romeo and Juliet," "You're between the two clarinets so you have to pick up something of the clarinet sound to get a blended tone from the section. And clarinets, watch the intonation. The bottom gets too low and the top gets too high." When the results were much improved, he smiled gratefully. "Very good, very nice."

As the session progressed, Bernstein grew more animated. With the NYP, he remained casual, seated on his conductor's stool, one hand often in his pocket. The younger players needed more urging. Little by little, Bernstein revealed the athletic podium style that made him famous, fists punching the air, body rocking from side to side.

He interrupted his dancing to comment on a misplaced rhythmic detail. "If American kids don't understand syncopation, who does?" he asked.

"They have the hard part here," he said later, gesturing toward the brass and percussion, "And they're doing it perfectly. All you have," he turned to the strings, "Are notes, a lot of notes. You're running away with them. It's insane, like a loony bin." Though Bernstein scowled, the remark got a faint smile from many string players, just as Bernstein knew it might.

An hour and a half passed and Bernstein prepared to do a final uninterrupted run-through before turning the rehearsal over to Avshalomov.

What followed wasn't perfect but it was magic. The PYP played with extraordinary dedication and commitment, spurred on by Bernstein's involved leadership.

"It will go well tomorrow," he concluded, "You'll be surprised . . . I'll be surprised."

He was right. The Tchaikovsky performance Wednesday was stunning, very likely one of the most remarkable sounds heard in Avery Fisher Hall for some time.

Avshalomov and the PYP began the program with a brisk performance of "Dance of the Clowns" from Tchaikovsky's little-known opera "The Maid of Orleans."

After a few introductory words from Roger Englander, long-time producer and director of the Young People's Concert telecasts, the PYP played the first movement from Schubert's "Unfinished" Symphony No. 8 and the fourth movement, entitled "The Glistening City," from Avshalomov's Symphony "The Oregon."

The Schubert went easily and effectively as it had during the hometown performance in Civic Auditorium. "The Glistening City," a dissonantly muddled score for which Avshalomov seems to have an unaccountable affection, didn't set well with the young audience members and was a poor showcase for the PYP.

It was "Romeo and Juliet" that truly climaxed the concert. With all 210 members of both orchestras assembled onstage, young musicians sharing the stands with their older counterparts, this chestnut had stunning impact. Winds, percussion and brass parts were all doubled producing a tidal wave of orchestral sound and the full complement of strings were brilliantly able to ride that wave.

With Bernstein commanding the podium in his most balletic style, the "Romeo and Juliet" was a smash hit that garnered a standing ovation and brought Bernstein back to the stage, and the orchestras to their feet many times.

No sooner had the PYP savored its triumph, however, briefly, it was time for the musicians to prepare to leave the country for a 10-day tour of Austria and Yugoslavia. For many of the orchestra members, the best moments, the most exciting moments were behind them.

Висок ниво музицирања

"Borba" Belgrade, April 3, 1984

A High Level of Music-Making

The concert of the Portland Youth Philharmonic (USA) in the Lisinski Concert Hall enraptured the audience and gave great encouragement to our young people devoted to classical music. The Orchestra, consisting of some 100 young men and women (age 12 to 22) was conducted by the skillful music master, Jacob Avshalomov; they played with the seriousness and precision of professional musicians with long years of experience.

The works of Copland, Barber, Gershwin and Shostakovitch's *Fifth Symphony* displayed the wondrous abilities of this orchestra which interpreted the various musical styles with ease. Enthusiastically applauding after each presentation, the audience regretted that we don't have an orchestra such as this.

K. Kovachevic

Нека нова, захвална публика

"Politika" Belgrade March 20, 1984

A New. Grateful Audience

The Sava Center was packed the day before yesterday (many even stood) at the concert of the Portland Youth Philharmonic. Judging by the response of the audience (over 4000, mostly young men and women) and the performance on stage—this was an extraordinary event in the musical life of Belgrade.

The young musicians (95 of them) and their conductor, Jacob Avshalomov, presented themselves with a professional, studious and successful performance of the Shostakovitch *Fifth Symphony* and shorter works by Barber and Copland. After each movement of the Symphony the hall resounded with applause. This was a sure sign that the piece and its performance found its way into the hearts of the listeners.

In the performance of Ravel's *Bolero* and Dvork's *Slavonic Dance #8,* the Portland philharmonists were joined by 116 members of the Youth Orchestra of Belgrade "Borislav Poscan", with their conductor Anton Kolar. Thus it was the largest orchestra that ever appeared in any Belgrade concert hall . . . and at the end this intercontinental integration of orchestras was greatly applauded.

THE OREGONIAN MAY 11, 1984

'Tis the season of the big concert

Music

Robert Lindstrom

For the Portland Youth Philharmonic, this is the year of the monster concert. Last March in New York City, the orchestra gave a joint concert with the New York Philharmonic in Lincoln Center. The climax of the evening was a collective playing of Tchaikovsky's "Romeo and Juliet" Overture-Fantasy conducted by Leonard Bernstein.

In Yugoslavia, the PYP appeared on the same stage with the Belgrade Youth Orchestra. More than 200 musicians comprised one huge symphony.

But they saved what may well be the best for last. To conclude the Philharmonic's 60th season as the oldest youth orchestra in the United States, Jacob Avshalomov will conduct 200 PYP members and former members in a spectacular reunion concert performance of Anton Bruckner's Symphony No. 7. This monster season-closer is heard at 8 p.m. Saturday in Civic Auditorium.

As the first U.S. musical ensemble ever to visit Yugoslavia, according to Avshalomov, the PYP attracted considerable attention including a televised press conference, banners hanging over city streets and an audience of over 4,000 in Belgrade's 3,700-seat Sava Center.

In Zagreb the orchestra "played in one of the most beautiful concert halls in Europe," Avshalomov said, though a bus driver with a poor sense of direction made the orchestra so late to the concert that there was barely time to get out of the bus and onto the stage before the downbeat. "The thing (that) really lit the kids up," added Avshalomov, "was the sound in the room."

The other memorable acoustics were in the Congress Hall in Graz, Austria, Avshalomov recalled. It was a renovated baroque hall with a small stage. "We only had four double-basses but there wouldn't have been room for more anyway. It was almost a church-like acoustic and it imposed a more leisurely tempo on Schubert's 'Unfinished' Symphony. I felt like I was bringing Schubert home." A few days later, a 31-hour airplane ride brought the PYP home.

THE OREGONIAN MAY 13, 1984

200 musicians give Bruckner depth, glow

By ROBERT LINDSTROM
of The Oregonian staff

Director Jacob Avshalomov chose Bruckner's Symphony No. 7 to conclude the 60th anniversary season of the Portland Youth Philharmonic Saturday in Civic Auditorium. This giant-sized performance included not only the 100 members of the youth orchestra but also 100 or more former members of the Philharmonic and the Portland Junior Symphony.

The symphony is one of Bruckner's most profound creations and a score whose epic proportions were enhanced by the doublings of a 200-plus member orchestra.

Avshalomov led a reverent interpretation, attentive to both the devotional and the rustic qualities of the music. He used his extra instrumental forces to add depth of sound to the volume. The opening string passages of the slow second movement glowed with warmth and body.

Also on the program was Tchaikovsky's "Romeo and Juliet" Overture-Fantasy performed by the current members of the PYP. This was the score that the orchestra performed in tandem with the New York Philharmonic last March in Lincoln Center. In the interim, Avshalomov and his musicians had improved even on that skillful performance.

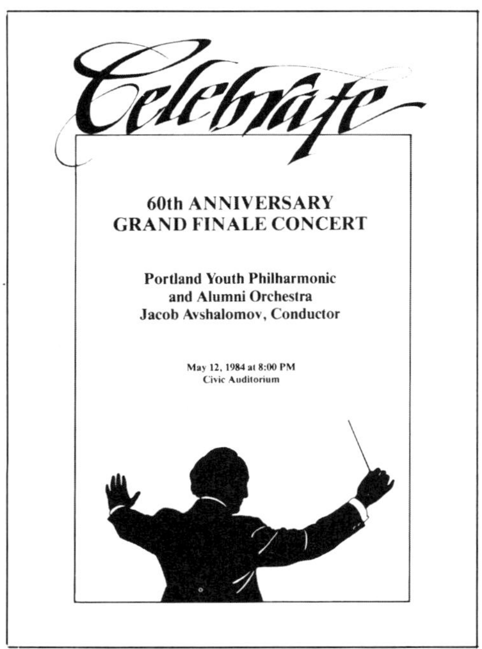

61st Season

Jacob Avshalomov, Conductor

May 4, 1985

SCHUBERT	Symphony NO. 9 in C
BROWN	Four by Three, NO. 3
BOCCHERINI	La Musica Notturno di Madrid
RAVEL	Daphnis & Chloe Suite NO. 2

March 18, 1985

Trinity Episcopal Church

VAUGHN-WILLIAMS	Fantasy on a Theme by Tallis
DVORAK	Mass in D

February 23, 1985

BERNSTEIN	Overture: "Candide"
IVES	The Unanswered Question
RUGGIERI	"if . . . then . . ."
FOSTER/LEYDEN	Medley of Songs
HOVHANESS	Fantasy on Japanese Woodcuts Jeff Peyton, *Marimba Soloist*
HUMMEL	Grand Concert for Bassoon Mary Ellen Harris, *Soloist*
KODALY	*Concerto for Orchestra

December 26, 1984

23rd Annual Concert at Christmas

December 7, 1984

SING-YOUR-OWN-MESSIAH

Civic Auditorium

November 27, 1984

GOULD	*Vivaldi Gallery
SCHUMANN	Piano Concerto, A minor Christina Su, *Soloist*
SIBELIUS	Symphony NO. 2, D major

* *Portland Premier*

THE OREGONIAN MAY 5, 1985

Final concert dazzling by Youth Philharmonic

By PHIL HUNT
of The Oregonian staff

In their final concert of the 1984–85 season the Portland Youth Philharmonic tackled Ravel's difficult and dazzling "Daphnis and Chloe Suite No. 2," and the orchestra came out the winner in an exciting finish to an evening of lush sounds and delightful music.

Conductor and musical director Jacob Avshalomov led his young players—105 of them—through the intricacies of the score, which gives an exceptional workout to all of the strings and woodwinds, with the brass and percussion sections not far behind. Flute principal Alisa Cross and concertmaster Ruth Sadilek both had the light touch to their solo parts in a performance that brought the full Ravel flavor to the fore.

Another highlight of the evening was Luigi Boccherini's "La Musica Notturno di Madrid," a light-hearted travelogue of the Spanish capital. Boccherini was a cellist, and in this number, which is for strings only (plus a snare drum), he had the cello section pick up their instruments and place them across the lap for strumming, guitar style. When there are 12 cellos doing this, the results are impressive.

The first half of the program was devoted exclusively to Franz Schubert's Symphony No. 9 in C. While it has many endearing qualities, such as melodic themes, sonorous trombones and French horns, and lovely woodwind runs and trills, the strings were a little overpowering.

Nevertheless, the vigorous third movement and the tension-filled fourth movement gave the orchestra an opportunity to show why this youth ensemble has won international acclaim for its performances.

THE OREGONIAN FEB. 24, 1985

Youth Philharmonic hits patriotic chord

By MARK MANDEL
of The Oregonian staff

Only a composer and enthusiastic proponent of modern music could have dared such bold programming.

The first tip-off that it would be an unusual evening in Arlene Schnitzer Concert Hall came long ago when the Youth Philharmonic's music committee chose a mallet percussionist and a bassoon player to appear as soloists with the orchestra.

Jeff Peyton, percussion principal, was superb on marimba—in a more demanding solo part than many concertos have—in the Fantasy on Japanese Woodcuts by Alan Hovhaness. His varied dynamics triumphed over Schnitzer Hall acoustics that do not enhance instruments of the pipe-resonating kind.

The bravura final section, with Peyton's prestissimo playing against the martial backdrop of his percussion cohorts, was a tour de force that drew bravos from the audience. Some of the cheering might have been for the composer, who maintains oriental flavoring through frequent use of the pentatonic scale.

The Bernstein not only was rousing but beautiful in its lyrical middle part based on "Oh Happy We," where the orchestra's fine string section played with great warmth; here the hall acoustics helped.

The strings glowed, too, in "The Unanswered Question," where they represent silence and the only answer to the question (What is the meaning of life?) propagated by Ken Aiken's flawless, off-stage trumpet solo. The woodwinds, which try to articulate a more meaningful answer, were effectively placed in the stage balcony.

THE LINFIELD REVIEW

Vol V, No. xv   Here's Harmony! Here's Repose!--Jane Austen   April 22, 1985

PYP'S MR. A

It's Wednesday evening again, 6:30 in the Glencoe School. From all over the metropolitan area 100 young musicians have come to rehearse in a grade-school cafeteria on Portland's east side, hard by Mt. Tabor. Jacob Avshalomov, once diving champion of his native northern China, emerges from his "office," the school nurse's station, and mounts the podium for a lesson in Sibelius, now just two weeks before the November concert. The orchestra responds to Mr. A's baton as a single committed being, probably exceeding in sound and interpretive acumen the sum of its talents. They are devoted to him and he to them: "Good rehearsal, my dears," he will say at 8:15, but that's time ahead of time. For the present: "Look up! The last bar has no additional information for you. I have the information locked up in my broken little wand."

The rehearsal is punctuated with constructive patter, talk of literature, trivia of musical history, art, notes on phrasing, bowing changes, geography ("Finest string section west of the Alleghenies--who knows where the Alleghenies are? No one? NO ONE? That's an assignment for next time!"), puns, opera, fashion, popular culture, unpopular culture. Some players wear T-shirts proclaiming fealty to one rock station or another, but in this, Mr. A's 31st year of directing the orchestra, they are all his, and they've come to conjure forth the spirit of the enigmatic bald Finn behind the Second Symphony. ". . .and the rhythm, the rhy-thm, the rhy-th-m, now dim. . . dee dee dee dee doo doo doo dooo--pump! Pump, celli, now dim. The truth is elsewhere than in the notes, my friends, and you're finding it. Resident orchestra--you've heard of it? Called the Portland Youth Philharmonic. Ssss! Ssss! Disappear! Do it now without my cheerleading. Hear it directly from Sibelius. . . .Now, celli, hit it! That's it! Easy, basses. Dee, dee, dee, now lift--fly! Rhythm! And a-one, good, good."

Twice a week they meet, to learn patience, devotion, tenacity, honesty, commitment, sensitivity, responsibility, responsiveness. About 5 percent go on as professional musicians. "I'm not training you to be professionals--I'm training you for life." Somehow we must all be artists. and Mr. A makes their Lehrjahre his business, before the Wanderjahre must begin. "Please write in an accelerando at the third bar of O. That's a tenuto, 'held back,' tenacious, 'holding on.'" The tension in the long pizzicato passage makes our eyes tear; do these kids really know how lucky they are? "Pizz! Pizz! Didn't you ever want to stamp your feet at someone?" (Stamps on floor) "Never mind--we'll get another one. . . .Sibelius, not Leroy Anderson's plink-plank-plunk. . . .Clarinets, I don't think I ever promised you anything, but violas are on your side. Sticky A's. and sep-a-rate that third beat. Patience, violins, your turn will come. . . .Sticky! Sticky! Frisk that last A! Once more at letter M, for Miserable."

Last year, during the orchestra's tour of Yugoslavia, someone asked Mr. A who the most talented players were. He refused to say. What father could single out one child above the others? "Move it, move it! Con moto! Don't be late moving, famous Aspen students (shall remain nameless). Russ, don't run out of bow. Letter N, for Nearly."

Occasionally his comments to the group are in Russian, the language he often spoke with his father. Last year he delighted in speaking Chinese with one of the players. Many would trade a limb for his command of English. "Two before C, as in Catch as Catch Can. Come on, you guys; Truth, truth--getting closer to Christmas every day--doo--doo--pom-pom. Patience, patience--Now firsts! Firsts! Keep it going, keep-it-going, ke-ep-it-go-ing." I have learned more about teaching from watching Mr. A than from practicing my own trade. Wise and fortunate Linfield, that awarded him an honorary degree some years ago. . . . "Martha! Don't let him loose like that--cage him up!" "This isn't meringue flim-flam, those 32nds are a part of the symphonic fabric. I want it better than the Philadelphia. It's already better than the Pittsburgh.. . . .Woops! We'll wait 'til Dominic finishes his yawning. Got it out of your system? . . .Tympani hold, now float--float. . ." The final concert is on Saturday, May 4, in the Schnitzer on Broadway. Do your soul a favor, folks.

PNR

62nd Season

Jacob Avshalomov, Musical Director

April 26, 1986
Eugene Kaza, Guest Conductor
Sabbatical Term

BACH	Toccata & Fugue, D minor
SAINT-SAENS	Violin Concerto NO. 3, B minor Emma Shook, *Soloist*
BRAHMS	Symphony NO. 4, E minor

March 15, 1986—5 p.m.
Jacob Avshalomov, Conductor
Trinity Episcopal Church

HAYDN	Mass in Time of War

March 1, 1986

ROSSINI	Overture: "Barber of Seville"
BERLIOZ	*Fantastical Choruses from "Lelio"

Linn Benton Community College, Portland State and Willamette Universities, Guest Choirs

TCHAIKOVSKY	Symphony NO. 5

December 26, 1985
24th Annual Concert at Christmas

Music of the Season, with Carol Singing,
The Preparatory Orchestra, Eugene Kaza *conducting*

PROKOFIEV	Peter & the Wolf
SURINACH	*The Trumpet of the Seraphim

November 23, 1985

MOZART	Overture: "Don Giovanni"
PACHELBEL	Magnificat, Fugue NO. 1
MENDELSSOHN	Symphony NO. 4
DOHNANYI	Variations on a Nursery Tune Edwin V. Le Barron, Jr., *Pianist*
KHATCHATURIAN	Dances from Ballet "Gayeneh"

*Portland Premier

THE OREGONIAN APR. 27, 1986

Young violinist shows sterling tone, stamina

MUSIC Robert Lindstrom

A confident Emma Shook, 15-year-old winner of the 1985–86 Portland Youth Philharmonic solo competition, appeared Saturday with the orchestra in a performance of Camille Saint-Saens' Violin Concerto in B Minor.

On the podium for the concert in Arlene Schnitzer Concert Hall was Portland violinist-conductor-teacher Eugene Kaza, who assumed leadership of the orchestra during Musical Director Jacob Avshalomov's sabbatical.

In the virtuoso challenges of the Saint-Saens concerto, Shook displayed a sterling tone in the upper range of the instrument and the stamina to bring the score to a forceful conclusion. Her precocious technique carried her through every difficulty of the score.

Kaza, a violinist himself, and the orchestra supported Shook at every turn, providing an accompaniment that reinforced yet never overwhelmed the soloist

Portland Youth Philharmonic
Conductor .... Eugene Kaza
Soloist ...... Emma Shook, violin
Playing.............. Saturday in Arlene Schnitzer Concert Hall

He opened the concert with a grandly conceived interpretation of Leopold Stokowski's romantic orchestration of J. S. Bach's Toccata and Fugue in D Minor. Stokowski didn't spare the horsepower in his instrumentation and neither did Kaza, eliciting a hefty string sound and dramatic phrasing.

THE OREGONIAN MAR. 2, 1986

Berlioz highlights youth concert

By ROBERT LINDSTROM
of The Oregonian staff

The Portland Youth Philharmonic is recognized by almost everyone as a beneficial asset for this city's young musicians. The early training and experience that student musicians receive in the PYP under Musical Director Jacob Avshalomov is invaluable whether the student intends a professional musical career or just wants to enjoy playing in an orchestra.

Not as frequently recognized is the role the orchestra consistently has played in introducing new works to Portland audiences. Avshalomov repeatedly has had the foresight and daring to take on projects with considerable musical value but considerably less box office appeal.

Hector Berlioz' "Lelio," the adventurous item on the program Saturday in Arlene Schnitzer Concert Hall, certainly qualifies. Under Avshalomov's lively leadership, all concerned made an overwhelmingly positive statement on behalf of, at least, these portions of the complete score.

Of special value was the PYP's vivid interpretation of the fantasia on "The Tempest." Stunningly and inventively orchestrated, the 14-minute work was a reminder of Berlioz' admiration for Shakespeare and made the listener wish that Berlioz had set "The Tempest" as an opera.

For those not interested in repertoire novelties, the PYP offered a bright account of Giacomo Rossini's "The Barber of Seville" Overture and a resonant, exciting version of Peter Tchaikovsky's Symphony No. 5 that must rank with the youth ensemble's most involving performances.

63rd Season

Jacob Avshalomov, Conductor

August 26, 1987

WATERFRONT CLASSICS

Retrospective Program from the Season

May 10, 1987

Reed College 75th Anniversary Concert

Retrospective Program from the Season

May 4, 1987

Coliseum

Montessori School Children's Fair

April 25, 1987

BRAHMS	Academic Festival Overture
HINDEMITH	Nobilissima Visione
MOZART	Mass in C minor, K.427

Bonnie Hensley, Barbara Custer, *Sopranos*; Kevin Skiles, *Tenor;* James Terrill, *Bass; Guest Choirs:* Western Oregon State College, Lewis and Clarke College & Community Chorale

---

March 15, 1987

Trinity Episcopal Church

BRITTEN	Rejoice in the Lamb
BACH	Cantata NO. 39 "Brich dem Hungrigen dein Brot"

February 28, 1987

REZNICEK	Overture: "Donna Diana"
FRANZ SCHMIDT	*Symphony NO. 4
IBERT	Concerto da Camera Eric Lindburg, *Saxophone Soloist*
FALLA	El Amor Brujo

December 5, 1986

5th Anniversary

SING-YOUR-OWN-MESSIAH

Civic Auditorium

	November 22, 1986
GLINKA	Overture: "Ruslan & Liudmilla"
BEETHOVEN	Symphony No. 7, A major, op. 92
WEBER	Concertstueck for Piano, op. 79
	Gita Karasik, *Soloist*
BARTOK	*Suite No. 1

* *Portland Premier*

Sketch of Jacob Avshalomov by Concertmaster Frieda Fehrenbacher.

Youth Philharmonic's season off to grand start

David Stabler

Despite a rain, dreary evening, a large and enthusiastic crowd turned out Saturday night for the season's opener of the Portland Youth Philharmonic. If any proof were needed of the philharmonic's place in this city's affections, such a crowd provided it.

There's something quite moving in watching this group of young people play with such excitement and commitment under the baton of the silver-haired maestro. Certainly, the program was well-chosen to demonstrate the group's strengths as an ensemble.

To begin with, there was Glinka's rowdy overture to the seldom performed opera "Ruslan and Ludmilla." Avshalomov has a great deal of confidence in his players. He lets them play without any badgering from the podium.

There are some great moments in the overture in which the lower strings have a noble-sounding theme. Instead of urging them over every note. Avshalomov simply opened the door and let them walk through. The result was delightful and engaging.

The emotional centerpiece of the concert was Beethoven's Symphony No. 7 in A Major, a huge work, full of detail and complexity for any orchestra. The Portland Youth Philharmonic did justice to the work.

The slow introduction to the first movement, which others have described as sounding like a forest just waking up, gave way, with just the right amount of tension, to the galloping Vivace section. Oboist Katherine E. Panaretos delivered some lickity-split playing.

For rhythmic intensity, the orchestra couldn't be beat in the second, mournful movement.

The concert closed with Bartok's Suite No.1, written when the composer was in his 20s. There was much to like about this performance, especially the playing of the violin sections. Concertmistress Ann Warton is terrific to watch. She sits up straight and has a wonderful bow arm and an energetic way of playing.

The music sounded well-rehearsed and incisive. The shifting rhythms were clearly articulated.

THE OREGONIAN DEC. 7, 1986

Conductor keeps sing-along 'Messiah' on track

As individuals and in groups they marched into the seats of Civic Auditorium Friday. With scores in hand, minds set and throats readied, they mustered themselves for the coming challenge. Their assignment? Sing-Your-Own-Messiah.

For the fourth year, a full house of

MUSIC

Robert Lindstrom

music enthusiasts joined conductor Jacob Avshalomov and the Portland Youth Philharmonic for a do-it-yourself version of G. F. Handel's oratorio "Messiah."

Vocalists of all kinds basked under the bright television lights as KGW-TV taped the event for a Dec. 24 broadcast. A few of the participants were serious vocalists. Some of them were regulars with their church choirs. Still others rarely perform without the accompaniment of running water and the acoustic enhancement of ceramic tile. Yet when the orchestra rang out the stentorian chords of "And the glory of the Lord," all were choristers for an evening.

A fine quartet of soloists took responsibility for the arias and recitatives. Notable were Barbara Custer's powerful soprano and tenor Scott Tuomi's light but impressively flexible vocalism. Alto Kristina Burbank and basso Donald Mead also contributed informed and musicianly singing.

Though Avshalomov wisely opted for expansive tempos overall, in the faster choruses the conductor occasionally resembled a later-day Sisyphus trying to push his choral boulder uphill. Instinctively, large choruses tend to drag tempos, and this audience-choir was no exception. Remarkably, Avshalomov and his orchestra overcame those laggardly instincts, held the shifting counterpoint in order and kept the entire performance firmly on track.

(Franz Schmidt's Original Sketch)

THE OREGONIAN

Youth orchestra shines in powerful exhibition

By DAVID STABLER
of The Oregonian staff

The Portland Youth Philharmonic ended its subscription season on a high note Saturday night with a performance of Mozart's Great Mass in C Minor. The work which took up the second half of the concert, featured two different orchestras. Because the size of the Philharmonic—112 members—is too large to perform Mozart, Avshalomov divided the group roughly in two and had half play the first part and half play the second. Some first chair players kept their seats for the entire performance.

Soloists were Bonnie Hensley and Barbara Custer, sopranos; Kevin Skiles, tenor; and James Terrel, baritone.

The music, composed in gratitude after Mozart's bride-to-be recovered from an illness, was a joy to hear. Soloists and orchestra offered a stylish performance that may have lacked polish in places, but still managed to communicate the composer's deep devotion to God.

Kudos to the three instrumentalists—bassoon, oboe and flute—for their fine work in the treacherous "Et incarnatus est."

THE OREGONIAN FEB. 29, 1987

Youth Philharmonic ends season in style

By PHIL HUNT
of The Oregonian staff

The saxophone is not a widely recognized solo instrument in the classical repertoire, but that instrument got a thorough airing Saturday night at the midseason concert of the Portland Youth Philharmonic in Arlene Schnitzer Concert Hall.

Twenty-one-year-old Eric Lindburg, who came to the orchestra as a bassoonist from Salem four years ago, was the soloist in Jacques Ibert's Concerto da Camera. He drew a standing ovation from the crowd of about 2200.

The program was an ambitious one, opening with a short, melodic Overture to "Donna Diana" by Emil Reznicek, and closing with the dramatic and exotic sounds of the ballet suite "El Amor Brujo" ("Love, The Magician") by Manuel De Falla. The haunting Ritual Fire Dance with its insistent rhythms is mesmerizing when fully realized, as it was Saturday night.

But the highlight of the evening was the Portland premier of the Franz Schmidt Symphony No. 4, written in 1933 and rediscovered by Jacob Avshalomov, the youth philharmonic's musical director, who journeyed to Schmidt's native Austria to learn more about the work.

It opens and closes with a melodic solo trumpet statement. The four movements are played continuously in a 40-minute development that moves to rollicking dance tempos, including a tarantella, and skips alone at high speed with full orchestra before beginning to wind down to the trumpet finale.

Principals Bryan Burkett on trumpet, Jason McComb on cello, several of the woodwinds and Concertmaster Ann Warton were singled out for their roles in bringing the work to a full reading, along with the entire viola and horn sections.

Avshalomov is convinced the work, reminiscent of Gustav Mahler, will take its place in musical literature of this century.

NATIONAL
ENDOWMENT
FOR
THE ARTS

WASHINGTON
D.C. 20506

A Federal agency advised by the
National Council on the Arts

July 9, 1986

Mr. Jacob Avshalomov
Conductor
The Portland Youth Philharmonic
1119 SW Park Avenue
Portland, Oregon 97205

Dear Jacob:

As you may know, the music panels of the Endowment regularly evaluate artists and ensembles for the USIA. Recently one of our panels met and heard your organization. I am pleased to inform you that the panel unanimously voted to give the Portland Youth Philharmonic its highest recommendation.

In addition, they were most enthusiastic about the continued high standards of this orchestra. While the NEA recommendation is not a guarantee that the USIA will use an organization, it is certainly my impression that they would like to do something with your group in regard to the new Soviet - U.S. Exchange.

I thought you would like to have this information and I am pleased to relay it to you.

With every good wish,

Sincerely,

Edward R. Birdwell
Director, Music Program

64th Season

Jacob Avshalomov, Conductor

August 25, 1988

WATERFRONT CLASSICS

Retrospective Program
from the Season

April 30, 1988

RAMEAU	Les Indes Galantes
DELIUS	*Appalachia
	Trinity Choir
CHAVEZ	Sinfonia India
DVORAK	Symphony No. 9
	"From the New World"

February 20, 1988

ALFVEN	Midsommarvaka
FRANCK	Symphony in D minor
RAVEL	Tzigane
	Jonathan Talbot, *soloist*
STRAVINSKY	Firebird Suite

December 1, 1987

SCANFEST

Selections from the Season

December 4, 1987

6th Annual

SING-YOUR-OWN-MESSIAH

Civic Auditorium

November 14, 1987

BERLIOZ	Corsair Overture
BEETHOVEN	Triple Concerto
	Florestan Trio
DEBUSSY	Nocturnes 1 & 2
BLOCH	Suite Symphonique

**Portland Premier*

THE OREGONIAN NOV. 15, 1987

Youth concert shows excellence

Musicians parade rich, strong sound

By DAVID STABLER

of The Oregonian staff

The annual fall concert by the Portland Youth Philharmonic began boldly Saturday night with the "Corsair" Overture by Hector Berlioz. There for all to hear were the zephyrs and ocean storms that alternately tossed the pirate's ship from wave to wave, or becalmed it.

The episodic overture is a favorite of conductor Jacob Avshalomov; he programmed it during his first season with the orchestra 34 years ago. As is his custom, Avshalomov kept a tight rein on the music as it surged past. Most notable in this regard was the brass section, which played brilliantly and with great force but did not drown the rest of the orchestra. Superb calculations.

What came next was in marked contrast to the Berlioz. Beethoven's Triple Concerto, for piano, violin and cello, was performed by the Florestan Trio, accompanied by the orchestra.

Pianist Harold Gray, violinist Carol Sindell and cellist Hamilton Cheifetz gave a gentle performance of the work, stressing interaction between soloists. The Triple Concerto gets pretty tedious during the third movement, but the players' ideas were so clear and carefully shared that the long moments passed quickly.

Memorable moments came from Cheifetz as he dashed off the treacherous beginning of the third movement with easy-looking skill. Throughout, he and Sindell provided some fine duet partnering, with rhetorical comments from Gray.

The piano sound, hampered by the instrument's lid, was not present enough to match the other soloists, but the orchestra was not to blame. Avshalomov knows how to accompany a concerto. The young players never intruded, yet provided ample support.

Woodwinds were featured in two of Debussy's three Nocturnes, "Nuages" ("Clouds") and "Fêtes" ("Festivals"). In "Nuages," flutist Vivian Hsiao spun her tone to silky lengths.

"Fêtes" was notable for its restless energy. In both pieces, the winds weave upper strands of sound that are often cruelly exposed. Despite some mishaps, the delicate tapestry did not tear.

Avshalomov chose Ernest Bloch's Suite Symphonique to close the concert. Bloch has a well-documented association with Oregon and, over the years since the composer's death in 1959, Avshalomov has helped cement that association. The philharmonic has played much Bloch and even recorded some, including Suite Symphonique.

The performance was led clearly and intently by Avshalomov and featured strong playing from each section, including a richly played quartet by the first-desk string players. The French horns, led by Ayden Adler, had some particularly fine moments.

THE OREGONIAN DEC.5, 1987

2,500 amateurs make joyful noise: 'Messiah'

By PHIL HUNT

of The Oregonian staff

For more than 2,500 amateurs—baritones to sopranos—it was the ultimate sing-along: the sixth annual "Sing-Your-Own Messiah," presented by the Portland Youth Philharmonic on Friday night at Portland Civic Auditorium.

Before the singing began, Conductor Jacob Avshalomov urged the singers "to be joyous but at the same time prudent—and keep your place." He said, "If disaster strikes, we'll stop and start over again.

On "Lift up your heads," Avshalomov stopped the music with "I can't take it anymore," noting that some of the singers were "lagging." He admonished them to "Lift up your music" and called for a repeat.

Avshalomov anticipated trouble on "Let us break their bonds asunder," and when the passage was over, he declared, "It was better than I feared."

From the front of Civic Auditorium, the fullness of sound in G. F. Handel's masterpiece was surprising; and if there were some who were singing off-key, it was hard to detect.

During the intermission Tom Nadal, an elementary school principal at Battle Ground, Wash., said, "It was wonderful, singing again after 19 years." He said he and his sister, Barbara Kuehner of Tigard, had been trying for five years to get together for the annual sing-along.

Carl Schenck, 56, a bass who moved to Portland to help put KGW (8) on the air in 1956, said he had taken part in every one of the six sing-alongs. "I like to sing."

Schenck's daughter, Susan, played violin in the Portland Youth Philharmonic for two years, and Schenck sings in the Christ Methodist Church choir in Cedar Mill.

Jim Finlayson, 42, brought his wife, Linda, and his mother-in-law, Katherine Hunt of Terrebonne, to the concert. They all sat together in the bass section, even though the two women sing soprano. Finlayson, a pharmacist, said he had played trumpet in high school in Missoula, Mont.

No one, including Avshalomov, expected a polished performance. But this "Messiah" did have power, and the singers seemed to follow his broad gestures, pointing up for the sopranos to reach a high note and shushing them all for a soft note in "Behold the Lamb of God."

For those who missed it, the entire program will be telecast by KGW 8 twice, at 9 p.m. Dec. 24 and at 10 a.m. Christmas Day.

THE OREGONIAN DEC. 12, 1987

Jane Powell wins hometown hearts

By PHIL HUNT
of The Oregonian staff

Jane Powell won the hearts of nearly 2,000 listeners Friday night at Arlene Schnitzer Concert Hall as she recalled her visits as a toddler to what was then the Paramount Theatre, when she was growing up in Portland more than 50 years ago.

Coming on stage at 10:15 p.m.—late in an extra-long program—in her brilliant red velvet, single-strap gown, the glamorous movie queen of the 1940s and '50s looked half her age—by the calendar, 58.

After a couple of songs, accompanied by the Portland Youth Philharmonic and her own conductor/pianist, John Lesco, Powell launched into recollections of the Paramount.

Powell was the guest star for the fourth annual Scanfest concert, a benefit for the Scandinavian Study Program at Portland State University. In honor of the program she sang a medley of song's by Norwegian composer Edvard Grieg. She also sang a medley of movie tunes and other favorites of hers; including her theme song, "It's a Most Unusual Day." But some of greatest applause came for numbers such as "Abba Dabba" and a gutsy rendition of "You Know I've Been a Liar."

In its second concert in a week, the Portland Youth Philharmonic was at its best, performing two movements from Grieg's "Peer Gynt Suite No. 1," the familiar "Morning" and "In the Hall of the Mountain King."

John Warton, the orchestra's principal trombonist, acquitted himself well in the third movement of Lars-Erik Larsson's "Concerto for Trombone," a movement that covers the complete range of the bass-clef instrument.

Warton also led a 12-member brass choir from the orchestra in Christmas music, including a bright rendition of "Silent Night" and "Hark, the Herald Angels Sing."

THE OREGONIAN OCT. 12, 1987

Music, setting combine perfectly at Timberline

By DAVID STABLER
of The Oregonian staff

The '30s tunes of "Jeepers, Creepers" and "I've Only Got Eyes For You" swirled lazily through the lobby of Timberline Lodge Sunday afternoon, taking listeners back 50 years to the days when a brand-new lodge with brand-new beams and fireplaces beckoned from the tree line of Mount Hood.

Listeners and tourists—in from a day of glittering sun and lip-cracking wind—heard "Up At Timberline," a 20-minute classical composition written by Jacob Avshalomov to celebrate Timberline's 50th anniversary.

The combination of music and setting was delightful, if not acoustically perfect.

Sunday's premier was a commission by the Friends of Timberline, and was taped by KGW (8) for broadcast in December.

As requested by the Friends of Timberline, the performers were all current or recent members of the Portland Youth Philharmonic, which Avshalomov has led for 34 years; Avshalomov stood in the balcony above the lobby to conduct the 15 players. One group sat opposite him on the other side of the balcony, about 40 feet away, and a second group sat below on the main floor.

The tunes from the '30s didn't come until the last of the work's three movements, but they were worth waiting for and provided the most inspired moments. Avshalomov wove each tune in and out of the sonic tapestry with great skill, creating, in effect, a dreamy reminiscence, now sharply in focus, now fading in the haze.

He was greatly helped by the trombone playing of John Warton and David Bryan, whose smooth, sexy sound in the many repetitions of "I've Only Got Eyes For You" rolled through the lobby's cavernous, yet acoustically dry areas.

Although the first two movements were less immediately appealing, they contained specific images.

When challenged with the commission—how do you write good, serious music for a building?—Avshalomov wisely decided that each of the three movements should tell a story. In the first, it is the mountain, with "ancient" sounding modal harmonies and pre-human twitterings in the woodwinds.

For the second movement, called "Lodge," the tom-tom readily evokes Indian tribal lodge celebrations. The third, of course, captures the human interaction in the present lodge.

As a whole, the piece would have had more impact if the sound had been more immediate and resonant. Timberline's lobby is not a place of subtlety. With a Stonehenge of a chimney and beams as thick as ship masts, how could it be? As a result, several places in the music, including the ending of the second Lodge movement, where the French horn and woodwinds hold long notes very quietly, didn't come off.

But the playing by these young musicians certainly did. This was not easy music; it was full of meter changes, quick flourishes and chromatic runs. Avshalomov knows what his players can handle and he asked a lot of them this time.

Beginning the concert was music by Handel, Lully, Pachelbel, Joplin and Susato. Saxophone player Eric Lindburg and bass player Allen Regnier offered some mellow jazz, too.

Young violinist shows expertise, composure during Philharmonic concert

By DAVID STABLER
of The Oregonian staff

Maurice Ravel's violin concerto, called "Tzigane," is dramatic enough without the soloist breaking a string in the middle of a performance. But that's exactly what happened Saturday night onstage at the Arlene Schnitzer Concert Hall.

Jonathan Talbott, a 17-year-old violinist with the Portland Youth Philharmonic, was flying through the concerto when he suddenly stopped, bent down and exchanged violins with concertmistress Emma Shook. That's what professionals do when they've broken a string or some other disaster strikes.

The concertmistress, in turn, passes the wounded violin to her partner who then passes it through the section to the poor person at the end. Without missing a pizzicato, Talbott continued on the borrowed instrument.

It wasn't just Talbott's grace under pressure that ensured a successful performance. He played mightily well, too. In fact, he played with more style and expression than many professionals. He showed a maturity and flair for the music that was quite winning. The audience was on its feet at the end.

Talbott is finishing six years with the philharmonic before heading off to college. Judging by Saturday's polished playing, he should do well.

The philharmonic's winter concert began under a guest conductor's baton, that of Dannette Warren, a former member and now a conductor-in-training in Houston. Warren's father bought the opportunity for Warren to lead the philharmonic at last year's fund-raising auction.

Warren conducted Hugo Alfvén's Swedish Rhapsody feelingly and the wind instruments had a chance to warm up for the following piece, César Franck's Symphony in D Minor.

Conductor Jacob Avshalomov led a highly charged performance of this romantic masterpiece, not too slow as to be sluggish, yet still majestic and large-scaled. Standout performances were heard from the English horn, Shannon Sprenger, oboist Heather Freck, flutist Vivian Hsiao, bassoonist Terry Ronsheimer and the French horn section, led by Ayden Adler.

A strong, brilliantly colored account of Igor Stravinsky's "Firebird" Suite ended the program. This was the piece that launched Stravinsky's career, followed soon after by two other 20th century landmarks: "Petrouchka" and "Rite of Spring." The philharmonic played the second of three versions Stravinsky arranged.

The music is hypnotic and still sounds exotic, lo these 80 years later.

Again, Adler's horn playing, together with the woodwind principals and cellist Jenny Roberts helped make it a memorable performance. The concert was broadcast live on radio station KBPS-FM.

Youth Philharmonic provides exciting 'New World'

By PHIL HUNT
of The Oregonian staff

Antonin Dvorak's "From the New World" Symphony No. 9 in E Minor proved a powerful vehicle for the Portland Youth Philharmonic to demonstrate its maturity Saturday night at the Arlene Schnitzer Concert Hall.

The "New World" filled the second half of a two-hour-plus program played to a near-capacity crowd. For nearly 40 minutes, conductor and musical director Jacob Avshalomov maintained a constant state of excitement, from the vigorous first movement to the heroic finale, Allegro con fuoco.

In the second movement the plaintive solo English horn statement of the "Going Home" theme was echoed softly through the woodwinds and strings, and a pizzicato walking bass accompanied a delicate restatement by the violins. Then it moved on to a brass choir and ended with soft arco sounds in the bass.

In the third movement the woodwinds were playful, the strings bouncy, the brass thunderous.

And in the last movement the orchestra builds to a stupendous climax only to drop down to a hush before the restatement of the noble theme and with a mightily volume of sound the orchestra drives to the final chord.

The Trinity Episcopal Choir joined the orchestra in the first half of the program for a Portland premier of "Appalachia" by Frederick Delius. The English composer lived in Florida in the 1880s and this work is a series of seven variations of an old slave song with a final chorus.

The variations provide opportunity for many tonal colors, including the opening evocation to daybreak, which the orchestra carried off well.

When the 49-voice choir was finally called into play it was with a long a cappella statement of a simple text. Baritone Kevin Walsh sang the solo section, "Oh Honey, I'm goin' down the river in the morning."

The Schnitzer Hall space provided for choral groups is less than satisfactory and in the closing section of "Appalachia," the Trinity Choir lost the battle to the orchestra.

The program opened with the orchestra performing Jean-Philippe Rameau's "Les Indes Galantes," beginning with a very sedate "Dance of the Savages" followed by the Chaconne. While he had in mind the West Indies when he wrote it, the music sounds more like a courtly dance than anything American "savages" might dance to.

Mexican composer Carlos Chavez was represented with his "Sinfonia India."

While it is a relatively short work—about 12 minutes—"Sinfonia India" covers a lot of ground. It fades to very soft at times and builds to a grand climax, maintaining its hypnotic effects to the very end.

Appendices

ROSTER OF PLAYERS, 1924–1959

Abbett, Barbara '32
Abbett, Betty '34
Abbot, Edith Cavell '36
Adamson, Shirley '46
Adams, La Vina '53
Addleman, Bonnie Jean '37
Adkins, Ronald L. '50
Alderson, George '58
Alexander, Ed '56
Allen, Charlotte M. '38
Allen, Eleanor '49
Allen, John '49
Alway, Thomas R. '37
Anderson, Carl '32
Anderson, Dan '56
Anderson, Doug '57
Anderson, Laurence W. '26
Anderson, Marilyn '46
Anderson, Naomi '42
Anderson, S. '28
Andreasen, Ray '44
Anthony, Shirley '39
Appelgren, Wilson '31
Appleman, Jerry '54
Arbour, Shirley '46
Arenz, Robert '37
Arledge, Gary '49
Arnold, Philip '38
Arns, Don L. '54
Aschenbrenner, Karl '31
Asvik, Charleen '47
Asvik, Mary Jo '47
Atwood, Beryl '30
Austin, Silva '49
Avery, Harriet '26
Avolesi, Gyrid '46
Avshalomov, David '59
Avshalomov, Jacob '38
Ayers, Brian '50

Babcock, Harriet '31
Babson, James '26
Babson, Ned '25
Badley, Tom W. '45
Bailey, Jimmy '34
Bailey, Page '46
Bailey, William R. '42
Bain, Bob '47
Baker, Howard '59
Baker, James '52
Baker, Janet L. '29
Baker, Joan '52
Baldra, Merle '34
Baldwin, Henry Wallace '33
Banister, Harold '39
Banks, William '42
Barchus, Dorothea '28
Barnard, Shirley M. '46
Barneburg, Bernice '28
Barry, Catherine '43
Barry, Harold '37
Barry, Lewis, Jr. '29
Barter, Martha Jane '44
Bass, Ollie Gene '53
Bate, Eleanor '46
Bate, Marcia '46
Beacock, Laverne '59
Beadles, David '48
Becker, Helen '27
Becker, Herbert '50
Becvar, Vlasta '39
Beetham, Anne '51
Belisle, Irma '39
Bell, Dennis '55
Bell, Walter E. '52
Belsher, Marcia '49
Benard, James '39
Benard, Martha '42
Bennett, Billy '36
Bennett, James E. '51
Bennett, John '50
Bennett, Melba '51
Berardinelli, H. '25
Berardinelli, J. '25
Bercovich, Florence '30
Berg, Lillian '32
Berg, Norma '41
Bergheim, Jeanne-Marie '44
Bergis, Don '41
Bergman, Norman A. '42
Berkshire, Joanne '50
Bermel, Muriel '46
Bermel, Paula '48
Berndt, Susan '52
Besson, Barbara '36
Besson, Mary Millicent '36
Beulter, John '40
Bevens, Jean '43
Bissco, Arthur '27
Bixby, Horace '30
Blakeslee, George '31
Blakeslee, LaRaine '31
Bland, Rodney '39
Blatner, Joe '34
Bledsoe, Gaylon J. '56
Bleything, Willard B. '44
Bliss, Albert '36
Blosser, Paul H. '32
Blumberg, Mary '29
Bocek, Mark '39
Bogard, Ann '46
Bohnenkamp, Mitzi '43
Bolik, Evelyn '34
Bolobonoff, Theodore '36
Bongard, Lois M. '43
Boone, Harold '39
Boone, Roberta '45
Boone, Walter '39
Borchers, Barbara '51
Borg, Rosalind '50
Boring, Erwin '50
Boster, Robert '46
Bottler, Grace '32
Bovey, Mary '58
Boyer, Bill '34
Boyer, Karen '55
Bowerman, Milton '50
Bowman, Carl '27
Bowman, Lucille '27
Boyce, Jean Ann '51
Braden, Mary Ellen '31
Bradley, Charles '55
Brady, Kathleen '28
Brandow, Claudine '53
Braunstein, Reuben '26
Braymen, Charles '37
Breckon, Lyall '51
Brennan, Glenna '53
Brenner, Edna '35
Brewster, Mary Jane '56
Bridgwater, Elizabeth '50
Brink, Harold C., Jr. '25
Brink, Holden '25
Brockway, M. '25
Brodie, Allan '46
Brodie, Eleanor '47
Brodie, Laird '37
Bromberg, Ruth '26
Bromberg, Stanley '30
Brookman Dorothy '43
Brown, Arlene '36
Brown, Frances '25
Brown, Mary Charlotte '56
Brown Robert B. '52
Bruce, Helen M. '28
Brunk, Joanne '48
Brunner, Helen '35
Buchanon, Bill '57
Buchmann, Maynard '59
Buffington, Jack '26
Bugbee, Jane '39
Bugher, Audrey '52
Bunch, Betty Ann '25
Burkhart, Donald '27
Burness, James '36
Burnett, George '28
Burns, Josephine K. '43
Bush, Maurice '26
Bushnell, Phyllis '48
Butler, Beverly '50
Butler, Helen '25
Butterfield, Dave C. '43
Butzien, Chester '25

Cady, Janice '35
Cairns, Doris '40
Cairns, Robert
Callison, John H. '36
Campbell, Helen '36
Canfield, Lee '32
Canfield, Mildred '31
Cannon, Jack '31
Carleson, David '56
Carlson, Diane '52
Carlson, Dorothy '44
Carlson, Harry '43
Carlson, Marjorie '44
Carlson, Robert '37
Carlson, Ruth '37
Carnes, Duane J. '29
Carpenter, Clyde A. '43
Carroll, Patricia '36
Carson, Ruth '37
Carter, Dorothy '26
Carter, Jack '37
Cartozian, Navere '35
Chapman, Marvel '31
Chapman, William '55
Charette, Margery '30
Charley, Jack T. '49
Chase, Lynne
Cheek, Robert '46
Chehak, Melba '39
Cheshire, Elinor '35
Christie, Bernice
Christie, Ed '57
Christy, David '48
Church, Verle '31
Churchill, Betty '46
Churchley, Edith '29
Cipolla, Barbara '41
Clarizeo, Mike '49
Clark, Ben '34
Clark, Tamara '57
Clark, Vincent '31
Clark, Virginia '30
Clarke, Dorothy
Clay, Ben H. '28
Cleaver, Carol Anne '44
Clifford, Happa Belle '40
Clifton, Jacob '29
Coates, Gary '58
Cockrum, H. Rebecca '44
Coffman, Helen '32
Cohen, Jerome '48
Cohn, Celia '25
Coie, Ralph '32
Coin, Mary '26
Cole, Amelia '48
Coleman, Mary Elizabeth '42
Collamore, Dorothy '30
Collamore, Margaret '26
Collamore, Mildred '25
Cone, Charles, Jr. '37
Cone, Fred '43
Conrath, Jerry H. '51
Cook, Gordon '41
Cook, Ivy '35
Cook, Murvyn '37
Cook, Scott H. '47
Cooley, Arlene '58
Cooper, Eric '30
Coppedge, Choice '29
Corlett, Tom '53
Cornford, Alfred '32
Cornford, Leslie '31
Costello, Harriet '25
Costello, Robert '25
Cotter, Dick '46
Cotton, Glenda '47
Coucher, Margaret '39
Couling, Leona '25
Cowen, Dale R. '26
Cowgill, Dorothy '25
Coxley, Bruce '50
Coy, Marjorie '39
Cramer, Gerald '47
Crane, Carolyn '48
Crane, Jo Ann '43
Crawford, Georgia '46
Crawford, Neva '37
Creekpaum, Christy '57
Critchlow, Victor '39
Crosby, Coralie '42
Cross, Eric Lionel '43
Cruson, Crystal C. '29
Cunningham, Robert '40
Curletto, Anna Mae '49
Curry, William '36
Curtin, Claire '37
Cykman, Harry '33

Danforth, Virginia '25
Darnielle, Jack '49
Davidson, Betsy Jean '42
Davis, Arthur '26

Davis, Leona '28
Davis, Madeline '26
Davis, Mary '26
Dawe, Sally '47
Dawe, Sidney '45
Day, Irval '37
Day, Ralph, Jr. '34
Deakin, Deloris '51
Deffenbaugh, John '38
de Gastyne, Sergei '49
De Harpport, Marie '50
Deiz, Robert '37
Delano, Lois '54
DeMoss, Catherine '44
DeMott, Wayne '48
Denkman, Kathleen '56
Derby, Ray '30
Derrick, Mary '28
Deutschman, Emmy '34
Deutschman, Paul '34
De Veny, Dewane '47
Dhanens, Betty '46
Dick, Gale '41
Dick, Robert '25
Dickson, Bill '52
Dickson, Gerald '50
Didek, Eugene '37
Dietz, Ellen '59
Dietz, Marie '52
Dillon, Anne '53
Dimm, Gwendolyn Mary '44
Ditto, Mary Lois '31
Dodd, Clyde Eugene '34
Dodd, Joe '26
Dodge, Edward '28
Dodge, Glenn '26
Dodge, Thomas C. '26
Dolan, Earl '30
Dotson, Mary Helen '38
Doty, Norma '43
Doughtery, Colleen '42
Dowling, Agnes '44
Downing, Carol '55
Doyle, Jean '25
Drake, Raleigh '53
Dressler, Naomi '35
Driscoll, Mary Elizabeth '37
Drummond, Walter S., Jr. '46
Dudley, Zana Mae '40
Du Fresne, Janette '44
Du Fresne, Nyle '43
Duke, Jacqueline '31
Dunkelberger, Dan '50
Dunn, Dorothy '45
Dunstan, Marvin '42
Durgan, Bonnie '44
Durgan, Donna May '43
Durham, Larry '58
Dwyer, Rosemary '25
Dyck, Vern '44
Dyer, Dick '48

Earl, Victor '27
Easley, Elizabeth '31
Easley, Norman '29
Easton, Elvera '44
Eaton, Margaret '43
Eby, Susan '55
Eckhardt, Bob '54
Eddy, Marie '38
Edlefson, Dorothy '25
Edmiston, Pat '54
Edmiston, Virginia '55
Edmunds, Arthur '38
Edmunds, Ralph '43
Egbers, Cheri Ann '48
Egbers, Joan '54
Elder, Nancy '57
Eller, Erma '25
Ellison, Mary '25
Ellman, Daisy Louise '31
Elmer, Antonette '55
Elsey, Roger '47
Elsing, Lorraine '34
Elssner, Eleanor '49
Emery, Larry '56
Engdahl, Corinne '41
Englehart, Gladys '47
Englehart, Mary '54
Englehart, Ruth '43
Englund, Eugene '41
Enyart, Lavelle '26
Eoff, James '25
Erickson, Gerald '53
Erickson, M. Joy '48
Erskine, David '38
Esterly, Henry '25
Esting, Fred, Jr. '28
Etchison, Dorothy '35
Etlinger, Joseph S. '47
Evans, Sheila '50
Ewen, Jean '34
Exskine, Martha

Fallkoff, Phyllis '38
Farrar, Edward '34
Farrell, Mary Carolyne '29
Faveluke, Eugene '29
Fearing, Donald '25
Fehrenbacher, Frieda '58
Fehrenbacher, Sigrid '54
Felde, Doris '39
Felde, Max '36
Fettick, June '35
Fetzer, Paul '39
Findley, Bob '57
Finley, Gordon '30
Finley, John T. '30
Fisher, Mary Ellen '40
Fisher, Samuel K. '29
Fitsgerald, Bill '45
Flatland, Kathy '56
Flisram, La Royce '42
Fogdall, Carol '53
Ford, Eleanor '59
Forncrook, Douglas '52
Forncrook, Ross '51
Forsyth, Carol '58
Fortier, Barbara '40
Foster, Elsie '29
Foster, Mark '57
Foth, Harland '25
Foust, Charles '40
Fowler, Don '37
Franzel, David '48
Freeburg, Mary '30
Freer, Christian '28
Frese, Catherine '43
Frey, Juanita '42
Friedman, Albert '30
Friedman, Martin, '58
Frost, Joyce '47
Frost, Larry '47
Fuhrmann, John '45
Fuller, Arthur '34
Fuqua, Carmen '39
Furrow, Robert '46

Gabriel, Stacia '53
Galbraith, Tom '25
Gardner, Georgia Mae '29
Gassie, Loretta '42
Gates, Frank '32
Gawer, William '59
Gearhart, Diane '51
Gentry, Gertrude '47
George, Mary '51
Georgeades, Penny '50
Gerow, James '51
Gevurtz, Martha '25
Gibbens, John E. '55
Gibson, Joan '45
Gilbert, Janee '37
Gilchrist, Alden
Gile, Vernon E. '41
Gill, Walker '30
Glanz, Arlene '54
Golden, Daniel '25
Golden, Kenneth '35
Goldstein, Betty '26
Goodfellow, Marion '28
Goodwin, Betty '32
Goodwin, Donald '44
Gordner, Helen '48
Gordon, Jeanette '32
Goss, George Edward
Grabovac, Lucille '46
Graham, Bob '44
Graham, Virginia '26
Graham, Wallace D. '26
Grant, Jeanette '41
Grantz, June '38
Gray, William '25
Graw, Ruth
Graziano, Agatha '38
Grebe, George '27
Green, Albert
Green, Philip '43
Greenberg, D. M. '28
Greenfield, David '50
Grenz, Ruby '35
Griesinger, Verda Mae '39
Griffis, Joan E. '51
Groth, C. Robert '44
Gulick, Greta Mae '45
Gumeson, Ted '52

Hacker, Laurene '43
Hadduck, Charles '46
Haeflinger, Donald '26
Hale, Arthur '33
Hale, Frank '55
Hall, Charles Louis '51
Hall, Richard '45
Hall, William '26
Halverson, Catherine M. '46
Halvorsen, Grant '29
Hamilton, Alexander '25
Hamilton, Brian '25
Hamilton, Linda Lou '55
Hamilton, Shirley '42
Hamilton, William '30
Hamman, Patricia '45
Hampton, Lesley '42
Hanks, Eileen '38
Hannam, William '34
Hansberger, Clarence '26
Hansen, Adell '52
Hansen, Bernice '30
Hansen, Charles '52
Hansen, Frances '31
Hansen, Marcia Ann '51
Hanson, Lorna '45
Hanthorn, Marilyn '48
Hardie, George '28
Hardwick, Mary Jo '48
Harris, Betty Jean '38
Harris, Clara '25
Harris, Jerry '51
Hart, Lowell '42
Harter, Betty '31
Harter, Jean '31
Hartford, Paul C. '31
Hartwick, Marcellaise '40
Harvey, Richard '45
Haslett, William '39
Hastings, Ross '27
Hawkins, Jeanne '35
Hayes, Bob '44
Hayes, Janet '37
Hays, Evelyn '32
Hays, Graydon '29
Hearne, Joe '57
Hedburg, Mavis '25
Hedeen, Lauren H. '46
Hedman, Carolyn '58
Hegge, Delores '32
Heineck, Gordon '37
Heitzhausen, Fred '47
Helmer, Eggert '27
Hemmila, Lewis '28
Henderson, Lyle '29
Henderson, Mary Lou '38
Hendricks, Joanne '51
Henricksen, Robert '55
Henriksen, George '45
Heppenstall, Jeanne '36
Heppner, Catherine '27
Hermann, Virginia '39
Hern, Clara Dell '25
Herndobler, Allan '38
Herndon, W. K. '31
Herse, Corvallis '25
Heywood, Barbara '45
Hiatt, Bill '51
Hicks, Gerald '42
Higgins, Elvery '25
Hill, Ralph '39
Hillwertz, Boyd '50
Hinman, Charles '29
Hinshaw, Barbara '56
Hodel, Donald '48
Hodes, Harry '28
Hodgkins, H. Claire '39
Hodgson, Keith '45
Hoelschen, Judith '58

Hoffman, Frank '27
Hoffman, Norman '53
Hogan, Hermine '34
Hogan, Phyllis '27
Hogan, Rozanne '58
Hollister, Helen '26
Hollister, Hestine '25
Hollister, Mary '26
Hollister, Robert S. '26
Holloway, Arline '26
Holloway, May '33
Holt, Mary Ann '34
Homann, Joe '58
Honsberger, C. '28
Hood, Robert George '47
Hopper, Bill '38
Horing, Donald '34
Howard, Josephine G. '25
Howard, Richard '53
Howell, Verle J. '26
Hoyt, Byron '26
Hoyt, Helen '40
Huebner, Naomi E. '48
Huebschwerlen, Alvin '40
Huget, Jack C. '25
Hughes, Doraliene '43
Hughes, Yvonne '49
Hull, Arlie Dale '46
Hull, Lawton '39
Hungerford, Rae '30
Hunt, Florence '40
Hunt, Frances '40
Hunt, Phil '34
Hunt, William '52
Hurst, George F. '38
Hurst, Mary '39
Hurt, Dorothy '58
Hutchinson, Dorothy '30
Hyland, Magar '27

Ireton, Tom Alan '51
Irvine, Carol '46
Irwin, Patricia '40
Isaacson, Gary '54
Isted, Leslie '29

Jackson, George '25
Jacobsen, Karen '31
Jacox, Douglas '52
Jagielski, Verna '29
Jali, Marie '45
Jaloff, Fay '25
James, Myron O. '36
James, Paul V. '35
James, Robert '35
James, Roger '35
Janinsky, Norman '31
Jeleniewski, Cazmir '29
Jellison, Tom '31
Jensen, Audrey '25
Jewell, Dana '40
Johnson, Carol '36
Johnson, Dorothy '26
Johnson, Lewis '27
Johnson, Robert L. '45
Johnson, Wendell A. '36
Johnston, Judy Lou, '52
Johnston, Norma '38
Johnston, Pat '54

Jones, Barbara Frances '31
Jones, Betty Yvonne '38
Jones, Millard '31
Jones, Pete '54
Jones, Warren '47
Jones, William '25
Jorgensen, Lotus '31
Jorgensen, Pauline '32
Jwayad, Mary Jo '54

Kacin, Joseph '51
Kaden, Jo Ann '51
Kafoury, Ann Elizabeth '41
Kalberer, Patricia '51
Kalinsky, Janet '26
Kallak, Harry '44
Karasick, Joe '34
Kattge, Ralph '28
Kaufman, Goldie '29
Kaump, Marian '48
Kavich, S. '53
Kean, Laurin '25
Kearn, Clara Dell '26
Keen, Carolyn '46
Keiney, Arthur '37
Keizer, Lewis '57
Keller, Evelyn '47
Keller, Marian '45
Kellmer, Charles '37
Kellmer, Lucille '35
Kellogg, Willis Dwight '46
Kelly, Mathew '32
Kelly, Roxallanne '58
Kelly, Stanley '29
Kelm, Marcine '53
Kelso, Gloria '38
Kemper, Dorman '29
Kemper, Douglas '33
Kemper, Stanley '30
Kennedy, Margaret '43
Keppinger, Cordelia '37
Keppinger, Leo '42
Kerby, Karolyn '59
Kerlee, Donald '43
Kerr, Lorn '31
Kerr, Marie '34
Kido, Katherine '40
Kilpatrick, Maxine '42
Kincaid, Clyde W. '25
King, Hermina '26
Kinnari, Sylvia '56
Kinnel, Fay '29
Kinnel, Hope '30
Kirch, Joseph I. '32
Kirk, Weldon '25
Kleep, Bill '33
Kline, Alice '34
Knight, Beth '34
Knight, Harwood '37
Knight, John T. '25
Knopes, Robert '39
Konrad, Catherine '32
Konrad, Ferdinand '32
Kontz, Martha '53
Koster, Harold '43
Kotchik, George '26
Kramer, Mildred '26
Kramer, O. F. '26
Kraus, Walter '34

Kregal, Anne '48
Kregal, Henrietta '45
Kregal, Jesse '43
Krick, Bob '55
Krieger, Willis '52
Kriger, Walter G. '29
Kruse, Jack '36
Kugel, Dale '44

Labby, Dr. Daniel H. '29
Lake, Virginia '59
LaMar, Dorothy, '34
Lamb, Betty Lou '38
Lamont, Lucille '39
Lamont, William G. '36
Lance, Marion T. '30
Lange, John '58
Langille, Cherie '49
Langille, Jim '53
Langman, Robert '50
Larkin, Pat '47
Larsen, Jerome '54
Larson, Roy '42
Lathrop, Jack '58
Laudan, Barbara '59
Lauinger, Robert '54
Laurin, Kean '25
LaValley, Dolores '42
Lawrence, Emma Lou '28
Lawrence, Lois '28
Leadbetter, Sterling '27
LeBeck, Beverly Jeanne '35
LeBeck, Einard '37
LeBeck, Majolaine '35
Lee, Charles A. '50
Lee, Ramona '28
Leech, Gary '50
LeFebre, Babette '49
LeFevre, Jeanne '35
Leihy, Virginia '25
Leison, Wilbur '28
LeMar, Jo Anne '50
Leslie, George '31
Leu, Elizabeth '29
Leuck, Frank L. '45
Leupold, Marcus '24
Leva, Jerome, Jr. '34
Levin, Carolyn '46
Lichty, Sally '45
Lichty, Suzanne '45
Lieberman, Melba '34
Lightner, Frank '53
Lightner, John '42
Liming, Jerry '50
Lincke, June Joy '44
Linden, Eugene '27
Lindquist, Judy '53
Linnett, Lois '30
Litton, Gordon Thomas '44
Loafbourow, Lee '37
Long, Severyn '43
Long, Truman '37
Long, Warner '55
Longtin, Dave '28
Lorenz, Raymond '54
Lotzenhiser, Jack B. '30
Lowell, Arthur '59
Luce, John '34
Luik, Harold F. '30

Lund, Bert '45
Lundell, Vivienne '29
Lusk, Catherine '32
Lutz, Norman '49
Lynch, Frances '30
Lynds, Edwin '25

MacKenzie, Kenneth '59
Mackey, Arvo '32
MacManiman, James '25
MacMickle, Eleanor '39
Maddox, Walter '50
Mahaffay, Mike '58
Main, Charles L. '31
Majovski, Marlene '48
Makino, Chiyoko '25
Mallett, Lin E. '39
Mallicoat, Everett '33
Malos, Nancy '59
Managhan, Robert '30
Mandell, Wayland '29
Mann, Robert '33
Mannel, Bette '50
Manners, Jean '30
Manning, Brad '51
Marshall, Eleanor '51
Marshall, Nancy '49
Martin, Connie '40
Martinjak, Anna '34
Marvin, John '55
Masco, Judi '59
Masco, Romana Marie '51
Mason, Dr. Charles '29
Mason, David '35
Matheson, Eileen '34
Matson, Gertrude '31
Matteson, Glynn Echo '45
Matthews, John '40
Matthews, Martha '45
Mattie, Dewey '36
Mayer, Arther '38
Mayer, Bernice E. '30
Mayer, Sharon '55
Maynard, Sylvia '48
Mayo, Patsy '32
Mays, Bob '59
Maxwell, Elizabeth Ann '52
McAfee, Lucy '39
McAllister, Eileen '35
McAvoy, Thomas '25
McCabe, Sharron '49
McCain, Doris '42
McCann, J. Louise '35
McCarley, Hazel '46
McClelland, Jerry '53
McConnell, Grant '32
McDonald, Lawrence '34
McGrew, Anna Marie '42
McGrew, Pat '48
McKeown, Marianne '50
McKrill, Edward '28
McLaughlin, Donald '38
McLaughlin, Muriel '26
McLean, Anne '36
McLean, Margaret '41
McMahon, Marion '34
McMahon, Mike '58
McMath, Joanne '48
McSparan, Leila '37

Meagher, Cecelia Frances '37
Meagher, Mary Agnes '32
Meagher, Winifred '31
Medak, Charles F. '32
Mehrer, Carol '36
Menzies, Jane '25
Merchant, Louis '30
Merrill, Jerry '44
Merritt, Pauline '25
Meserve, Gene Drexel '26
Messerli, Victoria '40
Metzger, Sarah '28
Meves, Lotte '37
Meyer, Marion '28
Michelsen, Eliot '26
Miles, Patricia '52
Miller, Alice '53
Miller, Jayne Alice '55
Miller, John '41
Miller, Marilyn '48
Miller, Stafford '47
Miller, Walter '28
Milligan, George F. '27
Milligan, James '25
Mills, Virginia '35
Missildine, Margaret '29
Missildine, Ruth '28
Mitchell, Carol Mae '43
Mitchell, Harold '25
Mitchell, Owen '48
Mitchell, Stanley '47
Moffit, Barbara Jean '40
Monge, Gloria Louise '44
Monson, David L. '32
Moore, Addie '33
Moore, Franklin '30
Moore, Jack '55
Moore, Lorraine '47
Moore, Teddy N. '48
Moore, Verne '56
Moran, Virginia '56
Morris, Kenneth '32
Morris, Lambert '57
Morris, Marjorie '27
Morris, Robert '25
Morrison, Barbara Jean '44
Mosher, Hal '26
Mosher, Paul H. '52
Mount, Jane '35
Muceus, Joanne '58
Muenchow, Albert '34
Mulharen, Robert '42
Mundel, Robert '57
Murawski, J. Edward '54
Murrell, Sally '45
Murthe, Phillip '49
Muscovitz, Alfred
Mussler, Dorothy '43
Myers, Leonore '39
Myers, Mary '44
Myers, Winifred '32
Myrick, David '53

Nabut, Amy '47
Nace, Rebecca '40
Nace, Robert '39
Naglee, Bob '53
Nash, Charlotte '27
Nash, Phyllis Jane '42
Nebergall, Jim '55
Neese, Marie '27
Nelden, Denton '31
Nelson, Edith '27
Nelson, Marshall '59
Nelson, Marvin D. '44
Nelson, Sandra '59
Nesbit, Emma Jean '51
Newberg, Joyce '34
Newcomer, Jim R. '51
Newman, Joseph '25
Newton, Connie '50
Newton, G. P. '25
Niblock, James '35
Nickelson, Judy '56
Nickerson, Margaret '37
Nielsen, Russell '26
Nieuwboer, Harry '53
Nolan, Anna May '25
Nolan, Paul F., Jr. '25
Noonan, Evelyn '27
Norgard, Ruby '25
Norman, Virginia Lee '44
Norton, Arthur '36
Norton, Carolyn '33
Norton, Clem '49
Noyes, Emily '32
Noyes, Humphrey F.
Nudelman, Marilynn '48
Nugent, Donna '48
Numbers, Leland '28
Nye, Alma '51

Oakland, Alberta '26
Obee, Jane '28
Odegard, Peter Sigurd '45
O'Donnell, Jack '27
O'Gara, Pat '59
Ogden, Carmen '42
Ohlemiller, Margaret '31
Oliver, John '25
Olleman, Lois '49
Olsen, Marvin '44
Olson, Arthur '34
Olson, Barbara '46
Olson, Bob '47
Olson, Karen '52
Olson, Kay '38
Olson, Leonard '34
Olson, Margaret '26
Olson, Ray '34
O'Neal, Patrick '51
O'Neill, Marjorie '51
Ono, Y. '26
Orman, Arnold '33
Orser, Howard '25
Orser, Owen '55
Osburn, Harry S. '24
Osgood, Bea '59
Osgood, Boyd '55
Owen, Barbara '53
Owens, Ken '46

Packer, Jean '41
Pailthorp, M. C. '25
Palacios, Dolores '32
Paladeaux, Peggy '25
Palladini, Gloria '37
Palmer, Ellen '55
Palmer, Esther '27
Palmer, Katherine '25
Pancheau, Marshall '56
Panzica, Sam '49
Parker, Barton '58
Parker, Tom '43
Parkinion, Bob '44
Parman, Judy '58
Parr, Peter '42
Parrett, Ruth '56
Parrott, Max H. '32
Parrish, Norma '24
Parrish, Valdera '27
Partipilo, Raymond '30
Partlow, Bill '45
Patterson, Jack '42
Paulsen, Georgia '30
Payne, Walter W., Jr. '43
Peake, Marilyn Eileen '43
Pearson, Rudolph '27
Peebler, Ethel Jane '33
Peery, Esther '53
Pelker, Rex '58
Pelz, Benny '25
Pelz, Misha '33
Perkin, Paul '54
Perkins, Margaret '42
Peters, Robert '45
Petersen, Carlotta '27
Petersen, Catherine '25
Peterson, Geraldine '25
Peterson, Robert '43
Peterson, William '26
Petrasso, Carol '56
Petrasso, David '35
Petrusich, Catherine '37
Pettingell, Bob '59
Pettys, Delmar '57
Pewtherer, Helen '34
Pfenning, Bernice '27
Pfingsten, Hal S. '48
Pharris, Betty '41
Phillips, Clarence '29
Pierre, Bob '43
Pietka, Genevieve '31
Pike, Patricia '43
Piland, Kenneth '55
Pilger, Betty Sabra '39
Pitila, David '28
Pittard, Rujean '51
Plaissand, Lawrence '40
Poe, Grover '37
Pohl, Robert L. '46
Polinoosky, Saul '26
Pollock, Leon '28
Pollock, Mrs. Richard W. '41
Porschman, Erich '25
Porter, Richie '49
Porter, Ed '38
Potter, Jeane '43
Potts, Gladys '26
Poullette, Vicki '58
Pozzi, Frances '25
Pozzi, Prospera
Pratt, Dustinn '45
Preston, Donna '53
Pride, Larry '58
Pulham, Harold '35
Putnam, Clyde '27
Putnam, Marjorie '31
Quinn, Russell '34

Rader, Miriam '54
Rahn, Betty '38
Ragnone, P. Edward '25
Randol, Carolyn '41
Range, George '59
Rankin, Earl '32
Rasmussen, Bob '47
Raudsep, Edwin '28
Reaksecker, Beverly '38
Reed, George '34
Reed, Virginia '25
Reeder, Bonnie Athleen, '35
Reeder, Delmer '34
Reeves, Glenn W. '25
Reierstand, Marcia '59
Reinmiller, George '52
Reith, Katherine Mae '43
Renfro, Robert '28
Reynolds, Charlotte '36
Reynolds, Craig '50
Rhadon, Beatrice '37
Rhisy, Wilbur '27
Rhodes, Beulah '27
Rigas, Elaine '54
Riley, Don '56
Rizor, George A., Jr. '43
Rocheleau, Elaine '46
Rodinsky, Ida '26
Roeckel, Shirley '49
Rogers, Anne '51
Rood, Joy '32
Roper, Steve '58
Roppel, Marilyn '36
Rose, Rowland, S. '25
Rosebraugh, Gail '56
Rosenbaum, Sue '50
Rosencrans, Robert '42
Rosenfeld, Alan '34
Ross, Charles '27
Ross, Kathryn '37
Roth, Neil '50
Rothchild, Frederic '28
Rouse, Carol '49
Rowan, Robert '28
Rowe, Tarrant J. '28
Rowland, John D. '29
Ruddie, Marilyn '37
Runquist, Dexter '25
Russell, Darlene '53

Samson, Raymond '30
Sanpietro, Elsie '26
Saunders, Ruth '25
Savage, David '40
Savan, Bruce '41
Sawyer, Virginia
Say, Margaret '37
Scarci, Secondo '30
Scarpelli, Ernest M. '38
Schacher, Walter C. '28
Schaer, Dorothy '40
Schaer, Ray '44
Schafer, Tillman '36
Schappacher, Norman '53
Schille, Janet '48
Schlatter, Adam J. '27

Schlavin, Lyle '43
Schlegel, Henry, Jr. '29
Schlieski, Josephine '34
Schmale, Fred '48
Schmidt, Dave '48
Schmidt, Rodney '55
Schmitt, Nancy '46
Schmoll, Erika '53
Schmoll, Gerhard '55
Schnoor, Carl '48
Schnoor, Jack '51
Schramm, Lawrence '26
Schultz, Trilby Mary '49
Scott, Elinor '35
Scott, Irving '32
Scott, Joe '34
Scott, Mildred A. '50
Searle, Adella '28
Seder, Leslie '54
Seeburger, Hildagard '34
Sellers, Betty Grace '47
Seltmann, John '49
Settlemier, Harold '51
Seymour, Charles '36
Shafer, Janet '37
Shanafelt, Laurel '40
Sharp, Elinore '38
Sharp, Morell '34
Sheets, Virginia '31
Sheldon, Charles '38
Shell, Jane '54
Shelton, Mary Louise '37
Sherman, Robert M. '30
Sherson, Jerrold '39
Sherwood, Wayne '33
Shipley, Lowell '34
Shirley, Beatrice '45
Shirley, Frances '41
Shirley, Virginia '44
Shojo, Midore '27
Short, Hugh A. '25
Shov, Lynden '32
Shove, Nancy Lee '37
Showerman, Harold '34
Shtoffer, Sarah '37
Sichau, Reinhold '28
Sievere, William '25
Sigell, Leonard '53
Sigell, Michael '51
Signor, Warren Basil '36
Simmons, Mary Dorothy '31
Simpson, John '34
Siner, Helen '42
Singletary, Craig E. '45
Skelton, Sarah Lee '41
Skibitzke, Benton '25
Skinner, Sara '46
Slayton, Kathe '52
Sloan, Beverly '45
Smith, Brice '35
Smith, Britt '34
Smith, Carol '32
Smith, Dan '34
Smith, Donald '29
Smith, Garrett '50
Smith, Holman C. '27
Smith, Howard '31
Smith, Lane '29
Smith, Lois Ann '42

Smith, Marjorie '32
Smith, Robert '28
Smith, Robert '41
Smith, Sid '59
Smith, Sol '43
Smith, Thomas '25
Smith, Wenda '55
Snedecor, Philip A. '37
Snook, Ruth Caryl '45
Snow, Janet '58
Snyder, Doralee '54
Sommers, Bernard '26
Sorber, Marjorie '28
Sorensen, B. '25
Sorensen, Hubert '25
Sorenson, Garland '54
Sorenson, Richard '25
Southard, Alice '27
Spady, Bill '53
Spande, Barbara '48
Sparlin, Evelyn '27
Speaker, Mary Lou '56
Speaker, Paul '55
Spellman, Wesley '47
Spencer, Alden '45
Spencer, John '32
Spies, Jane '26
Spooner, Richard '38
Spoor, Charles '44
Sprague, Frances '31
Springer, Bill '44
Springer, George '43
Sprouse, John '25
Stayner, Dale '27
Steele, Orvie '25
Steen, Patricia '43
Stehn, Leonard '55
Stein, Doris '38
Stell, Marion '43
Steres, Chris, Jr. '37
Stevens, Clarence '28
Stevens, Richard '53
Stevenson, Gladys '37
Stevenson, William '34
Stewart, Lynn '27
Stewart, Raymond Edw. '43
Stewart, Rosemary '50
Stewart, Wesley '27
St. Helen, Dorothy '38
Stilwell, Frances '37
Stilwell, Roy A. '34
Stolz, Fred '32
Stone, Virginia '43
Stoneburg, Audrey '43
Storli, Kerman
Stoskoff, G. P. '25
Stratton, Lois '46
Strech, Louella '26
Strode, Garen '53
Struntz, Kathryn '30
Studholme, Ernest '33
Stump, Glenna '36
Subotnick, Arthur '29
Sullivan, Audrey '49
Sumner, John '56
Sutton, Fred B., Jr. '41
Swanson, Irene '32
Swanson, Nellie '37
Swanson, Peggy '58

Swasey, Virginia
Swayze, Harold '45
Swire, Marvin '25

Tadino, Glen '56
Taraldson, James '43
Taylor, Eric '25
Taylor, Jane '48
Taylor, Margie W. W. '25
Teadtke, Lynn '49
Telford, Maxine '25
Teter, Sue '47
Thayer, Stephen '52
Thielsen, Bernard '25
Thiess, Paul '53
Thompson, Edward '25
Thompson, Lester '26
Thompson, Marilyn '42
Thomsen, A. '26
Thomsen, Christi '59
Thor, Marlene '48
Thornton, Elizabeth '27
Thureson, Glenn '52
Thurlow, Lawrence '29
Thurman, Jean '53
Tibbits, Douglas E. '47
Tichborne, Marigene '32
Tillson, Julie '57
Tinkleman, Isadore '37
Tobias, Helen '30
Todd, Horace '36
Tonkyn, Grace '34
Treesh, Nancy Anne '48
Tregaskis, Audrey '25
Trenholme, Anne '57
Trenholme, Arthur '53
Tretheway, Maurice '31
Trovas, Barbara
Trubey, Doris '37
Trueblood, Sam '40
Trullinger, Larry '44
Trump, Elizabeth Ann '41
Trump, William '43
Tujo, John '52
Turner, J. G. '47

Uchiyama, Matsui '38
Unruh, Albeth May '53
Updike, Olive '25
Urquhart, Don, Jr. '27

VanDemarr, Charles '51
Van Fleet, David '42
Van Fleet, Douglas '43
Van Fleet, Sarah '42
Van Gorder, John '30
Van Schoonhoven, Ruth '25
Varker, Elaine '36
Vernon, Louise '46
Versoza, Bonnie R. '54
Vincent, Douglas '52
Vincent, Ellis '25
von Ammon, Reinhard '50
Vreeland, Harold '57

Wagner, Edward '28
Wahlberg, Lois '45
Waitt, J. E. '43
Walker, Clay '37

Walker, Marilyn '45
Walkkey, John '35
Wall, Edwin '28
Wallin, Lewis '25
Walsh, Thomas '27
Walton, Eldon '48
Wanger, George '27
Ward, Sharron '56
Warner, Betty '37
Warnstrom, Mavis '56
Wary, Beverly '52
Wary, Dick '51
Washburn, Ruth '25
Watson, Marie '29
Wawrinofsky, Gloria '45
Webb, Audrey '38
Webb, Grace Louise '29
Weber, Leonard '43
Weeks, Larry '50
Weibel, Brenda '54
Weidel, Kathleen '51
Weiland, David '47
Weiland, Dorothy '35
Weinstein, Sheldon '39
(Wayne, Sheldon)
Weiss, Fred '30
Wellman, Paulette '58
Wenker, William '45
West, Charles G. '26
West, Rosalie '55
Westerman, Arnold S. '43
Westfall, Wade '37
Wetterborg, Gerald '35
Wheeler, Bradley '37
Wheeler, Martha '37
Wheeler, Ray F. '44
Wheeler, Tom '52
Whelchel, Maxine '50
Whechel, R. Carleton '52
White, Betty May '44
White, Frank '43
White, Harry '54
White, Judith Gene '51
White, Russell
Whitlock, Evan '25
Widmer, Margaret '41
Wier, Luannna '48
Wikander, Guilford '37
Wikander, Ruth '37
Wilde, Edith '30
Wildman, Doris '25
Wildman, Louis '52
Williams, Dawn '48
Williams, Larry '58
Williams, Roy Benjamin '42
Willis, Stanley '41
Willock, Elizabeth '27
Wills, Sharon '59
Wilson, Jay R. '29
Wilson, Lillian '34
Wilson, Paul '40
Wilson, Roscoe '31
Wilson, Ruth '39
Winer, Sadie '29
Winslow, Marilyn '55
Winter, Joanne Lee '48
Wintler, John '38
Wire, Sally '38
Witkowski, Donna '46

Wohler, Helen '41
Wolf, Pauline '25
Wolfe, Betty '36
Wolfe, Eleanor '46
Wolfenberger, Dolores '48
Wood, Dick '27
Wood, Mary Helen '25
Woodside, Gail '57
Wooton, Lorene
Word, Archie J. '58
Word, Maradick '36
Worth, Don '48
Wright, Marshall '42
Wright, Roderick '54
Wright, Virginia '35
Yager, Bill '46
Yates, Norma '34
Yates, Norris '40
Yeager, Geraldine '49
Yost, Margaret '25
Young, Delores '37
Yount, Leola '43
Zerzan, Margaret M. '26
Zgonc, Larry '59
Ziegler, Sidney '40
Zimmerman, Charles '57
Zornado, Richard Jim '54
Zwerenz, Elizabeth '35

ROSTER OF PLAYERS, 1959–1979

Abney, Brenda '67
Ackley, Linda '74
Aird, Samela '76
Albertson, Ivan '60
Alexander, Tina '72
Amato, Gerry '73
Armbruster, Sandra '64
Anderson, Bruce '74
Anderson, Coni '62
Anderson, Karen '78
Anderson, Pam '63
Anderson, Penny '63
Anderson, Susan '62
Angell, Michael '70
Arnold, Janice '71
Aungst, Joanne '62
Avshalomov, Daniel '65
Ayers, Bruce '72
Ayers, Kenneth '76

Babcock, Michael '61
Bachelder, Ann '62
Bachelder, Peggy '62
Baker, Margaret '68
Baker, Phil '76
Balch, Bill '65
Baldino, Phil '66
Baldridge, Larry '64
Barnes, Darlene '60
Barrett, Delmar '61
Bartels, Mel '71
Bass, Donavin '72
Bates, Jim '69
Bates, Natalie '77
Bauer, Kathy '66
Beale, Clare '61
Beckley, Ruth Ann '66
Becraft, Myra '78
Bell, Harry '67
Bennett, Edie '64
Bennett, Mary Helen '71
Bennett, Ruthanne '62
Benson, Melinda '76
Berdahl, Dacia '73
Berdahl, Emalie '62
Berdahl, Lawrence '62
Berdahl, Rebecca '73
Berg, Nancy '73
Berkshire, Judy '61
Bernhard, Barbara '62
Berton, Greg '71
Biehler, Connie '61
Bigelow, Jay '77
Bigelow, Mardi '66
Bishop, Diana '60
Bjerke, Janice '60
Bjorkman, Pam '72
Bleth, Jen '74
Blum, Lisa '77
Blume, Karl '78
Boer, Jon '66
Bonaparte, Ruth '76
Booher, Betty '74
Boone, Debra '61
Borgensgard, Sue '69
Boring, Ann '67
Borowiak, Sarah '78
Borst, David '64
Bose, Madelon '63
Boss, Bonnie '72
Boyer, Bette '63
Bradt, Claudia '71
Brady, Lavina '59
Bragg, Barbara '67
Brandenburg, Jacquie '60
Briggs, Kendall '75
Brodie, Carol '72
Brostoff, Eric '61
Brown, Rosalie '78
Browning, Daphne '64
Browning, Karren '65
Brumbaugh, Janet '61
Brunton, Blake '73
Bryan, David '76
Bryant, David '65
Bunce, Pat '62
Bunch, Jeff '70
Bunker, Suzanne '76
Burgstahler, Judy '75
Busch, Jon '61
Bush, Bernice '66
Bush, Janice '74
Butterfield, Brad '76
Butzer, Michelle '77
Butzin, Annette '62
Byers, Harold '61
Byers, Louise '62

Callaghan, Curtis '62
Campbell, Mary-Anne '69
Campbell, Patrick '70
Captein, David '72
Carlson, Harriet '65
Carroll, Kathy '68
Casale, Maria '77
Casler, John, Jr. '63
Casperson, Dean '60
Casperson, Debbie '67
Casperson, Mark '71
Casperson, Pam '60
Chambers, Mark '78
Chambers, Tamara '76
Chapman, Patricia '68
Choban, Maria '78
Chung, Paul '77
Clark, Ray '66
Closs, Christiane '61
Cochran, Sandra '60
Cochrane, Bonnie '64
Cogan, Leonard '77
Coggins, Mary Ann
Colburn, Charles '60
Colby, Stashia '67
Cole, Dan '65
Cole, Jim '67
Cook, Kathy '76
Cook, Robin '75
Cooper, Claudia '75
Cooper, Connie '72
Corkum, Anne '69
Cory, Mike '66
Couture, Jerry '76
Covert, Cathi '72
Craford, Mary '70
Craig, Jeff '66
Cramer, Anne '65
Cramer, Betsy '71
Cramer, Seldy '64
Cramer, Tom '77
Critchlow, Steven '69
Cropper, Janet '60
Crowley, Regan '64
Crumpacker, Charles '61
Cushman, Claire '73
Cushman, Sandra '61
Dafoe, Janet '65
Dana, Christy '68
Davies, Linda '77
Davis, Bill '60
Davis, Paul '77
Day, James '64
Delay, Myra '71
DeLessert, Irene '73
DeLorenzo, Anthony '61
DeLorenzo, Teresa '65
Derry, George '60
Derville, Susan '69
Desbrisay, Diana '65
deWald, Jane '66
Dewoina, Kathy '67
Dietz, Jeff '70
Dietz, Peter '69
Dillon, Damian '75
Dinsmore, Mary Alice '76
Dinsmore, Teresa '77
Dirks, Grant '61
Dobbins, Ron '69
Doerksen, Debora '73
Donoghue, Margaret '75
Donoghue, Maureen '76
Donoghue, Michael '67
Dorsey, Alan '65
Drysdale, Debbie '67
Dubay, Gregory '78
Dubay, Jonathon '78
Dubs, Ronald '73

Earl, Chris '67
Earley, Leslie '70
Eckard, Drew '78
Edens, Jeff '78
Egbers, Kathie '63
Eisert, Lynne '73
Eklof, Mark '77
Ellis, Dan '67
Ellis, Junko '61
Ellis, Sam '72
Eng, Sharon '67
Engel, Steve '74
Engleheart, Kathy '76
Ensworth, Deena '65
Eoff, James, Jr. '63
Eoff, Janet '61
Estep, Steven '69
Evans, David '72
Evens, Connie '77
Everett, Thomas '63
Ewart, David '70

Faruolo, Alarik '70
Faruolo, Andrius '69
Fay, Patrick '60
Fenimore, Diane '71
Ferguson, Gary '76
Feves, Julie '64
Feves, Rick '63
Fiasca, Ann '65
Fiebiger, Daniel '65
Fillis, Jeff '78
Fisk, Kent '68
Folkins, Doug '77
Follis, Kevin '78
Ford, Eric '68
Ford, Wanda '77
Foster, F. Mark '61
Frank, Judy '65
Friedhoff, Barbara '70
Friedhoff, Jolan '67
Friedhoff, Mark '64
Friedhoff, Paul '64
Frerichs, Marna '72
Fukabori, Hiroko '74

Gadeholt, Greg '74
Gander, Bill '66
Garlick, Bill '63
Garner, Gloria '64
Gatto, Teresa '76

George, Stan '60
Georges, Emily '70
Gerber, Leslie '72
Giles, Randall '66
Gill, Bonnie '65
Gillespie, Deda '78
Gillespie, Diane '71
Goldhaber, Shaindell '78
Goren, Neal '76
Graham, Russell '74
Gray, Tanya '61
Green, Sid '65
Grille, Ted '73
Groh, Janet '72
Groh, Linda '72
Gross, Joanne '62
Grube, Luise '74
Gruber, Dwight '63
Gruwell, Philip '74
Gunderson, Susan '62
Guthman, Eric '72
Guthman, Gary '69
Guthmann, Dave '73

Haines, Virginia '71
Hale, Charles '63
Hale, Marilyn '66
Halladin, Julie '74
Halling, Nancy '72
Hamilton, Herb, Jr. '62
Hamilton, Linda '62
Hanan, Steve '62
Handler, Susan '60
Handler, Terry '68
Hanna, Stephanie '74
Hanneman, Kathleen '74
Hansen, Beth '62
Hansen, Jill '72
Hanson, Crystal '74
Hanson, Martin '69
Hanson, Michael '69
Hardie, Sally '71
Hardie, Susan '67
Hardt, Anthony '76
Hatch, Carolyn '66
Hatch, Peter '62
Hatch, Warren '71
Hawkey, Doreen '72
Haworth, Ann '62
Haynes, Phillip '78
Heald, Jason '78
Heikkinen, David '70
Heitmeyer, Karen '71
Helton, Chris '65
Helton, Holly '70
Henrickson, Richard '62
Herigstad, Dale '67
Hess, Mike '70
Heubach, Karin '74
Hicken, Jim '66
Hicks, Martha '62
Higgins, Nancy '73
Hilley, Karen '72
Hillyer, Dirk '66
Hinds, John '62
Hinds, Tom '71
Hirsch, Mary '75
Hoelschen, Judie '62
Hoesly, Elizabeth '72

Hoesly, Jennifer '64
Hoesly, Veronica '71
Holcomb, Pam '76
Hood, Sally '76
Hooten, Carrie '75
Hopkins, Rick '66
Horowitz, Paul '76
Howard, Roger '60
Howe, Laurie '73
Howell, Marlene '75
Hudgins, Elizabeth '62
Hume, Lisa '77
Hurst, Gary '67

Iles, Randy '61
Irgens, Jeff '70
Izquierdo, Pablo '72

James, Dale '71
James, Valerie '68
Jester, Priscilla '68
Johansen, Linda '62
Johns, Debbie '69
Johnson, Audrey '75
Johnson, Gregg '76
Johnson, Jerry '67
Johnson, Kevin '78
Johnson, Larry '75
Johnson, Louisa '70
Johnson, Nancy '69
Johnson, Tobin '74
Johnston, Milton D. Jr. '60
Johnston, Randy '62
Johnston, Victoria '76
Jones, Alex '71
Jones, Dan '74
Jones, Robert '63
Jones, Timothy '70
Joseph, Aloysius '75
Jossy, Gerald '63

Kalk, Rae Louise '65
Karabut, Diana '62
Kay, Ronda '73
Kaza, John '63
Kaza, Roger '68
Kee, Lawrence '69
Kelly, Bridget '62
Kelly, Cathleen '62
Kelly, Randy '67
Keiser, Kari '78
Kerman, Debby '78
Kight, Jane '72
Kimmel, Marcia '66
Kindler, George '61
Kindler, Marilyn '61
Kindler, Robert '67
Kindler, Steve '68
King, Kimberly '70
Kjelgaard, Ellen '74
Klaner, Carolyn '69
Klevit, Lisa '72
Klobas, Patrick '75
Knight, Laraine '61
Koehler, David '69
Kohne, Marcia '75
Kraxberger, Allen '70
Kreger, Tom '72
Kroboth, Pat '64

Kudzia, Susan '67
Kuhns, Todd '76
Kullberg, Greg '66
Kummrow, Emma '70

Lambert, Phyllis '62
Lamoreaux, D'Anne '71
Lange, Carol '65
LaRochelle, Solange '77
Larson, Chris '64
Larson, Jon '70
Lathrop, Anne '61
Laughlin, Mark '65
Lee, Cecilia '74
Lee, Christopher '76
Leeb, Margaret '68
LeGuin, Elizabeth '71
Leigh, Barbara '66
Leitner, Bobbie '61
Levine, Gil '65
Levine, Peter '65
Levitt, Nathalie '63
Lim, Christina '64
Lindner, Jenny '71
Linke, Kathy '60
Litt, Barbara '76
Litt, David '76
London, Brad '68
Long, David '66
Long, Steve '60
Loomis, Harlan '60
Lorati, Kim '77
Lorati, Linda '72
Lotz, Mark '76
Lotz, Matt '70
Lotz, Michael '69
Ludwigsen, Sharon '62
Lushenko, Art '65
Lyons, Kenneth '67
Lyons, Lori '72

MacRae, Wendell '76
Madill, Emilee '60
Mahan, Eileen '74
Malbin, Diane '62
Malcolm, Keith '60
Malinas, Manuel '77
Malmstrom, Randall '71
Manly, Paul '65
Mann, Victoria '71
Marsh, Ross '66
Marshall, Larry '70
Martin, Jeff '76
Marvin, Toni '64
Masco, Marlene '60
Mason, Elizabeth '69
Mathews, Eleanor '62
Mathis, Nancy '63
Matthews, Billie Jean '63
Matthews, Pamela '78
Mattison, Bob '63
Mayeda, George '63
Mazzio, Paul '76
Mazzio, Toni '68
McCarthy, Tim '67
McComb, Flora '60
McConnell, Ronald '62
McDade, David '78
McDonald, Nyla '74

McEwen, Jamie '74
McGee, Barbara '60
McGee, Gary '66
McKinley, Don '77
McLennan, James '70
McMenemy, Jeanne '64
McMillin, Elena '75
Meadows, Christine '72
Meisenheimer, Darrel '65
Merriman, Rob '73
Metcalf, Carol '75
Meyer, Angela '76
Michel, James '71
Michel, Thomas '70
Mielke, Kathryn '78
Mindolovich, Catherine '74
Mindolovich, Paul '76
Mirel, James '65
Moffitt, David '72
Monda, Denise '72
Moore, Louise '76
Moore, Nadine '78
Moreland, Mark '75
Morgan, Donna '62
Mueller, Steve '68
Murphree, Gaen '77
Murphy, Janet '65
Murray, Jean '64

Naito, Larry '64
Neale, Linda '63
Neighorn, Richard '64
Nelsen, Craig '65
Nelsen, Kristine '67
Nelson, Georgia '63
Newman, David '69
Newman, Gail '75
Nicholson, Dick '68
Nielsen, Erling '75
Nikka, David '74
Nolte, Noelle '65
Nord, Tim '75
Nowels, Kent '73
Nowels, Lynn '68
Nowels, Nan '67
Nunn, Linda '71
Nussbaum, Fred '69

O'Brien, Robin '64
Oge, Robin '78
O'Hara, Ann '71
O'Hara, Joan '74
Oleksak, Sue '74
Olsen, Erik '70
Olsen, Laurie '65
Olsen, Marilyn '75
Olson, Dale '74
Olson, Janis '73
Orem, David '65
Oringdulph, Diane '72
Oringdulph, Judy '76
Oringdulph, Mary Ann '77
O'Shaw, Michael '68

Page, Cathy '73
Parker, Kelly '71
Parker, Rebecca '70
Parrish, RuthAnn '68
Pastorino, Nina '61

Pavlakovich, Catherine '75
Pelker, Ellen '62
Penk, Maria '74
Perry, Chris '72
Perry, Lisa '77
Peters, Judy '63
Petralli, Mary '67
Petrasso, Lorely '69
Phin, Elizabeth '72
Picchi, Virginia '77
Pierce, Alan '60
Pieters, Roberta '69
Pisotchi, Maurice '66
Pitkin, Paul '78
Potharst, Jasper '62
Poullette, Valerie '64
Powell, Lisa '73
Powell, Maria '73
Powers, Gary '69
Powers, Michael '69
Powloski, David '77
Price, Del '75
Price, Jim '73
Price, Steve '64
Prichard, Ruth '60
Puls, Dave '73
Puls, Georgienne '70

Quinby, Jack '76

Ramsey, Mack '74
Ranes, Evan '76
Redwill, Rick '70
Reed, Rob '71
Rees, Mary Ann '67
Reitz, John '63
Repsold, John '78
Reuter, John '66
Rice, Bart '64
Rice, Bill '67
Richardson, Janice '77
Richardson, Phil '76
Rickey, Alice '71
Rifas, Helen '71
Rispler, Maren '68
Ritzman, Mary '64
Robare, Steven '78
Robbins, Kay '61
Roberts, Jonnie '65
Roberts, Katy '70
Roberts, Larry '63
Robinson, Janet '69
Rogers, Cindy '77
Rogers, Mark '77
Rogers, Ron '65
Rose, Brian '75
Rosenberg, Kurt '71
Roth, Suzanne '76
Roundy, Lisa '74
Rowe, Ryan '77
Ruben, Bruce '67
Rugland, Andrea '66
Rupert, Jane '78
Rust, Kathy '73

Sadilek, Paul '76
Sadilek, Ruth '77
Saiger, Carla '69
Sanborn, Jane '67
Sandberg, James '60
Sanders, Pete '74
Sansregret, Anne '78
Sawyer, Cathy '70
Scarth, Kent '74
Schenck, Jim '68
Schleuning, Elizabeth '74
Schlichting, Joyce '74
Schlichting, Robert '76
Schroeder, John '76
Schuster, Teresa '66
Scott, Cathy '74
Scott, Cynthia '74
Scott, Kathleen '74
Seeber, Todd '78
Sellman, Mark '76
Sermol, Luisa '78
Severson, Gayle '67
Shaw, Michael '68
Shepard, Cathy '73
Shepard, Mark '70
Sheridan, Scott '78
Shirk, Kenneth '76
Sholkoff, Karen Sue '62
Silverman, Karen '77
Simmons, Kathy '70
Sisson, Paula '68
Sklower, Keith '70
Slater, Jeff '74
Small, Linda '65
Smesrud, Denise '77
Smesrud, Phil '74
Smith, Ann '72
Smith, Clay '75
Smith, Dwight '75
Smith, James '73
Smith,-Jess '69
Smith, Julie R. '72
Smith, Julie '72
Smith, Pam '67
Smith, Paula '70
Smith, Rex '66
Smith, Robert '67
Smith, Stephanie '63
Smith, Stephen '78
Soelling, Jonelle '67
Songer, Michael '66
Spellman, Robert '70
Spellman, Stephen '72
Spencer, Cheryl '67
Stahl, Terese '69
Starr, Eve '76
Starr, Jenny '78
Starr, Rollie '63
Starr, Sara '75
Steinfeld, Pat '71
Stelter, Monica '64
Stevens, Jan '71
Stohs, Luther '74
Storer, Margaret '68
Storer, Mary Ruth '68
Stromquist, Karen '67
Stromquist, Lee '63
Strong, Cathy '65
Sullivan, Mark '76
Swanson, David '66
Sweetman, Bruce '67
Sweetman, Per '64
Sweetman, Tyrrell '71
Swenson, Ted '72
Swope, Scott '67

Taggart, Erin '77
Taggart, Mark '73
Tank, Julie '76
Tatum, Kathy '72
Terman, Peter '74
Terrill, Debbie '74
Thomas, Hollis '65
Thompson, Tim '70
Thompson, Tom '67
Thornburg, Richard '63
Thurlow, James '68
Timmons, Mamie '73
Tollard, Carol '61
Toussaint, James '78
Trullinger, John '60
Tunstall, Julie '72
Tyle, Chris '72
Tyle, Shari '62

Utter, Becky '70

Vagt, William '71
Vahsholtz, Trina '77
Van Schoiack, Larry '61
Vasey, Vernon '76
Verbout, Karen '69
Vinikow, Patty '67
Vinikow, Van '68
Van Linsowe, Marina '71
Vore, Gail '78
Vorm, Dan '76
Vorm, Susan '67
Vose, Trudy '68
Waddington, Bob '65
Wagner, Kenneth '63
Walker, Claudia '67
Walker, David '71
Walker, Patty '77
Walker, Ruth '67
Walsh, Patrick '73
Walton, Vic '77
Wamble, Casey '66
Ward, Debbie '70
Ward, Dinah '69
Ward, Jeff '64
Warren, Danette '77
Washington, James '69
Wasser, Carolyn '72
Watson, Diane '62
Watson, Donna '60
Wayrynen, Wanda '69
Weber, Terese '69
Weinstein, John '67
Welch, Roger '63
Weller, John '66
Weller, Paul '66
Wenzel, Larry '77
Wess, Joanne '62
Westcott, Mark '65
Wetzel, Vicke '70
Wetzel, Wende '67
Whinton, Melet '72
White, Jim '60
White, Terry '78
Whitesides, Chip '78
Whitlow, Leo '73
Wick, Kimberly '76
Wick, Shannon '77
Wiley, John '61
Willey, Carter '66
Williams, Arlene '75
Williams, Christine '75
Willner, Sarah '78
Wilson, Janet '61
Wirt, Doug '74
Wirt, Ron '72
Wold, Michael '63
Wolters, Marc '63
Wong, Angela '72
Wood, Alison '63
Woodruff, Larry '74
Woodward, Judy '68
Wysham, Sarah '74

Yost, Cynthia '77
Yost, Lisa '77
Yost, Zilpha '73

Zalutsky, Diane '76
Zerbe, Patty '72
Zerbe, Ruth '72
Zimmerman, Karen '72

Concertmaster Robin Cook and Conductor in "Star Wars" masks at a Children's Concert.

ROSTER OF PLAYERS, 1979–1989

Adams, April '85
Adler, Ayden '85
Aikin, Ken '84
Akagi, Greg '89
Allred, Hilari '82
Altstadt, Louise '81
Anderson, Greg '81
Anderson, Kathy '82
Apodaca, Janeen '86
Artis, Shane '84
Asburry, Linda '86
Avedovech, Jonathan '86
Averill, Corey '86

Bailey, Linda '87
Barber, Doug '88
Barnett, Rand '89
Bennett, Christy '81
Benting, Steve '87
Bentley, Carlota '89
Bergau, Dan '81
Bergman, Mark '87
Bezdechi, Ivans '81
Blankenship, Dorothy '83
Boehr, Christy '79
Bonhorst, Lena '81
Bos, Jeff '89
Bowen, Elizabeth '81
Braden, Anne '88
Braich, Stephen '89
Brandon, David '85
Brenneman, Ava '85
Brenneman, Martha '84
Breuner, Creagh '84
Breuner, Mary '81
Brewster, Jason '87
Bristol, Lori '89
Broeren, Theresa '87
Brown, Catherine '87
Brucker, Mike '87
Brunelle, Russell '88
Brunette, Harold '82
Buist, Catriona '85
Bunch, Genji '87
Bunch, Kenji '87
Burkett, Bryan '86
Burton, Gene '81

Callahan, Eve '88
Capon, Kim '85
Capon, Steve '82
Casale, Elizabeth '82
Chadek, Dennis '82
Chamberlain, Charles '85
Charnholm, Diane '89
Cheng, Bonnie '86
Cheng, Jean '84
Cheng, John '81
Cheng, Paul '83
Chidester, Stuart '88
Chien, Tom '87
Choi, Aaron '86
Choi, Jennifer '88
Chong, Lisa '88
Chotocruz, Carlos '86
Chou, Hong '81
Chung, Sungil '89
Clark, Brian '81
Clark, Michelle '83

Coleman, Julie '87
Colvin, Aimee '87
Conover, Kelly '89
Conrow, Steve '81
Cooke, Jubilee '82
Cook, Darren '88
Cook, Kamela '86
Coulter, Anna '85
Covert, Jennifer '84
Cox, Chris '81
Craswell, Heather '89
Crisp, Tim '80
Critchett, Alan '88
Cross, Alisa '81

Dahlin, Johan '82
Dahlke, Lane '82
Daily, Curtis '80
Dakin, Mary '83
Davenport, Sandra '83
Davidson, Bruce '80
Davidson, Caryn '87
Davolt, Ami '86
Dawson, Denise '84
Day, Emily '87
Dennis, Suzanna '87
Detroit, Anna '87
Devine, Patrick '89
Diliberto, Jamie '85
Dinsmore, Anne '80
Dormier, Tracie '83
Duncan, Robin '86
Dunne, Julie '85
Dunn, Charles '89
Duplessie, Monica '88
Durland, Darcy '81
Durych, Robert '80
Dyer, Michael '82
Dzubay, David '82

Ellefson, Pete '81
Ellis, Chris '88
Elmore, Jack '88
Elston, Margareta '81
Emery, Anne '81
Eppick, Glen '84
Ewing, Brenda '80

Falconer, Wendy '87
Fergison, Drue '80
Ferries, Michael '83
Fields, Doug '85
Fisher, Sam '87
Fitzgerald, Pat '85
Flanery, John '84
Flynn, Justine '88
Fogle, Janet '80
Foley, Andrew '81
Folsom, Marc '89
Fordyce, Richard '82
Forsgren, Krista '89
Frampton, Teresa '86
Frankel, Steve '80
Frasca, Andrea '88
Freck, Heather '86
Freck, Scott '85
Freedman, Jessica '87
Fry, Patti '81
Fuller, Rob '89

Fussell, Kelly '87

Gee, Annie '86
Gerber, David '80
Gerdes, Hilary '80
Gerken, Stephen '89
Gerling, Chris '86
Gilbert, Melissa '87
Gilbert, Shannon '87
Gilmore, Pam '80
Girardeau, Cathy '81
Gomez, Bernardo '86
Gomez, Anneliese '89
Graven, Randy '85
Gray, Dana '83
Gray, Leslie '81
Griffin, P. Andrew '88
Gronke, Edward '81
Grose, Michael '80
Guild, Peter '85
Guthrie, Heidi Jo '89
Gygi, Kristen '84

Hacket, Jan '84
Hague, Renee '82
Hambourg, Corinne '80
Hambourg, Tanya '80
Hardt, Christopher '82
Harris, Mary Ellen '83
Harris, Sara '85
Hata, Jonathan '88
Hayward, Deneen '81
Ha, Sung '89
Ha, Young '89
Heidenreich, Florian '86
Heine, Sam '87
Hervey, Jennifer '85
Hofstad, Dawn '85
Hollingshead, Jeanne '82
Holt, Janna '89
Holz, Darbi '89
Homma, Hiroki '82
Hornick, Jeff '84
Hornof, Luke '86
Hsiao, Vivian '85
Hsu, Immanuel '89
Hsu, Israel '88
Humohrey, Sandra '89
Hunt, Craig '83
Hwee, Yin Kan '82

Inglis, Adrienne '80
Irlandez, Mimi '83
Isaac, Julie '82

Jacobs, Roberta '88
Jauregui, Laurita '87
Jellesma, Garrett '89
Jennings, Marty '82
Jin, Paul '85
Johnson, Eric '84
Johnson, Heather '84
Johnson, Heidi '84
Johnson, Kristina '86
Johnson, Peter '89
Johnson, Susan '81
Jones, Leslie '81
Jossy, Ted '84
Juza, Alan '80

Kan, Karla '82
Kartak, Stephanie '87
Kaye, Jeff '88
Keddie, Laurie '83
Keene, Edmund '86
Keivanzadeh, Reza '88
Kim, Heidi '89
Kim, Judy '79
Kiso, Tom '88
Kocher, Matt '87
Kocher, Tonya '88
Kracke, Susan '83
Krause, Cindy '80
Kremin, Athena '89
Kuffner, Jim Jr. '88
Kunz, Jennifer '87

Lahart, Heidi '88
Laird, Andy '84
Landstrom, John '82
Lannigan, Shannon '82
Larsen, Todd '81
Lauderdale, Mike '83
Ledoux, Monique '87
Lee, Hayne '87
Lee, John '86
Lee, Kristin '83
Lee, Lisa '84
Lemieux, Matthew '89
Leuthauser, John '81
Lindburg, Eric '85
Li, Mary Theresa '83
Li, Veronica '81
Lofquist, Shannon '85
Loontjens, Glenn '85
Luke, Jennifer '85
Lundquist, Paul '87
Lybeck, Tami '85

MacRae, Wendell '80
Maddox, Trent '88
Mahn, Jerry '86
Mankin, Bill '83
Marinier, Carolyn '88
Markham, John '80
Mathey, Matt '87
Matthews, Eric '87
Maxwell, Martha '88
Mazzio, Carl '80
McComb, Jason '83
McComb, Jody '81
McCormick, Dan '81
McIsaac, John '82
McMillan, Brad '82
McTaggart, Tom '81
Medack, Dan '80
Megyesi, Heather '85
Miller, Jim '80
Milliren, Paul '87
Millspaugh, Kristi '88
Mitch, Cindy '80
Moltmann, Jon '88
Monroe, Matt '89
Moreland, Bonnie '82
Morgenstern, Fred '82
Mosback, Craig '80
Mulder, Carol '80
Mullen, Elizabeth '86
Muller, Jeff '82

Mundorff, Emily '88
Mundorff, Lisa '86
Murphy, Christina '86
Muth, Karen '81
Muto, Angela '88
Myers, Mikylah '88

Naglee, Diane '82
Naze, Christopher '86
Neace, Anne '84
Nelson, Michelle '82
Neufeld, John '89
Newton, Barry '84
Nichols, Kathy '82
Nichols, Stacey '89
Norlen, Kim '87
Nutt, Stephanie '87

O Dierno, Dominic '85
Ohle, Bill '81
Ohnstad, John '88
Oldham, Catherine '85
Oldham, Collin '86
Oleksak, Lynn '80
Olsen, Richard '82
Olsen, Sonja '88
Otey, David '83

Panaretos, Katherine '86
Paredes, Dawn '83
Park, Cathy '89
Pearson, Rochelle '83
Peddicord, Meghan '82
Pedersen, Wendy '87
Peniston, Sara '82
Peterson, Erik '83
Peyton, Jeffrey '83

Qualls, Darin '81
Qualls, Kim '81

Ratzlaf, Amy '83
Ratzlaf, Dieter '86
Reeder, David '87
Regnier, Allen '82
Reynolds, Jeffrey '86
Rice, Melinda '87
Richardson, Cindy Lou '79
Richardson, Laura '87
Richards, Janice '84
Richen, Margaret '85
Rickard, Julia '85
Riggs, Doug '84
Riggs, Stephanie '87
Ritchie, Brad '86
Ritchie, Gregg '88
Roberts, Jenny '85
Roberts, Ken '89
Rochon, Alan '89
Ronsheimer, Terri '86
Ross, Clare '87
Roy, Todd '82
Rust, Dorothy '80
Rutkin, Rachael '88
Ryan, Dale '83
Ryan, Donna '80
Ryan, Julie '88

Salcedo, Isaiah '86
Sanders, Jay '83
Sato, Erik '88
Schell, Christopher '87
Schenck, Susan '85
Schleuning, Maria '79
Schliemenz, Susanne '83
Schulte, Dan '80
Schumacher, Theresa '82
Segerstrom, Suzie '87
Seifers, Joey '85
Selover, Vance '83
Sevetson, Erika '85
Sheetz, Melanie '86
Shin, Helen '84
Shin, Brian '85
Shiolas, George '80
Shook, Anna '85
Shook, Emma '85
Silver, Kimberley '85
Simmons, Yukiko '84
Smejtek, Dalibor '82
Smith, Denise '81
Smith, Doug '83
Smith, Laura '84
Snavely, Dean '86
Sokol, Tracy '86
Solomon, Ron '83
Spece, Richard '84
Sprenger, Shannon '88
Stalnaker, Trask '87
Stecker, Shelly '81
Stegmeier, Randy '88
Stevens, Leigh '84
Stiger, Jennie '81
Stodd, Michael '80
Stohs, Joanna '79
Strain, Katherine '81
Sturgeon, Tandy '88
St. John, Mark '87
Suzuki, Leo '89
Swafford, Matt '84
Sytman, Paul '80

Takasomi, Karla '80
Talbott, Jonathan '84
Toevs, Heidi '86
Turner, Elizabeth '83

Unger, Paul '88

VanFleet, Laura '83
Vergotis, Pekio '84
Vincent, Jennifer '88
Vukelich, Mike '80

Wagar, Donna '89
Wainright, Shannon '86
Waitt, Kim '83
Walczyk, Kevin '84
Wallace, Scott '84
Walthinsen, Karen '86
Warren, Cynthia '86
Warton, Ann '84
Warton, John '85
Warton, Margaret '84
Warton, Peter '85
Wathen, Lisa '86
Wells, Richard '85
Wharton, Ann '86
Whitehead, Mark '85
Whitesides, Vance '82
Williams, Shannon '88
Willoughby, Dean '81
Wilson, Doreen '83
Winston, Kevin '87
Wong, Aliza '89
Wong, Lennie '80
Wright, Allison '86

Yates, Jerry '85

Zupancic, Christian '88

Rick Olsen leading the oboes.

John, Margaret, Peter, and Ann Warton—all principals of their section.

NOTABLES

Concertmasters

1925–29	Dorothy Cowgill
1930–33	Anna May Nola
1934	Catherine Peterson
1933–35	Geraldine Peterson
1936	Marjorie Morris
1936–38	Robert Mann
1938–40	Dorothy Hutchison
1940–41	Elizabeth Zwerenz
1941–42	Victoria Messerli
1942–44	Margaret Say
1944–46	Elinore Sharp
1946–47	Robert Pierre
1947–49	William Bailey
1949–50	Nancy Schmitt
1950–52	Catherine DeMoss
1952–54	Eleanor Wolfe
1954–55	Walter Maddox
1955–57	Marlene Majovski
1957–58	Diane Carlson
1959	Adell Hansen
1959–61	Michael Sigell
1961–64	Marylou Speaker
1964–67	Frieda Fehrenbacher
1967	Mary Ann Coggins
1967–69	Nancy Mathis
1969–70	Valerie Poulette
1970–71	Robin O'Brien
1971–72	Paula Sisson
1972–74	Steven Kindler
1974–76	Michael Hanson
1976–77	Lynne Eisert
1977	Irene DeLessert
1977	Janet Groh
1981	Robin Cook
1982–83	Ruth Sadilek
1984	Maria Schleuning, Co-Concertmaster
1985–86	Ann Warton
1987	Emma Shook
1988–90	Dawn Hofstad

Assistants to the Conductor

1925–29	Mary V. Dodge
1929	Gertrude Peterson
1930–34	Eugene Linden
1934	Karl Aschenbrenner
1935–78	James Eoff
1981–84	Cline Otey
1985–90	Eugene Kaza

Presidents of the Board

1925	Robert Robinson
1925–30	John Edlefson
1930–32	Mrs M. Lloyd Frank
1932–36	Mrs Robert H. Noyes
1936–38	Blaine Coles
1938–41	Charles A. Hart
1941–43	Mrs Estes Snedecor
1943–46	W. P. Stalnaker
1946–48	Moe M. Tonkon
1948–53	L. R. Hussa
1953–55	E. R. Nudelman
1955–57	L. B. Staver
1957–58	Edmund P. Platt
1958–60	Waldo B. Taylor
1960–61	Mrs Simeon R. Winch
1961–64	Mrs Harold S. Hirsch
1964–66	Mrs Leslie Sherman
1966–68	Mrs Jan de Graaff
1968–70	Mrs A. Gordon Russell
1970–73	Henry T. Stanley, Jr.
1973–74	Edward H. Look
1974–76	Victor J. Critchlow
1976–77	Maurice Engleman
1977–78	William B. Webber
1978–79	Mrs Edward Rosenfield
1980–81	John Huisman
1982–83	Patricia Schleuning
1984	Sarah Wagster
1985–86	Edwin Schneider
1987–90	Joseph C. Blumel
1990	George Reinmiller

Executive Secretaries

1927	Josephine H. Forney
1927–28	Elizabeth K. Watson
1928–32	Mrs Elbert C. Peets
1932–38	Ruth Isherwood
1939–50	Helen M. Erskine
1951–58	Barbara M. Walker
1958–59	Cynthia H. Reid
1959–61	Doris H. Johnston
1961–70	Kim Angell
1970–71	Emmy Lou Roe
1971	Kay Young

Manager of Support Services

1986–90	Janet Fry

REVIEWERS

C. Hilton-Turvey, 1925–
J. L. Wallin, 1925–
David Tamkin, 1925–
Emil Enna, 1925–
Sam Raddon, Jr., 1926
Aaron Avshalomoff, 1926
Suzie Aubrey Smith, 1925–1951
Grant Showerman, 1927
Audred Bunch, 1927
David L. Piper, 1927
Joseph MacQueen, 1929–
Hilmar Grondahl, 1933–1976
Jean Macguire, 1937
Fred M. White, 1947
Herb Penny, 1949
Frederic Rothchild, 1954
Martin Clark, 1956–1982
Donald Dierks, 1961–
John Voorhees, 1962
Louis R. Guzzo, 1962
David Campbell, 1962
Joan Riggs, 1964
Douglas McConnell, 1964
Charlie Hanna, 1965
Sally Landauer, 1969
Phil Hunt, 1970–
Janet Goetze, 1971
JohnWendeborn, 1972–
Bob Michelet, 1975
Robert Lindstrom, 1977–1986
Elaine Cogan, 1977
Mark Mandel, 1978
Elsa F. McDowell, 1981
John Rockwell, 1984
K. Kovachevic, 1984
Peter N. Richardson, 1985
David Stabler, 1986–
T. Ursinyova, 1989
Gabor Valtinyi, 1989

PROGRAM COVER DESIGNERS

Lloyd Reynolds, February 1954
Jacob Avshalomov, September 1954
Paul Paxton, November 1955
Joe Erceg, November 1956
Raymond Olson, April 1957
Earl Cunningham, April 1958
Ronald Kincaid, November 1958
Jay Smith, February 1960
Darlene Diven, November 1961
Bob Selby, April 1962
Ken LeBack, March 1963
Douglas Lynch, April 1963
Mineko Hirayama, May 1963
Darrell Mingo, April 1964
Robin Rickabaugh, March 1965
Douglas Lynch, April 1965
Mel Ulven, November 1965
Ray Dodge, March 1966
Rosemary Opp, April 1966
Douglas Lynch, February 1967
Frieda Fehrenbacher, April 1967
Mariah Chu, November 1967
Penny Erler, March 1968
Paul Klax (D. Lynch), November 1969
Douglas Lynch, March 1970
Jere Harley, November 1970
Ben Shahn, April 1971
Victor Hartman, November 1971
Dale Ott, April 1973
Ken LeBack, November 1974
Douglas Lynch, April 1976

DISCOGRAPHY

Composers Recordings, Inc. New York

C.R.I. No. 140
DIAMOND: *The World of Paul Klee*
LEES: *Prologue, Capriccio and Epilogue*
BERGSMA: *Chameleon Variations*
HARRIS: *Reverie and Dance*

C.R.I. No. 192
WARD: *Divertimento*
JACOB AVSHALOMOV: *Phases of the Great Land*

C.R.I. No. 210 S
AARON AVSHALOMOV: *Peking Hutungs*
Piano Concerto in G
Margaret Moore, piano solo
JACOB AVSHALOMOV: *Cantata, How Long O Lord*
Neil Wilson, Baritone solo

C.R.I. No. 351 SD
BLOCH: *Symphony for Trombone and Orchestra*
Howard Prince, soloist
BLOCH: *Suite Symphonique*

Youth Philharmonic puts on dazzling performance

By DAVID STABLER
of the Oregonian staff

MUSIC REVIEW

The Portland Youth Philharmonic put on quite a show Saturday night at the Arlene Schnitzer Concert Hall. The concert offered a heaven-sent movement by S. A. Mozart; a young violin virtuoso from within the ranks, Lisa Chong; and the weighty beauty of a Brahms symphony.

First to come was a flashy soufflé in the form of Donizetti's overture to "Roberto Devereaux," an obscure opera. With lively accents by the wind players and lots of energy in the strings, the orchestra got the concert off to a crisp start.

Mozart's Adagio from the Divertimento in B-Flat Major (K.287) is inspired music and an inspired choice for a symphonic program. Avshalomov, who enjoys speaking to the audience about the music, described the spiralling motion of the first violins as they ascend to the upper limits of their instruments.

The string sound did not disappoint. The players phrased their lines elegantly, at the same time taking care to blend as sections. Such a performance comes from hard work and a conductor with an ear for Mozart's style. For the audience, the result was eight or so minutes of profound beauty.

Before intermission, Lisa Chong, a sophomore at Beaverton High School, took the spotlight for the Third Violin Concerto by Camille Saint-Saëns. George Bernard Shaw, who once dismissed the piece as "trivially pretty scraps of serenade music," might have been persuaded to change his mind if he'd heard Chong.

She is a talent with a bright future. Chong possesses a sure sense of intonation, a keen ear for the musical line and a flexible bow arm that brings out the tone. There were many pleasing moments, but she excelled at the close of the slow second movement where whe played ever so quietly without losing focus or momentum. The extra-high notes known as false harmonics were expertly controlled. Better controlled, in fact, thean Isaac Stern's harmonics, which audiences heard in the same hall a week ago.

Brahms' lengthy Second Symphony balanced the concert's first half. Avshalomov chose this big 19th century work wisely.

The French horn work of principal player Monica Duplessie was exemplary—round tone, evenly shaped notes, a real arch to the phrase. Shannon Sprenger's oboe playing was of equal caliber. It was quite easy, but nonetheless remarkable, to hear the fine training behind these young musicians.

As a whole, Brahms came across with much of his nobility and warmth intact.

The Continuing Way

An organization such as the Portland Youth Philharmonic is valuable to many more people in the community than those who come in direct contact with it. Echoing Mayor Carson's remark of 1934, Mayor Shrunk wrote in 1970:

> Congratulations on a most marvelous tour. The ovations you and the Orchestra received in Europe and at home are a matter of great pride to us all, and you are a credit to your city and your country. These are the warm, human, people-to-people relationships that develop strong international ties.

Without any of the trappings of a school—such as credits, grades, deans, dorms, or uniforms—this activity became the very essence of "school," attesting to the inscription above the Liepzig Gewandhaus: *Res severa est verum gaudium*: Serious things are the true joy.

Jacques Gershkovitch, and surely Mary V. Dodge, hoped that the Junior Symphony idea would spread, and it has. There are now over 300 such groups around the country; and the American Symphony Orchestra League has a separate division for youth orchestras.

I am often asked whether the students of today are any different from those of the past—when I played in the Orchestra, or when I became Conductor. The answer is, they are not. Those who gravitate to the Orchestra are still the ones who are drawn to music, have an aptitude for playing an instrument, and a family that encourages them and provides the instrument and lessons. When all of this is added to the known gratification of playing great music in a full orchestra—and the reputation of this one—a deep and genuine commitment develops. These students are in the PYP because they want to be.

However, the circumstances of their lives today *are* different. Many more activities are available to them; and in preparation for life in the modern world they feel they must participate in this broadened range. Outdoor school, computer camp, athletic competitions, band rallies, debating teams, religious groups, theater and ballet, wind-surfing, skiing, mock trial—all receive the students' time and energies.

The public school music programs which, as noted early in this book, contributed so strongly to the development of musical activity in America, have wound down to such a low level as to be eliminated from the school districts in many states. To outline the professional reasons for this decline would require a separate article. But some of the sociological reasons are plain to see: in the field of popular music, the inclination among the young toward individual expression, rather than group activity, has led to the proliferation of guitar and other solo players without precedent. The advent of electronic keyboards, with built-in chording capabilities, now makes it possible for anyone to "compose" by doodling—without any musical training whatsoever.

In this context amateur orchestras will become increasingly important to our society. They will continue to thrive because it is inherently rewarding to play music that is written to be played and to sound well after a reasonable amount of practice. But the function of orchestras will come to seem more curatorial as time goes on. We musicians are all custodians of the great musical literature created since 1700. Much of the music written between 1910 and 1950, once considered "difficult" both for audiences and performers, has been incorporated into the general repertoire. But I predict that very little of the music written after 1950 will ever find its way to "permanent" acceptance—despite its great increase in quantity.

I believe this because most of the new practices in "serious" compositions ignore playability and aptness for the traditional instruments in general use. Composers and sound technicians are turning in synthetic means of producing sounds—now widely channeled through computers—which bypass the performer and are produced in the studio/lab, and even desk top, emerging as final products that go directly to the consumer. From time to time composers will produce playable works which incorporate new elements devised by the avant-garde, and we, together with other interested orchestras, will seek them out and present them. The works, which gratify both the performers and the listeners, will enter the repertoire and stay a while. Not many. In a typical recent season 417 orchestras in the United States performed works by 1,027 composers, of which 834 were contemporary (mostly pre-1950); but two-thirds of all the music played was written by the 200 "standard" composers: the vast majority of the contemporary works were played just once!

In this period of unparalleled and unpredictable change the PYP continues its joyful work. This present account reaches print as the Orchestra we embark on our 67th Season. Some of the former players have children in the present Orchestra, some have grandchildren in it. Others see their pupils, and *their* pupils in it. Some, not too many, have come to serve on the Board of Directors—enough to provide continuity without inbreeding.

One former player returned 36 years ago, to serve as Conductor. It is his hope that the Orchestra will long continue to inspire and train young people so that they may gain a sense of personal as well as group achievement, and that their own efforts will form the basis of lasting joy in music.

In this period when the arts are so readily available and so often leveled for mass consumption, we must keep sanctuaries where our youth can learn to address themselves to the highest manifestations of the human spirit. This is a demanding exercise; and to fully experience the rewarding exaltation requires seriousness, devotion, and a good working method.

These we have had; and what a pleasure to all concerned.